OCEAN SENTINEL

The Short Sunderland

John F Hamlin

An AIR-BRITAIN Publication

Ocean Sentinel
The Short Sunderland
by John F Hamlin
Copyright © Air-Britain (Historians) Ltd 2012

Published in the United Kingdom by

Air-Britain (Historians) Ltd

Regd Office:
Victoria House, Stanbridge Park,
Staplefield Lane, Staplefield,
West Sussex RH17 6AS, England

Sales Dept:
41 Penshurst Road, Leigh,
Tonbridge, Kent TN11 8HL, England

Membership Enquiries:
Barry J. Collman,
1 Rose Cottages, 179 Penn Road,
Hazlemere, Bucks. HP15 7NE, England

Website: www.air-britain.co.uk

Correspondence regarding this publication to:
sunderland@air-britain.co.uk

All rights reserved. No part of this publication may be reproduced, stored in a retrieval system or transmitted, in any form or by any means, electronic, mechanical, photocopying, recording or otherwise, without the prior written permission of the author and of Air-Britain (Historians) Ltd.

ISBN 978-0-85130-400-7

Colour side-views by Peter G Coker

Origination by Dave Partington

Printed in Poland
www.polskabook.co.uk

Front Cover:

Sunderland Mk.III EK591 of 422 Squadron, based at Castle Archdale in Northern Ireland and captained by Flt Lt S W Butler, attacking U-625 on 10th March 1944 at approximately 1500 hours, west of Ireland. The U-boat sank some ninety minutes later. Flt Lt Butler was training a new crew on this occasion.
This Mk.III aircraft still carried early ASV equipment and an early nose turret with a single pan-fed Vickers VGO 0.303 machine gun but with four 0.303 Browning guns in the hull.
(Original artwork by Mike Bailey)

Back Cover:

A pre-delivery photograph of Tasman Empire Airways' Solent 4 ZK-AML "Aotearoa II" in the early colour scheme.
(Short Bros & Harland Ltd via Stephen Piercey Collection)

OCEAN SENTINEL

The Short Sunderland

John F Hamlin

with
Phil Butler, Peter Marson,
Dave Partington, Douglas Rough

Sting in the tail. The Nash & Thompson F.N.13 tail turret of the Sunderland prototype K4774 featured four Browning 0.303 machine guns.
(via P H Butler)

TABLE OF CONTENTS

Introduction: 6

Abbreviations: 8

Bibliography: 10

Chapter 1: Development and production, including specifications
and production batches: 11

Chapter 2: Operational overview: 23

Chapter 3: Operating units — RAF, RAAF, RNZAF, SAAF,
Aéronautique navale and Aviação Naval: 29

Chapter 4: RAF Sunderland bases: 73

Chapter 5: Individual aircraft histories: 91

Chapter 6: Civilian conversions and new-build aircraft: 159

Appendix 1: Sunderlands by military unit: 209

Appendix 2: Military serials / civil registrations cross-reference;
Civil aircraft names; Extant aircraft 217

Appendix 3: Roll of Honour: 219

Colour pages and side-views: 194

Don Schofield 1943 – 2012

This book is dedicated to the memory of Don Schofield, who passed away just before Christmas 2012, after a short and sudden illness. His many skills were evident in most areas of Air-Britain's operations, from his skilful and assiduous proof-reading of many of our prestige hard-cover titles, to his long-term role as Treasurer, which he pursued with vigour and vigilance for very many years – indeed our healthy financial position is a testament to his exceptionally high standards of conscientious perfectionism.

Don represented the very essence of backroom diligence and commitment and we remember him with great affection.

Sunderland MR.5s RN304 [D:M] of FBTS Pembroke Dock (Wing Commander J W Louw OBE DFC) and DP200 [B:Z] of 230 Squadron (Flight Lieutenant Stan Bowater DFC) escorting the Royal Yacht HMY Britannia *in the English Channel shortly before its arrival in London at the end of HM The Queen's Commonwealth Tour on 15th May 1954.* (P H T Green collection)

INTRODUCTION

The founders of what would become the largest and most respected British manufacturer of flying-boats were the three sons of Samuel and Emma Short: Horace Leonard, born in 1872, Albert Eustace, born in 1875, and Hugh Oswald, born seven years later. Apart from Horace, the boys were generally known by their second given names rather than their first, and are referred to thus in this introduction.

Eustace Short was the first of the three to become interested in aviation, when in 1898 he acquired a second-hand coal-gas balloon named *Queen of the West*. After he and Oswald had repaired it they flew it at a number of village fetes and other gatherings. Two years later, the brothers visited the Paris Exhibition and, spurred on by what they saw there, Eustace and Oswald began building their own 41 ft (12.5 m) diameter balloon in April 1901. Encouraged by its modest success and confident of a growth in ballooning, they soon opened a workshop off Tottenham Court Road in London and built a second balloon, which was not as successful as the first.

Nevertheless, the two brothers secured a contract in October 1903 to supply balloons to the Indian Government, and in the following year Horace, who had been working as an engineer in the north of England, returned to help design a large balloon for high-altitude work. As no sponsor was forthcoming this project had to be abandoned.

In 1907, the brothers constructed a glider in which J T Moore-Brabazon attempted to take to the air at Brooklands, and this event appears to have moved their interests towards heavier-than-air machines. Although the balloon business was thriving in two railway arches at Battersea, when the brothers heard, through the Aero Club, of Wilbur Wright's flights in France they decided to diversify into aeroplane production. Horace was approached and willingly agreed to take part, and in November 1908 Short Brothers was formed as a partnership, to build Wright aircraft under licence. On December 5th Eustace flew a Wright biplane at Le Mans, and early in 1909 work started on the first powered aircraft to be ordered from Short Bros, to be designed by Horace for Frank McClean. In unfinished state, this machine, Short Biplane No 1, was exhibited at Olympia in March 1909, but probably never flew.

As no manufacturing facility had been established in the United Kingdom by the Wright Brothers, an order was placed with Short Bros for six aircraft of a Wright design. Erection of a workshop on a new airfield being set out at Leysdown on the Isle of Sheppey for the Aero Club began in February 1909, but little more than a year later the site was abandoned in favour of a new one at nearby Eastchurch, where once again Short Bros set up a workshop. There they produced biplanes on which the first four Royal Navy officers learned to fly.

In 1912 Short Bros began the design of seaplanes, and this function expanded so rapidly that in a year or so extra production facilities had to be acquired. A site was found at Rochester, on the banks of the River Medway, where a large factory was built and placed under the control of Oswald Short. The First World War saw a huge increase in production of several types of aircraft, principally the Admiralty Type 184, the Short Bomber, the Short 320, the DH.9, the Felixstowe F.3 (which was the first flying-boat built by Short Bros) and the F.5. During the war, in October 1916, John Lankester Parker joined the company as test pilot, becoming the chief test pilot two years later and remaining as such until the end of the Second World War in 1945.

What might have been seen as a retrograde step was taken in 1917, when Short Bros received an Admiralty order for the construction of two rigid airships, and to accommodate them a huge shed was built at RAF Cardington in Bedfordshire. A further airship was added to the order in 1918, but in April 1919 the Cardington factory was taken over by the Admiralty.

In 1919 Eustace and Oswald formed a limited company, without Horace, who had died two years earlier. This company was to be known as Short Brothers (Rochester & Bedford) Ltd, and Oswald was appointed Chairman and joint managing director with Eustace.

INTRODUCTION

Trading conditions after the war ended were poor, but the company overcame them to an extent by manufacturing bus bodies and boats, while retaining an aviation division to await better times. In 1920 they built an experimental aircraft known as the Silver Streak in aluminium alloy, but otherwise there was little aviation activity until the Short Calcutta flying-boat emerged at Rochester as the company's first series production aircraft with a metal fuselage.

Eustace Short died in April 1932, leaving Oswald to run the business. In June 1936, as a result of an agreement to build both land and marine aircraft, Short & Harland Ltd was formed as a joint venture with Harland & Wolff Ltd, the well-known shipbuilders in Belfast, where the Air Ministry had agreed to establish a new factory. By the end of the year, the company's main offices had been moved to Belfast.

Meanwhile, the Mercury and Maia composite aircraft and the first Empire flying-boat had flown, with the prototype Sunderland not far behind. With land and sea facilities available at Belfast, production of Sunderlands and Stirling heavy bombers proceeded almost side-by-side.

In January 1943 Oswald resigned as managing director and Short Bros (Rochester & Bedford) Ltd was taken over by the Government as a temporary measure, during Sir Stafford Cripps' tenure as Minister of Aircraft Production. Management and shareholders alike were dispossessed of their interests, and many years passed before the shareholders received the compensation to which they were entitled.

After the war, in June 1946 the Rochester factory was closed and all production was transferred to Belfast. Short Bros (Rochester & Bedford) Ltd sold its design and production business to Short & Harland Ltd and became a holding company as S B (Realisations) Ltd. In November 1947 Short & Harland Ltd was retitled Short Bros & Harland Ltd, a name which survived until the title Short Bros Ltd superceded it in 1977, long after the last flying-boat had been built, refurbished or serviced.

Throughout its existence, the company founded by the three Short brothers enjoyed a reputation for quality of design and manufacturing, and it is unfortunate that the era of the flying-boat came to an end after such a relatively short time. If it hadn't, who knows what achievements Short Brothers might have attained? This book, published over 100 years after the establishment of Short Brothers, is an attempt to celebrate one of the Company's most significant products.

I wish to thank the following persons for helping with various aspects of the research — without them, the story could not have been completed.

Roger Andrews for information on Sunderland movements at Belfast; *John Austin-Williams, Stefaan Bouwer, Winston Brent, Tom Chalmers, Ken Smy* and *Brian Stockland* all for SAAF data; *Phil Butler* for information on contracts, Ministry of Supply aircraft, ground instructional airframes and other matters; *Mr P J Christopher* for providing an insight into a typical Sunderland sortie; *Peter Coker* for the side-view drawings; *Ernie Cromie* for Northern Ireland research; *Jean-Pierre Dubois* for Aéronautique navale histories; *John Evans* for his willing help on the subject of RAF Pembroke Dock; *Alan Faupel* for information on Aéronautique navale aircraft; *Robert Feuilloy* of ARDHAN for French Naval research; *Peter H T Green* for access to his library; *Keith Hayward* for information on BOAC; *Norman Hull* for access to his Aquila Airways information; *Allan King* for information on the Windermere factory; *Paul McMaster*, Bombardier Aerospace, Belfast for Short Bros information and photos; *Peter Marson* for his invaluable input on civil Sunderlands and derivatives; *Michael Magnusson* and *John M Davis* for information on Sunderlands used in Argentina; *Dave Partington* for access to the late *Jack Meaden's* photo collection; *Richard Poad*, ATA Museum, Maidenhead Heritage Centre; *Douglas Rough* for acting as facilitator and for providing additional information and contacts; *Graham Skillen*; *David J Smith*; the late *Ray Sturtivant* for his support; *Luis Tavares* for information on the Portuguese Sunderland; *Nathan Basher, David Duxbury, Simon Moody, Alan Taylor; Stewart Waring* and *Alan Willoughby* for RNZAF data; and with acknowledgements to the Air Force Museum of New Zealand.

John F Hamlin, 2012

Three Sunderlands Mk.V of 201 Squadron in 1945, with RN285 [NS:H] in the foreground and RN284 [NS:G] on the right, at low-level over Belleek, Co Fermanagh, Northern Ireland in what was the 7-mile long "Donegal Corridor" in WW2. This followed the course of the River Erne towards the Atlantic Ocean and involved flying across four miles of neutral Eire airspace. Instead of the long route North and then West, this short-cut had been agreed with Eire in January 1941 ...ostensibly only for air/sea rescue missions! (R C Sturtivant collection)

ABBREVIATIONS

AA	Anti-aircraft
AC1	Aircraftsman First Class
AC2	Aircraftsman Second Class
ACSEA	Air Command South East Asia
AD	Air Depot (RNZAF)
AFC	Air Force Cross
Air Cdre	Air Commodore
ALFA	Sociedad Mixta Aviación del Litoral Fluvial Argentino
ANA	Australian National Airways
ANSW	Airlines of New South Wales
AOC-in-C	Air Officer Commanding-in-Chief
ASR	Air/Sea Rescue
ASV	Air-to-Surface Vessel [radar]
ASWDU	Air-Sea Warfare Development Unit
ATA	Air Transport Auxiliary
BBOC	Brought Back on Charge
Bf	Bayerische Flugzeugwerke
BOAC	British Overseas Airways Corporation
BOC	Brought on charge (NZ)
CA	California
Cat	Category
CAUSA	Compania Aeronautica Uruguayana SA
CCIS	Coastal Command Instructors' School
CF	Communications Flight
C-in-C	Commander-in-Chief
cm	centimetre
CMG	Companion (of the Order) of St Michael & St George
c/n	construction number
CO	Commanding Officer
CofA	Certificate of Airworthiness
CofR	Certificate of Registration
Col	Colonel
Const.	Construction
(C) OTU	(Coastal) Operational Training Unit
CRP	Civilian Repair Party
c/s	radio call-sign
CSSA	Corporacion Sudamericana de Servicios Aereos SA
CTU	Commander Task Unit
DFC	Distinguished Flying Cross
DFC*	DFC and Bar
DFM	Distinguished Flying Medal [awarded to NCOs]
DH	de Havilland
DNL	Det Norske Luftfartselskap A/S
Do	Dornier
DSO	Distinguished Service Order
DUKW	Duplex Drive Amphibious Truck, 1942 model, on General Motors' 2.5-ton chassis
FAA	Fleet Air Arm / Federal Aviation Administration [USA]
FAMA	Flota Aerea Mercante Argentina
FBRD	Flying Boat Repair Depot (RAAF)
FBSU	Flying Boat Storage Unit (when un-numbered) or Flying Boat Servicing Unit (when numbered)
FBTS	Flying Boat Training Squadron
FE	Far East
Flg Off	Flying Officer
Flt Lt	Flight Lieutenant
FP	Ferry Pool
ft	feet
FTU	Ferry Training Unit
Fw	Focke-Wulf
gall	gallons
Gen	General
GI	Ground Instructional
Gp Capt	Group Captain
GR	General Reconnaissance
He	Heinkel
HH	His Highness
HMS	His/Her Majesty's Ship
HMT	His/Her Majesty's Troopship
HMY	Her Majesty's Yacht
hp	horsepower
HQ	Headquarters
HRH	His/Her Royal Highness
in	inches
inc	including / inclusive
Is	Island(s)
JG	Jagdgeschwader [Luftwaffe day fighter unit]
Ju	Junkers
KCB	Knight Commander of the Most Honourable Order of the Bath
kg	kilograms
km	kilometres
kph	kilometres per hour
LAC	Leading Aircraftsman
Ltd	Limited [Company]
LTS	Long Term Storage
m	metres
MAEE	Marine Aircraft Experimental Establishment
Maj Gen	Major General
MC	Military Cross
MCA	Ministry of Civil Aviation
MF/DF	medium frequency direction finder
Mk.	Mark
mm	millimetres
MOCU	Maritime Operational Conversion Unit (RNZAF)
mods	modifications
MoS	Ministry of Supply
MOTAT	Museum of Transport and Technology (NZ)
MR	Maritime Reconnaissance
MRSU	Maritime Reconnaissance & Support Unit (RNZAF)
MTB	Motor Torpedo Boat
MU	Maintenance Unit
MV	Motor Vessel
M&V	Meat & Vegetable
NAS	Naval Air Station [US]
NZNAC	New Zealand National Airways Corporation
OBE	Order of the British Empire
OCU	Operational Conversion Unit
P&O	Peninsular & Oriental Steam Navigation Company
PoW	Prisoner of war
Pty	Proprietary
pwfu	presumed withdrawn from use

Abbreviations

P.II	Pilot II [an RAF rank used for a short time only]	Sqn	Squadron
QANTAS	Queensland & Northern Territory Aerial Services	Sqn Ldr	Squadron Leader
RAAF	Royal Australian Air Force	SNCO	Senior Non-Commissioned Officer [Sergeant, Flight Sergeant, Warrant Officer]
RAF	Royal Air Force		
RAI	Réseau Aérien Interinsulaire	SOC	struck off charge
RCAF	Royal Canadian Air Force	SoTT	School of Technical Training
recat	recategorised	SS	Steamship
regd	registered	TEAL	Tasman Empire Airways Ltd
regn	registration	TOA	Trans-Oceanic Airways
RMS	Royal Mail Ship	TOC	taken on charge
RN	Royal Navy	TTS	Technical Training School (RNZAF)
RNoAF	Royal Norwegian Air Force	TX	Texas
RNAS	Royal Naval Air Station/ Royal Naval Air Service	USAAF	United States Army Air Force
		USAF	United States Air Force
RNZAF	Royal New Zealand Air Force	USS	United States Ship
RSU	Repair & Storage Unit (RAAF)	VA	Virginia
S.II	Signaller II [a rank in the RAF used for a short time only]	VE	Victory in Europe
		VIP	Very Important Person
SAAF	South African Air Force	VJ	Victory Against Japan
SBHL	Short Bros & Harland Ltd, Belfast	VVIP	Very Very Important Person
SBL	Short Bros Ltd	wfs	withdrawn from service
SB(R&B)L	Short Bros (Rochester & Bedford) Ltd	wfu	withdrawn from use
SB(W)L	Short Bros (Windermere) Ltd	Wg	Wing
Scot Avn	Scottish Aviation Ltd	Wg Cdr	Wing Commander
SFBTF	Sunderland Flying Boat Transport Flight (NZ)	W/T	wireless telegraphy
SFBTS	Sunderland Flying Boat Transport Squadron (NZ)	ZG	Zerstörergeschwader [Luftwaffe twin-engined fighter unit]
sq	square		

Sunderland GR.5 ML778 on the step as it makes a test flight from Belfast Lough, with Cave Hill in the background, in April 1951 before being delivered to the Aéronautique navale on 12th May 1951 as Sunderland 5 ML778. It is being observed from a de Havilland Dragon Rapide overhead, probably Short Bros' own G-AKDW. Earlier, whilst with 201 Squadron, ML778 made made the last official patrol of World War 2 on 3rd-4th June 1945. (SB&H via P H Butler)

BIBLIOGRAPHY

For further research, the following publications may be of interest:

Berlin Airlift by Robert Rodrigo (Cassell & Co Ltd 1960) (no ISBN)
The Berlin Airlift by Ann & John Tusa (Hodder & Stoughton Ltd 1988) ISBN 1-86227-044-9
British Civil Aircraft since 1919 by A J Jackson (Putnam & Co Ltd 1974) ISBN0-370-10014-X)
British Independent Airlines by A C Merton Jones (Aviation Hobby Shop 2000) ISBN0-907178-82-0
Flying-boat Queen by John Evans (Paterchurch Publications 1997-2005) ISBN1-870745-00-0
Flying-boat Queen Vol 2 by John Evans (Paterchurch Publications 1993) ISBN1-870745-03-5
Flying-boat Queen Vol 3 by John Evans (Paterchurch Publications 2004) ISBN1-870745-13-2
Merchant Airmen (HMSO 1946) (no ISBN)
Planemakers: 4 — Shorts by Michael J H Taylor (Jane's Publishing Co Ltd 1984) ISBN 0-7106-0237-5
Royal Air Force 1939-45:
    Vol 1 by Denis Richards, ISBN 0-11-771592-1;
    Vol 2 by D Richards & Hilary St G Saunders, ISBN 0-11-771593-X;
    Vol 3 by Hilary St G Saunders, ISBN 0-11-771594-8
    (all HMSO 1954)
The Royal Air Force in the World War by Capt N Macmillan MC AFC (George G Harrop & Co Ltd 1949/50) (no ISBN)
The Short Sunderland by Chaz Bowyer (Aston Publications Ltd 1989) ISBN 0-946627-34-7
The Short Sunderland — Profile No 189 (Profile Publications Ltd, undated) (no ISBN)
Short Sunderland in World War II by Andrew Hendrie (Airlife Publishing Ltd 1994) ISBN 1-85310-429-9
Shorts Aircraft since 1900 by C H Barnes (Putnam Aeronautical Books, rev.1989) ISBN 0-85177-819-4

Documents at The National Archives:

Ref	Sqn	Years
AIR27/2440	88 Sqn	1946 - 1954
AIR27/761	95 Sqn	1941 - 1943
762		1944 - 1945
AIR27/910	119 Sqn	1942 - 1943
AIR27/1177	201 Sqn	1940
1178		1941 - 1943
1179		1944 - 1945
2456		1946 - 1950
3158		1951 - 1955
3159		1951 - 1957
3356		8.54 >
AIR27/1182	202 Sqn	1941
1183		1942
AIR27/1208	204 Sqn	1939
1209		1940 - 1943
1210		1944 - 1945
AIR27/1216	205 Sqn	1945
AIR27/2461	205 Sqn	1946 - 1950
2660		1951 - 1954
AIR27/1295	209 Sqn	
1296		1945
2467		1946 - 1950
2663		1951 - 1954
AIR27/1298	210 Sqn	1938 - 1940
1299		1941
AIR27/1412	228 Sqn	1938 - 1939
1413		1940
1414		1941
1415		1942 -1943
1416		1944 - 1945
AIR27/1422	230 Sqn	1938 - 1942
1423		1943 - 1945
2477		1946 - 1950
2668		1951 - 1955
2848		1.56 - 2.57
AIR27/1461	240 Sqn	1945
1462		1945 - 1946
AIR27/1484		246 Sqn 1942 - 1943
AIR27/1533		259 Sqn 1945
AIR27/1571		270 Sqn 1943 - 1945
AIR27/1722		330 Sqn 1943
1723		1944 - 1945
AIR27/1830	422 Sqn	1942 - 1945
AIR27/1832	423 Sqn	1942 - 1945
AIR27/1912	461 Sqn	1942
1913		1943
1914		1944 - 1945
AIR27/1940	490 Sqn	1944 - 1945
AIR27/149	10 (RAAF) Sqn	1939 -1940
150		1941
151		1942
152		1943
153		1944 - 1945
AIR15/555	CCDU	
AIR29/609	4 (C) OTU	1940 -1943
AIR29/629	302 FTU	1942 - 1944
AIR29/696	131 (C) OTU	
AIR29/859	Special Duty Flt	1.40 - 3.40
AIR29/893	CF Iraq etc	12.40 - 8.46
AIR29/1014	57 MU	10.43 - 12.45
1511		1.46 - 9.51
1512		1.46 - 9.51
1513		1.49 - 4.50
1514		5.50 - 9.51
AIR29/1236	ASWDU	1.46 - 12.50
1237		1.46 - 5.46
1238		1.47 - 12.47
1239		1.48 - 12.48
AIR29/1554	272 MU	
AIR29/1639	235 OCU	
2170		

Nose-on view of the prototype Sunderland K4774 at Short Bros' factory at Rochester in November 1937. Note the beaching gear and the compartments in the leading edges of the wings open for inspection. (P H T Green collection)

Chapter 1
DEVELOPMENT AND PRODUCTION

While the Short Singapore Mk.III biplane flying-boat was still in production at the Rochester factory of Short Brothers, the Air Ministry issued Specification R.2/33, which called for a new maritime long-range reconnaissance aircraft to replace it. Chief designer Arthur (later Sir Arthur) Gouge began to prepare a tender without delay, in the knowledge that his design for a new passenger-carrying all-metal stressed-skin flying-boat was already well advanced. This design was the S.23 'C' Class, of which twenty-eight were ordered by Imperial Airways in 1935 for use on the burgeoning Empire routes. Short Brothers submitted their proposal for the new military aircraft, to be named the Sunderland, in 1934. The only competition to win the contract came from Saunders-Roe Ltd, which submitted a proposal powered by four Bristol Perseus engines which was known as the A.33, a parasol-winged aircraft of far less modern appearance than Gouge's design.

The S.25 Sunderland was to have a hull of much deeper cross-section than the civil S.23, and a long nose projecting forward from a flight deck located near the high wing. It was also to carry power-operated turrets as part of its armament, the first British flying-boat to do so. Originally, the armament was to consist of no more than one 37mm Coventry Ordnance Works gun in the bows and one Lewis gun in the tail, but during construction of the prototype it was decided to incorporate a Nash & Thompson FN.11 nose turret carrying one Vickers gas-operated machine gun, and four Browning .303 (7.7 mm) guns in a Nash & Thompson hydraulic turret. To allow an anchor to be passed through a bow hatch, the front turret was retractable. The offensive load, weighing up to 2,000 pounds (907 kg), could comprise bombs, depth charges or mines, and was suspended from carriers on lateral tracks beneath the centre section. Large hatches opened in the sides of the fuselage to allow the weapons to be run out under the wings, powered by an electric motor which cut out after full travel.

Powered by four Bristol Pegasus XXII engines of 1,010 horsepower, which were more powerful than those of the S.23, the Sunderland prototype, K4774, made its maiden flight from the River Medway at Rochester on 16th October 1937, captained by J Lankester Parker. For early trials, the Sunderland's wing was similar to that of the S.23 design, but the prototype then returned to Short's factory to have a wing of new profile with a swept-back leading edge fitted. Thus equipped, K4774 took to the air again on 7 March 1938.

A crew of seven was allocated to the Sunderland: two pilots, radio operator, navigator, flight engineer and two gunners, accommodated on two decks. There were six bunks for sleeping, a galley in which meals could be prepared, workshop areas in case repairs were needed, and ample stowage for such equipment as hand guns and three spare propeller blades.

The Sunderland's hull was efficiently shaped, causing a lower drag than that of the earlier and smaller Singapore Mk.III. Wing loading was, as expected, very much higher than other military aircraft of that decade, but Arthur Gouge incorporated his own patented flaps to provide an increased area and add 30% to the lift coefficient for landing. The planing bottom was brought to a vertical knife-edge at the rear and from there in a smooth line back to the underside of the tail.

The Saro A.33 did not make its first flight until 14th October 1938, by which time a contract for twenty-one Sunderlands Mk.I had already been placed and production was well under way at Rochester. Eleven days later, the A.33 suffered from porpoising, capsized and was damaged beyond repair, which prompted Saunders Roe to concentrate on the twin-engined Lerwick.

In June 1938 the first Sunderland for the Royal Air Force, L2159, was flown out to 230 Squadron at Seletar, Singapore. Orders for a further twenty-one aircraft were placed that year, and by the outbreak of the Second World War about forty were in service with 210 and 230 Squadrons. In production, Sunderlands were being improved in several ways, including the addition of two Vickers gas-operated guns in hatches on each side of the rear upper deck. A second gun was added to the nose turret, and rubber 'boot' de-icers were applied to the leading edges of wings and tailplanes. In addition, the de Havilland-made Hamilton propellers were replaced by 12ft 6in (3.81m) constant-speed propellers with spinners. From October 1941, ASV Mk.II radar with matched dipole aerials was mounted on the upper rear fuselage in groups of four, with horizontal poles under the wings for azimuth guidance, adding very significantly to the Sunderland's search capabilities.

By that time, output of the Sunderland Mk.I had reached its total of 73. Production then switched to the Mk.II, an interim version which featured Pegasus XVIII engines with superchargers. A second production site came into use at this time, run by Blackburn Aircraft adjacent to the Denny shipyard at Dumbarton, and the first fifteen Mk.II aircraft were produced there. A further 25 were built at a third site, Short Bros & Harland's factory at Queen's Island, Belfast. The relatively small number of Mk.IIs produced, 58, resulted from the testing on a Mk.I, T9042, of a modified planing bottom which gave reduced drag in the air and was incorporated in the Mk.III, for which T9042 effectively became the prototype aircraft.

Armament on the last few Mk.IIs was much heavier than on the Mk.I Sunderland. Apart from improved armour in a twin Browning nose turret, an FN.7 dorsal turret was installed above the trailing edge of the wing, slightly off-centre on the starboard side of the fuselage. This contained two more Browning machine guns and of course added to the crew number. In an FN.4A tail turret there were four Brownings, for which 1,000 rounds of ammunition each were provided. By this time the Sunderland had become a formidable fighting machine, able to fend off most attacks by lone enemy fighters and flak from submarines.

The 'standard' Sunderland during the Second World War was the Mk.III, of which 463 were produced, 35 of them built at a new site run by Short Bros on Windermere, 170 by Blackburn at Dumbarton, 71 at Belfast and 187 at Rochester. After U-boats were equipped with passive receivers able to receive warning of the approach of Allied aircraft, ASV Mk.III was installed, its aerials fitted in neat under-wing fairings. This effectively countered the enemy equipment and enabled Sunderland crews to increase the number of 'kills'. In retaliation, the submarines were fitted with batteries of flak, which the crews of Sunderlands, not having adequate forward-firing guns, found quite deadly. Four fixed .303 (7.7 mm) Brownings were then fitted to many Sunderlands, but much more effective were additional 0.5-inch (12.7 mm) Brownings in hatches be-

Sunderlands Mk.V under overhaul at Short Bros & Harland, Belfast. The nearest aircraft is coded WH and belonged to 330 Squadron. (V A Hodgkinson)

A magnificent view of the Belfast shipyards with four Sunderlands moored nearby. (Peter Davis collection)

hind the trailing edge. By this time, the Sunderland was carrying, it is believed, the largest number of guns of any British service aircraft.

Development of the Windermere factory was a prime example of what concerted efforts by all concerned could achieve. In order to sustain and increase output, the Ministry of Aircraft Production looked for sites well away from possible bombing and where there was already a skilled workforce on hand or nearby. As Short Bros' factory at Rochester was in the forefront of Luftwaffe activity, plans to build two more large hangars there were shelved and an alternative site was sought. Consideration was given to Dundee, Belfast and Lytham St Annes, but in the end Windermere, where there was sheltered deep water, was selected. Although there were doubts about the quantity of manpower available, construction work went ahead early in 1941 on an erection hangar, a component manufacturing building and a slipway on marshy land at White Cross Bay. Offices, a canteen and other sundry buildings completed the site.

Initially, the Windermere factory produced all the component parts of the Sunderland apart from engines and wings, which arrived from Rochester, but with the increasing risk of bombing there, duplication became necessary, and the trucks which brought the components took wing spars, engine nacelles and other parts back to Rochester. At its peak in 1942, 1,571 workers were employed at Windermere, 47% of whom were initially unskilled and had to be trained 'on the job'. In December 1941 conscription of women began, greatly easing the labour situation. At nearby Troutbeck Bridge, no less than 200 bungalows and a hostel to house the workers were completed by March 1942, with shops, a canteen, dance hall and a small school.

After the entry of Japan into the war and the subsequent increase in demand for reconnaissance aircraft, specification R.8/42 was issued for a more powerful long-range flying-boat. Short Bros submitted a design for the Sunderland Mk.IV, to be powered by four 1,700 hp Bristol Hercules XIX engines, with an improved hull, new tail configuration and heavier armament. As it was so different, the Mk.IV was renamed Seaford Mk.I. In the event, only ten were built, and none saw military service.

A requirement for greater power persisted, and the suggestion was made by

Four Sunderlands Mk.III on the hardstanding at Short Bros & Harland's Queen's Island factory, Belfast in 1944, including EJ168, EJ169 and EJ170. (V A Hodgkinson)

10 (RAAF) Squadron that the Sunderland could perhaps be powered by the reliable and ubiquitous 1,200 horsepower Pratt & Whitney R-1830-90 Twin Wasp engine. Trials carried out in March 1944 found that this version of the Sunderland had a significantly better climb factor and ceiling height than the Mk.III and could fly at cruising speed with two engines stopped on one side. Production of 154 aircraft as the Mk.V then went ahead at three sites, 60 being built at Dumbarton, 47 at Belfast and 47 at Rochester. In addition, 33 were modified from Mk.III aircraft. ASV radar Mk.III was fitted as standard to this Mark, which entered RAF service in February 1945, eventually becoming known as the Sunderland MR.5. In this form, the noble Sunderland remained in RAF service until May 1959, by which time it had been replaced by land-based aircraft such as the Neptune and Shackleton.

In 1944, the Windermere factory ceased production of Sunderlands, 35 of which had been built, and then concentrated on refurbishment work on 25 aircraft.

At the end of the Second World War the inevitable cancellation of many Sunderlands from production contracts took place, involving a total of 222 Sunderlands Mk.IV (Seafords) and 35 Sunderlands Mk.V.

Handling

Beaching a Sunderland was a tricky operation. The aircraft was moored to a buoy as close to the slipway as possible, and a pinnace stood by while the beaching gear was towed out by a dinghy. A gang of airmen stood on each side of the slipway, with one of them wearing a waterproof rubber suit and heavy boots ready to manhandle the huge chocks on the gear.

The beaching gear comprised a pair of twin-wheeled beams which carried cork flotation gear and a four-wheeled steerable trolley, which also floated, to support the tail. Attaching the gear to the hull of the Sunderland by special pins often demanded almost total immersion of at least one airman in cold and choppy water!

After the gear had been taken well below water level by means of the slipway, the pinnace crew attached a line to the nose of the Sunderland, which could then be slipped from its mooring. Until the aircraft was placed in a position opposite the cradle which would allow it to be drawn up, the pinnace was the only method of securing it. With the Sunderland poised above its beaching trolley, the waiting airmen could then gradually haul the heavy load towards the slipway by ropes.

From a mechanic's point of view, the Sunderland had many advantages, most particularly the easy accessibility of all services and the simple removal and replacement of sub-assemblies. Headroom was ample, and on the upper deck there was even a workbench. However, carrying out servicing on the engines of a Sun-

The 'Chariot' project

As part of the campaign to eliminate the German battleship *Admiral von Tirpitz*, experiments were carried out at Helensburgh, Dumbarton and Greenock into the possible use of two-man midget submarines. At the time, the was hiding in Asenfjord, near Trondheim in Norway, and an attempt was made in October 1942 to disable the ship by using midget submarines. Due to weather conditions, this failed, and so a scheme was hatched in which two of the midget submarines could be carried at night by a Sunderland to within ten miles (16 km) of the target, from where they would be launched to attach limpet mines to the hull of the battleship.

Each 'Chariot' was about 25 feet (7.6 m) long and weighed about 4,000 lbs (1.82 tonnes), very much more than a Sunderland was able to carry safely. The induced drag, method of release and available fuel were other factors to be considered. In the event, nothing came of this interesting attempt to overcome many problems, referred to at Rochester as the 'Large Lump' modification, but experiments continued almost to the end of the Second World War. The aircraft used was JM714, while four others, JM715 to JM718, were held in reserve at Wig Bay.

Short S.45 Seaford

Designed for military use, the Seaford was originally referred to as the Sunderland Mk.IV, although it was virtually a new design rather than a modified one. The tail unit was redesigned, the fuselage forward of the wings was lengthened by about three feet, a new planing bottom was incorporated and more powerful Bristol Hercules 130 engines were used.

All these factors combined to provide an aircraft suitable for use on the Empire routes. The resulting aircraft had seating for either 24 day-and-night passengers or 36 day passengers in six 'cabins', four on the lower deck and two on the upper. In the former case, during the day the lower cabins were used, the upper deck being used as a lounge and dining room, and both decks were converted to sleeping accommodation at night. Food and drinks were prepared in a spacious galley. The crew consisted of two pilots, navigator, radio operator, engineer and two stewards.

Technical specifications

Short S.25 Sunderland:

Mark I:
- Wingspan — 112 ft 8 in (34.35 m)
- Length — 85 ft 8 in (26.12 m)
- Height overall — 32 ft 10.5 in (10.01 m)
- Wing area, gross — 1,687 sq ft (156.73 sq m)
- Weight empty — 28,290 lbs (12859 kg)
- Max weight on take-off — 45,700 lbs (20772 kg)
- Maximum speed — 210 mph (338 kph)
- Cruising speed at 2,000 ft (609 m) — 178 mph (286 kph)
- Range at cruising speed — 2,880 mls (4,639 km)
- Service ceiling — 20,500 ft (6250 m)
- Fuel capacity — 1,720 galls with maximum bomb-load
- Engines —four Bristol Pegasus XXII (t/o rating 1,100 hp)

Mark II:
- Wingspan — 112 ft 8 in (34.35 m)
- Length — 85 ft 8 in (26.12 m)
- Height overall — 32 ft 10.5 in (10.01 m)
- Wing area, gross — 1,687 sq ft (156.73 sq m)
- Weight empty — 33,000 lbs (14,968 kg)
- Max weight on take-off — 58,000 lbs (26,308 kg)
- Maximum speed — 205 mph (330 kph)
- Cruising speed at 2,000 ft (609 m) — 144 mph (232 kph)
- Range at cruising speed — 1,780 mls (2,866 km)
- Service ceiling — 12,600 ft (3,841 m) at maximum weight
- Fuel capacity — 1,962 galls with maximum bomb-load
- Engines — four Bristol Pegasus XVIII (t/o rating 965 hp)

Mark III:
- Wingspan — 112 ft 9.5 in (34.39 m)
- Length — 85 ft 4 in (26.01 m)
- Height — 32 ft 10.5 in (10.01 m)
- Wing area, gross — 1,687 sq ft (156.73 sq m)
- Weight empty — 34,500 lbs (15,680 kg)
- Max weight on take-off — 58,000 lbs (26,308 kg)
- Maximum speed — 212 mph (341 kph)
- Cruising speed at 2,000 ft (609 m) — 143 mph (230 kph)
- Range at cruising speed — 2,880 mls (4,639 km)
- Service ceiling — 17,200 ft (5244 m)
- Fuel capacity — 1,862 galls with maximum bomb-load
- Engines — four Bristol Pegasus XVIII (t/o rating 965 hp)

Mark V:
- Wingspan — 112 ft 9.5 in (34.39 m)
- Length — 85 ft 3.5 in (26 m)
- Height — 32 ft 10.5 in (10.01 m)
- Wing area — 1,687 sq ft (156.73 sq m)
- Weight empty — 37,000 lbs (16,783 kg)
- Max weight on take-off — 60,000 lbs (27,273 kg)
- Landing weight — 47,500 lbs (21,591 kg)
- Maximum speed — 213 mph (343 kph)
- Cruising speed at 2,000 ft (609 m) — 133 mph (214 kph)
- Range at cruising speed — 1,880 mls (3,027 km)
- Service ceiling — 17,900 ft (5,457 m)
- Fuel capacity — 2,552 galls (5,614 litres) in 10 tanks
- Engines — four 1,200 hp P&W R-1830-90B/C/D Twin Wasp

CHAPTER 1 : DEVELOPMENT AND PRODUCTION

After four years' production of the type by Blackburn Aircraft Ltd at their Clyde Factory, Dumbarton, Sunderland Mk.V VB889 was the final one built by the company. Seen, left, on the slipway with the assembled workforce and, right, immediately following its launch on 19th October 1945 with the imposing Dumbarton Rock as a backdrop.

A Sunderland Mk.III ready for launching from the slipway at Short Bros' Windermere factory, almost certanly DP176, the first example to be completed there, in September 1942. (via Alan J King)

Sunderlands Mk.III under construction in the Windermere factory. (via Alan J King)

Sunderland armament

Mark I:
One (later two) 0.303-in (7.7 mm) machine guns in Nash & Thompson FN11 nose turret and four in FN13 tail turret; two 0.303-in (7.7 mm) Vickers 'K' gas-operated beam guns; bombs, depth charges, mines etc to total weight of 2,000 lbs (907 kg) carried on railed racks.

Mark II:
Two 0.303-in (7.7 mm) machine guns in Nash & Thompson FN7 dorsal turret, replacing the beam guns; two ditto in Fraser-Nash FN11 nose turret; four ditto in FN4a tail turret; bombs, depth charges, mines etc to total weight of 2,000 lbs (907 kg) carried on railed racks.

Mark III:
As Mk.II; later production also equipped with fixed guns in nose and side hatch guns; bombs, depth charges, mines etc to total weight of 2,000 lbs (907 kg) carried on railed racks.

A note in 201 Squadron's Operational Record Book in June 1944 states that the equipment of the unit's Mk.III Sunderlands was as follows: twelve 0.303-in (7.7 mm) fixed Browning guns - four fixed and two free firing forward, two in the mid-upper turret and four in the rear turret; two Vickers gas-operated 0.303 (7.7 mm) guns in the galley (one each side); and a free 0.5-in (12.7 mm) Browning firing forward. Bomb racks carried eight 250 lb (114 kg) Torpex depth charges Mk.I. In addition, 80 1.7-in (43 mm) flares were carried. A Mk.III low-level bombsight and ASV Mk.III were installed, and three dinghies provided some safety if the aircraft ditched.

Mk.V:
Two 0.303-in (7.7 mm) machine guns in Nash & Thompson FN11 nose turret and four in Nash & Thompson FN4a tail turret; two 0.5-in (12.7 mm) manually-operated beam guns; four remote-controlled Browning guns in bow (not always fitted); two-gun dorsal turret (later omitted

Short S.25 Sandringham:
Wingspan — 112 ft 9.5 in (34.39 m)
Length — 1: 85 ft 4 in (26.01 m)
2, 3, 5 and 7: 86 ft 3 in (26.3 m)
Height — 32 ft 10.5 in (10.01 m)
Wing area — 1,687 sq ft (156.73 sq m)
All-up weight — 1, 2 and 3: 56,000 lbs (25,454 kg)
5 and 7: 60,000 lbs (27,273 kg)
Maximum speed — 1: 216 mph (348 kph)
2 and 3: 238 mph (383 kph)
5 and 7: 206 mph (332 kph)
Range at cruising speed — 1: 2,550 mls (4,105 km)
2 and 3: 2,410 mls (3,880 km)
5 and 7: 2,440 mls (3,928 km)
Service ceiling — 1: 16,000 ft (4,878 m)
2 and 3: 21,300 ft (6,494 m)
5 and 7: 17,900 ft (5,457 m)
Engines — 1: four Bristol Pegasus 38
2, 4, 5, 6 and 7: four 1,200 hp P&W
R-1830-90B/C/D Twin Wasp

Short S.45 Seaford:
Wingspan — 112 ft 9.5 in (34.39 m)
Length — 88 ft 6.75 in (27 m)
Height — 34 ft 3.25 in (10.45 m)
Wing area — 1,687 sq ft (156.73 sq m)
Max weight on take-off — 75,000 lbs (34,091 kg)
Maximum speed — 242 mph (390 kph)
Range at cruising speed — 2,800 mls (4,508 km)
Service ceiling — 13,000 ft (3,963 m)
Fuel capacity — 2,916 galls (6,415 litres)
Engines — four Bristol Hercules 130

Short S.45 Solent:
Wingspan — 112 ft 9.5 in (34.39 m)
Length — 87 ft 8 in (26.73 m)
Height — 34 ft 3.25 in (10.45 m)
Wing area — 1,687 sq ft (156.73 sq m)
All-up weight: — 2: 78,000 lbs (35,454 kg)
3: 78,600 lbs (35,727 kg)
4: 81,000 lbs (36,818 kg)
Maximum speed — 2: 273 mph (440 kph)
3: 267 mph (430 kph)
4: 282 mph (454 kph)
Range at cruising speed — 2: 1,800 mls (2,898 km)
3: 2,190 mls (3,526 km)
4: 3,000 mls (4,830 km)
Service ceiling — 2: 17,000 ft (5,183 m)
3: 15,500 ft (4,726 m)
4: 17,100 ft (5,213 m)
Engines — 2 and 3: four Bristol Hercules 637
4: four Bristol Hercules 733

Left: Bomb racks inside a Sunderland loaded with depth charges which would be winched out of the hull sideways on rails for dropping.

Right: The Sunderland II was fitted with an FN7 two-gun dorsal turret. ASV aerials are visible on the top and side of the rear fuselage.
(via JM Collection)

CHAPTER 1 : DEVELOPMENT AND PRODUCTION

or removed); bombs, depth charges, mines etc to total weight of 2,000 lbs (907 kg) carried on railed racks.

Marine equipment

On the Sunderland Mk.V, rescue equipment consisted of a J-type dinghy in a blow-out compartment in the starboard wing and another in a valise usually located near the rear entrance door. Mooring facilities comprised a boat-hook, three drogues, a fog bell and a Mk.XIIa anchor attached by chain to a hand-operated winch. Other equipment included a crash axe stowed in the roof of the forward hull, leak stoppers and three first-aid outfits. For deliberate destruction of the aircraft, the crew had the use of two incendiary bombs stowed above the wireless operator's seat.

Sunderland MR.5 PP127 used for 1956 IFF and SARAH trials seen here at Short Bros & Harland Ltd Flight Shed at Sydenham on 16Jan56 along with Short Seamew AS.1s (XE172 ex RAF MR.2 trials, centre, and XE170, right) undergoing modifications and pre-service trials for the Royal Navy. (SB&H via Douglas Rough)

At Troutbeck Bridge Short Bros built an entire village, Calgarth Estate, to house an influx of workers for its Windermere factory. (via Alan J King)

Erection of the production hangar at Short Bros' Windermere site began in May 1941. (via Alan J King)

The production hangar at Windermere on 3rd June 1942. The first Sunderland built there was delivered that September. (via Alan J King)

Engine mechanics servicing a Sunderland at its moorings, demonstrating the difficult conditions in which these airmen often had to work. *(via Guy Warner)*

Looking forward from the aft interior of a Sunderland Mk.V. *(V A Hodgkinson)*

The hull of the Sunderland was nothing if not spacious, as demonstrated by the presence of the two RAF personnel in this picture.

CHAPTER 1 : DEVELOPMENT AND PRODUCTION

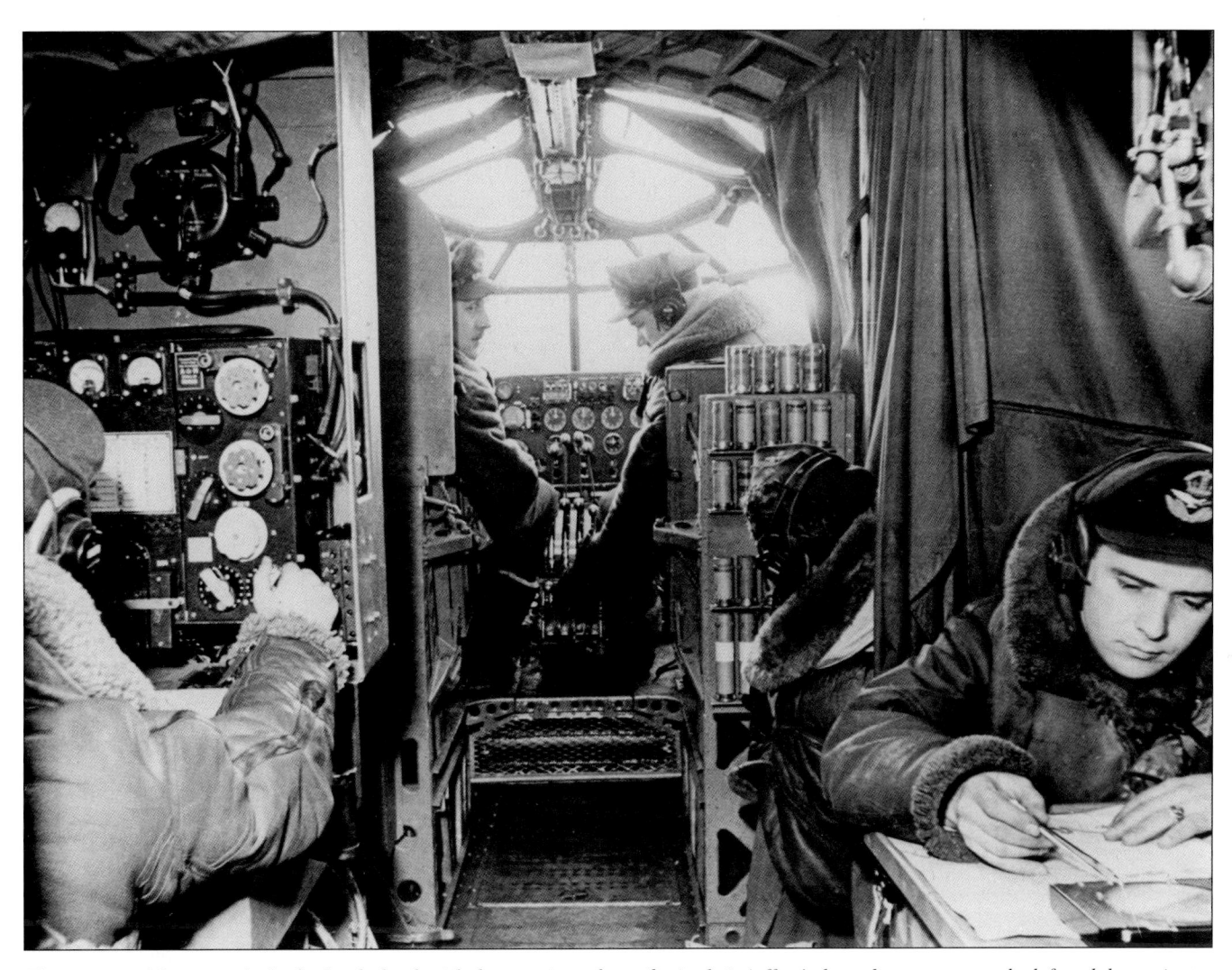

The interior of the upper deck of a Sunderland, with the captain and co-pilot in their 'office', the radio operator on the left and the navigator on the right, facing aft. (via Guy Warner)

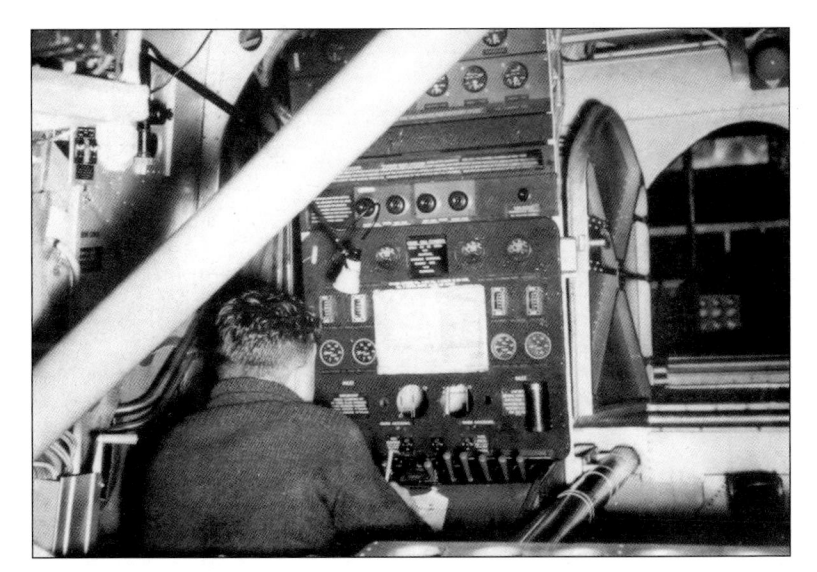

The radio operator's station in a Sunderland Mk.V. (V A Hodgkinson)

Viewed from the rear, this photograph appears to show a civilian instructor explaining the workings of a dorsal turret on a Sunderland Mk.II to three airmen. The aircraft may have been a Ground Instructional airframe. (P H T Green collection)

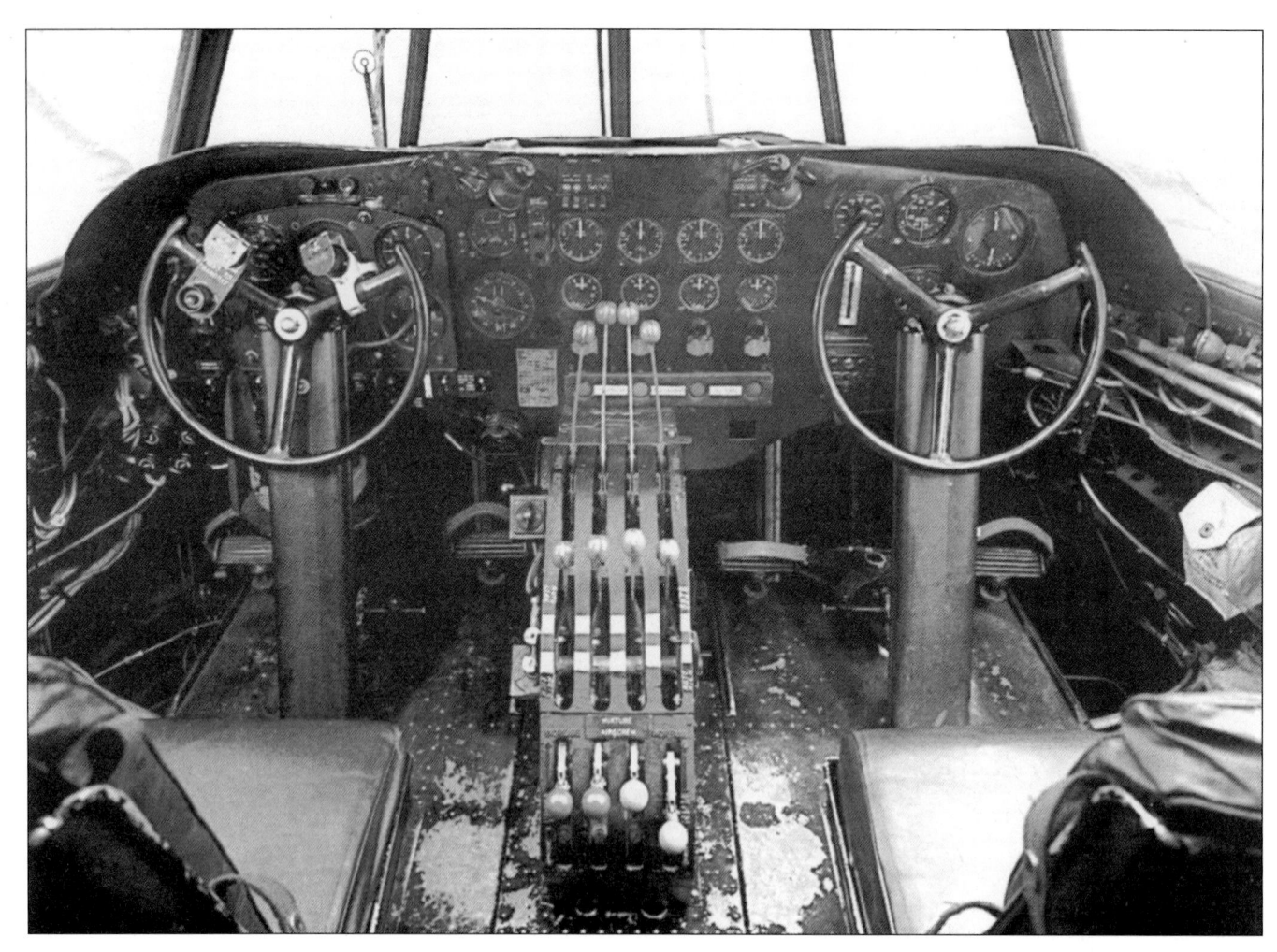

A view of the flight deck of a Sunderland Mk.V. (F Denyer via John Evans)

A BOAC radio officer encoding a message at his station in a Sunderland Mk.III

Sunderland production

Serials	Mark	c/n	Built at/by	Contract No.	Qty.	Remarks
K4774		S.803	Short Bros, Rochester	351564/34	1	Prototype
L2158-2168	I	S.860-870	ditto	533317/36	1	
L5798-5807	I	S.887-896	ditto	ditto	10	
N6133	I	S.897	ditto	774293/38	1	
N6135	I	S.898	ditto	ditto	1	
N6138	I	S.899	ditto	ditto	1	
N9020-9030	I	S.1004-1014	ditto	ditto	11	
N9044-9050	I	S.1015-1021	ditto	ditto	7	
P9600-9606	I	S.1028-1034	ditto	B.985038/39	7	
P9620-9624	I	S.1035-1039	ditto	ditto	5	
T9040-9050	I	S.1140-1150	ditto	B.18347/39	11	
T9070-9078	I	S.1151-1159	ditto	ditto	9	
T9083-9090	II	—	Blackburn Aircraft, Dumbarton	B.37753/39	8	
T9109-9115	II	—	ditto	ditto	7	
W3976-3998	II	S.1160-1182	Short Bros, Rochester	B.78939/40	23	Tfd from B.18347/39
W3999-4004	III	S.1183-1188	ditto	ditto	6	
W4017-4037	III	S.1189-1209	ditto	ditto	21	
W6000-6004	II	—	Blackburn Aircraft, Dumbarton	B.37753/39	5	
W6005-6016	III	—	ditto	ditto	12	
W6026-6033	III	—	ditto	ditto	8	
W6050-6064	II	SH.51-65	Short & Harland, Belfast	B.76674/40	15	
W6065-6068	III	SH.66-69	ditto	ditto	4	
W6075-6080	III	SH.70-75	ditto	ditto	6	
DD828-867	III	—	Blackburn Aircraft, Dumbarton	B.37753/40/C.20(b)	40	
DP176-200	III	—	Short Bros, Windermere	234/SAS/40/C20(b)	25	
DV956-980	III	—	Short Bros, Rochester	B.78939/40	25	
DV985-994	III	(see Chap 4)	Short & Harland, Belfast	B.76674/40	10	
DW104-113	III	(see Chap 4)	ditto	ditto	10	
EJ131-145	III	—	Short Bros, Rochester	B78939/40	15	
EJ149-158	III	—	Short Bros, Windermere	234/SAS/40/C20(b)	10	
EJ163-172	III	(see Chap 4)	Short & Harland, Belfast	B.76674/40	10	
EK572-596	III	—	Blackburn Aircraft, Dumbarton	B.37753/39	25	
JM659-689	III	—	Short Bros, Rochester	B.78939/40/C20(b)	31	
JM704-722	III	—	ditto	ditto	19	
ML725-774	III	—	ditto	Acft.2538	50	
ML777-795	III	—	ditto	Acft.2226	19	
ML796-801	V	—	ditto	Acft.2226	6	
ML807-831	III	(see Chap 4)	Short & Harland, Belfast	Acft.2227	25	
ML835-884	III	—	Blackburn Aircraft, Dumbarton	Acft.2228	50	
MZ269	IV	—	Short Bros, Rochester	Acft.2551	1	Seaford proto.
MZ271	IV	—	ditto	ditto	1	
NJ170-194	III	—	Blackburn Aircraft, Dumbarton	Acft.2228	25	
NJ200-207	IV	S.1292-1299	Short Bros, Rochester	Acft.2688	8	
NJ253-258	III	(see Chap 4)	Short Bros & Harland, Belfast	Acft.2227	6	NJ258 built as V
NJ259-277	V	(see Chap 4)	ditto	ditto	19	
PP103-132	V	—	Short Bros, Rochester	Acft.2226	30	
PP135-144	III	—	Blackburn Aircraft, Dumbarton	Acft.2228	10	
PP145-164	V	—	ditto	ditto	20	
RN264-273	V	—	Short Bros, Rochester	Acft.2226	10	
RN277-306	V	—	Blackburn Aircraft, Dumbarton	Acft.2228	30	
SZ559-584	V	(see Chap 4)	Short Bros & Harland, Belfast	Acft.4067	26	
SZ598, 599	V	(see Chap 4)	ditto	ditto	2	
TX293	V	—	Short Bros, Rochester	Acft.2226	1	
VB880-889	V	—	Blackburn Aircraft, Dumbarton	Acft.2228	10	
					Total 759	

The following Sunderlands were cancelled:

Serials	Mark	c/n	Built at/by	Contract No.	Qty.	Remarks
AX936-950	II	—	Short Bros, Rochester	B.78939/40	(15)	
AX973-997	II	—	ditto	ditto	(15)	
NE836-855	III	—	Short Bros, Rochester	Acft.2226	(20)	
NJ208-229	IV	—	Short Bros, Rochester	Acft.2688	(22)	Canx 6.10.45
NJ240-249	IV	—	Short Bros, Rochester	ditto	(10)	
NN941-990	IV	—	Blackburn Aircraft, Dumbarton	Acft.2828	(50)	
NP100-149	IV	—	Blackburn Aircraft, Dumbarton	ditto	(50)	
RN244-263	III	—	Short Bros, Rochester	Acft.2226	(20)	
SZ600-631	V	—	Short Bros & Harland, Belfast	Acft.4067	(32)	Canx 21.8.45
TK440-468	IV	—	Short Bros, Rochester	Acft.4287	(29)	
TK482-512	IV	—	Short Bros, Rochester	Acft.4287	(31)	
TW774-803	IV	—	Blackburn Aircraft, Dumbarton	Acft.3294	(30)	
TX294-296	V	—	Short Bros, Rochester	Acft.2226	(3)	
					Total 327	

A Biederman tractor unit of the USAAF, based at Langford Lodge airfield, hauling a Sunderland hull in Bradbury Place, Belfast on its way to Eastwood's scrap yard in Stockman's Lane. The hull was coded [YI:G] and thus was an aircraft of 423 Squadron, but which one is open to conjecture. The tramcar is on the route between Balmoral and Castle Junction, Belfast. *(via Noel Lynch)*

An evocative scene at Short Bros & Harland Ltd in June 1957. The five Sunderlands on the left, including one coded [NS:B] ex 201 Squadron, are destined for scrap. Four more, parked between the hangars, belong to the Aéronautique navale, while yet another five are visible over the bridge including one Seaford, the second prototype MZ271. *(via Noel Lynch)*

Sunderland I L5806 was delivered to the RAF in late 1938 and served pre-war with 228 Squadron operating from Pembroke Dock.
(via JM Collection)

Chapter 2
OPERATIONAL OVERVIEW

The outbreak of the Second World War

At the outbreak of war in September 1939, Coastal Command, under its AOC-in-C Air Chief Marshal Sir Frederick W Bowhill KCB CMG DSO, was something of a 'Cinderella' force within the Royal Air Force. Its equipment was generally obsolescent, and of its six squadrons of flying-boats only three, 204 at Mount Batten and 210 and 228 at Pembroke Dock, all under 15 Group, were operating the modern Sunderland. The primary task at that time was to maintain reconnaissance of the North Sea for surface vessels, which were expected to mount attacks on shipping bringing vital supplies to British ports, rather than submarines (U-boats). These enemy raiders would have to navigate through the North Sea on their way from Germany to the open waters of the North Atlantic, whether they then continued on a northerly heading to pass north of Scotland or south-westerly to run through the English Channel; in either case, the thinking was that they could be dealt with.

Patrols over the North Sea began, in fact, on 24th August 1939, three days after the heavy cruiser *Graf Spee* left Wilhelmshaven. The heavy cruiser *Deutschland* (later *Lützow*) also sailed before hostilities began, hiding in fog which kept RAF aircraft on the ground. Bad weather in September hindered the hunt for the battleships *Scharnhorst* and *Gneisenau*, and on only two days could the flying-boat crews at Pembroke Dock even reach their moored aircraft. In addition to the routine patrols, Coastal Command aircraft were soon involved in protecting east coast convoys, in cooperation with Fighter Command. In November, however, a serious threat became apparent in the form of the magnetic mine, laid by enemy aircraft and submarines. This problem was very rapidly dealt with by specially-equipped Wellington aircraft, but the U-boats themselves were quickly becoming a real menace, particularly in the Atlantic Ocean west of the British Isles.

This area was hardly covered by Coastal Command aircraft, which were all needed for the North Sea operations, and as the convoy system was not yet in use the scale of losses of shipping trying to reach Britain mounted alarmingly. Destroyers were unable to escort merchant vessels from further west than 13 degrees (about 300 miles or 480 km west of the Scilly Isles), and few aircraft were able to carry out this task beyond about 100 miles (160 km) west of the Scilly Isles (about 8.5 degrees west). The Royal Navy stepped into the breach with the aircraft carriers HMS *Ark Royal* and HMS *Courageous*, but when the latter was sunk by U-29 on 17th September 1939 with two squadrons of Swordfish aboard, that assistance ended.

The convoy system soon settled into a routine, however, and by October 1939 the range of convoy-escorting aircraft had increased to about 200 miles (320 km). Patrols over the North Sea had become highly successful, and the whereabouts of most enemy U-boats were being recorded. No effective attacks on the U-boats were yet possible, however, as the 250 lb (114 kg) anti-submarine bombs carried by the Mk.I Sunderlands could only inflict much damage if they burst within six feet (two metres) of the pressure hull of the vessel. Weaponry carried by land-based aircraft such as Ansons was even less effective. In December 1939, therefore, work began on developing depth charges suitable for dropping from the air.

By April 1940, due largely to the efforts of the Royal Navy, the situation in the North Sea and North Atlantic appeared to be under control, although U-boats were still a greater menace than expected.

Coastal Command continued to experience great difficulties caused by the persistent shortage of modern aircraft, a problem compounded by the failure of the Saro Lerwick flying-boat to come up to expectations. However, the Command was by then in the process of developing its own anti-U-boat strategies rather than continuing to be employed by the Navy for purely reconnaissance purposes.

July 1940's Order of Battle showed that 15 Group was controlling two squadrons of Sunderlands: 10 (RAAF) Squadron at Mount Batten and 210 Squadron at Oban. 18 Group, meanwhile, had 201 and 204 Squadrons at Sullom Voe — still only four UK-based squadrons, which were not enough to counter the growing threat to inbound merchant vessels, let alone to ships of the Royal Navy.

In addition, in October 1940 RAF Coastal Command was given the task of making strikes on enemy coastal convoys between Scandinavian ports and Germany and Holland, as well as blockade-runners in the English Channel. These operations were, however, carried out by land-based aircraft.

Overall responsibility for the anti-submarine campaign was given to the C-in-C Western Approaches, Admiral Sir Percy Noble, in February 1941, and 15 Group was subordinated to his new headquarters at Liverpool. In March the Luftwaffe formed several specialist units in France, flying Fw 200 Condor reconnaissance aircraft which would cooperate with the German Navy's U-boats in an all-out effort to wreak havoc among Britain-bound convoys of merchant ships.

In June, Air Marshal Sir Phillip B Joubert de la Ferté KCB CMG DSO took over as C-in-C Coastal Command, almost coinciding with a switch in tactics by the Wehrmacht, which was becoming more deeply involved with the war on the Eastern Front. A relative lull then developed in the Battle of the Atlantic, allowing Coastal Command some time to reinforce its fleet of land and sea aircraft and to develop more effective techniques. A major problem was that existing aircraft based in Northern Ireland or Iceland could not reach a point further than 27 degrees west, leaving an uncovered area of ocean 700 miles (1125 km) wide east of Newfoundland. If convoys took a route further south, the 'Atlantic Gap' became the 'Azores Gap', which was 1,250 miles (2,010 km) wide, where U-boats could operate with impunity as there was no air cover.

Based at Bathurst in The Gambia in 1941 and 1943, 95 Squadron was equipped with Mk.III Sunderlands of which [C] was one. (P H T Green collection)

Losses among convoys sailing north near the coast of West Africa were by now a serious problem, and in an attempt to counteract the U-boats involved, 95 Squadron's Sunderlands were moved to the area. Reinforcement later by 204 Squadron and by Hudson land-based aircraft ensured that a degree of success was attained, and the threat diminished somewhat.

Early in 1942, German U-boats began carrying a device known as Metox 600A (FuMB1), which enabled the operator to pick up transmissions of ASV Mk.II at a range of 40 miles (64 km), ample to allow the U-boat to crash-dive. In June of that year the 311 active U-boats sank 144 Allied ships, and in July Admiral Doenitz ordered them to concentrate in packs beyond the range of Allied aircraft in the 'Atlantic Gap'. At the same time, the first new IXD-2 U-boats sailed for South African waters to deal with convoys moving round the Cape of Good Hope.

In October 1942, a detachment of 210 Squadron Sunderlands was sent from Pembroke Dock to Gibraltar to join those of 202 Squadron in the work-up to Operation 'Torch', the invasion of northwest Africa. These squadrons then took part in the constant air patrols being made over the western Mediterranean.

The primary task of Coastal Command squadrons, however, remained that of carrying out anti-U-boat patrols over the Atlantic Ocean, the Bay of Biscay and between the Faeroe Islands and Norway. To counter the Metox equipment in U-boats, 10 cm ASV Mks.III and IV came into use in 1943, although for some time Coastal Command had to wait for it, as Bomber Command (to which it was known as H2S) had priority for supplies. This equipment successfully made Metox useless. Sunderlands Mk.III of 10 (RAAF) and 461 Squadrons made their first kills: *U-332* on 2nd May and *U-109* five days later.

On 24th May 1943, after the Kriegsmarine had suffered many U-boat losses to an increasing number of Coastal Command aircraft, Admiral Doenitz ordered the submarines to move from their North Atlantic patrol areas either to base or to the southern area. That day was crucial in winning or losing the Battle of the Atlantic: two months after sinking 21 ships in convoy HX.229 for the loss of one U-boat, Germany had almost handed over the initiative to Coastal Command and the Royal Navy.

Russia convoys

The first British convoy sailed to Russia on 21st August 1941, and others followed in September and October. Known as PQ convoys, they usually sailed west of Iceland through the Denmark Straits, round northern Norway and thence south to Murmansk or Archangel. During the first 150 miles (240 km) of the voyage they were shadowed by land-based aircraft from Iceland, but after that they were on their own. To counter the threat of German attacks on Murmansk, two squadrons of Hurricane fighters were despatched to Russia.

Up to the end of 1941 the enemy made little effort to interfere with the PQ convoys, relying instead on Russia's imminent defeat. Early in 1942, however, a change of tactic came about, and ships in the convoys began to fall victim to U-boats. In late May Sunderlands and flying-boats of the US Navy from Iceland failed to prevent heavy losses to convoy PQ16. After sailing from Iceland on 27th June, convoy PQ17 also came under heavy attack, with the loss of 23 of 37 vessels, survivors being picked from the sea by Catalinas based in Russia.

CHAPTER 2 : OPERATIONAL OVERVIEW

Sunderland Mk.II W3986 [RB:U] of No.10 (RAAF) Squadron was delivered in April 1942. The Squadron operated from Mount Batten and was tasked with patrol of the Western Approaches. Note background and ASV aerials removed by censor. (Crown RTP 10836B via P H Butler)

As at 15th February 1943, 15 Group controlled 201, 228, 246, 330, 422 and 423 Squadrons of Sunderlands, while 19 Group's Sunderland squadrons were 10 (RAAF), 119 and 461. Coastal Command's C-in-C from 5th February was Air Marshal Sir John C Slessor KCB DSO MC. In the Middle East 230 Squadron came under the control of 201 Group. By now, the Allies realised that the war could not be won until the U-boat menace was dealt with. In March at the Atlantic Convoys Conference in Washington DC a new system of convoy routes and escorts was mooted but not adopted, probably as it would have required a greater level of cooperation between the UK and the USA than was possible. At the time, the USA was more intent on the war in the Pacific than the Atlantic.

However, the Kriegsmarine was by now experiencing heavy opposition, and in May 1943 it recorded that losses to its U-boats had "....reached an impossible height." Admiral Doenitz then withdrew temporarily the remaining U-boat force from the North Atlantic to the relatively secure waters of the Bay of Biscay. The battle then intensified in that area, and when equipped with centimetric ASV radar and the Leigh Light, Coastal Command squadrons were able to locate and attack U-boats at any hour of the day or night. An area of sea 300 miles by 120 miles (480 x 190 km) had to be negotiated by 80% of the U-boats travelling to the north Atlantic from their French bases. It was found that they no longer crash-dived on being found by a Coastal Command aircraft, but remained on the surface to defend themselves with 37mm anti-aircraft cannon and 20mm heavy machine guns. This ploy was highly dangerous to an attacking aircraft such as a Sunderland, which was obliged to make a straight and steady run in order to drop its depth charges effectively. As a counter-measure, 10 (RAAF) Squadron Sunderlands were fitted with four additional .303 in. (7.7 mm) machine guns in the nose, and this idea was soon taken up by other Sunderland squadrons.

Then another device, the Schnorkel breathing tube, began to be fitted to U-boats, allowing them to remain below the surface of the water (and thus difficult to see with the naked eye) while battery-charging took place. This equipment undoubtedly helped the U-boat force to avoid many patrolling aircraft, but in September 1944, after the invasion of Normandy, all U-boats still in French ports were ordered to sail to Norway. At the end of the year a considerable effort by Coastal Command land-based aircraft was put into preventing newly-built larger U-boats equipped with Schnorkel from staging a last-ditch campaign. As part of this, aircraft of RAF Bomber Command and the US 8th Air Force successfully raided shipyards in Germany where U-boats were under construction.

This Sunderland Mk.V has just touched down somewhere in the Far East and a launch is about to begin the transfer of mail to HMS Belfast *in the left foreground.* (R C Sturtivant collection)

Air Chief Marshal Sir W Sholto Douglas KCB MC DFC took over as C-in-C Coastal Command on 20 January 1944 and remained in the post during the final days of hostilities.

D-Day, 6th June 1944

Although the number of Sunderlands available to Coastal Command at the time of the Allied invasion of Europe was substantial, only five took part in Operation 'Overlord'. The squadrons involved were 10 (RAAF), which fielded JM721; 201, which used ML760; 228, with ML763; and 461, which put up ML735 and ML747. At the time, 10 Squadron was based at Mount Batten, while the others were all at Pembroke Dock. For 201 Squadron, aided by 461 Squadron's ML747, 6th June was a highly satisfactory day, as the radar operators in ML760 spotted a U-boat after being in the air for just an hour. Six 250 lb (114 kg) Torpex depth charges eventually put paid to the U-boat, the squadron's first success of the year.

In the Far East

Flying-boats had long been an important factor in RAF operations in the Far East, due to the few land airfields available and to the fact that there were large numbers of suitable sheltered alighting areas around coastlines.

Before the outbreak of the Second World War, one squadron based in the Far East, 230, had started to equip with Sunderlands in June 1938. As soon as war in Europe was declared, they began patrolling the Malay Straits and Indian Ocean, but in February 1940 moved to Ceylon and in May to the Mediterranean, where their services were more urgently required.

By 1943, enemy submarines, both Japanese and German, were using Penang in Malaya as a base for anti-shipping operations. By that time, the Allies were making plans for a build-up during 1944, and an increased anti-submarine campaign was therefore instigated. The AOC-in-C Far East had ten squadrons of flying-boats at his disposal in the Indian Ocean, only one of which was flying Sunderlands. 230 Squadron was then moved from Dar-es-Salaam to Koggala in Ceylon and, with two Catalina squadrons, flew many anti-submarine sorties. By that time, however, it was believed that only two enemy vessels were still operating in the Indian Ocean.

In the spring of 1944, Allied troops advanced into Burma, and 230 Squadron played an important part in carrying supplies and evacuating the wounded. A second unit, 209 Squadron, re-equipped with Sunderlands in February 1945, and that summer saw 240 Squadron following suit. At the end of hostilities in August 1945, however, the Sunderlands were stripped of armaments and switched to courier and freight missions. To increase this role, 1430 Flight was formed in 1946 and was soon enlarged into a new 88 Squadron. Further reorganisation in 1946 resulted in the disbandment of 240 Squadron and an increase in the establishment of 230 Squadron.

Operation 'Firedog', the campaign against insurgents fighting under the banner of the Malayan Races Liberation Army, began in September 1948, and the surviving Sunderland squadrons (88, 205 and 209) made a useful contribution to the efforts of the combined services by dropping anti-personnel bombs. The Sunderland's long 'loiter' period over targets was seen as very useful.

Within a few days of the outbreak of the Korean War in June 1950, Sunderlands based at Seletar in Singapore were despatched to Iwakuni in Japan, primarily to patrol United Nations convoy routes. Working in close cooperation with Mariner flying-boat squadrons of the US Navy, the Sunderland crews also made weather reconnaissance flights and searched for enemy minefields off the east coast of Korea and for ditched aircrews, flying an average of eight sorties per week. When amphibious forces of the UN launched an attack on Inchon, flying-boat operations were increased from night-time reconnaissance flights three times each week to a full 24-hour watch on the approaches to Korea.

The Korean War ended in February 1954, after which the Sunderland squadrons began anti-piracy patrols and other ad hoc sorties, but the era of the flying-boat was clearly coming to an end, and 88 Squadron disbanded in October of that year. 209 Squadron was absorbed by 205 Squadron in January 1955, and this, the sole Sunderland unit, continued to fly maritime patrol missions until disbanding in May 1959, when Avro Shackleton landplanes began to arrive in the Far East to take over the task.

The Mediterranean area

Having been the first squadron to operate Sunderlands overseas (in the Far East), 230 Squadron moved to Alexandria in Egypt in May 1940, a month or so before Italy declared war on Great Britain. Prior to 230's arrival, 228 Squadron had been

An RAF marine craft speeds away after delivering the crew to a moored Sunderland [A] on Lough Erne (via Guy Warner)

present for a time at Alexandria and in Malta, but had returned to the UK, where its presence was considered to be of more use. However, 228 Squadron did make further appearances in the Mediterranean from time to time to augment 230 Squadron's almost lone efforts.

Patrols were flown from several detached operating bases, including Suda Bay in Crete and Lake Eleusis in Greece, but these bases rapidly became redundant when German forces invaded Greece and then Crete. The Sunderlands did, however, play a significant part in the evacuation of Allied troops from those areas.

The use of Sunderlands in the Mediterranean area came to an end in January 1943, when 230 Squadron moved to Dar-es-Salaam in East Africa.

A typical operational sortie

Details of a typical operational sortie were recalled by Mr P J Christopher, a former Sunderland captain in 95 Squadron at Bathurst in The Gambia.

After an early call in darkness, the crew was taken by truck from their quarters to the moorings at Half Die. There the men enjoyed breakfast in the mess, often tinned bacon, tomatoes and eggs, collected their flying rations for the long flight, and were briefed on the type of patrol, the signals to be used and the weather forecast. Then came a walk to the jetty to board a dinghy which took the crew to the waiting Sunderland, which was moored a few hundred yards away. After boarding by means of a door on the port side, they took up their positions and carried out routine checks.

Seating on the flight-deck for the captain (port side) and second pilot was roomy and comfortable. The wireless operator sat behind the captain, the navigator at his table behind the second pilot and the engineer behind him at his instrument panel.

The front turret was now wound back, usually by the gunner, who would use a

CHAPTER 2 : OPERATIONAL OVERVIEW

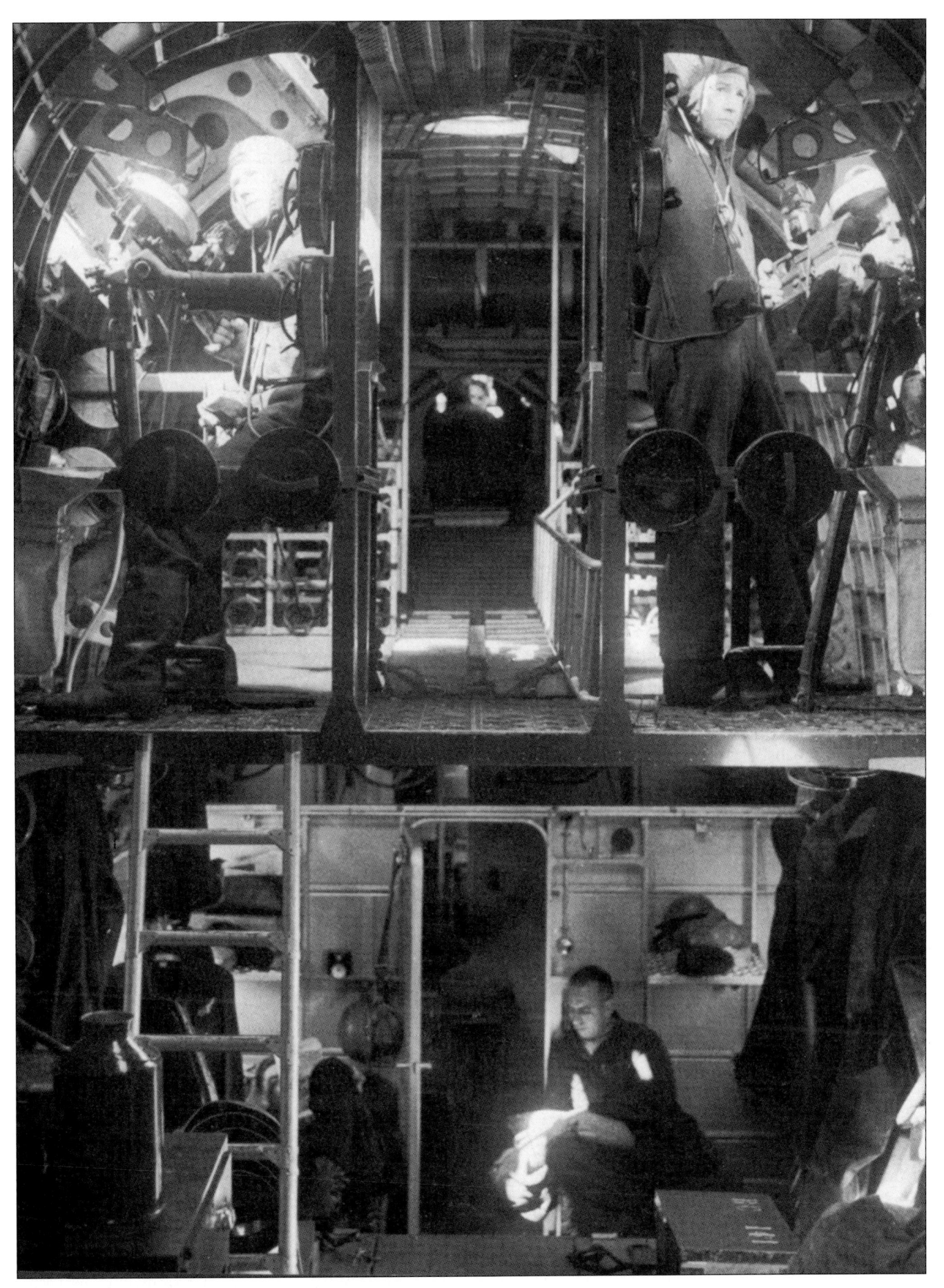

A wartime publicity photograph illustrating, or simulating, a Sunderland Mk.II crew on a patrol mission, showing on the upper deck of the mid-fuselage the waist gun positions manned by observers/gunners with their .303 Vickers gas-operated weapons at the ready. On the lower deck two crew members relax in the aft wardroom prior to taking their turn on watch or to handle the bombs and depth charges which were reached through the doorway between their bunks.
(via JM Collection)

boat-hook to haul in the straps on the buoy. These were unshackled and a short slip passed over the front bollard to hold the aircraft temporarily. When ready, the outer engines were started and left to tick over so that the aircraft did not pull on the buoy. The short slip was released and the Sunderland taxied forward, avoiding the buoy, which could cause damage to the hull. Then the front turret was wound back to the closed position, the inner engines were started and the aircraft taxied while the engines warmed up. All engines were then opened up fully and the magnetos checked by switching off individually. If there was no significant drop on the instruments, all was in order.

Ensuring that all hatches were closed, the crew turned the aircraft into wind and carried out final checks, for example one-third flaps for take-off. Ideal sea conditions were considered to be a 5 or 10 knot wind, which would break the water surface; a glassy calm acted like glue, making it more difficult to become airborne, especially with a heavy load. The Sunderland turned into wind automatically, as the large rudder produced a 'weather-cock' action. With the control column hard back, the outer engines were opened to full throttle, followed by the inners when the nose had risen and the spray had cleared, as spray could damage the propellers. Any swing to one side was controlled by throttling back slightly on one outer engine until rudder control was gained. When the Sunderland attained planing attitude (skimming the surface) take-off occurred at 75-85 knots. The aircraft then climbed at 200 feet per minute at about 105 knots up to our 2000 feet cruising height. Radio silence was maintained at all times. Although the aircraft was fitted with 'George' (the automatic pilot), it was seldom used as it was unreliable.

If the mission was to escort a convoy, which might be an hour or so from base, the Sunderland crew would identify their aircraft to one of the escort ships by Aldis lamp, a wireless operator/gunner usually signalling through the captain's sliding window. The Sunderland then set off on its defensive patrol, during which the crew members would change position every hour or so for a rest, while those on watch would spend their time searching the sea for any signs of enemy activity.

Navigation was by 'dead reckoning' based on a compass course modified by ever-variable wind speed and direction. The wind could be calculated at intervals according to the drift of the aircraft, obtained by using a drift sight in the front turret or by watching the white caps on the waves or yet again by smoke or flame floats dropped from the aircraft and measured from the rear turret. Radio or ASV bearings could be taken by the wireless operator, and the flight engineer kept watch on the instruments on his panel and switched from empty to full fuel tanks as necessary.

During the patrol, someone would supply food and tea from the galley amidships on the lower deck, which was equipped with three Primus hobs and a small stove. Close by were opening hatches, one on each side, which were useful for photography or when the crew wanted to catch fish while moored! Forward of the galley was a toilet with basin and mirror and a wardroom containing a bunk on each side and a portable table. Behind the galley was a vast open space, above which were eight depth charges and a hatch on each side for use when the DCs were run out under the wings. The rear gunner in his turret had a more remote position.

After several hours on patrol, the Sunderland returned to the convoy to signal its departure. When base was reached, the aircraft would land into wind (often identified by wind lanes on the water) or on the night flare-path, taxi to the buoy and switch off the inner engines. The outers were used for manoeuvrability until the aircraft drew up to the buoy on the port side. Mooring was sometimes tricky as the Sunderland could be affected by wind and tide. To assist in slowing down or guiding the aircraft, drogues, which were a sort of bucket on the end of a rope, could be slung out of the galley hatches. Depending on the relative strength of wind and tide, it was sometimes easy to miss the buoy with the boat-hook, which meant going round and through the whole process again, a frustrating and tiring process after a ten-hour sortie. Finally, when the engines were switched off and silence returned, all hatches were closed and the crew waited for the dinghy to take them to dry land for debriefing, a cooked meal and the truck to their quarters.

A Sunderland Mk.V of 201 Squadron coded [NS:Z] about to become airborne. This may be the aircraft which made the last official patrol of the war on 3-4 June 1945, ML778, or the example now preserved at Hendon, ML824, both of which carried this code in service. (via Guy Warner)

A Sunderland GR.5 of 88 Squadron at its moorings at Kai Tak. The fuel hose is being taken out to the aircraft by dinghy.
(P H T Green collection)

Chapter 3
OPERATING UNITS

PART 1: ROYAL AIR FORCE

88 Squadron

Unit code: (nil)

A late-comer to the Sunderland, 88 Squadron was re-formed at Kai Tak (Hong Kong) on 1st September 1946 from 1430 (Flying Boat Transport) Flight, itself formed only a month earlier to fly courier flights between bases in the Far East. The new squadron carried on these duties, using six Sunderland GR.5s flown by six crews who were tasked with providing a twice-weekly service to Iwakuni, a former Japanese Navy base on Honshu in Japan. Within days, however, a typhoon warning prompted the departure of three of the Sunderlands to the US Navy base at Okinawa, where crews were lodged on the depot ship USS *Salisbury Sound* overnight. Another typhoon warning was issued on 25th September and five of the aircraft moved to Seletar (Singapore), although due to fuel shortage one diverted to the Aéronautique navale base at Saigon in what was then Indo-China.

Affiliation with Seafires of the Fleet Air Arm took place twice in October 1946, the fighter pilots expressing some surprise at the Sunderland's manoeuvrability.

Still maintaining the transport service, the squadron fitted NJ272 with VIP seating, and the first passenger to make use of this improvement was Lord Tedder, the Chief of the Air Staff, on 28th November 1946. Just before Christmas, the CO, Wg Cdr Van der Kiste, took NJ272 to Iwakuni with the seasonal mail, but had to alight at Okinawa due to strong winds. This time, the crew were accommodated on the USS *Onslow*, but NJ272 developed a fault and the men spent Christmas at Okinawa.

Search and rescue also played a part in 88 Squadron's work. On 12th January 1947 a Sunderland was placed on alert after a C-46 Commando force-landed on a beach and a C-54 Skymaster ditched north of Luzon in the Philippines, but as all aboard were safe the search was called off. A missing Dakota of 48 Squadron was the subject of a search by RN297 on 28th February but bad weather forced a halt after three hours. Flt Lt Thomas, on his way to Iwakuni on 24th March 1947, encountered freak weather and so touched down on a lake at Miho, in the north of Honshu Island, where he disembarked the passengers for the night before refuelling. Next day the flight was completed safely. Another forced landing was made by the crew of SZ566, which alighted in Senzaki Bay on the north coast of Honshu on 7th May, again due to weather conditions. On that occasion the crew spent a night on board. Ten days later NJ272 alighted on the Inland Sea, 16 miles (25.5 km) from Iwakuni and completed the journey by taxying all the way!

Dummy attacks on HM submarines *Auriga* and *Affray* were made on 6th May 1947, but the transport operation continued, the 100th flight to Iwakuni taking place on 12th August 1947. However, demand for this service was decreasing, and it came to an end on 4th April 1948. 88 Squadron's Sunderlands had carried 2,368 passengers, 202,779 lbs (92.2 tonnes) of mail and 200,270 lbs (91 tonnes) of freight.

On 4th May 1948 a company of Sikh troops was flown to Castle Park Bay in Hong Kong to assist in an operation against armed pirates. As the squadron's transport days were now over, maritime matters became the main function. On 17th July 1948 Flt Lt Cosgrove's crew

Sunderland GR.5 ML772 [D] of 88 Squadron on the Whang Poo River in China on 24th April 1949 at the time of the Yangtze incident involving HMS Amethyst. *(P H T Green collection)*

Crew boarding a Sunderland GR.5 of 88 Squadron in preparation for a patrol over the Yellow Sea during the Korean War.

communist Chinese territory. Pilot and aircraft were picked up by HMS *Belfast*, with the help of 88 Squadron. On 18th March 1949 88 Squadron carried out its first bombing exercise since reverting to a maritime role.

88 Squadron's major claim to fame was its involvement in the Yangtze incident in April 1949. The frigate HMS *Amethyst* had been trapped on the Yangtze River by Chinese communists, and doctors and medical supplies were urgently needed. Sunderland GR.5 ML772 of 88 Squadron (with squadron letter D removed) was detailed to carry out the mission, and took off from Kai Tak on the morning of 21st April, carrying the Station Commander, Gp Capt J M Jefferson, two RAF doctors and two soldiers, but was diverted to Lung Wha, Shanghai, when it was found that the ship was under fire. This remained the case in the afternoon, but nevertheless ML772, piloted by Flt Lt Ken Letford DSO DFC, touched down close to the frigate, under heavy machine-gun fire. Leaving behind one doctor, the Sunderland beat a hasty retreat, and a second attempt next day was equally unsuccessful. Operating from Lung Wha again, ML772 made a further reconnaissance on 23rd April, only to receive a hole in the port main fuel tank. This aircraft was then flown back to Kai Tak and replaced at Lung Wha by NJ176, but no further attempts were made to reach the *Amethyst* safely. For his heroic attempts, Flt Lt Letford won a Bar to his wartime DFC.

Following the Yangtze incident, news came of the evacuation of British nationals from Shanghai, as Communist forces were closing on the city. 88 Squadron was notified that one Sunderland would be needed on 15th May and possibly three on the following day. The first five-hour trip was made by NJ176, captained by Sqn Ldr Gall, who brought back 26 passengers to Kai Tak. On 16th May Flt Lt Letford in DP199 collected 38 evacuees, while Flt Lt Dulieu in PP114 collected 35 and P.II Bartrum in NJ176 brought back 22.

After several naval cooperation exercises in late May 1949, four Sunderlands went south for armament practice at Seletar, a task which lasted three weeks. It was not until 31st July that the Amethyst finally escaped from the Yangtze river, and 88 Squadron stood by while it did so. Two aircraft left for a Japanese 'cruise' on 5th August 1949, the flight taking eight hours to Sasebo. For the next five weeks the crews took part in ASR, bombing, homing and search-and-shadow exercises.

made an ASR search for a Catalina of Cathay Pacific Airways which had crashed near Nine Pins Island, near Macao. A few days later, the CO, Sqn Ldr Gall, carried out a fleet escort and anti-submarine sortie for the British Pacific Fleet, which was on its way to Japan. On 23rd July he took the advance party of the Royal Inniskillen Fusiliers to Seletar to take part in dealing with civil unrest in Malaya.

After providing over-water escort to a number of Beaufighters flying from Ceylon to Malaya on 12th August, all the 88 Squadron Sunderlands flew to Seletar on 2nd September, with ground crews, to avoid a forecast typhoon. While there, three aircraft took part in Operation 'Firedog', the campaign against Malayan rebels. On return to Kai Tak, Flt Lt Letford and crew flew to Formosa (now Taiwan) to pick up the pilot of a P-47 which had crashed on a beach, only to find that he had left the area by train!

In January 1949 several naval cooperation sorties were flown, including some with HMS *Belfast*. More ASR patrols were also carried out, including one which involved covering Vampires flying from Singapore to Kai Tak via Saigon in what was then French Indo-China. On arrival, one of the Vampires overshot and force-landed on a beach at Bias Bay, in

1950 began with routine patrols, bombing exercises and naval cooperation sorties, complemented in June by flights to and from Japan carrying servicemen on leave. The outbreak of war in Korea, however, prompted the despatch of a detachment to Iwakuni in July to operate patrols off the Korean coast under US Navy control. By September many anti-shipping and anti-submarine patrols were being flown over the Yellow Sea and as far as Vladivostok. A few rescues were also effected, one eleven-hour sortie, by RN282, involving the pilot of a US Navy fighter in a dinghy off the enemy-held harbour at Wonsan. These operations were concentrated on until June 1951, when the squadron moved to Seletar to fly anti-terrorist operations over Malaya under Operation 'Firedog'. This again involved bombing and gunnery, coastal patrols and supply-dropping. The squadron still had some involvement in the Korean war, however, often detaching Sunderlands to Iwakuni to fly anti-submarine patrols and weather reconnaissance flights in Korean waters.

In August 1952 two aircraft flew to China Bay in Ceylon for fleet exercises, and on 10th September another Sunderland made what was described as 'a Top Secret ferry trip'. This flight, with a specially selected crew, was captained by Flt Lt Houtheusen and carried the OC Far East Flying Boat Wing, and it was later recorded to have been in connection with atomic bomb tests at Montebello. Similar trips were made on 12th, 18th and 20th September.

Further detachments to Iwakuni were made from 11th March to 12th April 1952, 4th June to 10th July 1952, 31st December 1952 to 29th January 1953, 31st March to 8th April 1953, 29th August 1953 to 28th September 1953 and from 21st November 1953. In May 1953 an extensive training programme, Exercise 'Mushroom', was held, in which 88 Squadron took part with US and French naval and air forces.

On 8th May 1954, 88 Squadron provided five Sunderlands to escort the SS *Gothic*, which was carrying HM Queen Elizabeth and HRH Prince Phillip to Ceylon on a state visit. The aircraft were positioned at China Bay for this mission, which also included a flypast at Colombo on 21st April and escorting the *Gothic* from the island on its departure next day.

One Sunderland acted as escort for C-124 Globemasters carrying troops to Indo-China on 7th May 1954, and on 23rd July the squadron provided ASR coverage for

RN293 [F] was one of four Sunderlands MR.5 of 88 Squadron which escorted the SS Gothic *carrying HM the Queen and HRH the Duke of Edinburgh on a state visit to Ceylon in April 1954.* (P H T Green collection)

a DC-4 of Cathay Pacific Airways which had ditched off Hainan. A raft with nine survivors was spotted by the crew of the Sunderland, which orbited until an SA-16 Albatross amphibian arrived from Clark Field in the Philippines.

Little work was now left for 88 Squadron, however, and a sudden decision to disband was made. This took place on 1st October 1954, with a formal ceremony next day.

95 Squadron

Unit code: **SE** (May 1941 to mid-1942, then single letter only)

95 Squadron was formed on 16th January 1941 at Pembroke Dock with a nucleus of three Sunderland Mk.Is and air and ground crews provided by Oban-based 210 Squadron. Its task was to be to protect shipping sailing in the South Atlantic off West Africa. At Pembroke Dock the Sunderlands were fitted with extra fuel tankage, bringing the total capacity to 2,400 gallons (4,267 litres), in readiness for the long flight to Freetown in Sierra Leone, the new squadron's intended base. On 31st January and 1st February, the three aircraft, N9027, P9623 and T9041, left Pembroke Dock for Mount Batten on the first stage of the journey. At Gibraltar, N9027 carried out some ASR searches before proceeding, but P9623 force-landed off Portugal and was interned, although its crew was released later. Meanwhile, on 7th February, the ground party boarded SS *Highland Brigade* at Gourock. Sunderland T9041 reached no further than Gibraltar, where its bows were damaged on 15th February, so it was sent back to Mount Batten for repair.

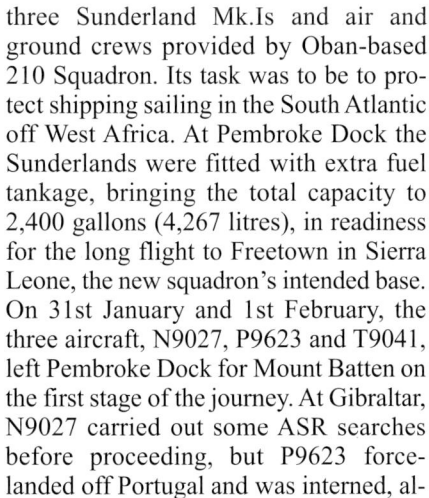

The troopship docked at Freetown on 2nd March 1941, and the squadron established a camp in primitive conditions at Fourah Bay, where further Sunderlands soon began to arrive. Anti-submarine patrols over the South Atlantic, where alarming numbers of vessels were being sunk, began on 24th March and became the daily routine for the squadron, protecting convoys sailing around the Cape of Good Hope to Egypt, with ASR searches if required. From time to time, 95 Squadron Sunderlands searched for enemy surface vessels and submarines as a result of finding survivors of torpedoed ships. Following a survey flight by a 95 Squadron Sunderland on 25th March, a detachment was set up at Bathurst in Gambia. From the end of August 95 Squadron began to work closely with 204 Squadron, which was also based at Bathurst.

An increase in activity by Vichy French Maryland reconnaissance aircraft resulted in a Flight of Hawker Hurricanes being added to the squadron in July 1941 to operate from Hastings (Sierra Leone), making 95 Squadron the only Sunderland squadron to fly fighters! These aircraft had been on a ship in Takoradi harbour when two of them were 'liberated' by 95 Squadron's CO. However, the Hurricanes were absorbed into 128 Squadron on 7th October.

The crew of 95 Squadron Sunderland Mk.III JM671 [Z] pose in front of their aircraft at Bathurst in November 1943, with maintenance personnel standing on the wing above. Note the ladder giving access to the front turret direct from a marine craft. (P J Christopher)

One of 95 Squadron's Sunderlands, L5805, began an extended survey cruise on 10th November 1941, covering Fernando Po, Libreville, Lagos and Angola, returning a week later. Another aircraft, T9046, being ferried from the UK to Freetown, had been pressed into delivering ten much-needed fighter pilots to Kalafrana, Malta. While there, it was shot up by enemy aircraft and sank, but its crew then ferried another Sunderland to Alexandria.

On 9th April 1942 the squadron left Freetown and moved to Jui, which is also in Sierra Leone, and three months later a number of Mk.III Sunderlands were added to the squadron's inventory. Detachments were sent to Gibraltar and Kalafrana to assist squadrons at these distant bases, but administration and servicing at such long distances soon became problematical. Not so far away was Bathurst, where a detachment was positioned from 26th October to 16th November. In October 1942 night patrols were added to the squadron's task.

Detachments were positioned at Port Etienne in French Morocco from 13th January 1943 to May 1945 and at Bathurst from October 1942. On 7th March 1943 squadron headquarters relocated to Bathurst, from where detachments were sent to Jui and Dakar. There was also an ASR element. On 31st March W6063's crew spotted survivors from a merchant vessel. Unfortunately the Sunderland then crashed into the sea and exploded, six of its crew being lost. The three survivors were picked up by HMS *Wastwater*.

The squadron's only contact with the enemy apart from a few U-boats sightings was made on 5th April 1943, when the crew of DV973 spotted one on the surface. The submarine opened fire but was silenced by the Sunderland's front gunner. Three depth charges were dropped, resulting in one near miss. Another pair of DCs was dropped, and the U-boat was believed to have suffered damage.

For the remainder of hostilities the squadron continued to patrol, and in addition flew other operations such as carrying yellow fever serum to the Cape Verde Islands on 22nd January 1944. In January 1944 central servicing was introduced at Bathurst, so that 95 Squadron's aircraft were effectively pooled with those of 204 Squadron. One Sunderland, DV964, was modified by 95 Squadron engineers to have twin 0.5-inch guns in the front turret, and left Bathurst on 21st March for the UK for inspection by the authorities.

Operational commitments began to decline in July 1944, and there were no U-boat sightings after October. Only ASR sorties and intensive training were carried out. However, in December 1944 U-boat patrols were resumed in case of a suspected sudden attack, 95 and 343 Squadrons each providing two aircraft. Surplus crews were posted to the UK in May 1945, and on 25th May all activities by 95 Squadron ceased. The squadron therefore disbanded officially on 30th June 1945.

119 Squadron

Unit code: (nil)

From 6th September 1942, 119 Squadron, under Wg Cdr D M Gordon AFC, converted from Catalinas to Sunderland Mks.IIs and IIIs at Pembroke Dock. An initial patrol was flown on 20th November, and the squadron was declared operational. Among the usual anti-

CHAPTER 3 : OPERATING UNITS (RAF, RAAF, RNZAF, SAAF, AÉRONAUTIQUE NAVALE)

submarine patrols, convoy escorts and general reconnaissance tasks, the crews continued training, and while on such a sortie over the Bristol Channel on 25th November Sunderland Mk.III DV972 was damaged when its own depth charges exploded. This caused the aircraft to ditch, but no injuries were sustained.

In December 119 Squadron carried out 33 operational sorties, during one of which DV971 was posted as missing, and no trace of it or its crew was ever found. During a patrol on 15th April 1943, DP176 had to ditch when both port engines caught fire after their propellers came off. In this mishap three crew members lost their lives and three were injured. Only two days later the squadron was disbanded, its Sunderlands being dispersed among other units.

201 Squadron

Unit codes: **ZM** (April 1940 to November 1943); **1** (November 1943 to July 1944); **NS** (July 1944 to c.1951); **A** (c.1951 to February 1957)

Sunderland Mk.II of 201 Squadron, W3981 [ZM:W], seen on 28th October 1941. Clearly visible are the ASV aerials on the rear fuselage and outer wing sections.
(P H T Green collection)

Handing over its Saro London flying-boats at Invergordon in April 1940, 201 Squadron ("Guernsey's Own") converted to the Sunderland Mk.I, of which P9608 was the first one flown by the squadron's crews. These it took to Sullom Voe in the Shetlands (where a detachment alrady existed) on 26th May 1940 to begin ferrying supplies and personnel to Iceland, which was being established as an Allied military base.

Serviceability became a problem, and on 1st December 1940 only two Sunderlands at Sullom Voe and one at Oban were operational, while four were at Pembroke Dock awaiting repair and one out of action at Sullom Voe. Between 8th March and 16th April and from 12th May to 2nd June 1941 a detachment was maintained at Reykjavik in Iceland. A notable part was played by the squadron in shadowing the battleship *Bismarck* and heavy cruiser *Prinz Eugen* in May 1941, but unfortunately squadron crews witnessed the demise of the battlecruiser HMS *Hood* on 24th May.

Leaving the Shetlands, the squadron moved on 9th October 1941 to Castle Archdale in Northern Ireland, aircrew personnel being billeted in the Charter School at Kesh until moving into accommodation at Castle Archdale on 1st April 1942. From the new base long-distance Atlantic patrols of up to fifteen hours were carried out. Mk.II aircraft had been received in May 1941 to supplement the earlier model, which were replaced by the definitive Mk.III in January 1942.

Another detachment of 201 Squadron aircraft and personnel was set up at Greenock from 23rd July to 28th August 1942.

201 Squadron's first 'kill' came about on 31st May 1943, when Flt Lt D M Gall and his crew in DD835 sank *U-440*. A notable event which took place on 27th December that year was the shadowing by Flt Lt L H Baveystock DFM in EJ137 of the enemy blockade-runner *Alsterufer*. He and his crew were the first to find the elusive vessel, and after many hours the Sunderland had to land at night off the Isles of Scilly in poor weather, with only 60 gallons of fuel in the tanks. Not damaged, the aircraft was towed into St Mary's harbour. In another 201 Squadron Sunderland the radio operator homed Liberators onto the *Alsterufer*, and they sank it. That second aircraft was in the air for 18 hours 36 minutes!

To help in preventing enemy submarines from sailing up the English Channel during the time of the forthcoming (but secret) Normandy landings in June 1944,

An extremely low pass by Sunderland Mk.V SZ567 [NS:B] of 201 Squadron, with the starboard engines apparently stopped.
(David Smith collection)

The same aircraft, SZ567 [NS:B] of 201 Squadron undergoing overhaul at Short Bros & Harland, Belfast, probably in mid-1949 when new sonobuoy equipment was fitted.
(P H T Green collection)

201 Squadron moved to Pembroke Dock between 28th March and 11th April. By the end of May eleven new Mk.III aircraft were on strength, but in the first five days of June only two sorties were flown. The first sortie after the landings, however, brought the first 'kill' of the year on the night of 6/7th June. This was *U-955*, which was sunk by ML760, captained by Flt Lt Baveystock. The first photograph taken with the benefit of 1.7-inch (43 mm) flares was acquired that night. During the peak period, 9th to 25th June, 55 sorties were flown and one Sunderland was lost, probably shot down by a U-boat it was attacking. Among the twelve men who lost their lives was Sqn Ldr W D B Ruth DFC*. Operational hours flown in June 1944 were 882, which included several patrols between the Isles of Scilly and Lundy Island in the Bristol Channel.

Denying U-boats access to the English Channel continued, and Flt Lt I F B Walters DFC and his crew in ML881 made a successful attack on *U-1222* on 11th July. August was the most strenuous month so far, over a thousand hours being flown by ten aircraft taking part in a gradual elimination of U-boat bases on the Bay of Biscay coast. Prominent again was Flt Lt Baveystock, whose crew sank *U-107*, a predator which had disposed of no less than 39 Allied ships. Patrols were now being flown closer to the coast and as far south as the Gironde estuary. One aircraft, ML742, was attacked by a Do 217 on 9th August. In September, however, far fewer operations were flown, as very few U-boats were evident.

Application of squadron code NS to the Sunderlands began early in August 1944, the letters being assumed (wrongly!) to stand for Nulli Secundus (Second to none).

In response to the growing use of Norwegian rather than French ports by U-boats, 201 Squadron was ordered to move back to Castle Archdale. An advance party left Pembroke Dock on 31st October 1944, and the main party, including 8201 Servicing Echelon, followed on 3rd November. On 16th November ML882 attacked, and probably sank, the first new 'prefabricated' Mk.XXI or XXIII U-boats discovered in Atlantic waters. Another 'probable' followed on 6th December, when the same Sunderland, captained by Flt Lt D R Hatton, found a U-boat schnorkelling in rough seas and attacked.

Extremely cold weather early in the new year prevented the squadron from flying between 25th January and 3rd February

A Sunderland coded [NS:Z] of 201 Squadron taking off against a dramatic sky. This may be compared with the photograph on page 28, but the NS:Z shown there is fitted with machine gun ports in the nose, not seen in the aircraft above. (R C Sturtivant collection)

1945, and only 35 sorties were possible that month. Examples of the final version of the Sunderland, the Mk.V, arrived in February for 201 Squadron, and by June the Mk.III had been disposed of.

A tragedy occurred on 14th March, when ML743 crashed on high ground 27 minutes after take-off, killing the entire twelve-man crew, including Flt Lt Hatton. They had set out on one of many sorties being flown to deal with an increasing number of U-boats reported in the Irish Sea, Western Approaches and North Atlantic. Even in April the U-boats were still in evidence, two or three being regular visitors to the Irish Sea. Flt Lt K H Foster of 201 Squadron was captain of ML783 on 30th April when he and his crew sighted a U-boat and after difficulties in winding out the bomb rack six depth charges were dropped. Three RN frigates were then guided to the scene and attacked the U-boat (*U-325*) and sank it.

201 Squadron's final attack was flown by Flt Lt Lillingstone and his crew in ML768. After VE Day (8th May 1945) patrols were flown as far as 150 miles (240 km) west of Ireland to shepherd U-boats to Loch Eriboll, the designated surrender point, in case of continued hostility by their crews. This task continued to the end of the month.

Coastal Command's operations in the Second World War officially ended on 4th June 1945. The last sortie was flown by Wg Cdr J Barrett DFC of 201 Squadron and crew in ML778 to provide an escort for an inbound convoy of fifty-one vessels. He landed at Castle Archdale at 03.21, and from that day just one Sunderland was on permanent readiness.

On 5th July 1945, Liberator JT982 of 231 Squadron was reported missing, and three of 201 Squadron's Sunderlands joined Liberators from Ballykelly in a five-day search which unfortunately proved unsuccessful. With a crew of six, this aircraft had been carrying nine passengers who had attended the San Francisco Conference to establish the United Nations.

Two flights were made in July to Murmansk in northern Russia. Freight was collected at Woodhaven and fuel was taken aboard at Sullom Voe before the Sunderlands flew across the North Sea and followed the coast of Norway to their destination. Another two transport trips were flown to Bergen and one to Gibraltar during that month.

At the time many personnel were leaving for demobilisation or were being posted elsewhere, leaving the squadron somewhat depleted. During the first week of August the squadron returned to Pembroke Dock, continuing for the time being the series of transport flights. On 17th August a pleasant task for the crews of PP114 and PP117 was to escort the Queen Mary at the beginning of a voyage in which she carried high-ranking American officers home. Flights were also made to Tromsø and Stavanger, during which the crews searched the Norwegian coast for any mines.

In September 1945 201 Squadron reverted entirely to peacetime activities, but was employed on a flight to north Norway to take senior officers to view the remains of the *Tirpitz*. Five tons of freight were carried to Reykjavik in Iceland, and on the return journey brought back RAF personnel who thought that they had been forgotten. One aircraft made three trips via Felixstowe to Schleswig in Germany, the first Sunderland to do so. Although servicing facilities were non-existent, the crews were delighted when they were provided with excellent food and drink!

Early in October 1945, six of the Sunderlands, plus others from 4 (C) OTU, flew 800 servicemen to Iceland and brought a thousand home. Similar trips were made to Gibraltar.

During October, ten Mk.V Sunderlands were transferred from 10 (RAAF) Squadron, which was in the process of disbanding as a unit under RAF control. Several repatriation sorties were flown in November, bringing home men from Cairo, Iceland and Norway, but these appear to have been almost the last of their type as far as 201 Squadron was concerned. Exercises in interception and night shadowing with the Home Fleet off Cornwall took up the squadron's time in December, and two of the Sunderlands made practice attacks on a former enemy U-boat with six Torpex depth charges under Operation 'Deadlight'. Four aircraft delivered freight, including spare parts for Lancaster aircraft, to Kasfareet in the Canal Zone just before Christmas, and a hundred men were very pleased to be passengers in the Sunderlands on the return journey.

Transport sorties continued during January 1946, with such destinations as Gibraltar, the Faeroe Islands and Bathurst in Gambia. During the first week of April, the squadron began to move to Calshot and transport work virtually came to an end, the emphasis now being put on training, with 18 Sunderlands on the books. A limit of 250 flying hours per month was determined in June, when activities included a detachment of two aircraft to Castle Archdale to take part in a successful naval anti-submarine exercise. More spectacular was the Victory flypast over London on 8th June, in which three of 201 Squadron's crews and aircraft took part.

By August 1946 the squadron had been reduced from twelve crews and ten aircraft to six crews and six aircraft, with serviceability being much affected by lack of personnel. Nevertheless, the squadron was called upon on 17th October to begin a series of meteorological sorties under Operation 'Epicure Able'. A 'hack' aircraft on the strength at the time was Sea Otter JM815, although in fact it was 'u/s'. In December, the squadron is recorded as having "....reached its lowest ebb", but was determined to regain its status. One notable mission flown by Wg Cdr Tremear in RN284 on 1st February 1947 was to escort HMS *Vanguard*, which was carrying the Royal party to South Africa for an official visit.

Meteorological sorties were again carried out in April 1947, and on 13th May two of the Sunderlands, NJ267 and PP113, flew to Guernsey on an official visit, the first visit by 'Guernsey's Own' since the end of the recent war. Two silver cups, hidden during the German occupation, awaited presentation to the officers and other ranks of the squadron, who much enjoyed the event.

In June 1947 the squadron was again detached to the Joint Anti-Submarine School at Londonderry, flying from Castle Archdale. Serviceability was excellent, due no doubt to the personal interest taken by the airmen in the Sunderlands allocated to them. Sadly, on 5th July, PP113 crashed off the north coast of Ireland after a simulated attack on a submarine, with the loss of four men, three more being posted as missing and five injured. The rest of the detachment returned to Calshot on 31st July.

During August, several coastal sorties were flown so that photographs could be taken for Town & Country Planning purposes, an unusual use for a Sunderland! A routine programme of training continued, with March 1948 a very good month, several fleet and merchant ship exercises and bombing and gunnery sorties being flown. In addition, fighter affiliation with Meteor jet fighters from Tangmere were enjoyed by the crews, who later saw the fighters' camera-gun films.

Nine crews and their aircraft, again based temporarily at Castle Archdale, were attending the Joint Anti-Submarine School at Londonderry when they received urgent orders on 2nd July 1948 to return to base next day. Personnel and equipment were loaded onto the aircraft by 05.00, the men not knowing what the panic was all about. At Calshot, the crews discovered that they were to take part in the newly-established Berlin Airlift, and so on 4th July an advance party comprising one of 201 Squadron's Sunderlands and three from 230 Squadron flew to the former Blohm und Voss shipyards at Finkenwerder in Hamburg, which was to be their base. More aircraft followed two days later.

The alighting area in Berlin was the Havel Lake, seventy minutes flying time from Finkenwerder along the air corridor. Practical difficulties involving mooring and refuelling were soon overcome, but the operation took time to establish, just eight sorties being flown on the first full day. Within ten days, the first three Sunderlands on each day's programme were each completing three sorties. Initially, cargoes carried included noodles, cigarettes, flour, yeast, 'spam' and tins of M&V. Morale among the ground crews was very high. By the end of July the air-

Seen at Gibraltar in 1954, this Sunderland [A:W] belonged to 201 Squadron and is moored to a buoy. With the front turret retracted, one of the crew is at work in the mooring bay. This aircraft may well be MR.5 PP117.
(P H T Green collection)

lift had become a long-term operation, the Sunderlands now being used largely to carry salt, as they were the only aircraft proofed against salt corrosion. 205 sorties were flown in August, during which several Russian fighters were spotted in the distance. Although the demand declined in September, with only 380 tons carried in 80 sorties, it built up again to produce 132 sorties (all carrying salt) in October. In very poor November weather, 159 trips were made, and on 22nd November the first batch of undernourished children was brought out of Berlin. By the end of the month, 683 children and 56 nurses had been carried.

With the possibility of the Havel Lake freezing over, it was decided to terminate the Sunderlands' activity on 15th December after 88 sorties in those two weeks. A further 237 children and 27 nurses were brought out. At the end of the detachment, 201 Squadron had set the record for the fastest turn-round: fifteen minutes loading and twelve minutes unloading. Four 201 Squadron captains and their crews achieved high rates of activity: Flt Lt Cooke (110 sorties), Flt Lt Hobden (95), Flt Lt Harkman (76) and Flt Lt Thomas (65). Most captains also acted as co-pilots for others, pushing up their flying hours even further. Recognition was given to those who took part when six of them were in a parade in London at the end of November 1949.

After the airlift, 201 Squadron returned to Calshot, where the Sunderlands were beached for much-needed servicing. Routine flying then continued with the six aircraft until, on 17th January 1949, an advance party left for Pembroke Dock, to where the squadron was to return. After settling in, training continued, with some night flying in Angle Bay, a difficult site due to its short flare-path. At the end of the month, two aircraft went to Gibraltar to take part in a search for a downed USAF B-29 Superfortress, but nothing was found.

A new HQ for the squadron was inspected on 7th April by Air Marshal Sir John Baker KCB MC DFC, the AOC-in-C of Coastal Command. The squadron CO then took the opportunity of interviewing every crew member to try to persuade them to sign on for further service, but most were reluctant to commit themselves, probably seeing greater opportunities in civilian aviation.

A recruitment drive in July 1949 involved 201 Squadron sending Sunderlands to seaside towns such as Bournemouth, Weymouth and Torquay to boost interest in the Royal Air Force, but what the result was is not recorded. Another event at which the RAF was prominent was the air show on 23rd July at Gatwick, where three of 201 Squadron's aircraft flew past. Included in that month's training was Exercise 'Varsity' with Western Union fleets, the Sunderlands being flown in a close escort role.

After the 'Yangtze incident', in which 88 Squadron had played the leading part, HMS *Amethyst* returned home. Two of 201 Squadron's aircraft flew to Calshot on 30th October 1949 to embark pressmen and next day intercepted *Amethyst*, with which greetings were exchanged. On board one of the Sunderlands was Sig I Moreby, who had flown in the Sunderland which alighted on the Yangtze River. One BBC reporter on the *Amethyst* remarked later that he had looked down on passing Sunderlands from the ship's bridge!

November 1949 activities included Exercise 'Porcupine', in which an 'enemy' convoy was shadowed down the west coast of Ireland. There was further involvement in the Joint Anti-Submarine School course in May/June 1950, when once again Castle Archdale was used by the Sunderlands. On 3rd July all four serviceable aircraft flew to Farnborough to lead the flypast of heavy aircraft at that year's air display, which must have been quite a sight.

That autumn, two of the crews were detailed to ferry Sunderlands out to Singapore, considered an enjoyable task, but one crew had to spend an uncomfortable month at Bahrain, where the aircraft had become unserviceable.

Routine operations continued at Pembroke Dock until 201 Squadron (along with 230) disbanded on 28th February 1957.

202 Squadron

Unit code: **TQ**

A long-term resident of Gibraltar, in 1941 202 Squadron acted as host to Sunderlands of other squadrons passing through Gibraltar on delivery. The squadron began adding Sunderlands Mk.I and II to its fleet of Catalinas in December 1941 and used them on patrols over the western approaches to the Straits of Gibraltar, a highly important area. Single Sunderlands of other units were often attached to 202 Squadron when required.

On 15th July 1942, one of the Sunderlands was patrolling off the coast of Majorca when the crew spotted a Cant Z.501 seaplane of the Spanish Air Force which had alighted and burst into flames. The Sunderland picked up the crew and took them to Gibraltar, from where they were allowed over the Spanish border.

A number of Mk.III aircraft were received in March 1942, but it was Mk.II W6002 that sank the Italian submarine *Alebastro* off Algiers on 14th September 1942. All the Sunderlands were withdrawn later that month, some at least being transferred to 119 Squadron, as it had been decided to concentrate on Catalinas. A few attachments of Sunderlands of other units continued for a time, however.

204 Squadron

Unit code: **RF** until Sep 1939; **KG** until end of 1941 or early 1942; then individual aircraft letters only.

Based at Mount Batten, 204 Squadron began receiving Sunderland Mk.Is in June 1939 to replace its obsolescent Saro London aircraft. On 2nd September the squadron was mobilised and began convoy escort work at once. By the end of September the squadron was fully equipped with eight aircraft, allowing patrols to be flown over the English Channel and Western Approaches. Seven attacks on submarines were made in the first month, the first one on 8th September, when a U-boat 30 miles (48 km) south-west of the Lizard was attacked. Another task was carried out by L5802, which carried secret documents to Brest in Brittany for discussion at the French Navy base there.

On 18th September, hearing distress signals from the *Kensington Court*, a tramp steamer carrying 8,000 tons of grain, which had been torpedoed 70 miles (112 km) off the Isles of Scilly, one of 204's aircraft (L5802 again) made for the reported position. On arrival, the Sunderland alighted, as did one from 228 Squadron, and between them they picked up all 34 seamen from the vessel and delivered them safely to dry land.

CHAPTER 3 : OPERATING UNITS (RAF, RAAF, RNZAF, SAAF, AÉRONAUTIQUE NAVALE)

Apparently being beached, this Sunderland of 202 Squadron was at Castle Archdale on Lough Erne in 1942. (P H T Green collection)

Unidentified Sunderlands Mk.II of 202 Squadron, coded [TQ:X] and [TQ:Y[] at Alexandria, Egypt. (R C Sturtivant collection)

One of the Sunderlands, N9045, had to be abandoned on 3rd October when after a U-boat search the captain, Flt Lt Hyde, saw that the fuel state was very low. He set it down on a heavy sea near the Scillies in a gale, losing the port float in the process. An SOS was sent to a Dutch vessel, the *Bilderdiyke*, which diverted from its voyage to New York to rescue the crew and supernumeraries, who were transferred later to the destroyer HMS *Icarus*. A subsequent enquiry found that the fuel consumption rate had been abnormal.

During November none of the seven aircraft on strength was fully serviceable due to lack of Vickers gunsights and camera mountings, which had been on order since July. Nevertheless, convoy escorts were flown whenever possible. Automatic pilots were being installed in January 1940, but the pilots considered them almost useless due to precession. The situation had improved by the end of February, when five aircraft were fit for operations and only three were unserviceable. Detachments were maintained at Falmouth from 1st to 26th March 1940 and at Pembroke Dock from 1st April 1940 to 26th August 1941.

After sending an advance party, on 2nd April 1940 the squadron moved to Sullom Voe in the Shetlands to carry out patrols off Norway. Personnel were at first accommodated on board HMT *Manela* as buildings were not ready. The next day, Sunderland N9046 was attacked by six Ju 86Ks off the Norwegian coast in the first of the type's aerial battles with enemy aircraft, but its gunners managed to shoot one down and badly damage another. The crew of L5799 was not so lucky, however, as it force-landed south of Bergen and they were interned.

Potential alighting areas at Balta Sound and Catfirth in the Shetlands were investigated by the crew of N9024 on 19th April, but by 4th May only one Sunderland was serviceable. By June this situation had been overcome, and a detachment was positioned at Reykjavik in Iceland for a week. On 21st June two of the Sunderlands shadowed the battleship *Scharnhorst*, escorted by three Blenheims from Sumburgh which returned to base after being attacked and damaged by a Do 18! Swordfish aircraft of the Fleet Air Arm then appeared on the scene and attacked the battleship and its escort of seven destroyers. Sunderland N9028 continued to shadow the German ships and was attacked by Bf 109 fighters, but although damaged was able to return to base.

Early in July 1940 more missions were flown from Reykjavik, with HMT *Manela* again in support. This ship sailed from Iceland on 17th July, however, and the Sunderlands flew to Pembroke Dock. In late August three or four of them made the journey to Gibraltar and on to Bathurst (Half Die) in Gambia, from where they carried out convoy escort work through September. In October, however, the squadron was back at Sullom Voe, with yet another detachment at Reykjavik from 9th to 19th November.

With *Manela* again in attendance, on 5th April 1941 Reykjavik became the

Sunderland Mk.I N9021 coded [KG:G] just after launching at Mount Batten. (V A Hodgkinson)

squadron's base. Whilst there, surveys of Iceland revealed several safe alighting areas and good anchorages, as well as possible airfield sites for land-based squadrons. However, on 15th July the Sunderlands, now including some Mk.II aircraft, flew south to the warmer waters of Gibraltar, where some escort sorties and trips to Malta were flown. Even this was only temporary, as the squadron continued southward to Bathurst, where the Sunderlands arrived on 28th August 1941. Squadron HQ was set up on board HMT *Dumana* at Bathurst until moving onto dry land on 21st May 1942.

From its new base, 204 Squadron flew patrols off the coast of West Africa to combat the high incidence of losses of Allied merchant shipping to enemy submarines. Some Sunderlands routinely escorted northbound convoys to Gibraltar, where they refuelled before giving similar protection to south-bound shipping. The intensity of operations increased in the autumn of 1942 with preparations for Operation 'Torch', which successfully eliminated opposition from Vichy French fighters. In addition, several missions were flown to look for survivors of shipping and downed aircraft. An RAF detachment was set up at Port Etienne in French Morocco in January 1943 under the control of 295 Wing, and remained in

Aircrews of 204 Squadron pose in front of a Sunderland at Bathurst (Half Die) in September 1943. The photograph may represent a farewell to the unit's Mk.Is which were retired in that month. This squadron was based at Bathurst from August 1941 to January 1944.
(R Birchell via John Evans)

place for some time to allow coastal reconnaissance sorties to cover a wider area.

In October 1942 Mk.III aircraft were received to add to the earlier models, but the Mk.II was relinquished in March 1943 and the Mk.I in September, thus creating a standardised fleet. For the remainder of that year and through 1943 204 Squadron maintained the tedious but essential task of searching for enemy submarines and escorting Allied convoys. One notable event took place on 15th October 1942, when DV959 landed on the open sea and picked up five survivors from Wellington HX636, which had ditched off Cape Roxo, Sénégal, the previous day while on a ferry flight. Another rescue was made on 5th March 1943, when one of the Sunderlands picked up the entire crew of a ditched USAAF B-24 Liberator and brought them to Bathurst before flying them on to Dakar.

On 28th January 1944, 204 Squadron moved to Jui in Sierra Leone, although the Sunderlands returned to Bathurst from 1st to 8th April in connection with a special operation. On 8th March the suitability of Fisherman's Lake in Liberia as a diversion area was investigated by Wg Cdr Hawkins, who landed there in DV959. Substantial use of the Lake was made subsequently, and detachments were also sent to Lagos and Freetown.

Curtailment of sorties due to the increasing unreliability of Pegasus XVIII engines was on the increase by May 1944, and fervent appeals for an alternative were made. For the time being, however, 204 Squadron had to soldier on at Jui, with a detachment at Abidjan from August 1944 to at least February 1945. In November 1944 the whole month was devoted to training, as the squadron had no other commitments. In March 1945, however, there was a new campaign to rid the South Atlantic of remaining U-boats, and the squadron experienced the best month for patrols since the previous May, flying 364 hours plus 98 hours in training. A few Mk.V aircraft had been placed into service in April 1945, and meteorological flights became part of the routine until the squadron's disbandment on 30th June 1945.

205 Squadron

Unit code: (nil)

Having flown Catalinas throughout most of the Second World War, 205 Squadron started converting to Sunderland Mk.Vs in June 1945 at Koggala, Ceylon. Training began in July, at which point the Canadian and Australian personnel of the squadron left for home. The first nine Sunderlands were used for navigational exercises, radar work, sea firing and other functions, but training was hampered by lack of spares.

On 4th August RN293 made the first trip by the squadron to the Cocos Islands, carrying among other freight an 'iron lung', and flights to the islands soon developed into a regular route. Other activity included meteorological flights and fighter afiliation with Hellcats of the Fleet Air Arm. A break was taken on 15/16th August to celebrate VJ Day, and on 25th August a Victory fly-past over Colombo by two of the Sunderlands and one from 209 Squadron was held. From 26th August one of the eleven aircraft was maintained on air-sea rescue standby every day.

On 3rd September RN293 began a tour of Malaya with Gp Capt Francis as Captain. Flying via Sabang, Penang (Georgetown) and Port Swettenham, the Sunderland arrived at Singapore (Seletar) on 8th September. There, Gp Capt Francis was to become the first postwar Station Commander, and RN293 was believed to be the first RAF aircraft to land in Malaya since the occupation. Operating conditions there were primitive and there were difficulties with refuelling, but on 14th September RN288 flew from Koggala to pick up an initial load of former prisoners of war. Other 205 Squadron aircraft followed, and the task grew rapidly into a regular service. All the Sunderlands on this mercy mission were fitted with bunks for any wounded men, fifteen of whom were carried on each trip, which took 23 hours out and back. A rudimentary reception building was provided at Koggala, with refreshment facilities for the 'passengers'.

During January 1946 the Singapore courier service was reduced to seven flights per week, of which four were flown by 205 Squadron. On 19th January one of the Sunderlands flew to Mombasa to collect the former Premier of Burma and return him to his liberated country. The regular Singapore flights were again reduced in April, to two per week, although some of them continued to Kai Tak in Hong Kong. Another task for the depleted squadron involved ferrying aircraft of its own and of 209 Squadron back to the UK. By the end of December 1946 there were only three navigators on the squadron, which meant that few missions could be undertaken.

In February 1947, one Sunderland was employed in a photographic survey of Addu Atoll in the Maldives, for which a base at Male was used. Whilst there, the aircraft struck a coral reef on take-off, but the damage was repaired by the ground crew.

CHAPTER 3 : OPERATING UNITS (RAF, RAAF, RNZAF, SAAF, AÉRONAUTIQUE NAVALE)

A Sunderland Mk.V of 205 Squadron moored at Koggala in 1945.
(P H T Green collection)

Coded [L], Sunderland MR.5 PP127 of 205/209 Squadron is airborne alongside another aircraft
(R A Walker collection)

September 1947 found three of the squadron's Sunderlands taking part in Operation 'Seahawk', a goodwill and training flight to South Africa. Their route took them to Male, Port Victoria, the Seychelles, Mombasa and Port Mozambique to Durban, returning via Lourenco Marques, Mozambique, Grand Port in Mauritius and Diego Garcia.

A move back to Seletar was completed on 14th September 1949, and RAF Koggala began to close down. At Seletar, the squadron began to take part in Operation 'Firedog', the anti-bandit campaign in Malaya, although difficulties were experienced due to a lack of personnel and equipment. In August 1950 three aircraft were sent to Kai Tak to ferry supplies to Japan, and, perhaps a forecast of things to come, all three were fired on by Communists near Hong Kong.

During the Korean conflict a detachment of three Sunderlands was sent to Iwakuni in Japan from 28th October 1950 to 6th May 1951 so that patrols could be flown over Korean coastal waters in conjunction with the US Navy. During these sorties, the crews looked for suspicious vessels and when possible they destroyed sea-mines. While returning to Kai Tak on 28th January 1951, Sunderland PP107 crashed on Mount Morrison in Formosa (now Taiwan), with the loss of the crew of five, a navigator from 88 Squadron and eight ground personnel, a sad loss to the squadron. At least eight further detachments to Iwakuni took place before the Korean War ended: 5th February to 11th March 1952, 9th May to 4th June 1952, 6th August to 3rd September 1952, 21st November to 31st December 1952, 25th February to 31st March 1953, 25th May to 8th July 1953, 8th August to 29th September 1953, 22nd October to 21st November 1953, and possibly others. Meanwhile, Operation 'Firedog' continued, the Sunderlands of 205 Squadron taking part whenever required.

In October 1952, Sunderland SZ578 was converted to VVIP configuration for use in carrying Their Royal Highnesses the Duke and Duchess of Kent on a ten-day tour of Borneo and Sarawak.

Sunderland MR.5 JM667 from 205 Squadron and still coded [M] became an instructional airframe as 7172M in Singapore after retirement in 1954. *(Roy Green)*

Five Sunderlands MR.5 of 205 Squadron, taking part in the King's birthday flypast over Singapore in 1951. Identifiable are PP148 [L], PP154 [N] and PP144 [P].
(Andrew Hendrie collection)

On 1st January 1955 205 Squadron absorbed 209 Squadron, an indication of the beginning of the end for the Sunderland. Maritime reconnaissance patrols continued, 205 Squadron now being the RAF's last flying-boat squadron. A requirement for a post-war island base in the Indian Ocean led to the selection of Gan, to where 205/209 Squadron Sunderlands established a transport service.

Use of the Sunderland was now coming to an end, and on 14th May 1959 205 Squadron made the final operational flight of an RAF Sunderland when DP198 took part in an exercise with naval vessels. Next day, ML797 was one of the aircraft which flew in formation around Singapore Island. The squadron then became land-based, converting to Shackletons.

209 Squadron

Unit code: **WQ**, June 1945 to April 1951, then nil

While it was operating Singapores in May/June 1938, a small number of early production Sunderlands were taken on charge by 209 Squadron at Felixstowe before being released to other squadrons.

Operationally, 209 Squadron was a latecomer to the Sunderland when it began to give up its Catalinas in February 1945 at Kipevu in Kenya in favour of the Mk.V version of the larger 'boat'. From Kipevu, detachments were sent to Mombasa and Diego Suarez in February and March. Soon after conversion was completed, the squadron began to move to Koggala in Ceylon, the main party embarking on HMT *Hunan* at Mombasa on 5th July 1945. Five days later the air party flew to the new base via the Seychelles.

From Koggala one Sunderland, PP159, was sent to Rangoon on 21st July to attack shipping along the coast of Burma and Malaya. The first armed reconnaissance off the Kra Isthmus in Siam (now Thailand) was flown on 26th July against Japanese coastal vessels, and five days later PP159 flew a sortie lasting 10 hours 15 minutes during which the Sunderland shot up junks and a train.

In September, the war over, work began on disarming the Sunderlands, and a number of freighting sorties were flown to such places as the Cocos Islands. On 12th September a flypast was staged at Seletar, Singapore, in the presence of Lord Louis Mountbatten to mark the Japanese surrender, and five of the six Sunderlands involved were 209 Squadron aircraft. Considerable effort then went into the repatriation of prisoners of war from Singapore.

A detachment soon took up residence at Kai Tak in Hong Kong, and on 27th October 1945 was joined by the remainder of the squadron. The work was now varied, but was mainly of a transport nature. Alighting areas were actively sought in hitherto unvisited places such as Saigon in what was then French Indo-China, where on 9th January 1946 Flt Lt G Mc Kendrick touched down, but found the river unsuitable due to its curvature. On 13th January a Sunderland left for Sydney via Darwin and Cairns, possibly the first one to fly this route. Arriving at Sydney, the aircraft was flown under Sydney Harbour Bridge before alighting

A formation flypast on 18th April 1945 by six Sunderlands Mk.V of 209 Squadron based at Kipevu before going to the Far East.
(P H T Green collection)

CHAPTER 3 : OPERATING UNITS (RAF, RAAF, RNZAF, SAAF, AÉRONAUTIQUE NAVALE)

at Rose Bay! There it remained until 30th January.

209 Squadron was actively involved in setting up the RAF's flying-boat operations in Japan, the first of its Sunderlands flying to Tokyo on 18th January 1946 carrying, among other passengers, Air Cdre W A Brook, the AOC at Hong Kong. It landed in Yokohama Bay and returned to base six days later.

Taking off from Seletar for Kai Tak on 23rd January 1946, PP150 swung due to overloading and struck a buoy, tearing a large hole in the fuselage. The captain managed to keep it in the air and flew it to Kai Tak, where it was landed and beached.

As the USS *Greenwich Bay* depot ship, which 209 Squadron crews had been using, was withdrawn early in March 1946, an alternative alighting area had to be found, and a site at Iwakuni was chosen. This had the advantage of a nearby RAAF airfield. By 3rd April detachment facilities had been established there, and the first routine flight left Kai Tak for Iwakuni on 16th April.

The squadron suffered a severe loss on 27th March 1946, when Sunderland PP103, taking off from Seletar at night, lost the power of both starboard engines. It crash-landed in the Johore Strait, but in doing so broke its back, and five crew and six passengers lost their lives.

On 15th April 1946 a detachment left for Seletar, most of the remainder of the squadron following on 18th May. However, part of the squadron was left behind at Kai Tak to become 1430 Flight on 5th August. Flying from Seletar, one of the Sunderlands visited Kallang on 22nd April to collect Admiral Lord Louis Mountbatten and take him on a visit to the Rajah of Sarawak at Kuching. More aggressively, Wg Cdr Ogle-Skan and his crew carried out a survey of the coasts of Malaya in late April to check for possible alighting areas. On 6th June, Sqn Ldr Ruston and his crew began another foray to Australasia, flying via Surabaya, Darwin and Cairns to Sydney, where they remained for three days, and finally to Auckland in New Zealand. On the homeward leg they carried Air Chief Marshal Sir Keith Park and a party of senior officers.

One of the Pacific Ocean's typical typhoons hit Kai Tak on 18th July 1946, and although two Sunderlands had been flown to Hainan as a precaution, severe

Sunderland Mk.V NJ261 [T] of 209 Squadron flying over Mombasa's busy harbour in 1945. (P H T Green collection)

damage was done. Aircraft R, already SOC, and S were firmly picketed on the slipway, but R was lifted bodily into the air by the wind and 15 feet (4.5 m) of the port wing broke off and the hull split. The port leg of the beaching gear attached to S was forced through the concrete slipway and the hull was extensively damaged. On the adjacent land airfield two Dakotas were lifted 20 feet (6 m) into the air. At Hainan, Sunderland P sprang a leak and was beginning to sink when the tail broke off. Aircraft O was beached with slight damage and was flown to Kai Tak ten days later, but with warped stringers and a crinkled skin it was then struck off charge.

Life for the 209 Squadron crews was not very arduous at this time, and involved such activities as air/sea exercises with Firefly aircraft from HMS *Venerable* on 21st October 1946 and searches for mines thought to remain in the vicinity of the Andaman and Nicobar Islands early in November.

On 11th November a fighter affiliation exercise with Fireflies and Seafires from RNAS Sembawang was held, and ten days later the Mosquitos of 84 Squadron had their chance to 'shoot down' a Sunderland during exercise 'Ginger Ale'. Strangely, 209 Squadron also had a landplane, a Harvard coded Z, though its

A fine over-water view of 209 Squadron's Sunderland MR.5 SZ577 [Y] in 1954. (Roy Green)

Named "Cromarty Firth", Sunderland Mk.V [WQ:O] of 209 Squadron but otherwise unidentified positively, was beached, presumably at Hainan in the typhoon of 18th July 1946. *(R C Sturtivant collection)*

Another unidentified Mk.V, [WQ:U] of 209 Squadron was moored at Hong Kong (Kai Tak) in 1945. *(Gerald Raggett collection via Rod Simpson)*

209 Squadron crew manning a Sunderland's side-hatch machine gun. *(Roy Green)*

Clear prop! Routine maintenance on a Seletar-based 209 Squadron Sunderland MR.5. *(Roy Green)*

Viewed from atop the wing the crew of this 209 Squadron aircraft are busy handling the mooring buoy. *(Roy Green)*

Sunderland MR.5 EJ155 [U] of 205/209 Squadron undergoing repairs in situ after losing its port float on 21st February 1955 alighting at a base in Borneo. *(Roy Green)*

identity remains questionable. At Seletar, 209 Squadron was named City of Hong Kong Squadron on 23rd January 1947.

Sorties under Operation 'Firedog' against the rebels in Malaya began on 7th July 1948, and in connection with hostilities in Korea a detachment was sent to Iwakuni from 11th September to 18th December 1950 to patrol off the Korean coast. Further detachments to Iwakuni were from 29th December 1951 to 5th February 1952, 12th April to 9th May 1952, 10th July to 6th August 1952, 29th January to 25th February 1953, 28th April to 25th May 1953, 8th July to 8th August 1953, 28th September to 22nd October 1953 and 8th August to October 1954.

Still headquartered at Seletar, 209 Squadron was absorbed by 205 Squadron on 1st January 1955.

210 Squadron

Unit codes: **VG** (to September 1939); **DA** (September 1939 to April 1941)

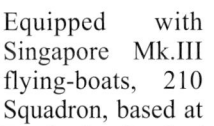

Equipped with Singapore Mk.III flying-boats, 210 Squadron, based at Pembroke Dock, began to convert to Sunderland Mk.Is in June 1938, the first two aircraft, L2162 and L2163, arriving from Short Bros at Rochester on 24th June. Conversion training had begun at Felixstowe in mid-May, and on 20th May Wg Cdr W N Plenderleith, the CO, had flown L2159 to Pembroke Dock to take part in the Empire Air Day display.

During June, several new Sunderlands were ferried out to Singapore by 210 Squadron crews for 230 Squadron, providing very useful experience. Conversion training was completed by December, and the squadron's crews busied themselves with preparations for the hostilities which many considered inevitable.

On 29th September 1938 six of the Sunderlands were sent to Tayport, the squadron's 'war station' but returned to Pembroke Dock on 8th October. Five Sunderlands again visited Tayport from 12th to 18th November for exercises with the Fleet.

From 12th to 21st August 1939 three of the Sunderlands were detached to Woodhaven for an exercise, during which the personnel were billeted in a Boy Scout hut. 210 Squadron flew its first operational mission, a convoy patrol ahead of seven destroyers patrolling the approaches to Milford Haven, on 3rd September 1939, the day hostilities began. On 9th September L2165 attacked a U-boat which was crash-diving, and two days later the crew of the same aircraft spotted survivors from a British merchantman 200 miles (320 km) north-west of Ireland, and directed a US vessel to pick them up. Survivors from MV *Vancouver City* were also located and were rescued by a Dutch ship while Sunderland L2167 remaining on station.

210 Squadron's first fatal loss occurred on 17th September 1939, when L2165 crashed on St Ann's Head, killing all nine crew members.

Detachments were sent to Invergordon from 23rd October to 6th November 1939 and 23fd November 1939 to June 1940, to Oban from 16th November 1939 to 17th July 1940 and to Sullom Voe from 24th November 1939 to 21st May 1940 to carry out patrols over the northern North Sea. One of the more significant sorties from Sullom Voe was made on 12th April 1940 by L5798, its mission being to bomb troopships in Hardanger Fjord, Norway. Anti-aircraft fire over Haugesund pierced two fuel tanks and damaged the tailplane, but the Sunderland was able to return to Sullom Voe safely after an abortive six-hour flight.

A switch of emphasis brought about a move on 13th July 1940 to Oban (where there was already a detachment) to fly patrols over the North Atlantic. These were largely inconclusive, but on 16th August the crew of P9624 spotted a U-boat and

Sunderland Mk.I L2163 saw service with 210 Squadron from June 1938 to December 1941 and is seen here as DA:G with a distinct paint loss from the planing hull and a full height fin flash. In October 1946 it became instructional airframe 4891M. (P H T Green collection)

attacked with depth charges. The submarine was blown out of the water and sank, but no trace was found by a nearby destroyer. On 6th January 1941 Flg Off R Baker, flying P9624, attacked and sank an Italian submarine, *Nani*, one of a fleet of eighteen which were operating out of Bordeaux under German control.

On 16th January 1941 three of the squadron's Sunderlands, L2163, N9027 and P9623, were ordered to fly to Pembroke Dock to be fitted out for service in West Africa, but of these P9623 was blown well off course over the Bay of Biscay and force-landed off the coast of Portugal (see Chapter 4). The reason behind the deployment was to rid the area of seven U-boats which were causing havoc, having sunk 74 Allied ships in four months.

In April 1941, however, the squadron gave up its Sunderlands in favour of Catalinas, the first of which arrived on the 15th of the month.

228 Squadron

Unit codes: **TO** (November 1938 to June 1939); **BH** (June 1939 to September 1939); **DQ** (September 1939 to February 1945); **UE** (March 1942 to June 1945); **1** (May 1943 to June 1945)

Based at Pembroke Dock, 228 Squadron had been flying Stranraer Mk.I flying-boats, and on 30th October 1938 had been nominated to help in ferrying new Sunderlands to the Far East. Only a small

Sunderland Mk.Is of 228 Squadron in 1939 with L5806 [Q] nearest. Note the serial carried on the rudder as well as on the rear fuselage.
(Andrew Hendrie collection)

number, among them L5803 and L5804, were in fact dealt with in this way before on 20th November the order was received for the squadron to re-equip with Sunderlands itself on the basis of six Initial Equipment and two Immediate Reserve. The first one, Mk.I L5806, was collected from Rochester on 10th December.

On 18/19th January 1939 228 Squadron took part in a combined forces exercise to test the defence of the Western Approaches against surface vessels and submarines, and a similar exercise followed in March.

There was a slight delay in receiving Sunderlands, but the last Stranraer left in April 1939, and at the end of May the squadron began to move to Alexandria in Egypt, an operation completed on 12th June. The squadron's HQ was established on board SS *Balmaha* and HMT *Dumana*. A concentrated schedule of night-flying practice was soon evolved, and took place at Aboukir from 21st July. A survey flight of the lower River Nile was flown on 27th July by Sunderland N9020, partly to find fresh-water washing facilities for the aircraft. Other activities included an exercise, in which five of the Sunderlands took part, in shadowing an 'enemy' fleet which had simulated the bombardment of Cyprus.

On the outbreak of war five of the squadron's aircraft were at Alexandria and three were detached to Kalafrana in Malta, all serviceable, fully armed and ready to go. However, a recall to the UK was issued, and on 9th September L5805, L5806, N9020 and N6135 flew to Kalafrana, carrying a large number of ground personnel and equipment, and flew on to Pembroke Dock next day.

Safely established at Pembroke Dock, 228 Squadron aircraft began to fly anti-submarine sorties west of Ireland and to escort convoys as required. On 18th September Consolidated Model 28 Catalina flying-boat P9630 was added to the squadron's inventory, possibly so that it could be given a thorough operational trial in advance of a production order being placed.

An unusual event took place on 14th September, when Sunderland N9023 suffered engine trouble and alighted in Dingle Bay in Eire. After taxying to Ventry Bay, the crew found a garage mechanic who was persuaded to repair a fractured pipe. Negotiations then had to be made with the local Garda (police) before the Sunderland was allowed to return to Pembroke Dock.

Two prominent rescue missions were flown by 228 Squadron that September. The first was on the 18th, when N9025 alighted on the sea to pick up survivors of SS *Kensington Court*, which had been torpedoed, and the second was six days later, when N9020 made a similar rescue of survivors from the torpedoed SS *Hazelside* south-west of Ireland. Sunderland N9023, meanwhile, was attacking and sinking a U-boat at point 51°10'N 09°22'W.

In general, life for 228 Squadron maintenance personnel had been difficult during 1939, largely due to a shortage of spares. One success, however, had been a local training scheme under which aircraft captains were responsible for producing efficient crews.

One of 228 Squadron's Sunderlands, N9025, attacked an already damaged U-boat, *U-55*, on 30th January 1940, and after losing his nerve the vessel's Captain scuttled it, the victim of a Sunderland by default!

Contact with the enemy became much more of a reality on 3rd April 1940, when the crew of N6133, on convoy patrol, spotted a He 111K and pursued it at maximum speed, but failed to come within range. Ten miles east of the convoy, four Ju 88s were spotted, and the convoy opened fire, sending three of the enemy aircraft away, although one dropped bombs nearby. The same Sunderland carried Maj Gen C de Wiart from Invergordon to Nansen Fjord in Norway on 15th April to meet a Tribal Class destroyer. Fifteen minutes later, this ship was attacked by four Ju88s and two He111s, which dropped bombs but failed to hit it. The Sunderland was machine-gunned and bombed but managed to escape and flew back to Invergordon and two days later to Pembroke Dock.

Meanwhile, on 10th April, L5806 moved to Stranraer in order to carry out a reconnaissance of Trondheim Fjord. After making a landfall at Vikten Island, it flew eastward over Trondheim, the crew noticing several German ships. Course was then set for Sullom Voe in the Shetlands. Two days later the same aircraft flew another sortie to determine the strength of enemy naval vessels in several fjords. Carrying out yet another risky mission, L5806 and its crew transported 1.5 tons of explosives from Invergordon to Romsdals Fjord on 19th April, after all superfluous equipment had been removed from the aircraft. On arrival, the crew found cloud at sea level, so alighted ten miles (16 km) away and taxied for four miles (6.4 km) before taking to the air again and touching down close to the intended place. After the cargo had been transferred to the sloop HMS *Bittern*, the Sunderland returned safely to Invergordon.

Still working to try to help Norwegian resistance fighters, 228 Squadron sent N9025 to one of the fjords on 25th April, carrying naval personnel and radio equipment for transfer to HMS *Calcutta*. Repeating the mission on 27th April, this time carrying RAF men, the crew of N9025 crossed the coast at Allesund and spotted enemy aircraft attacking a W/T station at Sala. They made for Molde Fjord, where the Sunderland was first attacked by three Ju 88s and, after alighting, by twelve! Amidst the bombing, the captain, Flt Lt Craven, accompanied the men when they transferred to a whaler in order to assess the situation. He was then marooned, as the co-pilot, realising that the Sunderland's engines were becoming very hot, carried out avoiding action and took off, only to be attacked by a Bf 110. The Sunderland's gunners, however, shot it down, and the Sunderland alighted at Aandalsnes, where they took army officers on board and flew them back to Invergordon via Sullom Voe. Finally, N9025 carried other army officers from Invergordon to Namsos on 20th April.

When Italy entered the war on 10th June 1940, 228 Squadron was again posted to the Mediterranean area, leaving behind, for the time being, its maintenance crews. Three aircraft, L5806, L5807 and N9025, left Pembroke Dock that day for Alexandria via Marseilles (Marignane) and Kalafrana, carrying seven officers, seven SNCOs and 28 other ranks, together with a large quantity of equipment. L5806 was delayed at Marignane, and after a night at Kalafrana the other two Sunderlands were forced out by a warning of an air raid. They then flew to Aboukir, where L5806 joined them On arrival, personnel were accommodated on HMT *Dumana* and offices and stores were set up on the former Imperial Airways site. By now, the squadron's main party had reached Gibraltar, and on 26th June it reached Cape Town. At Aboukir, anti-submarine patrols began at once, as well as searches for the Italian fleet, elements of which were seen and reported.

From Pembroke Dock, two of the squadron's other Sunderlands, P9621 and P9622, were sent to Gibraltar on 30th June on a four-week attachment to 202 Squadron. Whilst there they carried out reconnaissance sorties over Oran in Algeria and Malaga and Almeria in Spain. Over Algeria on 4th July, P9621 was attacked by four Curtiss 75A Hawk fighters being operated by Vichy France. The Sunderland's gunners were able to shoot down one of them, probably two, after which the badly damaged flying-boat returned safely to Gibraltar. Next day, the crew of P9622 took photographs of French shipping which had been beached and destroyed. By 27th July 1940 both aircraft had returned to Pembroke Dock for repairs.

On 5th July 1940 three Sunderlands were put on standby for special fleet duties to last six days. This turned out to consist of concentrated sweeps for enemy surface vessels between Alexandria and Malta, but at first there were no sightings. On 9th July, however, Flt Lt D Mc Kinley DFC and his crew in L5807 spotted two battleships, four cruisers and six destroyers and shadowed them. Later, another six cruisers and eleven destroyers were seen east of the first fleet and then seven cruisers to the west. In nine hours of shadowing, many enemy aircraft were seen but none attacked the Sunderland. Seven aircraft were in fact seen to bomb their own ships! In the same action, Sqn Ldr G L Menzies in N9020 was repeatedly subjected to intense AA fire but remained undamaged. A number of He 115 floatplanes were fired on, but without result. The Sunderland's crew witnessed the first stage of action between the Royal Navy and the Italian fleet, which eventually fled under cover of a heavy smokescreen. Both 228 Squadron aircraft spent the night at Kalafrana.

Further very long patrols engaged the squadron over the next few days. Flying from Kalafrana on 12th July, N9020 was patrolling between Sicily and the Ionian Islands when a surfaced U-boat was seen and attacked from 2,000 feet. A large amount of air came to the surface, indicating that the submarine had sunk.

Aboukir became the squadron's advanced base on 14th July 1940, and patrols continued from there. Unfortunately, on 6th August N9025 was lost. It had alighted on the open sea after being damaged by enemy action, but the radio operator was able to maintain W/T contact with base until the Sunderland was taken in tow by an enemy destroyer, at which point the crew, apart from one member who lost his life, were made prisoners of war. The Sunderland is thought to have sunk during the towing operation.

At last, on 25th August 1940, the squadron's main party arrived at Aboukir, but another move was afoot. This time the new base was Kalafrana in Malta, to where the squadron moved on 13th September, leaving a detachment to operate from Gibraltar. The maintenance personnel caught up with the squadron in October, and operations over the Mediterranean from Malta continued.

Airborne from St Paul's Bay in Malta on 12th October, L2164 received a signal from HMS *Illustrious* to the effect that a Cant Z.501 floatplane of the Italian Air Force had been shot down by a Fulmar of the Fleet Air Arm, and survivors were in a rubber dinghy. The Sunderland crew

At Kalafrana in Malta during September 1940, Sunderland Mk.I L5806 [DQ:Q] of 228 Squadron was moored next to a Latécoère 298B floatplane which was flown in RAF colours by French crews on reconnaissance missions and leaflet dropping. Originally HB2.5 of Flottille 6F, Karouba, the Latécoère was sunk in an air attack on Kalafrana in February 1941.

(P H T Green collection)

Set on fire by Bf 109s during an attack on Kalafrana on 25th April 1941, Sunderland Mk.1 L5807 of 228 Squadron sank two days later. (R C Sturtivant collection)

found them, alighted to pick them up and flew them to Kalafrana. On 1st November, L5806 was attacked by a CR.42 and a Macchi MC.200 while on patrol. Two crew members were wounded and mattresses in the hull were set alight, causing the aircraft to fill with smoke. Although badly damaged below the waterline, the Sunderland managed to return to Kalafrana.

228 Squadron was involved on 11th November in the operation mounted to deal with Italian battleships in the port of Taranto. Until 22.30 one of the Sunderlands, equipped with ASV Mk.I, maintained a reconnaissance patrol over the Gulf of Taranto and was able to report a sixth vessel entering the harbour to join the five already there. Subsequently, intensive attacks by RAF and FAA aircraft and the Mediterranean fleet succeeded in crippling half the Italian ships.

In a slightly different mission, L5803 escorted twelve Hurricanes and two Skuas to Malta on 17th November, although two of the Hurricanes ditched, with the loss of one of the pilots, the other being picked up by the Sunderland.

Concentrated efforts were being made to deal with enemy shipping, and on 2nd December 1940 Operation 'X' was put into force. This involved Sunderlands using ASV to search for Italian convoys between the Italian coast and Benghazi in Libya and to intercept Italian radio signals. A special force of Fleet Air Arm torpedo-bombers was held in readiness to attack the ships. From the middle of December, L5803 carried out trials to determine the fitness of crews to carry out medium-level night bombing of merchant shipping. However, the outcome of this exercise is not recorded.

Another example of the versatility of the Sunderlands and their crews came about on 13th January 1941, when Wg Cdr Nicholetts flew to the coast of Tunisia, taxied to within half a mile (800 m) of the shore and landed several agents by rubber dinghy.

From 23rd January to 25th March 1941 two Sunderlands (referred to as Detachment 2) were kept at St Paul's Bay permanently, as the alighting area at Kalafrana was subject to an almost continuous swell. An officers' mess was established in the house of one Dr Piro, which was then renamed Pembroke House. The enemy must have learned of this, as on 11th February two Ju 88s and a Ju 87 made an attack, although no damage was caused. Two Bf 109s made a further attack on 7th March, causing the death of the guard stationed on Sunderland L2164 and severe damage to the aircraft. A formation of the same type of enemy fighter returned on 10th March, damaging T9046 and setting on fire L2164, which by then had been beached and which eventually sank.

A move was made on 25th March 1941 back to the much less vulnerable base at Aboukir, although a small maintenance party was left behind in Malta. The advance party flew in T9046, while the main party sailed in HMS *Bonaventure*, *Calcutta* and *Greyhound* to Alexandria. Most of the squadron's stores, however, had to be abandoned in Valletta docks, where a lorry loaded with personal kit caught fire in an air raid. At Aboukir, squadron offices were set up in a beach hut and the workshops in old Blenheim packing cases.

Having settled in, 228 Squadron crews began a series of patrols from Suda Bay in Crete and Scaramanga in Greece. On 23rd April the evacuation of RAF personnel from Greece began when T9046 made two trips from Scaramanga to Suda Bay. Further sorties were made by the same aircraft next day, carrying forty men from Scaramanga and twenty-five from Nauplia Bay, the latter trip involving a very difficult take-off due to smoke from burning ships.

Ordered to look for a party of RAF men believed to be in the Githeon area, Flt Lt Lamond flew T9048 and alighted in the harbour, but was then told that the men would be found a little to the south-west. On arrival, he found 101 men of 112 Squadron, which had been flying Gladiator biplane fighters from Heraklion. He took 52 on board and told the officer in charge that he would try to return by 22.00 hours that evening. If he did not do so, the men were to evacuate in a caique. In fact Flt Lt Lamond was later directed to Kalamata instead of Githeon. There no fewer than 72 men boarded the Sunderland, a record number, but with a light load of fuel, the crew found that the aircraft's stability was not affected and the take-off run was only average. However, disaster was not far away for the crew of T9048. They took off again from Suda Bay and alighted at Kalamata at 23.15, but on doing so the Sunderland crashed and broke up, all but four of the crew losing their lives. The survivors clung to the wreckage and were rescued by a fishing boat and taken to hospital, after which at least three of them became prisoners of war.

Flt Lt Frame's crew in T9046, meanwhile, had also been sent to Kalamata, where on 25th April they found fifty RAF men who for some reason fired on the Sunderland before emerging from hiding-places and boarding it and being flown to Suda Bay and thence to Alexandria.

The evacuation of Allied personnel from Greece and its islands was by no means over yet. On 30th May Flt Lt Frame flew the same aircraft to evacuate 25 personnel of all three services from Sphakia Bay in Crete, a small fishing village with a shingle beach. He had difficulty in finding the bay, but alighted so that two members of his crew could row ashore to ask for directions. On their return, a bearing was taken on a flickering light on Gavdo Island, giving the Sunderland's position as six miles (9.6 km) south-west of Sphakia Bay. The Sunderland taxied there and found 25 men in a boat, loaded them aboard and flew them to Alexandria. Next day the same aircraft returned to collect six Greek VIPs and an RAF officer, who were flown to Aboukir. Thus ended the humiliating withdrawal from Greece and Crete, in which a significant part was played by the Sunderlands of 228 Squadron.

Meanwhile, on 27th April 1941 L5807 escorted eight Hurricanes and a Fulmar from a rendezvous point to Malta, but on alighting at Kalafrana during a raid it was attacked by two Bf 109s and destroyed. Back at Pembroke Dock, L5806, now fitted with ASV Mk.II, was air-tested on 28th April and left for the Middle East next day.

Reduced to two aircraft without ground crews, 228 Squadron received an order on 4th June 1941 to move to Bathurst (Half Die) in Gambia. Sufficient personnel and equipment were to be taken to allow the squadron to operate on arrival but the remainder, such as it was, became absorbed into other Middle East units. The two Sunderlands were to leave at once, while personnel would sail on HMT *Dumana* and would be reinforced from the UK. The ground party boarded *Dumana* at Port Tewfik on 17th June, but next day it was learnt that all the squadron's equipment had been destroyed in a fire on SS *Georgic*.

The two Sunderlands, L5803 and T9046, began their 8,908-mile (14,342 km) journeys on 23rd June and 25th June. Their route to Bathurst was via Khartoum, Port Bell, Stanleyville, Leopoldville, Libreville, Lagos and Freetown, and on arrival an operations room was established at Half Die and a Flying-Boat Control Unit in Bathurst itself. This allowed both aircraft to commence patrols on 1st August.

228 Squadron's sojourn at Bathurst turned out to be a short one, however. On 20th August the order was given for all personnel to return to the UK, as 204 Squadron was to replace 228. Overload tanks were to be fitted to both Sunderlands for the long flight, which began on 24th August and ended at Mount Batten two days later. HMT *Dumana*, carrying some of the squadron's ground crews, was diverted to Pembroke Dock, where it arrived on 28th August. Others were left behind, however, not beginning the sea voyage until September and arriving at Avonmouth on the SS *Oronsay* on 20th October. From there the men went to Stranraer, where the squadron had been reunited on 9th October 1941, soon to became operational again.

Early in November 1941 some Mk.II and Mk.III Sunderlands were received for training purposes, but on 15th January 1942 two of them sank in a gale. Convoy escort and anti-submarine patrol work began early in March, but on 10th March the squadron moved to Oban to begin routine patrol flying. Just before the move, however, one of the crews took part in the notable official film Coastal Command, with Wg Cdr Johnnie Hyde DFC brought in from 201 Squadron to act as skipper.

Operations from Oban began at once, but were interrupted by the loss on 13th May of Sunderland T9084, which ran ashore on the island of Gasey, two crew being killed and the other ten injured. Another loss was suffered on 29th May, when T9089 crashed on alighting near Kerrera Island, when five of the crew lost their lives.

A certain amount of mystery still surrounds the loss on 25th August 1942 of HRH the Duke of Kent, who was airborne in Sunderland W4026 of 228 Squadron, on his way from Invergordon to Reykjavik in Iceland. In command was Flt Lt Frank Goyen, with the CO, Wg Cdr Thomas Moseley, as co-pilot. The Sunderland left Invergordon at 13.10 to fly almost 900 miles (1450 km), after a forecast of low cloud and poor visibility. Fitted in the aircraft was a new gyro magnetic compass, on which the magnetic variation had to be set by the navigator. At 13.42 the Sunderland hit a hill known as Eagle Rock in Caithness at a shallow angle, rolled and burst into flames, killing all on board except the tail gunner. Search parties who found the wreckage, and all others involved, including the weather forecasters, were sworn to secrecy, but at a Court of Enquiry the dead pilot was blamed for poor airmanship.

Another accident, just as sad but perhaps of a lower profile, occurred on 4th September 1942, when W4032 alighted in Vaul Bay, Tiree, on return from patrol, due to shortage of fuel. A radio message reported that it was on the water, but nothing further was heard, and it transpired that the Sunderland had hit rocks and broken up, with the loss of eight of the crew, some of whom were in a dinghy which was swept out to sea.

During October, Sunderland DV970 of 228 Squadron was employed to search for possible flying-boat bases in the Hebrides, but nothing appears to have come of this.

228 Squadron stayed at Oban only until 11th December, when Castle Archdale in Northern Ireland became its base. However, the squadron was soon on the move again. After an advance party had left on 27th April 1943, this much-travelled squadron returned to Pembroke Dock on 4th May. The method of movement used was most unusual: gliders, escorted by a

Alighting alongside a launch is Sunderland Mk.I L5806 [BH:Q] of 228 Squadron which later served with 230 Squadron also in the eastern Mediterranean. (P H T Green collection)

Sunderland Mk.II W3996 [DQ:R] of 228 Squadron was hit by a bomb while on the slipway at Kalafrana on 2nd February 1942. The lack of rear fuselage and tailplane seems to indicate that this is a post-raid photograph and that the camouflage netting was not effective. (P H T Green collection)

Sunderland, were towed from St Angelo to Talbenny by Albemarle aircraft carrying the ground crews and equipment.

Returning to the routine task of patrolling the Western Approaches, 228 Squadron enjoyed a partial success on 31st May, when DD838 attacked U-boat *U-563* at position 4700N 0940W after it had already been attacked by others. Eight depth-charges were dropped and many crew members were seen in the water, but the U-boat returned fire and dived out of harm's way. This U-boat was finally despatched by the joint efforts of Halifax HR774 of 58 Squadron, Sunderland DV969 of 10 (RAAF) Squadron and of course DD838 of 228 Squadron. A good result was obtained on 13th July, when the crew of JM708 sank *U-607* with seven depth-charges, blowing the conning tower off. A dinghy was dropped for survivors, and the Sunderland returned to base after being shadowed by a Ju 88. The crew of JM679 sighted three U-boats on the surface on 30th July, and Liberators and Catalinas soon appeared on the scene, upon which the Sunderland provided top cover. There was no decisive result to this incident. On 1st August Flt Lt S White and his crew in JM678 was able to sink *U-383*. Next day JM708 attacked U-boat *U-106* in cooperation with a Sunderland of 461 Squadron, and the enemy submarine was seen to explode.

Anti-submarine patrols formed almost all of 228 Squadron's work during this period. During March 1944, 19 Group aircraft broke all records for flying hours, largely due to very good weather. This placed, of course, a great deal of hard work on all personnel, particularly the ground crews. In May 39 sorties were flown, as the crews took part in a number of 'Viking' and 'Oasthouse' radar exercises. June 1944, the month of the Allied invasion of Normandy, resulted in 77 sorties, although only one, ML763, operated on D-Day. On D+1, ML877, captained by Flt Lt G D Lancaster, sank *U-970*, some of the crew of which were later picked up by rescue boats. Special patrols were organised by Coastal Command to flood the Western Channel and approaches with patrolling aircraft, which meant meticulous time-keeping on patrol, an extra burden on the very efficient navigators. Two of the squadron's aircraft failed to return from patrol during this period, with the loss of fifteen lives.

In July, 68 operational sorties were flown but only one sighting was made. August followed the same pattern, but when Allied troops occupied Brittany the patrol area was moved to the west of Brest. Then, when the enemy U-boat bases at Brest, St Nazaire and Lorient were cut off the U-boats were moved to the Bordeaux area. Due to the almost complete absence of the Luftwaffe from the area, the Sunderlands were then able to work close to the coast and the ports, and flew 85 sorties during the month.

During the middle weeks of September 1944 patrols were flown just off the southern coast of Ireland, as Allied convoys were now using that route. After this, the patrol area moved again, to the north and west of Co Donegal, but there were no sightings. October followed the same pattern, but orders were given that any Spanish fishing vessels outside their territorial waters were to be threatened by a burst of gunfire over the bows! There were no sightings during 46 sorties in November, and this state of affairs continued until 19th December. Then, however, U-boats again began to operate in considerable numbers in the English Channel, sometimes close inshore, and also off Ireland. Their use of the schnorkel breathing device made them difficult to locate, although much use of radar was made.

Re-equipment with the Mk.V Sunderland began in February 1945, and patrols, mainly uneventful, remained the squadron's main task. U-boat activity continued, and some merchant ships were sunk. Attacks were made by 228 Squadron aircraft, and on 27th April RN283 crashed into the sea after being severely damaged by the explosion of its own depth-charges, with some loss of life.

After VE-Day, patrols continued to ensure that all U-boat commanders surrendered, until the squadron disbanded on 4th June 1945.

230 Squadron

Unit codes: **NM** (September 1939 to March 1942); **DX** (March 1942 to December 1942); nil (January 1943 to April 1946); **4X** (April 1946 to March 1951); **B** (March 1951 to February 1957)

Another unit based at Seletar in Singapore, 230 Squadron began receiving Sunderland Mk.Is in June 1938 to replace Short Singapores. The first one, L2159, left Pembroke Dock on 9th June and made its way via Gibraltar, Malta (Calafrana), Alexandria, Lake Habbaniya in Iraq, Bahrain, Karachi, Gwalior, Calcutta, Dalar River and Rangoon to Seletar, arriving on 22nd June. Later, four of the new aircraft were named *Selangor*, *Pahang*, *Negeri Sembilan* and *Perak* in response to a gift of £300,000 from the Sultans of those Malayan states.

With the possibility of war in the air, three of the Sunderlands were despatched on 3rd December 1938 on a Colonial Development cruise to Ceylon, part of which was devoted to examining potential flying-boat bases at Trincomalee, Colombo and Galle.

By the end of that year conversion had been completed, and from the outbreak of the Second World War patrols over the Indian Ocean and the approaches to Malaya were flown. A mobile detachment was based at Penang (Glugor) from 15th October 1939, moving to Trincomalee in Ceylon on 27th October and Colombo on 30th October. That day, two of the Sunderlands visited Koggala Lagoon, which had been recommended as an alternative to Trincomalee. On 3rd November it was proposed that four aircraft would operate from China Bay as Colombo was too congested. However, in November it was decided that Koggala was a practical proposition, and on 23nd November three of the squadron's Sunderlands flew in as a detachment. Koggala was confirmed as 230 Squadron's base in Ceylon on 13th February 1940, and there it was joined by the remainder of the aircraft. Ground-based personnel remaining in Singapore were then posted to 205 Squadron.

Koggala was not used by 230 Squadron for long, however. In advance of the anticipated forthcoming involvement of Italy in the war, four aircraft, each carrying seventeen personnel, left for Egypt on 2nd May 1940. They flew via Cochin, Bombay, Karachi, Bahrain and Lake Habbaniya and arrived at Alexandria four days later, and three more Sunderlands followed. From Alexandria reconnaissance missions for the Mediterranean fleet were flown, as well as anti-submarine patrols and convoy escorts. Some bombing and machine-gunning of enemy merchant ships also took place. During a mission over Tobruk harbour, Sunderland L2160 was attacked by four Fiat fighters, of which one was shot down. Bullet damage to the Sunderland was repaired in flight by the use of Plasticene! Two Italian submarines fell victim to 230 Squadron aircraft during this period, the *Argonauta* on 28th June and the *Rubino* next day, both dealt with by Sunderland L5804. Having sunk the *Rubino*, Flt Lt W W Campbell landed and rescued four of the surviving crew.

The defence of Greece was now becoming a problem, and 230 Squadron Sunderlands shepherded eight Gladiator biplane fighters from Heraklion in Crete on 1st December. A detachment at Suda Bay in Crete was maintained from 3rd November 1940 to 20th January 1941. The role of 230 Squadron at that time was seen as providing assistance west of Crete to convoys in the Aegean Sea and searching in the northern part of the eastern Ionian Sea when the Mediterranean Fleet was present.

On 14th January 1941, the forward alighting area at Suda Bay was closed except in emergency, and a detachment of 230 Squadron there was moved to Scaramanga in Greece, 15 miles (24 km) west of Athens on Lake Eleusis, where it remained until 18th April. At the time, Gladiator fighters were still being escorted to Greece by the squadron. However, Germany invaded Albania and Greece on 6th April 1941 and within a week enemy attacks on Scaramanga made the place very dangerous for the Sunderlands. A retreat to Suda Bay was therefore ordered and was completed by 18th April.

Evacuation of important personnel then became a major task for 230 Squadron. On 16th April two Sunderlands flew to Kotor in Albania and brought out 48 passengers to Greece, and two days later one aircraft flew King Peter of Yugoslavia, members of his family and military staff from Suda Bay to Alexandria. Further evacuation missions were flown to recover Allied personnel and members of the Greek Royal Family from Crete after the enemy airborne invasion of the island. (For more detailed information on this campaign see *Flat Out*, the history of 30 Squadron, published by Air-Britain).

As part of the evacuation of Greece, naval personnel were flown to Scaramanga on 21st April with a stock of pyrotechnics, the sailors forming a shore party for the embarkation of Greek personnel. Over the next ten days, the intensive evacuation of troops and the Greek Royal Family continued, the Sunderlands often escorting BOAC flying boats. One Sunderland, attempting to take off from Scaramanga for Alexandria on three engines, had to return to its moorings, where it was attacked by seven

Two camouflaged Sunderlands Mk.I of 230 Squadron in 1941; [X] in the foreground has an L serial and may be L2160. (P H T Green collection)

Seen at Argos in Greece, this Sunderland Mk.I coded [NM:X] of 230 Squadron took part in the evacuation of British troops to Egypt. (P H T Green collection)

A Sunderland Mk.V of 230 Squadron coded [W] undergoing maintenance, with a purpose-made rig around the starboard wing. (P H T Green collection)

Ju87s, and it caught fire and was destroyed. One of the Stukas was, however, shot down by the Sunderland's top gunner.

On 1st May 1941 the detachment at Suda Bay was withdrawn to Alexandria. Two days later, a Sunderland was sent to Lake Habbaniya in Iraq to rescue members of the BOAC staff, who were reported to be on a boat, but as nothing was found the aircraft returned to base. Similarly, L2160 was despatched to Eremopoli on 9th June to investigate a report that a thousand British troops were still there. It landed east of Paxmadra Island, where a machine gun opened fire but, as no troops were seen, the Sunderland returned to Alexandria.

Patrolling above a slow-moving line astern group of Royal Navy vessels post-war is a Sunderland GR.5 of 230 Squadron, possibly RN270 [4X:V]. (R C Sturtivant collection)

As Alexandria was now suffering frequent air raids, 230 Squadron moved to Aboukir on 19th June 1941, taking over buildings used previously by 228 Squadron. The first Sunderland Mk.IIIs were received in April, and Kasfareet (Fanara) became the squadron's base on 3rd July 1942, but a return was made to Aboukir on 28th July. One U-boat, U-577, was sunk by 230 Squadron during this period, going down north-west of Mersa Matruh on 9th January 1942 after an attack by W3987.

Early in June 1941, 230 Squadron took over the administration of 2 (Yugoslav) Squadron, the eight Do 22 seaplanes of which had escaped from their home country, and this arrangement lasted until February 1942. During those few months, a large number of patrols were carried out by the Dorniers.

230 Squadron left Aboukir for nearby Kasfareet / Fanara on 3rd July 1942 but stayed there only until 28th July before returning. A complete change of scenery was appreciated on 9th January 1943, when the squadron began to move to Dar-es-Salaam in Tanganyika, leaving the Mk.II Sunderlands behind. It was, however, 25th March before the main party of personnel arrived on SS *Takliwa*! From their new base, the Sunderland crews patrolled over the Indian Ocean to look for Japanese submarines, with detachments in Madagascar. Another detachment was positioned at Aboukir on 1st June to await instructions, following the successful end of the North African campaign. On 11th June this detachment was ordered to begin operating from Bizerta in Tunisia to carry out transport flights to Malta. In addition, many air/sea rescue sorties were flown. On 18th July, the crew of EJ141, which was escorted by fifteen P-38 Lightning fighters, rescued the entire crew of a B-26 of the 320th Bombardment Group USAAF, based in Tunisia. On the same day, JM659 took off on an air-sea rescue mission off Naples, again escorted by P-38s, which promptly shot down fifteen Ju 52 transport aircraft!

The Bizerta detachment returned to Dar-es-Salaam on 29th July, and the squadron then detached four Sunderlands to Pamanzi for anti-U-boat operations in the Mozambique Channel in cooperation with the Royal Navy. This lasted until 25th October, when the detachment returned to Dar-es-Salaam.

From 14th September 1943, several sorties were flown to the former Italian island of Castelorosso in the Dodecanese Islands with freight and passengers, and whilst there W4021 was attacked by Ju 88s, but was not damaged. In the second half of November, daily shuttle services were flown between Khartoum and Kisumu by aircrews under training. By December,

A 230 Squadron Sunderland Mk.V identified only as [P] undergoing maintenance at Seletar in 1945. (R C Sturtivant collection)

A magnificent picture of Gibraltar airfield in 1950, with a Sunderland GR.5 of 230 Squadron making a low pass above the runway.
(R C Sturtivant collection)

230 Squadron was flying a mixture of operational, transport and training sorties, and it was while carrying out a radio calibration task on 29th December that Sunderland EJ140 crashed into a hill near Voi, with the loss of the entire crew.

In February 1944, by which time no more Japanese submarines were being reported in the Indian Ocean, 230 Squadron began to move back to Koggala in Ceylon. Squadron members regretted leaving Dar-es-Salaam as they felt that they had been instrumental in creating the base. However, nine Sunderlands left on the long flight via Kisumu, Khartoum, Aden, Masirah, Korangi Creek, Bombay and Cochin. The sea party travelled in late March on HMT *Manela*, not arriving in Ceylon until 9th April. Only minimal maintenance, therefore, was carried out on the aircraft in a two-month period. There was little, if any, enemy activity in the Indian Ocean in May and June, in which month two of the Sunderlands evacuated almost 500 casualties belonging to the 3rd Indian Division from Lake Indawgyi in north Burma when monsoon rain made airstrips unserviceable. A short renewal of U-boat activity took place in July 1944, but the situation again became quiet in August.

During this period, detachments of 230 Squadron were located at Diego Garcia, Addu Atoll, Kelai, Lake Indawgyi, Bally and Trombay.

Sunderland Mk.Vs began to arrive in January 1945 to replace Mk.IIIs, the last of which left for 374 MU at Korangi Creek in March. During February, two Sunderlands flew to Bombay, where arrangements were made to carry urgently-needed heavy equipment from Calcutta to Burma. Next day, Sqn Ldr S W Deller took one aircraft to Shweggin, on the Chindwin River, where he selected an alighting area and organised yellow-painted oil drums to mark the spot. He then returned to Calcutta and three days later began the airlift, which necessitated flying over the treacherous Chin Hills. The second Sunderland soon made a similar sortie and two more were drafted in to build up the operation. After the fifth day, the task began to include repatriating troops for leave, until on 9th March the operation was completed, 400,000lbs of freight having been carried to an area where no flying-boat had ever been seen before.

On 15th March all sections of the squadron packed half of their equipment and took it to Colombo for loading on HMT *Manela*, which would take it to Akyab so that attacks on Japanese coastal shipping could be carried out. *Manela* would also be used as living accommodation. Sunderlands PP145 and PP158, the first of seven, left for Akyab on 16th April, and personnel remaining at Koggala then became a detachment. Squadron HQ was established on board *Manela* on 17th April, and Operation 'Dracula' was implemented for the recapture of Rangoon. Between 9th and 17th May all the aircraft were flown to Koggala or Redhills Lake while the squadron HQ moved once more, this time to newly-freed Rangoon on 23rd May. From 31st May two Sunderlands operated from Dibrugarh on the Brahmaputra River, delivering supplies and carrying 500 troops out. During this operation one of the flying-boats was wrecked.

In June, several small ships were sunk or damaged, while other ships were reported to the bomber force, to be dealt with later by Liberators. However, June was recorded as being "...one of the most trying months in the squadron's history." Conflicting orders were received, and the repatriation of Dominion personnel depleted aircrew numbers by about a third.

From Rangoon the squadron began to move to Redhills Lake in India on 26th July 1945, just before the end of hostilities. There the squadron's main function became the transport of freight and personnel, including released prisoners of war, to and from Singapore. For this the Sunderlands were hurriedly fitted with seats for twenty passengers and bunks for twelve. At the end of August the Koggala detachment was closed and the squadron was reunited. On 12th September a Sunderland which had been lent to Station Flight Koggala left for Seletar to take part in a VJ Day flypast, and returned next day with nine former prisoners of war. A daily service to Seletar began at once and a detachment of three Sunderlands went to Seletar for air-sea rescue duties and local transport flights. The schedule was completed at the end of October, by which time 315 former prisoners of war

A post-war visit to Tower Bridge, London, by Sunderland GR.5 RN299 [4X:P], probably in 1948.   (R C Sturtivant collection)

230 Squadron Sunderlands moored in Young Sound on Greenland's east coast, from where supplies were flown to the British North Greenland Expedition base at Britannia Lake, August 1952.

had been carried on the first stage of their repatriation, 112 medical personnel had been flown to Seletar and 68,429 lbs (31.1 tonnes) of Red Cross parcels had been carried.

In the early days of peace, 230 Squadron completed a move back to Seletar on 30th November 1945, and from there took part in the release of prisoners of war and women and children from Java, a task which came to an end on 4th January 1946. A photographic reconnaissance of Borneo coastal waters was carried out that month, as well as air-sea rescue sorties in support of Spitfires covering a native uprising in Sumatra. At the end of January one aircraft carried 37 Japanese war criminals to Pontianak from Kuching for trial and eventual execution.

At Seletar, the squadron servicing crews found themselves responsible for maintaining the Sunderlands of 209 and 240 Squadrons in addition to their own, a considerable strain on resources. To provide some leave for the hard-pressed men, it was decided to fly them in two Sunderlands each month to India or Ceylon. Nevertheless, all airmen at Seletar ceased work on 26th January in protest at the slow rate of demobilisation and remained idle for two days in what was seen as a mutiny.

The servicing task proved to be a temporary one, as the squadron left the Far East in March 1946 to return to the United Kingdom, arriving on 15th April to settle at Pembroke Dock for the first time in ten years. There, the aircraft establishment was increased to twelve, and the squadron was able to take part in summer exercises with the Fleet in June. After a short spell at Castle Archdale from 10th August 1946, 230 Squadron moved to Calshot on Southampton Water between 16 and 19th September, the aircraft flying in formation to their new base.

During the early part of 1947 aircraft serviceability was poor, with sometimes only two of five being ready for use. More Fleet exercises were indulged in during June, and in September a goodwill tour to Oslo, Copenhagen and Kiel took place.

Like those of 201 Squadron, crews of 230 were taking part in an anti-submarine course in Northern Ireland when the unexpected call to return to Calshot came on 2nd July 1948. There they discovered that they would be involved in the Berlin airlift, and four of 230's Sunderlands flew out to Hamburg (Finkenwerder) on 4th July. The squadron's first sortie was undertaken by VB887 next day. Operating to the Havel Lake in Berlin, the Sunderlands built up a remarkable effort, and those of 230 Squadron set a record for carrying out three complete sorties in seven hours twenty-five minutes. Although accommodation in the former Blohm und Voss aircraft factory, now in the hands of the Army's 22 Heavy Workshops, was basic, morale was high.

Standard loads of 10,000 lbs (4,545 kg) of freight and 700 gallons (3,179 litres) of fuel were carried at first, but before long salt became the Sunderlands' main cargo, with large quantities of documents making return loads. Children and disabled people were also evacuated from Berlin. Highly successful though they were, the Sunderlands were withdrawn on 18th December, by which time it was considered that land-based aircraft were able to cope. After returning to Calshot, 230 Squadron moved to Pembroke Dock once more on 16th February 1949.

During August 1952 230 Squadron was involved in the Greenland Expedition, and maintained a daily airlift into the Arctic Circle. The first of five Sunderlands left Pembroke Dock on 21st July and staged through Reykjavik to rendezvous with the ship carrying the main expeditionary party. In total, the Sunderlands, their crews under the command of Sqn Ldr J S Higgins, flew approximately 150 tons of stores from Young Sound on the east coast of Greenland to Britannia Lake, 190 miles (306 km) to the northwest and 888 miles (1430 km) from the North Pole.

A mission of mercy in which 230 Squadron took part was Operation 'Ionia', the relief of Greek islands after an earthquake. For this, two Sunderlands were detached on 16th August 1953 to Kalafrana in Malta, where three others joined them to form a composite unit.

230 Squadron remained at Calshot until disbanding on 28th February 1957, the Sunderland having by then become something of an anachronism.

240 Squadron

Unit code: (nil)

On 1st July 1945 212 Squadron, which had been flying Catalinas from Redhills Lake in India, was renumbered 240 Squadron, which in turn had been operating similar aircraft from the same base! The new 240 Squadron, which absorbed the old squadron's Special Duties Flight, took over the Sunderland Mk.Vs which had been arriving for 212 Squadron, but

CHAPTER 3 : OPERATING UNITS (RAF, RAAF, RNZAF, SAAF, AÉRONAUTIQUE NAVALE)

Yes, the Sunderland could fly on one engine! Here is MR.5 SZ560 taking part in a Battle of Britain air display at RAF West Freugh on 18th September 1954 while in the hands of the nearby Wig Bay FBSU [later with 209 and 230 Squadrons], with Sqn Ldr Weaver at the controls. An Avro Lincoln B.2 of the Bombing Trials Unit, West Freugh, stands on the ground below. (Andrew Hendrie collection)

continued to fly a number of Catalinas. A new establishment was for twelve ASR Sunderlands and three Catalinas for special duties.

With detachments at China Bay and Bally, the 'new' squadron carried out meteorological sorties, air-sea rescue patrols and anti-locust missions from Korangi Creek. Despite the end of the war, there was no relaxation in the squadron's efforts. A detachment was set up at Rangoon in Burma, and another aircraft establishment, this time for twelve Sunderlands for ASR work and three Catalinas for special duties, came into force. Conversion to Sunderlands began on 1st August.

Special ferry flights to Bangkok, Hong Kong and Melbourne occupied the Sunderland crews in September, as well as daily trips to Singapore (Seletar) in conjunction with 230 Squadron which began on 29 September. On 17rh September the crew of NJ273 rescued the crew of a Liberator of 355 Squadron, who were no doubt grateful for the service. Air-sea rescue sorties were by now mainly made from Penang and Rangoon for the benefit of Transport Command crews flying in the area.

240 Squadron moved to Koggala in Ceylon on 10th January 1946 to concentrate on the Singapore route. However, maintenance of the Sunderlands by personnel who were anxious to be demobilised was becoming a major problem, and 240 Squadron disbanded at Koggala on 31st March 1946.

246 Squadron

Unit code: (nil)

After being reformed on 5th August 1942 at Bowmore, 246 Squadron received Sunderland Mk.IIs and IIIs in October and began making anti-submarine patrols on 12th December. Severe gales caused havoc in mid-February 1943, but the task continued until 28th April, when operations were suspended. 246 Squadron was disbanded on 30th April 1943, its aircraft being dispersed among 228, 330 and 422 Squadrons.

259 Squadron

Unit code: (nil)

A very short-term user of the type, 259 Squadron at Dar-es-Salaam in Tanganyika began receiving Sunderland Mk.Vs on 3rd March 1945 to supplement its Catalinas. Conversion training began at Mombasa on 13th March and by early April several crews were proficient. However, a change of policy meant that the squadron was to disband. Before the end of April six Sunderlands had been despatched to Durban for use by the South African Air Force and the squadron was no more.

270 Squadron

Unit code: (nil)

Based at Apapa in Nigeria, with a detachment at Jui in Sierra Leone, 270 Squadron received its first Sunderland Mk.IIIs in December 1943, but retained some Catalinas until May 1944. Conversion training began soon after Christmas, and anti-submarine patrols and convoy escort work off the west coast of Africa began as soon as the crews were familiar with the aircraft. Advanced bases such as Abidjan in the Ivory Coast, Pointe Noire on the coast of the Congo, Banana on the mouth of the River Congo and Libreville in Gabon were used quite extensively.

Routine operations formed the squadron's task until October and November 1944, when a significant number of meteorological sorties were flown. Continuation training followed, but on 8th March 1945 four Sunderlands were detached to Jui for ten days for anti-submarine operations. However, on 15th May all training ceased and soon afterwards a signal announcing the squadron's imminent move back to the United Kingdom for disbandment was received, with effect from 30th June.

A very dirty Sunderland Mk.III of 270 Squadron, based at Apapa, Nigeria, taking to the air at an unknown location. (P H T Green collection)

330 Squadron

Unit code: **WH**

Formed at Reykjavik in Iceland on 25th April 1941 from Norwegian personnel who had escaped from their homeland when it was overrun, 330 Squadron was based at Oban when in February 1943 the first Sunderland Mk.IIIs arrived to replace Catalinas. Conversion training occupied most of March and April, but anti-submarine work then began.

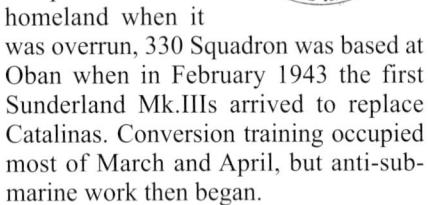

Squadron personnel were inspected by Crown Prince Olaf of Norway on 7th June. Ten days later two Northrop N-3PB floatplanes arrived from Reykjavik and although destined for storage they became useful additions to the squadron's fleet. Patrols over the North Atlantic were the squadron's routine, before and after a move to Sullom Voe on 12th July 1943. From there the squadron flew protection sorties over Russian convoys and hunted for submarines between the Shetlands, Iceland and Norway. The first sighting was on 30th August, but the first success did not come until 16th May 1944, when JM667 attacked *U-240* on the surface and sank it. In addition, 330 Squadron made clandestine flights to carry Allied agents to operate in German-occupied Norway.

The Mk.III Sunderlands were replaced by Mk.V aircraft in May 1945. On 7th May ML827 flew to Woodhaven to collect members of the Allied Military Mission and fly them to Norway to accept the German surrender of that country. Four days later ML814 escorted five ships of the Royal Navy and one of the Royal Norwegian Navy to Norway, after which the Sunderlands began regular transport flights to Oslo, Bergen, Stavanger and Trondheim.

330 Squadron's final parade at Sullom Voe was held on 29th May 1945, and the squadron then began to move to Stavanger (Sola). The last Sunderland left on 14th June, and the squadron passed to the control of the Royal Norwegian Air Force on 21st November 1945.

343 Squadron

Unit code: (nil)

On 29th November 1943, Flottille 7FE of the French naval air arm, which had been formed by an amalgamation of 'Free French' Flottilles 3E and 4E, also became 343 Squadron, RAF. Based at Dakar (Bel Air) in French West Africa, the squadron flew Sunderland Mk.IIIs on anti-submarine and convoy escort sorties. In June 1945 several of the Sunderlands were transferred to Aéronautique navale before the squadron's disbandment as an RAF unit and reversion to its original status as Flottille 7FE on 27th November 1945, becoming Flottille 7.F under a new designation system. Further details will be found in the Aéronautique navale section of this chapter.

422 Squadron (RCAF)

Unit code: **DG** (November 1942 to 1943); **2** (November 1943 to November 1944)

422 Squadron converted to Sunderland Mk.IIIs from Catalinas after moving from Lough Erne to Oban on 5th November 1942, and by the end of December seven Sunderlands were on strength. Initially the squadron was employed on transport tasks, including carrying Hurricane spare parts to Russia. On 10th January 1943 three Sunderlands, W6027, W6030 and W6031, were made ready for special operations in West Africa, and by the end of the month their crews were carrying out coastal reconnaissance missions from Bathurst in Gambia. During the same month the squadron carried out a number of transport and mail flights to Lagos in Nigeria, for which a servicing detachment was positioned at Jui in Sierra Leone.

On 25th February 1943 routine patrols over the Western Approaches were resumed, the squadron moving to Bowmore on 7th May in six tank landing craft. Accommodation there was primitive in the extreme until four Nissen huts were built in June. A spectacular incident, from which all twelve crew members were rescued, occurred on 3rd September, when an engine of DD861 caught fire in the air and fell off, taking a wingtip float and part of the wing with it. The Sunderland rapidly hit the water and sank, but fortunately the crew escaped into dinghies.

The location of this Sunderland Mk.III, NJ188 [WH:G] of 330 Squadron, is not known but may well have been the waters close to Oban. (P H T Green collection)

CHAPTER 3 : OPERATING UNITS (RAF, RAAF, RNZAF, SAAF, AÉRONAUTIQUE NAVALE) 55

Seen at Skattöra Stöflyhavn, Trömso, Norway, in 1945 is a 330 "Norwegian" Squadron Sunderland Mk.V ML824 [WH:T]. The Norwegian flag is painted on the nose above the crew door. (Andrew Hendrie collection)

By September it had become clear that basing an operational squadron at Bowmore was very difficult and would become more so during the winter. Frequent gales, lack of proper maintenance facilities, particularly a slipway, and poor accommodation meant that 422 Squadron personnel hoped that a move would be forthcoming. The move came about at the end of October, when Castle Archdale became the squadron's operating base, although its headquarters was established temporarily at St Angelo airfield, where it remained until joining the squadron at Castle Archdale on 3rd February 1944. On 27th December 1943 one of the Sunderlands attacked an enemy merchant vessel 500 miles (800 km) west of Cape Finisterre, and was damaged in the operation. The vessel was later destroyed by a Liberator.

Only one U-boat was claimed as sunk by 422 Squadron. This was *U-625*, which perished at the hands of Flt Lt S R Butler and his crew in EK591 on 10th March 1944. After the attack, the U-boat surfaced and its commander signalled "Fine bombish" before sinking.

Routine anti-submarine patrols and convoy escort duties continued through 1944, although July and August were quiet months, a detachment being located at Sullom Voe. Squadron personnel had soon settled down at Castle Archdale, many of them making use of the 'Bothwell de Luxe Dinery' at nearby Irvinestown, where a large steak, up to four eggs and a pile of chips could be enjoyed for 3/6 (17.5p in today's money)!

However, on 28th October a move to Pembroke Dock began, 422 Squadron

A Sunderland Mk.III of 330 Squadron on the waters of the Orkney Islands and about to be taken in tow by a high-speed launch.

Sunderland Mk.III, possibly ML759 [M] of 422 Squadron in late 1944, seen approaching a mooring buoy, manoeuvering with inner engines shut down. (Andrew Hendrie collection)

exchanging places with 201. Early in 1945 the squadron participated in a number of actions over the Western Approaches. At Pembroke Dock, a recreation room named Canada House was opened on 5th March 1945 for the use of both Canadian and British personnel. Although hostilities ended, patrols continued until 27th May, and special reconnaissance flights over the Bay of Biscay and Irish Sea and convoy escorts went on until 2nd June.

On 1st June 1945 422 Squadron was transferred to Transport Command to fly Liberators from Bassingbourn, and repatriation to Canada of time-expired personnel began.

423 Squadron (RCAF)

Unit codes:
AB (May 1942 to September 1942);
3 (November 1942 to August 1945);
YI (1944 to May 1945)

Commanded by Wg Cdr F J Rump, the other Canadian-manned Sunderland squadron, 423, was formed at Oban on 18th May 1942 and received its first two aircraft, W6000 and W6001, on 17/18th July. From 23rd August, patrols over the Western Approaches became routine, with a move to Lough Erne (Castle Archdale) on 3rd November 1942 intervening. Some of the patrols were flown over the Bay of Biscay to Gibraltar, where the Sunderlands refuelled before making the hazardous return flight.

On 13th May 1943 Sunderland W6006 attacked *U-456*, but was damaged by a cannon shell; before long, however, HMS *Lagan* destroyed the U-boat and W6006 was able to return to base. One of the Sunderlands, DD859, was shot down on 4th August while dropping Torpex depth charges onto *U-456*. The captain, Flg Off A H Russell, attempted a landing, but the port wing dropped, causing the aircraft to nose in. Fifteen minutes later, the U-boat's crew took to rafts before it exploded, and after a further ten minutes the destroyer HMS *Castleton* picked up the six injured survivors from DD859.

HQ Coastal Command, aware of aircrew frustrations, sent the squadron a signal on 31st October to the effect that although the crews might be disappointed at not seeing many U-boats they could be assured that their patrols were keeping the enemy at bay. At about the same time, special training was provided to allow crews to combat the enemy use of the Schnorkel device.

Operations increased in number in the early part of 1944, and the squadron was particularly busy during the invasion of Normandy. Soon afterwards, a detachment was set up at Sullom Voe. In October 1944 many of the navigators went to nearby Mullaghmore to be trained in the use of Gee and/or Loran systems in an effort to counteract the advantage that enemy submarines were gaining by the use of the Schnorkel breathing tube. An intensive training programme was arranged in which two Royal Navy submarines were used as targets. When, however, a lull in U-boat activity was found in November, training for night operations began. For this, radio altimeters were fitted in the Sunderlands.

In January 1945, ice four inches (100 mm) thick encrusted the wings of the flying boats at Castle Archdale, preventing any flying for several days. Soon after flying was resumed, tragedy hit the squadron when on 11th February NJ183 crashed near Irvinestown, with the loss of all eleven men on board. A mass funeral took place in the local cemetery five days later, and many businesses closed as a mark of respect.

March and April 1945 were taken up mainly by training. The final sortie was made on 31st May 1945, and on 5th June the squadron was told that it would be transferred to Transport Command to fly Liberators. No flying took place that month, repatriation of personnel began and the Sunderlands were flown away. On 6th August the main party of personnel left Northern Ireland via Larne and arrived at Bassingbourn two days later.

By the end of hostilities in Europe, 423 Squadron had sunk five submarines.

461 Squadron (RAAF)

Unit codes: **UT** (April 1942 to June 1945); **2** (April 1943 to June 1945)

Formed at Mount Batten on 25th April 1942 from a nucleus provided by 10 (RAAF) Squadron, 461 Squadron also absorbed experienced land-plane pilots who con-

Taking off from Lough Erne, this Sunderland Mk.III NJ184 [YI:C] was in use by 423 Squadron at Castle Archdale. On 8th May 1945 it overshot the Lough on landing and was not permanently repaired. (Andrew Hendrie collection)

Ground crews of 423 Squadron take a break from servicing a Sunderland's engines at Castle Archdale. Note the ingenious scaffolding designed for use when servicing had to be carried out over water. (P H T Green via Andrew Hendrie collection)

CHAPTER 3 : OPERATING UNITS (RAF, RAAF, RNZAF, SAAF, AÉRONAUTIQUE NAVALE)

After rescuing sixteen survivors from a ditched aircraft early in 1944, this Sunderland Mk.III ML758 [E] of 461 Squadron was taken in tow by Free French warship L19 La Combattante, *the former Hunt-class Escort Destroyer HMS* Haldon. *(P H T Green collection)*

verted to Sunderlands. The squadron began to receive Sunderland Mk.IIs immediately and local flying began on 5th May. It was not long before one of the aircraft, T9111, was attacked by a Bf 109 while searching for a dinghy in the water north of Eddystone lighthouse.

461 Squadron became operational on 1st July 1942. Its routine was to fly patrols over the Western Approaches and the Bay of Biscay. It was not long before the ill-fated T9111 was attacked again, this time by three Ar 196 floatplanes on 30th July. One of these was shot down by T9111's gunners and the others hurriedly made off, leaving the Sunderland slightly damaged. The squadron's first fatalities were caused by the crash of T9090 on 12th August, when it failed to return from an air-sea rescue mission over the Bay of Biscay. Only one of the eleven crew was rescued.

Shipping congestion in Plymouth Sound compelled the squadron to move to Hamworthy in Poole Harbour at the end of August 1942, by which time Mk.III aircraft had been received. Night flying, however, was still carried out at Mount Batten.

In October 1942 461 Squadron was relieved of patrol duties and was tasked with carrying passengers and freight to and from Gibraltar in connection with the forthcoming Operation 'Torch', after which Biscay patrols were resumed.

Another move, to Pembroke Dock, was made on 21st April 1943, and soon afterwards the last Mk.II Sunderland left. Patrols were maintained, particularly over the Bay of Biscay in the hope of intercepting submarines bound for or from their French bases. On 29th April Flg Off R de V Gipps, on his first patrol as captain, and his crew, seriously damaged a U-boat but failed to sink it. On board the Sunderland that day was Air Vice Marshal Baker. Better still, on 2nd May DV968, captained by Flt Lt E C Smith, sank *U-332*.

A spectacular rescue was made on 26th May 1943 by the crew of UT:E, which had gone to the rescue of another Sunderland, JM675, the crew of which had taken to their dinghy after their aircraft had sunk. After transferring the men to a destroyer, UT:E was hit by a huge wave, which made a hole 7ft by 4ft (2.1m by 1.2m) in the hull. In flight, the captain decided not to try a landing on water, and signalled that he would crash-land on Angle airfield, which he did with perfect precision on all four engines!

During a patrol on 30th July 1943 Sunderland 'U' of 461 Squadron (W6077) destroyed U-boat *U-461*! Earlier, on 2nd June, EJ134, patrolling at 200 feet over the Bay of Biscay, was spotted by the leader of eight Ju 88s. Realising this, the Sunderland's crew made for the cover of cloud, but were quickly attacked. The gunners put up a heroic resistance, shooting down three of the enemy aircraft before the Sunderland could escape to safety. Eventually it was beached, with one gunner dead and all the others wounded.

More success came on 2nd August, when the crew of DV968 attacked *U-106* in conjunction with a Sunderland of 228 Squadron, and saw the submarine explode and about thirty of its crew take to the water.

In August, experiments with two-gun belt-fed turrets in place of single-gun magazine-fed turrets in the bows were made. Galley guns designed by the squadron were by then being fitted to all Sunderlands.

The weather in January 1944 was so bad that no flying could take place for eleven days. However, at the end of the month the squadron's usual patrol area was altered from the Bay of Biscay to an area off the north-west coast of Ireland in the vicinity of Fastnet Rock. Large numbers of ships were moving in that area, and the Sunderlands were needed to cover them. On 28th January an enemy submarine (*U-571*) was sunk by the crew of EK577, the first such victory for several months. It was some time before a similar achievement was enjoyed. On 10/11th August ML741 sank *U-385* and two days later ML735 sank *U-270*. First location was by radar, and then the U-boats were illuminated by 1.7-inch (29.7mm) flares. This was the final U-boat success for the crews of 461 Squadron.

In an attempt to determine the true weight of a Sunderland Mk.III, ML771 was flown to Short Bros factory at Windermere on 1st September, and the results can be taken as accurate. The weight empty, but including all 'tare' weight items, was found to be 35,866 lbs (16.303 tonnes); the weight of the crew was estimated at 2,200 lbs (1 tonne); depth

The aircrews of 490 Squadron posed for the camera at Jui, Sierra Leone, in 1945 with one of the Squadron's Sunderland Mk.IIIs and the flag of New Zealand forming a backdrop. *(P H T Green collection)*

charges accounted for 2,136 lbs (971 kg); oil was 1,080 lbs (491 kg); fuel was 14,677 lbs (6.671 tonnes), making the take-off weight 58,680 lbs (26.672 tonnes).

From 28th September to 29th October 1944 a detachment was positioned at Sullom Voe in the Shetlands, from where many patrols were flown over the North Sea.

461 Squadron received Mk.V Sunderlands in March 1945, and conversion was completed by the end of April. After the end of hostilities, the squadron continued to fly patrols and convoy escorts, but carried on only until 20th June, when disbandment took place. During its service, squadron crews had sunk seven U-boats and damaged five others, had destroyed four enemy aircraft, probably accounted for seven more and had damaged eight.

490 Squadron (RNZAF)

Unit code: (nil)

Based at Jui in Sierra Leone for almost its entire existence, 490 Squadron was flying Catalinas on patrols over the South Atlantic when Sunderland Mk.IIIs began arriving in May 1944. The first two started operating anti-submarine missions on 17th May. Several other landing areas in West Africa were used as required, the most prominent being Fisherman's Lake in Liberia. This routine pattern continued until the squadron disbanded on 1st August 1945.

Servicing Echelons

Within many RAF squadrons, Servicing Echelons were formed to provide maintenance facilities, and were generally numbered in line with their parent units. Those involved in Sunderland maintenance were as follows:

4422 SE: renumbered from 8422 SE at Pembroke Dock on 5th June 1945; continued when parent 422 Squadron became land-based in July 1945.

4423 SE: renumbered from 8423 SE at Castle Archdale on 5th June 1945; continued when parent 423 Squadron became land-based in August 1945.

6330 SE: renumbered from 8330 SE on arrival of parent 330 Squadron at Stavanger on 30th May 1945; taken over by RNoAF on 21st November 1945.

7001 SE: formed at Bathurst on 1st April 1944 to service 95 Squadron; renumbered 7095 SE on 18th April 1944.

7002 SE: formed at Jui on 1st April 1944 to service 204 Squadron; renumbered 7204 SE on 18th April 1944.

7003 SE: formed at Apapa on 1st April 1944 to service 270 Squadron; renumbered 7270 SE on 18th April 1944.

7004 SE: formed at Jui on 1st April 1944 to service 490 Squadron; renumbered 7490 SE on 18th April 1944.

7095 SE: renumbered from 7001 SE on 18th April 1944; disbanded with parent 95 Squadron on 30th June 1945.

7204 SE: renumbered from 7002 SE on 18th April 1944; disbanded with parent 204 Squadron on 30th June 1945.

7270 SE: renumbered from 7003 SE on 18th April 1944; disbanded with parent 270 Squadron on 30th June 1945.

7490 SE: renumbered from 7004 SE on 18th April 1944; disbanded with parent 490 Squadron on 1st August 1945.

8010 SE: formed at Mount Batten on 23rd June 1943 to service 10 (RAAF) Squadron; disbanded when Sunderlands were withdrawn on 20th June 1945.

8201 SE: formed at Castle Archdale on 23rd June 1943 to service 201 Squadron; disbanded on 1st August 1949.

8202 SE: formed at Gibraltar on 23rd June 1943 to service 202 Squadron; disbanded on 4th June 1945.

8228 SE: formed at Pembroke Dock on 23rd June 1943 to service 228 Squadron; disbanded on 4th June 1945.

8230 SE: formed at Pembroke Dock on 15th April 1946 to service 230 Squadron; disbanded on 25th February 1949.

8330 SE: formed at Oban on 23rd June 1943 to service 330 Squadron; renumbered 6330 SE on 30th May 1945.

8422 SE: formed at Bowmore on 23rd June 1943 to service 422 Squadron; renumbered 4422 SE on 5th June 1945.

8423 SE: formed at Castle Archdale 23rd

June 1943 to service 423 Squadron; renumbered 4423 SE on 5th June 1945.

8461 SE: formed at Pembroke Dock on 23rd June 1943 to service 461 Squadron; disbanded on 4th June 1945.

Air-Sea Warfare Development Unit

Unit code: **P9**
Headquartered at Thorney Island, the ASWDU was formed on 1st January 1945 from the Coastal Command Development Unit, and had a detachment of Sunderland Mk.IIIs and Vs at Calshot.

4 (Coastal) Operational Training Unit

Unit code: **TA**
Formed at Stranraer from 1 Flying Boat Training Squadron on 16th March 1941, this important unit was tasked with training crews to fly flying boats, and at first was equipped with Singapores, Stranraers, Londons, Lerwicks and Catalinas. Sunderlands began to arrive on 3rd December 1941 to augment the fleet, which had been based at Invergordon since 21st June, and five of them were dispersed to Wig Bay on 20th February 1942 due to the threat of air attack.

On 28th February 1942, the training programme was split so that the number of aircraft at Invergordon could be reduced. Initial training would be carried out at Stranraer with seven Londons, three Sunderlands and three Catalinas, while advanced training would continue at Invergordon. This system continued until 10th November 1942, when the detachment returned to Invergordon.

An unusual operation carried out on 21st April 1942 involved three of the Sunderlands alighting on Loch Lochy, each carrying 35 commandos, in order to train them in embarking in and disembarking from flying-boats.

Routine maintenance was carried out on a floating dock at Dalmore pier, while the slipway and hardstandings around Alness were used for major servicing. Five hangars were erected to give cover to personnel working on the exposed site. RAF Invergordon was renamed Alness on 10th February 1943.

In December 1942 there was an establishment of 44 Catalinas and Sunderlands seventeen Sunderlands were serviceable, owing to a lack of skilled fitters and a shortage of spare parts. In August 1943, by which time 4 (C) OTU had become an efficient unit, the establishment for Sunderland Mk.IIs and IIIs was 31. In October the Catalinas were transferred to 131 (C) OTU, leaving Sunderlands as the sole equipment. By March 1944 the aircraft establishment was 41, but by January 1945 this had reduced to 19 operational and twelve non-operational Mk.IIs and Vs.

With the end of their courses in sight, trainee crews often took part in operational patrols, and it was during one of these, on 25th May 1944, that Sunderland ML736, captained by Flt Lt T F Frizzell DFC, dropped depth-charges on surfaced U-boat *U-240*, destroying it.

There were, unfortunately, several serious accidents to 4 (C) OTU aircraft operating from Invergordon / Alness. During the last week of November 1943, for example, three Sunderlands crashed on the flarepath. A year later, one of the aircraft hit debris on alighting, made another circuit and crashed, killing all twelve men aboard. Only two weeks later, eleven men lost their lives when an engine of DD851 caught fire and fell out, the Sunderland then crashing on a nearby railway.

In October 1944 Operation 'Uplift' was mounted to repatriate time-expired personnel from Iceland and replace them with others. Nine Sunderlands of 4 (C) OTU took part, carrying 1,115 men from Reykjavik to Alness and 593 on the outbound journeys.

Flying continued after the end of hostilities, although on a much-reduced scale. After the CO had investigated and rejected the idea of a move to Killadeas in June 1946, 4 (C) OTU moved to Pembroke Dock on 15th August. From there a number of trips were made to Fornebu in Norway to collect RAF ground crew men who had been stationed there. Finally, on 31st July 1947, 4 (C) OTU was redesignated 235 Operational Conversion Unit.

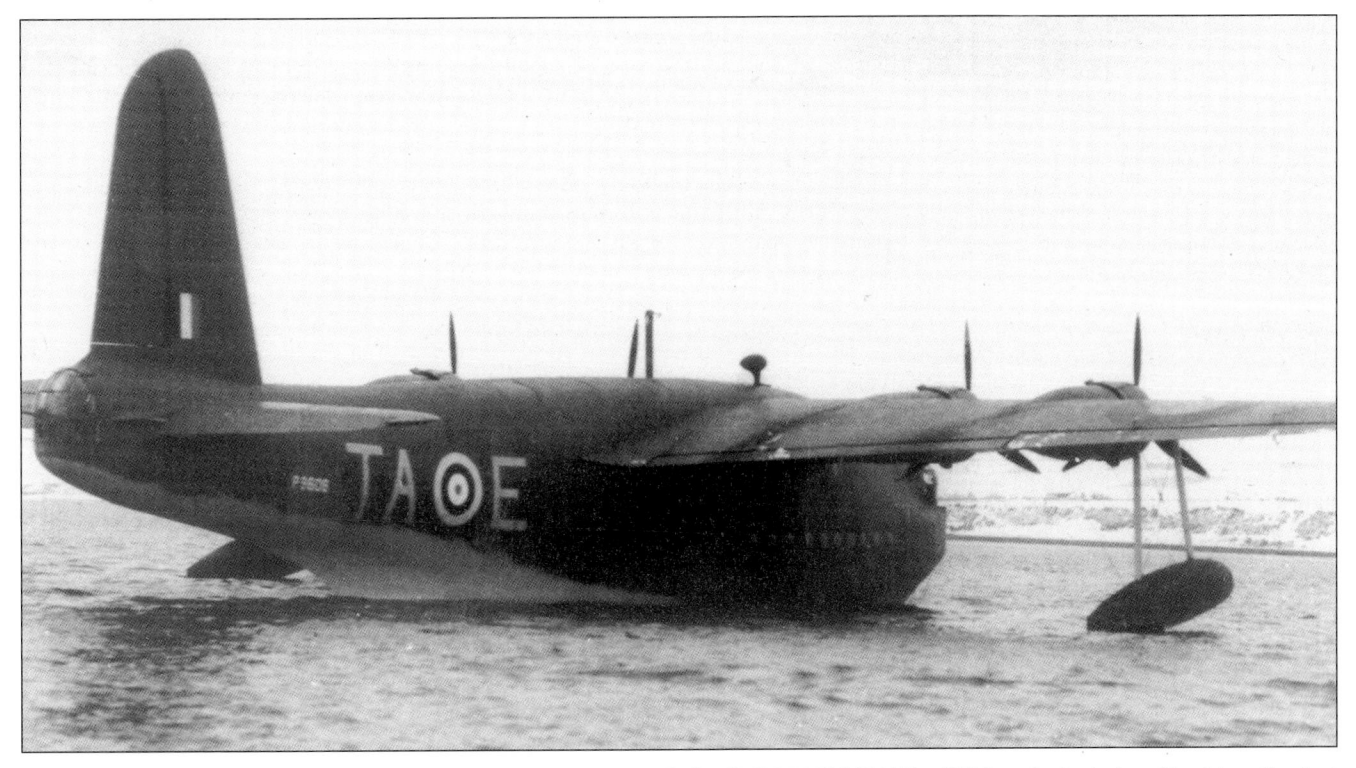

4 (C) OTU used code letters TA, which were carried by this drab Sunderland Mk.I P9606 [TA:E]. (E Edwards via Andrew Hendrie collection)

131 (Coastal) Operational Training Unit

Unit code: (nil)
This unit was formed at Killadeas on 20th July 1942, with its HQ at St Angelo while proper accommodation was being built. Sunderlands did not appear until May 1944 to operate alongside Catalinas, and by January 1945 there were 22 Sunderland Mk.IIIs on strength. On 13th February, however, the Sunderland commitment was transferred to 4 (C) OTU, and the unit closed down in June 1945.

235 Operational Conversion Unit

Unit codes: **TA** (1947 to 1951); **D** (1951 to 1953)
Retitled from 4 (C) OTU on 31st July 1947, 235 OCU used five Sunderland GR.5s to train crews at Calshot. Crews so trained included, in 1952/53, several for the Royal New Zealand Air Force, which was about to receive Sunderlands. In August 1953 two Sunderlands were sent to Kalafrana in Malta to take part in Operation 'Ionia', in which they carried supplies to Greek islands affected by an earthquake.

The unit was disbanded on 17th October 1953 and its personnel and aircraft were handed over to the reformed Flying Boat Training Squadron at Pembroke Dock.

Flying Boat Training Squadron

Unit code: (nil)
Inheriting three Sunderland GR.5s from 235 OCU on 17th October 1953, the FBTS carried on the training programme on a reduced scale at Pembroke Dock until 5th October 1956, by which time no more crews for Sunderlands were required.

302 Ferry Training Unit

Unit code: (nil)
This unit was one of two which gave further training to flying-boat crews who would ferry the aircraft overseas. Formed on 30th September 1942 at Lough Erne, 302 FTU flew both Catalinas and Sunderlands.

Moves were made to Stranraer on 1st December 1942, and on 22nd July 1943 to Oban, where it operated from Ganavan Sands. Trainee crews flew many hours on Atlantic patrols until they were judged proficient, when they ferried Sunderlands and Catalinas to bases in the Middle East, Far East or West Africa. On 12th January 1944 the other unit, 308 FTU, was absorbed, and a detachment was sent to Alness from March to June 1944.

Another move, to Killadeas, was completed on 28th April 1945, but the unit did not stay long before moving on 1st July to Alness, although no more training was carried out. The unit was not formally disbanded, however, until 1st April 1946.

308 Ferry Training & Test Flying Unit

Unit code: (nil)
Formed at Pembroke Dock on 22nd March 1943 specifically to train crews to ferry Sunderlands to overseas squadrons, this unit lost the 'test flying' part of its title on 7th May 1943. It was absorbed into 302 FTU on 12th January 1944.

1430 (Flying Boat Transport) Flight

Unit code: (nil)
Five Sunderland Mk.Vs equipped this unit, which was formed at Kai Tak on 5th August 1946. Its first aircraft was SZ564, which did not arrive at Kai Tak until 23rd August. The Flight's existence was very short, as on 1st September 1946 it was redesignated 88 Squadron.

Coastal Command Flying Instructors School

Unit code: (nil)
A combined landplane and flying-boat unit, CCFIS based its Sunderland Mk.IIIs at Killadeas, where its predecessor, 12 Flying Instructors School, had been based until redesignation on 23rd February 1945. The unit's HQ, until then at St Angelo, moved to Turnberry on 9th June 1945, and the Sunderlands to Alness on 16th July. There they were used until the unit was redesignated Coastal Command Instructors School on 29th October 1945.

Coastal Command Instructors School

Unit code: **EJ** (use on Sunderlands not confirmed)
Remaining at Alness after the minor change of title, the Sunderlands of CCIS carried on their task until the unit disbanded on 1st April 1946.

11 Flying Boat Fitting Unit

Unit code: (nil)
This unit was formed at Wig Bay on 15th July 1943 and was absorbed into 57 MU on that unit's formation on 8th October that year.

Flying Boat Storage Unit

Unit code: (nil)
This post-war unit was formed at Wig Bay on 1st October 1951 to store Sunderlands after the disbandment of 57 MU. The unit was operated by Short Bros & Harland Ltd and disbanded on 31st October 1957.

1 Flying Boat Servicing Unit

Unit code: (nil)
Formed at Wig Bay on 12th March 1942, this unit, not numbered until 25th September 1942, worked alongside 57 MU until being absorbed by it on 1st February 1944. In its early days, 1 FBSU was the main reception point for deliveries of new Sunderlands from the various factories.

2 Flying Boat Servicing Unit

Unit code: (nil)
This unit was formed at Greenock on 25th September 1942, to service mainly Catalinas. It was May 1944 before preparations were put in hand for dealing regularly with Sunderlands. Work was disrupted by stacks of building materials on site awaiting use, but a new hangar came into use in August, easing the situation. By the end of the year some conversions of Sunderlands from Mk.III to Mk.V had been carried out, but then the workload began to diminish, and on 13th August 1945 the unit closed down. The last aircraft, ML819, had taken off for Calshot on 25th July.

3 Flying Boat Servicing Unit

Unit code: (nil)
This unit was formed at Pembroke Dock on 25th September 1942 and disbanded in December 1944.

4 Flying Boat Servicing Unit

Unit code: (nil)
Formed on 25th September 1942 from the Flying Boat Servicing Unit at Oban (Ganavan Sands), this unit disbanded in April 1944.

5 Flying Boat Servicing Unit

Unit code: (nil)
Formed on 25th September 1942 at Invergordon, which was renamed Alness on 10th February 1943, 5 FBSU was disbanded in August 1945. Its task seems to have been servicing for units based in the area, particularly 4 (C) OTU.

6 Flying Boat Servicing Unit

Unit code: (nil)
Formed from the Flying Boat Repair Section at Calshot on 13th September 1943, this unit concentrated on Sunderland repairs and modifications. Disbandment took place in August 1945.

12 (Flying Boat) Aircraft Preparation & Modification Unit

Unit code: (nil)
This short-lived unit with a self-explanatory title was formed at Calshot on 1st September 1945, probably from 6 FBSU personnel, and disbanded on 25th May 1946.

57 Maintenance Unit

Unit code: (nil)
Responsible for the acceptance of most new Sunderlands from the manufacturers, the supply of airworthy aircraft to the squadrons, for modifications not carried out by the manufacturers, and for storage, 57 MU was formed at Wig Bay on 8th October 1943. Unfortunately, at the end of January 1944 ten Sunderlands fell victim to a freak gale which blew them over. On 1st February 1944 57 MU absorbed 1 FBSU, and the unit became very busy in its work on all types of marine aircraft. By January 1945 over 1000 personnel were on 57 MU's books.

When hostilities ended in May 1945, the pressure on 57MU did not ease, as the unit was given the task of disposing of numerous landplanes through Sub-Storage Units at RAF Castle Kennedy and West Freugh. At the same time, large numbers of flying-boats were present at Wig Bay for scrapping or disposal. In 1945 the unit dealt with the modification of a number of Sunderland Mk.IIIs to Mk.V standard, the first taking to the air on 18th May.

By the end of 1948 most of 57 MU's activities involved the preparation of Sunderlands for further service at the rate of six per month, three of them for use in the Far East. Four Sunderlands for the New Zealand Air Force were also refurbished.

57 MU disbanded on 1st October 1951 and the site was taken over by Short Bros & Harland Ltd under contract, although a small number of RAF personnel of the Flying Boat Test Unit remained until 1st November 1955, when they moved to RAF Pembroke Dock. The last of a further sixteen Sunderlands was flown out in June 1954 by a RNZAF crew which had arrived at Wig Bay via RAF West Freugh. There being no more work to do, on 11th September 1957 the site closed and Short's workers began to leave for Belfast.

272 Maintenance Unit

Unit code: (nil)
On 1st August 1945 there were 13 Sunderlands and 26 Catalinas on charge to RAF Killadeas and being prepared for long-term storage. 272 MU came into being on 17th August and took over this task. Work was often held up by the demobilisation of personnel, but many Sunderlands were dealt with until on 24th May 1946 the order was given to fly all remaining aircraft to 57 MU at Wig Bay, an operation which was completed on 14th November, when ML769 took to the air.

Marine Aircraft Experimental Establishment

Unit code: (9J)
A very old-established unit, MAEE was based at Felixstowe until 21st September 1939, when a move was made to Helensburgh (Rhu) in Scotland, considered to be a much safer area. Its task was the testing and evaluation of service and civilian flying-boats and seaplanes, their engines and equipment, and Sunderlands were among the many types which passed through the hands of the MAEE. Control of the Establishment was transferred to the Ministry of Aircraft Production in 1940, and the unit returned to Felixstowe on 1st August 1945. The RAF element disbanded on 31st March 1953.

Air Headquarters Iraq Communications Flight

Unit code: (nil)
For a period in 1945, 'B' Flight of this large unit operated Sunderland Mk.IIIs from Habbaniya Lake, conveniently close to its headquarters at the land airfield.

Station Flight, Kallang

Unit code: (nil)
Kallang was a flying-boat base pre-war, being used for Imperial Airways services. It was used by Japanese Navy flying-boats in wartime and by the RAF after the Japanese surrender in Singapore.

Station Flight, Koggala

Unit code: (nil)
Three Sunderlands are known to have been used at various times postwar by this Flight — ML865, RN280 and RN302.

Station Flight, Pembroke Dock

Unit code: (nil)
This Flight is believed to have used one or more Sunderlands, but no identities are recorded.

Far East Flying-Boat Wing

This unit was formed on 1st February 1950 at Seletar to administer 88, 205 and 209 Squadrons of Sunderlands, which were providing support for the Army in Malaya and United Nations forces in Korea, for which an advanced HQ was set up at Iwakuni in Japan on 11th September 1950. The Wing was disbanded on 31st December 1954.

86 (General Reconnaissance) Wing

Purely an administrative unit, 86 Wing was formed aboard MV *Dumana* on 5th May 1939. Five days later the vessel sailed from London to Malta, where the staff were to administer 202 and 228 Squadrons. From Malta the *Dumana* proceeded to Alexandria, arriving on 2nd June, but in November a return to Malta was made, the vessel docking at Marsaxlokk. From there it sailed to Gibraltar on 10th December, and on 16th February 1940 the Wing was renumbered 101 (GR) Wing.

100 (General Reconnaissance) Wing

Another administrative unit, 100 Wing was set up on board the depot ship HMT *Manela* in London Docks on 12th May 1939. It then sailed to Calshot, but soon moved to Scotland, and by 9th August was at Garth Voe in the Shetlands, controlling 209 and 210 Squadrons, and soon 240 Squadron. Some time was then spent in Icelandic waters, and in September of 1941 the Wing was scheduled to go to West Africa, but this plan was cancelled, and the unit disbanded on 9th September 1941.

101 (General Reconnaissance) Wing

Formed from 86 (GR) Wing on 16th February 1940 at Gibraltar, 100 Wing spent its time on MV *Dumana* in control of 202 and 230 Squadrons in the Mediterranean until disbanding in July 1941.

102 (General Reconnaissance) Wing

This Wing HQ was formed on 14th April 1941 on board MV *Batavier II* at

Gourock, which then took over from HMT *Manela* as the depot ship for UK-based flying-boat squadrons. Although the ship spent some time in Northern Ireland waters, the HQ never became fully operational and disbanded on 31st January 1942.

116 (Transport) Wing

Formed on 1st January 1944 at Hendon Hall Hotel in north London, this unit took over the operation of scheduled services to India from 44 Group. As such, it was responsible for the Sunderland flying-boat services between Hamworthy and India, but was redesignated 47 Group on 1st January 1945.

295 (General Reconnaissance) Wing

Established on 1st March 1942 at Marine Camp, Bathurst in Gambia, this HQ unit controlled squadrons in West Africa, initially including 204 Squadron and later 95 Squadron. On 1st May 1943 the unit moved to Dakar in Sénégal and assumed control of Free French units operating in the area, but on 21st September 1944 returned to Gambia to be based at Yundum airfield. 295 (GR) Wing disbanded on 1st August 1945.

297 (General Reconnaissance) Wing

Based at Freetown in Liberia, 297 (GR) Wing controlled locally-based reconnaissance squadrons, including Sunderlands. It came into being on 7th October 1942 but lasted only until 15th February 1943.

Two additional formations existed, which, although civilian in nature, aided the war effort to such an extent that they became indispensable.

Air Transport Auxiliary

Although not a military unit, the ATA was an essential component of the overall war effort by virtue of delivering aircraft between factories and operating units and to and from Maintenance Units. Sunderlands were among the aircraft types ferried by ATA pilots, who were given a conversion course by the RAF, initially on a Catalina at Largs, and after that aircraft had been written off, at Alness. There, a comprehensive course was arranged on both Catalinas and Sunderlands. Later, the two-week training course was moved to 131 OTU at Killadeas.

It is believed that about fifteen pilots and their crews qualified to fly the two types of flying-boat. In ATA terms, flying-boat crews were unusually comprehensive, consisting of the pilot, co-pilot, flight engineer and two Sea Cadets, who helped during mooring. The crews were allocated to one of three Ferry Pools: 4 FP at Prestwick, 6 FP at Ratcliffe, or 8 FP at Belfast. From these bases they were flown by taxi aircraft to the land airfield nearest to the flying-boat base and thence by road.

Between 1943 and 1945, 560 Sunderlands were ferried by ATA crews, many of whom are said to have found the experience highly enjoyable.

Civilian Repair Parties

Among the many unsung heroes in the story of the Sunderland are the personnel of Short Bros Civilian Repair Parties (CRPs), under the manager of the Repairs Department at Rochester, W David Main. Controlled by the Ministry of Aircraft Production, Shorts maintained several such parties, which comprised five or six men under a Firm's Representative, or 'gaffer', and their task was to carry out major repairs and some modifications, often under arduous conditions, at flying-boat bases around Great Britain.

One of the more difficult of these expeditions took place when a CRP was sent to the Faeroe Islands on 9th November 1942 to repair a Sunderland of 228 Squadron, then based at Oban. While alighting on Lake Sorvaagvata on the island of Vaaga, the Sunderland had struck a rock and was partly submerged a mile or so offshore. The men of the CRP, under their 'gaffer', Frank Freeman, travelled overnight by rail to Stranraer, from where they flew in a Sunderland of 246 Squadron to Oban to spend the night before the last leg of their journey to Vaaga. Still wearing clothing suitable for the south of England, they were ferried ashore, where they were taken aback when they met RAF men in full Arctic kit! The weather on the Faeroes, which lie about halfway between Scotland and Iceland, was extremely cold and the hours of daylight very limited.

Even after its engines had been removed, lifting the Sunderland proved to be a major problem, but eventually airbags were acquired from Scotland and used successfully. The work was still in progress at Christmas, but disaster struck in January 1943, when a violent storm wrecked the Sunderland on which the men had been working for so long. Before leaving for home, however, the CRP men managed to repair a Sunderland on which a landing light had been damaged by a bird strike.

Members of the CRPs were responsible for their own tools and light equipment, and one man remembers being obliged to buy replacements from a local hardware shop after his toolbox was damaged in transit to a repair job at Dumbarton.

RAF Sullom Voe in the Shetlands was regarded by the CRPs as being little better than the Faeroes. Frank Freeman's party worked mainly for 330 (Norwegian) Squadron while at the Voe, and although the men found the work interesting they were not sorry to leave for the warmer and drier south of England. Permanent bases such as Pembroke Dock were the natural favourite places for the CRP men, but even there they had to find their own lodgings and food. Among the jobs carried out by a CRP which worked mainly for 461 Squadron was the removal of Sunderland T9114 from

T9114 was the 461 Squadron Sunderland Mk.II which made a forced landing on Angle airfield on 29th May 1943, requiring ingenuity from the CRP to restore it. (R C Sturtivant collection)

Angle airfield, where it had crash-landed. Before repairs could be made, the aircraft had to be dragged to the shore of Angle Bay. This involved crossing fields, going through hedges and across roads, moving telegraph poles if necessary. Nobody could claim this as a run-of-the-mill project!

Another fine piece of work carried out by a CRP was the joining together of the serviceable portions of Sunderlands DV962 and DV980 (see Chapter 4). This had to be done very precisely, so specially-built wooden jigs were used. A pilot, Flt Lt Young, watched part of the work in progress, offered to fly the completed aircraft, and reported that it flew better than some new Sunderlands!

Little has been recorded about the activities of the Civilian Repair Parties, but it is clear that without their practical support far fewer Sunderlands would have been available for active service.

PART 2: ROYAL AUSTRALIAN AIR FORCE

10 (RAAF) Squadron

Unit code: **RB**

Unique in being a fully-manned RAAF unit operating from the United Kingdom, this squadron had been formed on 1st July 1939 at Point Cook in Australia to operate Sunderlands which had been ordered by the RAAF. It was planned that these aircraft would be flown from Rathmines, on Lake Macquarie, New South Wales. To undergo a conversion course, crews were sent by Imperial Airways flying-boat to England, where at Calshot they flew Singapores at first, moving on 12th August to Pembroke Dock to receive their Sunderlands, an event scheduled for 11th September. However, war was declared on 3rd September, and on 7th October the detachment, including a small number of ground personnel, was ordered to stay at Pembroke Dock.

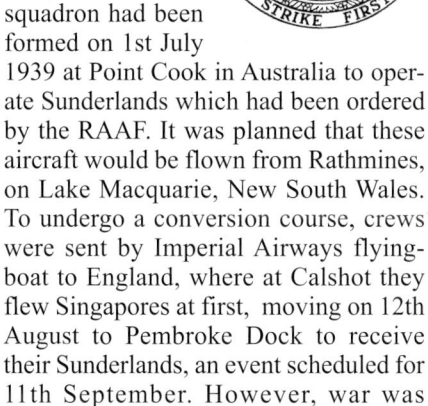

RAF Sunderland Mk.Is were then provided for what was developing into a squadron, and a first operational flight was made on 10th October, a trip by Sunderland N9049 to Bizerta in Tunisia with a spare engine for another squadron.

Making a low pass over the water is W3984 [RB:S], a Sunderland Mk.II of 10 (RAAF) Squadron. Underwing aerials have been removed on the print. (P H T Green collection)

More crews and ground personnel left Australia in RMS *Orontes*, which set sail on 27th November, and after transferring to the SS *Duke of Argyll* at Cherbourg, the men arrived at Pembroke Dock on 6th December.

On 9th December a number of army officers were flown from Calshot via Marseilles and Bizerta to Cairo, but bad weather delayed the flight at Cadzu and Biscarosse, and on the return trip at Marseilles.

10 Squadron's first operation took place on 6th February 1940, when Flt Lt Pearce and crew carried out a convoy escort mission, alighting off Penrhos in north Wales due to bad weather. Escort work and continuation training occupied the squadron for the next few months.

A move to Mount Batten was made on 1st April 1940, with nine Sunderlands on strength. During the course of a patrol on 24th April, one of the captains was asked to search for a submarine reported off Start Point in Devon, but no trace of it was seen. A close encounter with the enemy was experienced by the crew of N9050 on 28th May when it was fired on by AA guns off Boulogne and, two minutes later, six Me 110 fighters passed close by. The first attack on an enemy submarine occurred on 17th June 1940, when Sqn Ldr Pearce spotted one six miles (9.6 km) away and was able to drop six bombs just in front of it. While oil and bubbles were seen on the water, there was no proof of a 'kill'.

In addition to normal patrol duties, the squadron flew special sorties carrying VIPs to France during the last days before the Germans overran the northern part of the country, and to Malta. A notable trip was made by Flt Lt Cohen and crew in P9602, with Lord Gort and Mr Duff-Cooper as passengers, to Rabat in French Morocco on 25th June. French officials at Rabat were very obstructive, only allowing Flt Lt Cohen ashore to give an urgent message to Lord Gort when he threatened the local boatmen with his revolver. A safe return to base was made next day via Gibraltar.

On 1st July 10 Squadron celebrated its first U-boat 'kill'. Flt Lt W N Gibson and his crew in P9603, spotting *U-26* on the surface at position 4803N 1130W, dropped two sticks of four bombs, which damaged the submarine so severely that the crew abandoned it, and it then sank. The 41 survivors were picked up later by HMS *Rochester*. Two days later Sunderland N9049 carried out a photo-reconnaissance sortie over Bordeaux and St Nazaire and was fired on by AA without serious damage. A similar mission, to ensure that the coast of the Irish Republic did not harbour any enemy vessels, took place on 22nd July. A U-boat had been reported to be taking refuge in Dingle Bay on 29th July, but was not found.

That same day, the crew of Sunderland P9602 sighted a Do 18 flying-boat and attacked it, scoring some hits. The enemy aircraft retaliated, wounding the Sunderland's front gunner, but after the rear gunner managed to hit the Dornier again it departed hastily.

Two Sunderlands, P9600 and P9605, were sent to Gibraltar on 8th July 1940 to carry out reconnaissance and anti-submarine duties, and while present there they

An attractive photograph of an unidentified Sunderland Mk.I code [RB:Z] of 10 (RAAF) Squadron alighting, probably on Milford Haven.
(P H T Green collection)

This 10 (RAAF) Squadron Sunderland Mk.I T9071 [RB:M] has a damaged starboard wing tip as a result of a collision with a tanker at Alexandria on 4Jun41.   (Gerald Raggett collection via Rod Simpson)

The Sunderlands of 10 (RAAF) Squadron wore large clear codes on their camouflage, in this case [RB:A].   (P H T Green collection)

Sunderland Mk.I N9050 [RB:D] of 10 (RAAF) Squadron, moored in front of HMS Hood. *The photograph must pre-date 24th May 1941 which was the date on which the battlecruiser was sunk by the* Bismark.   *(Gerald Raggett collection via Rod Simpson)*

cooperated with HMS *Argus*, on board which were twelve Hurricanes and two Skuas bound for Malta. Apart from shadowing the aircraft carrier, the Sunderlands carried personnel to service the fighters on arrival on Malta. Initially, the Sunderlands could not locate *Argus* in the dark, and were shadowed by a twin-engined Caproni aircraft, so had to take avoiding action. The fighters took off from *Argus* and reached Malta safely, as did the Sunderlands. P9600 continued to Alexandria next day to collect a number of VIPs, including Gen Sir Archibald Wavell, the C-in-C Middle East, and fly them home via Crete, Malta and Gibraltar, and both Sunderlands arrived at base on 7th August.

A detachment of two Sunderlands was sent to Oban on 1st August 1940, and while there one crew carried out a significant humane mission. Sqn Ldr Bill Garing, flying N9050 on 25th September, spotted a solitary lifeboat 400 miles (nearly 650 km) out in the Atlantic, with a boy frantically signalling by semaphore the words '*City of Benares*'. Garing tried three times to alight on the rough sea, but without success. Eventually, HMS *Anthony*, an escort destroyer, was guided to the spot and the 46 survivors of the ill-fated ship were rescued. The detachment returned to Mount Batten on 10th April 1941.

Another rescue was effected on 17th October 1940, this time by Flt Lt I Podger, who spotted a faint light which proved to be from a lifeboat carrying survivors of the MV *Stagrant*. With great difficulty, Podger alighted and picked up 21 crew members who had been adrift for four days. A third attempt at saving lives was made on 16th November, when Flt Lt Bruce Courtney took off from Oban to search for the SS *Camita*, a tanker. It was not found, but the SS *Planter* was discovered alone and vulnerable. After trying to arrange for an escort vessel, Courtney abandoned the attempt, and it was then learnt that *Planter* had sunk.

Plymouth, including RAF Mount Batten, was the subject of many heavy air raids at this time, and a particularly damaging one occurred on 27th November 1940. Standing on the apron, Sunderland N9048 was destroyed by fire, while P9601, at its moorings, was also burnt out. Other Sunderlands were damaged but repairable, and much damage was caused to buildings and oil storage tanks, prompting the move of two Sunderlands to Pembroke Dock for safety. Another severe raid took place on 13th January 1941, during which three Sunderlands were damaged, and yet another on 20/21st March. At the end of March, three of 10 Squadron's aircraft were operating from Oban and four from Mount Batten, and a month later the three at Oban had moved to Pembroke Dock.

On 28th April 1941 T9075 took off from Pembroke Dock for a routine patrol in the hands of Flg Off V A Hodgkinson. In bad weather and believing the aircraft to be over Eire, the captain gave his crew the choice of baling out or remaining on board; all chose to stay. A sea landing was then attempted, but the port float hit the water, the hull broke in two and three engines fell off. Five of the crew managed to clamber out onto the wing and climb into a dinghy to paddle towards a visible shore. They were rescued next day by a vessel named *Buziras* nine miles (15 km) north-north-west of Bardsey Island and were landed at Holyhead, but unfortunately six of the crew had to be posted as missing.

One aircraft, P9600, flew to Malta on 27th April with personnel and spares for a squadron of Beaufighters, and returned on 4th May, when air raids on the island were intense. Other overseas flights followed, and on 10th May N9049 was attacked at its moorings in Malta by a Bf 109 fighter and set on fire. Attempts to tow it ashore failed, and it soon sank, luckily without any injuries to personnel.

There was a heavy air raid on Pembroke Dock on 11/12th May, and mines were dropped into Milford Haven, so aircraft were dispersed in Angle Bay for a few days while the mines were removed. 10 Squadron's headquarters returned to Pembroke Dock on 28th May 1941 and Mk.II aircraft were received in June, although some of the earlier version were retained. However, Mount Batten continued in use as an advanced base for patrols over the Bay of Biscay.

In June 1941 the gunners on board P9603 shot down one of two floatplanes described as similar to the Ar 196 but single-seaters. The same Sunderland searched unsuccessfully on 20th June for Short G-Class flying-boat G-AFCJ *Golden Fleece*, which was eventually found to have sunk off Cape Finisterre, Spain, while on a flight from Mount Batten to Gibraltar. This active Sunderland unfortunately came to grief itself on 24th June, when it overshot the flarepath after a patrol and crashed in Milford Haven, seriously injuring three pilots, two of whom died later.

While attempting to pick up four men from a dinghy on 9th July, Sunderland T9047 hit a heavy swell, which tore the port outer engine away. The crew then removed and threw overboard the 'special equipment' (ASV radar), recovered the dinghy and began taxying towards the shore on three engines. The flying-boat crew, together with the four men from the dinghy, were picked up by HMS *Brockleby*, after which the Sunderland was sunk by shellfire from the navy ship.

On 17th July a Catalina Mk.I, AH561, was taken on squadron charge, but the reason for this is not stated. It was handed over to 415 Squadron on 13th August.

Special flights to the Middle East continued as required by higher authority, one of which took place on 7th August, when Gen Auchinleck, Air Marshal Tedder and other VIPs were taken to Malta via Gibraltar.

Another sad loss of personnel and aircraft was sustained on 5th December, when T9072, flying from Oban to Pembroke Dock, crashed into the sea about 15 miles (24 km) north-west of Holyhead. An engine malfunction had caused the Sunderland to go out of control, enter a steep dive and break up on hitting the water. Four men were missing, presumed drowned, but survivors were rescued by MV *Kilkenny*.

Mount Batten once again became 10 Squadron's home from 31st December 1941, all personnel and equipment being present by 5th January. There, in January 1942, Sunderland Mk.IIIs were received, and in June the last of the original Mk.I aircraft departed. In April, a nucleus of personnel and aircraft was separated from 10 Squadron to form 461 Squadron.

During June 1942, Flt Lt Martin's crew in W3983 attacked an Italian submarine on the surface and badly damaged it, after which it sought refuge at Santander in Spain, only to be interned. Ten days later, on 21st June, W3999, on an ASR search for survivors from a Wellington of 172 Squadron, was attacked by an Ar 196, shot at and forced down onto the sea. Soon afterwards, the Sunderland exploded, with the sad loss of the eleven crew members. Some retribution was made on 28th July, when the rear gunner in T9110 shot down a Bf 109.

A tour of flying-boat bases was made in early August 1942 by Air Chief Marshal Sir Philip Joubert de la Ferté, who was carried by 10 Squadron in Sunderland W3983. From Mount Batten he was flown to Stranraer, Iceland, Invergordon, Stranraer and back to Mount Batten over a seven-day period.

Few U-boats were spotted by 10 Squadron crews in the Bay of Biscay in the early part of 1943, but on 14th April the crew of W3993 saw one and attacked, without result. On 18th April a U-boat was attacked on the surface by DV969, and on 29th April the crew of DP177 joined a Sunderland of 461 Squadron to attack *U-119*, but without success.

While on patrol at 1,700 feet over the Bay of Biscay on 1st August 1943, the crew of Sunderland W4020 saw five sloops and a Catalina hunting for a U-boat. They decided to join in, but then spotted a U-boat (*U-454*) two miles (3.2 km) away. Approaching to drop its depth-charges, the Sunderland's port inner engine and main tank were hit by flak, and fuel poured into the cockpit onto the wounded crew. However, six depth-charges were dropped, and the U-boat was seen to lift out of the water and sink. The Sunderland then force-landed, bounced heavily and sank, but six of the crew were rescued from the broken-off starboard wing by the sloop HMS *Wren*. The other six aboard the aircraft sadly lost their lives in the ditching, which was approximately at position 45°39'N 10°15'W.

Two days later, a Sunderland went on an operation carrying, for the first time, four fixed Browning .303 (7.7 mm) guns firing forward and controlled by the pilot. On 15th August an order was received to the effect that one 270lb (123kg) depth charge was to be removed, along with all parachutes and harnesses, in an effort to reduce weight so that fuel capacity could be increased.

It was noted during that month that the quality of replacement engines being received had fallen below an acceptable level, causing serviceability of the Sunderlands to suffer. However, this fact was probably hidden when two Russian officers of the Soviet Military Mission visited Pembroke Dock and 10 Squadron on 24th August.

From 1st October 1943, 10 Squadron was detailed for night missions only. The apparent success of the new armament evaluated by the squadron was discussed at a conference at Mount Batten on 5th October, when it was decided that all Sunderlands in Coastal Command would be so equipped. On 24th October a ruling came into force that all the aircraft would carry five depth charges and would fly thirteen-hour sorties with 2,040 gallons of fuel.

Routine patrols continued, with Mk.III Sunderlands totally equipping the squadron from December 1943 until Mk.V aircraft supplemented them from May 1944. Early in March 1944 Pratt & Whitney Twin Wasp engines were installed in Sunderland ML839, complete with propellers formerly used on an Albemarle aircraft, with nine inches (225mm) chopped off! ML839 made its first flight with its new engines on 4th May, after which 10 Squadron recorded that it was hoped that all Sunderlands could be fitted with Twin Wasps, as the Pegasus Mk.XVIII engines were "...most unsatisfactory".

When D-Day (6th June 1944) arrived, the distant rumble of heavy guns across the Channel could, it is said, be heard at Mount Batten. At 05.21 JM721 took off on a special patrol, the crew reporting a strange feeling of 'calm before the storm'. Anti-U-boat patrols were flown during the next few days, but little was seen.

During 1944, 10 (RAAF) Squadron flew 741 operational sorties in 8,540 hours, plus 2,940 non-operational hours, and two U-boats were sunk. Most of the work early in 1945 consisted of convoy escorts. On 9th May, the day after the end of hostilities in Europe, ML828 escorted ships which visited harbours in the Channel Islands to free the people. Five of the Sunderlands took part in a Victory flypast over Plymouth on 13th June, but the squadron continued U-boat patrols until 27th May, just in case!

10 (RAAF) Squadron became non-operational on 1st June 1945, but continued to train until 20th June. Although many of the Sunderlands were being flown away for disposal, others were being taken on charge by the squadron from 461 Squadron (RAAF) which was disbanded at that time. On 20th June, the squadron was transferred to Transport Command, although most of the personnel were posted to other Coastal Command squadrons until 31st October, when they returned to the RAAF.

Since its formation in 1939, 10 (RAAF) Squadron had flown 43,116 hours, and its crews had destroyed seven submarines and six enemy aircraft.

Wg Cdr V A Hodgkinson (right), CO of 40 Squadron RAAF in 1945, on the flight deck of one of the six Sunderlands flown by the squadron. (V A Hodgkinson)

40 Squadron

Unit code: **HF**
(allocated but not carried)

Formed at Townsville in Queensland on 31st March 1944, 40 Squadron was equipped with six Sunderlands, numbered in the A26 series, which were delivered to and moored at Rathmines due to lack of space. These aircraft had been flown out from the UK via Gibraltar in January and February, crewed by Australians who had served their time on one or other of the UK-based squadrons. The squadron moved ten days later to Port Moresby in New Guinea, where personnel, after living in tents for a time, moved into requisitioned houses which they repaired.

From Port Moresby a daily return service to Townsville was established, and once each week, after stopping at Townsville overnight, a Sunderland carried on to Darwin via Karumba. The service was mainly organised for the benefit of US forces, for whom a 10,000lb (4545 kg) load of fruit and vegetables was usually carried. The RAAF at Karumba was also catered for as required. Returning to Port Moresby, the Sunderlands often carried

Chapter 3 : Operating Units (RAF, RAAF, RNZAF, SAAF, Aéronautique Navale)

Code [KN:B] signifies that this Sunderland MR.5, captured just a few feet above the water, belonged to 5 Squadron of the RNZAF.
(R C Sturtivant collection)

meat, fish and canned goods for hungry 40 Squadron personnel. At first, two crews were allocated to each aircraft, but this was later reduced to one.

During the active life of the Sunderlands, major maintenance was carried out by QANTAS at Rose Bay, Sydney. However, in 1945, replacement by Martin Mariners began, and the last flight of a 40 Squadron Sunderland took place on 12th March 1946, when A26-2 flew from Cairns to Rathmines. During their service, the Sunderlands had carried nearly 5,400 tons of freight and passengers. Subsequently, five of the Sunderlands were bought by Trans-Oceanic Airways.

PART 3: ROYAL NEW ZEALAND AIR FORCE

Four Sunderland Mk.IIIs were provided to the RNZAF from RAF stocks in 1944 and were numbered NZ4101 to NZ4104. They left the UK in October that year via West Africa, South America, the West Indies, the United States and thence to Fiji. Some of 490 Squadron's New Zealand personnel were involved in the ferrying, and on arrival the aircraft were allocated to the Flying Boat Transport Flight at Hobsonville.

In 1953 sixteen former RAF Sunderlands which had been reconditioned and upgraded to MR.5 standard were bought by the RNZAF and numbered NZ4105 to NZ4120. The first of these arrived in New Zealand on 13th June 1953 and the last one, NZ4117, on 9th May 1955.

5 Squadron

Unit code: **KN**

Based at Hobsonville, with a detachment of two aircraft at Lauthala Bay in Fiji, 5 Sqn replaced its last two Catalinas in August 1953 with Sunderlands the first two of which arrived in June. Four more Sunderlands completed the allocation to 5 Squadron, and were used mainly for reconnaissance missions.

5 Squadron made a vital contribution to the search for the MV *Joyita* in October 1955, which was one of the most intense air searches ever made in the South Pacific. The vessel was not found for 36 days, and no trace has ever been found of the 25 people on board.

The squadron's allocation was reduced from six aircraft to four on 1st April 1962. On 2nd April 1967 the last of 5 Squadron's, by then, two-ship Det Flt in Fiji returned to Hobsonville marking the RNZAF MR.5 finale. Radio call-signs used by 5 Squadron are thought to have been ZMZG followed by an individual aircraft letter.

6 Squadron

Unit code: **XX**

Part of the Territorial Air Force and based at Hobsonville in April 1954 when its first Sunderland MR.5 was received. 6 Squadron's life was short, as it disbanded on 1st August 1957. 6 Squadron is reported to have used radio call-signs ZMZH followed by an individual aircraft letter.

Flying Boat Transport Flight

Unit code: None

Formed on 21st November 1944 at Mechanics Bay, Auckland, this unit used the first four Sunderlands, NZ4101 to NZ4104, to carry freight and passengers between New Zealand (Hobsonville Bay) and Fiji, New Caledonia and the New Hebrides.

Flying Boat Transport Squadron

Unit code: None

Established 29th November 1945 as successor to the Flight. Operated passenger and freight flights from Hobsonville and Mechanics Bay until an, as yet, unknown date, possibly November 1947. Thereafter, this task completed, the four Sunderlands were loaned to NZNAC from November 1947 to 1951, when they were stored to await scrapping in 1954.

Maritime Operational Conversion Unit

Unit code: **XX**

Formed in May 1955 at Hobsonville to train complete Sunderland crews. From May55 - Aug57 used 6 Sqn aircraft; thereafter using single-letter coded MR.5s from the central pool. On 1st May 1962

RNZAF Sunderlands at rest on 9th December 1963 NZ4116 [S] nearest.
(Andrew Hendrie collection)

NZ4112 as [L] of MRSU afloat at Hobsonville in December 1964 wearing a 'fern leaf' roundel.
(R A Walker collection)

RNZAF Sunderland MR.5 NZ4114 overhead Hobsonville showing the 6 Squadron / MOCU code [XX:A]. Pier and slipway are visible on the right.
(Andrew Hendrie collection)

CHAPTER 3 : OPERATING UNITS (RAF, RAAF, RNZAF, SAAF, AÉRONAUTIQUE NAVALE)　　　　　　　　　69

it became **Maritime Reconnaissance & Support Unit (MRSU)**, remaining in being until at least cFebruary 1965. Radio call-signs appear to have been ZMZJ and an individual aircraft letter.

PART 4: SOUTH AFRICAN AIR FORCE

35 Squadron

Unit code: **RB**

Formed on 15th February 1945 at Congella, Durban, from 262 Squadron RAF, most of the personnel of which was South African, 35 Squadron inherited its predecessor's Catalinas. In April, however, Sunderland Mk.Vs began to arrive, the first six coming from the RAF's 259 Squadron via Tulear. At first they continued to carry their RAF serial numbers, but eventually most (although probably not all) were renumbered in the SAAF 1700 series. Unfortunately, the first Sunderland to arrive, PP153, was written off immediately in a landing accident, but the other fifteen arrived safely.

35 Squadron's first major operation was to repatriate South African troops from the Canal Zone, and in order to save weight the upper turrets were removed from the aircraft concerned. Three flights were made per week until 1,786 soldiers and 655 tons of equipment had been brought back to South Africa.

In February 1947 a Sunderland of 35 Squadron flew 1,000 miles (1,610 km)

Sunderland V [L] of 35 Squadron SAAF still wearing RAF serial NJ259 unloading troops into 24-foot marine tender 3140 at Durban-Congella after a repatriation flight from the Suez Canal Zone between November 1945 and March 1946. *(via Stefan Bouwer)*

Sunderland GR.5 SAAF 1703 [RB:H] of 35 Squadron based at Congella, Durban,, wearing the Springbok roundel. *(SAAF via JM Collection)*

out into the Atlantic Ocean to meet and escort HMS *Vanguard*, which was carrying the Royal Family to tour South Africa.

During December 1947 it was announced that all but five of the Sunderlands would be put into storage as they were not required, while the remainder continued to carry out routine maritime patrol sorties and to take part in many air displays. The first non-stop flight around the Union of South Africa was made on 29/30th July 1948 by Sunderland 1701, flown by the squadron CO, Col D A du Toit, a distance of 2,880 miles (4,637 km) in 19 hours 50 minutes flying time.

Apart from its base at Congella, 35 Squadron made use of alighting areas at Saldanha Bay and Umsingazi, particularly during exercises. Introduced on August 24th 1950, the new Springbok roundel was applied to the five remaining operational Sunderlands and the squadron badge was applied above the entrance door.

35 Squadron SAAF Sunderland MR.5 1710 [RB:D] being prepared for mooring, outer engines only running. *(via JM Collection)*

In 1952, after a visit by three Avro Shackletons, the SAAF placed an order for a batch of these aircraft to replace the Sunderlands. However, the five airworthy flying-boats soldiered on for several more years, while the stored examples were sold for scrap in 1955. The final flight of a SAAF Sunderland took place on 8th October 1957, when 1710, by then the only one left, took to the air for the last time in the hands of Capt A J Cooney; soon afterwards, it was broken up.

PART 5:
FRENCH NAVY
(Aéronautique navale)

The success of the Allied landings in North Africa in November 1942 (Operation 'Torch') with the former Vichy French forces in Africa soon joining the Allied cause prompted, in February 1943, a decision to allocate some Sunderlands to the naval aviation of the Fighting French. Initially referred to as 'France libre' from 1940, it became 'France combattante' from 1943 when merging with the former Vichy French forces until a legal provisional government of the French Republic based in Algiers was established.

Most French crews were sent to the UK for training, after which two Sunderlands, DP182 and JM674, were despatched to Dakar in Sénégal, French West Africa, where Escadrille 4E, part of 1st Flottille (1FE), took them on charge for crew conversion. On 10th October 1943, 1FE was renumbered Flottille 7FE, (7th Flottille d'Exploration, ie. maritime patrol) and was attached to 295 Wing of the RAF. For administrative purposes which suited both sides, from November 29th 1943 this Flottille (until then known to the RAF as No.1 (French Naval) Squadron) was redesignated 343 Squadron of the RAF (q.v.) and had by then received a dozen Sunderlands. The escadrilles within the squadron were also discarded to make up a single 7FE.

In June 1945 many war-weary RAF Sunderlands in West Africa, and the previous wartime transfers to the French Navy, officially became French property. These surplus aircraft would otherwise have been scrapped by the RAF and indeed several were SOC by the French and used for spares. After the end of the war, on 27th November 1945, the re-equipped Aéronautique navale, which, besides US trained and equipped units going back to former Free French Gaullist personnel, had amalgamated the former Vichy French crews, maintained the Sunderland Squadron now referred to as flottille 7.F. Karouba, a major naval base at Bizerta, Tunisia, was responsible for major inspections of the Sunderlands prior to redelivery to Dakar or being SOC. To these were added two in 1947 obtained from Britain.

Under the pre-cold war Western Union agreement, more Sunderlands were purchased for the French Navy, this time the safer GR.5 variant with American powerplants and feathering propellers. Fourteen came in 1951, four in 1952 and a final five in 1957, the last example was withdrawn in 1960. They completely replaced the old wartime Mk.III models in the squadron then renamed Flottille 27.F in June 1953, still in Western Africa. These soldiered on until the late fifties when replaced by MDAP-supplied Martin P5M-2 Marlins.

During the fifties, some Mk.V Sunderlands were also diverted to training squadrons, escadrille 50.S at St-Mandrier near the major naval harbour of Toulon, for sonobuoy practice; escadrille 50.S at Lanvéoc-Poulmic in Brittany, attached to the naval academy; and escadrille 53.S at Dakat, Tunisia, then West Africa for flying-boat training. All surviving aircraft were struck off charge on 30th January 1962, but luckily one ex-French Sunderland was returned to the UK for preservation at Pembroke Dock, and later at the RAF Museum, Hendon.

Note on French units and codes:
Until 1944 a French naval aviation squadron, called a *flottille*, usually containing two *escadrilles*. Thus Flottille 7F (7FE) consisted of escadrilles 3E and 4E, these identifiers being followed by an individual aircraft number within each flight and a single code letter, usually tied to that number, eg. 3E-2 'B', 3E-5 'E'. There were some exceptions, possibly with former RAF code letters being retained for some time.

From late 1945 individual letter codes were dropped and a dot inserted in the Flottille serial, eg. 7.F-2. Flottilles were then fighting squadrons whereas the Escadrilles became support or training squadrons. While Coastal Command in the UK was manned by RAF personnel, the French Sunderlands were a naval responsibility and always manned by naval personnel.

PART 6:
PORTUGUESE NAVY
(Aviação Naval)

As will be found in Chapter 5, the Portuguese Navy took over and refurbished one Sunderland, P9623, which had force-landed on its way to West Africa in February 1941. However, as serial 136 it flew just once operationally but unsuccessfully, in 1944 as described above, after which it languished for some time before being scrapped.

There have been rumours about a second Portuguese Navy Sunderland and a photograph found of one wearing serial 120 at the Lisbon naval base of Bom Sucesso. So far this has not been identified although W6065 which ditched off Oporto in 1943 has been suggested as a candidate but without proof, see page 158.

The Portuguese Navy Sunderland I, 136 was formerly 95 Squadron's P9623 which force-landed near Troia beach south of Lisbon on 15th February 1941 due to hurricane-strength winds. It was taken over by the Portuguese, test flown in 1942 and was tasked with a flight to Portuguese Guinea on 8th March 1944 during which the propeller of no.3 engine fell off and no.4 engine was also shut down, forcing the aircraft to return to Lisbon in the condition in which it can be seen above.
(via Luis Tavares)

CHAPTER 3 : OPERATING UNITS (RAF, RAAF, RNZAF, SAAF, AÉRONAUTIQUE NAVALE)   71

Formerly RAF ML796, this Sunderland 5 went to France in 1957 but in 1962 , as ML796/ 50.S-3, was SOC and eventually taken to La Baule for use as a bar, later being acquired by the IWM at Duxford.
(via JM Collection)

Sunderland 5 ML800 seen at Wig Bay on 18th June 1957 a few days prior to delivery to Brest for the Aéronautique navale, with whom it served for three and a half years.
(Bill Broadfoot via JM Collection)

A close-up of the bow of ML799 / 27.F-5, showing the mooring arrangements. The unit badge of Flottille 7F is shown in the inset, as worn by this Sunderland when arriving at SB&HL in March 1956.
(Bombardier/Shorts via Noel Lynch)

Sunderland 5 ML824 last served with Escadrille 50.S as 50.S-9 whose unit badge appears above. Departing Brest on 24th March 1961, it was escorted to Pembroke Dock by Shackletons of 201 Squadron as seen, right. Looking immaculate at Pembroke Dock on 7th August 1961, above, it was later to find a permanent resting place at the RAF Museum; Hendon.
(Phil Butler (top) & P H T Green Collection)

After major maintenance, Sunderland 5 ML778 is seen on the slipway at Belfast ready to return to Brest on 28th April 1956 to become 27.F-3 once more. The French crew is most probably from the Escadrille de Réception et Convoyage (ERC), the FN ferry squadron.. In the inset is the unit badge of Escadrille 50.S showing a newly-hatched duckling.
(Bombardier/Shorts via Noel Lynch)

Built on a strip of land at the southern end of Southampton Water, the flying boat base at Calshot was a major maintenance centre for Sunderlands during the war but its significance had declined by the early 1950s when this photograph was taken. (F Denyer via John Evans)

Chapter 4
RAF SUNDERLAND BASES

In this chapter, the information relates specifically to the use of each base by Sunderlands rather than to its general use. Some details of infrastructure are also given.

Section 1:
THE UNITED KINGDOM

Alness (see Invergordon)

Boa Island (Co Fermanagh)

Sometimes known as Rock Bay, this site was never more than a satellite alighting area and as such was used by Sunderlands of 131 (C) OTU, based at Killadeas, from the end of May 1944 to April 1945.

RAF Bowmore (Isle of Islay)

Previously used by 119 Squadron's C-class and G-class flying boats, Bowmore was first used by Sunderlands in September 1942, after 246 Squadron formed there. That unit disbanded on 30th April 1943, but on 7th May 422 Squadron sent its Sunderlands from Oban. Official use of Bowmore by Sunderlands finished when 422 Squadron moved to Castle Archdale on 4th November 1943, due to the difficulty in carrying out operations with Bowmore's limited facilities.

The marked alighting area on Loch Indaal, about five miles (8 km) north of Port Ellen airfield, measured 1.5 miles (2.4 km) in all directions, and a flarepath comprising three launches was available. Sixteen moorings were provided off Bowmore pier, but there was no slipway. The Station closed in July 1945.

RAF Calshot (Hampshire)

This famous flying-boat base was opened by the RNAS in March 1913 on a strip of land projecting into the Solent, at the southern end of Southampton Water. The main feature of the Station was Calshot Castle, which was absorbed into the Station during WW2 and later had a control building sited on its roof (see photo above). Another unusual feature was the narrow-gauge railway built to transport stores and personnel. Patrols were flown from Calshot throughout the First World War, but between the wars the Station was best known for its participation in the Schneider Trophy competitions. The site is now a leisure complex.

During the early part of the Second World War RAF Calshot carried out servicing of marine craft and training of personnel to man them. Calshot was also responsible for major servicing of the Sunderlands of 201, 209 and 240 Squadrons, and to achieve this 6 Flying-Boat Servicing Unit was formed in September 1943.

Not until peace had returned were any Sunderland units based at Calshot. The first was 201 Squadron, which arrived from Pembroke Dock in March 1946, and this was joined by 230 Squadron from Castle Archdale in September of the same year. Finally, 235 OCU was formed at Calshot, under the command of Gp Capt D B Fitzgerald OBE AFC, at the end of July 1947 from 4 (C) OTU at Pembroke Dock. The two squadrons both left for Pembroke Dock early in 1949, leaving 235 OCU to continue training crews. Activity at Calshot was still quite intense, with a total of 673 aircraft movements in March 1949, 114 of which were at night and 31 were civilian aircraft. However, on 1st May 1949 Calshot relinquished its status as a Master Diversion station in favour of Pembroke Dock, and movements then declined.

235 OCU disbanded in October 1953 and handed its training commitment over to a smaller unit at Pembroke Dock. At Calshot there was also a detachment of two Sunderlands of the Air Sea Warfare Development Unit, headquartered at Thorney Island.

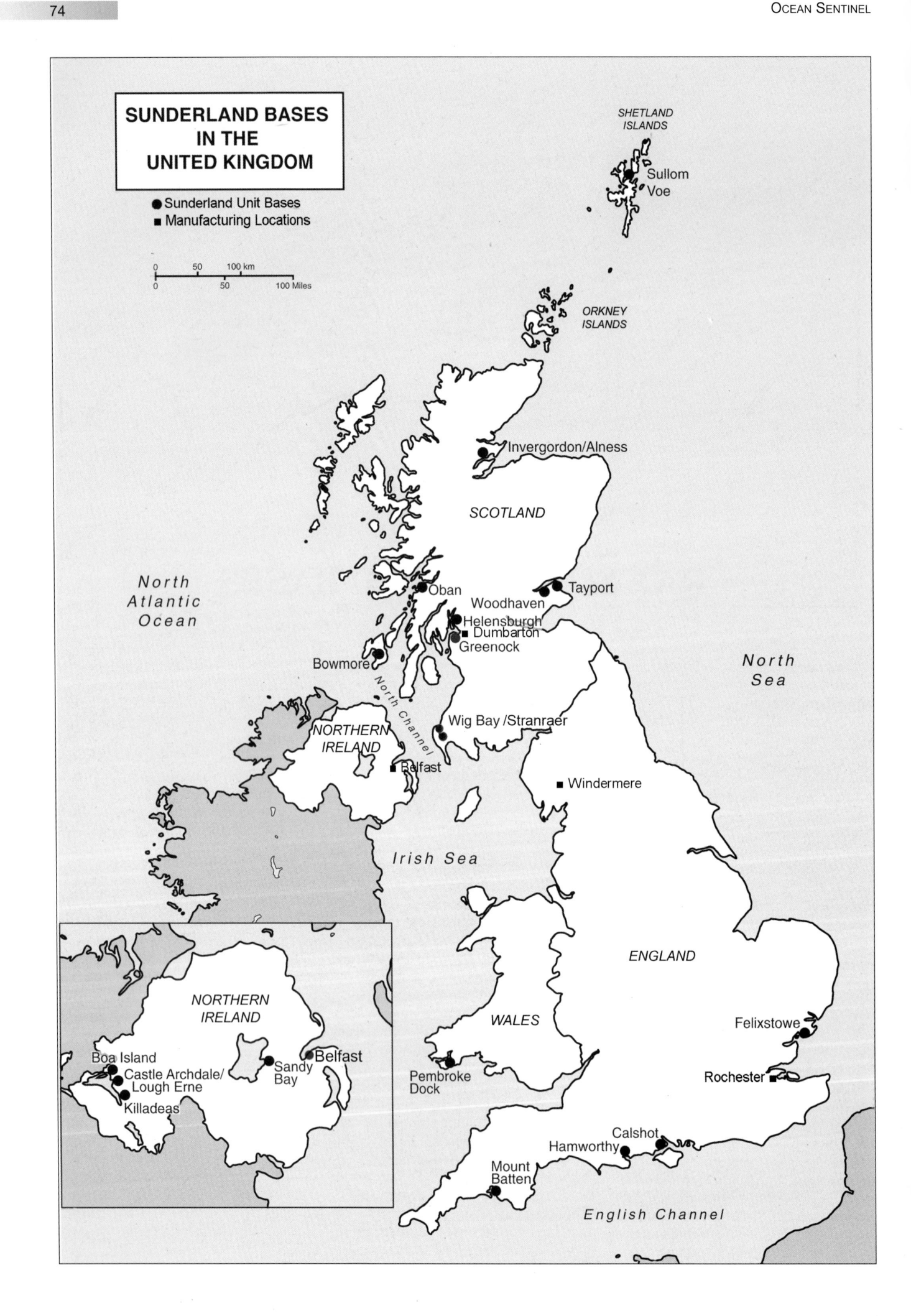

SUNDERLAND BASES IN THE UNITED KINGDOM

- Sunderland Unit Bases
- Manufacturing Locations

Shetland Islands — Sullom Voe
Orkney Islands

Scotland
- Invergordon/Alness
- Oban
- Woodhaven
- Tayport
- Helensburgh
- Dumbarton
- Greenock
- Bowmore
- Wig Bay/Stranraer

Northern Ireland
- Belfast
- Boa Island
- Castle Archdale/Lough Erne
- Killadeas
- Sandy Bay

England/Wales
- Windermere
- Pembroke Dock
- Felixstowe
- Rochester
- Hamworthy
- Calshot
- Mount Batten

North Atlantic Ocean · *North Channel* · *Irish Sea* · *North Sea* · *English Channel*

CHAPTER 4 : RAF SUNDERLAND BASES

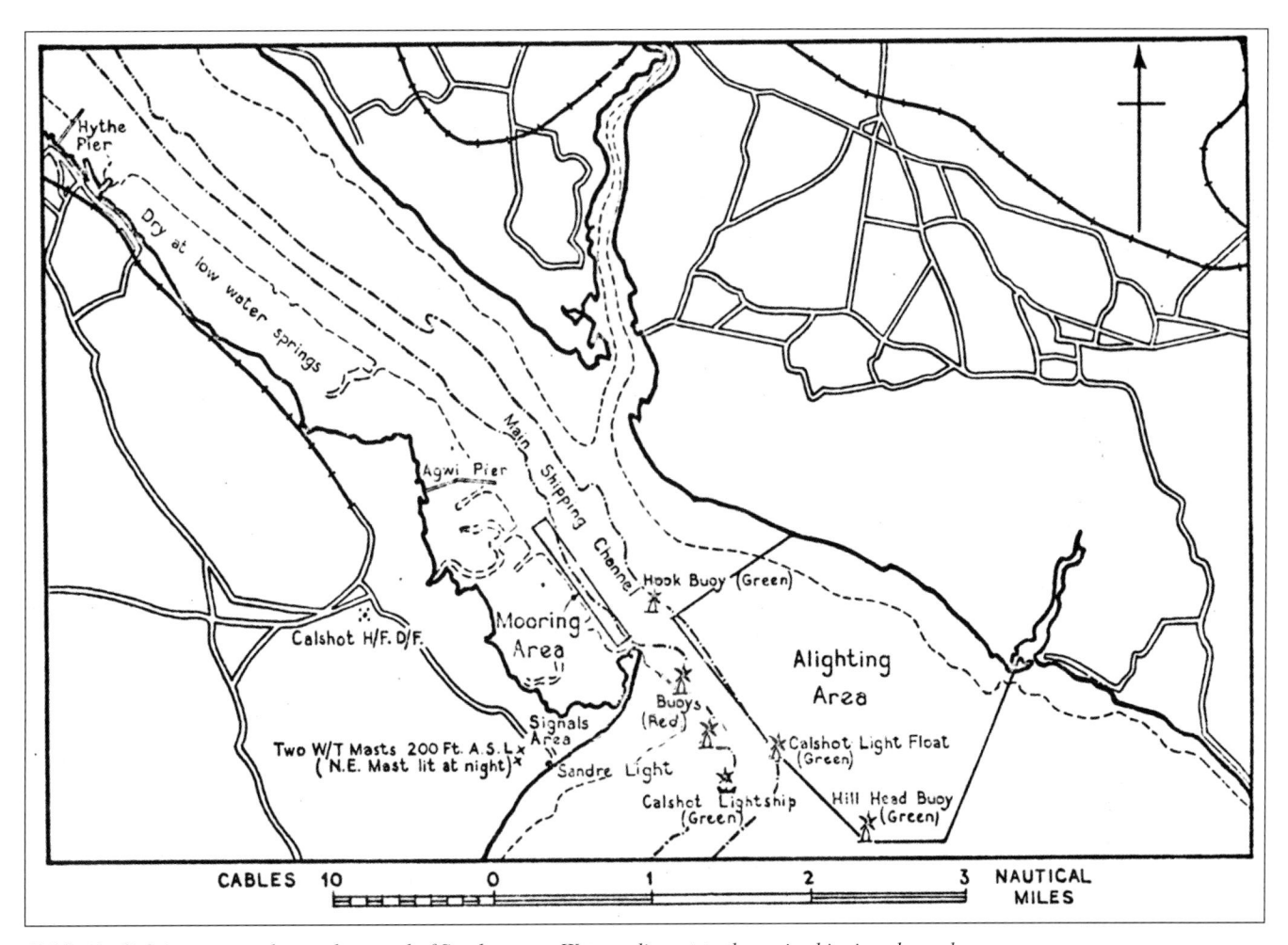

Calshot's alighting area at the southern end of Southampton Water, adjacent to the main shipping channel.

An aerial view of RAF Calshot in 1948 with Sunderland GR.5s of 201 and 230 Squadrons and 235 OCU in evidence. Note the ample hangarage and the air traffic control building on top of Calshot Castle.

The alighting area in Southampton Water was very large; from north to south a run of 15,840 feet (4830 m) was available, while from east to west the dimension was 5280 feet (1610 m). Six dinghies carried the lighting, and there were fifteen Short type buoys for mooring.

Facilities at Calshot were of a high standard. Hangarage, all built in the 1916 to 1918 period, was considerable, and comprised 'E' shed 130 ft by 75 ft (396 m by 22.9 m); 'F' shed, 100 ft (33 m) span; 'G' shed of 60 ft (18.2 m) span; and 'H' shed, an enormous building 625 ft (190.5 m) long by 120 ft (36.5 m) wide. Of these, 'E' shed was demolished in the 1950s, but the others remain as part of the Calshot Activities Centre. The control tower, of 1936 design, was unique in that it was perched on top of the old castle, and a controller in a tender directed waterborne aircraft. Adjacent to a beach were the slipway and apron, which is now a car park. The single-storey 1914-vintage officers' mess is now the 'Flying Boat Inn'.

RAF Castle Archdale / Lough Erne (Co Fermanagh)

When a critical requirement for bases for flying-boat patrols over the North Atlantic became clear in 1939/40, Lough Erne in Northern Ireland was surveyed by 119 Squadron in December 1940. Although the report was unfavourable, the site was selected for development and work began on the Castle Archdale estate. There was one major problem with the location of this base: the aircraft would have to cross County Donegal in the Irish Free State (now Irish Republic) if on a direct route out into the Atlantic. High-level negotiations took place to resolve the matter, and permission was granted by Eamonn de Valera, the Irish Prime Minister, in time for the opening of the base. Stipulations were that no low-level flights would be allowed and the Irish Army camp near Ballyshannon was not to be overflown.

Opened in February 1941, Castle Archdale suffered a change of name almost immediately, becoming known as Lough Erne on 14th February. The first Sunderland-equipped unit to be based there, 201 Squadron, arrived from Sullom Voe at the end of October 1941 and stayed for much longer than was usual, not leaving until April 1944, when it moved to Pembroke Dock. Lough Erne's new slipway was used by a Sunderland for the first time in February 1942, when a Sunderland of 228 Squadron which had run aground was beached.

Following 201 Squadron, a unit that would become very important, 302 Ferry Training Unit, formed at Lough Erne in September 1942, but left for Stranraer two months later, soon after 423 Squadron had arrived from Oban. Next to arrive was 228 Squadron from Oban in December 1942, taking space previously occupied by 302 FTU.

In January 1943 the Station's name reverted to Castle Archdale, to avoid confusion with Kildeas, also on Lough Erne, and the occupants remained static until November of that year, when 422 Squadron arrived from Bowmore. 201 Squadron left in April 1944, and was replaced in the September by 202 Squadron from Gibraltar. Two months later, there was an exchange of squadrons, when 422 Squadron left for Pembroke Dock in exchange for 201 Squadron.

Early in 1945, the weather was so cold that crews could walk across the ice to their aircraft. As far as Sunderlands were concerned, 1945 was a year of disbandment or movement. 202 Squadron disbanded in June, while 423 Squadron transferred to Transport Command and 201 Squadron returned to Pembroke Dock in August.

RAF Castle Archdale was placed on a Care & Maintenance basis on 25th September 1945, and came under the control of RAF Killadeas on 1st January 1946.

An evocative picture of the flying-boat maintenance area at RAF Castle Archdale in Northern Ireland in 1945. Identifiable Sunderlands appear to be Mk.III EJ150 [NS:W] of 201 Squadron and Mk.V ML825 [YI:D] of 423 Squadron. (R C Sturtivant collection)

The very crowded maintenance area at RAF Castle Archdale with both Sunderlands and Catalinas visible. In addition to standard hangarage, four 'nose-in' shelters are in evidence. (P H T Green collection)

Some Sunderland activity continued, however, including visits by a detachment of 201 Squadron in December 1945 and by 230 Squadron from Pembroke Dock in August 1946, which left for Calshot a month later. During exercises, 201 Squadron was still using the site in June 1949.

Castle Archdale was well equipped, with full-size hangars and with 'nose-in' shelters for engine maintenance, but domestic accommodation was not so comprehensive. Station HQ was in the 'big house' itself, and originally the air traffic control function was handled from a small glasshouse on the roof. However, a replacement control tower on stilts was built later on Gay Island, in the middle of the Lough, from where visibility was much better.

An aerial view of RAF Greenock, located in Gourock Bay, in 1940. (via Peter Berry)

Falmouth (Devon)

During the early days of the Second World War, moorings in the outer harbour at Falmouth were used by Sunderlands based at Mount Batten and Pembroke Dock. A detachment of 204 Squadron, for example, used the facilities between 1st and 26th March 1940. On 1st December 1942, however, the moorings were closed, as other diversionary alighting areas had become available.

RAF Felixstowe (Suffolk)

Although no Sunderland-equipped operational squadrons were ever based at Felixstowe, the type was seen there frequently. From 1924 the Marine Aircraft Experimental Establishment had been based there, carrying out development work on all types of flying-boats and floatplanes, becoming part of Coastal Command on 1st May 1936.

Before 21st September 1939, when the MAEE moved from its prominent position on the River Orwell to Helensburgh on the River Clyde for safety reasons, Sunderlands were often on charge. Likewise, after the unit's return on 1st August 1945, the type was again in evidence. A number of former BOAC Solents retired to Felixstowe for storage, and the two Seaford prototypes underwent trials there, but were eventually abandoned. The unit became civilianised in March 1953, and closed down on 31st March 1956, its task completed.

The site of RAF Felixstowe has now been completely swallowed by a huge container depot, said to be the largest in the United Kingdom.

RAF Greenock (Renfrewshire)

Located on the River Clyde, RAF Greenock was opened on 20th October 1940 by a party of men who arrived the previous day from RAF Calshot. Initially the station concentrated on servicing Lerwick flying-boats. On 24th December 1940, however, the first Sunderland arrived from Malta for maintenance at the outstation of Scottish Aviation Ltd which had been set up at Caird's Shipyard in June. That area was the location of a heavy air raid on 7th May 1941 in which Sunderland L2159 was damaged beyond repair. Three days later, all aircraft at Caird's shipyard were transferred to a new site at Gourock Bay.

In September 1942, 2 Flying Boat Servicing Unit was established to handle work on Catalinas, to the exclusion of most Sunderlands. Until the end of 1942, when Largs came into use, Greenock was also the terminus of transatlantic flying-boat services of RAF Ferry Command. A stored reserve of Sunderlands also existed there.

More Sunderlands were seen at Greenock between 23rd July and 28th August 1942, when a detachment of 201 Squadron from Lough Erne was present.

Work on Catalinas ended in April 1944, and specialisation in Sunderlands began. New buildings were badly required, but work was slow, and it was not until August that new hangars came into use. In October conversion of Mk.III Sunderlands to Mk.V started, and carried on until 25th July 1945, when the last aircraft took off. The Station officially closed down on 13th August 1945 and went onto Care & Maintenance, although there was some activity until the early 1950s.

A slipway 230 ft long by 66 ft wide (70 m by 20 m) was provided, and moorings consisted of two trots of four buoys each. Marine craft were used as tugs.

RAF Hamworthy (Dorset)

In 1942, congestion at Pembroke Dock and Mount Batten flying-boat bases forced the authorities to look for additional facilities. After considerable discussions between the Air Ministry and BOAC, which had been using the area since 1939, Poole Harbour was selected, although it was far from ideal as it was very busy already. A spot about 1.5 miles (2.4 km) west of Poole, on the northern side of the Wareham Channel, was decided upon, and work on a slipway began in June 1942. As there was no space for hangars or other buildings, requisitioned houses in the Lake Estate area came into use as workshops, while properties in Poole and Parkstone were put into use for administrative purposes.

RAF Hamworthy came into being on 1st August 1942, and approval was granted for the operational area to move to Salterne Pier, in the Lilliput area of Parkstone, although BOAC was still in residence and the best moorings were up to four miles (6.4 km) away from the pier. There was not room to park the aircraft properly on the makeshift slipway, and every maintenance job was fraught with difficulty.

Hamworthy's only operational unit was 461 Squadron, which arrived from Mount

Batten on 31st August to continue with the task of patrolling the Bay of Biscay. For night take-offs, however, 461's Sunderlands returned to Mount Batten.

Later in 1942, the Army vacated Salterne Pier, an operations room was established in the Harbour Yacht Club and the Harbour Heights Hotel became the officers' mess.

461 Squadron left for Pembroke Dock on 21st April 1943, and in December the Air Ministry, aware of Hamworthy's operational shortcomings, decided to vacate the site. On 13th January 1944 RAF Hamworthy was transferred to 116 Wing of Transport Command, which would control BOAC services to India which had been operated since October 1943 by Sunderlands carrying RAF markings.

In February 1944 much of the local accommodation was de-requisitioned, but Salterne Pier, the yacht club and Harbour Heights hotel were handed over to the DGCA on the closure of RAF Hamworthy on 1st May. Renamed Poole, the site continued in use by BOAC for services to the Far East until 31st March 1946, when they were transferred to Southampton Water.

RAF Helensburgh / Rhu (Dunbartonshire)

Helensburgh was a single-unit Station, with the Marine Aircraft Experimental Establishment in residence from 21st September 1939, when it moved from Felixstowe, a much more vulnerable location. In 1940 MAEE came under the control of the Ministry of Aircraft Production, and carried on with the work of trialling and improving flying-boat design and equipment. MAEE returned to Felixstowe on 1st August 1945 to continue its work.

Dumbarton-built Sunderlands were flown to Rhu for hand-over to the RAF, and thence by ATA ferry pilots to RAF units.

RAF Invergordon / Alness (Ross & Cromarty)

Probably one of the finest natural harbours in the United Kingdom, the Cromarty Firth comprises a twenty-mile (32.2 km) deep-water channel with a sheltered entrance. It was used as a naval base from the early 19th century, and in the First World War seaplanes of the RNAS used a shore site for a time. During the 1920s and 1930s, flying-boat moorings were established at Invergordon naval dockyard, but they were used only for exercises and by aircraft in transit.

Although not of the best quality, this is a rare picture of an RAF floating dock. It contains Sunderland Mk.I L2165 and was probably in use at Invergordon in 1939. When the aircraft was in the dock, mechanics were able to work on engines and hull in much easier conditions than normal. *(D Teague via D Jago and John Evans)*

Development of Invergordon as a flying-boat base seems to have been somewhat half-hearted. In September 1938, at the time of the Munich crisis, Singapore, London and Stranraer aircraft of three squadrons were present for a few days, their ground crews living in tents as no other accommodation was available. More arrived just before the outbreak of hostilities, and when most of the Royal Navy ships left for battle stations the area effectively began to come under RAF control. Buildings in the nearby town were requisitioned as stores and offices and Station HQ was set up in the Masonic Hall, although it was soon moved to an address in the High Street. Most RAF personnel were billeted in private houses and the Academy, but some still lived in tents.

The first Sunderlands to use Invergordon flying-boat base were a detachment of 210 Squadron from Pembroke Dock, which arrived on 23rd October 1939 and left two weeks later. Many other flying-boats visited Invergordon on their way to or from other bases. 210 Squadron returned on 24th November for another period of detachment, which lasted until 21st May 1940. By that time, 201 Squadron, already based at Invergordon, had begun to receive Sunderlands to replace its elderly Saro Londons.

Detachments of 204 Squadron from Sullom Voe in September 1940 and from 201 Squadron, also from Sullom Voe, in May 1941 brought Sunderlands to Invergordon, but it was in June 1941 that the Station's long-term resident unit arrived from Stranraer. This was 4 (C) OTU, which was fully established by 21st June, with an officers' mess at Dalmore House. A mixed bag of flying-boat types was used, including Sunderlands. Early in 1942, the basic training section of the OTU was sent back to Stranraer, as conditions at Invergordon were becoming crowded. By June, however, seventeen Sunderlands were included in the fleet at Invergordon.

In another move to relieve the overcrowding at Invergordon, a new slipway was constructed at Alness, about a mile (1.6 km) to the west, and this came into use in December 1941. By the summer of 1942, routine servicing was being carried out in a floating dock at Dalmore pier, while major servicing was dealt with at Alness slipway, where there were one Bellman and five modified T.2-type hangars and an adjacent hardstanding. This area now became known as 5 Flying Boat Servicing Unit, which seems to have devoted its efforts to the aircraft of 4 (C) OTU. In the same area a Nissen hut was allocated as a watch office, but as it was not possible to see aircraft movements from that spot a control tower of local design was built on the Admiralty pier at Invergordon.

On 10th February 1943 the Station was renamed RAF Alness, and 4 (C) OTU's work continued unabated. The unit was joined by 302 FTU from Killadeas on 1st July 1945, but this unit's task was completed early in 1946 and it disbanded on

1st April. Also at Alness in the immediate postwar period was the marine section of the Coastal Command Flying Instructors' School, which had its headquarters at Turnberry.

4 (C) OTU abandoned Alness on 15th August 1946 to move to Pembroke Dock, but Alness continued to be used spasmodically by Sunderlands from other bases until January 1957. A Marine Craft Unit operated there until the mid-1980s.

Administrative and domestic buildings on this Station were widely scattered. One communal site contained, in Nissen huts, an airmen's mess for 1200 and a sergeant's mess for 450, while Station HQ, having moved from the town, occupied another Nissen hut in the maintenance area. Nine domestic sites housed NCOs and airmen in 161 Nissen huts, while officers used 29 similar buildings.

The alighting area was about six miles (10 km) long in an east to west direction and up to half that length from north to south. There were 42 moorings.

RAF Killadeas (County Fermanagh)

After prolonged talks between the British and United States governments early in 1941 (before the USA entered the war but when it seemed inevitable), it was decided that two flying-boat bases would be made available to the US Navy. One was to be on Lough Erne and the other on Loch Ryan in Scotland. Construction was to be in the hands of American engineers, and if the need arose the bases were to be completely under American control.

Work started in August 1941 on the Lough Erne site, which was given a headquarters at Ely Lodge and technical facilities at Killadeas, after which the base was named. It was commissioned by the US Navy early in 1942 but not in fact brought into use. The technical site was transferred to the RAF in June 1942, while the remainder went into US Army control. In RAF hands, the Station's main function was operational training, carried out by 131 (C) OTU, which was formed in July 1942 and operated Catalinas and Sunderlands. For the benefit of trainee gunners, a detachment of target-towing aircraft was based at nearby St Angelo airfield. From July 1944, a detachment of Sunderlands of 12 Flying Instructors School was based at Killadeas, using the aircraft of 131 (C) OTU. This unit became the Coastal Command Flying Instructors School in February 1945 and continued until July 1945. A satellite alighting area at Boa Island was used from May 1944 to April 1945.

302 Ferry Training Unit arrived from Oban in April 1945, and 131 (C) OTU disbanded in the July, its task completed, as all future crews would go to 4 (C) OTU. At the same time, 302 FTU moved to Alness, leaving Killadeas devoid of Sunderlands for a month or so until 272 Maintenance Unit was formed to store and dispose of redundant aircraft. This task ended in February 1947.

Lough Erne (see Castle Archdale)

RAF Mount Batten (Devonshire)

Opened during the First World War as RNAS Cattewater, this flying-boat Station was provided with four large hangars, two 200ft x 100ft (61m x 30.5m) and two 180ft x 60ft (55m x 18m), and three slipways in the following year. Between 1922 and 1925, however, the Station was closed and in fact was little used until 1928. It was renamed Mount Batten on 1st October 1929.

The first Sunderlands arrived in June 1939 for 204 Squadron, which had been flying Saro Londons since 1936, and shared the facilities with the Shark floatplanes of 2 Anti Aircraft Cooperation Unit. Relieving 204 Squadron on 1st April 1940 came 10 (RAAF) Squadron from Pembroke Dock, and 204 left for Sullom Voe the next day. When France fell in June 1940, 10 Squadron was involved in long-range transport duties for a time.

RAF Mount Batten was within easy reach of enemy aircraft based in northern France, and raids began on 15th July 1940, when two Ju 88s dropped bombs, although damage was slight. A heavier attack took place on 27th November, when one of 10 Squadron's hangars was destroyed. One Sunderland in the hangar was written off, as was one on the water. More enemy aircraft dropped bombs on Mount Batten on 13th January 1941, causing slight damage to three Sunderlands, and on 20/21st April the operations room was destroyed and the breakwater damaged.

Enemy activity, coupled with congestion on the water and the proximity of barrage balloons, made a move necessary for 10 Squadron, which flew to Pembroke Dock in May 1941. For a time, Mount Batten served as a forward operating base for several squadrons of Sunderlands and other types until 10 Squadron returned on 5th January 1942. Crews of 10 Squadron took under their wing those of 461 Squadron, which was formed on 25th April 1942, and once operational the new unit moved to Hamworthy in August.

10 (RAAF) Squadron remained at Mount Batten for a considerable time. In January 1944 six Sunderlands were prepared for the Royal Australian Air Force and were flown out by time-expired Australians of 10 and 461 Squadrons. Those left behind took an active part in the D-Day operations.

The war in Europe over, 10 Squadron left for Australia on 31st October 1945 and the Station was placed on a Care & Main-

A close-up of damage to a Sunderland and hangar sustained during the raid on RAF Mount Batten on 27-28th November 1940. *(via Aldon P Ferguson)*

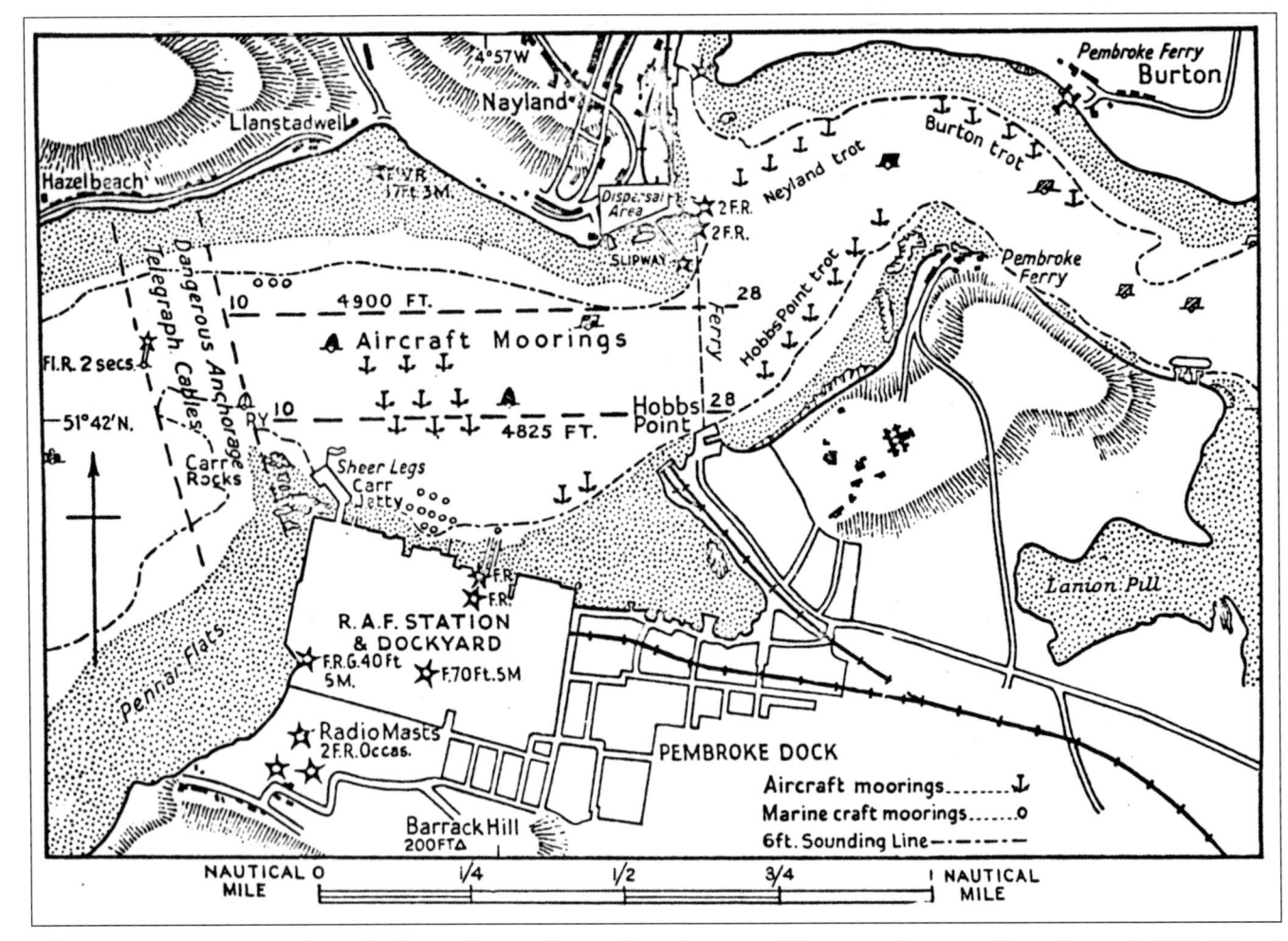

The flying-boat base at Pembroke Dock, showing the many dispersed moorings around the estuary. Open water lies to the west in Milford Sound.

tenance basis. Sunderlands from Calshot and Pembroke Dock still visited occasionally until the last ones were withdrawn from service in the UK in 1957. The last flight was made in 1958, when a Sunderland of the Aéronautiqu Navale touched down. 19 Group Coastal Command left the base in 1968 but the RAF Marine Branch remained there until 1986. Two large hangars remain but the site is now used for commercial and leisure purposes.

At Mount Batten the alighting area was between Drake's Island and the coastline from Cattewater and Stadden Heights, in Plymouth Sound. Hangarage consisted of F-Type and G-Type buildings similar to those at Calshot.

RAF Oban (Argyllshire)

Work on the construction of a permanent flying-boat base at Oban began in September 1938, after earlier use had been made of the site as a refuelling point. RAF Oban came into being on 2nd October 1939, with a slipway and fuel dump on Kerrera Island. Station HQ was in Dungallan House, a requisitioned Victorian villa from where good views over the alighting area and across to Kerrera Island could be obtained.

The first Sunderlands to appear were those of 210 Squadron, a detachment of which arrived in May 1940 from Pembroke Dock. This was followed by the squadron's headquarters on 13th July 1940, but the Sunderlands left when the squadron converted to Catalinas in April 1941. A detachment of 10 (RAAF) Squadron arrived from Mount Batten on 1st August 1940 and left in April 1941.

It was the spring of 1942 before more Sunderlands were based at Oban. These belonged to 228 Squadron, which moved from Stranraer on 10th March and left for Castle Archdale on 11th December. 423 Squadron was formed at Oban on 18th May 1942, and changed places with 422 Squadron from Castle Castle Archdale in the first week of December 1942. From Reykjavik in Iceland to convert from Catalinas to Sunderlands came Norwegian-manned 330 Squadron on 28th January 1943, but 422 Squadron left for Bowmore on 7th May and 330 Squadron for Sullom Voe on 12th July.

These moves left Oban clear for 302 Ferry Training Unit, which arrived from Stranraer on 22nd July 1943 and stayed until moving to Killadeas in April 1945. This important unit actually operated from Ganavan Sands, where a ground-crew training unit was also located. RAF Oban was then placed on a Care & Maintenance basis.

Today, the slipway and hard-standings at Ganavan Sands are used as a caravan site. The former SHQ is now Dungallan House Hotel, while the sergeants' mess is now the Regent Hotel. On Kerrera Island the slipway and jetty still exist, as do several minor buildings.

RAF Pembroke Dock (Pembrokeshire)

Opened as an RAF Station on 1st January 1930, Pembroke Dock was probably the best-known flying-boat base in the United Kingdom. At first, work on the flying-boats of the time was carried out in the open pending construction of hangars.

It was at Pembroke Dock that 228 Squadron received its first Sunderlands

Chapter 4 : RAF Sunderland Bases

in November 1938, and it was where 10 Squadron RAAF came into being on 12th August 1939. After a period in Egypt, 228 Squadron returned to 'PD' as it was known to many of those who served there, and stayed a year before leaving for Malta. Another new unit was 95 Squadron, formed in January 1941 before leaving for West Africa in the March. 10 Squadron left for Mount Batten in April 1940, but returned a year later, finally vacating Pembroke Dock at the end of the year. By that time, 228 Squadron had returned, but left again in October.

From Lough Erne came 119 Squadron in September 1942, but this unit disbanded the following March. Filling the vacated space, 461 Squadron arrived from Hamworthy and remained until disbanding in June 1945. Another unit at Pembroke Dock was 308 Ferry Training Unit, formed on 22nd March 1943 to carry out test flying as well as crew training, although within a few weeks the testing task was dropped. This unit was absorbed by 302 FTU at Oban on 12th January 1944. 228 Squadron put in a final appearance in May 1943 and remained in place until disbanding in June 1945. Present in 1944 were 201 and 422 Squadrons, which came from Castle Archdale in April, 201 returning there in November and 422 transferring to Transport Command to fly land-planes in July 1945.

Post-war, RAF Pembroke Dock remained open, and hosted 201 Squadron from August 1945 to March 1946, when it moved to Calshot, and 230 Squadron, which brought its Sunderlands back from Seletar in Singapore in April 1946 before moving to Castle Archdale four months later. 201 Squadron returned in January 1949 and 230 Squadron in February, and both carried on the business of flying Sunderlands until disbanding in February 1957, the last UK-based Sunderland units.

Her Majesty the Queen paid her first visit to RAF Pembroke Dock in August 1955 and was welcomed by the AOC of 19 Group and by the last Station Commander, Gp Capt P A Lombard DFC. A flypast by eight Sunderlands of 201 and 230 Squadrons and the FBTS was the Station's way of saying goodbye to Her Majesty.

On 1st February 1957 a ceremony was held to mark the end of Sunderland operations from the UK. Present were a former AOC-in-C Coastal Command (AM Sir Alick Stevens), the AOC 19 Group (AVM G I L Saye) and the AOC 18 Group (AVM P L Cracroft). Also present were the COs of 201 Squadron, Sqn Ldr D Baird, and 230 Squadron, Sqn Ldr P Adams, but due to heavy rain and strong winds a flypast had to be cancelled.

The Station was then put onto a Care & Maintenance basis and 'ownership' of the site passed to the Admiralty. However, on 24th March 1961 former Aéronautique navale Sunderland ML824 alighted in Milford Sound and remained at Pembroke Dock for about fifteen years before being transported to the RAF Museum in 1976 as a permanent exhibit.

Pembroke Dock RAF Station viewed from the west in May 1943, with fourteen white-liveried Sunderlands visible. The two pre-war hangars were well-camouflaged.
(Gp Capt A M Carey via John Evans)

Two B-type Aeroplane Sheds of 160 ft (49 m) span and 90 ft (27 m) length were built in 1934 to accommodate flying-boats during maintenance work. A T2-type hangar was built in 1943 for the use of 78 Maintenance Unit, which carried out major repairs on Sunderlands. At Pembroke Dock there were two slipways, one 36 ft (11 m) wide and 1121 ft (342 m) long, the other 68 ft (21 m) wide and 199 ft (61 m) long, while at Neyland was a third slipway, 30 ft (9 m) wide and 525 ft (160 m) long. There were two separate alighting areas in Milford Sound, one for day and the other for night use. A perma-

A group of RAF personnel unloading petrol from jerry-cans at the Pembroke Dock rail sidings. Note the well-camouflaged hangar disguised as housing and the two Sunderlands in the background.
(via A P Ferguson)

nent flarepath of Type I marker buoys was provided, and there were sodium lead-in lights and traffic control lights on Stack Rock and Popton Point. Aircraft moorings were about 440 yds (400 m) north of the Station and during hostilities were also located along both banks of the river for about one mile (1.6 km) to the east. To oversee the complicated business of taxying, a control pinnace was used.

Sandy Bay / Lough Neagh (County Antrim)

Between May and October 1944, the US Navy's Air Transport Command used an alighting area on Lough Neagh for a regular service from Botwood in Newfoundland and on to Port Lyautey in Morocco. A single Sunderland could often be seen there when detached for gunnery practice with RAF Aldergrove.

Stranraer (see Wig Bay)

RAF Sullom Voe (Shetland)

The most northerly RAF Station in the United Kingdom, Sullom Voe was located 25 miles (40 km) north of Lerwick, and was regarded as a very bleak spot "...at the back of beyond." The first RAF influence was the arrival on 27th June 1939 of the HMT *Manela*, a former P&O vessel which had been impressed to serve as a depot ship for squadrons under the control of 100 Wing. The site came into use for the Londons of 201 Squadron, which arrived from Calshot on 9th August that year to carry out patrols between Norway and Iceland.

Sunderlands appeared at Sullom Voe on 24th November 1939, when a detachment of 210 Squadron flew up from Pembroke Dock, remaining until returning home on 21st May 1940. They were joined on 2nd April 1940 by 204 Squadron from Mount batten, which carried out patrols until moving to Iceland on 5th April 1941. As soon as the 210 Squadron detachment left, it was replaced by 201 Squadron, which brought its Sunderlands to Sullom Voe from Invergordon on 26th May and stayed until moving to Castle Archdale on 9th October.

Facilities at Sullom Voe were very limited in the early days, although a floating dock which arrived in May 1940 aided the servicing of the flying-boats. A large bulk fuel installation in the side of a hill at Graven was completed in late June 1941.

Sullom Voe was often disturbed by false alarms of enemy action, but on 23rd March 1941 two Bf 110s from a Norwegian base attacked at low level, causing damage in the nearby village before one was shot down.

Shetland's proximity to Norway encouraged a number of Norwegians anxious to leave their country to avoid the German occupation. They used a number of floatplanes, some of Norwegian origin, some German, to fly to Sullom Voe in April 1940.

It was 12th July 1943 before another Sunderland unit was posted to Sullom Voe. This was 330 Squadron, manned largely by Norwegian crews, which arrived from Oban and stayed until leaving on 30th May 1945 to be absorbed into the postwar Royal Norwegian Air Force. Joining them from 28th September to 29th October 1944 was a detachment of 461 Squadron from Pembroke Dock. After 330 Squadron left, there was little activity at Sullom Voe apart from an occasional visit by a Sunderland of 4 (C) OTU from Alness. Although the Station was closed on 10th July 1945, it was used for a short time by US Navy PBM-5 Mariners in September 1946 and by 201 Squadron's Sunderlands during Exercise 'Mainbrace' in 1952.

Facilities at Sullom Voe comprised 22 moorings in Garth's Voe, plus three buoys at Heinkel gap, two at Voxter Voe, five off the Bight of Haggrister and five barge moorings in Scatsta Voe. The slipway was 260 ft (79 m) wide and there were three hangars, two of them Bellman-type. A flarepath consisted of three pram dinghies and a pinnace. As in other flying-boat bases, accommodation, both domestic and technical, was scattered, the airmen's living quarters in particular being about three-quarters of a mile (1.2 km) from the hangars and slipway.

Tayport (Fife)

A seldom-used alighting area, Tayport was frequented by the Sunderlands of 210 Squadron from Pembroke Dock early in October 1938.

RAF Wig Bay / Stranraer (Wigtownshire)

One of the busiest flying-boat bases in the UK could be found on the shores of Loch Ryan, where two RAF Stations, Stranraer and Wig Bay, functioned for many years. Their alighting areas were effectively the same.

RAF Stranraer was opened on 1st August 1940, but it was 9th October 1941 before the first Sunderland-equipped unit appeared. This was 228 Squadron, which moved in from Pembroke Dock and stayed until 10th March 1942, when it went to Oban. Just before it left, a detachment from 4 (C) OTU at Invergordon arrived on 28th February and continued with its task of crew training, specifically the prelim-inary part of the course, using three Sunderlands among other types. This continued until the detachment returned to Invergordon on 10th November.

After 4 (C) OTU had left, 302 Ferry Training Unit moved in from Castle Archdale on 1st December 1942, and trained crews

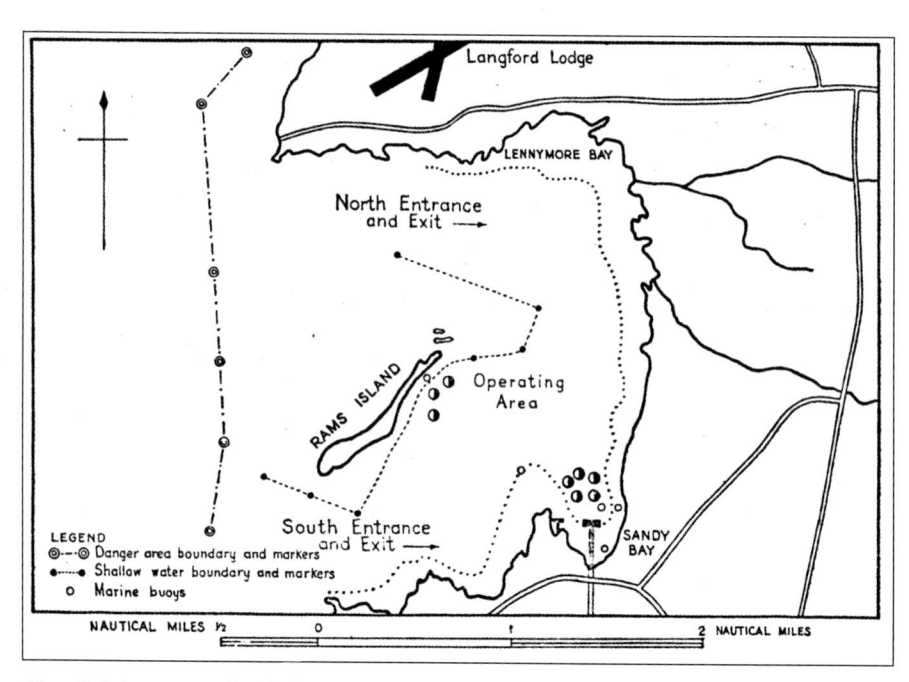

The alighting area at Sandy Bay, Lough Neagh which was used occasionally by Sunderlands.

CHAPTER 4 : RAF SUNDERLAND BASES

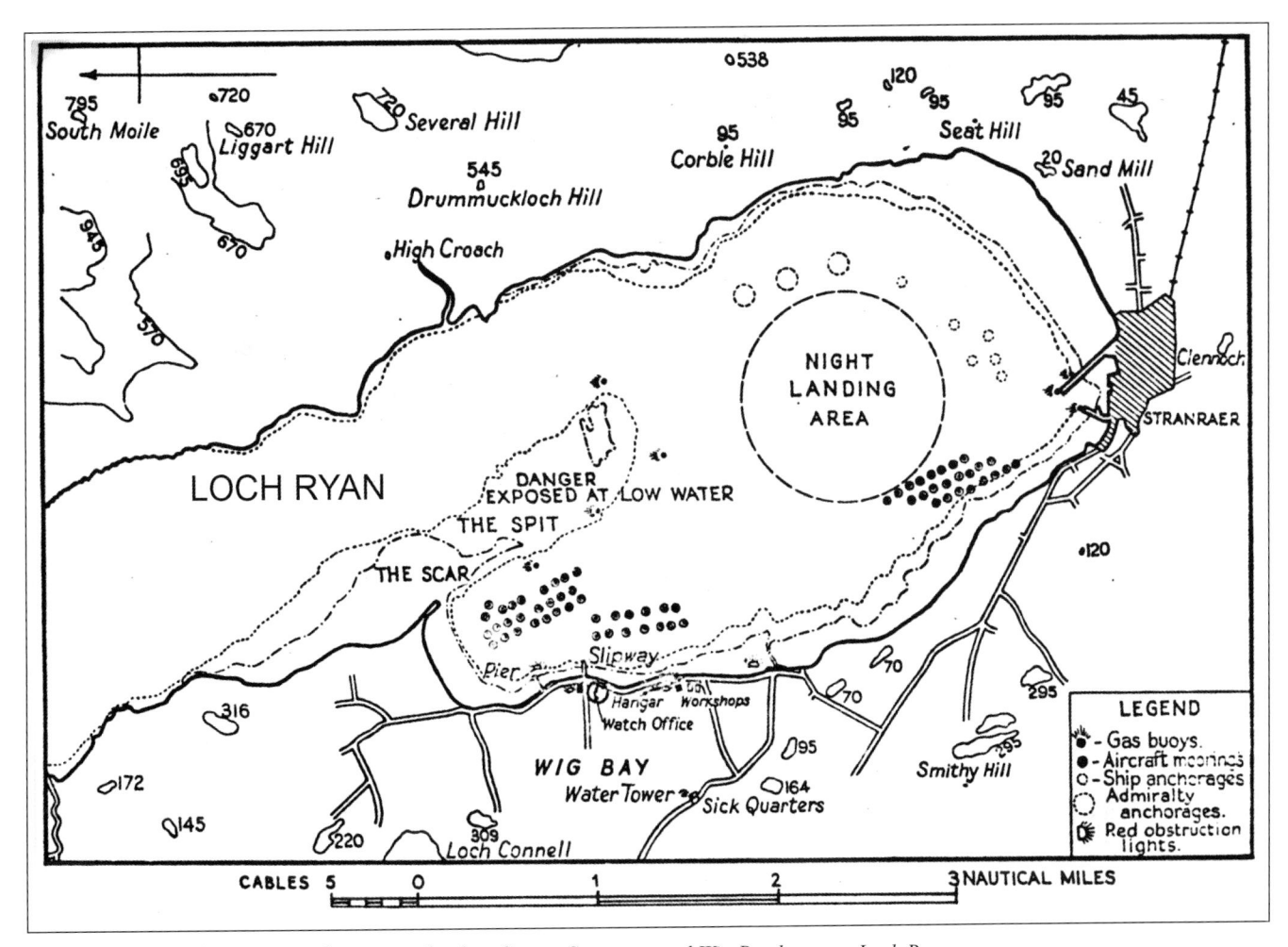

Location of the alighting area and moorings for the adjacent Stranraer and Wig Bay bases on Loch Ryan.

A typical Wig Bay 'hangar' which on 9th February 1957 contained Sunderland MR.5 ML817 [230:X] of 230 Squadron prior to its being SOC in the following October. (J R Grant via Douglas Rough)

Sunderland MR.5 PP151 had already been reduced to a bare hulk at the former 57MU Wig Bay when photographed on 1st August 1955. (Bill Broadfoot via JM Collection)

in the routine of ferrying Sunderlands and Catalinas to mainly overseas bases. This function came to an end on 22nd July 1943, when 302 FTU moved to Oban. RAF Stranraer closed on 15th February 1944.

Wig Bay's main task was to be the acceptance of new aircraft, their fitting out and delivery to operational units. To this end, 1 Flying Boat Servicing Unit was formed on 12th March 1942. This took the pressure off RAF Stranraer. The fitting-out function was placed in the hands of 11 Flying Boat Fitting Unit on 15th July 1943, but on 8th October of that year 57 Maintenance Unit came into being and absorbed 11 FBSU. Soon afterwards, on 1st February 1944, 1 FBSU was itself merged into 57 MU, which then became the main acceptance, fitting-out, modification, servicing and storage unit for Sunderlands in the UK. On that date, 57 MU was transferred from Coastal to Maintenance Command, and RAF Stranraer disbanded as a separate entity. By January 1945 57MU had over 1,000 personnel employed in the unit.

At nearby Carsewall, non-airworthy Sunderlands were used by the Marine Craft Training Unit to provide mooring practice for trainee ground crews.

Heavy gales in April and November 1944 caused damage to Sunderlands and Catalinas at Wig Bay at a time when the staff were at their busiest. After VE-Day the unit's main function became the storage and eventual disposal of withdrawn Sunderlands and other types, although a number were prepared for handing over to other forces, such as the RNZAF, the last of which left in June 1954. 57 MU disbanded in October 1951, when the unit's task was taken over by civilians employed by Short Bros & Harland Ltd, although a few RAF personnel remained until September 1957, by which time there were few Sunderlands in service.

There were two 'Shetland'-type and one J-type hangars at Wig Bay, as well as numerous 'nose-in' shelters. Air traffic control was carried out from a control tower on the west side of the bay and from a control pinnace.

Woodhaven (Fife)

210 Squadron Sunderlands were based at Woodhaven for a few days at the beginning of October 1939, when they left for Pembroke Dock.

Section 2:
THE MEDITERRANEAN AREA

RAF Aboukir (Egypt)

A long-established airfield and flying-boat base, Aboukir became the short term home of 204 Squadron's Scapa aircraft in 1935. After a gap of several years, 228 Squadron set up an advanced base at Aboukir on 14th July 1940 from which its Sunderlands could carry out patrols over the eastern Mediterranean, and the main party arrived from Pembroke Dock on 25th August. On 13th September 1940, however, the squadron moved to Kalafrana in Malta. After returning to Aboukir on 25th March 1941, 228 Squadron patrolled over Greece and took part in the evacuation of Crete.

In June 1941 the squadron left to take up duties at Bathurst in The Gambia, and was replaced by 230 Squadron from Alexandria, where air raids had become too intense. Apart from a short period when the squadron was detached to Kasfareet on the Great Bitter Lake, in July 1942, it remained at Aboukir until leaving for Dar-es-Salaam in East Africa on 9th January 1943.

After the departure of 230 Squadron, flying-boat activity at Aboukir consisted only of transit flights.

RAF Alexandria (Egypt)

Early flying-boat activity at Alexandria in the Suez Canal Zone of Egypt consisted of the use of Short 184 aircraft by two units: 270 Squadron between October 1918 and September 1919, and 202 Squadron, reformed there in April 1920 and disbanded in May 1921.

204 Squadron's Scapas were stationed at Alexandria from 22nd October 1935, when they arrived from Aboukir, until leaving for Mount Batten on 5th August 1936, as were the Singapores of 230 Squadron. 202 Squadron was again present at Alexandria from 26th September to 13th October 1938, when it returned to Kalafrana.

The first Sunderlands to be based at Alexandria were those of 228 Squadron, which arrived from Pembroke Dock on 5th June 1939, but they returned to the UK on 10th September. Subsequently, Sunderlands of 230 Squadron were based at Alexandria from 6th May 1940, when they moved in from Koggala in Ceylon, until 19th June 1941, when Aboukir became their base.

RAF Gibraltar

Both a land airfield and a flying-boat base, Gibraltar was first used in 1915, when ten aircraft of different types were sent there to fly submarine-spotting sorties. During the inter-war years the Royal Navy used the airfield on the racecourse, but on the outbreak of the Second World War Gibraltar became a vital staging post as well as a useful base for maritime reconnaissance aircraft. Among these were Sunderlands of 228 Squadron which were sent from Egypt to assist.

From mid-July to the end of August 1941 204 Squadron's Sunderlands were at Gibraltar, from where they flew convoy escorts before proceeding to Bathurst in Gambia, their intended base. In the reverse direction, 95 Squadron sent a detachment of Sunderlands from Freetown in February 1942, soon after which, in May, RAF North Front and RAF New Camp were formed, the latter controlling the activities of transient flying-boats.

Subsequently, Sunderlands continued to be seen at Gibraltar during transit flights to other bases in the Middle and Far East.

RAF Kalafrana (Malta)

Work on the construction of a seaplane base at Calafrana [sic] began in 1915 and in July 1916 the first Curtiss America flying-boats arrived. The base expanded during the First World War, and was the home of numerous floatplane-equipped units between the wars. Visiting aircraft were also frequently seen there.

The only Sunderland-equipped unit to be based at Kalafrana was 228 Squadron, which arrived from Pembroke Dock in October 1940 after being detached to the Maltese base on several earlier occasions. On 10th June three of the squadron's Sunderlands flew from Pembroke Dock to Alexandria via Marseilles and Kalafrana, returning on 9th July to carry out a dawn patrol of the Adriatic Sea. While at Kalafrana, 228 Squadron carried out routine anti-submarine patrols, using St Paul's Bay as a forward alighting area, until moving to Aboukir in March 1941.

Subsequently, Kalafrana received many visiting Sunderlands, but the last recorded touch-down was on 12th September 1957, when RN303 staged through on its way to Tobruk. The Station closed at about this time, and the site is now a fuel tank farm serving the island's requirements.

Scaramanga (Greece)

Used by Sunderlands during the evacuation of Greece in 1941, the alighting area at Scaramanga was on Lake Eleusis, about 15 miles 24 km) west of Athens.

Suda Bay (Crete)

Located on the northern coast of Crete, Suda Bay was and is a Greek Navy base, and was used by RAF and civil flying-boats during the evacuation of that island.

Section 3:
AFRICA

RAF Apapa (Nigeria)

The only RAF squadron ever to be based at Apapa was 270 Squadron, which brought its Catalinas from Jui in Sierra Leone on 23rd July 1943. An advanced base was established at Banana, at the mouth of the Congo river by September.

Sunderlands began to replace the Catalinas in December 1943, and by May 1944 no Catalinas remained. Banana closed down on 2nd October 1944, but a site at Owendo, Libreville, was still in use as an advanced base until 24th February 1945. Disbandment of 270 Squadron and 7270 Servicing Echelon came in June 1945, after which there was probably no more use for the base.

In addition to RAF use, there was a small amount of BOAC flying-boat activity at Apapa.

RAF Bathurst (The Gambia)

From 1934 almost to the outbreak of war in 1939, Bathurst, at the mouth of the Gambia River, had been one end of an unusual flying-boat service operated by

CHAPTER 4 : RAF SUNDERLAND BASES

The important flying-boat base at Kalafrana, Malta, with two slipways, an expanse of hangarage and high-quality domestic accommodation. The tall radio mast (centre) must have been a considerable hazard to aircraft in poor weather. (Author's collection)

A Sunderland at Kalafrana post-war being readied by a ground crew brought out by pinnace, with the aircrew looking on. (via F Galea)

Moored in Kalafrana Bay, a Sunderland in company with a Saro London. (via F Galea)

This vertical shot illustrates the slipway and maintenance area at Bathurst with a Sunderland and a Walrus on view. At centre left are a number of beaching trolleys for RAF launches, four of which are visible. The small hangar on the right still exists. (P H T Green collection)

A Sunderland Mk.II of 204 Squadron at its moorings at Bathurst, Gambia, in March 1942. (R C Sturtivant collection)

A parade to mark the visit of Lord Swinton taking place at RAF Bathurst in 1944. Visible are the main buildings (apart from a B-type hangar out of view on the left) and the jetty. None of the three Sunderlands in view have propellers fitted. (P J Christopher)

the German flag-carrier, Lufthansa. Originally, Dornier Wal aircraft took off and flew to a depot ship in mid-Atlantic, where they were hoisted aboard, refuelled and catapulted on their way to Natal in Brazil. Before long, larger Dornier flying-boats were making the complete journey without refuelling. To provide a landplane link to Germany, Lufthansa built an airfield at Jeswang, about 6 miles (10 km) west of Bathurst. Why the Colonial Office, representing the British Government, allowed this service to operate at a time when the Royal Air Force in the UK was undergoing a huge expansion scheme to defend the country against Germany remains a mystery.

Only three RAF flying-boat squadrons, all equipped with Sunderlands, were ever based at Bathurst. The first was 228 Squadron, which was established at Bathurst by the beginning of August 1941 but stayed only four weeks before returning to Pembroke Dock. Next came 204 Squadron, which arrived on 28th August 1941 and stayed until 28th January 1944. To administer the squadron and other units, RAF Bathurst was established on 1st September 1942, with Wg Cdr J P Cecil-Wright in command.

95 Squadron, which was at Bathurst from March 1943 to June 1945 after moving from Jui, had already been detached to Bathurst in 1941 and from October 1942 until the HQ arrived on 7th March 1943. 204 Squadron returned on 1st April 1944 as a detachment which remained for just a week.

In addition to RAF flying-boat activity, Bathurst was, from March 1943, a staging post for aircraft of BOAC on the UK to Lagos route and also regularly played host to Sikorsky flying-boats of American Export Airlines and Aeromaritime and Boeing 314s and Coronados of Pan American Airways. During December 1943 and the early part of 1944, numbers of Martin Mariner flying-boats for the RAF passed through Bathurst on delivery flights to the UK, only to return later when they were found to be unacceptable. Commencing in October 1944, substantial numbers of Catalinas bound for Russia were ferried through Bathurst.

The alighting area for Bathurst was in the mouth of the Gambia River, which allowed three miles (4.8 km) of open water in all directions. Buildings, including an operations room and eventually half a B-type hangar, were at Half Die, quaintly named as the result of an earlier epidemic of tropical disease which killed half the population. Another operations room, controlling the airfields at Jeswang and Yundum, was established at Cape St Mary.

Bathurst, now known as Banjul, has become a popular tourist destination, and a war cemetery which includes 48 RAF graves is located nearby. A quay for container traffic now functions where the slipway and hangars once stood.

Dakar / Bel Air (Sénégal)

Located in the French colony of Sénégal, Dakar (Bel Air) was the base for 343 Squadron, formed on 29th November 1943 from 'Free French' naval elements with a joint French identity as Flottille 7F. Detachments were sent to Port Etienne by January 1944, and were still there until shortly before 343 Squadron reverted to Flottille 7F on 27th November 1945.

RAF Dar-es-Salaam (Tanganyika — now Tanzania)

Catalinas were operated by 259 Squadron at Dar-es-Salaam from September 1943, and Sunderlands were added in March 1945, but the squadron disbanded on 30th May 1945.

RAF Freetown / Fourah and Jui (Sierra Leone)

In 1941 a flying-boat base was established at Fourah, in Freetown harbour, but as the harbour rapidly became congested it was decided that a site at Jui, six miles (10 km) south-east of Freetown, would be more appropriate.

Fourah was initially home to 95 Squadron, which brought three Sunderlands, fitted with extra tankage, on detachment from Pembroke Dock in February 1941. The ground party arrived on board ship on 2nd March, and accommodation for them was found at Fourah Bay College and at the Essex Regiment's Lumley Camp. More Sunderlands followed, and the squadron was officially complete at Fourah on 17th March 1941.

Jui was built to house two flying-boat squadrons, the first of which, 95 Squadron, moved in from Fourah on 9th April 1942. The RAF Station was officially formed on 12th July 1942, and next to take up residence were the Catalinas of 270 Squadron, which was formed there on 12th November 1942. 95 Squadron, however, left for Bathurst on 7th March 1943, to be replaced when 490 Squadron was formed on 28th March with Catalinas.

On 23rd July 1943 270 Squadron moved to Apapa, leaving 490 Squadron in sole charge. Soon afterwards, on 1st September, Jui took over the responsibility for the satellite alighting area at Fisherman's Lake.

204 Squadron, the final arrival at Jui, moved in from Bathurst on 28th January 1944 and apart from a week in April 1944 spent the rest of its time at Jui, disbanding there on 30th June 1945. 490 Squadron, which had taken delivery of Sunderlands in May 1944, followed suit on 1st August 1945, ending the working life of this RAF Station, which went onto a Care & Maintenance basis on 11th August.

Considerable use was also made of the facilities by flying-boats of BOAC.

RAF Kipevu (Kenya)

Catalinas were the most prominent type of flying-boat based at Kipevu, 209 Squadron being present from 15th June 1942 to 12th July 1945, when a move was made to Koggala, and 259 Squadron from 16th February to 14th September 1943. Sunderlands began to arrive for 209 Squadron in February 1945.

Port Etienne (French Morocco - now Mauretania)

Although no Sunderland squadrons were ever based at Port Etienne, small detachments were often sent there from Bathurst, 550 miles (885 km) to the south. Detached duty was organised to include routine patrols on the flights to and from Port Etienne, and crews enjoyed

Early in 1945, three Sunderlands are seen moored in the river estuary at Kipevu, inland from Mombasa, Kenya. (P H T Green collection)

the experience due to the site's pleasant sunny climate and lack of regulations. The location was on a south-facing sandy bay on the edge of the Mauretanian desert, backed here and there by a low sandstone cliff. Nearby was a sardine-canning factory and a desalination plant, while half a mile (800 m) inland was the RAF quarters, a small group of Nissen huts.

Section 4:
INDIA and CEYLON

RAF China Bay / Trincomalee (Ceylon — now Sri Lanka)

Opened on 1st August 1939, RAF China Bay eventually became a joint land/marine airfield, although permanent facilities for flying boats did not exist when 230 Squadron sent Sunderlands there in October of that year for a short detachment. A slipway was built in June 1941, and by 1943 the site was suitable for use by two squadrons of flying-boats. Although no Sunderland squadrons were ever headquartered at China Bay, 205 Squadron had detachments there from September 1949.

RAF Koggala (Ceylon — now Sri Lanka)

Said by some to be an idyllic location, the flying-boat alighting area at Koggala was in a long palm-fringed lagoon on the south coast of Ceylon (now Sri Lanka). A coastal road led westwards fifteen miles (24 km) to the town of Galle, where eventually RAF personnel were accommodated, and on to Colombo, the capital city.

RAF Koggala, situated at the head of a lagoon near Galle in Ceylon, with three Sunderlands at the moorings. The presence of these aircraft and of the runway of the land airfield date this photograph as post-1945. (Andrew Hendrie collection)

Flying low on 14th November 1945 over Redhills Lake where 240 Squadron was based, are two Sunderlands Mk.V of that squadron.
(P H T Green collection)

A brief survey of the lagoon was made in June 1939 and another, by two Sunderlands of 230 Squadron, on 30th October 1939. After a detailed survey on 7th November it was decided that the site would be suitable as a base for RAF flying-boats, and two weeks later two moorings were laid in the lagoon. A detachment of three Sunderlands of 230 Squadron arrived on 23 November, and two days later the Government of Ceylon gave formal approval to the use of the site. A proviso was that great care was to be taken to avoid offending or harming local people.

230 Squadron left Koggala in May 1940, and the base appears to have fallen into disuse until March 1942, when Catalinas of 413 Squadron arrived, followed by those of 205 Squadron in July. 230 Squadron returned for a short time in the spring of 1944, and 205 Squadron converted to Sunderlands in June 1945. They were joined in July by 209 Squadron and in January 1946 by 240 Squadron, another Sunderland operator, although the latter disbanded in March.

Koggala was the scene of a minor mutiny among RAF personnel on 25th January 1946, when all airmen below the rank of corporal marched around the Station after pay-parade to express their discontent at the rate of demobilisation. On 205 Squadron's hardstanding, they were addressed by the Station Commander and by a Labour MP who happened to be visiting. He promised to raise the men's grievances in the House of Commons, but work did not recommence for three or four days.

Koggala was still being used by 205 Squadron until September 1949, when Seletar became the squadron's base. It was also the terminus of BOAC's Ceylon to Australia service, flown by Catalinas.

RAF Redhills Lake (India)

This was a very busy flying-boat base, but Catalinas were the commonest type from July 1942, when the first unit, 240 Squadron, arrived. This unit disbanded on 1st July 1945 and reformed the same day from 212 Squadron, another Catalina unit. Sunderlands then began to arrive, and the squadron moved to Koggala on 10th January 1946, the last squadron to leave the base.

A good view of the flying-boat base at Seletar in 1954, with two Sunderlands on their hardstandings. The land airfield was some distance away to the right.   (Sqn Ldr Bryn Evans)

Section 5: FAR EAST

RAF Iwakuni (Japan)

A detachment of 209 Squadron was established at Iwakuni, 30 miles (48 km) from Hiroshima, as early as 3rd April 1946, and the first routine flight from Kai Tak arrived on 16th April. Adjacent was a land airfield used by the RAAF, and this is probably where personnel were accommodated.

Following the establishment of an Advanced HQ by the Far East Flying Boat Wing on 11th September 1950, RAF Iwakuni in Japan was formed on 1st November 1951 to act as a forward base for detachments of squadrons, although no servicing facilities were to be provided. Close by, the USAF assumed responsibility for the land airfield on 1st April 1952.

The detachments involved 88, 205 and 209 Squadrons, which rotated every five or six weeks until October 1954, by which time the Korean War had come to an end.

RAF Kai Tak / Hong Kong

Opened in 1927, Kai Tak was used by Fleet Air Arm land-based aircraft, but an adjacent alighting area enabled occasional visits by flying-boats of the RAF. In December 1941 the Japanese invaded, and the Colony surrendered on Christmas Day.

On 6th September 1945 Catalinas of 240 Squadron were the first RAF flying-boats to fly to the newly-liberated colony, but on 27th October 209 Squadron's Sunderlands moved in from Koggala, remaining until 18th May 1946 but leaving a detachment behind. 1430 Flight, comprising five Sunderlands, formed at Kai Tak on 5th August 1946, but within a month was redesignated 88 Squadron, which remained as the only flying-boat unit at Kai Tak until it moved to Seletar on 12th June 1951. During this period, 88 Squadron had taken part in the Korean war with a detachment at Iwakuni in Japan, and was prominent in the Yangtze incident.

RAF Seletar (Singapore)

Established in 1927 as a joint marine/land airfield, Seletar came to prominence as a flying-boat alighting area when the Far East Flight of Southamptons arrived there from Felixstowe. The airfield opened officially as RAF Base Singapore on 1st January 1930, gaining gradual importance over the next few years. In November 1936 it was renamed RAF Seletar.

Sunderlands began to arrive at Seletar in June 1938, when 230 Squadron took its first deliveries of the new aircraft. Some of them remained at Seletar until 13th February 1940, when the squadron HQ left to catch up with a mobile detachment which had found its way to Koggala. Due to the Japanese occupation, no more Sunderlands were based at Seletar until 1st December 1945, when 230 Squadron returned from India, but left on 15th April 1946, when a detachment of 209 Squadron arrived from Kai Tak, its HQ following on 18th May. With land airfields on Singapore Island in a bad state of repair, the Sunderland crews found themselves flying food and medicines around the area and repatriating Allied troops, both vital tasks.

This squadron was joined on 14th September 1949 by 205 Squadron, and on 12th June 1951 by 88 Squadron, the three becoming components of the Far East Flying Boat Wing, which flew operationally in the Korean conflict. 88 Squadron disbanded in October 1954, however, and the other squadrons merged to form 205/209 Squadron in January 1955. In May 1959 at Seletar the the RAF's final Sunderland flight was made from Seletar.

Section 6: ICELAND and THE FAEROES

RAF Reykjavik (Iceland)

Only one Sunderland squadron was based at this station — 204 Squadron, which made an initial appearance in May 1940, when it arrived from Sullom Voe on a week's detachment. In July and November of that year, more sorties were flown from Reykjavik, and in April 1941 HMT *Manela* was positioned there to act as squadron HQ. However, a change of plan found the squadron moving to Gibraltar in July 1941, to be replaced by Catalinas of 209 Squadron.

Other units based at Reykjavik were 330 Squadron, which was crewed by Norwegian personnel and had used Northrop N-3PB floatplanes before they were replaced by Catalinas, and 162 Squadron RCAF, which brought Canso aircraft from Nova Scotia in January 1944 and in June 1945 were the last to leave the base.

Midvag (Faeroes)

Located on the island of Vaaga in the Faeroes was an alighting area on Lake Sorvaagvata, and although no RAF squadrons were ever based there it was used from time to time from June 1942 by Sunderlands as a refuelling and rearming location while carrying out patrols over the North Atlantic.

Five Sunderlands beached at Seletar including MR.5 NJ193 [P] labelled 'Lot 47', before being scrapped on the disbandment of 205/209 Squadron. (Gerald Raggett collection)

Standing at the end of a hangar at Seletar is an unidentified Sunderland MR.5, possibly coded [X]. (P H T Green collection)

Sunderland MR.5 ML797 [P] of 205/209 Squadron being hauled up the slipway at Seletar for the last time on 22nd May 1959, after its final flight two days earlier. In true nautical tradition, it carries a 'paying-off' pennant. (J Power via John Evans)

The prototype Sunderland, K4774, on the hardstanding at Felixstowe in August 1938 with, on the left, Walrus L2179 keeping it company.
(P H T Green collection)

Chapter 5
INDIVIDUAL AIRCRAFT HISTORIES

Important note: Information on individual Sunderlands given in the following summaries has been gleaned from a number of sources, principally the Aircraft Record Cards (Form 78). However, the Form 78s provide 'paper' dates, which often differ from actual dates, and therefore more accurate sources have been employed when possible. Where the word 'delivered' is used, it signifies the actual arrival date on that unit as recorded in the unit Operational Record Books (Forms 540 and 541) and other sources. **Also of note**: as of 1st July 1948, Roman numeral Mark Numbers gave way to Arabic numbers. Rôle prefix letters, GR, were also introduced then before changing to MR as of 1st February 1951.

Part 1: ROYAL AIR FORCE

K4774 c/n S.803; prototype, built by Short Bros Ltd at Rochester under Contract 351564/34; first and second flights 16Oct37 with Pegasus X engines, subsequent flights 21 and 28Oct37; re-engined with Pegasus XXIIs; flight tests resumed 7Mar38; full load test 31Mar38; MAEE 11Apr38; damaged when depth charge exploded at Helensburgh 13Feb42; last known flight Sep42; SOC .44

11 Sunderlands Mk.I built by Short Bros Ltd, Rochester under Contract B.533317/36:

L2158 c/n S.860; first flight 21Apr38; full load test 9May38; TOC MAEE 2Jun38; Shorts 12Apr40; returned to MAEE 25Apr40; BOAC for overhaul 11Mar41; 204 Sqn [KG:M] 30May41; Calshot 16Feb42; returned to 204 Sqn 26May42; during convoy escort off Sierra Leone 17Aug42, struck water nose-down and exploded (4 killed, 5 survivors reached land and were rescued later)

L2159 c/n S.861; first flight 4May38; TOC 209 Sqn for ferry preparation 9May38; left Pembroke Dock 9Jun38; delivered to 230 Sqn [FV:W, NM:W] 22Jun38; force-landed in Nikolo Bay, Kythera (an island between the southern tip of Greece and Crete) 26Aug40, temporarily interned; left Egypt 21Dec40 for overhaul by Scottish Aviation; damaged beyond repair in air-raid on Scottish Aviation at Greenock 7May41; SOC 12May41

L2160 c/n S.862; first flight 18May38; TOC 209 Sqn for ferry preparation 22May38; overload test 3Jun38; left Pembroke Dock 22Jun38; delivered to 230 Sqn [NM:X] 4Jul38; named *Selangor* by HH Sultan of Selangor 19Oct38; damaged by four Fiat CR.42 fighters 20Jun40; 228 Sqn [DQ:X] 1Oct40; 230 Sqn ?; left for UK 18Sep41; Mount Batten stored reserve 25Nov41; repaired on site 31Dec41; 4 (C) OTU 2Apr42; became GI airframe **3372M** at 4 (C) OTU 21Sep42, renumbered **4005M** 27.7.43

L2161 c/n S.863; first flight 23May38; TOC 209 Sqn May38; delivered to 210 Sqn from Felixstowe 11Jun38 for preparation for 230 Sqn; delivered to 230 Sqn [NM:Y] 26Jul38; named *Negeri Sembilan* by HH Sultan of Sembilan 25Nov38; badly damaged 12Dec38 when two propellers detached and damaged hull; aircraft diverted to Nancowry (Nicobar Is) for repair, after which it flew to Penang (Malaya) 11Jan39; Calshot 7Jul40; BOAC, Hythe, 26Jul40; 204 Sqn 19Aug40; 230 Sqn [NM:P] 24Aug40; 228 Sqn [DQ:P] by Oct40; sunk at moorings at Scaramanga (Greece) by Ju.87s 23Apr41 (no casualties); SOC 26Apr41

L2162 c/n S.864; first flight 1Jun38; delivered to 210 Sqn [DA:G] 21Jun38; broke in two during night landing at Angle Bay, Milford Haven, 20Sep38 (2 killed, 6 injured)

L2163 c/n S.865; first flight 17Jun38; delivered to 210 Sqn [C, later DA:G] 24Jun38; attacked by Fw.200 29Jan40, rear turret damaged; lost float on alighting in heavy seas at Oban 25Sep40; 95 Sqn [SE:G] 16Jan41; 228 Sqn 18Dec41; broke from moorings and driven ashore in gale at Stranraer 15Jan42; S&HL 21Apr42; 57 MU 17Feb44; became GI airframe **4891M** at 1 MCTU, Corsewall, 12Oct44

L2164 c/n S.866; first flight 30Jun38; TOC 210 Sqn 5Jul38 for preparation for 230 Sqn; delivered to 230 Sqn [FV:Z, NM:Z, NM:R] 16Aug38; named *Pahang* by HH Sultan of Pahang 21Oct38; lost propeller in forced landing at Aboukir (Egypt) 19Jul40; delivered to 228 Sqn [DQ:Z, DQ:M] by Oct40; severely damaged in raid, St Paul's Bay, Malta, 7Mar41; destroyed by fire in further raid by Bf.109s of 7/JG26 10Mar41 and sank; SOC 27Mar41

L2165 c/n S.867; first flight 12Jul38; delivered to 210 Sqn 16Jul38; crashed near St Anne's Head, Pembrokeshire, 17Sep39 while attempting to alight at night after fuel exhausted (all 10 killed)

Apparently brand new and moored at Rochester, Mk.I L2158 was the first production Sunderland and went to MAEE for trials on 1st June 1938.
(P H T Green collection)

Seen alighting at Bathurst in The Gambia is Sunderland Mk.I L2158 [KG:M] of 204 Squadron which was lost during a convoy escort on 17th August 1942.
(P H T Green collection)

Sunderland Mk.I L2159 of 209 Squadron took part in tropical trials at Kalafrana, Malta, in June 1938 before delivery to 230 Squadron. Clearly visible under the wing, the fuselage bomb door is open. This aircraft was unfortunately destroyed in an air raid on Greenock on 7th May 1941.
(R C Sturtivant collection)

CHAPTER 5 : INDIVIDUAL AIRCRAFT HISTORIES

L2166 c/n S.868; first flight 27Jul38; TOC 210 Sqn 29Jul38 for preparation for 230 Sqn; delivered to 230 Sqn 5Sep38; named *Perak* by HH Sultan of Perak 30Sep38 and carried white / yellow / black fin flash of State of Perak; Egypt to UK via Gibraltar 25Jun40; BOAC for overhaul 27Jun40; Calshot 10Aug40; returned to 230 Sqn [NM:U] 17Aug40; sank Italian submarine *Gondar* 30Sep40; shot down by flak from Italian submarine *Delfino* at 32°12N 14°46E in Gulf of Sollum (Egypt) 1Aug41; crew taken PoW; SOC 3Aug41

L2167 c/n S.869; first flight 27Jul38; delivered to 210 Sqn [DA:H] 12Aug38; attacked by two Bf.110s over Oslofjord (Norway) 1Aug41, caught fire and exploded (1 crew member survived after falling 3000 ft (915 m) without parachute!)

L2168 c/n S.870; first flight 10Aug38; delivered to 210 Sqn 27Aug38; 201 Sqn [ZM:Z] 13May40; BOAC 19Jun40; Calshot 4Jul40; returned to 201 Sqn; overshot night landing and ran aground, Sullom Voe, 11Mar41; returned to 201 Sqn 11Aug41; Pembroke Dock 4Sep41; returned to 201 Sqn [ZM:Z] 6Nov41; delivered to 228 Sqn 28Jan42; engine cut on air test, hit shoal on alighting at Stranraer 7Feb42; repaired on site; 4 (C) OTU 22Apr42; 1 FBSU 14Dec42; 4 (C) OTU 26Jun43; moorings broke, drifted ashore at Alness 20Jul43; caught fire in air and crashed near Nigg, Ross & Cromarty, 21Nov43 while on night training flight (1 killed, 4 missing)

10 Sunderlands Mk.I built by Short Bros Ltd, Rochester under Contract B.533317/36:

L5798 c/n S.887; first flight 1Sep38; TOC 210 Sqn 8Sep38 [DA:A]; BOAC (servicing) 4Apr41; delivered to 201 Sqn [ZM:Z] 22Apr41; Pembroke Dock 12Jun41; 201 Sqn [ZM:Z] 31Jul41; 204 Sqn [Z] same day; Calshot 27Dec41; 204 Sqn [KG:B] 19Feb42; struck by refueller at Bathurst (The Gambia) 4Dec42; damaged in gale while moored at Gibraltar 20Sep43; flown to Calshot 1Oct43; SOC 25Oct43

L5799 c/n S.888; first flight 12Sep38; delivered to 210 Sqn 19Sep38; 204 Sqn [KG:D] 19Jun39; damaged by He.111 during reconnaissance 7Apr40 and crashed in sea S of Bergen (Norway); crew interned

L5800 c/n S.889; delivered to 210 Sqn 29Sep38; 201 Sqn [ZM:S] by 1May40; BOAC 26Oct40; Pembroke Dock 24Feb41; BOAC for repair 11Apr41; returned to 201 Sqn 23Apr41; 204 Sqn [KG:L] 1Aug41; Calshot 11Dec41; returned to 204 Sqn [KG:J] 22Jan42; Mount Batten 17May42; Cat B to S&HL 10Jan43; 4 (C) OTU [TA:U] 22Apr43; repaired on site by Shorts 13Nov43; SOC 2Jul44

L5801 c/n S.890; TOC 210 Sqn 15Oct38 for ferrying; delivered to 230 Sqn 15Nov38; ditched in Johore Straits (Malaya) 5Jun39 due to control problem after take-off (4 killed, 4 injured); taken under tow but sank

L5802 c/n S.891; del 210 Sqn 24Oct38; damaged on alighting at Pembroke Dock 21Apr39; repaired on site; 204 Sqn [RF:F, KG:F, KG:G] 19Jun39; Pembroke Dock 1Apr40; delivered to 201 Sqn [ZM:U] 3Jun40; UK to Bathurst via Gibraltar 1/2Jun41; delivered to 95 Sqn [SE:F] 5Jun41; BOAC 17Jul42; 461 Sqn 26Jul42; 4 (C) OTU [TA:J] 16Nov42; bounced on alighting at Alness at night, stalled and hit water, 16Jan43 (no casualties); SOC same date

L5803 c/n S.892; collected from Rochester by 228 Sqn crew for 210 Sqn 3Nov38; delivered to 230 Sqn [NM:T] 5Dec38; delivered to 228 Sqn [DQ:T] 6Nov40; left Kalafrana for UK via Gibraltar 21Dec40 for overhaul by Scottish Aviation, Greenock (arrived 24Dec40); left for Aboukir via Gibraltar 10May41; delivered to 228 Sqn [DQ:T] 13May41; left Alexandria (Egypt) for Bathurst 23Jun41 (delivered to 30Jul41); Calshot 26Aug41; 95 Sqn [SE:H] 14Oct41; Calshot 12Nov41; 204 Sqn 30Jan42; Calshot 24Apr42; 95 Sqn [H] 26Apr42; Cat AC at Mount Batten 1May42; repaired on site by SBL 20May42; destroyed by fire while refuelling at Jui 22Aug42 and depth charges exploded

L5804 c/n S.893; collected from Rochester by 228 Sqn crew 9Nov38; delivered to 210 Sqn 10Nov38 for ferrying; left Pembroke Dock 8Dec38; delivered to 230 Sqn [NM:S] 22Dec38; sank Italian submarines *Argonauta* 28Jun40 and *Rubino* 29Jun40; while on patrol over Sicily on 28Jul40, was attacked and badly damaged by four Macchi MC.200 fighters but flew to Kalafrana for repair and thence to base at Alexandria; hit felucca (wooden sailing-boat) on take-off from Alexandria 21Oct40; repaired on site; broke loose from mooring in gale at Scaramanga (Greece) 25Feb41, driven ashore and abandoned in evacuation; SOC 15Jun41

Sunderland Mk.I L2160 "Selangor" (a Malayan State) of 230 Squadron moored on a river in Malaya, probably at the time of its naming ceremony. (P H T Green collection)

Named "Negeri Sembilan" after a Malayan State and wearing its flag on the fin in November 1938, this Sunderland Mk.I L2161 was later-destroyed on 23rd April 1941 at Scaramanga, Greece. (Gerald Raggett collection via Rod Simpson)

Seen here in its original finish, L2163 [C] saw service with 210 Squadron in 1938 and 228 Squadron from the end of 1941. (R C Sturtivant collection)

L5805 c/n S.894; delivered to 228 Sqn 24Nov38; engine cut while taxying at Calshot, swung and struck barge, 12Dec38; repaired on site; Pembroke Dock 2Jul40; left Alexandria for Pembroke Dock via Kalafrana 9Sep39; Pembroke Dock 2Jul40; 201 Sqn [ZM:Y] 16Jul40; 95 Sqn 12Mar41; Calshot 26May41; flew UK to Bathurst via Gibraltar 17Jun41; delivered to 95 Sqn [SE:B] 17Jun41; Calshot 26Aug41; 95 Sqn 26Sep41; Calshot 28Nov41; 95 Sqn 14Dec41; Calshot 20Mar42; 95 Sqn 6May42; 202 Sqn 7May42; 95 Sqn 11May42; crashed during patrol over South Atlantic 8Oct42 (at least 4 killed)

L5806 c/n S.895; delivered to 228 Sqn 10Dec38; 210 Sqn 13Jul39; 228 Sqn [DQ:Q, BH:Q] 22Aug39; left Alexandria for Pembroke Dock via Kalafrana 9Sep39; flew Kalafrana to Pembroke Dock via Gibraltar 8/9Apr41 for fitting with ASV Mk.II; flew Pembroke Dock to Gibraltar 29Apr41; 230 Sqn [DX:Q, Q]; bounced on alighting at Kalafrana at night 23Sep41 and float collapsed; repaired on site; failed to return from anti-submarine patrol off Egyptian coast 25Jul42; SOC 14Aug42

L5807 c/n S.896; delivered to 228 Sqn 14Jan39; left Pembroke Dock for Alexandria via Malta 29Apr39; delivered to Pembroke Dock 5Aug39 for mods by Short Bros; 210 Sqn 17Aug39; 228 Sqn [DQ:R] 22Aug39; Calshot 8Oct40; BOAC 10Oct40; 228 Sqn [DQ:F] 18Oct40; Calshot 29Oct40; Pembroke Dock 1Nov40; destroyed by fire in attack by Bf.109s of 7/JG26 at Kalafrana 27Apr41 and sank

Six interested parties, apparently non-service personnel, gaze upon new Sunderland Mk.I L2164. The location is probably MAEE, Felixstowe, although there is no record of it being allocated to that unit. (P H T Green collection)

How did he get there? An airman on the tailplane of Sunderland Mk.I L2164 [FV:Z] of 230 Squadron in the 1938 scheme with the flag of Pahang Malayan State on the fin. (Andrew Hendrie collection)

In late 1938, or not later than 17th September 1939, Sunderland Mk.I L2165 [B] of 210 Squadron accompanied by two others, is shadowing what appears to be a French warship and merchantman flying their national flags; location and occasion unknown. (P H T Green collection)

Sunderland Mk.I L5798 of 210 Squadron seen at Oban in May 1941 with two crewmen at the nose attempting to manoeuvre the mooring buoy and one offering helpful advice from the cockpit window. (P H T Green collection)

CHAPTER 5 : INDIVIDUAL AIRCRAFT HISTORIES

L5802 of 204 Squadron, with paintwork a little worn around the waterline, carried code [RF] and a duplicate display of its serial on the rudder. (R C Sturtivant collection)

Seen at Pembroke Dock in late May 1941, Sunderland Mk.I L5802 was being worked on before despatch to 95 Squadron in West Africa, whose [SE:F] code it already carried. In the background is 10 (RAAF) Squadron's P9603 [RB:H]. (P H T Green collection)

Sunderland Mk.I L5804 [NM:S] of 230 Squadron sank in a gale at Scaramanga, Greece, on 25th February 1941 and is seen here being salvaged. (R C Sturtivant collection)

A somewhat specialised piece of engineering enables Sunderland Mk.I L5803 to be hauled out of the water at Pembroke Dock.
(Sir Robert Carver via Andrew Hendrie collection)

In the summer of 1939, Sunderland Mk.I N9020 [TO:W] of 228 Squadron was photographed at its moorings somewhere in the Mediterranean.
(P H T Green collection)

3 Sunderlands Mk.I built by Short Bros Ltd, Rochester under Contract B.774293/38:

N6133 c/n S.897; delivered to 228 Sqn 12Feb39; left Pembroke Dock for Alexandria via Malta 29May39, arrived 5Jun39; Pembroke Dock 27Aug39; 201 Sqn [ZM:Y]; shot down by Bf.110 90 mls (145 km) SW of Sumburgh 8Jul40 (10 killed); SOC 11Jul40

N6135 c/n S.898; delivered to 228 Sqn 17Feb39; left for Malta 26Apr39; 210 Sqn 13Jul39; 228 Sqn [TO:U, BH:U] 22Aug39; left Alexandria for Pembroke Dock via Kalafrana 9Sep39; alighted downwind at Pembroke Dock 10Sep39 and lost both floats, later capsized and sank while under tow; salvaged but SOC

N6138 c/n S.899; delivered to 228 Sqn 22Feb39; left Pembroke Dock for Alexandria via Malta 29May39, arrived 5Jun39; 201 Sqn [ZM:V] 12Apr40; hull badly damaged in attack by Do.215 near Ranna Stacks; Calshot 7Aug40; BOAC for repair 10Aug40; Pembroke Dock 10Oct40; 201 Sqn 12Oct40; broke moorings at Pembroke Dock and drifted ashore 12Nov40 (2 drowned); 4 (C) OTU 19Dec41; BOAC 9Jul42; 4 (C) OTU 22Aug42; 4 FP, ATA, 9Oct42 for ferrying to Scottish Aviation; 4 (C) OTU 20Oct42; force-landed after engine caught fire on take-off from Alness 17Feb43; repaired on site; swung on alighting at Alness 17Jul43 and lost float

18 Sunderlands Mk.I built by Short Bros Ltd, Rochester under Contract B.774293/38:

N9020 c/n S.1004; delivered to 228 Sqn [TO:W/DQ:W] 9Mar39; left Pembroke Dock for Alexandria via Kalafrana 6Jun39, arrived 12Jun39; left Alexandria for Pembroke Dock 9Sep39 but remained at Kalafrana; shot down by Macchi 200 fighters during reconnaissance over Ionian Sea 1Nov40

N9021 c/n S.1005; delivered to MAEE 17Mar39; 204 Sqn [KG:C, KG:G] 19Aug39; damaged when being towed off mudbank by powerboat at Falmouth, Cornwall, 25Mar40; repaired on site; stored Pembroke Dock 16Jul40; 201 Sqn 19Oct40; stalled on alighting at night at Invergordon after patrol 13Dec40 (no casualties); capsized and sank while being salvaged

N9022 c/n S.1006; delivered to 210 Sqn 29Mar39; 204 Sqn 19Jun39; 210 Sqn [DA:B] 26Sep39; engine cut while taxying at Pembroke Dock 28Mar40 and collided with ship; repaired on site; struck object in water just off Maiden Island while alighting at Oban 27Dec40 and flipped onto back (10 drowned, 1 survived)

N9023 c/n S.1007; delivered to 228 Sqn 6Apr39; made heavy landing on port float while avoiding another aircraft at Rochester 2May39; repaired on site; left Pembroke Dock for Alexandria via Malta 13Jun39, arrived 14Jun39; Calshot stored reserve 7Jun40; BOAC 19Jun40; 204 Sqn 16Jul40; on return from patrol over Fragjadalsfjall, SE of Reykjavik (Iceland), on 24Apr41, flew into mountain and exploded (3 killed, 10 injured); SOC 1May41

N9024 c/n S.1008; delivered to 210 Sqn 21Apr39; delivered to 204 Sqn [KG:A] 10Feb40; Pembroke Dock 1Apr40; 201 Sqn; 204 Sqn [KG:H] 11Nov40; Pembroke Dock 7Aug41; 204 Sqn; engine lost power, lost height due to heavy load and struck water 1 ml N of Cape St Mary (Gambia) 28Dec41; repaired on site; BOAC 5Jul42; Pembroke Dock 23Aug42; Cat B 24Aug42; BOAC 5Sep42; Pembroke Dock 9Jan43; 204 Sqn [KG:H] 10Jan43; 4 (C) OTU [HH] 4Jul43; SOC 16Aug44

N9025 c/n S.1009; delivered to 228 Sqn 6May39; 210 Sqn 18Jul39; delivered to 228 Sqn [DQ:Y] 10Aug39; sank U-55 30Jan40 (first success for any Sunderland); forced down due to severe damage by Fiat CR.42s at 32°19'N 23°42'W (in central Mediterranean) 6Aug40; alighted on sea and taken in tow by enemy destroyer but sank (1 killed, remainder PoW)

N9026 c/n S.1010; delivered to 210 Sqn [DA:D] 17May39; port wing damaged in taxying accident 3May40; repaired on site by Shorts; failed to return from Atlantic convoy patrol off south-west Ireland 29Jun40 (9 killed); SOC 27Aug40

N9027 c/n S.1011; delivered to 228 Sqn 30May39; 210 Sqn [DA:J] 19Jun39; attacked by Fw.200 14Aug40 and damaged; 95 Sqn [SE:N] 16Jan41; sank at moorings in gale at Devil's Tongue Bay, Gibraltar, 16Feb41; SOC 26Feb41

N9028 c/n S.1012; delivered to 204 Sqn [KG:A] 10Jun39; Pembroke Dock 1Apr40; shot down by Bf.110s near Linaero [sic] 21Jul40 during reconnaissance of Trondheim (Norway) (all 12 killed, inc CO of squadron, Wg Cdr E S C Davis)

N9029 c/n S.1013; delivered to 204 Sqn 25Jun39 for ferrying; delivered to 230 Sqn [NM:V] 25Jul39; damaged at moorings by Fiat CR.42 6Nov40; Malta to UK via Gibraltar 14/15Jun41; missing from anti-submarine patrol 1Jan43; wreckage found at 31°45N 32°28E, about 100 mls (160 km) N of Damietta, Egypt (no survivors)

N9030 c/n S.1014; delivered to 204 Sqn 9Jul39; crashed outside Plymouth breakwater during night of 15/16Oct39 in poor visibility on return to Mount Batten from patrol (4 killed, 7 injured)

N9044 c/n S.1015; delivered to 204 Sqn [KG:C] 11Jul39; Pembroke Dock 1.40; damaged by He.115 9Apr40; repaired on site; Pembroke Dock 14Aug41; Calshot 31Oct41; Cat AC 18Nov41; 204 Sqn [KG:C] 22Feb42; 4 (C) OTU [CC] 3Jul43; SOC 24Jul44

N9045 c/n S.1016; delivered to 204 Sqn [KG:J] 24Jul39; after anti-sub patrol on 3Oct39, sank after alighting near Scilly Isles in gale and heavy seas due to abnormal fuel consumption (crew rescued)

N9046 c/n S.1017; delivered to 204 Sqn [KG:F] 2Aug39; damaged by Ju.88s 3Apr40; Pembroke Dock 8Apr40; returned to 204 Sqn 15Apr40; damaged by Bf.109 off Norway 21Aug40; repaired on site; destroyed by fire at moorings, Sullom Voe, 28Oct40; SOC 11Dec40

N9047 c/n S.1018; delivered to 210 Sqn 18Aug39; BOAC 13Oct39; 204 Sqn [KG:B] 26Oct39; damaged by flak 8Apr40; repaired on site; engine cut while taxying on two engines 6Nov40 and ran aground on reef off Oban; after refuelling, caught fire at moorings at Skerjafjordur, near Reykjavik (Iceland) 10Jun41 and sank; SOC 17Apr42

CHAPTER 5 : INDIVIDUAL AIRCRAFT HISTORIES

Sunderland Mk.I N9021 visited Kalafrana, Malta on a demonstration tour while on charge to the MAEE. (P H T Green collection)

N9048 c/n S.1019; delivered to 210 Sqn 5Sep39; 10 (RAAF) Sqn [RB:A] 30Nov39; destroyed by fire in air raid at Mount Batten, 27/28Nov40; SOC 4Feb41

N9049 c/n S.1020; delivered to 210 Sqn 9Aug39; del to 10 (RAAF) Sqn [RB:B] 18Sep39; damaged in air-raid on Mount Batten 13Jan41; UK to Malta via Gibraltar 1May41; damaged at moorings by Bf.109s of 7/JG26 and sank, Kalafrana, 10May41 (no casualties); SOC 1Jul41

N9050 c/n S.1021; TOC 4 MU at Pembroke Dock 9Aug39 for preparation for RAAF in Australia; delivered to 210 Sqn 3Oct39; 10 (RAAF) Sqn [RB:D] 30Nov39; first 10 Sqn aircraft to encounter enemy aircraft, a Bf.110 in Jul40; delivered to 95 Sqn [SE:D] 14Mar41; force-landed 12 mls (19.2 km) from Bathurst after engine failure 10Apr41; drifted aground but repaired; Calshot 5Jul41; returned to 95 Sqn 9Aug41; Calshot 24Oct41; returned to 95 Sqn 1Dec41; 202 Sqn 10Feb42; 95 Sqn 3Apr42; Pembroke Dock 21Jul42; Scottish Aviation, Greenock, 21Jul42; SOC; BBOC; 4 (C) OTU [TA:C] 16Apr43; SOC 29Jul44

12 Sunderlands Mk.I built by Short Bros Ltd, Rochester under Contract B.985038/39:

P9600 c/n S.1028; TOC 4 MU at Pembroke Dock Oct39 for preparation for RAAF in Australia; 210 Sqn 27Oct39; delivered to 10 (RAAF) Sqn [RB:E] 27Oct39; hit wreckage in Firth of Lorne, Scotland, while alighting at night 10Jan41; repaired on site; flew UK to Malta via Gibraltar 27/28Apr41, returned 3/4May41; flew UK to Gibraltar 6Jun41; damaged by Fw.200 30Jun41; 228 Sqn [DQ:T] 19Nov41; 4 (C) OTU 2Mar42; lifting gear failed and engine dropped at Wig Bay, 25May42; repaired on site; Scottish Aviation 26Oct42; returned to 4 (C) OTU 5Jul43; hit by drifting Sunderland at moorings, Alness, 29Sep43; overshot and ran aground, Alness, 9Jun44; 57 MU 22Jun44; SOC and scuttled 11Dec46

P9601 c/n S.1029; TOC 4 MU at Pembroke Dock 3Nov39 for preparation for RAAF in Australia; delivered to 10 (RAAF) Sqn [RB:F] 3Nov39; destroyed by fire in air-raid at Mount Batten and sank 27/28Nov40; SOC 4Feb41

P9602 c/n S.1030; TOC 4 MU at Pembroke Dock for preparation for RAAF in Australia; delivered to 10 (RAAF) Sqn [RB:G] 13Nov39; ran into Island of Lismore, Firth of Lorne, Scotland, 2Sep40 while alighting in high winds at night, when flarepath drifted towards cliffs (1 injured); broken up at Ardentrive, Argyll; SOC 25Sep40

P9603 c/n S.1031; TOC 4 MU at Pembroke Dock for preparation for RAAF in Australia; delivered to 10 (RAAF) Sqn [RB:H] 28Nov39; with HMS *Gladiolus* sank *U-26* off Bishop Rock 3Jul40; overshot flarepath at Pembroke Dock 24Jun41 and crashed on rocks off Popton Point in Milford Haven (2 crew died later, 10 injured); SOC 4Jul41

Drab-looking Sunderland Mk.I N9027 at its moorings on the River Medway near Rochester. (Mrs M Main)

At some time during its service with 230 Squadron, N9029 carried the full code [NM:V]. (P H T Green collection)

Sunderland Mk.I N9029 of 230 Squadron at low level wearing only code letter [V] and a short fin flash. (P H T Green collection)

Brand-new Sunderland Mk.I N9046 on the River Medway at the Short Bros works at Rochester in 1939. Note the front turret retraction to allow for the mooring operation and the lack of a dorsal turret.
(P H T Green collection)

Sunderland Mk.I P9623 being hoisted out of the water at Lisbon after its unfortunate mishap on its way to West Africa (above). Once on land its RAF markings were obliterated (below) and it subsequently became 136 of the Portuguese Navy but made only one operational flight before being scrapped.
(via Luis Tavares)

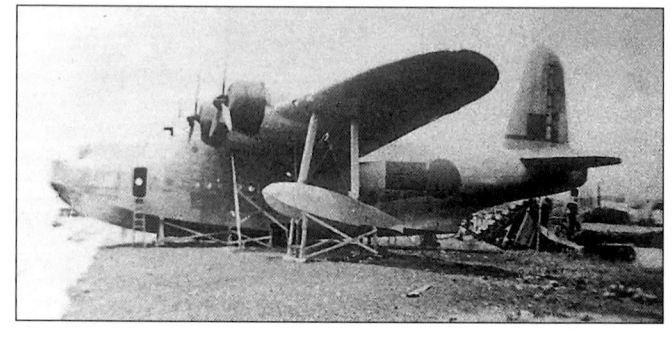

No 'Health & Safety at Work' apparent here! The airman standing above the Fraser-Nash tail turret looks particularly vulnerable. This Sunderland Mk.I P9603 was in use by 10 (RAAF) Squadron at the time and the photo was taken at Mount Batten. (P H T Green collection)

P9604 c/n S.1032; TOC 4 MU at Pembroke Dock 29Nov39 for preparation for RAAF in Australia; delivered to 10 (RAAF) Sqn [RB:J] 15Dec39; bounced on alighting in gale in Firth of Lorne 21Aug40; repaired on site; damaged in air-raids on Mount Batten 13Jan41 and 20/21Mar41; UK to Gibraltar 25May41, to Malta 31May41; returned to UK via Gibraltar 5/6Jun41; engine failed, force-landed at Coverack, Cornwall, 27Aug41; repaired on site; 201 Sqn [ZM:S] 29Oct41; MAEE 17Dec41; 4 (C) OTU [TA:A] 19Dec41; refueller damaged hull, Invergordon, 24Dec41; repaired on site 28Dec41; Scottish Aviation 7Jan42; returned to 4 (C) OTU 28Jan42; BOAC 7Apr42; Pembroke Dock 9Jun42; engine cut on take-off, dropped wing and hit water at Wig Bay 11Jun42 (5 killed); SOC 1Jul42

P9605 c/n S.1033; TOC 4 MU at Pembroke Dock 29Nov39 for preparation for RAAF in Australia; delivered to 10 (RAAF) Sqn [RB:K] 21Dec39; slightly damaged in air-raid at Mount Batten 27/28Nov40; float torn off while alighting in Plymouth Sound at night, 25Dec40; repaired on site; 4 (C) OTU 14Mar42; damaged a float when alighting in cross-wind at Invergordon 30Apr42; repaired on site; 1 FBSU 2Sep42; returned to 4 (C) OTU 21Oct42; flying accident Cat AC 26Oct42; repaired on site; damaged when alighting in heavy seas 27May43; repaired on site; returned to 4 (C) OTU 4Sep43; float torn off when alighting in cross-wind at Alness 20Oct43; repaired on site by SBL 26Oct43; returned to 4 (C) OTU 18Dec43; RTP 12Feb44; SOC 3May44

CHAPTER 5 : INDIVIDUAL AIRCRAFT HISTORIES

P9606 c/n S.1034; TOC 4 MU at Pembroke Dock 1Dec39 for preparation for RAAF in Australia; Pembroke Dock stored reserve 23Dec39; 10 (RAAF) Sqn 2Jan40; 201 Sqn [ZM:R] 13Apr40; Pembroke Dock 6Aug41; BOAC for repair 11Aug41; 4 (C) OTU [TA:E] 29Dec41; featured in film *Coastal Command*, released Oct42; 1 FBSU 14Aug42; 4 (C) OTU 30Oct42; struck by drifting W4034 while moored at Invergordon 3Dec42, then engine cut while taxying to slipway and aircraft struck W3980; repaired on site; returned to 4 (C) OTU 25Jan43; float hit refueller while taxying at Alness 19Mar43; Shorts 4Feb44; returned to 4 (C) OTU 5Feb44; SOC 10May44

P9620 c/n S.1035; TOC Calshot 15Feb40; Calshot stored reserve; 204 Sqn [KG:K] 4Apr40; ran out of fuel and ditched in Atlantic at night in rough seas 29Oct40 (3 killed); SOC 31Oct40

P9621 c/n S.1036; TOC Calshot 15Feb40; Calshot stored reserve; 228 Sqn 7Jun40; on loan to 202 Sqn 30Jun40; left Gibraltar for Pembroke Dock 9Jul40; 201 Sqn [ZM:W] 30Sep40; force-landed in bad weather and ran aground at Scalasaig Bay, Colonsay, 9Oct40; SOC 4Dec40

P9622 c/n S.1037; TOC Calshot 7Mar40; Calshot stored reserve; 228 Sqn 7Jun40; on loan to 202 Sqn 30Jun40; left Gibraltar for Pembroke Dock 27Jul40; on loan to 210 Sqn 8Oct40; delivered to 201 Sqn [ZM:W] 27Oct40; flew into hill at night, Houstry, near Dunnet Head, Caithness, 29Oct40, while attempting to alight (4 killed, 5 injured); SOC 7Jan41

P9623 c/n S.1038; TOC Pembroke Dock 14Apr40; Pembroke Dock stored reserve; 210 Sqn [DA:E]; 95 Sqn [SE:E *The Lazy E*] 16Jan41; left Pembroke Dock 13Feb41 for West Africa via Gibraltar, found hurricane-force winds over Bay of Biscay which blew aircraft well off course; force-landed off Troia beach near Setubal in the Sado estuary, south of Lisbon, 15Feb41; crew interned; SOC 20May41; taken over by Portuguese Navy and towed to Tagus estuary, where it was put on supports at Bom Sucesso Naval Air Station; overhauled by 1943 and given serial number **136** (see Part 6)

P9624 c/n S.1039; TOC Pembroke Dock 19Apr40; 210 Sqn [DA:H] 19Apr40; trialled new step design; lost float while avoiding oil drum in Angle Bay 1May40; repaired on site; sank Italian submarine *Nani* 6Jan41; bounced on alighting at Oban 6Feb41 and damaged float; BOAC for repair 8Feb41; returned to 210 Sqn [DA:H]; stalled on alighting at Oban 15Mar41 and broke back (4 killed); wreck beached on South Pier, Oban; SOC 1Apr41

20 Sunderlands Mk.I built by Short Bros Ltd, Rochester under Contract B.18347/39:

T9040 c/n S.1140; TOC Pembroke Dock 31Jul40; Pembroke Dock stored reserve; 204 Sqn 21Aug40; 95 Sqn 16Apr41; flew UK to Bathurst via Gibraltar 22/23Apr41; Calshot 19Jul41; returned to 95 Sqn [SE:E] 16Sep41; Calshot 1Dec41; returned to 95 Sqn 9Jan42; engine cut while on convoy escort 9Feb42, force-landed and towed to land; Calshot 27Mar42; returned to 95 Sqn 6May42; 202 Sqn 7May42; Gibraltar to Bathurst 11May42; delivered to 95 Sqn 12May42; Cat B 14Sep42; BOAC for repair 15Sep42; returned to 95 Sqn [J] 26Feb43; 57 MU 10Jul43; Cat B 16Jul43; Scottish Aviation 1Sep43; 4 (C) OTU 23Dec43; damaged beyond repair when engine caught fire while taxying at Alness 2Jul44; SOC 9Aug44

T9041 c/n S.1141; TOC Pembroke Dock 9Aug40; Pembroke Dock stored reserve; 210 Sqn 9Sep40; 95 Sqn [SE:D] 16Jan41; bow damaged by pinnace at Mount Batten 26Feb41; repaired on site; 10 (RAAF) Sqn 28Feb41; 201 Sqn 24Jun41; 204 Sqn [KG:V, KG:A] 11Sep41; Calshot 14Apr42; returned to 204 Sqn 20May42; while on patrol 28Jun42, ditched off West Africa after complete engine failure; 10 crew rescued next day by HMS *Velox* and landed at Freetown (Sierra Leone), but 2 crew were dead; SOC 30Jun42

T9042 c/n S.1142; SB(R&B)L 20Feb41 for mods to become prototype Mk.III; first flight as Mk.III 28Jun41; MAEE 31Dec42; repaired in works by Scottish Aviation 9Jul43; 4 (C) OTU 6Mar44; 57 MU; SOC 20Feb45

T9043 c/n S.1143; TOC Pembroke Dock 19Aug40; 210 Sqn 20Aug40; failed to return from convoy escort 2Sep40 (11 killed)

T9044 c/n S.1144; TOC Pembroke Dock 1Sep40; 210 Sqn 9Sep40; sank at moorings at Pembroke Dock during severe gale 12Nov40; SOC 9Apr41; one engine and parts recovered by 2012 and proposal exists from the Pembroke Dock Sunderland Trust to raise the wreck

T9045 c/n S.1145; TOC Pembroke Dock 20Aug40; 204 Sqn [KG:K] 30Sep40; after searching for crew of P9620 on 29Oct40, was diverted to Invergordon but could not locate it, so alighted on water in darkness, smashing starboard float; tow by trawler *A76* was abandoned, and aircraft sank 5 mls (8 km) SE of Strathy Point, Sutherland (5 killed, 4 injured)

T9046 c/n S.1146; TOC Pembroke Dock 8Oct40; 201 Sqn 6Nov40; delivered to 228 Sqn 6Dec40; damaged in raid, St Paul's Bay, Malta, 10Mar41; left Alexandria for Bathurst 25Jun41, arrived 31Jul41; 95 Sqn

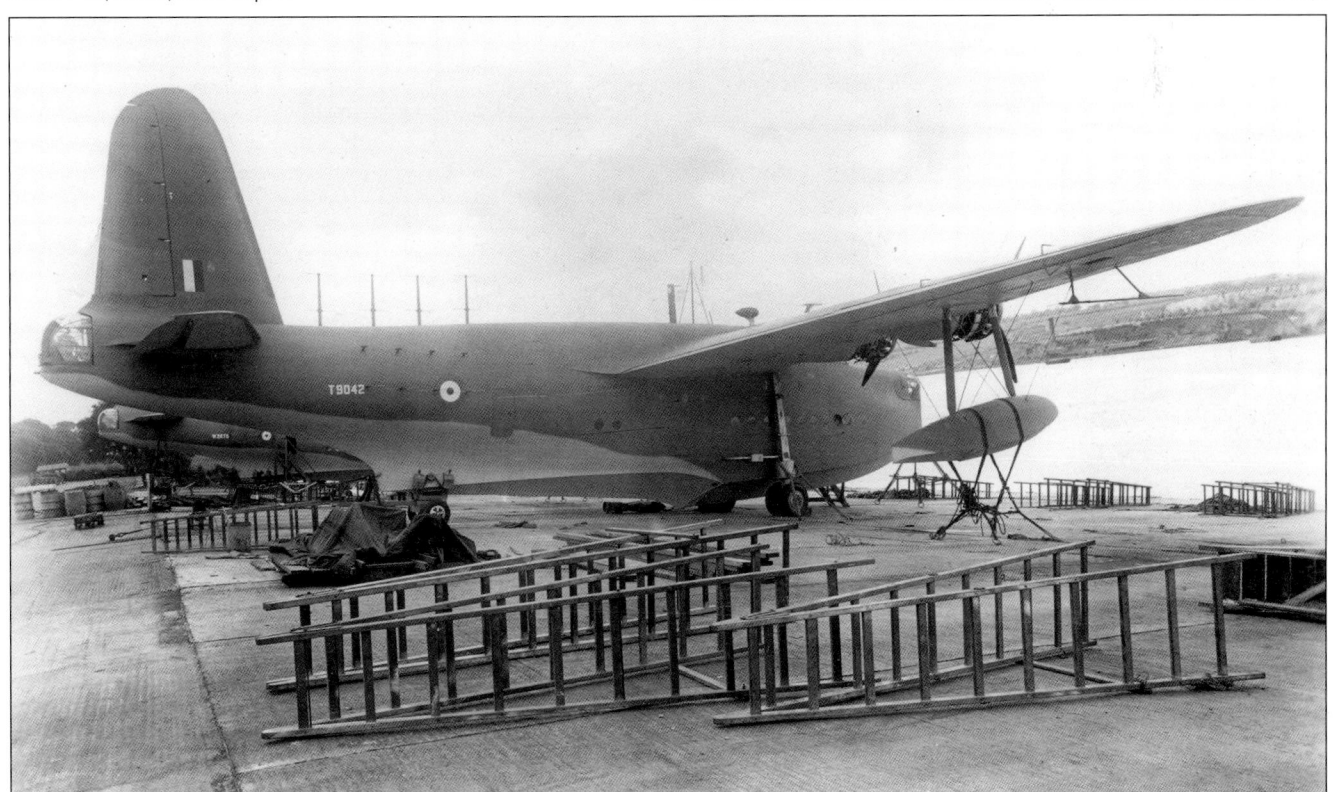

The Sunderland Mk.III prototype, T9042, complete with ASV aerials, sits on the slipway at Rochester in June 1941. Behind is Sunderland Mk.II W3979 which was about to be delivered to 10 (RAAF) Squadron at Pembroke Dock. (P H T Green collection)

[SE:J] 21Aug41; Calshot 28Aug41; returned to 95 Sqn 15Oct41; Calshot 28Dec41; returned to 95 Sqn 5Jan42; damaged at moorings at Kalafrana by Bf.109s 21Feb42 and sank in storm 23Feb42; SOC 11Mar42

T9047 c/n S.1147; TOC 10 (RAAF) Sqn [RB:L] 21Oct40; slightly damaged by shrapnel in air-raids on Mount Batten 27/28Nov40 and 20/21Mar41; on 9Jul41, landed on sea 160 mls (258 km) W of Brest to rescue crew of 206 Sqn Hudson but port outer engine fell out of wing so taxied 30 mls (48 km) towards Isles of Scilly and crew rescued by HMS *Brocklesby*; sunk by Naval gunners at 48°15'N 08°45'W next day

T9048 c/n S.1148; TOC Pembroke Dock 1Nov40; 204 Sqn 6Nov40; 228 Sqn [DQ:N/DQ:X] 9Nov40; crashed on alighting at night at Kalamata, Greece, 25Apr41 and broke up (6 killed); SOC 30Apr41

T9049 c/n S.1149; TOC 204 Sqn 14Nov40; 201 Sqn [ZM:O] 16Nov40; after carrying out recce and bomb-dropping sortie on Fagernes Point, near Narvik, on 21Jan41 encountered storm over Shetlands and W/T was unserviceable, so force-landed at Herma Ness, damaging wing-tip; taxied to Woodwick for anchorage, but drifted onto rocks and hull was holed; was towed to Culli for salvage a few days later but was repaired on site; 201 Sqn [ZM:S] 7Aug41; repaired on site, Felixstowe, 7Sep41; Pembroke Dock 1Nov41; 4 (C) OTU [TA:A] 3Dec41; Pembroke Dock 7Mar42; returned to 4 (C) OTU; 1 FBSU 27Mar43; returned to 4 (C) OTU 24Jul43; repaired on site Shorts 16Oct43; returned to 4 (C) OTU 17Nov43; flying accident Cat AC 28May44; 57 MU 23Jun44 for storage; scuttled in Wig Bay 11Dec46

T9050 c/n S.1150; TOC Pembroke Dock 28Nov40; delivered to 230 Sqn [NM:Y] 10Dec40; Malta to UK via Gibraltar 22/23May41; crashed on alighting at Aboukir 30Sep41 after patrol along Egyptian coast (3 killed, 9 injured)

T9070 c/n S.1151; TOC Pembroke Dock 7Dec40; 204 Sqn [KG:E] 9Dec40; on 21/22Jan41, alighted at Muckle Flugga (Scottish island) in bad weather, drifted onto rocks and suffered punctured hull; salvaged and engines removed; towed to Sullom Voe 8Feb41; Felixstowe 9.41; Calshot 7Dec41; BOAC 29Dec41; 204 Sqn [E] 12Feb42; hit by yawl while moored at Bathurst 15Jun43; repaired on site; caught fire at moorings at Bathurst 16Aug42 and depth charges exploded (1 injured); SOC 8Oct42

T9071 c/n S.1152; TOC Pembroke Dock 9Dec40; del 10 (RAAF) Sqn [RB:M] 23Dec40; damaged in air-raid on Mount Batten 13Jan41; flew UK to Gibraltar 25May41, to Malta 31May41; caught by gust while taxying at Alexandria 4Jun41 and struck tanker; repaired on site; Calshot 17Sep41; 230 Sqn [NM:M] 9.41; Calshot 27Oct41; Mount Batten 1Nov41; returned to 230 Sqn 22Dec41; crashed 3 mls (4.8 km) NW of Ras-el-Amr (Egypt) 22Dec41 after attack by two Bf 110 fighters of III/ZG26; SOC 2Jan42

T9072 c/n S.1153; TOC 204 Sqn [KG:F] 4Jan41; on returning from anti-submarine sweep on 4Apr41, alighted at Reykjavik and struck uncharted rocks while taxying, causing 12 ft (3.6 m) of hull to be torn; repaired on site by SBL; returned to UK 29Aug41; 10 (RAAF) Sqn [RB:V] 29Sep41; while flying from Oban to Pembroke Dock 5Dec41, engine malfunction caused aircraft to go out of control and crash into sea 15 mls (24 km) NW of Holyhead, Anglesey, (near Skerries) 5Dec41 (4 killed, 11 injured)

T9073 c/n S.1154; TOC Pembroke Dock 29Dec40; 210 Sqn 19Jan41; left Pembroke Dock for West Africa via Gibraltar 29Apr41; delivered to 95 Sqn [SE:G] 3May41; Mount Batten 11Jun41, Calshot 15Jul41; returned to 95 Sqn 3Nov41; Calshot 22Jan42; returned to 95 Sqn [G] 21Feb42; damaged tailplane while alighting in bad weather in Kumbrabe Creek (Gambia) 2Sep42; repaired on site; returned to UK and SOC; BBOC 57 MU 30Jan44; destroyed by fire at moorings at Scar Point, Wig Bay, 22Jun44

T9074 c/n S.1155; TOC Pembroke Dock 4Feb41; delivered to 201 Sqn from Reykjavik 1Apr41; 204 Sqn [KG:L] 2Jun41; engine cut, force-landed and towed to Bathurst by HMS *Challenger* 23Oct41; Calshot 27Nov41; 95 Sqn 3Jan42; 204 Sqn [L] 19Jan42; Pembroke Dock 11May42; 204 Sqn 7Jul42; Pembroke Dock 5Nov42; returned to 204 Sqn 19Feb43; 343 Sqn 19Apr43; Greenock 16Aug43; repaired in works by Scottish Aviation 8Sep43; SOC 25Oct43

T9075 c/n S.1156; TOC Pembroke Dock 25Jan41; 210 Sqn 15Feb41; 10 (RAAF) Sqn [RB:N] 4Apr41; low on fuel, became lost in bad weather and ditched 9 mls (14.5 km) WNW of Bardsey Is (N Wales) 29Apr41; (5 survivors, 6 missing); SOC 1Jul41

T9076 c/n S.1157; TOC Pembroke Dock 23Feb41; 210 Sqn 7Mar41; 201 Sqn 23Apr41; Pembroke Dock 12Sep41; returned to 201 Sqn [ZM:O] 21Sep41; Pembroke Dock 12Oct41; 4 (C) OTU 3Dec41; Greenock 21May42; repaired in works by Scottish Aviation 29May42; 4 (C) OTU [TA:D] 10Jan43; float damaged during maintenance at Alness 10Jun43; repaired on site by SBL 31Jan44; SOC 57 MU 11Jul44

T9077 c/n S.1158; TOC Pembroke Dock 9Mar41; 201 Sqn [ZM:Y] 30Mar41; Pembroke Dock 5Dec41; 201 Sqn 8Dec41; delivered to 228 Sqn 26Jan42; 4 (C) OTU 19Feb42; Greenock 27Apr42; repaired in works by Scottish Aviation; returned to 4 (C) OTU 26Oct42; repaired on site 24Aug43; repaired on site 4Feb44; SOC 29Jul44

T9078 c/n S.1159; TOC Pembroke Dock 21Mar41; left for W Africa 31Mar41 via Gibraltar; delivered to 95 Sqn [SE:A] 3Apr41; Bathurst to Calshot via Gibraltar 23/25Jun41; returned to 95 Sqn 20Jul41; Calshot 16Oct41; returned to 95 Sqn 18Nov41; Calshot 3Mar42; Wig Bay 7Mar42; Calshot 19Mar42; returned to 95 Sqn 22Apr42; Pembroke Dock 7Aug42; returned to 95 Sqn 23Aug42; Mount Batten 23Dec42;

Sunderland Mk.I T9070 [KG:E] was in the hands of 204 Squadron, its sole RAF unit, at Bathurst (Half Die) where, at its moorings on 16th August 1942, it caught fire and exploded after igniting on-board depth charges. (P H T Green collection)

CHAPTER 5 : INDIVIDUAL AIRCRAFT HISTORIES

Two views of Sunderland Mk.I T9072 [KG:F] of 204 Squadron, seen on the left at Bathurst in 1941 in rather dirty condition with its servicing crew clambering over it and on the right beached and under repair, almost certainly in Iceland following damage after striking an uncharted rock on 4th April 1941. A cartoon character is painted above the entry hatch. (P H T Green collection)

BOAC 26Jan43; returned to 95 Sqn 1Feb43; returned to UK; 4 (C) OTU [TA:B] 18Jul43; gunner fired onto tailplane 28Aug43; repaired on site by SBL 3Sep43; repaired on site by SBL 16Feb44; repaired on site by SBL 21Mar44; SOC 24Jul44

15 Sunderlands Mk.II built by Blackburn Aircraft Ltd, Dumbarton under Contract B.37753/39:

T9083   TOC MAEE as Mk.II prototype 1Nov41; Short Bros 27Jan42; delivered to 201 Sqn [ZM:Q] 31Oct42; 1 FBSU 20Mar43; returned to 201 Sqn 5May43; 230 Sqn 7Jul43; 330 Sqn 9May43; 4 (C) OTU 19May44; damaged beyond repair in heavy landing at Alness same day; SOC 10Jun44

T9084   TOC Pembroke Dock 5Dec41; Pembroke Dock stored reserve; 201 Sqn 10Dec41; caught balloon cable on approach to Pembroke Dock 19Dec41; repaired on site; left on transfer to 202 Sqn, Gibraltar, 22Dec41; Pembroke Dock 9Jan42; 228 Sqn [DQ:N] 16Feb42; stalled on alighting at Lochboisdale, South Uist, 3May42 and ran ashore on island of Gasey (2 killed, 10 injured); SOC 12Jul42

T9085   TOC Pembroke Dock 9Jan42; Pembroke Dock stored reserve; 228 Sqn 10Feb42; ran aground at Scar Point, Stranraer, while taxying 10Feb42; Scottish Aviation 22Feb42; returned to 228 Sqn 27Mar42; Pembroke Dock stored reserve 15Apr42; 461 Sqn [UT:A] 24Apr42; crashed in bad weather over Western Approaches 21Jan43 during anti-submarine mission with 'special equipment' (entire crew of 11 killed)

T9086   TOC Pembroke Dock 19Jan42; 228 Sqn 3Feb42; 10 (RAAF) Sqn 2Mar42; 228 Sqn 11Mar42; delivered to 461 Sqn 2May42; 1 FBSU 18Jun42; 228 Sqn [DQ:S] 13Aug42; while delivering equipment to Vaagar (Faeroes) 6Oct42, struck uncharted rock in Sorvaag Vath and beached with holes in keel; repaired on site; Cat B 6Jan43; recat E 25Feb43; SOC 28Feb43

T9087   TOC Pembroke Dock 23Jan42; delivered to 201 Sqn [ZM:O] 23Mar42; engine caught fire on start-up at Lough Erne 27Jun42; repaired on site; Scottish Aviation 2Jul42; SBL 19Nov43; SOC 4Feb44

T9088   TOC Pembroke Dock 7Mar42; Pembroke Dock stored reserve; 228 Sqn [DQ:R] 9Mar42; 461 Sqn by 2May42; 228 Sqn 8May42; ran aground in Lough Neagh 15Jul42; 1 FBSU 29Jul42; 228 Sqn 26Sep42; overshot flarepath and struck shoal in Lough Erne 15Jan43; repaired on site; 4 (C) OTU 25Aug43; failed to return from exercise off Orkneys 17Dec44 (8 killed)

T9089   TOC 228 Sqn [DQ:O] 26Mar42; ran into mist on approach to Oban and hit water on alighting in Firth of Lorne, just off north coast of Kerrera, in very bad weather 29May42 and broke back (5 killed when depth charges exploded, 3 injured); SOC 4Sep42

T9090   TOC Pembroke Dock 3Apr42; delivered to 461 Sqn [UT:B] 22Apr42; attempting on 12Aug42 to aid survivors of Wellington of 172 Sqn, made for the scene in the Bay of Biscay escorted by three Beaufighters but was attacked by a Fw 200; attempted to alight in bad weather, hit wave, bounced and lost starboard wing-tip; a starboard engine burst into flames and aircraft nosed in and sank; crew escaped into dinghy, which then burst, throwing crew into water (10 drowned, 1 rescued)

T9109   TOC Pembroke Dock 7Apr42; Pembroke Dock stored reserve; delivered to 461 Sqn [UT:D] 24Apr42; swung into wall in gust while taxying at Mount Batten 28Apr42; repaired on site; struck rocks on take-off from Scillies 16Aug43; repaired on site; 228 Sqn 28Sep43; 1 FBSU 11Nov43; damaged beyond repair in collision with JM720 in gale at Wig Bay 25Jan44; 57 MU and SOC 1Feb44

T9110   TOC Pembroke Dock 21Apr42; Pembroke Dock stored reserve; delivered to 10 (RAAF) Sqn [RB:C] 7Jul42; damaged by Bf.109 while bombing trawlers in Bay of Biscay 28Jul42; repaired on site; swung on take-off and hit buoy at Mount Batten 8Sep42; repaired on site; repaired in works 6Jul43; lost float in heavy landing at night in Plymouth Sound 5Jan44; SOC 16Aug44; to SB(W)L 22Aug44 for RTP

T9111   TOC Pembroke Dock 1May42; delivered to 461 Sqn [UT:C] 30May42; dropping leaflets to fishing vessels 30Jul42, was attacked by three Ar.196 floatplanes and damaged; repaired on site; 1 FBSU 21Oct42; returned to 461 Sqn 31Dec42; crashed on take-off from Hamworthy 21Mar43 (4 injured); SOC 31Mar43

T9112   TOC Pembroke Dock 7May42; 228 Sqn [DQ:N] 13May42; 1 FBSU 8Oct42; returned to 228 Sqn 17Jan43; 330 Sqn 25Apr43; 228 Sqn 6May43; Scottish Aviation 1Jul43; SOC 12Apr44

T9113   TOC Pembroke Dock 19May42; delivered to 461 Sqn [UT:F. K] 12Jul42; shot down by two Ju.88s in Bay of Biscay 1Sep42 (11 killed)

T9114   TOC Pembroke Dock 1Jun42; delivered to 461 Sqn [UT:E] 7Jul42; rescued crew of JM675 and a Whitley in the Bay of Biscay on 29May43, but these were transferred to French vessel; T9114 took off from very rough seas on seventh attempt but was struck by huge wave which made large hole in hull; captain (Flg Off G Singleton) decided not to alight in open sea but crash-landed on Angle airfield; recovered to the water and repairs attempted but SOC 31Jan44; was to become GI airframe **4446M** at 4 SoTT, St Athan but cancelled and SOC 30Apr44 at Pembroke Dock; M serial reallocated to W6050

T9115   TOC Pembroke Dock 4Jul42; Pembroke Dock stored reserve; delivered to 461 Sqn [UT:G, UT:K] 1Aug42; during air-sea rescue search 22Feb43, two engines failed; force-landed in darkness 8 mls (12.8 km) S of Plymouth and was towed to Mount Batten next day; repaired in works by SBL 5Apr43; 4 (C) OTU 10Jul43; SOC 16Aug44

23 Sunderlands Mk.II built by Short Bros Ltd, Rochester under Contract B.78939/40 (transferred from Contract B.18347/39):

W3976   c/n S.1160; TOC Pembroke Dock 19May41; MAEE 16Jul41; crashed on alighting off Rhu, Gareloch, on moonlit night 28Nov41 and sank (2 killed, 7 injured); SOC 1Jan42

W3977   c/n S.1161; TOC 201 Sqn [ZM:Q] 26May41; Gibraltar to UK 13Jun41; Pembroke Dock 27Oct41; 201 Sqn 29Nov41; crashed in sea off coast of Donegal (Irish Republic) 5Feb42 (no survivors); SOC 6Feb42

W3978   c/n S.1162; TOC Pembroke Dock 2Jun41; 204 Sqn 9Jun41; BOAC 25Jun41; 204 Sqn 2Jul41; lost a float in heavy landing at Rochester 9Jul41, took off again and alighted; SBL same day; Pembroke Dock 24Jul41; delivered to 201 Sqn [ZM:Z] 27Jul41; crashed on alighting at Sullom Voe at dusk 11Aug41 (5 killed)

W3986 was a Sunderland Mk.II operated by 10 (RAAF) Squadron and coded [RB:U]. Although the background and the ASV installation have been removed by the censor, this photograph, taken at Mount Batten in April 1942, clearly profiles the Sunderland and its beaching gear. In May 1943, W3986 crashed near the Eddystone lighthouse, Devon, following an in-flight fire. (P H T Green collection)

W3979 c/n S.1163; TOC Pembroke Dock 1Jun41; 10 (RAAF) Sqn [RB:Q] 19Jun41; ran out of fuel in bad weather, ditched in heavy seas off St Govan's Head, Pembrokeshire 1Mar42 (2 injured); damaged by trawler during towing and sunk by naval guns as hazard to navigation; SOC 2Mar42

W3980 c/n S.1164; TOC 10 (RAAF) Sqn 11Jun41; Pembroke Dock 26Jun41; 201 Sqn 16Oct41; Cat AC 21Oct41; Pembroke Dock stored reserve 5Jan42; 201 Sqn [ZM:P] 10Jan42; to Pembroke Dock 5Jun42; 4 (C) OTU [TA:S] 8Jun42; struck by P9606 while moored at Invergordon 3Dec42; Scottish Aviation 19Feb43; 57 MU 17May44; became GI airframe **4908M** 23Oct44

W3981 c/n S.1165; TOC Pembroke Dock 28Jun41; 204 Sqn 4Jul41; 201 Sqn [ZM:R] 1Aug41; Pembroke Dock 4Sep41; returned to 201 Sqn [ZM:W] 5Oct41; left for Alexandria, Egypt, for transport duties 11Dec41, returned 5Feb42; wing-tip hit trees while taxying at Lough Erne 12Feb42; repaired on site; delivered to 4 (C) OTU [TA:S] 5Jun42; 1 FBSU 20Jul42; returned to 4 (C) OTU 30Sep42; float collapsed on take-off from Invergordon in rough seas 15Dec42 and further damaged on alighting; broke away from moorings in gale at Alness 10Mar43 and collided with pinnace; repaired on site; 57 MU 27Jun44; SOC 1Jul44

W3982 c/n S.1166; TOC Pembroke Dock 14Jul41; 201 Sqn 22Jul41; ditched NNW of Shetlands 21Aug41 while on patrol

W3983 c/n S.1167; TOC Pembroke Dock 14Jul41; delivered to 10 (RAAF) Sqn [RB:R] 27Jul41; after attacking U-boat on 15May42, force-landed on sea after fuel ran out and was then towed to Gibraltar; repaired in works by SBL 14Feb44; became GI airframe **4603M** 3Mar44 at SB(W)L, Windermere; reduced to produce 16Jun44;

W3984 c/n S.1168; TOC Pembroke Dock 19Jul41; delivered to 10 (RAAF) Sqn [RB:S] 1Aug41; Mount Batten 3Jan42; returned to 10 (RAAF) Sqn 28Feb42; overshot landing at Pembroke Dock 28May42 and ran aground; repaired on site; repaired in works by SBL 3Dec43; SOC 20Jun44

W3985 c/n S.1169; TOC 10 (RAAF) Sqn [RB:U/RB:T] 11Aug41; damaged by unidentified ship while moored at Mount Batten 13Jan42; repaired on site; Shorts 11Jun42; barge drifted into aircraft at Mount Batten 15Jul42; missing over Bay of Biscay 18Aug43, believed shot down by Luftwaffe (12 killed); SOC 31Aug43

W3986 c/n S.1170; TOC 10 (RAAF) Sqn 29Aug41; Mount Batten 5Jan42; 228 Sqn 19Feb42; Pembroke Dock 6Apr42; 10 (RAAF) Sqn [RB:U] 8Apr42; crashed on fire 4 mls NW of Eddystone lighthouse 20May43 after take-off from Mount Batten (12 killed)

W3987 c/n S.1171; TOC 201 Sqn 7Sep41; 230 Sqn [NM:X] 30Sep41; landed downwind at night at Aboukir, Egypt, 28Nov41; repaired on site; crashed near Fort Burg, Egypt, on take-off from Aboukir 7Sep42 after engine cut and smoke filled cockpit (8 killed, 6 Injured)

W3988 c/n S.1172; TOC Pembroke Dock 13Sep41; 201 Sqn [ZM:P] 1Oct41; on return from patrol on 3Dec41, dropped flares near Carrowmore Point, Co Clare, Irish Republic, and ditched after two attempts to land (all crew evacuated safely but 9 drowned 2 or 3 miles from shore)

W3989 c/n S.1173; TOC Pembroke Dock 18Sep41; delivered to 228 Sqn [DQ:L] 3Nov41; Pembroke Dock 5Nov41; 202 Sqn 20Dec41; 228 Sqn same day; Pembroke Dock stored reserve 31Dec41; 228 Sqn same day; 202 Sqn 4Jan42; 228 Sqn 7Feb42; Iceland 4Jan43; repaired in works by SBL 6Apr43; 4 (C) OTU 5Sep43; 302 FTU 6Sep44; ran onto rocks at Castle Archdale and beached 7Oct44; repaired on site; 302 FTU 13Jan45; SOC 23Feb45

W3990 c/n S.1174; TOC Pembroke Dock 30Sep41; delivered to 228 Sqn 7Nov41; Pembroke Dock 11Nov41; 228 Sqn 17Dec41; 202 Sqn 20Dec41; 228 Sqn 25Dec41; 202 Sqn 4Jan42; 228 Sqn 7Feb42; struck submerged obstruction while taxying at Lochboisdale, South Uist, 8May42; repaired in works by Scottish Aviation, Greenock, 14May42; Oban 22Sep42; 4 (C) OTU [TA:V] 2Oct42; sank in gale at Alness 15Feb43 after a float was carried away by pinnace; SOC 31Mar43

W3991 c/n S.1175; TOC Pembroke Dock 3Oct41; delivered to 228 Sqn [DQ:P] 11Nov41; sank at moorings during gale 15Jan42 but recovered; ran aground on Troublesome Rocks, Lough Erne, 10Jan43; salvaged next day but one civilian killed; 1 FBSU 17Nov43; repaired on site SBL11Jan44; 57 MU 29Jan44; became GI airframe **5016M** at 1 MCTU, Corsewall 22Jan45

W3992 c/n S.1176; TOC Pembroke Dock 12Oct41; delivered to 228 Sqn 11Nov41; taxied onto rocks at Lough Erne 17Feb42; repaired in works by Scottish Aviation 22Feb42; 4 (C) OTU [TA:R] 7.42; sank in gale at Alness 13Feb43; SOC 31Mar43

W3993 c/n S.1177; TOC Pembroke Dock 20Oct41; 10 (RAAF) Sqn [RB:W, RB:G] 15Nov41; a float struck buoy during night take-off from Mount Batten 17Mar43; repaired on site; sank U-465 off Cape Ortegal (NW Spain) 7May43; struck by W4024 at Mount Batten moorings 7Oct43; ferried to S&HL but beyond economic repair; SOC 3Jul44

W3994 c/n S.1178; TOC Pembroke Dock 29Oct41; 10 (RAAF) Sqn [RB:X] 15Nov41; 202 Sqn 17Jun42; 10 (RAAF) Sqn [RB:X] 6Jul42; missing off Spain 30Jul42

CHAPTER 5 : INDIVIDUAL AIRCRAFT HISTORIES
103

Low over the water, Sunderland Mk.II W3989 [DQ:L] of 228 Squadron carries out a routine patrol. In this photo the ASV aerials are clearly visible, as is the crew member waving from the dorsal hatch.
(P H T Green collection)

Sunderland Mk.III W4004 spent two periods in service with 10 (RAAF) Squadron as [RB:Z] and is seen below taxying at speed for its mooring. Note the barrage balloon above the cliff.
(P H T Green collection)

W3995 c/n S.1179; TOC Pembroke Dock 4Nov41; Pembroke Dock stored reserve; 228 Sqn [DQ:P] 28Nov41; 1 FBSU 22Aug42; returned to 228 Sqn 13Oct42; ran aground in Lough Erne 10Jan43 and sank during salvage next day; SOC 25Feb43

W3996 c/n S.1180; TOC Pembroke Dock 18Nov41; Pembroke Dock stored reserve; 228 Sqn [DQ:R] 28Nov41; hit by bomb on Kalafrana slipway 2Feb42; SOC 20Mar42

W3997 c/n S.1181; TOC Pembroke Dock 20Nov41; Pembroke Dock stored reserve; 201 Sqn [ZM:S] 3Dec41; 10 (RAAF) Sqn 13Feb42; damaged by fire from convoy at 54°26'N 18°46'W 1Mar42; Wig Bay 2Jun42; 201 Sqn 12Jul42; Wig Bay 7Nov42; 4 (C) OTU [TA:R] 31Dec42; crashed 17 mls (27 km) E of Lossiemouth and 4 mls (6 km) N of Portsoy, Banff, 13Oct43 (cause unknown)

W3998 c/n S.1182; TOC Pembroke Dock 7Dec41; Pembroke Dock stored reserve; 201 Sqn 10Dec41; left on transfer to 202 Sqn, Gibraltar 17Dec41; crashed 200 yds from Breakwater Fort, Plymouth Sound, 20Dec41 after take-off from Mount Batten (12 killed, 4 injured)

27 Sunderlands Mk.III built by Short Bros Ltd, Rochester under Contract B.78939/40 (transferred from Contract B.18347/39):

W3999 c/n S.1183; first flight 15Dec41 as first production Mk.III; TOC Pembroke Dock 5Jan42; delivered to 10 (RAAF) Sqn [RB:Y] 5Jan42; damaged a float on alighting in squall at Mount Batten 1Mar42; repaired on site; while on ASR mission over Bay of Biscay 8Jun42, shot at by Ar.196 floatplane, forced to alight and exploded (11 killed); SOC 21Jun42

W4000 c/n S.1184; TOC 201 Sqn [ZM:R] 9Jan42; ditched 5 mls (8 km) from convoy WS.21 1Aug42, exploded and sank (11 killed)

W4001 c/n S.1185; TOC Pembroke Dock 26Jan42; Pembroke Dock stored reserve; delivered to 201 Sqn [ZM:V] 5Feb42; hit rock in Lough Erne while taxying near Castle Archdale 4Oct42 and SOC

W4002 c/n S.1186; TOC Pembroke Dock 11Jan42; delivered to 201 Sqn [ZM:U] 16Feb42; detached to Gibraltar 8Jul42 to 30Jul42; 1 FBSU 17Dec42; 201 Sqn [ZM:U] 31Dec42; 1 FBSU 15Jul43; 201 Sqn 20Aug43; flying accident Cat AC 21Aug43; 57 MU 9Mar44; delivered to 302 FTU 16Nov44; delivered to Greenock for scrapping 13Feb45; SOC 22Feb45

W4003 c/n S.1187; TOC Pembroke Dock 11Jan42; 10 (RAAF) Sqn 10Jan42; delivered to 201 Sqn [ZM:Y] 7Feb42; struck by W6000 while moored in Lough Erne 4Nov42; repaired on site; 1 FBSU 5Dec42; 461 Sqn 31Mar43; 201 Sqn 29May43; BOAC 29Jun43; Wig Bay 18Sep43; Cat B 22Sep43; Calshot 26Sep43; 1 FBSU 29Nov43; 57 MU 23Jan44; tail trolley collapsed while aircraft being towed at Wig Bay 2Aug44; repaired on site; 57 MU 16Sep44; 302 FTU 9Dec44; damaged in gale at Killadeas 21Sep45; 272 MU 10Oct45; SOC as beyond economic repair 16Nov45; 226 MU for scrapping 10Dec45

W4004 c/n S.1188; TOC Pembroke Dock 19Jan42; delivered to 10 (RAAF) Sqn [RB:Z] 6Feb42; 202 Sqn 14May42; force-landed in bad weather in open sea off Plymouth during delivery flight 22May42; repaired on site at Mount Batten; returned to 10 (RAAF) Sqn [RB:Z] 31Dec42; missing over Bay of Biscay 17May43 (11 killed); SOC 31May43

W4017 c/n S.1189; TOC Pembroke Dock 7Feb42; Pembroke Dock stored reserve 23Feb42; struck buoy while taxying 26Feb42; repaired on site; 228 Sqn [DQ:T] 19Mar42; 1 FBSU 23Sep42; 228 Sqn 20Nov42; BOAC 9Aug43; 57 MU 8Mar44; 302 FTU 19Sep44; despatched to ACSEA 22Oct44; lost propeller on ferry flight, damaging wing and float, same day; SOC 19Jan45

W4018 c/n S.1190; TOC Pembroke Dock 7Feb42; delivered to 201 Sqn [ZM:Z] 10Mar42; 1 FBSU 27Nov42; broke away from moorings in gale at Wig Bay 13Dec42; 1 FBSU 19Feb43; 201 Sqn [ZM:O] 1Apr43; 1 FBSU 8Jun43; 201 Sqn 10Jul43; 8 FPP; ran aground at Castle Archdale while taxying for ferry flight 28Sep43; S&HL 13Oct43; 57 MU 25Aug44; SB(R&B)L, Rochester 23Feb45 for scrapping

W4019 c/n S.1191; TOC Pembroke Dock 8Feb42; delivered to 10 (RAAF) Sqn [RB:A] 17Feb42; 202 Sqn 29Mar42; 10 (RAAF) Sqn [RB:A] 24Apr42; missing over Bay of Biscay 8Aug42 (12 killed); SOC 9Aug42

W4020 c/n S.1192; TOC Pembroke Dock 4Feb42; del 10 (RAAF) Sqn [RB:B] 7Mar42; tested new galley gun mounting; damaged by flak from trawler in Bay of Biscay 16Apr42; repaired at Mount Batten; badly damaged by gale while moored at Mount Batten (or Isles of Scilly ?) 27May42; repaired on site by Shorts 10Jul42; returned to 10 (RAAF) Sqn [RB:R] 8Apr43; shot down off Cape Finisterre (NW Spain) by flak from *U-454* 1Aug43 (6 killed, 6 survivors rescued by HMS *Wren*); SOC 31Aug43

W4021 c/n S.1193; TOC Pembroke Dock 14Mar42; delivered to 230 Sqn [NM:W] 15Apr42; hit uncharted reef while attempting three-engined take-off from Castelorosso (Italy) 7Nov43; taxied out to deep water and allowed to sink; SOC 1Jan44

W4022 c/n S.1194; TOC Pembroke Dock 13Mar42; delivered to 230 Sqn [NM:Z] 16Apr42; a float collapsed on alighting at Port Reitz (Kenya) at dusk 23Mar43; repaired on site; to ACSEA 29Jun44 but no record of use; SOC 3Jan45

W4023 c/n S.1195; TOC Pembroke Dock 10Apr42; 230 Sqn [NM:U] 25Apr42; SOC 29Aug46

W4024 c/n S.1196; TOC Pembroke Dock 10Apr42; 202 Sqn [TQ:N] 31May42; 119 Sqn [J] 12Sep42; delivered to 10 (RAAF) Sqn [RB:G] 16Apr43; engine cut during taxying at Mount Batten 7Oct43 and aircraft swung into buoy; aileron controls jammed on take-off 14Dec43, aircraft force-landed in Plymouth Sound; Cat B 27Jun44; SB(W)L, Windermere, for major repairs 6Jul44; 57 MU 21Nov44; sold for scrap to Phoenix & Clifton Ironworks, Coatbridge, Lanarkshire,10Mar47

W4025 c/n S.1197; TOC Pembroke Dock 22Apr42; delivered to 201 Sqn [ZM:P] 14Jun42; shot down by AA fire from convoy *WS.21* 31Jul42 (12 killed)

W4026 c/n S.1198; TOC Pembroke Dock 24Apr42; 228 Sqn [DQ:M] 13May42; tailplane damaged on take-off from Oban 11Aug42; repaired on site; with HRH Duke of Kent on board, took off from Oban 25Aug42 on flight to Iceland but crashed on Eagh Rech [Eagle Rock], above village of Berriedale, Caithness (all killed except rear gunner)

W4027 c/n S.1199; TOC Pembroke Dock 22Feb42; Pembroke Dock stored reserve 14May42; 4 (C) OTU [TA:M] 6Jun42; 1 FBSU 22Sep42; returned to 4 (C) OTU [M] 4Dec42; repaired on site by Shorts 24Sep43; propeller flew off and engine caught fire during take-off from Alness 5Mar44; fire spread to hull and aircraft sank

W4028 c/n S.1200; TOC Pembroke Dock 28Apr42; delivered to 202 Sqn [TQ:B] 7Jun42; 1 FBSU 16Sep42; 119 Sqn [O] 20Sep42; 1 FBSU 31Dec42; returned to 119 Sqn 3Jan43; 4 (C) OTU [AI] 28Jun43; hull damaged while taxying at Alness 15Oct43; repaired on site by SBL 20Oct43; damaged in heavy landing at Alness 11Jul44; repaired on site; 57 MU 22Jun45; SOC 12Jul45

W4029 c/n S.1201; TOC Pembroke Dock 5May42; delivered to 202 Sqn [A, later M] 4Jun42; after being menaced by enemy aircraft during ferry flight; flew into sea on approach to Gibraltar flarepath 21Aug42, burst into flames and two depth charges exploded (11 killed, 1 injured)

W4030 c/n S.1202; TOC Pembroke Dock 8May42; 202 Sqn 16Jun42; a float torn off on alighting in Angle Bay 2Jul42; repaired on site by SBL 4Jul42; 119 Sqn [C] 16Sep42; struck by EJ141 at moorings, Pembroke Dock, 13Jan43; repaired on site; delivered to 10 (RAAF) Sqn [RB:H] 16Apr43; sank *U-243* 8Jul44; hit pinnace on take-off from Mount Batten 16Sep44; delivered to 57 MU 6Nov44; SOC 30Nov44

W4031 c/n S.1203; TOC Pembroke Dock 14May42; 1 FBSU; 4 (C) OTU [TA:N] 8Jun42; 1 FBSU 23Oct42; returned to 4 (C) OTU 14Feb43; undershot landing at Alness 23Feb43, lost a float and ran aground; repaired on site 28Feb43; Calshot 17Apr44; returned to 4 (C) OTU 31May44; 2 FBSU 11Aug44; SOC 12Jul45

W4032 c/n S.1204; TOC Pembroke Dock 24May42; 228 Sqn [DQ:O] 31May42; damaged during taxying in rough water in Lough Erne 12Aug42; repaired on site; on return from patrol on 4Sep42, in bad weather and short of fuel, alighted in Vaal Bay, Tiree; on taking off again, struck rocks 5 mls (8 km) N of Scurnish Light and broke up (8 killed); SOC 5Sep42

Sunderland Mk.III W4029, wearing code [A:1], shows off an impressive ASV aerial display. This aircraft served with 202 Squadron for less than three months before it came to grief off Gibraltar on 21st August 1942.
(Peter Davis collection)

W4033 c/n S.1205; TOC Pembroke Dock 27May42; 4 (C) OTU [TA:O] 8Jun42; 1 FBSU 24Mar43; returned to 4 (C) OTU 26Nov43; SOC 28Feb45

W4034 c/n S.1206; TOC Pembroke Dock 29May42; 4 (C) OTU 8Jun42; broke from moorings at Invergordon and drifted into P9606 2Dec42; repaired on site; flying accident Cat AC 26Mar43; flying accident Cat AC 14Jun44; repaired on site by SBL; delivered to 2 FBSU 11Aug44; returned to 4 (C) OTU 28Oct44; propeller detached damaging another engine 20Nov44; repaired on site 27Nov44; 57 MU 15May45; sold for scrap to Phoenix & Clifton Ironworks, Coatbridge, 10Mar47

W4035 c/n S.1207; TOC Pembroke Dock 5Jun42; 4 (C) OTU [TA:Q] 8Jun42; bounced on alighting at Invergordon 11Aug42, stalled and sank

W4036 c/n S.1208; TOC Wig Bay 8Jun42; delivered to 201 Sqn [ZM:W] 7Jul42; 1 FBSU 25Sep42; returned to 201 Sqn 18Dec42; 1 FBSU 28Jan43; returned to 201 Sqn by end of May43; overshot flarepath, wing dug in on alighting at Castle Archdale 18Nov43 and sank (3 killed, 5 injured)

W4037 c/n S.1209; TOC Pembroke Dock 16Jun42; delivered to 202 Sqn 3Jul42; collided with barges while taxying at Gibraltar 22Jul42; repaired on site; 1 FBSU 26Jul43; 4 (C) OTU 28Jul43; 1 FBSU 1Aug43; 57 MU 23Jan44; SB(W)L, Windermere, 15Aug44; MAEE 21Sep44; 57 MU 19Nov44; sold to S&HL 21Aug47 for conversion to Sandringham 6 **LN-LAI** (see Chapter 5)

5 Sunderlands Mk.II built by Blackburn Aircraft Ltd, Dumbarton under Contract B.37753/39:

W6000 TOC Wig Bay 11May42; 423 Sqn [AB:A, 3:A] 18Jul42; taxied into W4003 at Lough Erne 4Nov42; repaired on site; 1 FBSU 4Dec42; sank in gale at Wig Bay 13Dec42; SOC 12Jan43

W6001 TOC Wig Bay 28May42; delivered to 423 Sqn [B] 17Jul42; force-landed 23Sep42 after an engine cut; damaged on take-off after restarting; repaired in works by BOAC 1Oct42; 119 Sqn 29Nov42; 4 (C) OTU 5Dec42; broke from moorings and sank in gale at Alness 17Apr43; SOC 19May43

W6002 TOC Pembroke Dock 23Jun42; delivered to 202 Sqn [AX:R] 17Jul42; sank Italian submarine *Alabastro* off Majorca 14Sep42; delivered to 119 Sqn [R] 29Sep42; 4 (C) OTU 30Apr43; lost prop in flight 26Jun44 and Cat AC; recat E 14Jul44 and SOC

W6003 TOC Pembroke Dock 30Jun42; delivered to 202 Sqn [S] 8Jul42; developed engine trouble during hunt for U-boat 12Aug42, alighted at Gibraltar, lost a float and capsized; SOC 13Aug42

W6004 TOC Wig Bay 7Jul42; delivered to 228 Sqn [DQ:U] 6Aug42; 1 FBSU 17Dec42; struck by drifting Catalina FP100 and sank, Wig Bay, 29Dec42

20 Sunderlands Mk.III built by Blackburn Aircraft Ltd, Dumbarton under Contract B.37753/39:

W6005 TOC Wig Bay 2Aug42; Bristol Engine Co 13Aug42; 201 Sqn [ZM:P] 21Aug42; damaged in downwind landing at Lough Erne 11Sep42; repaired on site by S&HL 15Sep42; 1 FBSU 14Jul43; 201 Sqn 2Sep43; engine caught fire 18Feb44; repaired on site; 4 (C) OTU 18May44; Cat AC 27Mar45; recat E 10Apr45 and SOC

W6006 TOC Wig Bay 16Aug42; 423 Sqn [AB:F] 26Aug42; 1 FBSU 18Feb43; 423 Sqn [3:F] 17Apr43; 4 (C) OTU 4Jul43; lost propeller during test flight 24Aug43; repaired on site by SBL 3Sep43; returned to 423 Sqn 23Oct43; 4 (C) OTU 31Oct43; repaired on site by SBL 17Nov43; damaged during mooring in Cromarty Firth 26Mar44; repaired on site 4Apr44; engine cut in circuit, undershot and struck beacon on alighting at Alness 13Aug44; caught fire and sank 3.5 mls (5.6 km) E of Invergordon (1 killed, 1 injured)

W6007 TOC Wig Bay 26Aug42; 423 Sqn [AB:G] 8Sep42; 1 FBSU 3Apr43; returned to 423 Sqn 5May43; 1 FBSU 20Aug43; returned to 423 Sqn 20Sep43; struck by truck on Castle Archdale slipway 20Oct43; repaired on site 24Oct43; 131 OTU 29May44; damaged by ice at Killadeas 30Jan45; repaired on site by Shorts 3Mar45; 57 MU 10Apr45; sold for scrap to Phoenix & Clifton Ironworks, Coatbridge, 10Mar47

W6008 TOC Wig Bay 1Sep42; 423 Sqn [AB:H] 3Sep42; took off in heavy swell and fell back into water at Oban 14Dec42; repaired in works by Shorts; 1 FBSU 8Jun43; returned to 423 Sqn [3:H] 29Jun43; 1 FBSU 31Oct43; returned to 423 Sqn 8Dec43; three engines cut while on patrol 12Mar44, ditched at 53°00'N 14°00'W (200 mls/322 km W of Ireland); crew rescued

W6009 TOC Wig Bay 9Sep42; 423 Sqn [AB:J] 14Oct42; 1 FBSU 17Mar43; returned to 423 Sqn [3:J] 6Apr43; 1 FBSU 5May43; returned to 423 Sqn 8Jun43; 4 (C) OTU [DD] 4Jul43; repaired on site by SBL 27Apr44; Calshot Servicing Wing 27May44; returned to 4 (C) OTU 6Jul44; struck water during low-level bombing practice off Ferrytown 14Jan45, crashed on Dornoch bombing range and destroyed by fire (5 killed, 5 injured); SOC 25Jan45

W6010 TOC Wig Bay 11Sep42; del 201 Sqn [ZM:V] 16Oct42; lost propeller 18 mls (29 km) SW of Bowmore 26Jan43; 1 FBSU 14Mar43; returned to 201 Sqn 18Apr43; 4 (C) OTU [AA] 8Jul43; repaired on site by SBL 14Dec43 and 23Dec43; flying accident Cat AC 24Mar44; repaired on site by SBL 28Mar44; crashed at Allerton Farm, Cromarty, 27Jul44 on approach to Alness at night; hit HT cables and slid for half a mile (800 m) downhill into stone-built farmhouse (1 killed on ground, 7 injured)

W6011 TOC Wig Bay 22Sep42; 423 Sqn [3:F] 3Oct42; engine lost power while taxying at Lough Erne 26Nov42, swung and ran aground; repaired on site by SBL 29Nov42; struck by DD831 while moored at Castle Archdale 7Mar43; repaired on site; 1 FBSU 28Jul43; returned to 423 Sqn 14Sep43; Castle Archdale Servicing Wing 20Dec43; returned to 423 Sqn; ran aground while taxying at Castle Archdale 24Jul44; repaired on site; 131 (C) OTU 8Sep44; delivered to 2 FBSU for maintenance 24Dec44; returned to 131 (C) OTU 4Feb45; 57 MU 16Feb45; sold for scrap to Phoenix & Clifton Ironworks, Coatbridge, 10Mar47

W6012 TOC Pembroke Dock 27Sep42; delivered to 204 Sqn [KG:E] 22Oct42; Cat B 13Apr43; Wig Bay 14Jun43; 4 (C) OTU 28Jul43; lost propeller in flight 17Jul44; repaired on site by SBL 23Apr45; SOC 12Jul45

W6013 TOC Wig Bay 1Oct42; 423 Sqn [3:B] 12Nov42; 1 FBSU 14Jun43; returned to 423 Sqn 28Jul43; flew into Nochlaine Mountain, nr Ballycastle, Co Antrim, 5Dec43 while on ferry flight (9 killed, 7 injured)

W6014 TOC Wig Bay 11Oct42; 201 Sqn [ZM:S] 9Nov42; bollards pulled out at mooring, Castle Archdale, 26Mar43; repaired on site; 1 FBSU 28May43; returned to 201 Sqn 24May43; 1 FBSU 4Sep43; returned to 201 Sqn 28Oct43; 461 Sqn 25Apr44; 4 (C) OTU same day; engine caught fire in Alness circuit 12Aug44; repaired on site; SOC 12Jul45

W6015 TOC Wig Bay 22Oct42; 204 Sqn 21Nov42; delivered to 95 Sqn [M] 2Dec42; returned to UK; Pembroke Dock stored reserve 4Mar43; Scottish Aviation 20Apr43; 1 FBSU 14Jul43; 4 (C) OTU [Q] 28Jul43; 1 FBSU 1Aug43; 6 FBSU 27Sep43; ferried Calshot to Wig Bay 11Dec43; 57 MU 23Jan44; SB(R&B)L, Rochester, 23Jan45; sold for scrap 3Sep47

W6016 TOC Wig Bay 20Oct42; 95 Sqn 21Nov42; missing over Bay of Biscay 24Nov42 while in transit from Mount Batten to Bathurst for 204 Sqn (14 killed)

W6026 TOC Wig Bay 24Oct42; 422 Sqn [DG:A] 17Nov42; BOAC 26Jan43; returned to 422 Sqn 10May43; ran aground in gale at Wig Bay 23Jun43; repaired on site; 1 FBSU 3Sep43; returned to 422 Sqn [2:A, 2:C] 23Oct43; swung on take-off from Castle Archdale and struck buoy 2Jan44; repaired on site 6Jan44; 4 (C) OTU [V] 18Jul44; crashed when port wing fractured on alighting at Alness 22Mar45; repaired on site by SBL 27Mar45; 57 MU; SOC 31May45

W6027 TOC Wig Bay 26Oct42; 422 Sqn [DG:B] 19Nov42; damaged during launching at Lamora slipway, Oban, 16Mar43; repaired on site; 1 FBSU 30Sep43; returned to 422 Sqn [2:N] 29Nov43; collided with another aircraft after engine lost power while taxying at Castle Archdale 27Jan43; repaired on site; 330 Sqn 20May44; Calshot 21Jun44; returned to 330 Sqn 29Jun44; 4 (C) OTU [AD] 8Jul44; delivered to 2 FBSU 25Aug44; Cat B 28Apr45; recat E and SOC

W6028 TOC Oban 1Nov42; 422 Sqn [DG:C] 1Nov42; flying accident Cat A 20Dec42; BOAC 28Jan43; 1 FBSU 30May43; returned to 422 Sqn [2:C] 26Jun43; 1 FBSU 6Nov43; returned to 422 Sqn 4Jan44; crashed nr St Angelo, Fermanagh, 19Feb44, when a wing broke up during fighter affiliation exercise (2 killed, 8 injured)

Seen at Belfast about January 1942 with a Stirling in the background, Sunderland Mk.II W6050 was in the hands of MAEE Helensburgh at the time. *(P H T Green collection)*

Another view of Sunderland Mk.II W6050 of MAEE as it digs its nose in on alighting. *(P H T Green collection)*

Launching the first Sunderland built at Belfast, Mk.II W6050, on 10th April 1942.

W6029   TOC Oban 3Nov42; 422 Sqn [DG:D, 2:D] 30Nov42; inbound from Sullom Voe on 19Dec42 with 22 passengers and crew, alighted in lee of Kerrera Island in heavy swell, causing bow to collapse (7 killed, 14 injured); SOC 31Aug43

W6030   TOC Wig Bay 18Nov42; delivered to 422 Sqn [2:F] 2Dec42; slipped off tail trolley while running-up at Ganavan Sands 3May43; repaired on site; 330 Sqn [WH:M] 19Jun43; hull damaged by debris when alighting in Firth of Lorne at night 1Sep43; repaired on site; Cat B at Sullom Voe 15Jun44; for repair in works by SBL 24Jun44 but recat E 10Jul44 and SOC

W6031   TOC Wig Bay 18Nov42; 422 Sqn [2:G] 12Dec42; 1 FBSU 3Sep43; returned to 422 Sqn 6Oct43; forced to ditch 150 mls (240 km) W of Gibraltar 20Nov43 after attacking *U-618* (11 killed)

W6032   TOC Wig Bay 22Nov42; 422 Sqn [2:H] 9Dec42; 1 FBSU 17May43; returned to 422 Sqn 19May43; ran aground while taxying at Reykjavik 13Aug43; repaired on site by S&HL 11Jun44; returned to 422 Sqn 11Aug44; 131 OTU 31Oct44; ground accident Cat AC 27Mar45; repaired on site 29Mar45; 57 MU 10Apr45; sold for scrap to Phoenix & Clifton Ironworks, Coatbridge, 10Mar47

W6033   TOC Wig Bay (date unknown); 422 Sqn [2:J] 27Dec42; 1 FBSU 14Aug43; returned to 422 Sqn 21Sep43; crashed on alighting in Hvalfjord, Iceland, in snowstorm 28Sep43, drifted onto rocks and caught fire (2 injured); SOC 11Nov43

15 Sunderlands Mk.II built by Short & Harland Ltd, Belfast under Contract B.76674/40:

W6050   c/n SH.51; first flight 10Apr42; TOC MAEE 17Apr42; 1 FBSU 5Aug42; 461 Sqn [UT:L] 14Aug42; 1 FBSU 22Apr43; returned to 461 Sqn 28Jun43; struck submerged object on take-off from Pembroke Dock at night 21Sep43; repaired on site by Shorts; damaged in severe gale at Pembroke Dock 24Jan44 when tail trolley collapsed; repaired on site 14Feb44; became GI airframe **4446M** at 4 SoTT, St Athan 2Feb44 (replacing T9114 with the same number); SOC 7Mar44

W6051   c/n SH.52; TOC MAEE 4Jun42; 1 FBSU 10Jul42; 201 Sqn [ZM:T] 3Aug42; 4 (C) OTU 2Jun43; repaired on site 8Aug43; 57 MU 10Jul44; SOC same day

W6052   c/n SH.53; TOC Pembroke Dock 5Jul42; Pembroke Dock stored reserve; 423 Sqn [AB:D] 22Jul42; grounded while taxying in Lough Neagh 24Aug42; repaired on site; 330 Sqn [WH:D] 8May43; missing over North Atlantic 5Jun43, last heard from when 22 mls (35 km) SSE of St Kilda (off Outer Hebrides) (12 killed)

W6053   c/n SH.54; TOC Wig Bay 10Jul42; 423 Sqn [AB:E] 7Aug42; 1 FBSU 23Nov42; struck by tender while moored at Wig Bay 4Mar43; repaired on site; 330 Sqn [WH:E] 6May43; lost propeller while on patrol 21Jul43; repaired on site; struck by pinnace at night at Sullom Voe 29Jan44; repaired on site by SBL 8Feb44; 57 MU 10Apr44; SOC 30Apr45

W6054   c/n SH.55; TOC Pembroke Dock 23Aug42; delivered to 10 (RAAF) Sqn [RB:D] 29Aug42; short of fuel in bad weather 12Nov42, overshot Mount Batten flarepath and crashed into sea 1.5 mls (2.4 km) from breakwater lighthouse, turned over and broke up; (10 crew and passengers injured and picked up by surface vessel, but 3 RN officers, 1 army officer and 1 other killed); SOC 13Nov42

W6055   c/n SH.56; TOC Wig Bay 6Aug42; delivered to 201 Sqn [ZM:R] 18Sep42; damaged by gale while picketed at South Ford, Benbecula 5Oct42; repaired on site by Shorts 27Oct42; returned to 201 Sqn [ZM:X] 5Jun43; 57 MU 27Mar44; at 1 MCTU, Corsewall, 4Nov44; to become GI airframe **4909M** but not taken up; scuttled 11Dec46

W6056   c/n SH.57; TOC Wig Bay 3Sep42; 246 Sqn [A] 16Sep42; a float damaged on take-off in choppy sea at Wig Bay 15Oct42; repaired on site; 4 (C) OTU 19May43; repaired in works by Scottish Aviation, Greenock, 9Jul43; 57 MU 27Apr44; became GI airframe **4782M** at 131 (C) OTU 10May44

W6057   c/n SH.58; TOC Wig Bay 6Sep42; 246 Sqn [B] 16Sep42; damaged while being taxied out of floating dock at Loch Indaal, Islay, 9Mar43; repaired on site by Shorts 16Mar43; engine cut while taxying at Alness 22Jul43; repaired on site; returned to 246 Sqn 2Oct43; 1 FBSU 6Nov43; 57 MU 29Jan44; scuttled 16Mar45

W6058   c/n SH.59; TOC Wig Bay 29Sep42; 246 Sqn [O] 28Oct42; port float filled with water, cast off from mooring and beached in Loch Indaal (Islay) 12Feb43; repaired on site by Shorts 16Mar43; lost propeller while on patrol 7Jun43; repaired on site; 1 FBSU 16Oct43; 57 MU 29Jan44; Greenock 28May44; became GI airframe **4798M** at 1 MCTU, Corsewall 17May44; SOC 1Feb45

Beached on Scottish sands at Loch Indaal, Islay, on 12th February 1943 was Sunderland Mk.II W6058 of 246 Squadron but fortunately it was largely undamaged and repaired on site.

CHAPTER 5 : INDIVIDUAL AIRCRAFT HISTORIES

In what appears to be distinctly cold weather, Sunderland Mk.III W6066 of 131 OTU takes a reflective rest at Killadeas on Lough Erne in 1945. Its code is CL, which did not form part of the formal promulgated RAF code letters system and perhaps should have been painted as [C:L]. W6066 was sold for scrap in 1947.
(R C Sturtivant collection)

W6059 c/n SH.60; TOC Wig Bay 8Oct42; delivered to 201 Sqn [ZM:R] 27Oct42; Ganavan Sands, Oban, 31Jan43; repaired on site by BOAC 13Mar43; 330 Sqn [WH:P] 29Apr43; flying accident Cat AC 7Jun43; 57 MU 13Feb44; SOC 5Apr44

W6060 c/n SH.61; TOC Wig Bay 13Oct42; 246 Sqn [D] 16Oct42; 4 (C) OTU 10May43; force-landed in Beauly Firth, Inverness, 14May43; repaired on site by SBL 10Nov43; crashed on alighting at Alness 27Nov43 and broke back (5 killed, 6 injured)

W6061 c/n SH.62; TOC ?; 423 Sqn [3:K]; 330 Sqn [WH:X] 9May43; 1 FBSU 13Jul43; returned to 330 Sqn 17Jul43; 57 MU 16Feb44; presumed SOC 21Jun47

W6062 c/n SH.63; TOC Wig Bay 7Dec42; 95 Sqn [H] 8Jan43; severe damage to port wing, dorsal turret and fin caused by Sunderland JM680 of 204 Sqn at Bathurst moorings 31May43; SOC 11Nov43

W6063 c/n SH.64; TOC Wig Bay 6Dec42; 204 Sqn 10Jan43; 95 Sqn [N] 9Apr43; crashed into sea at 04°30'N 17°12'W 29Mar43 (6 killed, 3 injured); SOC 30Nov43

W6064 c/n SH.65; TOC Wig Bay 31Dec42; 1 FBSU same day; 423 Sqn 26Jan43; 330 Sqn [WH:R] 9Feb43; Oban 27Aug43; 330 Sqn 2Oct43; Oban 15Dec43; 330 Sqn 25Jan44; 4 (C) OTU 28Feb44; repaired on site by SBL 10Mar44; delivered to Pembroke Dock 30Sep44 to become GI airframe **4881M** but not taken up; SOC 13Nov44

10 Sunderlands Mk.III built by Short Bros & Harland Ltd, Belfast under Contract B.76674/40:

W6065 c/n SH.66; engine cut while taxying for ferry flight 30Jan43, swung into jetty in Musgrove Channel, Belfast; Pembroke Dock stored reserve 6Feb43; 95 Sqn 11Feb43; engine cut, ditched off Oporto (Portugal) 5Mar43 on ferry flight to Bathurst, crew rescued and interned; aircraft destroyed in heavy seas

W6066 c/n SH.67; TOC Pembroke Dock 18Feb43; 246 Sqn [F] 4Mar43; 422 Sqn [2:F] 30Apr43; dinghy struck aircraft in heavy seas at Loch Indaal 12Jun43; repaired on site; 1 FBSU 4Jul43; beached in rough weather in Wig Bay 10Jul43; repaired on site; returned to 422 Sqn 12Aug43; repaired on site by S&HL 3Sep43; 131 (C) OTU 30May43; lost a float on take-off in rough water at Castle Archdale 30Aug43; repaired on site; 422 Sqn 29Feb44; 131 (C) OTU [C:U] 30May44; delivered to Greenock 11Oct44; returned to 131 (C) OTU 26Nov44; ground accident Cat AC 3Mar45; repaired on site by S&HL 8Mar45; 57 MU 9Apr45; sold for scrap to Phoenix & Clifton Ironworks, Coatbridge, 10Mar47

W6067 c/n SH.68; TOC Wig Bay 27Feb43; 330 Sqn [WH:I] 16Mar43; lost propeller in flight 19Aug43; Oban 26Aug43; returned to 330 Sqn [WH:T] 20Oct43; Calshot 6Aug44; repaired on site 1Sep44; hit submerged rocks on alighting at Sullom Voe after patrol 5Feb45; SOC 15Feb45

W6068 c/n SH.69; TOC Pembroke Dock 4Mar43; 330 Sqn 2Apr43; 423 Sqn [3:N] 9May43; 6 FBSU 19Sep43; returned to 423 Sqn 6Nov43; struck buoy while being moored at Stornoway 19May44; repaired on site by Shorts 24May44; 131 (C) OTU 31Aug44; damaged by ice at Killadeas 30Jan45; repaired on site by S&HL 27Feb45; 57 MU 8Apr45; sold for scrap to Phoenix & Clifton Ironworks, Coatbridge, 10Mar47

W6075 c/n SH.70; TOC Pembroke Dock 4Mar43; 330 Sqn [WH:Z] 2Apr43; crashed on alighting on Lough Neagh 12May43 after training flight and sank off Rams Island; SOC 8Jun43

W6076 c/n SH.71; TOC Pembroke Dock 15Apr43; 95 Sqn [D] 1Jul43; SOC 21Jun45

W6077 c/n SH.72; TOC Pembroke Dock stored reserve 6Apr43; 461 Sqn [UT:U] 5May43; damaged while sinking *U-461* 30Jul43; Shorts 27Aug43; 57 MU 10Mar44; SOC 20Dec45

W6078 c/n SH.73; TOC Pembroke Dock stored reserve 19Apr43; delivered to 230 Sqn [DX:N] 19Aug43; SOC 16Aug45

W6079 c/n SH.74; TOC Pembroke Dock stored reserve 28Apr43; delivered to 204 Sqn [KG:C] 10May43; crashed on take-off from Port Etienne 2Oct43 after third attempt; swung to port and struck beach (1 killed, 7 injured); SOC 11Nov43

W6080 c/n SH.75; TOC Pembroke Dock 30Apr43; 308 FTU 10Jun43; to Free French at Dakar 20Jul43; SOC 3Sep43

40 Sunderlands Mk.III built by Blackburn Aircraft Ltd, Dumbarton under Contract B.37753/40/C.20(b):

DD828 TOC Wig Bay 12Dec42; 423 Sqn [3:B] 16Dec42; 1 FBSU 20Apr43; returned to 423 Sqn 10May43; an engine lost power while taxying at Castle Archdale 22Jun43 and aircraft ran aground; repaired on site; 201 Sqn [ZM:N] 30Jun43; 1 FBSU 4Oct43; returned to 201 Sqn 21Nov43; struck by dinghy while moored at Castle Archdale 19Jan44; repaired on site; 4 (C) OTU 13Apr44; Cat B 25Mar45; 57 MU; SOC 31Mar45

DD829 TOC Wig Bay 19Dec42; 201 Sqn [ZM:Z] 22Dec42; 1 FBSU 6Jul43; returned to 201 Sqn 12Aug43; 131 (C) OTU 10May44; flying accident Cat AC 14Apr45; repaired on site; 57 MU 3May45; sold for scrap to Phoenix & Clifton Ironworks, Coatbridge, 10Mar47

DD830 TOC Wig Bay 19Dec42; 1 FBSU 20Dec42; 228 Sqn 30Dec42; engine cut, hit wave on alighting in Firth of Clyde 2 mls (3.2 km) W of Ailsa Craig 3Feb43 (1 injured)

DD831 TOC Wig Bay 28Dec42; 422 Sqn [2:K] 2Jan43; 1 FBSU 17May43; returned to 422 Sqn 9Jun43; broke adrift and blown ashore in gale at Bowmore 24Jan44 and damaged beyond repair (4 injured)

DD832 TOC Wig Bay 31Dec42; MAEE 8Jan43; 4 (C) OTU [V] 18Feb43; mooring rope broke, aircraft drifted into DD842 at Alness 28Jun43; repaired on site; flying accident Cat AC 5Apr44; repaired on site 11Apr44; struck submerged obstruction on alighting at Alness 24Dec44; repaired on site 30Dec44; 272 MU 11Jul45; sold for scrap 25Mar47

DD833 TOC Wig Bay 29Dec42; 204 Sqn [KG:M] 24Jan43; loaned to Aéronautique navale Flottille 7FE at Port Etienne 18Mar43; Scottish Aviation, Greenock, 30May43; returned to RAF Aug43; float collapsed on alighting at Wig Bay 10Sep43; 1 FBSU14Sep43; damaged beyond repair during salvage and SOC

DD834 TOC Wig Bay 24Jan43; taxied onto rocks at Wig Bay during delivery flight 11Feb43; repaired on site by Shorts 17Feb43; 1 FBSU 3Apr43; 204 Sqn 30Mar43; delivered to 228 Sqn [S] 15Apr43; Cat B 16Nov43; repaired on site by SBL 23Nov43; repaired in works by SBL 4Apr44; ferried Belfast to Windermere 12Apr14 for repairs; 57 MU 30Sep44; sold to SB(R&B)L, Rochester, 29Jun45 and converted to Sandringham 2 **G-AGPT** (see Chapter 5)

DD835 TOC Wig Bay 13Jan43; 330 Sqn [WH:H, WH:P] 11Feb43; 201 Sqn [ZM:R] 6May43; sank *U-440* 31May43; 1 FBSU 18Jun43; returned to 201 Sqn 19Jul43; flying accident Cat AC 15Nov43; repaired on site by S&HL 18Nov43; 228 Sqn 27May44; 131 (C) OTU 10Aug44; delivered to 2 FBSU 29Dec44; returned to 131 (C) OTU 16Feb45; 228 Sqn 6Mar45; 422 Sqn 12Mar45; 57 MU 21Jun45; SOC 12Jul45

DD836 TOC 1 FBSU 28Jan43; delivered to 228 Sqn 25Feb43; taxied into W6011 at Castle Archdale 7Mar43; repaired on site; engine cut while on patrol at night, force-landed and struck small boat off Scilly Isles 23Dec43; lost a float in gale and sank at St Mary's, Isles of Scilly, 24Jan44 while being recovered; SOC 29Feb44

DD837 TOC Wig Bay 25Jan43; delivered to 228 Sqn [DQ:V] 8Mar43; shot down by Ju 88s over Bay of Biscay, near Spanish northern coast 15May43 (11 killed)

DD838 TOC Wig Bay 28Jan43; 228 Sqn [DQ:X] 3Feb43; 423 Sqn [3:X] 12May44; 4 (C) OTU [AB] 28Jul44; SOC 28Jun45

DD839 TOC 1 FBSU 13Feb43; 4 (C) OTU 23Mar43; undershot on alighting at Alness 27Nov43 and overturned (3 killed, 5 injured)

DD840 TOC Wig Bay 16Feb43; 4 (C) OTU 24Feb43; force-landed on Loch Ness in bad weather 2Aug43; flying accident Cat AC 15May44; repaired on site by Shorts 18May44; 272 MU 21Mar46; SOC 26Mar47

DD841 TOC Wig Bay 22Feb43; 4 (C) OTU [J] 2Mar43; Oban 13Jan44; Cat B 18Mar44; repaired in works by SB(W)L, Windermere, 27Mar43; 57 MU 13Aug44; sold to SB(R&B)L 13Jun45 and converted to Sandringham 3 **G-AGPY** (see Chapter 5)

DD842 TOC Wig Bay 22Feb43; 4 (C) OTU [AL] 2Mar43; struck by drifting DD832 at Alness moorings 28Jun43; repaired on site; struck buoy on take-off from Alness 22Oct43; repaired on site by SBL 13Nov43; flying accident Cat AC 9Feb44; Calshot 21Apr44; returned to 4 (C) OTU 14Jun44; 57 MU 18Jun45; SOC 12Jul45

DD843 TOC Wig Bay 21Feb43; 330 Sqn [WH:S] 14Mar43; 423 Sqn [3:E] 10May43; 1 FBSU 11Jun43; 423 Sqn 10Jul43; damaged a float on alighting at Calshot 29Nov43; repaired on site by SBL 6Dec43; 131 (C) OTU 25Jun44; 4 (C) OTU [F] 23Aug44; damaged on ground 24Jan45; repaired on site by SBL 30Jan45; 57 MU 20Jun45; SOC 12Jul45

DD844 TOC Wig Bay 5Mar43; 330 Sqn [WH:Y] 9Mar43; Calshot 11Feb44; returned to 330 Sqn 30Mar44; 4 (C) OTU [BE] 15Jul44; damaged in heavy landing at Alness 26Sep44; repaired on site 2Oct44; SOC 14Jun45

DD845 TOC Wig Bay 11May43; 246 Sqn 30Mar43; 422 Sqn [2:B] 30Apr43; 1 FBSU 30Jul43; returned to 422 Sqn 30Aug43; struck rock while taxiing at Castle Archdale 14Sep43; repaired on site by S&HL 14Sep43; 131 (C) OTU 25Jun44; repaired on site by S&HL 20Apr45; 57 MU 15May45; sold for scrap to Phoenix & Clifton Ironworks, Coatbridge, 10Mar47

DD846 TOC Wig Bay 6Mar43; 246 Sqn 23Apr43; 422 Sqn [2:O] 30Apr43; crashed on Beetle Head, Clare Island, Co Mayo (Irish Republic) 25May43 (7 bodies recovered, 5 missing); SOC 10Jun43

DD847 TOC 1 FBSU 13Mar43; 228 Sqn 29Mar43; an engine cut while taxiing at Castle Archdale 15Apr43 and aircraft ran aground; repaired on site by SBL; taxied into DP191 at Castle Archdale 21May44; repaired on site; 131 (C) OTU 12Jun44; repaired on site 22Aug44; flying accident Cat B 2Nov44; at 2 FBSU for repairs 29Nov44 to 21Dec44; damaged by ice at Killadeas 30Jan45; repaired on site by S&HL 20Feb45; 57 MU 8Apr45; sold for scrap Phoenix & Clifton Ironworks, Coatbridge, 10Mar47

DD848 TOC 1 FBSU 21Mar43; 201 Sqn [ZM:N] 20Apr43; while returning from night patrol in low cloud, flew into hill at Brandon Head, Co Kerry (Irish Republic) 22Aug43 (8 killed, 4 injured); SOC 31Aug43

DD849 TOC 1 FBSU 19Mar43; 423 Sqn [3:M] 28Apr43; 1 FBSU 3Jul43; returned to 423 Sqn 23Jul43; repaired on site by S&HL 1Jan44; 131 (C) OTU [C:K] 28Jul44; 57 MU 4Mar45; sold for scrap Phoenix & Clifton Ironworks, Coatbridge, 10Mar47

DD850 TOC 1 FBSU 23Mar43; 422 Sqn [2:M] 18May43; 1 FBSU 11Sep43; returned to 422 Sqn 6Nov43; Calshot 14Jul44; 4 (C) OTU 16Aug44; collided with barge while taxiing at night at Alness 22Oct44; repaired on site; 57 MU 20Jun45; sold for scrap Phoenix & Clifton Ironworks, Coatbridge, 10Mar47

DD851 TOC 1 FBSU 6Apr43; 330 Sqn [WH:Z] 17May43; Castle Archdale Servicing Wing 25Nov43; returned to 330 Sqn 29Dec43; Calshot Servicing Wing 15Apr44; returned to 330 Sqn 25Apr44; 4 (C) OTU 20Jul44; engine failed on take-off from Alness 22Nov44, caught fire and fell out; aircraft crashed on railway line 2 mls (3.2 km) NE of Invergordon station (all 11 killed)

DD852 TOC 1 FBSU 3Apr43; 10 (RAAF) Sqn [RB:J] 24May43; attacked by seven Ju.88s and badly damaged 3Aug43 (1 killed); repaired on site; lost propeller while on patrol over Bay of Biscay 6May44; repaired on site by Shorts 11May44; struck shoal, damaging keel and chine, during take-off from Mount Batten 4Jul44; repaired on site by SBL 5Jul44; hit uncharted obstruction S of Drake Is 17Jul44; repaired on site by SBL 19Jul44; struck by vessel which had dragged anchor in Plymouth Sound during fierce gale 2Sep44, then blown onto rocks in Jennycliffe Bay; later wrecked in salvage operation

DD853 TOC 1 FBSU 15Apr43; 423 Sqn [3:K] 30May43; 6 FBSU 23Oct43; returned to 423 Sqn 27Dec43; struck flare on landing at Castle Archdale 15Jan44; struck by DP178 at Castle Archdale moorings 28Feb44; repaired on site by Shorts 7Mar44; Calshot 30Aug44; 131 (C) OTU 27Oct44; delivered to Greenock 2Jan45 for maintenance; returned to 131 (C) OTU 10Feb45; 461 Sqn [Y] 6Mar45; accident 21Jun45; SOC 13Jul45

DD854 TOC 1 FBSU 17Apr43; 422 Sqn [2:P] 30May43; ran aground while taxiing in squall at Castle Archdale 18Jun43; repaired on site; 131 (C) OTU 25Jun44; taxied onto rocks in Lough Erne 15Aug44; repaired on site; damaged float while taxiing in rough water at Castle Archdale 6Dec44; not repaired and SOC 14Jun45

DD855 TOC 1 FBSU 19Apr43; 201 Sqn 30May43; ran aground after alighting at Castle Archdale10Jun43; Castle Archdale Servicing Wing 25Nov43; 201 Sqn 2Feb44; 422 Sqn [2:Y] 12Feb44; two engines cut over Irish Sea, force-landed and towed to Belfast 19Jun44; repaired in works by S&HL 22Jun44; 4 (C) OTU [AJ] 12Jul44; engine caught fire on take-off from Alness 20Apr45, alighted and sank (1 injured); SOC 26Apr45

DD856 TOC 1 FBSU 24Apr43; 330 Sqn [WH:G] 6Jun43; 4 (C) OTU [AR] 21Jul44; taxied into NJ177 in gale at night, Sullom Voe, 27Nov44; repaired on site; cylinder flew off in flight and struck hull 3May45; 57 MU 22Jun45; not repaired; became GI airframe **5716M** at 1 MCTU, Corsewall, 13Oct45; to 12 SoTT, Melksham then SOC14Jun46

DD857 TOC 1 FBSU 4May43; delivered to 201 Sqn [ZM:V] 24Jun43; flew into glassy calm water on alighting at Castle Archdale 30Jun43 (2 killed); Shorts 31Aug43; presumed SOC 21Jun47

DD858 TOC 1 FBSU 3May43; 201 Sqn [ZM:Y] 12Jun43; ran aground while taxiing in rough water at Castle Archdale 25Sep43; repaired on site; while being flown by 423 Sqn crew, alighted heavily on Lough Neagh 23Oct43, hull split and aircraft overturned (7 injured); no SOC date

DD859 TOC Wig Bay 7May43; 423 Sqn [3:G] 14Jun43; shot down by flak from *U-489* 4Aug43 while sinking it at 61°11'N 14°38'W; force-landed but cartwheeled (5 killed, 6 rescued); SOC 30Aug43

DD860 TOC Wig Bay 14May43; 423 Sqn [3:J] 19Jun43; Cat AC 23Jul43; 201 Sqn [ZM:O] 25Sep43; Shorts, Windermere, 29Feb44; 57 MU 23Jun44; delivered to BOAC 2Mar45 and regd **G-AHEP** (see Chapter 5); returned to RAF at 57 MU 24Sep47; sold for scrap to John Dale & Co, London Colney, Herts, 12Jan50

Chapter 5 : Individual Aircraft Histories

The first Sunderland built at Windermere was Mk.III DP176 which was taken on charge by the RAF at Pembroke Dock on 28th September 1942. It survived only six months before ditching in the Bay of Biscay on 15th April 1943. (via Alan J King)

DD861 TOC 1 FBSU 19May43; 422 Sqn [2:P] 26Jun43; during Bay of Biscay patrol 3Sep43, ditched at 44°05'N 10°30'W (about 100 mls/160 km W of Cape Finisterre, NW Spain) after starboard outer engine caught fire and fell off; starboard inner engine failed, aircraft alighted and sank; crew rescued after three days by Sunderland JM679 of 228 Sqn and flown to Pembroke Dock

DD862 TOC 1 FBSU 22May43; 423 Sqn [AB:A] 5Jul43; 6 FBSU 7Oct43; returned to 423 Sqn 19Dec43; float damaged by vehicle on slipway at Castle Archdale 14Jan44; repaired on site; Cat B 24Apr44; repaired on site by S&HL 5May44; returned to 423 Sqn [3:A]; destroyed by fire on alighting at Castle Archdale 31May45 after an engine caught fire 10 mls (16 km) from base; SOC 6Jul45

DD863 TOC Wig Bay 27May43; Wig Bay stored reserve; 423 Sqn [3:J] 30Jul43; after reported engine failure, ditched at 54°30'N 09°30'W (200 mls/320 km W of Ireland) 13Nov43; SOC 30Nov43

DD864 TOC 1 FBSU 29May43; 228 Sqn [K] 1Aug43; missing over Bay of Biscay 24Dec43

DD865 TOC 1 FBSU 12Jun43; delivered to 10 (RAAF) Sqn [RB:L] 11Aug43; struck buoy in Plymouth Sound while taxying at night 18Oct43; repaired on site; badly damaged by six Ju 88s over Bay of Biscay 30Nov43; repaired on site; engine cut while taxying, hit obstruction at Mount Batten 30Jan44; repaired on site by SBL 5Feb44; delivered to Scottish Aviation, Largs, 5Jan45 for disposal; but 302 FTU 6Jan45; reported to have been ferried to the Far East; SOC 5Jun45

DD866 TOC Wig Bay 12Jun43; Wig Bay stored reserve; 461 Sqn [B] 14Aug43; damaged by pinnace while being towed in Angle Bay 31Aug43; repaired on site; damaged on striking rocks when alighting at Pembroke Dock 4Mar44; repaired on site by Shorts 7Mar44; repaired in works by SB(W)L, Windermere, 23Mar44; 57 MU 2Aug44; 302 FTU 8Nov44; delivered to 230 Sqn [NM:T] 18Dec44; SOC 16Aug45

DD867 TOC 1 FBSU 15Jun43; 10 (RAAF) Sqn 8Aug43; 1 FBSU 12Aug43; 423 Sqn [3:G] 20Aug43; 131 (C) OTU 2Aug44; 57 MU 10Feb45; SOC 5Mar45

25 Sunderlands Mk.III built by Short Bros (Windermere) Ltd, Windermere under Contracts/Acft/234/SAS/40/C.20(b):

DP176 TOC Pembroke Dock 28Sep42; 119 Sqn [D] 1Oct42; drifted into EJ133 while taxying at Pembroke Dock 22Mar43; repaired on site; lost both port propellers and ditched in Bay of Biscay 15Apr43 (3 killed, 12 survivors picked up by *Wensleydale*)

DP177 TOC Pembroke Dock 7Nov42; 10 (RAAF) Sqn [RB:K] 31Dec42; bounced on alighting at Pembroke Dock and float collapsed 17Jan43; repaired on site; while alighting in gusty conditions at Pembroke Dock 4Mar43, starboard float collapsed; missing over Bay of Biscay 11Aug43, believed to have been shot down by Ju.88s (12 killed); SOC 31Aug43

DP178 TOC 1 FBSU 15Dec42; 422 Sqn [2:L] 21Dec42; struck by tender while moored at Kerrera, Oban, 15Apr43; repaired on site; 1 FBSU 9Jun43; returned to 422 Sqn 5Jul43; 1 FBSU 25Nov43; returned to 422 Sqn 15Jan44; collided with DD853 while taxying at Castle Archdale 29Feb44; repaired on site; 330 Sqn [WH:L] 7Jun44; 4 (C) OTU 6Jul44; failed to return from night training exercise 14Mar45 (11 missing); SOC 22Mar45

DP179 TOC Pembroke Dock 13Jan43; 119 Sqn [V] 30Jan43; overshot down-wind approach and ran ashore at Mount Batten 29Mar43, salvaged and beached 31Mar43; recovered and repaired by 10 (RAAF) Sqn; 10 (RAAF) Sqn [RB:M] 12Aug43; ditched (possibly 20 mls/32 km S of Isles of Scilly) 2Oct43 after engine trouble (11 killed); SOC 31Oct43

DP180 TOC Pembroke Dock 2Feb43; 230 Sqn [NM:O] 7Mar43; bounced on alighting at Gibraltar and lost a float 7Apr43; repaired on site; returned to 230 Sqn [NM:O] 13May43; overshot when alighting from ferry flight and ran ashore at Aboukir 7Jun43; Korangi Creek (India) 29Jan45; SOC 31Jan46

DP181 TOC Wig Bay 27Feb43; 1 FBSU 7Mar43; 330 Sqn [WH:U] 16Mar43; 423 Sqn [3:D] 3May43; 1 FBSU 4Jul43; returned to 423 Sqn 9Jul43; hull split on alighting on rough water at night at Castle Archdale 11Nov43 and sank (5 killed, 6 injured); SOC 12Nov43

DP182 TOC 1 FBSU 27Mar43; final camouflaged Windermere-built Sunderland; 204 Sqn [KG:J]; Free French at Dakar (Sénégal) Sep43 (see Part 5)

DP183 TOC 1 FBSU 15Apr43; 330 Sqn [WH:W] 6Jun43; tail trolley collapsed during compass swing 12Sep43; repaired on site Shorts; Calshot Servicing Wing 17Feb44; returned to 330 Sqn 10Mar44; missing from patrol, 20Mar44 (11 missing)

DP184 TOC Wig Bay 2May43; 330 Sqn [WH:F] 6Jun43; Calshot Servicing Wing 6Apr44; Sullom Voe 2May44; 4 (C) OTU [AG] 6Jul44; struck buoy while taxying at Alness 24Sep44; repaired on site 28Sep44; repaired in works by Shorts, Rochester, 15Mar45; returned to 4 (C) OTU 17Mar45; 57 MU 18Jun45; SOC 12Jul45

Above is MR.5 DP200 [230:Z] at Wig Bay in 1957 prior to sale for scrap. Last operator was Station Flight Pembroke Dock in 1956. Left is a view of 423 Squadron's Sunderland Mk.III DP191 [3:L].
(J Wright via Andrew Hendrie collection)

Sunderland MR.5 DP198 [W] of 209 Squadron over Seletar in 1959. Note the underwing fairings for ASV Mk.VIc equipment.

An 88 Squadron Sunderland GR.5 DP199 [C] resting at Kai Tak, Hong Kong.
(J Nance via Andrew Hendrie collection)

DP185 TOC 1 FBSU 21May43; 201 Sqn [ZM:V] 12Jul43; 4 (C) OTU 28Apr44; repaired on site by SBL 22May44; 57 MU 25Mar45; SOC 31May45; sold for scrap to Phoenix & Clifton Ironworks, Coatbridge, 10Mar47

DP186 TOC 1 FBSU 3Jun43; 95 Sqn [J] 1Sep43; 57 MU 14Jun45; sold for scrap to Phoenix & Clifton Ironworks, Coatbridge, 10Mar47

DP 187 TOC Wig Bay 26Jun43; Wig Bay stored reserve; 308 FTU 12Aug43; Free French at Dakar 1Oct43 (see Part 5)

DP188 TOC 1 FBSU 24Jul43; 204 Sqn [KG:L, later KG:C] 20Aug43; struck buoy while taxying in Angle Bay 6Sep43; delivered to West Africa 12Nov43 (squadron not recorded); 57 MU 19Jun45; sold for scrap to Phoenix & Clifton Ironworks, Coatbridge, 10Mar47

DP189 TOC Wig Bay 6Aug43; 1 FBSU 12Aug43; delivered to 230 Sqn [NM:L] 16Nov43; struck obstruction at Kelai (Burma) 29Mar44; repaired on site; Korangi Creek 30Jan45; SOC 16Aug45

DP190 TOC 1 FBSU 14Aug43; delivered to 270 Sqn [G] 11Jan44; 204 Sqn [G] by 1Oct44; SOC 21Jun45

DP191 TOC 1 FBSU 30Aug43; 423 Sqn [3:L] 24Oct43; struck by DD847 at Castle Archdale moorings 21May44; repaired on site by S&HL 24May44; 131 (C) OTU 29Jul44; at 2 FBSU for maintenance 25Nov44 to 17Dec44; ground accident Cat AC (ice on water) 7Feb45; repaired on site; 57 MU 21Mar46 for storage; to SB&H 29May52 for conversion to MR.5; test-flown 9Jun53 as RNZAF **NZ4109**; delivered to Wig Bay 19Jun53 for RNZAF as **NZ4109** (see Part 3)

DP192 TOC Wig Bay 3Oct43; 10 (RAAF) Sqn 11Nov43; left for Australia via Gibraltar 14Feb44; to RAAF as **A26-6** (see Part 2)

DP193 TOC Wig Bay 3Oct43; 201 Sqn 21Nov43; 1 FBSU 25Nov43; 423 Sqn 1Dec43; Calshot 3Aug44; 131 (C) OTU 6Sep44; damaged by ice at Killadeas 30Jan45; repaired on site by SBL 12Feb45; 272 MU 8Jul45; SOC 26Mar47

DP194 TOC 1 FBSU 26Oct43; 57 MU 6Dec43; 302 FTU 30Jan44; despatched to West Africa 24Mar44; 95 Sqn [F] by 3May44; bows damaged on alighting at Bathurst 12Apr45; repaired on site but SOC 21Jun45

DP195 TOC Wig Bay 6Nov43; 57 MU 8Jan44; damaged in gale at Wig Bay 25Jan44; repaired on site by SBL 2Feb44;57 MU 14Feb44; 4 (C) OTU (? date); flying accident Cat AC 20May44; conv Mk.V; 57 MU 21Mar46; sold to SB&HL 22Jan48; became **CX-AKR** (see Chapter 5)

DP196 TOC 6 FBSU 22Nov43; 57 MU 14Jan44; 461 Sqn [K] 16Feb44; damaged when taxied into moored vessel after alighting at

Rochester-built Sunderland Mk.III DV960 [2:H] photographed when serving with 461 Squadron in 1944.
(Gerald Raggett collection via Rod Simpson)

Mount Batten 18Mar44; repaired on site 22Mar44; 201 Sqn [NS:K] 16Sep44; propeller detached in flight 19Apr45; repaired on site by S&HL 24Apr45; 57 MU 3Jul45; Castle Archdale 4Jul45; delivered to 272 MU 1Nov45; sold for scrap 26Mar47

DP197   TOC Wig Bay 2Dec43; 57 MU 20Jan44; 4 (C) OTU 30Mar44; during radar homing in low cloud at night, flew into hill, Creag a' Chrionaich, near Lothbeg, Sutherland, 15Aug44 (15 killed)

DP198   TOC Wig Bay 3Dec43; damaged in gale at Wig Bay 25Jan44; repaired on site by SBL 1Feb44; Calshot 17Aug44; Castle Archdale Reserve Pool 24Aug44; 423 Sqn [J] 3Sep44; repaired on site by S&HL 11Apr45; delivered to Greenock 10May45 for conversion to Mk.V; 57 MU 30May46; SB&HL 1Jul49; 57 MU 1Mar50; 209 Sqn [V, W] 5Aug50; 205 Sqn [O] 1Jan53; FBSU 29Apr53; delivered to SB&HL 28Oct53; test-flown 1Mar55; delivered to FBSU 11Mar55; 201 Sqn [A:B, 201:A] 2May56; last RAF aircraft to land on River Thames during a Battle of Britain week, Sep56; FBSU 11Feb57; 205/209 Sqn [W] 10Jul57; SOC 1Jun59 (the RAF Sunderland on charge the longest, at 14 years 9 months); scrapped by Chinese metal dealers

DP199   TOC Wig Bay 4Jan44; 57 MU same day; Calshot 28Jan44; 57 MU 24Feb44; delivered to 461 Sqn [UT:U] 27Mar44; struck obstruction on night take-off from Castle Archdale 16Mar45; repaired on site by S&HL 21Mar45; S&HL for conversion to Mk.V 19Jun45; 57 MU 13Sep45; S&HL 19Aug47; 57 MU 16Mar48; left for Far East via Calshot 29Apr48; delivered to 88 Sqn [C] 19May48; left for UK 12May50; 57 MU 23May50; SB&HL 25May50; test-flown 29May51; 57 MU 6Jun51; FBSU 7Jul53; non-effective stock 22Feb54; sold for scrap to BKL Alloys, King's Norton, Birmingham, 30Jun55

DP200   TOC 57 MU 14Jan44; delivered to 461 Sqn [2:X] 28Mar44; collided with ML878 while moored at Sullom Voe 1Oct44; Shorts for conversion to Mk.V 26Jan45; 423 Sqn 9Jun45; 4 (C) OTU [TA:T] 30Jun45; delivered to 272 MU 9Feb46; delivered to 57 MU 3Oct46; delivered to SB&HL 30Jan52; delivered to FBSU 27Jun52; 230 Sqn [B:Z/230:Z] 11Feb54; via Kalafrana to Far East May55; returned Jul55; Station Flight Pembroke Dock 5Oct56; FBSU 18Dec56 and noted there 9Feb57 devoid of fin and engines, coded 230:Z in red; non-effective stock 11Mar57 and noted again 17Aug57; sold for scrap to International Alloys, Aylesbury, Bucks 4Oct57

25 Sunderlands Mk.III built by Short Bros Ltd, Rochester under Contract B.78939/40:

DV956   TOC Pembroke Dock 19Jun42; delivered to 95 Sqn [L] 7Jul42; 302 FTU 18Jan44; despatched to 95 Sqn 29Feb44; delivered to 95 Sqn [L] 6Mar44; delivered to 343 Sqn 22Mar44; 95 Sqn [H] (? date); lost propeller on approach to Bathurst 15Feb45; repaired on site; ditched at 12°51'N 21°56'W 30Apr45 after engine failure; crew rescued by MV *Guine* and taken to Cape Verde Is; SOC 6May45

DV957   TOC Pembroke Dock 27Jun42; delivered to 95 Sqn [K] 17Jul42; flew into hill 1 ml (1.6 km) W of Wellington, Sierra Leone, 3Sep42 and destroyed by fire (whole crew killed)

DV958   TOC Pembroke Dock 30Jun42; delivered to 202 Sqn [AX:T] 12Jul42; delivered to 119 Sqn 29Sep42; approaching to land at Pembroke Dock 26Jan43, starboard engines failed at 600 ft, aircraft bounced on alighting, losing port float; repaired on site; broke from mooring at Pembroke Dock and drifted onto rocks 26Apr43; repaired on site by SBL; 228 Sqn 19Oct43; flying accident Cat AC 1Dec43; repaired on site by SBL 3Dec43; Calshot 10Jun44; delivered to 10 (RAAF) Sqn [RB:E] 24Jul44; delivered to Scottish Aviation, Largs, 29Nov44 for disposal; delivered to 272 MU 2Oct45; scrapped 3Dec45; SOC 26Apr46

DV959   TOC Pembroke Dock 6Jul42; delivered to 204 Sqn 17Jul42; Pembroke Dock 11Dec42; 204 Sqn [KG:F]; SOC 21Jun45 and scuttled at Jui

DV960   TOC Pembroke Dock 9Jul42; delivered to 461 Sqn [UT:H, later 2:H] 26Jul42; Cat AC 17May43; fell off tail trolley when engines being run up 2Feb44, damaging hull; repaired on site; delivered to Greenock 14Jun44; delivered to 131 (C) OTU 9Aug44; pilot throttled back on take-off from Killadeas 9Oct44 when he noticed pitot head cover had not been removed, aircraft ran onto rocks; repaired on site; SOC 31May45

DV961   TOC Pembroke Dock 14Jul42; delivered to 461 Sqn [A, later I] 18Jul42; 1 FBSU 14Nov42; returned to 461 Sqn 31Dec42; practice bomb fell off rack and exploded on floor 11Jun43; damaged at Pembroke Dock moorings 9Mar44 by tow-rope between tanker and tug; delivered to 4 (C) OTU 11Mar44 to become GI airframe **4666M**; SOC 18Dec44

DV962   TOC Pembroke Dock 23Jul42; Pembroke stored reserve; 202 Sqn [TQ:Q] 14Aug42; 119 Sqn [Q] 28Sep42; 461 Sqn 26Apr43; caught fire at moorings (or in hangar?) at Pembroke Dock 7Jun43 while being cleaned with fuel and partially destroyed; rear half of aircraft married to front half of DV980 and returned to service as DV980

DV963   TOC Pembroke Dock 30Jul42; delivered to 95 Sqn [B] 21Aug42; swung by squall at Gibraltar 14Jun45 while being towed, and struck dinghy; SOC 13Jul45

Sunderland Mk.III DV963 [B] of 95 Squadron alights on the calm waters of the Gambia River at Bathurst. (P J Christopher)

DV964 TOC Pembroke Dock 1Aug42; Pembroke Dock stored reserve; delivered to 95 Sqn [C] 20Aug42; left for UK 21Mar44; SB(W)L, Windermere, 9Apr44; 57 MU 12Oct44; sold to SB(R&B)L 21Jun45; converted to Sandringham 2 **G-AGPZ** (see Chapter 5)

DV965 TOC Pembroke Dock 11Aug42; Pembroke Dock stored reserve; damaged by three Vichy French fighters on ferry flight to West Africa; delivered to 204 Sqn [A] 17Aug42; force-landed on sea between Bathurst and Freetown 24Sep42 and towed to Freetown by corvette 26Sep42; suggested to Free French at Dakar Oct43 (but see Part 5)

DV966 TOC Pembroke Dock 11Aug42; collided with boom while taxying at Mount Batten 4Sep42; repaired on site by SBL 9Sep42; delivered to 204 Sqn [KG:D] 16Sep42; 57 MU 12Jun45; damaged beyond repair in gale at Wig Bay 21Sep45; SOC 13Oct45

DV967 TOC MAEE 12Sep42; struck by *LCT395* in gale at Helensburgh 15Sep42; repaired on site SBL 30Sep42; 1 FBSU 20Mar43; 228 Sqn [U] 2Apr43; shot down by flak from *U-564* over Bay of Biscay 13Jun43 (11 killed)

DV968 TOC Wig Bay 22Aug42; 461 Sqn [2:M] 24Sep42; 1 FBSU 27Mar43; 461 Sqn [UT:M] 27Apr43; sank *U-332* 2May43; with JM708, helped sink *U-106* 2Aug43; shot down by Ju.88s over Bay of Biscay 13Aug43 (11 killed); SOC 31Aug43

DV969 TOC Pembroke Dock 26Aug42; 10 (RAAF) Sqn [RB:E] 6Sep42; helped sink *U-563* 31May43; attacked and damaged by four Ju.88s 27Jul43; shot down by Ju.88s over Bay of Biscay 21Sep43 (11 killed)

DV970 TOC Pembroke Dock 25Aug42; delivered to 228 Sqn [DQ:E] 17Sep42; damaged in blizzard at Reykjavik 16Mar43; repaired in works by SBL14Apr43; 1 FBSU 21Sep43; ran aground at Wig Bay while taxying during ferry flight 26Sep43; repaired on site by SBL 29Sep43; returned to 228 Sqn 12Nov43; struck by pinnace at Pembroke Dock 10Jan44; repaired on site; 422 Sqn [2:T] 15May44; 4 (C) OTU 11Jul44; SOC 26Jun45

DV971 TOC Pembroke Dock 1Sep42; 119 Sqn [A] 16Sep42; struck buoy on alighting in Angle Bay 30Nov42; repaired on site; failed to return from patrol approx 200 mls (320 km) SW of Land's End 15Dec42 (11 killed)

DV972 TOC Pembroke Dock 10Sep42; 119 Sqn 16Sep42; ditched in Bristol Channel 25Nov42 after own depth charges exploded (no casualties); SOC 26Nov42

DV973 TOC Pembroke Dock 23Sep42; delivered to 95 Sqn [J, later P] 15Oct42; crashed on alighting at Bathurst 13Apr44 (3 killed); SOC 18May44

DV974 TOC 204 Sqn 21Sep42; 95 Sqn 28Sep42; delivered to 204 Sqn [KG:G]14Oct42; crashed on alighting at Bathurst from Port Etienne at night 1Oct43 and sank (3 killed, 7 injured); SOC 11Nov43

DV975 TOC Pembroke Dock 23Sep42; delivered to 95 Sqn [H] 15Oct42; crashed in Bunce River (Sierra Leone) and destroyed by fire at Jui 28Nov42 after direction-finding exercise with high-speed launch (7 killed, 4 injured); remains later blown up

DV976 TOC SBL DTD 31Dec43; repaired in works by SBL 21Mar44; 57 MU 8Jul44; SBL for conversion to Mk.V 22Mar45; 57 MU 14Jul45; delivered to MAEE 13Nov46; engine caught fire in air and fell off 21Oct47, aircraft ditched and overturned 2.5 mls (4 km) WSW of Southend-on-Sea, Essex (4 killed, 6 injured)

DV977 TOC Pembroke Dock 30Sep42; delivered to 228 Sqn [DQ:V] 29Oct42; shot down by Ju.88s over Bay of Biscay 12Jul43 (11 killed); SOC 31Jul43

DV978 TOC Pembroke Dock 6Oct42; delivered to 246 Sqn [E] 18Feb43; ferried to Pembroke Dock 30Apr43; 228 Sqn 5May43; collided with JM678 while under tow at Pembroke Dock at night 30Oct43; repaired on site by SBL 2Nov43; 423 Sqn [3:N, later 3:P] 15May44; 131 (C) OTU 31Jul44; delivered to 2 FBSU for maintenance 2Dec44; damaged in gale, overturned and sank while being towed to shore at Duross Point, Greenock, 4Dec44

DV979 TOC Pembroke Dock 5Oct42; 246 Sqn [F] 27Oct42; crashed on alighting off Black Rock, Loch Indaal, Islay, 24Jan43, on return from operational sortie (9 killed, 3 injured)

DV980 TOC Pembroke Dock 12Oct42; 246 Sqn [G] 27Oct42; damaged in gale at Loch Indaal, Islay, 5Feb43; repaired on site; struck by EJ137 at Loch Indaal moorings 15Apr43; ferried to Pembroke Dock 30Apr43; 228 Sqn [DQ:G, G] 5May43; fell off beaching trolley while being towed 1Jun43, damaging rear hull and fuselage; front half of aircraft married to rear half of DV962; resulting aircraft flown as DV980 *Half & Half*; struck flotsam on take-off from Pembroke Dock 6Feb44; repaired on site by Shorts 11Feb44; 423 Sqn [A] 11May44; 131 (C) OTU 4Aug44; flying accident Cat AC; repaired on site 13Nov44; SOC 14Jun45

20 Sunderlands Mk.III built by Short & Harland Ltd, Belfast under Contract B.76674/40:

DV985 c/n SH.76; TOC Pembroke Dock 4May43; 461 Sqn 9May43; 308 FTU 10Jun43; bounced on alighting at Gibraltar 4Aug43, damaging a float; repaired on site; to Free French at Dakar 9Aug43 (see Part 5)

DV986 c/n SH.77; TOC 461 Sqn 19May43; 308 FTU 10Jun43; flying accident Cat AC 4Aug43; to Free French at Dakar 27Aug43 (see Part 5)

DV987 c/n SH.78; TOC Pembroke Dock 31May43; 308 FTU 11Jun43; to Free French at Dakar 1Sep43 (see Part 5)

DV988 c/n SH.79; TOC Pembroke Dock 29May43; 228 Sqn 20Jun43; struck by refueller at Pembroke Dock moorings 13Oct43; repaired on site by SBL 21Oct43; 422 Sqn [2:D] 15May44; delivered to Greenock for maintenance 6Jul44; delivered to 4 (C) OTU 9Sep44; 272 MU 13Jul45; SOC 26Mar47

DV989 c/n SH.80; TOC Pembroke Dock 3Jun43; 1 FBSU 20Jul43; 461 Sqn [F] 3Aug43; struck anti-submarine defence boom off Mount Batten 30Nov43 while taxying at night; repaired on site 12Dec43; 131 (C) OTU 27Oct44; repaired on site by S&HL 10May45; 57 MU 12Jun45; SOC 28Jun45

DV990 c/n SH.605; TOC Pembroke Dock 16Jun43; 422 Sqn [2:R] 8Sep43; damaged by flak while attacking blockade runner 27Dec43; repaired on site; ran aground at Castle Archdale 23Jan44 while taxying at night; repaired on site; shot down by flak from U-boat at 63°34'N 03°02'E 24May44 (12 killed)

DV991 c/n SH.615; TOC Pembroke Dock 30Jun43; 3 FBSU 18Jul43; 1 FBSU same day; delivered to 204 Sqn [KG:G, KG:Q] 1Nov43; crashed on take-off from Bathurst for operational sortie 13Jul44, lost a float in heavy swell, wing dragged in water and aircraft began to sink; some crew climbed onto wing but depth charges exploded (7 killed, 2 missing)

DV992 c/n SH.632; TOC Pembroke Dock 30Jun43; 1 FBSU 20Jul43; 330 Sqn [WH:H] 23Sep43; Calshot 21Jul44; 4 (C) OTU [AA] 29Aug44; during heavy rain at night, hit buoy on second attempt to alight at Alness 6Nov44 and sank in Nigg Bay (12 killed)

DV993 c/n SH.639; TOC Pembroke Dock 7Jul43; 1 FBSU 20Jul43; 10 (RAAF) Sqn [RB:T] 23Sep43; shot down by enemy aircraft over Bay of Biscay 17Nov43 (11 killed)

DV994 c/n SH.647; TOC 1 FBSU 13Jul43; 422 Sqn [2:T] 5Oct43; 4 (C) OTU 29Apr44; lost propeller, damaging float and aileron, force-landed at Alness and drifted into barge 7Aug44; repaired on site; lost propeller and engine caught fire 26Nov44; repaired on site; 272 MU 21Mar46; SOC 26Mar47

DW104 c/n SH.663; TOC 1 FBSU 8Aug43; delivered to 204 Sqn [KG:K] 12Nov43; force-landed in open sea 9Apr44; crew of 10 transferred to launch, aircraft towed to Bathurst by pinnace; force-landed short of fuel 18Dec44, taken in tow 22Dec44, all crew safe; 57 MU 15Jun45; SOC 25Oct45

DW105 c/n SH.671; TOC Wig Bay 9Aug43; delivered to 95 Sqn [T] 22Oct43; 8 mins after take-off from Port Etienne on 5Jan44, turned back with starboard inner engine on fire and smoke filling flight deck; failed to alight and crashed into water just S of Cansado Point (9 killed, 1 injured)

DW106 c/n SH.679; TOC 1 FBSU 20Aug43; allocated to 270 Sqn 5Dec43; despatched to West Africa 12Dec43 but lost between UK and Gibraltar 18Dec43 (19 killed)

DW107 c/n SH.689; TOC Wig Bay 31Aug43; 1 FBSU 3Sep43; 308 FTU ; delivered to 95 Sqn [R] 14Dec43; sank in severe storm at Bathurst 15Oct44 but dragged to slipway and scrapped

DW108 c/n SH.706; TOC 1 FBSU 2Sep43, delivered Belfast - Wig Bay 16Sep43; 270 Sqn 5Dec43; 308 FTU; struck by EK584 at moorings in Angle Bay 11Jan44; delivered to 270 Sqn [Y] 14Feb44; crashed on alighting at Jui 27Sep44 (4 killed)

DW109 c/n SH.714; TOC 1 FBSU 7Sep43; 270 Sqn [Q] 5Dec43; struck by JM683 while moored at Pembroke Dock 29Dec43; repaired on site 31Dec43; delivered to 270 Sqn 13Feb44; Mount Batten at unknown date; 57 MU 24Jun45; sold for scrap to Phoenix & Clifton Ironworks, Coatbridge, 10Mar47

DW110 c/n SH.721; TOC 1 FBSU 18Sep43; 228 Sqn 20Nov43; struck buoy while taxying at Pembroke Dock at night 28Dec43; repaired on site 31Dec43; in bad weather, flew into Blue Stack Mountains, Co Donegal (Irish Republic) 31Jan44 after being diverted to Castle Archdale (7 killed, 5 injured)

DW111 c/n SH.730; TOC 1 FBSU 5Oct43; 270 Sqn 8Dec43; 1 FBSU 21Dec43; 57 MU 23Jan44; 423 Sqn [3:S] 13May44; 4 (C) OTU 29Aug44; 57 MU 21Jul45; sold for scrap to Phoenix & Clifton Ironworks, Coatbridge, 10Mar47

DW112 c/n SH.744; TOC 1 FBSU 7Oct43; 423 Sqn 8Dec43; 1 FBSU 28Dec43; 57 MU 25Jan44; 302 FTU 15Apr44; despatched to Ceylon 19May44; 230 Sqn; Iraq Communications Flight; SOC 29Aug46

DW113 c/n SH.750; TOC 1 FBSU 6Oct43; delivered to 10 (RAAF) Sqn [RB:V] 10Jan44; delivered to Scottish Aviation, Largs, 29Nov44 for disposal; SOC 28Dec45

15 Sunderlands Mk.III built by Short Bros Ltd, Rochester under Contract B.78939/40:

EJ131 TOC 230 Sqn [NM:T] 11Dec42; while escorting naval force off East Africa on 20Aug43, probably ran out of fuel; captain transmitted SOS saying it was force-landing; searches over three days found nothing but later found to have crashed in Mozambique (9 killed)

EJ132 TOC Pembroke Dock 27Oct42; 461 Sqn same day; delivered to 230 Sqn [NM:X] 31Dec42; SOC 29May45

EJ133 TOC Pembroke Dock 21Oct42; 119 Sqn [F] 11Nov42; struck by DP176 while moored at Pembroke Dock 22Mar43; repaired on site; 461 Sqn [T] 26Apr43; repaired on site by SBL 2May43; 4 (C) OTU [AQ] 13Apr44; struck tender on alighting at Pembroke Dock 9Dec44; 57 MU; SOC 3May45

Sunderland Mk.III DV980 [G] of 228 Squadron suffered a handling accident at Pembroke Dock on 1st June 1943 but eventually formed the front half of a composite airframe with DV962, returning to service as DV980. (Andrew Hendrie collection)

Sunderland Mk.III EJ143 [S] of 230 Squadron in SE Asia markings taking off on a patrol from Diego Garcia. (P H T Green collection)

Another view of EJ143[S], here being serviced in rough-and-ready conditions at Koggala, Ceylon in 1944/45. (P H T Green collection)

EJ144 [A] was a Sunderland Mk.III of 95 Squadron, at Port Etienne in French Morocco on 8th June 1943. (P H T Green collection)

EJ134 TOC Pembroke Dock 2Nov42; 461 Sqn [N] 31Dec42; damaged by six Ju.88s over Bay of Biscay 2Feb43 and beached at Praa Sands, Marazion, Cornwall (1 killed, 3 injured); heavy seas then reduced aircraft to wreck

EJ135 TOC Pembroke Dock 6Nov42; 230 Sqn [N] 29Nov42; an engine cut while taxying at Pembroke Dock 12Dec42 and aircraft struck W4030; a float collapsed while taxying at Pembroke Dock 26Dec42; Pembroke Dock stored reserve 6Jul43; 1 FBSU 12Aug43; 57 MU 20Jan44; delivered to Greenock for mods 12Jun44; delivered to 302 FTU 15Jun44; despatched to West Africa 28Jun44; 490 Sqn [N] 7.44; 343 Sqn 4Jul44;(see Part 5)

EJ136 TOC Pembroke Dock 10Nov42; 230 Sqn [NM:Y] 4Dec42; ferried to Middle East 31Jan43; SOC 15Apr45

EJ137 TOC Pembroke Dock 12Nov42; 246 Sqn [K] 24Nov42; engine cut while taxying in Loch Indaal, Islay, 15Apr43, drifted into DV980; repaired on site; ferried to Pembroke Dock 30Apr43; 330 Sqn 1May43; 201 Sqn [ZM:T] 8May43; 1 FBSU 17May43; 201 Sqn [ZM:T] 22May43; 1 FBSU 7Sep43; 201 Sqn 22Oct43; struck obstruction while taxying at night at Castle Archdale 2Dec43; repaired on site by S&HL 6Dec43; 4 (C) OTU 12Apr44; depth charges released in error while inboard 10May44; repaired on site by S&HL 15May44; delivered to 2 FBSU 17Sep44; returned to 4 (C) OTU 5Mar45; SOC 28Jun45

EJ138 TOC Pembroke Dock 26Feb43; 308 FTU 3Jul43; 461 Sqn [J] 6Nov43; struck buoy at Pembroke Dock 30Jul44, damaging mainplane and radar; delivered to 2 FBSU 29Dec44 for conversion to Mk.V; delivered to 330 Sqn [WH:Y] 21Apr45; delivered to 2 FBSU for maintenance 24Jun45; broke loose and ran onto rocks at Trondheim, Norway, 2Nov45; SOC 16Nov45

EJ139 TOC Pembroke Dock 21Nov42; delivered to 246 Sqn [L] 3Jan43; repaired on site by SBL 16Mar43; ferried to Pembroke Dock 30Apr43; 228 Sqn [L] 5May43; shot down by flak from *U-441* over Bay of Biscay 24May43 (11 killed); SOC 30May43

EJ140 TOC Pembroke Dock 28Nov42; 230 Sqn [NM:V] 10Dec42; delivered to Middle East 21Jan43; flew into Sangala Hill (3500 ft/ 1067 m), near Voi (Kenya) 29Dec43, during MF/DF calibration flight (entire crew of 9 killed and buried near crash site)

EJ141 TOC Pembroke Dock 2Dec42; 230 Sqn [NM:R] 10Dec42; taxied into W4030 at Pembroke Dock 13Jan43; repaired on site; 205 Sqn 1Mar45; force-landed off Maldive Islands 31Mar45 after engine failure; SOC 2Jun45

EJ142 TOC Pembroke Dock 4Dec42; 119 Sqn [B] 18Dec42; 461 Sqn [UT:S] 26Apr43; struck by ML875 while moored at Pembroke Dock 27Apr44; repaired on site; delivered to 4 (C) OTU 12May44; 57 MU 16Jun45; SOC 12Jul45

EJ143 TOC Pembroke Dock 16Dec42; delivered to 230 Sqn [NM:S] 10Feb43; SOC 12Mar45

EJ144 TOC Pembroke Dock 18Dec42; 95 Sqn [A *Archimedes*] 10Jan43; delivered to Jui 1Mar43; sank in severe storm at Bathurst 15Oct44

EJ145 TOC Pembroke Dock 22Dec42; Pembroke Dock stored reserve; delivered to 204 Sqn KG:[P] 4Mar43; damaged in heavy landing at Bathurst 20Jun43; repaired on site; failed to return to Port Etienne after patrol 17Jul43 (engine failure); last position reported as 23°03'N 17°46'W; crew picked up by Spanish fishing boat and landed at Villa Cisneros, Rio de Oro

10 Sunderlands Mk.III built by Short Bros (Windermere) Ltd, Windermere under Contract 234/SAS/40/C.20(b):

EJ149 TOC Calshot 10Feb44; 57 MU 5Mar44; 4 (C) OTU [RR] 29Apr44; delivered to 272 MU 20Sep44; SOC 26Mar47

EJ150 TOC 57 MU 6Mar44; 201 Sqn [NS:W] 30Mar44; sank *U-107* 18Aug44; an engine cut while taxying at Castle Archdale, struck ML783,

CHAPTER 5 : INDIVIDUAL AIRCRAFT HISTORIES

Sunderland MR.5 EJ155 [U] of 205/209 Squadron receiving routine attention on the slipway at Seletar in 1955. (Roy Green collection)

19Jan45; repaired on site by S&HL 3Feb45; 57 MU 3Jul45; 272 MU 31Oct45; SOC 23Mar47

EJ151 TOC 57 MU 23Mar44; 201 Sqn 6Apr44; 228 Sqn 20Apr44; 422 Sqn [DG:H, H] 11Nov44; 57 MU 3Jun45; SOC 28Jun45

EJ152 TOC 57 MU 12Apr44; 4 (C) OTU [TT] 3May44; 57 MU 15Jul44; allotted to Saro, East Cowes, 15Apr45 for trials of automatic mooring pick-up device, arrived from Wig Bay 8Oct45; re-allotted for mock-up and ground trials of power-operated controls equipment for Saro Princess; damaged by fire 16Jul47; disposed of 9Sep48

EJ153 TOC 57 MU 10May44; Calshot Servicing Wing 24May44; Pembroke Dock stored reserve 7Jun44; delivered to 461 Sqn [S] 12Jun44; S&HL 13Apr45 for conversion to Mk.V; 57 MU 4Jul45; SB&HL for mods 24May48; 57 MU 7Oct48; 235 OCU [D:Q] 1Nov49; flying accident Cat 5c 1Nov49; skimmed top of hill, piercing hull, Jun51, but alighted safely; subsequently nicknamed *The Ploughman*; repaired on site SB&HL 19Jun51; recat 3R 21Jun51; SB&HL 15Oct53; test-flown 14Oct54; repaired in works 27Oct54; delivered to FBSU 1Nov54; 230 Sqn [B:R, 230:R] 7Jan55; via Kalafrana to Far East May55, returned Jul55; struck rock while taxying at Castle Archdale 30Oct56; 278 MU 2Nov56 and SOC

EJ154 TOC Wig Bay 13May44; Calshot Servicing Wing 24May44; Pembroke Dock stored reserve 7Jun44; 461 Sqn [T] 31Jul44; struck marine craft on alighting at Pembroke Dock 13Dec44, beached in Angle Bay and later submerged

EJ155 TOC Wig Bay 2Jun44; Calshot 25Jun44; 330 Sqn [WH:O] 11Jul44; delivered to Greenock 2Jan45 for repair to float; returned to 330 Sqn 7Jan45; damaged in collision with Northrop N-3PB 306 of RNoAF during photo session at Sullom Voe 25Jan45; repaired on site; S&HL 24Jun45 for conversion to Mk.V; 4 (C) OTU 7Jul45; Wig Bay 10Jul46; SB&HL 8Feb52 for mods; delivered to FBSU 12Aug52; left for Far East 30Nov52 but became unserviceable at Kalafrana; delivered to 88 Sqn [D] 31Dec52; 209 Sqn 9Oct54; 205/209 Sqn [U] 1Jan55; lost port float on alighting in Borneo 21Feb55, damaging propeller; repaired on site by local labour; FBSU 16Nov55; non-effective stock 8Aug56; noted stored at FBSU 9 & 17Aug57 coded U in black; sold for scrap to International Alloys Ltd, Aylesbury, 4Oct57

EJ156 TOC 57 MU 23Jun44; Calshot 11Jul44; 423 Sqn 25Jul44; depth charges dropped off racks onto deck in flight 4Aug44; repaired on site; depth charges exploded on impact during practice attack and damaged aircraft 11Aug44; repaired on site by S&HL; sold to S&HL 3Jan46 and regd **G-AGWW** (see Chapter 6)

EJ157 TOC Wig Bay 4Jul44; Calshot 22Jul44; 423 Sqn [YI:K] 14Aug44; damaged when engine caught fire on take-off from Castle Archdale 12May45; repaired on site by S&HL but SOC 3Aug45

EJ158 TOC 57 MU 2Aug44; Calshot 24Aug44; 423 Sqn [YI:M] 9Sep44; engine cut on take-off from Castle Archdale 15Jan45, swung and struck buoy; repaired on site by S&HL; hull damaged while taxying at Castle Archdale 10Jun45; repaired on site by S&HL; 272 MU 30Oct45; SOC 26Mar47

10 Sunderlands Mk.III built by Short & Harland Ltd, Belfast under Contract B.76674/40:

EJ163 c/n SH.762; TOC Wig Bay 21Oct43; 57 MU 6Dec43; 302 FTU 16Apr44; despatched to West Africa 13May44; delivered to 95 Sqn [K] 15May44; 343 Sqn; to Aéronautique navale 15May45 (see Part 5)

EJ164 c/n SH.774; TOC Wig Bay 11Nov43; 308 FTU 24Dec43; Calshot 29Jan44; delivered to 270 Sqn [E] 16Feb44; ditched in S Atlantic at 04°57N 03°35W 3Oct44; crew rescued by hospital ship *Chantilly*

EJ165 c/n SH.793; flying accident Cat AC before delivery; repaired on site by S&HL 30Nov43; TOC Wig Bay 1Dec43; 57 MU 23Jan44; 302 FTU 19Feb44; despatched to West Africa 30Apr44, arrived 7May44; delivered to 490 Sqn [R] by 11Jun44; 57 MU 22Jan45; sold for scrap to Phoenix & Clifton Ironworks, Coatbridge, 10Mar47

An earlier photograph of Sunderland GR.5 EJ155, bound for service with 88 Squadron at Seletar, which suffered technical problems and spent most of December 1952 at Kalafrana. (P H T Green collection)

Just off the slipway and with outer engines running is Sunderland Mk.III EK575 of 423 Squadron at Castle Archdale wearing the Coastal Command Squadron code [2:C].
(P H T Green collection)

Sunderland Mk.III EK595 of the Iraq Communications Flight was damaged by a barge at Basra on 5th March 1946 and is seen here being scuttled at Khor Kuwai, Oman on 1st April.
(P H T Green collection)

No more than a couple of feet above the water, Sunderland Mk.III EK591 [2:U] of 422 Squadron. *(P H T Green collection)*

EJ166 destroyed by fire at Queen's Island factory, Belfast, Nov43 before delivery; formally SOC 1Dec44

EJ167 c/n SH.818; TOC Wig Bay 30Nov43; damaged in gale at Wig Bay 25Jan44; repaired on site by SBL 1Feb44; 57 MU 25Nov44; SB&HL for conversion to Mk.V 9Jul52; test-flown 12May53 as **NZ4116**; delivered to Wig Bay 4Jun53 for RNZAF as **NZ4116**, to Belfast 11Jun53, to Calshot 12Jun53 on first leg of ferry flight, using radio callsign MCVLC (see Part 3)

EJ168 c/n SH.833; TOC 57 MU 4Jan44; 302 FTU 2Feb44; despatched to West Africa 15Mar44; 343 Sqn 29Mar44; to Aéronautique navale Jun45 (see Part 5)

EJ169 c/n SH.847; TOC 57 MU 9Jan44; delivered to 302 FTU 31Mar44; despatched to West Africa 25Apr44, arrived 30Apr44; delivered to 490 Sqn [Y] by 2Jun44; 343 Sqn; 57 MU 18Jun45; sold for scrap to Phoenix & Clifton Ironworks, Coatbridge, 10Mar47

EJ170 c/n SH.868 ?; TOC 57 MU 16Feb44; conv Mk.V; sold to S&HL 13May47 and conv to Sandringham 3 **G-AGTZ** (see Chapter 6)

EJ171 c/n SH.869; TOC 57 MU 5Feb44; SBL 12Sep44 for conversion to Mk.V; 302 FTU 10Apr45; 57 MU 25Jul47; sold to SB&HL 22Jan48 and later regd **LV-AHH** (see Chapter 6)

EJ172 c/n SH.870; TOC 57 MU 16Jan44; converted to Mk.V 7Nov44; 302 FTU 4May45; 57 MU 30Jul45; Short Bros & Harland 4Jun47 for conversion to Sandringham 7 **G-AKCP** (see Chapter 6)

25 Sunderlands Mk.III built by Blackburn Aircraft Ltd, Dumbarton under Contract B.37753/39:

EK572 TOC Wig Bay 19Jun43; Wig Bay stored reserve; 228 Sqn [V] 12Aug43; ditched near Estaca de Bares, northern coast of Spain, 10Oct43 (12 killed, of whom six bodies were recovered by Spanish authorities)

EK573 TOC Wig Bay 23Jun43; Wig Bay stored reserve; 10 (RAAF) Sqn [RB:P] 14Aug43; lost a propeller, which struck another one, and ditched off Isles of Scilly 11Nov43 (1 injured); ditched in open sea 17Sep44 after an engine caught fire and fell off; towed to shore by motor torpedo boat; repaired on site 21Sep44; 4 (C) OTU 17May45; 272 MU 8Sep45; SOC 23Mar47

EK574 TOC 1 FBSU 28Jun43; 10 (RAAF) Sqn [RB:Q] 16Aug43; engine caught fire on take-off from Mount Batten 1Jun44, hit buoy and sank

EK575 TOC 1 FBSU 29Jun43; 461 Sqn [2:C] 20Aug43; 228 Sqn 1Mar44; 423 Sqn 12May44; Calshot Servicing Wing 14Aug44; 10 (RAAF) Sqn [RB:G] 24Sep44; delivered to Scottish Aviation, Largs, 29Nov44 for disposal; delivered to 272 MU 20Sep45; scrapped 7Nov45; SOC 30Nov45

EK576 TOC 1 FBSU 2Jul43; 422 Sqn [2:Q] 30Aug43; 4 (C) OTU 23Jul44; flying accident Cat AC 30Oct44; flying accident Cat AC 5May45; repaired on site by SB(R&B)L 11May45; 57 MU 20Jun45; SOC 12Jul45

EK577 TOC 1 FBSU 7Jul43; 461 Sqn [D] 21Aug43; sank *U-571* 28Jan44; delivered to 4 (C) OTU 12Apr44; depth charge dropped off inside fuselage 16Jun44; repaired on site by SBL 27Jun44; bounced on alighting at Alness 25Nov44 and lost a float; repaired on site by SBL 30Nov44; SOC 18Jul45

EK578 TOC 1 FBSU 12Jul43; 461 [E] Sqn 21Aug43; on anti-submarine patrol over Bay of Biscay 16Sep43, was attacked by six Ju.88s of 5/KG.40 and ditched with three engines out of action; crew took to dinghies and were rescued by HMS *Starling* after being found by crew of a 210 Sqn Catalina

EK579 TOC 1 FBSU 14Jul43; 201 Sqn [ZM:U] 29Aug43; Calshot 16Jun44; 131 (C) OTU 4Aug44; delivered to Greenock for maintenance 19Dec44; damaged by ice at Killadeas 30Jan45; repaired on site by S&HL 12Feb45; S&HL 8Apr45 for conversion to Mk.V; 57 MU 21Jun45; sold to SB&HL 22Jan48 and later regd **LV-AHG** (see Chapter 6)

CHAPTER 5 : INDIVIDUAL AIRCRAFT HISTORIES

A 205 Squadron Sunderland MR.5, JM667 [M], formed the background to the parade marking the disbandment of 88 Squadron at Seletar on 2nd December 1954.
(P H T Green collection)

EK580 TOC Wig Bay 31Jul43; 1 FBSU 8Aug43; 204 Sqn [KG:B] 7Sep43; diverted to Bathurst after operational sortie due to bad weather during night of 9Oct44, but overshot flarepath; on second attempt, struck water, nose dug in and aircraft turned over and caught fire (4 killed, 6 injured); wreck blown up later

EK581 TOC 1 FBSU 11Aug43; 95 Sqn 7Sep43; 1 FBSU 8Sep43; 423 Sqn [3:D] 13Nov43; Cat AC 27Dec43; repaired on site 4Jan44; an engine cut while running up at Castle Archdale 21Feb44, aircraft swung and struck trees; repaired on site 24Feb44; 4 (C) OTU 23Aug44; 272 MU 21Feb46; SOC 26Mar47

EK582 TOC 1 FBSU 12Aug43; delivered to 204 Sqn [KG:L] 4Dec43; SOC and scuttled at Jui 21Jun45

EK583 TOC 1 FBSU 16Aug43; 423 Sqn [3:J] 15Nov43; ran onto shoal while taxying at Hamworthy 2Jan44; repaired on site; 131 (C) OTU 3Aug44; repaired on site 25Sep44; delivered to Greenock 11Dec44; repaired on site by S&HL 24Jun45; 57 MU 25May46; sold for scrap to Phoenix & Clifton Ironworks, Coatbridge, 10Mar47

EK584 TOC 1 FBSU 2Sep43; 308 FTU; collided with DW108 while being towed in Angle Bay 11Jan44; repaired on site 14Jan44; delivered to 270 Sqn [D] 4Feb44; returned to UK on unknown date; SOC 2Jun45

EK585 TOC 1 FBSU 25Aug43; del 270 Sqn [A, later V] 28Dec43; caught fire at moorings at Apapa (Nigeria) 7Jun44 and depth charges exploded when aircraft sank (3 ground crew slightly injured)

EK586 TOC 1 FBSU 27Aug43; 10 (RAAF) Sqn [RB:U] 6Oct43; sank *U-426* 8Jan44; abandoned take-off from Mount Batten 30Jun44 and damaged tail; repaired on site; delivered to Scottish Aviation, Largs, 7Dec44 for disposal; SOC 31Dec45

EK587 TOC 1 FBSU 3Sep43; delivered to 95 Sqn [F] 27Oct43; delivered to 204 Sqn [KG:J] 9Nov43; 343 Sqn; to Aéronautique navale 15May45 (see Part 5)

EK588 TOC Wig Bay 8Sep43; 1 FBSU 11Sep43; 270 Sqn 5Dec43; missing on ferry flight to West Africa 8Jan44

EK589 TOC Wig Bay 11Sep43; 1 FBSU 14Sep43; delivered to 270 Sqn [V] 9Jan44; an engine over-ran on take-off from Apapa 15Feb45 and aircraft swung into launch; repaired on site; SOC 9Jul45

EK590 TOC Wig Bay 16Sep43; 1 FBSU 18Sep43; 422 Sqn 21Sep43; 1 FBSU 22Sep43; 201 Sqn [ZM:Y] 30Sep43; delivered to 461 Sqn [D] 14May44; Calshot 7Jun44; 4 (C) OTU [AW] 21Jul44; repaired on site by S&HL 22Feb45; 272 MU 8Sep45; SOC 26Mar47

EK591 TOC 1 FBSU 17Sep43; 422 Sqn [2:U] 3Oct43; sank *U-625* 10Mar44 but damaged; repaired on site; 4 (C) OTU 22Jul44; 57 MU 21Jul45; SOC 4Nov45

Handed over to BOAC on 29th January 1943, Sunderland Mk.III JM665 is seen here at Kasfareet in Egypt. Coded W, which relates to the last digit of radio call-sign OQZW, it was later civil registered as G-AGEW.
(P H T Green collection)

EK592 TOC 1 FBSU 25Sep43; 270 Sqn 5Dec43; delivered to West Africa 3Jan44; to UK 2Jun44; SB(W)L 4Jun44 for conversion to Mk.V; 57 MU 24Oct44; sold for scrap Phoenix & Clifton Ironworks, Coatbridge, 10Mar47

EK593 TOC Wig Bay 7Oct43; 57 MU 6Dec43; 302 FTU 22Apr44; 204 Sqn [KG:P] 12Jun44; 57 MU 17Jun45; sold for scrap Phoenix & Clifton Ironworks, Coatbridge, 10Mar47

EK594 TOC Wig Bay 8Oct43; 201 Sqn [W] 8Dec43; 422 Sqn [2:W] 6Apr44; delivered to 10 (RAAF) Sqn [RB:D] 24Jun44; delivered to Scottish Aviation, Largs, 5Jan45 for disposal; SOC 28Dec45

EK595 TOC Wig Bay 16Oct43; 57 MU 6Dec43; 302 FTU 10Feb44; ran aground on Ganavan Sands, Oban, 24Mar44 while being towed; repaired on site 2Apr44; 201 Sqn 4Apr44; 422 Sqn 6Apr44; despatched to ACSEA 29Sep44; Iraq Communication Flight 30Sep44; delivered to 230 Sqn [NM:Q] by 13Dec44; damaged at Fanara moorings (Egypt) 14Nov45; repaired on site; Iraq & Persia Communication Flight; damaged in collision with barge at Basra (Iraq) 5Mar46; scuttled at Khor Kuwai (Oman) 1Apr46; SOC 11Apr46

EK596 TOC Wig Bay 11Oct43; 57 MU 6Dec43; 302 FTU 15Apr44; repaired on site by SBL 12Jan45; 272 MU 21Mar46; SOC 16Mar47

50 Sunderlands Mk.III built by Short Bros Ltd, Rochester under Contract B.78939/40:

JM659 TOC Pembroke Dock 29Dec42; Pembroke Dock stored reserve; lost float while landing at Pembroke Dock in bad visibility 22Feb43; despatched to East Africa 26Feb43; delivered to 230 Sqn [NM:Q] 24Mar43; to SEAC with squadron 1Mar44; struck by army

Painted black, Sunderland Mk.III JM673 [P] of 230 Squadron was named "Black Peter" and was usually flown by Wg Cdr Dundas-Bendall, the Squadron's CO. (P H T Green collection)

204 Squadron's Sunderland Mk.III JM680 [KG:J] which was struck by another Sunderland, Mk.II W6050, on take-off at Bathurst on 31st May 1943. After becoming airborne, JM680's depth charges and fuel were jettisoned but when it alighted it rapidly sank, without crew injuries. (S Ellams voa John Evans)

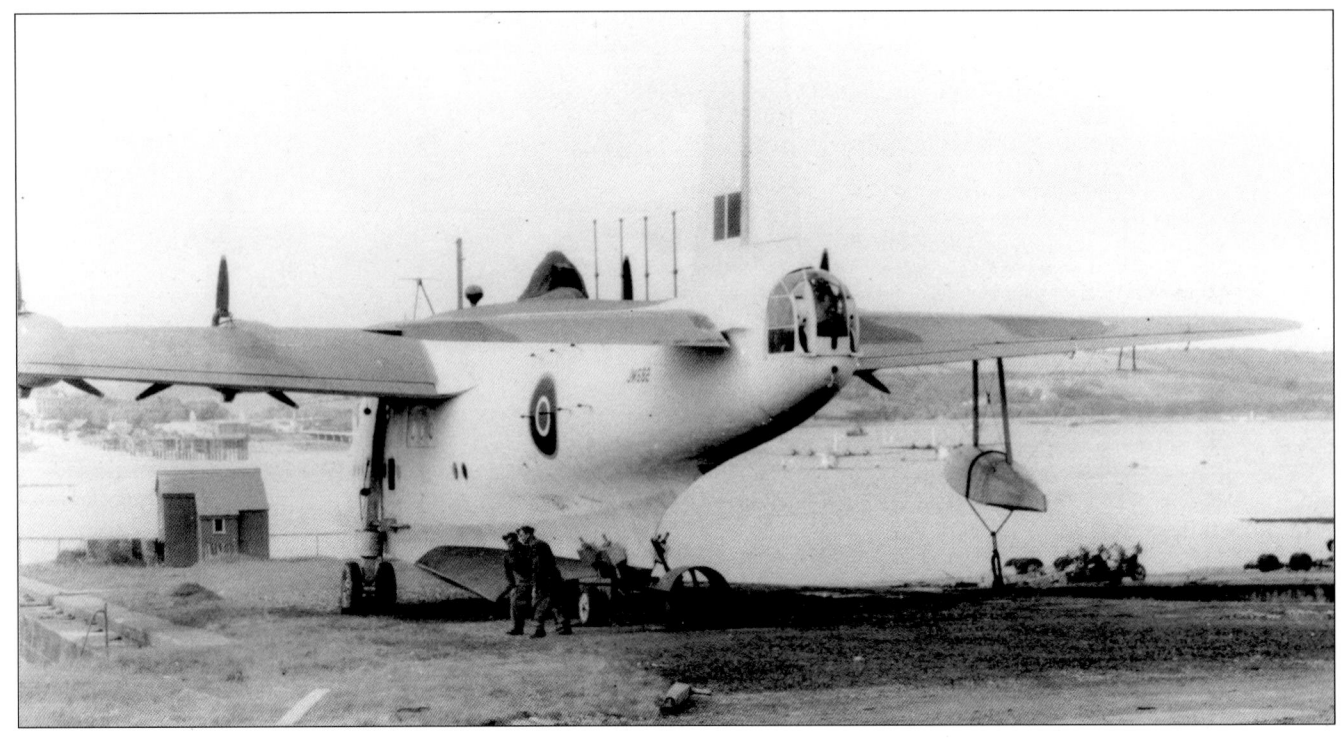

Sunderland Mk.III JM682 of 204 Squadron on a slipway at an unidentified location. It would appear that the slipway is being rolled level by two groundcrew. Other Sunderlands are visible moored offshore and near the opposite bank. (P H T Green collection)

DUKW on Brahmaputra River (India) 20Jun44; repaired on site; struck by whirlwind at Dibrugarh, on Brahmaputra River, 4Jul44 and sank

JM660 direct to BOAC, Hythe, 8Jan43; radio call-sign OQZR; later registered **G-AGER** (see Chapter 6)

JM661 direct to BOAC, Hythe, 15Jan43; radio call-sign OQZS; later registered **G-AGES** (see Chapter 6)

JM662 direct to BOAC, Hythe, 16Jan43; radio call-sign OQZT; later registered **G-AGET** (see Chapter 6)

JM663 direct to BOAC, Hythe, 21Jan43; radio call-sign OQZU; later registered **G-AGEU** (see Chapter 6)

JM664 direct to BOAC, Hythe, 29Jan43; radio call-sign OQZV; later registered **G-AGEV** (see Chapter 6)

JM665 direct to BOAC Hythe, 29Jan43; radio call-sign OQZW; later registered **G-AGEW** (see Chapter 6)

JM666 TOC Pembroke Dock 14Feb43; 330 Sqn [WH:Q] 1Mar43; 201 Sqn [ZM:Q] 23May43; 1 FBSU 12Aug43; 201 Sqn [ZM:Q] 14Aug43; struck rock while taxying at Castle Archdale 9Feb44; repaired on site 17Feb44; 423 Sqn 10May44; 131 (C) OTU 26May44; yawed after take-off from Lough Erne 29May44 due to trim tab defects; repaired on site; delivered to 2 FBSU for maintenance 13Nov44; returned to 131 (C) OTU 5Dec44; ground accident Cat AC 3Mar45; repaired on site by S&HL 8Mar45; 57 MU 15Apr45; sold for scrap Phoenix & Clifton Ironworks, Coatbridge, 10Mar47

JM667 TOC Pembroke Dock 16Feb43; 330 Sqn [WH:V] 1Mar43; blown onto Kerrera beach, Oban, after slipping moorings 5Mar43; repaired on site; ran aground while taxying in Lough Neagh 28Nov43; repaired on site; damaged by hangar door, Sullom Voe, 23Jan44; repaired on site; bounced on alighting at Sullom Voe 6Mar44 and a float torn off; repaired on site; sank *U-240* 16May44 but badly damaged by flak (1 killed); repaired on site; two engines cut, force-landed 6 mls (10 km) NE of Noup Head, Caithness, 6Jul44; SBL 11Sep44; converted to Mk.V; 302 FTU; struck by refueller at Oban moorings 14Apr45; repaired on site by SBL 22Apr45; 57 MU 21Mar46; delivered to FBSU 29May52; to FEAF via Wig Bay and return then Pembroke Dock 30Apr53; 209 Sqn [M] 29May53; FEFBWg 4Jun53; 205 Sqn [M, Q] 11Jul53; SOC 8Oct54; became GI airframe **7172M** in Far East 31Dec54; SOC 1Nov55

JM668 TOC Pembroke Dock 23Feb43; flying accident Cat AC same day; Pembroke Dock stored reserve 26May43; Wig Bay stored reserve 24Jul43; 1 FBSU 30Jul43; 4 (C) OTU 1Aug43; 1 FBSU same day; Calshot 27Sep43; 1 FBSU 25Nov43; 57 MU 20Jan44; damaged in gale at Wig Bay 25Jan44; repaired on site by SBL 1Feb44; 57 MU 30Sep44; sold for scrap to Phoenix & Clifton Ironworks, Coatbridge, 10Mar47

JM669 TOC Pembroke Dock 27Feb43; 204 Sqn [KG:A] 7Mar43; left Gibraltar at night 14Apr43; presumed to have encountered violent storm and sent message "Landing on sea"; wreckage found at 20°26'N 17°30'W, S of Port Etienne (10 killed)

JM670 TOC Pembroke Dock 25Feb43; 95 Sqn [M] 4Mar43; delivered to W Africa 1May43; 343 Sqn 17Jul44; destroyed by fire in hangar at Port Etienne 11Jan45; SOC 21Jun45

JM671 TOC Pembroke Dock 26Feb43; 95 Sqn [Z] 7Mar43; delivered to W Africa 1May43; SOC 21Jun45

JM672 TOC Pembroke Dock 1Mar43; delivered to 204 Sqn [KG:E] 12Apr43; crashed after night take-off from Jui for operational sortie 28Aug44 (3 killed, 6 including 1 passenger picked up)

JM673 TOC Pembroke Dock 4Mar43; Pembroke Dock stored reserve; delivered to 230 Sqn [NM:P] 1May43; painted black as personal aircraft of CO, Wg Cdr D Bednall and known as *Black Peter*; missing during patrol in bad weather 28Nov44, possibly hit by cyclone (10 killed)

JM674 TOC Pembroke Dock 8Mar43; 204 Sqn [KG:X] 11Apr43; to Free French at Port Etienne 30Apr43; 343 Sqn Jul43; to Aéronautique navale cFeb43; SOC 21Jun45 (see Part 5)

JM675 TOC Pembroke Dock 19Mar43; delivered to 461 Sqn [UT:O] 28Mar43; struck by refueller at Pembroke Dock 26Apr43; repaired on site 2May43; attempting to alight in Bay of Biscay to rescue men in dinghy 26May43, stalled and dived in (captain killed, remainder of crew rescued by another Sunderland, which transferred them to a destroyer)

JM676 TOC Pembroke Dock 19Mar43; 119 Sqn [H] 6Apr43; 461 Sqn [P] 26Apr43; shot down over Bay of Biscay 29Nov43 (all 12 crew killed)

JM677 TOC Pembroke Dock 26Mar43; Pembroke Dock stored reserve; 95 Sqn [S] 11Apr43; damaged a float on take-off from Port Etienne in rough seas 21Jun43; repaired on site; SOC 21Jun45

JM678 TOC Pembroke Dock 2Apr43; 228 Sqn [V] 21May43; sank *U383* 1Aug43 but damaged by flak; repaired at base; 461 Sqn [G, 2:G] 28Sep43; damage to port wing when struck by DV978, which was being towed by pinnace at Pembroke Dock 30Oct43; repaired on site by SBL 4Nov43; 228 Sqn 25Feb44; delivered to 10 (RAAF) Sqn [RB:B] 14May44; caught fire and sank at Mount Batten moorings 19Jun44 during daily inspection (3 injured); salvaged but SOC

JM679 TOC Pembroke Dock 3Apr43; Pembroke Dock stored reserve; delivered to 228 Sqn [DQ:R] 1May43; 422 Sqn [2:E] 20May44; bounced on alighting at Castle Archdale 18Jul44 and lost float; repaired on site; 4 (C) OTU 29Aug44; Blackburn, Dumbarton 14Dec44; Greenock 12May45; SOC 6Jul45

JM680 TOC Pembroke Dock 18Apr43; delivered to 204 Sqn [KG:J] 25Apr43; hit moored Sunderland W6062 of 95 Sqn on take-off from Bathurst 31May43, tearing large hole in hull; stayed airborne and circled for nearly four hours, jettisoning depth charges and fuel; alighted at end of slipway but sank immediately (crew escaped)

JM681 TOC MAEE 19Jun43; Scottish Aviation 13Jan45 for conversion to Mk.V; Greenock to Wig Bay 25Jul45; 57 MU 29Jul45; sold to S&HL 8May47 for conversion to Sandringham 5 **G-AJMZ** (see Chapter 5)

JM682 TOC Pembroke Dock 19Apr43; Pembroke Dock stored reserve; 204 Sqn [KG:H] 10May43; delivered to West Africa 1Jul43; on 15Jan45, starboard float fell off, aircraft became difficult to control but returned to base safely; 57 MU 17Jun45; sold for scrap to Phoenix & Clifton Ironworks, Coatbridge, 10Mar47

JM683 TOC Pembroke Dock 20Apr43; Pembroke Dock stored reserve; 461 Sqn [W] 6Jun43; taxied into DW109 at night at Pembroke Dock 29Dec43; repaired on site; delivered to 4 (C) OTU 13Apr44; Cat AC, repaired on site by SBL 16May45; 57 MU 19Jun45; SOC 12Jul45

JM684 TOC Pembroke Dock 30Apr43; delivered to 10 (RAAF) Sqn [RB:K] 28May43; damaged keel 5Aug44; delivered to 57 MU 18Jun45; SOC 15Jul45

JM685 TOC Pembroke Dock 3May43; 461 Sqn [X] 6Jun43; flying accident Cat B 15Aug43; Isles of Scilly to Mount Batten 10Sep43 for repair; returned to 461 Sqn 6Nov43; 228 Sqn 27Nov43; delivered to 10 (RAAF) Sqn [RB:Z] 10May44; delivered to Scottish Aviation, Largs, 7Dec44 for disposal; SOC 7Dec45

JM686 TOC Pembroke Dock 4May43; 461 Sqn [Y] 1Jun43; struck by Catalina at Pembroke Dock moorings 6Aug43; repaired on site; damaged by refueller while moored 30Nov43; delivered to 4 (C) OTU 22Apr44; delivered to 2 FBSU for maintenance 1May44; returned to 4 (C) OTU 30Jun44; SOC 28Jun45

JM687 TOC Pembroke Dock 11May43; 204 Sqn 11Jun43; missing from patrol 18Jul43 (14 killed)

JM688 TOC Pembroke Dock 21May43; 308 FTU 10Jun43; Free French at Dakar 24Jul43; 343 Sqn 29Nov43; to Aéronautique navale 21Jun45 (see Part 5)

JM689 TOC Pembroke Dock 25May43; 308 FTU 11Jun43; Free French at Dakar 1Sep43; 343 Sqn 29Nov43; to Aéronautique navale 21Jun45 (see Part 5)

JM704 TOC Pembroke Dock 24May43; Pembroke Dock stored reserve; 308 FTU 10Jun43; Free French at Dakar 7Aug43; 343 Sqn 29Nov43 (see Part 5)

JM705 TOC Pembroke Dock 28May43; Pembroke Dock stored reserve; 308 FTU 10Jun43; Free French at Dakar [3E-1/ F1]1Sep43 (see Part 5)

JM706 TOC Pembroke Dock 29May43; 308 FTU 11Jun43; delivered to W Africa 1Aug43; Free French at Dakar 25Jul43; 343 Sqn 29Nov43; (see Part 5)

JM707 TOC Pembroke Dock 5Jun43; 461 Sqn [Z] 13Jun43; shot down by Ju.88s over Bay of Biscay at 46°21'N 11°35'W 30Aug43 (11 killed); SOC 31Aug43

JM708 TOC Pembroke Dock 10Jun43; Pembroke Dock stored reserve; 228 Sqn [N] 10Jul43; sank *U-607* NW of Narvik (Norway) 13Jul43; shared sinking of *U-106* with DV968 NW of El Ferrol (Spain) 2Aug43; ditched after engine fire and foundered in Bay of Biscay 17Jan44 (crew rescued)

JM709 TOC Pembroke Dock 12Jun43; Pembroke Dock stored reserve; 228 Sqn 23Jul43; missing over Bay of Biscay 6Jan44 (11 killed)

JM710 TOC Pembroke Dock 12Jun43; 1 FBSU 19Jul43; 204 Sqn 8Aug43; 308 FTU 25Aug43; 204 Sqn [KG:L]; after patrol of Cape Verde Is on 22Sep43, flew over Bathurst flarepath at 800 feet, stalled in LH turn and crashed into sea (3 killed, 6 missing)

JM711 TOC Pembroke Dock 22Jun43; 1 FBSU 22Jul43; 308 FTU 8Aug43; hit small boat while alighting off Isles of Scilly 26Aug43; repaired on site; delivered to 230 Sqn [NM:M] by 7Oct43; Iraq Communication Flight; despatched to SEAC 1Mar44; 230 Sqn [Z] 4.46; SOC 29Aug46

JM712 TOC Pembroke Dock 25Jun43; 3 FBSU (? date); 1 FBSU 19Jul43; 422 Sqn [2:S] 3Sep43; damaged by flak from *U-470* 17Nov43 and ditched at 59°00'N 29°00'W, approx 250 mls (400 km) S of Iceland (7 survivors)

JM713 TOC MAEE 31Mar44; 4 (C) OTU 10Jul44; 57 MU 3Aug45; sold to Shorts 25Aug47 for conversion to Sandringham 6 but conversion not carried out

JM714 TOC MAEE 4Jul43; 57 MU 18Feb44; conv to Mk.V; 302 FTU 18May44; 57 MU 12Jul44; sold to Shorts 25Jan48 for conversion to Sandringham 6 **LN-LMK** (see Chapter 6)

JM715 TOC 1 FBSU 8Jul43; 57 MU 18Jan44; Scottish Aviation, Greenock, 6Apr45 for conversion to Mk.V; 57 MU 30Jul45; blown off beaching trolley at Wig Bay 21Apr47; sold to Tasman Empire Airways 30Apr47 and converted to Sandringham 4 **ZK-AMH** (see Chapter 6)

JM716 TOC 1 FBSU 21Jul43; 57 MU 8Jan44; delivered to BOAC, Hythe, 2Mar45; sold to BOAC 20Apr47 and registered **G-AHEO** (see Chapter 6)

JM717 TOC 1 FBSU 30Jul43; 57 MU 8Jan44; damaged in gale at Wig Bay 25Jan44; repaired on site 1Feb44; repaired in works 22Aug44; 302 FTU 10Feb45; delivered to 490 Sqn [O] 15Mar45; 57 MU 21Jun45; delivered to SB&HL 21Feb52 for conversion to MR.5; FBSU Wig Bay 9Jul52; to and from Belfast 23Oct53; to non-effective stock 27Oct53; SOC 31Dec53

JM716 was a Sunderland Mk.III which was supplied to BOAC after long-term storage at Wig Bay, with front turret removed and rear and dorsal turrets faired over. The significance of the letter P, not a prototype in this instance, is not known. (P H T Green collection)

JM718 TOC Wig Bay 3Aug43; 1 FBSU 8Aug43; 57 MU 8Jan44; damaged in gale at Wig Bay 25Jan44; repaired on site by Shorts 1Feb44; Shorts 20Jul44 for conversion to Mk.V; 4 (C) OTU [BY] 3Feb45; repaired in works by SB(R&B)L 3May45; bounced on alighting at Alness 5Aug45 and lost a float; repaired on site by SBL 21Aug45; delivered to 272 MU 10Jan46; delivered to 57 MU Wig Bay 11Nov46; delivered to SB&HL 10Apr49 for conversion to GR.5; test-flown Sydenham Oct49; delivered to 57 MU 6Jan50; 230 Sqn [B:Y] 10Mar50; SB&HL for mods 21Nov50; 235 OCU [D:L] 9Dec50; Cat 3R 4Apr51; repaired on site by SB&HL 5Feb52; Cat 3R 4Feb52; repaired on site by SB&HL 5Feb52; Cat 3R 7Jun52; repaired on site by SB&HL 9Jun52; SB&HL 28Sep53; test-flown 30Jul54; FBSU 9Aug54 until 27Aug54; FBTS 7Sep54; 230 Sqn [B:Y] 30Oct54; noted at Wig Bay as complete aircraft carrying code 230:Y in red 9Feb57; FBSU 5Jun57 and noted there 17Aug57; sold for scrap to International Alloys Ltd, Aylesbury, Bucks, 4Oct57

JM719 TOC 1 FBSU 23Aug43; 57 MU 8Jan44; damaged in gale at Wig Bay 25Jan44; repaired on site by SBL 1Feb44; converted to Mk.V; 302 FTU 25Apr45; 57 MU 29Apr45; 302 FTU 2May45; 57 MU 12Jul45; sold to S&HL 26May47 for conversion to Sandringham 7 **G-AKCO** (see Chapter 6)

JM720 TOC 1 FBSU 12Aug43; 228 Sqn [P] 3Dec43; 1 FBSU 8Dec43; 57 MU 8Jan44; damaged in gale at Wig Bay 25Jan44; repaired on site by SBL 1Feb44; Scottish Aviation, Greenock, 14Sep44 for conversion to Mk.V; 57 MU 1May45; 302 FTU 4May45; repaired on site by SBL 24Jul45; 57 MU 21Feb46; sold to S&HL 1Oct46 for conversion to Sandringham 6 **LN-IAW** (see Chapter 6)

JM721 TOC 1 FBSU 11Aug43; delivered to 10 (RAAF) Sqn [RB:W] 20Jan44; stalled on alighting at Mount Batten 21Oct44 and lost float; delivered to 57 MU 6Nov44; sank in Loch Ryan during gale 17Nov44, but salvaged; became GI airframe **4909M** at 1 MCTU, Corsewall

JM722 delivered direct to BOAC, Hythe, 21Aug43; radio call-sign OQZB; later registered **G-AGHV** (see Chapter 6)

50 Sunderlands Mk.III built by Short Bros Ltd, Rochester under Contract Acft.2226:

ML725 delivered direct to BOAC, Hythe, 27Aug43; radio call-sign OQZC; later registered **G-AGHW** (see Chapter 6)

ML726 delivered direct to BOAC, Hythe, 2Sep43; radio call-sign OQZX; later registered **G-AGHX** (see Chapter 6)

ML727 delivered direct to BOAC, Hythe, 3Sep43; radio call-sign OQZZ; later registered **G-AGHZ** (see Chapter 6)

ML728 delivered direct to BOAC, Hythe, 8Sep43; radio call-sign OQZA; later registered **G-AGIA** (see Chapter 6)

ML729 delivered direct to BOAC, Hythe, 15Sep43; later registered **G-AGIB** (see Chapter 6)

ML730 TOC Wig Bay 2Oct43; Mount Batten 5Dec43; left for Australia via Gibraltar 27Jan44; to RAAF as **A26-1** (see Part 2)

ML731 TOC Wig Bay 7Oct43; Mount Batten 27Jan44; left for Australia via Gibraltar 14Feb44; to RAAF as **A26-2** (see Part 2)

ML732 TOC Wig Bay 15Oct43; Mount Batten 5Dec43; left for Australia via Gibraltar 27Jan44; to RAAF as **A26-3** (see Part 2)

ML733 TOC Wig Bay 18Oct43; 57 MU 26Jan44; Mount Batten 16Feb44; left for Australia via Gibraltar 1Mar44; to RAAF as **A26-4** (see Part 2)

ML734 TOC Wig Bay 18Oct43; 57 MU 26Jan44; Mount Batten 20Feb44; left for Australia via Gibraltar 1Mar44; to RAAF as **A26-5** (see Part 2)

ML735 TOC Wig Bay 3Nov43; MAEE 27Nov43; delivered 461 Sqn [A] 27Mar44; sank *U-270* off La Pallice (France) 12Aug44; missing 30 mls (48 km) NW of Bergen (Norway) 1Oct44 (11 killed); SOC 18Oct44

ML736 TOC Wig Bay 17Nov43; 4 (C) OTU [AY] 20Nov43; repaired on site 19Feb44; sank *U-675* off Aalesund (Norway) 24May44; repaired on site 10Nov44; delivered to 272 MU 20Sep45; SOC 26Mar47

A much-used Sunderland Mk.III, ML739 [NS:N] was with 201 Squadron as seen here, then went to 461 Squadron before being converted to a Mk.V for use by 4 (C) OTU and eventual post-war service with the Aéronautique navale. (R C Sturtivant collection)

Frozen into the waters of Lough Erne in January 1945 was Sunderland Mk.III ML742 [NS:Q] of 201 Squadron, which was the only operational unit to have this aircraft on its books.
(P H T Green collection)

Coded 2:N, Sunderland Mk.III ML747 [2:N] of 461 Squadron sits high and dry on a beach.
(Andrew Hendrie collection)

ML737 TOC Wig Bay 3Nov43; 4 (C) OTU [R] 24Nov43; repaired on site 19Feb44; flying accident Cat AC 21Dec44; two engines failed, damaged beyond repair in heavy touch-down at Alness 3Feb45; SOC 13Feb45

ML738 TOC Wig Bay 7Nov43; 4 (C) OTU [B:H] 20Nov43; 57 MU 29Jan44; 4 (C) OTU 10Feb44; struck by EJ142 at Alness moorings 28May44; repaired on site by Shorts 2Jun44; control lost on take-off from Alness 3Jan45, swung, hit water and sank off Dalmore (5 killed, 2 injured); SOC 11Jan45

ML739 TOC Wig Bay 10Nov43; 57 MU 23Jan44; 201 Sqn [N, later NS:N, later NS:X] 6Apr44; 461 Sqn [W] 11Nov44; Shorts 13Apr45 for conversion to Mk.V; 4 (C) OTU 19Jun45; 302 FTU 9Apr46; 57 MU 18Jun47; SB&HL for mods 12Apr51 to 12Jan52; to Pembroke Dock 20Feb52 for Aéronautique navale (see Part 5)

ML740 TOC 6 FBSU 28Jan43; 57 MU 28Jan44; delivered to 461 Sqn [M] 19Feb44; ditched in Bay of Biscay 23Mar44 after damage by nine Ju.88s of V/KG40 (5 killed, 7 rescued after 2 days)

ML741 TOC Calshot 21Jan44; 57 MU 11Feb44; delivered to 461 Sqn [2:P, later X] 17Mar44; collided with ML757 on taxying for night take-off 28Oct44; SBL for conversion to Mk.V 6Apr45; 422 Sqn 2Jun45; 4 (C) OTU 16Jun45; CCIS 18Feb46; Cat AC at SB(R&B)L, Rochester, 20Feb46; 4 (C) OTU 1Apr46; 302 FTU 9Apr46; 57 MU 3May46; sold for scrap 13Apr50

ML742 TOC 1 FBSU 12Dec43; 57 MU 23Jan44; 201 Sqn [Q, later NS:Q] 30Mar44; swung and ran aground at Castle Archdale 15Nov44 after engine lost power; repaired on site; 423 Sqn [YI:P] by 1.45; 57 MU 3Jul45; Castle Archdale same day; delivered to 272 MU 2Nov45; SOC 26Mar47

ML743 TOC Wig Bay 4Dec43; 57 MU 23Jan44; 461 Sqn [O] 24Mar44; damaged while being launched 20May44 when beaching trolley collapsed; repaired on site 22May44; Pembroke Dock stored reserve 13Aug44; 201 Sqn [NS:A] 16Sep44; after take-off from Castle Archdale 14Mar45, flew into mountain 5 mls (8 km) NW of Killybegs, Co Donegal (Irish Republic) (12 killed); SOC 31Mar45

ML744 TOC 1 FBSU 5Dec43; 57 MU 23Jan44; delivered to 461 Sqn [UT:B] 6Apr44; 422 Sqn [2:B] 11Mar45; taxied into obstruction at Castle Archdale 27Apr45; 272 MU 29Oct45; SOC 26Mar47

ML745 TOC 6 FBSU 10Dec43; 57 MU 5Feb44; 228 Sqn [Z] 27Apr44; flying accident Cat B 1Oct44; Scottish Aviation, Greenock, 11Apr45 for conversion to Mk.V; 57 MU 21Feb46; delivered to SB&H 2Nov49; test-flown 22Jun50; delivered to 57 MU 4Jul50; delivered to 88 Sqn [B] 31Aug50; 205 Sqn [M] 1Jan53; FBSU 24Jun53; delivered to SB&HL 4Oct53; test-flown 4Nov54; delivered to FBSU 24Nov54; Cat 3R 20Aug56; repaired on site 16Sep56; Pembroke Dock 30Jan57; 205/209 Sqn [V] 21Feb57; damaged beyond repair when slipped off tail trolley 16May57; SOC 24May57

ML746 TOC Pembroke Dock 23Dec43; Calshot 16Jan44; 57 MU 5Feb44; delivered to 461 Sqn [R] 17Mar44; struck by mooring vessel at Pembroke Dock while under tow 3Oct44; repaired on site; force-landed at Pembroke Dock 14Nov44 after cockpit filled with smoke; 423 Sqn [O] 18Dec44; 272 MU 2Nov45; SOC 26Mar47

A rather poor but rare photograph of a Sunderland Mk.V ML763 of the ASWDU, wearing code [P9:Q]. *(P H T Green collection)*

When this photograph was taken, Sunderland Mk.V Prototype ML765 was in the hands of the MAEE for evaluation and experimental work. *(P H T Green collection)*

ML747   TOC Pembroke Dock 23Dec43; Calshot 10Jan44; 57 MU 29Jan44; 461 Sqn [UT:N], later [2:N] 24Feb44; S&HL 26Mar45 for conversion to Mk.V; 4 (C) OTU 15Jun45 Alness; SOC 26Aug46

ML748   TOC 57 MU 9Jan44; 6 FBSU 29Jan44; 57 MU 9Feb44; 461 Sqn [C] 6Apr44; after anti-submarine patrol on 10Jun44, force-landed on sea in lee of St Mary's, Isles of Scilly, tearing off starboard float; overturned while being towed by air-sea rescue launch and sunk by gunfire 4 mls (6.5 km) SE of St Mary's after crew had been taken on board

ML749   TOC 57 MU 4Jan44; 6 FBSU 29Jan44; 57 MU 29Feb44; 201 Sqn [O] 26Mar44; 228 Sqn [O] 22Apr44; 4 (C) OTU [B:J] 5Sep44; flare exploded inboard 13Dec44; repaired on site by SBL19Dec44; Cat AC, repaired on site 29Feb45; repaired on site by SBL 21Jun45; 57 MU 21Mar46; sold for scrap to Phoenix & Clifton Ironworks, Coatbridge, 10Mar47

ML750   TOC MAEE (date unknown); 422 Sqn [J] 6.45; 57 MU 6Jul45; Castle Archdale 8Jul45; 272 MU 22Oct45; delivered to S&HL 4Feb46 for mods; 57 MU 8Sep46; to Aéronautique navale 26Jul47 (see Part 5)

ML751   delivered direct to BOAC 13Jan44; radio call-sign OQZJ; later registered **G-AGJJ** (see Chapter 6)

ML752   FF 19Jan44; delivered direct to BOAC 21Jan44; radio call-sign OQZK; later registered **G-AGJK** (see Chapter 6)

ML753   delivered direct to BOAC 23Jan44; radio call-sign OQZL; later registered **G-AGJL** (see Chapter 6)

ML754   delivered direct to BOAC 2Feb44; radio call-sign OQZM; later registered **G-AGJM** (see Chapter 6)

ML755   delivered direct to BOAC 3Feb44; radio call-sign OQZN; later registered **G-AGJN** (see Chapter 6)

ML756   delivered direct to BOAC 3Feb44; radio call-sign OQZO; later registered **G-AGJO** (see Chapter 6)

ML757   TOC Calshot 10Feb44; 57 MU 5Mar44; delivered 461 Sqn [2:Z] 6Apr44; collided with ML741 on taxying for night take-off at Sullom Voe 28Oct44; repaired on site 3Nov44; S&HL 26Mar45 for conversion to Mk.V; 4 (C) OTU 26May45; damaged while taxying at Alness 1Nov45; repaired on site by S&HL9Nov45; 302 FTU 9Apr46; 57 MU 3May46; delivered to SB&HL for mods 19May50 (crew ferry by SZ571); ex mods 12Jun51; to Aéronautique navale 19Jun51 (see Part 5)

ML758   TOC Calshot 24Feb44; 57 MU 30Mar44; 461 Sqn [E] 6Apr44; struck by NJ189 at Pembroke Dock moorings 8Apr45; repaired on site; 330 Sqn [WH:O] 2May45; delivered to 2 FBSU for maintenance 24Jun45; sometime conv Mk.V; 57 MU 17Jun46; SOC 23Sep46; sold for scrap to Phoenix & Clifton Ironworks, Coatbridge, 10Mar47

ML759   TOC Calshot 28Feb44; 57 MU 31Mar44; 201 Sqn [T] 17Apr44; on special search west of Isles of Scilly 21Jul44, aircraft was at 50 feet above water when pilot was startled by red flare from corvette; aircraft hit sea but recovered and returned to base with hull completely out of alignment; repaired on site; 422 Sqn [M, G] 15Dec44; Cat AC 28Jan45; repaired on site by 71 MU 1Feb45; 57 MU 2Jul45; 272 MU 30Oct45; SOC 30Mar47

ML760   TOC Calshot Servicing Wing 7Mar44; 57 MU 31Mar44; 201 Sqn [S] 24Apr44; sank *U-955* in Bay of Biscay 7Jun44; shot down over the North Atlantic at 48°15'N 05°45'W by flak from U-boat 12Jun44

ML761   TOC Calshot Servicing Wg 7Mar44; 57 MU 9Apr44; CRD Helensburgh 24Apr44; 57 MU 23Jul45; S&HL (date unknown) for conversion to Mk.V; 57 MU 2Jan46; sold to S&HL 18Mar46 for conversion to Sandringham 4 **ZK-AMB** (see Chapter 6)

ML762   TOC Calshot 8Mar44; 57 MU 6Apr44; 228 Sqn 30Apr44; failed to return from patrol over Bay of Biscay 10Jun44 (8 missing)

ML763   TOC Calshot 20Mar44; 57 MU 23Mar44; 228 Sqn [UE:J, later UE:R] 4May44; Shorts 23Jun45 for conversion to Mk.V; 57 MU 7Oct45; SBL for mods 11Nov46 to 7Apr49; 57 MU 9Apr49; delivered to SB&HL 27Apr49; delivered to Folland Aircraft Ltd, Hamble, 20May49, on 3-month loan for installation of sonobuoy equipment for trials overseas; flown to ASWDU, Calshot, [P9:Q, later Q] 6Sep49; bounced on alighting in swell at Gibraltar 18Apr51 repaired on site; Calshot to SB&HL 17Mar52; test-flown 29Aug52; delivered to FBSU 12Sep52; 230 Sqn [B:R] 13Nov52; repaired on site 34 MU 5Mar54 and 21May54; FBSU 6Dec54; to non-effective stock 3Aug56; noted at FBSU 9Feb57 and 17Aug57 still coded B:R but with nose section cut off; sold for scrap to International Alloys Ltd, Aylesbury, 20Sep57; remains seen there 15Feb58

ML764   TOC 57 MU 26Mar44; 201 Sqn [V, later NS:V] 22Apr44; repaired on site by S&HL 12Mar45; 57 MU Wig Bay 4Aug45; delivered to SB&HL 12Jun50 for conversion to GR.5; ex mods 5Jul51; to Aéronautique navale 26Jul51 (see Part 5)

ML765   Shorts, Rochester, completed as Mk.V prototype, flown 3.44; TOC MAEE 22Apr44; 57 MU 27Sep44; Wig Bay 28Sep44; repaired on site by Shorts 3Nov45; MAEE 21Mar46; BOAC, Poole, 22Apr46; 57 MU 2May46; SOC 6Nov47

ML766   TOC 57MU Wig Bay 6Apr44; 57 MU 6Apr44; 228 Sqn [R] 22May44; lost float while taxying at Pembroke Dock 14Nov44 and damaged beyond repair

ML767   TOC 57 MU 30Mar44; 228 Sqn 24Apr44; struck buoy while being towed at Pembroke Dock 3Oct44; repaired on site; 4 (C) OTU [B:W] 28Oct44; 272 MU 21Mar46; SOC 26Mar47

ML768   TOC 57 MU 12Apr44; 201 Sqn [B] 23May44; Calshot 6Jun44; 201 Sqn [NS:B] 20Jun44; S&HL 15Jun45 for conversion to Mk.V; 57 MU 8Sep45; S&HL 30Jul47 for mods; 57 MU 14Jan48;crew ferry for PP144 Wig Bay - Sydenham 31Mar50; Cat 3R, repaired on site by SB&HL 26Jul51; FBSU 2Oct52; to non-effective stock 22Feb54; sold for scrap to British Aluminium Co 25Aug55

ML769   TOC Wig Bay 14Apr44; 57 MU 15Apr44; 201 Sqn [C, later NS:C] 23May44; Calshot 5Jun44; Pembroke Dock same day; 228 Sqn 16Sep44; struck by naval craft in gale at Pembroke Dock 11Oct44, struck ML876; repaired on site 17Oct44; 422 Sqn [S] 12Mar45; SOC 6Jul45 but to 272 MU 22Oct45; BBOC 21Mar46; delivered to 57 MU 14Nov46 (last Sunderland flown out of Killadeas); sold to S&HL 25Aug47

ML770 TOC 57 MU 20Apr44; 228 Sqn [UE:P, later 1:P] 22May44; hit rock while taxying after alighting off Isles of Scilly 21Feb45 and sank; SOC 22Feb45

ML771 TOC Calshot 24Apr44; 57 MU 14May44; delivered to 461 Sqn [UT:G] 28May44; broke from moorings in gale at Carr Spit, Angle Bay, 18Jan45 and drifted onto mud bank but eventually brought onto slipway; repaired on site by SBL 20Feb45; flying accident Cat B 24Jun46; BOAC 31Jul46; 57 MU 19Oct46; sold for scrap to Phoenix & Clifton Ironworks, Coatbridge, 10Mar47

ML772 TOC Calshot 27Apr44; 57 MU 28May44; 201 Sqn [S, later NS:S] 17Jun44; engine caught fire during run-up at Castle Archdale 7Jan45; repaired on site by Shorts 10Jan45; S&HL 16May45 for conversion to Mk.V; 57 MU 13Aug45; S&HL 22Aug47; 57 MU 23Feb48; left for Far East via Calshot 31Mar48; delivered to 88 Sqn [D] 7Apr48; damaged by Communist gunfire 5 mls (8 km) SE of Chiang Yin (Hunan Province, China) 23Apr49; repaired on site; left for UK 11Mar50; 57 MU 30Mar50; SB&HL 14Apr50; test-flown 28Jun51; deld to 57 MU 6Jul51; to non-effective stock 22Feb54; sold for scrap to BKL Alloys 30Jun55

ML773 TOC Calshot 18May44; 57 MU 28May44; 422 Sqn [2:R] 16Jun44; 57 MU 6Jul45; Castle Archdale 8Jul45; 272 MU 6Nov45; SOC 26Mar47

ML774 TOC Calshot 17May44; 57 MU 31May44; 228 Sqn 15Jun44; Calshot 2Nov44; 461 Sqn [F] 11Nov44; struck by merchant vessel in Angle Bay during gale 18Jan45 and sank; SOC 25Jan45

19 Sunderlands Mk.III built by Short Bros Ltd, Rochester under Contract Acft.2226:

ML777 TOC 57 MU 18May44; Calshot 5Jun44; 422 Sqn [2:M, 2:N] 18Jun44; ran aground while taxying at Castle Archdale 21Sep44; repaired on site 25Sep44; 423 Sqn [F] 24Dec44; float torn off during night take-off from Castle Archdale 19Feb45; repaired on site by S&HL 24Feb45; 272 MU 20Oct45; sold for scrap to Mr McKenny, Belfast, 24Jan47

ML778 TOC Wig Bay 24May44; Calshot 16Jun44; 422 Sqn [2:S] 23Jun44; damaged 14Aug44; 461 Sqn [R] 24Dec44; S&HL 9Mar45 for conversion to Mk.V; 201 Sqn [NS:Z] 10May45; made last official patrol of Second World War 3/4Jun45, with Wg Cdr J Barrett DFC at controls; delivered to 4 (C) OTU [TA:P] 15Jul45; 57 MU 26Jul46; S&HL for mods 11May50; test-flown at Belfast Apr51; ex mods 10May51; to Aéronautique navale via Pembroke Dock 12May51 using call-sign FXCGC (see Part 5)

ML779 TOC 57 MU 30May44; Wig Bay 1Jul44; Calshot 7Dec44; delivered to Greenock 30Dec44 (crew ferry by SZ560); conv Mk.V; 4 (C) OTU 17May45; delivered to 272 MU 4Feb46; delivered to 57 MU 21Sep46; delivered to SB&HL for mods 5May50; ex mods 26Apr51; to Aéronautique navale 27Apr51, but delivered via Pembroke Dock 14Apr51? call-sign FXCGB (see Part 5)

ML780 TOC Wig Bay 2Jun44; Calshot 23Jun44; 330 Sqn [WH:A] 6Jul44; delivered to Greenock for maintenance 9Feb45; returned to 330 Sqn 16Mar45; S&HL 14Apr45 for conversion to Mk.V; 4 (C) OTU 22Jun45; 235 OCU 31Jul47; sold for scrap to J H Connell Ltd, Coatbridge,12Aug48

ML781 TOC 57 MU 8Jun44; Calshot 22Jun44; 422 Sqn [Q] 3Jul44; ran aground while taxying at Pembroke Dock 9Dec44; repaired on site; 461 Sqn [Q] 21Jan45; S&HL 9Apr45 for conversion to Mk.V; 4 (C) OTU 6Jul45; CCFIS 22Feb46; 57 MU 20May46; blown off tail trolley in gale at Wig Bay 6Dec48; repaired on site by 63 MU 6Jan49; SB&HL for mods 27Apr50; test-flown 28 & 30Mar51; to Pembroke Dock 14May51 for Aéronautique navale, using radio call-sign FXGCA (see Part 5)

ML782 TOC Calshot 12Jun44; 57 MU 22Jun44; Pembroke Dock stored reserve 22Jul44; 201 Sqn [NS:X] by 30Jul44; 228 Sqn [UE:X] 16Sep44; bounced on alighting at Mount Batten 10Dec44 and lost float (2 killed); raised next day by civilians but depth charges exploded, killing several civilians and two RAF men; SOC 12Dec44

ML783 TOC Wig Bay 24Jun44; Calshot 18Jul44; 201 Sqn 23Jul44; 423 Sqn [3:H] 25Jul44; struck by EJ150 at Castle Archdale moorings 19Jan45; repaired on site byS&HL 3Feb45; 201 Sqn [H] 20Mar45; shared in sinking of U-325 30Apr45; ; S&HL 12Jun45 for conversion to Mk.V; 57 MU 20Aug45; sold to S&HL 15Apr46 for conversion to Sandringham 5 **G-AHZA** (see Chapter 6)

After being struck by a naval craft at Pembroke Dock on 11th October 1944, Sunderland Mk.III ML769 [I:C] of 228 Squadron was repaired and put back into service. (R Power via Andrew Hendrie collection)

Sunderland Mk.III ML771 [UT:G] of 461 Squadron at Pembroke Dock after being damaged in a gale in Angle Bay, Pembrokeshire on 18th January 1945. (Gerald Raggett collection via Rod Simpson)

ML784 TOC 57 MU 23Jun44; Calshot 19Jul44; 423 Sqn [L] 30Jul44; hit rock at Castle Archdale while taxying 6Jan45; repaired on site by S&HL 10Jan45; 201 Sqn 15Mar45; S&HL 13Jun45 for conversion to Mk.V; 57 MU 20Aug45; sold to S&HL 12Apr46 for conversion to Sandringham 5 **G-AHYZ** but destroyed by fire in Belfast works 18Jan47

ML785 TOC Wig Bay 9Nov44; ASWDU 12Jan45 (or 4Feb45?); delivered to 272 MU 3Sep45; repaired on site by SBL 22Nov45; 57 MU 7Nov46; sold to S&HL 22Aug47

ML786 delivered direct to BOAC 13Jul44; radio call-sign OQZD; later registered **G-AGKV** (see Chapter 6)

ML787 delivered direct to BOAC 21Jul44; radio call-sign OQZE; later registered **G-AGKW** (see Chapter 6)

ML788 delivered direct to BOAC 27Jul44; radio call-sign OQZF; later registered **G-AGKX** (see Chapter 6)

ML789 delivered direct to BOAC 28Jul44; radio call-sign OQZG; later registered **G-AGKY** (see Chapter 6)

ML790 delivered direct to BOAC 3Aug44; radio call-sign OQZH; later registered **G-AGKZ** (see Chapter 6)

ML791 delivered direct to BOAC 12Aug44; radio call-sign OQZI; later registered **G-AGLA** (see Chapter 6)

ML792 TOC 57 MU 20Aug44; 302 FTU 9Sep44; despatched to New Zealand 18Oct44; to RNZAF as ML792, later to **NZ4101** (see Part 3)

ML793 TOC 57 MU 18Sep44; 302 FTU 6Oct44; despatched to New Zealand 23Oct44; to RNZAF as ML793, later to **NZ4102** (see Part 3)

ML794 TOC 57 MU 12Sep44; 302 FTU 6Oct44; despatched to New Zealand 18Oct44; to RNZAF as ML794, later **NZ 4103** (see Part 3)

A rather battle-stained Sunderland Mk.III ML778 [2:S] of 422 Squadron. (P H T Green collection)

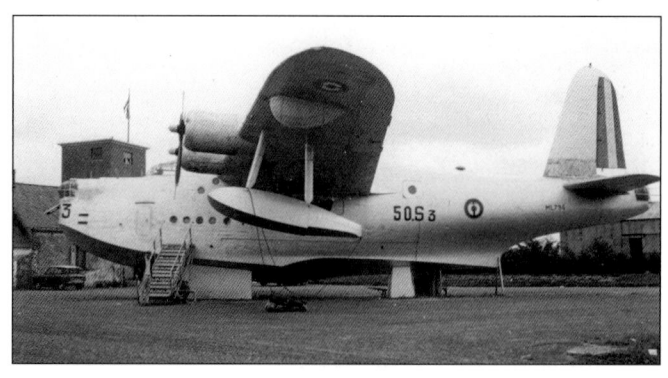

Seen at Lorient, France, in 1967, Sunderland 5 ML796 had been operated by the Aéronautique navale as 50.S 3 and in 2012 is currently on static display at the IWM at Duxford. (P H T Green collection)

With two RAF Sunderlands at the rear, Sandringham I ML788 carrying the BOAC Speedbird logo and Transport Command call-sign OQZF, taxies on the River Medway at Rochester after a trial flight on 28th November 1945. (P H T Green collection)

ML795 TOC 57 MU 27Sep44; 302 FTU 6Oct44; despatched to New Zealand 27Oct44; to RNZAF as ML795, later **NZ 4104** (see Part 3)

6 Sunderlands Mk.V built by Short Bros Ltd, Rochester under Contract Acft.2226:

ML796 TOC Calshot 16May45; 201 Sqn [NS:F then F] by 30Sep45; 4 (C) OTU 4Mar46; Wig Bay 10Jul46; SB&HL 23Jun50 for fitting updated anti-submarine equipment and refurbishment; ex mods 29Jul51; to Aéronautique navale 3Aug51 (see Part 5)
Currently on display at IWM, Duxford as ML796 [NS:F]

ML797 TOC Wig Bay 12Oct44; 308 FTU 5Dec44; delivered to 230 Sqn [NM:Q] 3Feb45; despatched to UK 26Jun47; 57 MU 11Jul47; S&HL 31Jul47; 57 MU 11Nov48; repaired on site by SB&HL 26Jul51; FBSU 20Feb53; delivered to SB&HL 15Jun53; test-flown 29Apr54; delivered to 57 MU 11May54; 230 Sqn 11Sep56; 205/209 Sqn [P] 9Mar57; flew final official Sunderland sortie 20May59; SOC 29Jul59; scrapped at Seletar by Chinese

ML798 TOC Wig Bay 23Oct44; despatched to East Africa 25Mar45, arrived 8Apr45; to SAAF 31May45, later **1709** (see Part 4)

ML799 TOC Wig Bay 30Oct44; 302 FTU 21Dec44; ran aground while taxying at Wig Bay 21Dec44; repaired on site; despatched to ACSEA 13Feb45, arrived 7Mar45; 230 Sqn [W] 4Jun45; despatched to UK 9Mar46; 57 MU 24Apr46; delivered to SB&HL for mods 12May50 (crew ferry by RN282); to Pembroke Dock 25May51 for Aéronautique navale, using radio call-sign FXCGD (see Part 5)

ML800 TOC 57 MU 9Nov44; 302 FTU 23Dec44; despatched to ACSEA 4Feb45, arrived 21Feb45; 230 Sqn [X]; 57 MU 24Apr46; SB&HL for mods 9Dec49 to 7Sep50; 57 MU 14Sep50; Cat 3R 3May51; repaired on site 19Jul51; delivered Wig Bay to SB&HL 20Jun52; to non-effective stock 23Feb54 but cancelled, FBSU 10Jun54; Cat 3R, repaired on site by SB&HL 13Jan56; to non-effective stock 19Oct56; delivered to SB&HL 1Jun57; test-flown 2Jun57; to Aéronautique navale at Brest 26Jun57, using radio call-sign FYBUA (see Part 5)

ML801 TOC 57 MU 1Nov44; beaching leg collapsed while being towed at Oban 12Jan45; repaired on site; Wig Bay 31May45; 4 (C) OTU 18Jul45; damaged 9Nov45; repaired on site 1Jan46; 302 FTU 9Apr46; 57 MU 3May46; sold for scrap to Phoenix & Clifton Ironworks, Coatbridge, 10Mar47

25 Sunderlands Mk.III built by Short & Harland Ltd, Belfast under Contract Acft.2227:

ML807 c/n SH.882; TOC 57 MU 6Feb44; Scottish Aviation 27Oct44 for conversion to Mk.V; 57 MU 6Jun45; sold to S&HL 19Sep46 via MoS for conversion to Sandringham 6 **LN-IAU** (see Chapter 6)

ML808 c/n SH.899; TOC 57 MU 8Feb44; 131 OTU 22Apr44; damaged by ice at Killadeas 30Jan45; repaired on site by S&HL 8Feb45; delivered to 2 FBSU 13Feb45; 272 MU (? date); delivered to 57 MU 1May46; sold to S&H 22Aug47

ML809 c/n SH.915; TOC 57 MU 3Mar44; SBL 21Oct44 for conv to Mk.V; 302 FTU 18May45; 57 MU 5Jul45; sold to S&HL 7Sep46 via MoS for conversion to Sandringham 6 **LN-IAV** (se Chapter 6)

ML810 c/n SH.918; TOC 57 MU 4Mar44; 302 FTU 22Apr44; despatched to West Africa 18May44; 490 Sqn [W] 25May44; SOC 21Jun45 (scuttled)

ML811 c/n SH.928; TOC 57 MU 7Mar44; 302 FTU 22Apr44; despatched to S E Asia 20May44 via West Africa; left Apapa for Libreville (Belgian Congo) 3Jun44 but crashed and destroyed by fire near Lakka (Belgian Congo) in tornado (10 killed)

ML812 c/n SH.940; TOC Calshot 18Mar44; 57 MU 15Apr44; Pembroke Dock 14Jun44; 228 Sqn [K] 15Aug44; S&HL 16Mar45 for conversion to Mk.V; 201 Sqn 27Apr45; 4 (C) OTU 8Jul45; Cat AC 9Feb46; repaired on site by SBL 14Feb46; 302 FTU 9Apr46; 57 MU 8May46; delivered to SB&HL for mods 23Mar50; delivered to 57 MU 7Dec50; Wig Bay to SB&HL and return 17Apr51 as crew ferry for NJ190; to non-effective stock 22Feb54; sold for scrap to BKL Alloys 30Jun55

ML813 c/n SH.967; TOC 57 MU 6Apr44; 201 Sqn [U, later NS:U] 22Apr44; struck flare on take-off from Castle Archdale 13Feb45 and drifted onto rocks; repaired on site by S&HL 26Mar45; delivered to 272 MU 3Nov45; SOC 26Mar47

ML814 c/n SH.974; TOC 57 MU 25Mar44; 201 Sqn [R, later NS:R] 24Apr44; ran aground while under tow at Pembroke Dock 11Oct44; repaired on site; 422 Sqn [2:N] 1Dec44; S&HL 20Feb45 for conversion to Mk.V; 330 Sqn [WH:A] 18Apr45; delivered to 272 MU 6Feb46; delivered to 57 MU 8Nov46; FBSU 15Apr52; delivered to SB&HL 16May52; Cat 4R 19May52; repaired in works by SB&HL 22May52; test-flown 1 & 4May53 as **NZ4108** for RNZAF; delivered to Wig Bay 21May53 as RNZAF **NZ4108** (see Part 3)

ML815 c/n SH.988; TOC 57 MU 6Apr44; 228 Sqn [W] 26Apr44; S&HL 30Jun45 for conversion to Mk.V; 57 MU 26Sep45; delivered to SB&HL for mods 13Oct49; ex mods 15Jun50; delivered to FBSU 22Jun50; crew ferry from Wig Bay to SB&HL and return 4-5Jul50 for ML745 & ML816; Cat 3R, repaired on site SB&HL 31Jan53; to non-effective stock 3Aug56; noted stored at FBSU uncoded 9Feb57 and 17Aug57; sold for scrap to International Alloys 20Sep57

ML816 c/n SH.1004; TOC 57 MU 22May44; Calshot same day; 422 Sqn [2:X] 30Jun44; lost float on alighting across wake of tanker 20Dec44 and ran onto rocks in Angle Bay; repaired on site by Shorts 29Dec44; delivered to Scottish Aviation 8Mar45 for conversion to Mk.V; damaged by refueller in strong wind 13Jun45; 4 (C) OTU 16Jun45; 272 MU 4Feb46; delivered to 57 MU 11Oct46; delivered to SB&HL for mods 5Jul50 (crew ferry by ML815) ; ex mods 29Aug51; to Aéronautique navale 10Aug51 (see Part 5)

ML817 c/n SH.1016; retained by S&HL as pattern for conversion to Mk.V; TOC MAEE 27Oct44; 57 MU 18Nov44; Calshot 10Feb45; 201 Sqn [NS:O] 12Feb45; 423 Sqn [X] 20Feb45; 330 Sqn [WH:X] 17Apr45; 57 MU 17May46; delivered to SB&HL for mods 29Sep49; ex mods 1Jun50; 57 MU 5Jun50; 235 OCU [D:P] 28Feb51; delivered to SB&HL for mods 25Oct51 as [L]; returned to 235 OCU 22Nov51; Cat 3R 18Jan52; repaired on site 12Feb52; Wig Bay to Calshot 9Jul53 as [P]; detached to Kalafrana 16Aug53 for Operation 'Ionia'; FBSU 27Oct53; 230 Sqn [B:X]; Wig Bay - SB&HL 6Jan54; Sydenham - Wig Bay 7Jan55; via Kalafrana to Far East May55; returned Jul55 and noted at Tower Bridge, London, 15Sep55, still coded B:X; FBSU 6Feb57 and noted there 9Feb57 coded 230:X in red; to non-effective stock 11Mar57; noted at FBSU 17Aug57; sold for scrap to International Alloys 15Oct57

ML818 c/n SH.1018; TOC 57 MU 7Jun44; Calshot 23Jun44; 330 Sqn [WH:X] 11Jul44; taxied into DP200 1Oct44; repaired on site 10Oct44; delivered to Greenock 8Dec44; returned to 330 Sqn 12Jan45, last op 20Apr45; S&HL 26Apr45 for conversion to Mk.V; 57 MU 4Jul45; S&HL 30May46 for conversion to Sandringham 5 **G-AHZE** (see Chapter 6)

ML819 c/n SH.1030; TOC 57 MU 15Jun44; Calshot 6Jul44; 330 Sqn [WH:V] 28Jul44; mooring rope broke, drifted into Tay Bridge, Woodhaven, 14Nov44; repaired on site 21Nov44; delivered to Scottish Aviation 11May45 for conversion to Mk.V; last aircraft to leave Greenock, 25Jul45; Calshot; 57 MU 20May46; delivered to SB&HL 2Aug50 for conversion to GR.5; ex mods 23Aug51; to Aéronautique navale 30Aug51 (see Part 5)

ML820 c/n SH.1036; retained by Shorts 22Jul44 for conv to Mk.V; TOC 4 (C) OTU 16Mar45; 272 MU 22Jan46; delivered to 57 MU 30Aug46; Cat 3R repaired on site by SB&HL 17Aug50; SB&HL Dec50 for mods; ex mods 1Nov51; test-flown 22Nov51; to Pembroke Dock 23Nov51 for Aéronautique navale, initially using radio call-sign FYBAC (see Part 5)

ML821 c/n SH.1041; TOC 57 MU 21Jun44; Calshot Servicing Wg 8Jul44; 422 Sqn [T] 21Jul44; Castle Archdale reserve pool 28Jul44; SB(W)L, Windermere, 4Feb45 for conversion to Mk.V; 201 Sqn [NS:C] by end of Jun45; delivered to 4(C) OTU 15Jul45; 57 MU 31Jul45; SB&HL for mods 18Aug50; ex mods 14Sep51; to Pembroke Dock 26Sep51 for Aéronautique navale, initially using radio call-sign FYBAA (see Part 5)

ML822 c/n SH.1055; TOC 57 MU 27Jun44; Calshot 23Jul44; 10 (RAAF) Sqn [RB:D] 17Oct44; delivered to 57 MU 15Jun45; SOC 12Jul45

ML823 c/n SH.1058; TOC 57 MU 23Jun44; Calshot 19Jul44; 423 Sqn 27Jul44; lost height after three engines failed during anti-submarine sweep 6Sep44; crashed while ditching NW of Donegal Bay (9 killed, 1 rescued)

Seen in the final days of Sunderland operation at Seletar is MR.5 ML797 [P] of 205/209 Squadron.   (Phillip Sharrat via Dave Welch)

230 Squadron's Sunderland Mk.V ML800 at Koggala in 1945 with its crew posed in the foreground. It carries no code letter so it had probably only recently arrived.   (G O'Neill)

ML817 [B:X] was a Sunderland MR.5 of 230 Squadron, seen here on 15th September 1955 while visiting the Pool of London during Battle of Britain Week.   (R C Sturtivant collection)

ML824 c/n SH.1071; retained by S&HL 6Jul44 for conv to Mk.V; TOC 57 MU 16Nov44; Calshot 4Feb45; 201 Sqn [NS:Z, later T] 11Feb45; 330 Sqn [WH:Z, later WH:T] 17Apr45; SOC 14Sep45; BBOC at Alness 20May48; 57 MU same day; SB&HL for mods 25Aug50; ex mods 4Oct51; to Pembroke Dock 26Oct51 for Aéronautique navale, using radio call-sign FYBAB (see Part 5);
Delivered to Pembroke Dock from Brest 24Mar61 for preservation [A:Z]; currently on display in RAF Museum, Hendon

ML825 c/n SH.1073; TOC 57 MU 1Aug44; Calshot 2Aug44; 423 Sqn [YI:D, 3:D] 14Aug44; delivered to 272 MU 1Nov45; SOC 26Mar47

ML826 c/n SH.1095; retained by S&HL 2Aug44 for conversion to Mk.V; 4 (C) OTU 7Mar45; repaired on site by S&HL 20Apr45; delivered to 272 MU 4Feb46; allotted GI airframe **6100M** at Alness 5Sep46

ML827 c/n SH.1104; TOC 57 MU 9Aug44; Calshot 26Aug44; Pembroke Dock 3Oct44; 461 Sqn [C] 5Oct44; converted to Mk.V; 330 Sqn

In pristine condition is Sunderland Mk.III ML818 which went into service with 330 Squadron before being converted to a Mk.5 in 1945. It was later transformed in 1946 into Sandringham 5 G-AHZE for BOAC and named Portsea. (R C Sturtivant collection)

Sunderland Mk.III ML865 [J] of 230 Squadron on patrol over the Indian Ocean in 1944. (P H T Green collection)

[WH:G] 18Apr45; ditched 12May45 after both starboard engines failed while flying at 600 ft about 100 mls (160 km) SW of Faeroes at 61°09'N 09°14'W; taken in tow by trawler from Aberdeen but sank (crew rescued)

ML828 c/n SH.1115; TOC 57 MU 28Aug44; Calshot 17Sep44; 10 (RAAF) Sqn [RB:C] 15Oct44; collided with PP142 when taxying in poor visibility 11Feb45; delivered to 57 MU 15Jun45; S&HL 16Sep45 for conversion to Mk.V; 57 MU 19Nov45; to S&HL via MoCA 13Jul46 for conversion to Sandringham 5 **G-AHZG** (see Chapter 6)

ML829 c/n SH.1126; TOC 57 MU 24Aug44; Calshot 16Sep44; Pembroke Dock 8Oct44; damaged 20Oct44; repaired on site 24Oct44; Pembroke Dock stored reserve 2Dec44; delivered to 10 (RAAF) Sqn [RB:K] 11Dec44; failed to become airborne on three-engined take-off from Mount Batten 9Feb45, struck boom defences, broke up and sank (2 killed, 6 injured); SOC 22Feb45

ML830 c/n SH.1130; TOC 57 MU 9Sep44; delivered 10 (RAAF) Sqn [RB:A] 14Oct44; flare caught fire in aircraft 15Nov44; repaired on site 20Nov44; delivered to 57 MU 19Jun45; sold for scrap to Phoenix & Clifton Ironworks, Coatbridge, 10Mar47

ML831 c/n SH.1139; TOC 57 MU 12Sep44; 10 (RAAF) Sqn 15Oct44; 461 Sqn [UT:H] 30Nov44; hit by drifting merchant vessel in gale in Angle Bay 18Jan45 and driven onto rocks; SOC 25Jan45

50 Sunderlands Mk.III built by Blackburn Aircraft Ltd, Dumbarton under Contract Acft.2228:

ML835 TOC Wig Bay 18Oct43; 57 MU 8Jan44; 302 FTU 31Jan44; despatched to West Africa 22Apr44, arrived 28Apr44; delivered to 490 Sqn [Z] 12May44; 343 Sqn; to Aéronautique navale 21Jun45 (see Part 5)

ML836 TOC Wig Bay 26Oct43; 422 Sqn [S] 24Nov43; 131 (C) OTU 25Jun44; struck pontoon while taxying at Castle Archdale 7Jan44; repaired on site 20Jan44; force-landed after engine lost power 14Jan45; SOC 31May45; sold for scrap to Phoenix & Clifton Ironworks, Coatbridge, 10Mar47

ML837 TOC 1 FBSU 24Oct43; 57 MU 6Dec43; 302 FTU 29Mar44; despatched to West Africa 6Apr44, arrived 12Apr44; 95 Sqn [G] by 7.44; SOC 21Jun45

ML838 TOC 1 FBSU 29Oct43; 57 MU 8Jan44; damaged in gale at Wig Bay 25Jan44; repaired on site 1Feb44; conv Mk.V; S&HL 5Apr46 for conv to Sandringham 5 **G-AHYY** (see Chapter 6)

ML839 TOC Wig Bay 3Nov43; 10 (RAAF) Sqn [RB:A] 8Dec43; partial conversion to Mk.V with Twin Wasp engines carried out at Mount Batten May44; returned to 10 (RAAF) Sqn 1Jul44; sank in gale at Mount Batten 12Oct44; SOC 25Oct44

ML840 TOC Wig Bay 8Nov43; 57 MU 8Jan44; damaged in gale at Wig Bay 25Jan44; repaired on site 1Feb44; Scottish Aviation, Greenock, 14Nov44 for conversion to Mk.V; 57 MU 24Jun45; sold to S&HL 24Jun47 for conversion to Sandringham 7 **G-AKCR** (see Chapter 6)

ML841 TOC Wig Bay 9Nov43; 4 (C) OTU 3Jan44; 57 MU 8Jan44; delivered to 302 FTU 15May44; despatched to West Africa 18Jun44 for 490 Sqn but damaged at Gibraltar 19Jun44; returned to Oban 18Sep44; delivered to West Africa 10Mar45; 343 Sqn; to Aéronautique navale 21Jun45 (see Part 5)

ML842 TOC 1 FBSU 15Nov43; 57 MU 8Jan44; damaged in gale at Wig Bay 25Jan44; repaired on site 1Feb44; 131 (C) OTU 22Apr44; damaged 25Nov44 (gale ?); SOC 6Sep45

ML843 TOC 1 FBSU 15Nov43; 57 MU 20Jan44; damaged in gale at Wig Bay 25Jan44; repaired on site 1Feb44; Calshot Servicing Wing 31Jul44; 57 MU 30Sep44; sold to S&HL 23May46 for conversion to Sandringham 2 **G-AHRE** (see Chapter 6)

ML844 TOC Wig Bay 18Nov43; delivered to 270 Sqn [X, later H] 4Mar44; Calshot Servicing Wing 29Sep44; 270 Sqn; on 10Mar45 a propeller flew off and made large gash in side of aircraft, which went out of control; control regained and landed safely but damaged beyond repair; SOC 21Jun45

ML845 TOC Wig Bay 22Nov43; 57 MU 20Jan44; 302 FTU 5Jul44; despatched to West Africa 18Jul44; arrived Gibraltar 20Jul44; took off for Port Etienne 24Jul44 but ditched off Canary Islands when engines lost power due to fuel contamination; foundered at 27°58'N 12°51'W while under tow and sunk by gunfire

ML846 TOC 1 FBSU 26Nov43; 57 MU 20Jan44; 302 FTU 22Apr44; struck rocks while taxying and beached at Ganavan Sands, Oban, 10May44; repaired on site 16May44; despatched to ACSEA 15Nov44, arrived 1Dec44; 230 Sqn [W] 13Dec44; force-landed 14Feb45 after an engine failed; SOC 13Sep45

ML847 TOC 1 FBSU 3Dec43; 57 MU 20Jan44; 302 FTU 15Apr44; despatched to West Africa 19May44, arrived 25May44; 95 Sqn [C] by 7.44; SOC 21Jun45

ML848 TOC 1 FBSU 4Dec43; 57 MU 23Jan44; 10 (RAAF) Sqn [RB:X] 22Feb44; struck balloon cable on take-off from Mount Batten 7May44; repaired on site; float struck boat while taxying at Mount Batten 29Sep44; delivered to Scottish Aviation, Largs, 5Jan45 for disposal; delivered to 272 MU 20Sep45; SOC 26Mar47

ML849 TOC 57 MU 30Dec43; 302 FTU 19Feb44; despatched to West Africa 30Mar44; 270 Sqn [K] 4.44; crashed on take-off from Port Lyautey (Morocco) during ferry flight to UK 16Jun45; repaired on site and resumed flight 1Jul45; 57 MU 6Jul45; sold for scrap to Phoenix & Clifton Ironworks, Coatbridge, 10Mar47

ML850 TOC 57 MU 30Dec43; 302 FTU 5Feb44; damaged 7Mar44; despatched to West Africa 22Apr44; 490 Sqn [S, B] by 17May44; 57 MU 17Jun45; sold for scrap to Phoenix & Clifton Ironworks, Coatbridge, 10Mar47

ML851 TOC 57 MU 3Jan44; 302 FTU 5Feb44; despatched to West Africa 11Apr44, arrived 20Apr44; 343 Sqn; to Aéronautique navale 21Jun45 (see Part 5)

ML852 TOC 57 MU 3Jan44; 302 FTU 8Feb44; despatched to W Africa 25Apr44; delivered to 490 Sqn [P] by 12Jun44; taking off from Bathurst on anti-submarine patrol 14Jul44, both port engines lost power; aircraft ditched and sank off Cape St Mary, The Gambia (2 killed, 8 rescued next day)

ML853 TOC 57 MU 4Jan44; 302 FTU 18Feb44; damaged float on alighting in Firth of Lorne 16Mar44; repaired on site 21Mar44; despatched to West Africa 23May44; delivered to 270 Sqn [B] 6Jun44; 57 MU 16Jun45; sold for scrap Phoenix & Clifton Ironworks, Coatbridge, 10Mar47

ML854 TOC 57 MU 7Jan44; 302 FTU 5Feb44; despatched to West Africa 13Apr44, arrived 25Apr44; 204 Sqn [KG:M] by 4Jun44; 343 Sqn; to Aéronautique navale 21Jun45 (see Part 5)

ML855 TOC 57 MU 9Jan44; delivered to Greenock for mods 12Jun44; delivered to 302 FTU 2Jul44; despatched to West Africa 5Jul44; 490 Sqn [R]; crashed 30 mls (48 km) N of St Louis (Sénégal) 17Jul44 during flight from Bathurst to Port Etienne; no casualties

ML856 TOC 57 MU 9Jan44; Calshot Servicing Wg 4Mar44; 1 FBSU; delivered to 10 (RAAF) Sqn [RB:Y] 19Mar44; delivered to Scottish Aviation, Largs, 29Nov44 for disposal; delivered to 272 MU 2Oct45; SOC 30Nov45; scrapped 3Dec45

ML857 TOC 57 MU 5Feb44; delivered to 302 FTU 17May44; delivered to 2 FBSU for maintenance 8Jun44; accident 14Jun44; repaired on site 17Jun44; stalled and damaged on alighting at Oban 6Oct44; repaired on site 11Oct44; 302 FTU 3Nov44; delivered to West Africa 30Dec44; delivered to 490 Sqn 17Jan45; 270 Sqn ???; SOC 21Jun45

ML858 TOC 57 MU 14May44; delivered to 302 FTU same day; flew into Hirta Island, St Kilda, 8Jun44 during night navigation exercise in bad weather (10 killed); wreckage found 10Jun44 by Vickers Warwick of 281 Sqn

ML859 TOC 57 MU 8Feb44; delivered to 302 FTU 8Jun44; despatched to West Africa 25Jun44, arrived 4Jul44; 490 Sqn [T]; SOC 21Jun45 (scuttled)

ML860 TOC 57 MU 8Feb44; delivered to 2 FBSU 19Jun44; 302 FTU 21Jun44; despatched to West Africa 19Jul44; lost power due to fuel contamination, ditched at 27°25'N 13°20'W, 23Jul44; later sunk by gunfire

ML861 TOC 57 MU 8Feb44; delivered to 2 FBSU for mods 12Jun44; delivered to 302 FTU 17Jun44; delivered to 2 FBSU 21Jun44; delivered to 302 FTU 25Jun44; despatched to Ceylon 26Jun44; delivered to 230 Sqn [NM:K] 19Jul44; SOC 28Jun45

ML862 TOC 57 MU 23Feb44; delivered to 302 FTU 16May44; despatched to West Africa 16Jun44; delivered to 490 Sqn [Q] late Jun44; major fire in port outer engine 17Feb45 caused force-landing 60 mls (96 km) W of Jui; high-speed launch took aircraft in tow and it was moored at Jui next day; SOC 21Jun45

ML863 TOC 57 MU 27Feb44; delivered to 302 FTU 14May44; despatched to West Africa 13Jun44; delivered to 490 Sqn [X] 27Jun44; SOC 21Jun45 (scuttled)

ML864 TOC 57 MU 18Mar44; delivered to Greenock 19Jun44; 302 FTU 22Jun44; despatched to West Africa 15Jul44; delivered to 490 Sqn 25Jul44; SOC 16May45

ML865 TOC 57 MU 27Feb44; 302 FTU 4Jul44; despatched to Ceylon 21Jul44; 230 Sqn [NM:J]; Station Flight Koggala; SOC 28Jun45

ML866 TOC MAEE 4Mar44; Calshot Servicing Wing 12Mar44; 57 MU 12Mar44; converted to Mk.V 9Aug44; 4 (C) OTU 20Mar45; 272 MU 22Jan46; delivered to 57 MU 5Sep46; delivered to SB&HL for mods 6Oct50; ex mods 25Oct51; to Pembroke Dock for Aéronautique navale 19Nov51 (see Part 5)

ML867 TOC Calshot Servicing Wing 2Mar44; 57 MU 15Mar44; delivered to 302 FTU 18May44; despatched to West Africa 20Jun44, arrived 29Jun44; 270 Sqn [N]; SOC 21Jun45

ML868 TOC Calshot Servicing Wing 2Mar44; 57 MU May44; delivered to 302 FTU 18May44; delivered to Greenock for maintenance 30May44; despatched to ACSEA 4Jun44, arrived 27Aug44 (!!!); 230 Sqn [NM:H]; SOC 31Jan46

Another 230 Squadron Sunderland Mk.III, ML868 [H], was also active in the ACSEA region towards the end of the war.

Sunderland Mk.III ML876 [NS:O] of 201 Squadron moored at Belfast with an aircraft carrier in the background. This aircraft appears to have been dogged by several collision incidents on water during 1944-45! (Peter Davis collection)

ML869 TOC Calshot Servicing Wing 2Mar44; 57 MU 19Mar44; delivered to 302 FTU 13May44; despatched to West Africa 17Jun44; delivered to 490 Sqn [V, N] 26Jun44; 57 MU 22Jun45; sold for scrap to Phoenix & Clifton Ironworks, Coatbridge, 10Mar47

ML870 TOC 57 MU 8Mar44; delivered to 302 FTU 8Jun44; despatched to West Africa 30Jun44; 490 Sqn [V] 7.44; 343 Sqn; SOC 21Jun45

ML871 TOC 57 MU 12Mar44; delivered to 302 FTU 8Jun44; despatched to West Africa 26Jun44, arrived 2Jul44; 343 Sqn [L]; to Aéronautique navale 2Jul44 (see Part 5)

ML872 TOC 57 MU 21Mar44; SB(W)L, Windermere, 21Jul44 for conversion to Mk.V; 302 FTU 18Jan45; delivered to West Africa 15Feb45; 204 Sqn [KG:B]; delivered to 57 MU 21Jun45; SB&HL for mods 26Oct50 to 6Dec51; to Pembroke Dock for Aéronautique navale 13Dec51 (see Part 5)

ML873 TOC 57 MU 21Mar44; S&HL 21Jul44 for conv to Mk.V; 57 MU 9Jan45; 4 (C) OTU 12Jan45; delivered to 272 MU 9Feb46; delivered to 57 MU 29Oct46; SB&HL for mods 29Sep49; 57 MU 16May50; repaired on site by SB&HL 11Dec52; FBSU 1Apr53; to non-effective stock 22Feb54; sold for scrap to British Aluminium Co 25Aug55

ML874 TOC 57 MU 27Mar44; delivered to 302 FTU 20May44; despatched to West Africa 7Jun44, arrived 12Jun44; 270 Sqn [L]; 343 Sqn; to Aéronautique navale 21Jun45 (see Part 5)

ML875 TOC 57 MU 27Mar44; 201 Sqn [M, later NS:M] 10Apr44; delivered to Greenock 10Jan45 for conversion to Mk.V; delivered to 4 (C) OTU 14Jun45; tail fell off trolley while being towed at Wig Bay 31Oct46; delivered to 57 MU 7Nov46; Cat B 13Mar47; SOC 6Nov47

ML876 TOC 57 Mu 6Apr44; 201 Sqn [O, later NS:O] 17Apr44; struck by ML769 at Pembroke Dock moorings during gale 11Oct44; repaired on site; while mooring at Pembroke Dock 9Jan45, engine ran away, aircraft struck ML772 ; repaired on site by S&HL 11Jan45; taxied into ML825 at night at Castle Archdale 28Feb45; repaired on site; 57 MU 3Jul45; Castle Archdale 4Jul45; sold to Shorts 3Jan46 and registered **G-AGWX** (see Chapter 6)

ML877 TOC 57 MU 10Apr44; 228 Sqn [G] 26Apr44; sank *U-970* in Bay of Biscay 7Jun44; SB(W)L, Windermere, 5Apr45 for conversion to Mk.V; 57 MU 23Sep45; delivered to SB&HL for mods 7Dec50; test-flown 9 & 18Nov51; ex mods Dec51; to Pembroke Dock for Aéronautique navale 12Jan52 (see Part 5)

ML878 TOC 57 MU 12Apr44; 228 Sqn 27Apr44; bounced in heavy landing and lost float at Pembroke Dock 14Aug44; repaired on site; S&HL 20Feb45 for conversion to Mk.V; 330 Sqn [WH:R] 14May45; delivered to 2 FBSU 19Jun45 for maintenance; drifted into RN267 at Stavanger, Norway, 2Dec45; repaired on site; delivered to 272 MU Killadeas 1Mar46; S&HL for mods 1Nov46; while in works, SOC 18Aug49

ML879 TOC 57 MU 18Apr44; 228 Sqn [UE:M] 10May44; Calshot 2Nov44; 461 Sqn [Y] 10Nov44; damaged when leg of beaching trolley collapsed at Pembroke Dock 19Dec44; repaired on site by SBL 29Dec44; 422 Sqn [P] 13Feb45; 57 MU 6Jul45; Castle Archdale 8Jul45; 272 MU Killadeas 3Nov45; delivered to 57 MU 24May46; sold to SB&HL 17Nov47

ML880 TOC 57 MU 20Apr44; 228 Sqn [U] 10May44; shot down by flak from *U-333* over Bay of Biscay 11Jun44

ML881 TOC Calshot Servicing Wing 27Apr44; 201 Sqn [P, later NS:P] 18May44; sank *U-1222* 11Jul44; struck by tender at Castle Archdale 6Mar45; repaired on site by S&HL 17Mar45; S&HL for conversion to Mk.V then deld 57 MU 7Aug45; S&HL for mods 12Aug47; 57 MU 21Apr48; 209 Sqn [X *Rajang River*] 6Aug48; bounced on alighting at Seletar 2Sep48; repaired on site; engine cut on take-off from Seletar 13Jul49; repaired on site; 57 MU 27Apr50; repaired on site by SB&HL 16Jun52; to non-effective stock 6Aug56; Sydenham to Wig Bay 1Dec56; noted at FBSU 9Aug57, still coded X; sold for scrap to International Alloys Ltd, Aylesbury, 20Sep57; remains seen there 15Feb58

ML882 TOC Calshot Servicing Wing 28Apr44; 201 Sqn [Y, later NS:Y] 18May44; struck buoy while taxying at night at Castle Archdale 15Feb45; S&HL 9Mar45 for conversion to Mk.V; 4 (C) OTU 2Jun45; delivered to 272 MU 4Feb46; delivered to 57 MU 9Oct46; delivered to SB&HL for mods 25Nov49, crew ferry by SZ573; ex mods 24Aug50; Sydenham to and from Wig Bay 21-23.Nov50; 88 Sqn [A] 20Dec50; 209 Sqn [X] 1Jan53; FEFBW reserve 14Dec53; to UK 19Jan54; FBSU 3Feb54; to non-effective stock 22Feb54; sold for scrap to Motherwell Eng Co, Lanarkshire, 19Oct56

ML883 TOC Calshot Servicing Wing 6May44; 57 MU 24May44; 422 Sqn [V] 9Jun44; damaged a float in heavy landing at Castle Archdale 20Jun44; repaired on site 27Jun44; 423 Sqn [F] 8Aug44; sank at moorings in gale at Calshot 17Dec44; salvaged but scrapped

ML884 TOC Calshot Servicing Wing and ferried Rhu to Calshot 8May44; 57 MU 24May44; 422 Sqn [2:Z] 7Jun44; 57 MU 6Jul45; 272 MU 29Oct45; SOC 26Mar47

2 Sunderland Mk.IV prototypes (later renamed Seaford Mk.I) built by Short Bros Ltd, Rochester under Contract Acft.2551:

MZ269 first flight 30Aug44; TOC MAEE Mar45; engine caught fire while taxying at Felixstowe 15Jul47; became GI airframe **6416M** at 1 MCTS, Felixstowe 22Aug49

CHAPTER 5 : INDIVIDUAL AIRCRAFT HISTORIES

One of the two prototypes of the Seaford Mk.I (originally known as the Sunderland Mk.IV) was MZ269 which first flew on 30th August 1944. (P H T Green collection)

330 Squadron Sunderland Mk.V conversion NJ172 [WH:F] flying from Sullom Voe in 1945 was originally delivered as a Mk.III to the Canadian crews of 422 Squadron in June 1944..

The second prototype Seaford Mk.I, MZ271, moored on the River Medway outside the Rochester works. (P H T Green collection)

MZ271 TOC MAEE Apr45; returned to makers; ferried from Belfast to MAEE Felixstowe 1Sep50 [C]; returned to SB&H prior to MAEE closure (ie.Mar53); presumed scrapped Sydenham

25 Sunderlands Mk.III built by Blackburn Aircraft Ltd, Dumbarton under Contract Acft.2228:

NJ170 TOC 57 MU 10May44; 422 Sqn [Y] 17Jun44; S&HL 16Mar45 for conversion to Mk.V; 330 Sqn 20May45; delivered to 272 MU 15Dec45; delivered to 57 MU 3Jul46; SB&HL for mods 11May50 to 17May51; to Aéronautique navale 25May51 (see Part 5)

NJ171 TOC 57 MU 12May44; Calshot for mods 27May44; Pembroke Dock 10Jun44; 228 Sqn [UE:A] 20Jun44; Windermere to S&HL 18Jul45 for conversion to Mk.V; 57 MU 18Oct45; S&HL 8May46 for conversion to Sandringham 5 as **G-AHZB** (see Chapter 6)

NJ172 TOC 57 MU 15May44; Calshot 11Jun44; 422 Sqn [2:O] 18Jun44; damaged 23Sep44; S&HL for conversion to Mk.V; 330 Sqn [WH:F] 10May45; overshot landing at Calshot and wing struck sailing boat 8Sep45; repaired on site by Shorts 14Sep45; repaired on site 15Nov45; 57 MU 17Jun46; delivered to SB&HL for mods 17Mar50; ex mods 28Dec50; 57 MU 4Jan51; to non-effective stock 8Aug56; noted with FBSU, uncoded, 9Feb57 and 17Aug57; sold for scrap to International Alloys Ltd, Aylesbury, 26Sep57

NJ173 TOC 57 MU 21May44; Calshot for mods 7Jun44; 422 Sqn [2:W] 21Jun44; 57 MU 6Jul45; Castle Archdale 8Jul45; 272 MU 24Oct45; SOC 26Mar47

NJ174 57 MU 25May44; Calshot 17Jun44; 422 Sqn [2:U] 29Jun44; 57 MU 6Jul45; Castle Archdale 8Jul45; 272 MU 29Oct45; SOC 26Mar47

NJ175 TOC 57 MU 29May44; Calshot 14Jun44; 422 Sqn [2:T] 29Jun44; on 12Aug44, engine cut after take-off for patrol, propeller broke off and lodged in float; lost height and flew into ground at Belleek, Co Donegal (Irish Republic) and destroyed by fire (3 killed, 6 injured)

NJ176 TOC 57 MU 30May44; Calshot 16Jun44; 422 Sqn [2:P] 23Jun44; Greenock stored reserve 1Feb45; repaired in works by Scottish Aviation 2Feb45; SB(W)L, Windermere, 19Jun45 for conversion to Mk.V; 57 MU 21Aug45; S&HL for mods 26Aug47; 57 MU 5Mar48; left for Far East via Calshot 21Apr48; delivered to 88 Sqn [F] 15May48; swung during night take-off from Seletar in overloaded condition in a storm 20/21Nov49 (5 killed, 2 seriously injured); SOC 24Nov49

NJ177 TOC 57 MU 12Jun44; Calshot 25Jun44; 330 Sqn [WH:F] 6Jul44; struck by DD856 at Sullom Voe moorings 27Nov44; repaired on site; S&HL 2May45 for conversion to Mk.V; 57 MU 6Jul45; SB&HL for mods 30Sep51 to 1May52; FBSU 1May52; to Far East via Pembroke Dock 16Apr53; 209 Sqn 29Apr53; FEFBWg 6May53; 209 Sqn [V] 5Jun53; wrecked in gale at Opama (Japan) 19Aug54, while on detachment to Iwakuni; SOC 20Aug54; remains purchased by Japanese toy manufacturer for equivalent of £600

NJ178 TOC 57 MU 12Jun44; Calshot 29Jun44; 330 Sqn [WH:H, later WH:L] 21Jul44; delivered to Greenock for maintenance 15Nov44; returned to 330 Sqn 11Dec44; hit submerged rocks on landing at Sullom Voe 7Mar45; repaired on site by SBL 19Mar45; delivered to 272 MU 20Aug45; SOC 26Mar47

NJ179 TOC 57 MU 12Jun44; Calshot 27Jun44; 330 Sqn [WH:Y] 21Jul44; struck by drifting Catalina JV931 at Sullom Voe 18Mar45; repaired on site; S&HL 3May45 for conversion to Mk.V; Belfast to Wig Bay 24Jul45; 57 MU 27Jul45; sold to S&HL 11Apr46 for conversion to Sandringham **ZK-AME** (see Chapter 6)

The remains of Sunderland MR.5 NJ172 at Wig Bay in 1957.

422 Squadron Sunderland Mk.III NJ176 [2:P] at Castle Archdale in 1944 was converted in 1945 to Mk.V and served with 88 Squadrons in the Far East. (J Eadie via Andrew Hendrie collection)

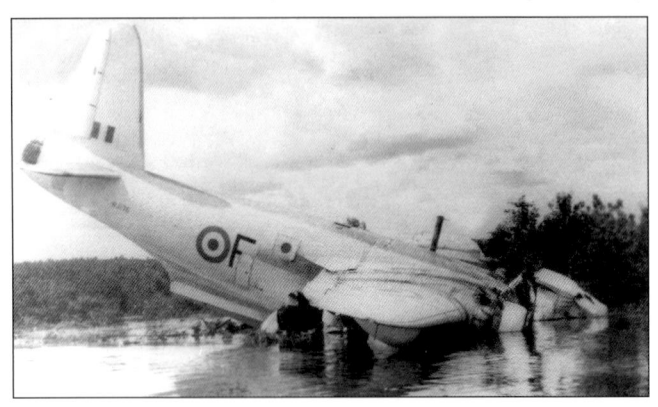

Sunderland GR.5 of 88 Squadron, NJ176 [F] crashed on take-off from Seletar on 21st November 1949 with the loss of five lives and serious injury to another two crew. (P H T Green collection)

Sunderland MR.5 NJ191 [W] of 205/209 Squadron seen taking off at Seletar in 1955-56. (Gerald Raggett collection via Rod Simpson)

Sunderland MR.5 NJ193 served with several squadrons, its fourth operational unit being 205 Squadron with which it was coded P. (P H T Green collection)

NJ180 TOC 57 MU 13Jun44; Calshot 29Jun44; 330 Sqn [WH:R] 21Jul44; engine caught fire on start-up at Sullom Voe 12Mar45, aircraft drifted onto island; repaired on site by SBL 15Mar45; S&HL 14May45 for conv to Mk.V; 57 MU 3Aug45; damaged 18Jan51; repaired on site 22Feb51; 57 MU 18May51; delivered to SB&HL 30Jul51; damaged 28Feb52; to Wig Bay 5Mar52; 57 MU 15Mar52; SB&HL to Wig Bay and return 1Aug52; to non-effective stock 31Aug52; fWig Bay ti SB&HL and return 13Sep 52; delivered Wig Bay to SB&HL 7Nov52; test-flown 17Nov52 & 27Nov52; delivered to FBSU 10Dec52; Wig Bay to SB&HL and return 12-13Dec52; FBTS 4Nov53; hit buoy during attempted overshoot at Pembroke Dock 23Feb54; SOC 28Apr54; became GI airframe **7146M** at Pembroke Dock 12May54; scrapped 21Sep54

NJ181 TOC 57 MU 22Jun44; Calshot 6Jul44; 330 Sqn [WH:Z] 27Jul44; missing from patrol 4Oct44 (10 killed)

NJ182 TOC 57 MU 22Jun44; Calshot 10Jul44; 422 Sqn [2:N] 27Jul44; 423 Sqn [N, 3:G] by 12.44; delivered to Scottish Aviation, Greenock, 5Apr45 for conversion to Mk.V; Calshot 17Jul45; ASWDU 26Oct45; 57 MU 27May46; SB&HL for mods 9Jan51 to 31Dec51; 57 MU 12Jan52; to Pembroke Dock for Aéronautique navale 12Jan52 (see Part 5)

NJ183 TOC 57 MU 23Jun44; Calshot 21Jul44; 423 Sqn [2:G] 30Jul44; practice bomb fell off inside aircraft and exploded 22Dec44; repaired on site; engine caught fire after take-off for patrol 11Feb45 and fell out; aircraft crashed at Knocknagor, 3 mls (4.8 km) E of Irvinestown, Co Tyrone (11 killed); SOC 1Mar45

NJ184 TOC 57 MU 26Jun44; Calshot 23Jul44; 423 Sqn [C] 9Aug44; overshot touch-down on Lough Erne 8May45 and grounded; repaired on site by S&HL 14May45; SOC 3Aug45

NJ185 TOC 57 MU 6Jul44; Calshot 27Jul44; 423 Sqn [E] 14Aug44; 272 MU 6Nov45; SOC 26Mar47

NJ186 TOC 57 MU 7Jul44; Calshot 23Jul44; 423 Sqn [A] 5Aug44; hit highest point of Mountains of Mourne, N Ireland, while descending in cloud 20May45, damaging hull; crash-landed on Jurby airfield, Isle of Man, and exploded, causing large crater but no loss of life; SOC 9Jun45

NJ187 TOC 57 MU 8Jul44; Calshot 22Jul44; 423 Sqn [B] 9Aug44; swung to avoid another aircraft at Castle Archdale 3Sep44 and lost float; repaired on site; S&HL 24Apr45 for conversion to Mk.V; 57 MU 5Aug45; S&HL for mods 2Jul47 to 18Dec47; 57 MU 19Dec47; FBSU 20Feb53; delivered to SB&HL 30Mar53; test-flown 26Mar54; delivered to FBSU 7Apr54; FBTS 5Aug55; FBSU 5Feb57; noted there 9Feb57 coded 201:W in blue; to non-effective stock 30Apr57; seen again, still coded, 17Aug57; sold for scrap to International Alloys Ltd, Aylesbury, 15Oct57

NJ188 TOC 57 MU 1Aug44; Calshot 17Sep44; 330 Sqn [WH:G] 13Oct44; first patrol 22Oct44; last operation 11Apr45; S&HL 14Apr45 for conversion to Mk.V; 57 MU 6Jul45; sold to S&HL 20May46 for conversion to Sandringham 5 **G-AHZF** (see Chapter 6)

NJ189 TOC 57 MU 1Aug44; Calshot 18Aug44; 422 Sqn [2:V] 3Oct44; taxied into ML748 at Pembroke Dock 8Apr45; repaired on site; 57 MU 6Jul45; Castle Archdale 8Jul45; 272 MU 3Nov45; SOC 26Mar47

NJ190 TOC 57 MU 15Aug44; Calshot 1Sep44; delivered to Scottish Aviation, Greenock, 9Oct44 for conversion to Mk.V; air-tested 21Feb45 (first Mk.V conversion at Greenock); delivered to 330 Sqn 14Apr45; ground accident 12Apr46; repaired on site by SBL 17Apr46; 57 MU 9Jul46; delivered to SB&HL for mods 17Apr51 (crew ferry by ML812); ex mods 14Feb52; to Pembroke Dock for Aéronautique navale 20Feb52 (see Part 5)

NJ191 TOC 57 MU 15Aug44; Calshot 31Aug44; Pembroke Dock pool 3Oct44; 228 Sqn [E] 5Oct44; SB(W)L, Windermere, 15Feb45 for conversion to Mk.V; 4 (C) OTU 11Jul45; 57 MU 8Jul46; delivered to SB&HL 15Oct51 for mods; delivered to FBSU Wig Bay 4Jun52; Wig Bay- Sydenham and return 4Jun53; despatched to Far East via Pembroke Dock 7Jul53; FEFBWg reserve 21Jul53; 209 Sqn [W] 1Dec53; 205/209 Sqn [W] 1Jan55; SOC 13Nov56

NJ192 TOC 57 MU 24Aug44; Calshot 6Sep44; Pembroke Dock pool 9Oct44; 228 Sqn [Y] 13Oct44; S&HL 16Mar45 for conversion to Mk.V; 201 Sqn [L] 15May45; 4 (C) OTU (date unknown); ground accident 20Feb46; SOC 28Feb46

CHAPTER 5 : INDIVIDUAL AIRCRAFT HISTORIES

Sunderland Mk.IV / Seaford Mk.I NJ203 on the Medway at Rochester in April 1946, clearly showing the increased fin and rudder area and the long dorsal fairing of this model which distinguish it from other Marks of Sunderland. (via Phil Butler)

NJ193 TOC 57 MU 28Aug44; Calshot 13Sep44; SBL 28Feb45 for conversion to Mk.V; Calshot 8Mar45; 461 Sqn [F] 14Mar45; delivered to 10 (RAAF) Sqn [RB:F] 15Jun45; 201 Sqn [X] 30Oct45; 57 MU 29Apr46; delivered as [B] to SB&HL for mods 17Aug51; ex mods 10Apr52; FBSU 19Apr52; to Pembroke Dock for Far East 20Mar53 but postponed; FBSU 30Apr53; repaired on site by SB&HL 8May53; test flight Wig Bay 4Jun53; despatched to Far East 5Jun53; 205 Sqn [P] 24Jun53; 205/209 Sqn 1Jan55; SOC 28Feb57

NJ194 TOC 57 MU 28Aug44; Calshot 23Sep44; 201 Sqn [NS:F] 9Oct44; engine cut and propeller detached 30Mar45; repaired on site by SBL 5Apr45; SB&HL 15Jun45 for conversion to Mk.V; 57 MU 19Sep45; S&HL for mods 23Jul47 to 18Dec47; 57 MU 19Dec47; FBSU 8May52; to non-effective stock 22Feb54; sold for scrap to British Aluminium Co 25Aug55

8 Sunderlands Mk.IV (Seafords Mk.I) built by Short Bros Ltd, Rochester under Contract Acft.2688:

NJ200 c/n S.1292; not TOC by RAF; became Seaford 1 **G-ALIJ** (see Chapter 6)

NJ201 c/n S.1293; not TOC by RAF; to MoS 12.45 as **G-AGWU**; radio call-sign OZZA; TOC by RAF 2.46; ferried Belfast to MAEE Felixstowe 1Sep50 {D}; still present there 2Nov52; later registered **G-ANAJ** (see Chapter 6)

NJ202 c/n S.1294; not TOC by RAF; became Solent 3 **G-AKNO** (see Chapter 6)

NJ203 c/n S.1295; not TOC by RAF; became Solent 3 **G-AKNP** (see Chapter 6)

NJ204 c/n S.1296; not TOC by RAF; became Solent 3 **G-AKNR** (see Chapter 6)

NJ205 c/n S.1297; not TOC by RAF; became Solent 3 **G-AKNS** (see Chapter 6)

NJ206 c/n S.1298; not TOC by RAF; became Solent 3 **G-AKNT** (see Chapter 6)

NJ207 c/n S.1299; not TOC by RAF; became Solent 3 **G-AKNU** (see Chapter 6)

6 Sunderlands Mk.III built by Short Bros & Harland Ltd, Belfast under Contract Act.2227:

NJ253 c/n SH.1159; TOC 57 MU 6Sep44; delivered to 10 (RAAF) Sqn [RB:B] 15Oct44; hull damaged on Mount Batten slipway 24Oct44; repaired on site 26Oct44; struck by NJ254 at Mount Batten moorings 16Apr45; repaired on site by SBL 16May45; delivered to 57 MU 15Jun45; S&HL 8Sep45 for conversion to Mk.V; 57 MU 1Nov45; S&HL 3May46 for conversion to Sandringham 5 **G-AHZC** (see Chapter 6)

Seaford Mk.I NJ201 wearing Transport Command call-sign OZZA at its moorings. (P H T Green collection)

Seaford Mk.I NJ207 seen in flight prior to being civilianised as Solent 3 G-AKNU. (P H T Green collection)

NJ254 c/n SH.1171; TOC 57 MU 21Sep44; delivered to 10 (RAAF) Sqn [RB:J] 1Nov44; delivered to 57 MU 19Jun45; taxied into NJ253 at Mount Batten 16Apr45; repaired on site; S&HL 25Jul45 for conversion to Mk.V; 57 MU 2Oct45; S&HL for mods 5Sep47; 57 MU 10Apr48; despatched to Far East via Calshot 8Jul48; 209 Sqn [V] 6Aug48; 57 MU (overhaul) 31Aug50; test-flown Apr51; to Wig Bay 2May51; to non-effective stock 22Feb54; sold for scrap to British Aluminium Co 25Aug55

NJ255 c/n SH.1173; TOC 57 MU 23Sep44; delivered to 10 (RAAF) Sqn [RB:G] 21Nov44; delivered to 57 MU 15Jun45; S&HL 4Sep45 for conversion to Mk.V; 57 MU 25Oct45; sold to S&HL 9Apr46 for conversion to Sandringham 4 **ZK-AMD** (see Chapter 6)

NJ256 c/n SH.1191; TOC 57 MU 30Sep44; delivered to 10 (RAAF) Sqn [RB:F] 28Oct44; engine lost power during taxiing at Mount Batten 19Jan45, aircraft swung and struck Catalina JX428; repaired on site; delivered to 57 MU 18Jun45; SOC 12Jul45

NJ257 c/n SH.1195; TOC 57 MU 4Oct44; 4 (C) OTU [B:I] 28Oct44; SBL 26Apr45 for conversion to Mk.V; 57 MU 14Nov45; sold to S&HL 30Apr46 for conversion to Sandringham 5 **G-AHZD** (see Chapter 6)

NJ258 c/n SH.1212; completed as Mk.V; TOC 57 MU 24Oct44; 302 FTU 3Nov44; 4 (C) OTU 26Dec44; 57 MU 11Feb45; 302 FTU 20Mar45; despatched to East Africa 9Apr45; arrived at Kisumu (Kenya) 19Apr45; to SAAF 31May45, later **1707** (see Part 4)

19 Sunderlands Mk.V built by Short & Harland Ltd, Belfast under Contract Acft.2227:

NJ259 c/n SH.1243; TOC 57 MU 10Nov44; 302 FTU 20Feb45; despatched to East Africa 17Mar45; to SAAF 26Apr45, later **1713** (see Part 4)

NJ260 c/n SH.1259; TOC 57 MU 19Nov44; 302 FTU 4Feb45; despatched to East Africa 5Mar45; 209 Sqn [V] Apr45; flew into high ground 20 mls (32 km) SW of Mombasa 14May45 while on radar exercise in heavy rain (3 killed)

NJ261 c/n SH.1270; TOC 57 MU 24Nov44; 302 FTU 4Feb45; despatched to East Africa 27Feb45; arrived 8Mar45; 209 Sqn [T]; practice bomb exploded inside aircraft 20May45, force-landed and lost float; repaired on site; ACSEA 19Jul45; two engines failed while taxying at Syriam, Rangoon (Burma) 3Aug45, drifted onto PP105; repaired on site; SOC 30May46

NJ262 c/n SH.1296; TOC 57 MU 28Dec44; 302 FTU 15Feb45; despatched to East Africa 15Mar45; arrived at Kisumu 29Mar45; to SAAF 31May45, later **1701** (see Part 4)

NJ263 c/n SH.1320; TOC 57 MU 2Feb45; 302 FTU 10Mar45; despatched to East Africa 2Apr45; arrived at Kisumu 21Apr45; to SAAF Apr45, later **1708** (see Part 4)

NJ264 c/n SH.1331; TOC Calshot 25Feb45; 461 Sqn [G] 14Mar45; delivered to 10 (RAAF) Sqn [RB:G] 18Jun45; damaged, repaired on site by SBL27Sep45; 201 Sqn [R] by 31Oct45; delivered to 230 Sqn [B:R] 19Jul46; ground accident 6Jun47; SOC 28Oct48

NJ265 c/n SH.1338; TOC 57 MU 28Feb45; 302 FTU 23Mar45; despatched to ACSEA 18May45, arrived 8Jun45; 209 Sqn [WQ:M]; struck submerged object while taxying off Cocos Islands 3Sep45 repaired on site; despatched to UK (? date); 57 MU 17Apr46; S&HL for mods 9Mar48; 57 MU 9Jul48; 235 OCU [TA:F, D:F, D:J] 30Sep48; struck pier while being beached at Calshot 11Apr49; repaired on site; repaired on site by SB&HL 22Jun50; delivered Wig Bay to SB&HL 8Dec50 as [F]; SB&HL for mods 1Nov51; test-flown 21Dec51; delivered to 57 MU 30Jan52; 235 OCU [D:F/D:J] 26Feb52; Wig Bay to Sydenham and return as crew ferry [J] 7May52; Calshot to Sydenham and return [J] 19May52; Calshot to Sydenham and return [J] 27Aug53 as crew ferry for RN284 [G]; FBSU 8Oct53; to non-effective stock 10Jun54; sold for scrap to British Aluminium Co 25Aug55

NJ266 c/n SH.1342; TOC 57 MU 1Mar45; 302 FTU 4Apr45; despatched to South Africa 6May45 via Kasfareet 12May45, Kisumu 25May45, Kipevu 26May45; arrived at Durban via Pamanzi 1Jun45; to SAAF 8.45, later **1711** (see Part 4)

NJ267 c/n SH.1351; TOC Calshot 12Mar45; 461 Sqn 19Mar45; struck by refueller at Pembroke Dock 18Apr45; repaired on site; delivered to 10 (RAAF) Sqn [RB:H] 18Jun45; 201 Sqn [P] 19Oct45; struck by refueller at Calshot 3Apr46; repaired on site by S&HL 10Apr46; 57 MU 13Nov47; SB&HL for mods 25Nov48 to 31Mar49; test flown Mar49; delivered to 57 MU Wig Bay 5Apr49 (crew ferry VB882); despatched to Far East 9Feb50; 209 Sqn [W] 30Mar50; returned to UK; delivered to 57 MU 11Jul50 (heavily corroded); SB&HL 2Feb51; FBSU 7May52; 201 Sqn [A:B] 4Jun53; Pembroke Dock to Sydenham and return 25Feb54 as [F]; porpoised on take-off from Pembroke Dock 3Mar54, nosed in and sank (7 killed); SOC 5Mar54; salvaged and sold for scrap to D V Howells Ltd, Milford Haven

NJ268 c/n SH.1371; TOC Calshot 26Mar45; 461 Sqn [M] 3Apr45; delivered to 10 (RAAF) Sqn [RB:M] 19Jun45; 201 Sqn [Z] 1Nov45; CCIS 4Mar46; 57 MU 20May46; S&HL for mods 26Sep47; 57 MU 16Apr48; despatched to Far East via Calshot 28Jun48, arrived 17Jul48; 205 Sqn [B] 29Jul48; returned to UK; 57 MU 31Aug50; to non-effective stock 31Oct50; sank in gale at Wig Bay, 28Feb51

NJ269 c/n SH.1390; TOC Calshot 29Mar45; 4 (C) OTU 5Apr45; became GI airframe **5753M** at Alness 10Dec45

NJ270 c/n SH.1400; TOC 57 MU 7Apr45; damaged while being towed at Wig Bay 20Apr45; repaired on site by SBL 25Apr45; 302 FTU 10May45; despatched to ACSEA 31May45, arrived 13Jun45; 205 Sqn [K]; returned to UK; 57 MU 25Apr46; sold for scrap to Phoenix & Clifton Ironworks, Coatbridge, 10Mar47

NJ271 c/n SH.1414; TOC 57 MU 14Apr45; 302 FTU 15May45; despatched to ACSEA 30May45, arrived 9Jun45; 205 Sqn; swung on alighting at Koggala 30Aug45, broke in two and sank (10 injured); SOC 20Sep45

NJ272 c/n SH.1417; TOC 57 MU 24Apr45; 302 FTU 5Jun45; despatched to ACSEA 30Jun45, arrived 14Jul45; 240 Sqn [B/N] 8.45; 1430 Flt; 88 Sqn [A] 1Sep46; left for UK after 17May47; 57 MU 19Jul47; S&HL for mods 27Oct47; 57 MU 27Feb48; despatched to Far East via Calshot 25Mar48; delivered to 209 Sqn [Z] 29Apr48; returned to UK; 57 MU 29Sep49; SB&HL13Oct49; 57 MU 7Aug50; despatched to Far East (? date); 88 Sqn [F] 30Nov50; 205 Sqn [N] 15Mar54; returned to UK; FBSU 7Apr54; repaired in works by SB&HL 26May54; Sydenham to Wig Bay and return 30May55; delivered to FBSU Wig Bay 8Jun55; despatched to Far East via Pembroke Dock 14Oct55; 205/209 Sqn [N] 10.55; SOC 24May57

NJ273 c/n SH.1422; TOC 57 MU 20Apr45; 302 FTU 9Jul45; despatched to ACSEA 4Aug45, arrived 31Aug45; 240 Sqn [D] 9.45; 209 Sqn; returned to UK; 57 MU by 5May47; SOC 6Nov47

NJ274 c/n SH.1430; TOC 57 MU 10May45; 302 FTU 16Jun45; despatched to ACSEA 8Jul45, arrived 21Jul45; 205 Sqn [B]; returned to UK (? date) ; delivered to 57 MU 17Jan47; SOC 4Nov47

NJ275 c/n SH.1432; TOC 57 MU 18May45; 302 FTU 5Jun45; despatched to ACSEA 20Jun45, arrived 18Jul45; 240 Sqn [N]; 1430 Flt; 88 Sqn [C] 1Sep46; left for UK after 30Jun47; 57 MU 30Sep48; Wig Bay to SB&HL 31Jan50 for mods 9Feb50 to 19Oct50; 57 MU 20Oct50; Wig Bay to Sydenham 9Oct52; and return visits 10, 14 and 15Oct52; to non-effective stock 22Feb54; returned to effective stock 29Apr54; to non-effective stock 8Aug56; noted uncoded at FBSU 9Feb57 and 17Aug57; sold for scrap to International Alloys Ltd, Aylesbury, 20Sep57; remains seen there 15Feb58

NJ276 c/n SH.1438; TOC 57 MU 25Apr45; 302 FTU 3Jul45; despatched to ACSEA 27Jul45, arrived 6Aug45; 240 Sqn [M] 8.45; 209 Sqn [U] 11Nov47; engine cut for practice on take-off from Seletar 14Jul48; bounced on alighting, nosed in and sank

NJ277 c/n SH.1456; TOC 57 MU 7Jun45; 302 FTU 3Aug45; despatched to ACSEA 29Aug45, arrived 11Sep45; 230 Sqn; flew into hill at 01°36'N 10°33'E, Johore (Malaya) 15Oct45 in bad visibility while on prisoner of war evacuation sortie and destroyed by fire (22 killed); SOC 25Oct45

30 Sunderlands Mk.V built by Short Bros Ltd, Rochester under Contract Acft.2226:

PP103 TOC 57 MU 25Nov44; 302 FTU 13Feb45; despatched via East Africa 1Mar45; delivered to ACSEA 19Jul45; 209 Sqn [U]; both starboard engines cut during night take-off from Seletar 27Mar46; crashed while attempting to alight on Johore Straits and broke back (5 crew + 6 passengers killed); SOC 13May46

PP104 TOC 57 MU 25Nov44; 302 FTU 9Feb45; despatched to East Africa 28Feb45, arrived 10Mar45; to SAAF 31May45, later **1715** (see Part 4)

209 Squadron Mk.V PP103 [U] on a detachment at Rangoon in September 1945 later suffered a fatal crash in the Johore Straits on 27th March 1946. (Gerald Raggett collection via Rod Simpson)

CHAPTER 5 : INDIVIDUAL AIRCRAFT HISTORIES

PP117 [4X:W], a Sunderland GR.5 of 230 Squadron in 1949, wearing differing roundel presentations on the wings and fuselage. It later served with 201 Squadron before being SOC for scrap at FBSU Wig Bay in October 1957. *(R C Sturtivant collection)*

PP105   TOC 57 MU 29Nov44; 302 FTU 2Feb45; despatched to East Africa 15Mar45, arrived 24Mar45; delivered to ACSEA 19Jul45; 209 Sqn [Y]; struck by NJ261 at moorings, Syriam, Rangoon (Burma) 3Aug45; repaired on site; left for UK 27Apr46; 57 MU 17Jun46; sold for scrap to Phoenix & Clifton Ironworks, Coatbridge, 10Mar47

PP106   TOC Wig Bay 5Dec44; 302 FTU 13Feb45; despatched to East Africa 13Mar45, arrived 24Mar45; delivered to ACSEA 19Jul45; 209 Sqn [X]; 205 Sqn 28Apr46; returned to UK; 57 MU 14May46; sold for scrap to Phoenix & Clifton Ironworks, Coatbridge, 10Mar47

PP107   TOC 57 MU 12Dec44; 302 FTU 15Feb45; despatched to East Africa 15Mar45, arrived 23Mar45; delivered to ACSEA 19Jul45; 209 Sqn [W]; returned to UK (? date); 57 MU 17Jun46; SB&HL for mods 27Jan49; delivered to 57 MU 2Nov49; 205 Sqn 31May50; while flying from Iwakuni to Kai Tak on 28Jan51, drifted off course at 2000 ft altitude and flew into Mt Morrison, nr Hwalien, Taiwan (crew of 5, 1 supernumerary and 8 ground personnel killed)

PP108   TOC 57 MU 18Dec44; 302 FTU 13Feb45; despatched to East Africa 4Mar45; delivered to ACSEA 19Jul45; 209 Sqn [Z]; struck launch while taxying at Bally 6Dec45; returned to UK (? date); 57 MU 8May46; sold for scrap to Phoenix & Clifton Ironworks, Coatbridge, 10Mar47

PP109   TOC MAEE 17Jan45; flying accident Cat AC 20Feb45; repaired on site 26Feb45; 302 FTU 13Apr45; despatched to South Africa 7May45; arrived at Kisumu 19May45; arrived at Durban 13Jun45; to SAAF, later **1703** (see Part 4)

PP110   TOC 57 MU 15Jan45; delivered to SB&HL for mods 5Apr52; test-flown 25Feb53; test flights as **NZ4105**, eg 12 & 18Mar53; 1, 12, 17 &24Apr53; to Wig Bay 12May53 for RNZAF as **NZ4105**; (see Part 3)

PP111   TOC 4 (C) OTU 13Jan45; undershot, bounced and struck flares at Alness 22/23Apr45; repaired on site by SBL 26Apr45; flash cartridge exploded in flight 6/7May45; repaired on site by SBL 16May45; airframe overstressed when control lost in cloud and aircraft inverted (!) 5Dec45; SOC 29Jan46

PP112   TOC 4 (C) OTU 5Feb45; 228 Sqn [UE:U] 11Feb45; 201 Sqn [G/X] 16Jun45; damaged 13Dec45; repaired on site by SBL 20Dec45; damaged 25Mar46; repaired on site 2Apr46; 57 MU 30Jan47; SB&HL for mods 27May48 to 4Oct48; 57 MU 14Oct48; Wig Bay to Sydenham and return 1Apr49, 10Jun49, 5, 13 and 8Jul49; despatched to Far East via Pembroke Dock 15Apr51; 209 Sqn [Q] 3May51; FEFBWg 30Jun51; damaged 27Sep52; 209 Sqn 21Jan53; ground accident 17Mar53; returned to UK; FBSU 28Apr53; to SB&HL for repair 19Jun53 to 31May54; test flown 27May54; delivered to FBSU 11Jun54; repaired on site by SB&HL 31Jan56; despatched to Far East Feb56; 205/209 Sqn [O] 27Feb56; SOC 27Jun58

PP113   TOC 4 (C) OTU 6Feb45; 461 Sqn 11Feb45; delivered 10 (RAAF) Sqn [RB:D] 16Jun45; 201 Sqn [W, Z] 20Oct45; damaged 12Nov45; repaired on site by SBL 22Nov45; damaged 20Aug46; repaired on site 26Aug46; during simulated attack on submarine HMS *Sentinel* on 5Jul47, slowly sank into sea 20 mls (32 km) N of Inistrahull Is, Co Donegal (Irish Republic) on even keel (4 killed, 3 missing, 5 injured)

PP114   TOC Wig Bay 9Feb45; delivered to 10 (RAAF) Sqn [RB:A] 15Jun45; damaged 18Jul45; repaired on site by SBL 24Jul45; delivered to 201 Sqn [Q] by 31Oct45; delivered to 57 MU 13Nov47; SB&HL for mods 9Feb48; delivered to 88 Sqn [B] 12Dec48; still there 31Aug50; Wig Bay to SB&HL 22Sep50 (crew ferry by PP148); 57 MU 4Sep51; SB&HL to Wig Bay and return 14Nov51; FBSU 2Mar54; to non-effective stock 12Mar54; sold for scrap British Aluminium Co 25Aug55

Sunderland MR.5 PP122 [A:E] of 201 Squadron flew to St Peter Port, Guernsey on 15th September 1954 to deliver a football team as part of the squadron's long association with the island. It hit a submerged rock in the harbour and sank, fortunately without loss of life.
(P H T Green collection)

PP115 TOC 461 Sqn 3Mar45; delivered to 10 (RAAF) Sqn [RB:B] 19Jun45; damaged; repaired on site by SBL 27Sep45; 272 MU 2Dec45; SB&HL for mods 12Feb48; 57 MU 8Jul48; 230 Sqn [4X:X] 12Aug48; 201 Sqn [A:C] 27Jan49; SB&HL from Wig Bay 24Feb49; struck by tender at Pembroke Dock 17Mar49; repaired on site by SB&HL 5Apr49; delivered to SB&HL for mods to sonobuoy equipment 14Apr49; test-flown 30May49; to Pembroke Dock as [G] 31May49; Pembroke Dock to SB&HL as [C] 8Feb50 (crew ferry by SZ567 [B]); Castle Archdale 31May50; lost float during three-engined take-off from Belfast Lough 14Jun50; repaired on site by SB&HL 1Jul50; 230 Sqn 19Sep50; 201 Sqn [NS:C, A:C] 1Oct50; SB&HL to Wig Bay and return 31Nov50; Wig Bay 4Sep51; repaired in works by SB&HL 21Aug53; repairs cancelled; to non-effective stock 10Aug54; sold for scrap to BKL Alloys Ltd 30Jun55

PP116 TOC 461 Sqn [K] 16Feb45; beaching trolley collapsed, damaging hull and floats, Calshot, 20Feb45; repaired on site by SBL 27Feb45; swung on take-off from Pembroke Dock 16May45, porpoised and nosed in (1 member of 8461 Servicing Echelon killed, 4 injured); SOC 24May45

PP117 TOC 228 Sqn [UE:P] 24Feb45; 201 Sqn [A:D] 15Jun45; struck by drifter while moored at Pembroke Dock 20Sep45; repaired on site by SBL 1Oct45; ground accident 29Apr46; repaired on site by SBL 6May46; 230 Sqn [P] 21Jul46; repaired in works by S&HL 10Jun47; 57 MU 6Aug48; collided with dinghy in gust at Pembroke Dock 26Feb49; repaired on site by SB&HL 5May49; delivered to SB&HL for mods 12May49 [W] (crew ferry by RN299 [P]); ex mods 13Jun49 [W]; 230 Sqn [4X:K, 4X:W, B:W] 13Jun49; damaged while under tow at Pembroke Dock 5Sep49; repaired on site by SB&HL 8Sep49; fell off tail trolley at Pembroke Dock 26Nov49; repaired on site; 201 Sqn [A:W] 4Jan51; repaired in works by SB&HL 12Feb53; test-flown 24Jan54; delivered to FBSU 8Mar54; 201 Sqn [201:W] 26Apr54; from and to Pembroke Dock - Sydenham 6Sep54 as [H]; from and to Pembroke Dock 17May56 using radio call-sign MJXWV; from and to Pembroke Dock 14Aug56; FBSU 13Sep56; noted there 9Feb57 and 17Aug57 coded 201:W in blue; sold for scrap to International Alloys Ltd 7Oct57

PP118 TOC 228 Sqn [UE:P] 28Feb45; 201 Sqn [J] 17Jun45; swung on take-off from Port Victoria, Seychelles, 11Jul45; repaired on site; 57 MU 7Feb46; repaired on site by SB&HL 5Feb48; SB&HL for mods 9Apr48; 57 MU 6Aug48; 230 Sqn [Z] 30Sep48; damaged float when it struck buoy at Pembroke Dock 29Jan49; beached next day and repaired on site by SB&HL; 235 OCU [TA:G] 11Aug49; damaged 22Oct49; repaired on site by SB&HL 3Nov49; sank at moorings in gale at Calshot 3Feb50; SOC 8Feb50; salvaged but destroyed by fire 23Feb50

PP119 TOC Calshot 3Mar45; 461 Sqn [E] 10Mar45; delivered to 10 (RAAF) Sqn 19Jun45; delivered to 201 Sqn [Y/V] by 31Oct45; Wig Bay 12Feb46; blown over while picketed at Wig Bay 23Apr47; SOC 6Nov47

PP120 TOC Calshot 10Mar45; 228 Sqn 14Mar45; float struck debris on alighting in Milford Haven 19May45 and wing hit sea; repaired on site by SBL 25May45; 201 Sqn [Y] 1Nov45; wings found to be wrinkled 18Mar46; repaired on site by SBL 27Mar46; SOC 27Mar47

PP121 TOC Calshot 16Mar45; 228 Sqn [UE:W] 21Mar45; 201 Sqn [B] 15Jun45; 57 MU 7Feb46; dragged moorings in gale at Wig Bay 19Feb46; SOC 28Apr46

PP122 TOC Calshot 27Mar45; 461 Sqn 5Apr45; delivered to 10 (RAAF) Sqn [RB:L] 19Jun45; delivered to 201 Sqn [O] by 31Oct45; struck by refueller at Calshot 9May46; repaired on site by SBL 14May46; delivered to 230 Sqn [4X:O, O] 19Jul46; struck buoy while taxying at Castle Archdale 22Oct46; repaired on site by SBL 28Nov46; ground accident 18Dec47; 57 MU 7Jan48; SB&HL for mods 28Oct48; delivered to 57 MU 7Apr49; delivered to Folland Aircraft Ltd, Hamble, 17May49 on loan for 3 months for installation of sonobuoy equipment for trials overseas; delivered to ASWDU, Calshot [P9:S] 15Sep49; damaged 9Jan52; repaired on site by SB&HL 17Jan52; Calshot to SB&HL [S] 4Mar52; repaired in works by SB&HL 1May52; Sydenham to Wig Bay and return 27Sep52; 201 Sqn Pembroke Dock [A:D, A:E] 30Oct52 as [E]; to Sydenham and return 12Mar53 as crew ferry; and again 27Mar53 and 3Jul53; Pembroke Dock - Sydenham and return 12Mar54 and 13Sep54; hit submerged object on alighting in St Peter Port harbour, Guernsey, 15Sep54 and sank

PP123 TOC 57 MU 10Apr45; 302 FTU 4May45; despatched to ACSEA 25May45, arrived 23Jul45; 205 Sqn [M] ; returned to UK (? date); delivered to 57 MU 4Dec46; SB&HL for mods 21Jun48 to 30Sep48; 57 MU 4Oct48; sank at moorings in gale at Wig Bay 2Dec48; SOC 27Jan49

PP124 TOC 57 MU 15Apr45; 302 FTU 11May45; despatched to ACSEA 9Jun45, arrived 12Jul45;205 Sqn [O]; returned to UK (? date); 57 MU 4Feb49; FBSU 2Apr52; damaged; delivered to SB&HL 12Aug52 for repaired in works; to RNZAF 14Oct53 as **NZ4113** (see Part 3)

PP125 TOC 57 MU 25Apr45; 302 FTU 10May45; despatched to South Africa 25May45; arrived at Durban 18Jun45 via Kasfareet 29May45 and Kisumu 8Jun45; to SAAF 10.45, later **1702** (see Part 4)

PP126 TOC 57 MU 22Apr45; 302 FTU 15May45; despatched to ACSEA 28May45, arrived 9Jun45; 212 Sqn [K] 6.45 (only Sunderland

CHAPTER 5 : INDIVIDUAL AIRCRAFT HISTORIES

to be TOC by this squadron, which then converted to Catalinas instead); 240 Sqn [K] 1Jul45; returned to UK (? date); 57 MU 7May47; SOC (extensive corrosion) 27Sep47

PP127 TOC Short Bros 27Apr45; S&HL 23May47; authority to transfer to Wig Bay for preparation for trials of IFF and SARAH equipment 15Mar56; test flights at Sydenham 4Aug55 and 25Mar56; to Wig Bay 28Mar56; trials at Calshott then to Sydenham 24Apr56; to RAF on transfer terms (repayment) 25Jul56; test flown at Sydenham 14Sep56; FBSU 16Sep56; Pembroke Dock 1Mar57; despatched to Far East Mar57; 205/209 Sqn [L, W] 1Apr57; SOC 1Jun57, scrapped at Seletar

PP128 TOC 57 MU 14May45; 302 FTU 1Jun45; despatched to ACSEA 30Jun45, arrived 12Jul45; 205 Sqn [V]; returned to UK (? date); 57 MU 8May46; sold for scrap to Phoenix & Clifton Ironworks, Coatbridge, 10Mar47

PP129 TOC 57 MU 18May45; 302 FTU 3Jun45; despatched to ACSEA 28Jun45, arrived 13Jul45; 205 Sqn [L/Q]; returned to UK (? date); 57 MU 30Jun49; FBSU 15Apr52; damaged; delivered to SB&HL 10Jun52 for repairs in works; test-flown 19Jun53 as **NZ4110**; to Wig Bay 1Jul53 for RNZAF; Belfast to Wig Bay 6Jul53 as crew ferry for NZ4111 (see Part 3)

PP130 TOC 57 MU 29May45; 302 FTU 21Jun45; despatched to ACSEA 13Jul45, arrived 23Jul45; 205 Sqn [A] Aug45; 209 Sqn [A, N] ?; returned to UK (? date); 57 MU 15Nov46; SB&HL for mods 12Aug48 to 16Dec48; 57 MU 12Jan49; 235 OCU [D:F] 15Mar51; 57 MU 19Oct51; Wig Bay to SB&HL and return 3Jul52 as crew ferry for RN293, and again 4Jul52 for RN288to non-effective stock 22Feb54; sold for scrap to BKL Alloys Ltd 30Jun55

PP131 TOC 57 MU 8Jun45; 302 FTU 12Jul45; despatched to ACSEA 20Jul45, arrived 10Aug45; 240 Sqn [J] 8.45; 209 Sqn [F, WQ:J] ?; returned to UK (? date); 57 MU 8Sep47; FBSU 12Apr52; allocated to RNZAF but not taken up; to non-effective stock 21May53; sold for scrap to Henry Bath & Sons, Liverpool, 1Sep53

PP132 TOC 57 MU 19Jun45; 302 FTU 14Jul45; despatched to ACSEA 3Aug45, arrived 13Aug45; 209 Sqn; overshot touch-down at Kai Tak 21Apr46 and beached; damaged beyond repair and SOC 11Jul46

10 Sunderlands Mk.III built by Blackburn Aircraft Ltd, Dumbarton under Contract Acft.2228:

PP135 TOC 57 MU 30Aug44; delivered to 10 (RAAF) Sqn [RB:E] 30Nov44; 57 MU 29Jun45; SOC 12Jul45

PP136 TOC MAEE (? date); 57 MU 2Sep44; Calshot 23Sep44; 228 Sqn 9Oct44; damaged by ship drifting in gale and blown ashore in Angle Bay 18Jan45; SOC 25Jan45

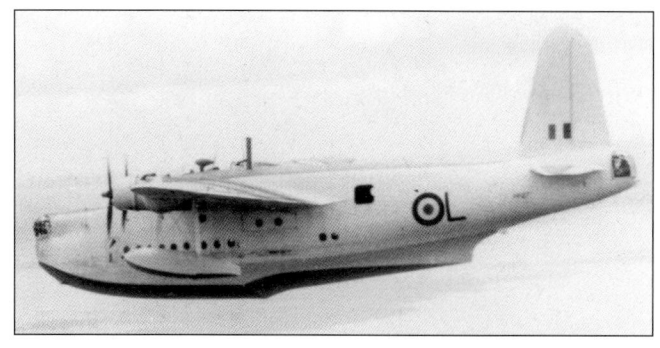

205/209 Squadron in the Far East in 1957 was the sole user of this Sunderland MR.5 PP127 [L]. (R C Sturtivant collection)

PP137 TOC 57 MU 16Sep44; SB(W)L, Windermere 17Jan45 for conversion to Mk.V; 4 (C) OTU 28May45; 57 MU 1Aug46; repaired in works by SB&HL 6Mar52; del Wig Bay 4Mar52; FBSU 21Aug52;Wig Bay to Sydenham and return 4, 8 and 12May53; despatched to Far East via Pembroke Dock 18May53; 205 Sqn [O] 27May53; 205/209 Sqn [O] 1Jan55; SOC 11Feb57

PP138 TOC 57 MU 18Sep44; delivered to 10 (RAAF) Sqn [RB:M] 9Nov44; lost propeller, which hit a second engine, lost height and ditched in Irish Sea 4Mar45; taken under tow by high-speed launch to Pembroke Dock; repaired on site by SBL 9Mar45 but not returned to service; delivered to 57 MU 19Jun45; sold for scrap to Phoenix & Clifton Ironworks, Coatbridge, 10Mar47

PP139 TOC 57 MU 18Sep44; delivered to 10 (RAAF) Sqn [RB:H] 30Nov44; delivered to 57 MU 18Jun45; sold for scrap to Phoenix & Clifton Ironworks, Coatbridge, 10Mar47

PP140 TOC 57 MU 30Sep44; 330 Sqn [WH:V] 19Dec44; repaired on site by Scottish Aviation, Greenock, 26Dec44; delivered to Calshot 4Jan45; 330 Sqn [WH:V] 26Jan45; hit sea in attempted ditching after engine lost power 100 mls (160 km) NW of Faeroes at 63°12'N 09°12'E 5Apr45, overturned and exploded (12 killed)

PP141 TOC 57 MU 30Sep44; conv to Mk.V; 4 (C) OTU [TA:B] 20Jun45; 235 OCU [TA:B] 31Jul47; 57 MU 26Sep47; SB&HL for mods 19Aug48 to 9Dec48; 57 MU 16Dec48; repaired on site by SB&HL 30Mar53; FBSU 11Aug53; to non-effective stock 22Feb54; sold for scrap to British Aluminium Co 25Aug55

PP142 TOC 57 MU 4Oct44; 10 (RAAF) Sqn [RB:L] 31Dec44; struck by ML828 while moored at Mount Batten 14Feb45; repaired on site by SBL 17Feb45; MAEE 9Jul45; loaned to BOAC 1Mar46; sold to BOAC 22Jun49 and registered **G-AHER** (see Chapter 6)

An air-to-air shot of Sunderland MR.5 PP137 of 205/209 Squadron in the mid-1950s when operating from Seletar. (Roy Green collection)

Sunderland Mk.5 PP151 was used by Short Bros from November 1950 to May 1951 to evaluate the enlarged tail of the Short Sperrin. The scene is Belfast harbour, with the 1935 Belfast-built SS Duke of York *in the process of conversion from 2 funnels to a single stack. Later the ship had to have a completely new bow fitted following a collision in the North Sea on 6th May 1953.*
(R C Sturtivant collection)

PP144 [A] was a Sunderland MR.5 used by 205 Squadron in the early 1950s.   (P H T Green collection)

Seen already stripped at Wig Bay on 7th June 1956, PP154 [X] was a Sunderland MR.5 formerly of 209 Squadron.(R C Sturtivant collection)

PP143 TOC 57 MU 9Oct44; converted to Mk.V; repaired in works by Scottish Aviation 2Feb45; 57 MU 28Jun45; FBSU; delivered to SB&HL 18Oct52 for repair in works; test-flown 11 & 12Jan54 as **NZ4119**; to FBSU storage 19Jan54 as RNZAF **NZ4119**; from Pembroke Dock to Belfast and return 17Jun55 (see Part 3)

PP144 TOC 57 MU 12Oct44; SBL 21Dec44 for conversion to Mk.V; Calshot 19Apr45; 228 Sqn [A] 30Apr45; 201 Sqn [NS:A] 16Jun45; 57 MU 7Feb46; SB&HL for mods 25Aug49 to 30Mar50; to Wig Bay 31Mar50 (crew ferry by ML768); 57 MU 4Apr50; despatched to ACSEA 31Oct50; 205 Sqn [P] 25Dec50; 88 Sqn [A] by Sep52; left for UK 1Feb54, delivered to Pembroke Dock 7Feb54; FBSU 2.54; to non-effective stock 22Feb54; sold for scrap to BKL Alloys Ltd 30Jun55

20 Sunderlands Mk.V built by Blackburn Aircraft Ltd, Dumbarton under Contract Acft.2228:

PP145 TOC 57 MU (? date); Saunders Roe, Beaumaris, 21Oct44; delivered to 302 FTU 20Nov44; despatched to to ACSEA 27Dec44; delivered to 230 Sqn [NM:O] 28Jan45; struck by PP117 while moored at Pembroke Dock 29Apr46, Cat AC; repaired on site by SBL 6May46; became GI airframe **6103M** at Pembroke Dock 9Sep46

PP146 TOC 57 MU 27Oct44; ferried Wig Bay to (302 FTU) Oban 1Nov44; delivered to 302 FTU 25Nov44; despatched to ACSEA 22Dec44, arrived 4Jan45; 230 Sqn [V, U]; damaged in squall at Pegu moorings 1Jul45; repaired on site; returned to UK, still with 230 Sqn; struck by refueller at Pembroke Dock moorings 25May46; repaired on site by SBL 12Jun46; 57 MU 6Dec46; SOC 6Nov47

PP147 TOC 57 MU 3Nov44; delivered to 302 FTU 25Nov44; despatched to ACSEA 28Dec44, arrived 4Jan45; 230 Sqn [V]; returned to UK, still with 230 Sqn; delivered to 57 MU 17May46; delivered to SB&HL for mods 11Jan50; ex mods 12Oct50; delivered to 57 MU 16Oct50; SB&HL 17Aug53; FBSU 1Mar54; noted there, uncoded, 9Feb57 and 17Aug57; SOC 16Oct57; sold for scrap to International Alloys Ltd, Aylesbury, 4Oct59

PP148 TOC 57 MU 8Nov44; 302 FTU 8Dec44; despatched to ACSEA 31Dec44; delivered to 230 Sqn [NM:P] 28Jan45; 209 Sqn [B]; returned to UK; Wig Bay 8May46; 57 MU 2Jul46; SB&HL for mods 25Aug49; test-flown 24Mar50; 57 MU 14Apr50; Wig Bay to SB&HL and return 22Sep50 (crew ferry for PP114); Wig Bay to SB&HL and return 6Oct50; Pembroke Dock 16Oct50; to Far East; 205 Sqn [L] 31Oct50; delivered to 88 Sqn [F] 1Aug52; bow dug in on alighting at night in storm at Iwakuni (Japan) 25Mar53 and overturned (5 killed)

PP149 TOC 57 MU 18Jan4; 302 FTU 30Dec44; despatched to ACSEA 1Feb45, arrived 18Mar45; 230 Sqn [R]; returned to UK, still with 230 Sqn; delivered to 57 MU 30May46; was to become GI airframe **6031M** at Halton 1Aug46 but not taken up; FBSU 2Apr52; to non-effective stock 21May53; noted on scrap heap at 63 MU, Edzell, 2Feb54; sold for scrap to Motherwell Machinery & Scrap Co Ltd

PP150 TOC 57 MU 20Nov44; 302 FTU 9Jan45; despatched to East Africa 11Feb45, arrived 7Mar45; to Far East 19Jul45; 209 Sqn [S]; SOC 26Sep46

PP151 TOC 57 MU 25Nov44; 302 FTU 5Jan45; despatched to East Africa 11Feb45, arrived 21Feb45; to Far East; 209 Sqn [R]; hull damaged by debris at Kai Tak 26Sep45; repaired on site; left for UK 6Apr46; 57 MU 17Apr46; delivered to SB&HL for mods 16Jun49; ex mods 2Feb50; SB&HL on free loan 3Feb50 for trials of enlarged fin of Short Sperrin Nov50; test-flown 6Feb50, 21Nov50 and Apr51; delivered to 57 MU 4Mar52; Wig Bay to SB&HL 4Mar52 then Sydenham - Wig Bay and return 5Mar52; to non-effective stock 22Feb54 Sydenham; sold for scrap to BKL Alloys Ltd 19Oct56

PP152 TOC 57 MU 5Dec44; 302 FTU 28Jan45; swung while being towed in windy conditions at Oban 7Feb45; repaired on site by SBL12Feb45; despatched to ACSEA 2Mar45, arrived 25Mar45; 209 Sqn; 122 R&SU; delivered to 230 Sqn 5.45; damaged in squall at Pegu moorings (Burma) 1Jul45; repaired on site; ground collapsed under tail trolley while being towed at Koggala 27Jul45; repaired on site; SOC 26Sep46

PP153 TOC MAEE 7Dec44; 57 MU 11Dec44; 302 FTU 9Jan45; despatched to East Africa 28Feb45, arrived 9Mar45; to SAAF 24Apr45 (no serial) (see Part 4)

PP154 TOC MAEE 7Dec44; 57 MU 11Dec44; 302 FTU 8Jan45; despatched to ACSEA 10Feb45, arrived 19Feb45; 230 Sqn [Y]; returned to UK; 57 MU 31May46; SB&HL for mods 16Dec48 to 30Jun49; 57 MU 6Jul49; Pembroke Dock 15Apr51; to Far East; 205 Sqn [X, N] 30Apr51; 209 Sqn 1Jan53; FEFBWg reserve 30Apr54; returned to UK; FBSU 22Jun54; noted there, coded X in black, 9Feb57 and 17Aug57; to non-effective stock 8Aug56; sold for scrap to International Alloys Ltd, Aylesbury, 20Sep57

PP155 TOC MAEE 11Dec44; 57 MU same day; 302 FTU 11Jan45; despatched to ACSEA 11Feb45, arrived 5Mar45; 230 Sqn [Z]; returned to UK, still with 230 Sqn; delivered to 57 MU 31May46; SB&HL for mods 24Feb49 to 3Nov49; test flown Oct49; delivered to 57 MU 16Nov49 (with RN788 as crew ferry); left for Far East via Calshot 29Dec49; delivered to 88 Sqn [D] 8Jan50; FEFBWG 30Jun50; 88 Sqn [D, possibly sometime F] 15Oct51; left for UK 23Oct52; FBSU 31Oct52; Wig Bay to Sydenham and return 14Jan53; repaired in works by SB&HL 15Jan53; test-flown 21Dec53; delivered to FBSU 6Jan54; Pembroke Dock to SB&HL and return 29Jun54 [O] as crew ferry for RN299[P] and SZ581[V]; 230 Sqn 7Jul54; hit swell on alighting in Transgigvaag Fjord (Faeroes) 23Oct54, bounced, nosed in and sank

PP156 TOC 57 MU 18Dec44; 302 FTU 5Feb45; despatched to South Africa 4Mar45; to SAAF 31May45, later **1712** (see Part 4)

PP157 TOC 57 MU 29Dec44; 302 FTU 28Jan45; despatched to ACSEA 2Mar45, arrived 12Mar45; 230 Sqn [S]; hit coral reef while taxying at Jesselton (N Borneo) 19Jan46 and damaged beyond repair; SOC 25Apr46

PP158 TOC 57 MU 29Dec44; 302 FTU 5Feb45; despatched to ACSEA 6Mar45, arrived 18Mar45; 230 Sqn [T]; hit underwater obstruction on alighting on Kuantan river (Malaya) 3Oct45 and damaged beyond repair; SOC 8Nov45

PP159 TOC 57 MU 28Dec44; 302 FTU 15Feb45; despatched to East Africa 25Mar45, arrived at Kisumu 4Apr45; to ACSEA 19Jul45; 209 Sqn [Q]; returned to UK; delivered to 57 MU 10Dec46; SOC 6Jan47

PP160 TOC Calshot 10Jan45; 4 (C) OTU 16Jan45; damaged 15Feb46; repaired on site by SBL 20Feb46; SOC 24Apr47

PP161 TOC Calshot 17Jan45; 4 (C) OTU same day; propellers and float damaged by buoy at Alness 24Sep45; repaired on site by Avro 19Jun46; 57 MU 21Sep46; 230 Sqn 30Oct47; SOC 6Nov47

PP162 TOC Calshot 9Feb45; 461 Sqn 19Feb45; delivered to 10 (RAAF) Sqn [RB:C] 16Jun45; 201 Sqn [S] 20Dec45; 57 MU 22Feb46; SB&HL for mods 4Mar48; 57 MU 9Sep48; MAEE 20Oct48 for experiments on pressure plotting, water loads on hull, etc; Felixstowe to SB&HL 24-26Oct49; struck by MV *The Wrangler* at Felixstowe moorings 21Aug51; repaired on site; damaged on alighting heavily at Felixstowe 14Mar52; Pembroke Dock to Sydenham 30Oct52 as [A]; to Wig Bay 31Oct52; SB&HL 1Nov52; returned to Felixstowe 2Nov52; sold to Aquila Airways 18Jun53 and registered **G-ANAK** (see Chapter 6)

PP163 TOC Calshot 9Feb45; struck by refueller at Milford Haven moorings 10May45; repaired on site by SBL 16May45; 228 Sqn 30May45; 201 Sqn [N, D] 16Jun45; chine damaged during defuelling at Calshot 31Dec46; repaired on site by SBL 17Jan47; delivered to 57 MU 8Aug47; SB&HL for mods 26Aug48 to 23Dec48; 57 MU 17Jan49; 235 OCU [D:K] 26Jan50; 57 MU 26Oct51; FBSU 13Dec52; test-flown 29Jan54; to Wig Bay 8Feb54; to Sydenham and return 16Aug54; delivered to FBTS Pembroke Dock 19Aug54; FBTS to Sydenham 2Jan56; test-flown 6Jan56; delivered to FBSU Wig Bay 13Jan56; to non-effective stock 8Aug56; noted there, still coded, 9Feb57 and 17Aug57; sold for scrap to International Alloys Ltd, Aylesbury, SOC 4Oct57

PP164 TOC 228 Sqn 9Feb45; 201 Sqn [A:L] 16Jun45; swung by gust and struck refueller at Pembroke Dock 31Jan46; repaired on site by SBL; delivered to 230 Sqn [4X:X] 19Jul46; 57 MU 21Oct47; SB&HL for mods 9Sep48 to 3Feb49; 57 MU 9Feb49; Calshot 13Oct49; to Far East; 209 Sqn [Z] 27Oct49; blown off moorings in gale at Yokohama (Japan) 19Jul50 and damaged beyond repair during salvage

10 Sunderlands Mk.V built by Short Bros Ltd, Rochester under Contract Acft.2226:

RN264 TOC 57 MU 25Jun45; 302 FTU 14Jul45; despatched to ACSEA 4Aug45, arrived 5Sep45; 209 Sqn [R]; broke from moorings in typhoon at Sana Bay, Hainan Province (China) 18Jul46 and damaged beyond repair; SOC 25Aug46

RN265 TOC 57 MU 3Jul45; 302 FTU 9Aug45; despatched to ACSEA 1Sep45, arrived 11Sep45; 209 Sqn [WQ:S]; swung on take-off from Seletar 23Jan46 and struck ship's buoy; flown to Kai Tak and beached; SOC 13Jun46

RN266 TOC 57 MU 14Jul45; 302 FTU 24Aug45; despatched to ACSEA 9Sep45, arrived 16Sep45; 209 Sqn [Q]; returned to UK; 57 MU

One of 235 OCU's Sunderlands, MR.5 PP163 [D:K] ended its days at FBSU Wig Bay where it was SOC for scrap on 4th October 1957.
(R C Sturtivant collection)

Seen in the c1947-49 post-war markings of 235 OCU is Sunderland GR.5 RN271 [TA:J]. *(P H T Green collection)*

6Aug47; SB&HL for mods 8Jan48; 57 MU 11May48; 201 Sqn [M] 16Dec48; struck by dinghy while moored at Calshot 17Dec48; repaired on site 13Jan49; SB&HL for mods to sonobuoy equipment 28Apr49; delivered SB&HL to Pembroke Dock for 201 Sqn [M] 8Jun49; struck by launch at Pembroke Dock moorings 30Jun49; repaired on site by SB&HL 21Jul49; flew Wig Bay - Sydenham - Pembroke Dock 21Feb50 [NS:M, later M]; Pembroke Dock to SB&HL 6Jun51 [M]; repaired in works by SB&HL 7Jun51; 57 MU 15Mar52; 235 OCU [D:K] 1Aug52; detached to Kalafrana 16Aug53 for Operation 'Ionia'; FBTS 16Oct53; Pembroke Dock to Sydenham and return 18May54 [K]; to non-effective stock 8Aug56; noted at FBSU coded D:K in black 9Feb57 and 17Aug57; sold for scrap to International Alloys Ltd, Aylesbury, 20Sep57; remains seen there 15Feb58

RN267 TOC Calshot 19Jul45; 330 Sqn 9Aug45; struck by ML878 while moored at Stavangar/Sola 2Dec45; repaired on site; from Norway to 272 MU 25Feb46; delivered to 57 MU 15Oct46; SOC 6Nov47

RN268 TOC 57 MU 4Aug45; 302 FTU 21Sep45; despatched to ACSEA 2Oct45, arrived 10Oct45; 205 Sqn [R]; returned to UK; 57 MU 30Sep48; FBSU 2Apr52; for RNZAF but not taken up; ground accident 17Dec52; sold for scrap to Henry Bath & Sons Ltd, Liverpool, 4May53

RN269 TOC 57 MU 4Aug45; 302 FTU 14Sep45; despatched to ACSEA 6Oct45, arrived 15Oct45; 205 Sqn [P]; returned to UK; 230 Sqn [T] 23Apr46; 57 MU 16Jun46; SB&HL for mods 19Jan48; 57 MU 26May48; 201 Sqn [K] 29Jul48; struck submerged object while taxying at Finkenwerder, Hamburg, 23Nov48; repaired in works by SB&HL 25Nov48; 57 MU 16Sep48; to Far East; 205 Sqn [M] 27Sep50; holed on alighting at NAS Sangley Point (Philippines) 28Jun53, overshot and foundered in shallow water

RN270 TOC 201 Sqn [K] 27Aug45; 57 MU 11Feb46; S&HL for mods 9Oct47; 57 MU 28Apr48; 230 Sqn [4X:O] 11Nov48; delivered Pembroke Dock to SB&HL [O] for mods 25Apr49; returned [C] to 230 Sqn 9Jun49; [B:O]; delivered SB&HL to Pembroke Dock for 230/240 Sqn 19Jul50 (crew ferry by RN299 [D]); SB&HL for mods 30Nov51; 230 Sqn [4X:V, 4X:O] 15Dec51; SB&HL to Wig Bay 29Feb52; Pembroke Dock to SB&HL and return 30Jun53 [O]; test-flown Sydenham 6Apr55; to Wig Bay 15Apr55; FBSU 25May55; to SB&HL 20Aug56; despatched to Far East via Pembroke Dock 9Oct56; 205/209 Sqn [K] 26Oct56; SOC 25Sep58

RN271 TOC 57 MU 25Sep45; 1430 Flt; 88 Sqn [G] 1Sep46; still present 30Jun47; S&HL for mods 12Jul47; 235 OCU [TA:H, TA:J, D:L] 26Aug47; hit buoy at Calshot 24Sep48 while avoiding ship; repaired on

Sunderland MR.5 RN273 [L] of 205 Squadron at Seletar and SOC there on 12th March 1957. *(Roy Green collection)*

Beached Sunderland MR.5 RN278 [N] of 205 Squadron in the Far East, mid 1950s. *(Gerald Raggett collection via Rod Simpson)*

Moored on the Thames during a Battle of Britain Week visit to the Pool of London in September 1948 is Sunderland GR.5 RN270 [4X:O] of 230 Squadron. *(R C Sturtivant collection)*

site by SB&HL 7Oct48; struck by tender at Calshot moorings 3Mar49; delivered to SB&HL 1Apr52 for repair in works; FBSU 9Oct52; 201 Sqn [A:E] 16Mar54; struck rock in St Peter Port harbour, Guernsey, 15Sep54 and sank; salvaged and to FBSU 5Nov54; to non-effective stock 8Aug56; noted at FBSU 9Feb57 and 17Aug57; sold for scrap to International Alloys Ltd, Aylesbury, 20Sep57

RN272 TOC CRD, Rochester, 15Oct45; 201 Sqn [G] 19Aug46; 4 (C) OTU [TA:D] 4Apr47; 235 OCU 31Jul47; became GI airframe **6534M** 16Apr48 at 235 OCU; SOC 22Oct51

RN273 TOC 57 MU 30Nov45; S&HL for mods 18May47; delivered to 201 Sqn [L] 3Sep47; test flown at Sydenham Feb49; to Pembroke Dock 19Feb49; SB&HL for mods 8Jun49 to 22Jun49 returned Pembroke Dock; 201 Sqn [NS:W, L, A:A] 24Jun49; damaged when alighted heavily at Mount Batten 16Feb50; repaired on site by SB&HL 1Jun50; test-flown 4 & 5Jun53; delivered to FBSU Wig Bay 23Jun53; to Sydenham and return 24Jun53; despatched to Far East via Pembroke Dock 29Sep53; FEFBWg reserve 6Oct53; 205 Sqn 14Dec53; 205/209 Sqn [L] 21Apr55; SOC 12Mar57

30 Sunderlands Mk.V built by Blackburn Aircraft Ltd, Dumbarton under Contract Acft.2228:

RN277 TOC 228 Sqn 9Feb45; 201 Sqn [NS:S, NS:O, A:F] 15Jun45; damaged at Alness moorings 9Aug45; repaired on site by SBL 21Aug45; 201 Sqn [A:D] 26Oct45; flying accident 12Apr46; repaired on site by SBL 17Apr46; struck by small craft at Calshot moorings 15Aug46; delivered to 57 MU 10Sep46; SB&HL for mods 30Sep48 to 3Mar49, test-flown Feb49; to Far East ; delivered to 88 Sqn [D] 23Apr50; 209 Sqn [D] 8.51; blown ashore in typhoon at Iwakuni (Japan)14Oct51 and damaged beyond repair; SOC 15Oct51

RN278 TOC 228 Sqn 22Feb45; 201 Sqn [M] 17Jun45; taxied into pinnace at Castle Archdale 26Jun45; repaired on site by S&HL 2Jul45; damaged during mooring at Rod-el-Faraq, Cairo, 22Nov45; repaired on site by S&HL 5Dec45; delivered to 230 Sqn [S] 17Jul46; ground accident 5Feb47; repaired on site by S&HL 20Feb47; 57 MU 13Nov47; delivered to SB&HL 26Mar52 for repair in works; test-flown 28Aug52; SB&HL for mods 4Sep52; delivered to FBSU 8Sep52; despatched to Far East via Pembroke Dock 22Feb54; delivered to FEFBWg reserve 28Feb54; 205 Sqn [N] 29Apr54; 205/209 Sqn [N] 1Jan55; SOC 11Sep56

RN279 TOC 461 Sqn 7Mar45; 57 MU 10Mar45; 302 FTU 1May45; despatched to South Africa 22May45; delivered to Durban 13Jun45 via Kasfareet (27May45) and Kisumu (3Jun45); to SAAF, later **1704** (see Part 4)

RN280 TOC 461 Sqn 24Feb45; 57 MU 14Mar45; 302 FTU 29Apr45; despatched to ACSEA 15May45, arrived 28May45; Station Flight Koggala; damaged while taxying in heavy swell at Direction Is (Cocos Is) 7Aug45; repaired on site; 205 Sqn; returned to UK; 57 MU 21Jun48; FBSU 2Apr52; delivered to SB&HL 1May52 for repair in works; test-flown 9 & 11Dec52 as **NZ4106**; delivered to FBSU 5Jan53 (crew ferry by SZ599) for storage; delivered to SB&HL for mods 4Sep53; test-flown 5Dec53; delivered to FBSU storage 21Dec53 for RNZAF as **NZ4106**; still at Wig Bay 18Mar54 when flown Belfast return (see Part 3)

RN281 TOC Calshot 24Feb45; 57 MU 10Mar45; 302 FTU 29Apr45; despatched to South Africa 17May45; delivered to Durban 1Jun45 via Kasfareet (20May45) and Kisumu (24May45); to SAAF, later **1710** (see Part 4)

RN282 TOC Calshot 16Mar45; 461 Sqn [UT:N] 21Mar45; delivered to 10 (RAAF) Sqn [RB:N] 19Jun45; 201 Sqn [U] 20Oct45; 57 MU 15Apr46; delivered to SB&HL for mods 24May49; delivered to 57 MU 31Jan50; Wig Bay to Sydenham and return 12May50 as crew ferry for ML799; likewise 25May50 for DP199; to Far East 8Jun50; delivered to 88 Sqn [C] by 30Jun50; FEFBWg 1Jan53; 209 Sqn 12Mar53; returned to UK; Wig Bay to FBSU 30Oct53; Wig Bay 6Sep54; Pembroke Dock 17Sep56; to Far East; 205/209 Sqn [N] 6Oct56; SOC 13May58

CHAPTER 5 : INDIVIDUAL AIRCRAFT HISTORIES

An excellent air-to-air close-up of Sunderland MR.5 RN284 [A:F] seen during its third spell with 201 Squadron in the mid-1950s. Note the squadron badge above the crew door.
(P H T Green collection)

The first user of Sunderland Mk.V RN282, in 1945, was 461 Squadron at Hamworthy which coded it UT:N. As the war ended shortly after the squadron was re-equipped, this Sunderland was moved on to 10 (RAAF) Squadron at Mount Batten.
(P H T Green collection)

RN283   Ferried Rhu to Calshot and TOC Calshot 16Mar45; 228 Sqn [DQ:F] 28Mar45; crashed in sea at 50°12'N 05°47'W 27Apr45 after dropping depth-charges from 50 feet, which exploded and blew tail off (3 killed, 4 missing); SOC 10May45

RN284   TOC Calshot 23Mar45; 201 Sqn [NS:C] 15Jun45; ground accident 6May47; repaired on site 15May47; delivered to 57 MU 18Sep47; SB&HL for mods 23Sep48 to 17Feb49; delivered to 57 MU 24Feb49; 201 Sqn [A:C/A:G] 15Jun51; struck flotsam while alighting at Pembroke Dock 29Oct51; repaired on site by SB&HL 8Nov51; Pembroke Dock to SB&HL and return 4Mar52 [E] as crew ferry for SZ568; 235 OCU [D:G] 31Mar52; repaired on site by SB&HL 1May52; Calshot to SB&HL 27Aug53 [G] (with NJ265 [J] as crew ferry); test-flown 30Jun54; delivered to FBSU Wig Bay 8Jul54; 201 Sqn [A:F/201:F] 20Jun55; test-flown 30Aug55 at Sydenham; FBSU 5Feb57; to non-effective stock 30Apr57; noted at FBSU, still coded 201:F in blue, 9Feb57 and 17Aug57; sold to SB&HL 2Jul57; test flown 12 and 19Dec57; to Brest for Aéronautique navale 21Dec57 with call-sign F-VBUE (see Part 5)

RN285   TOC Calshot 16Mar45; 228 Sqn 28Mar45; 201 Sqn [NS:H] 16Jun45; bounced on alighting at Calshot and lost float 12Apr46; repaired on site by SBL 23Apr46; 4 (C) OTU 24Apr47; ground accident 3Jul47; repaired on site by SBL; 57 MU 26Feb48; fell off tail trolley at Wig Bay 26Apr49; repaired on site by SB&HL 19May49; ground accident 17Dec52; FBSU 11Feb53; sold for scrap to H Bath & Sons Ltd 4May53

RN286   TOC Calshot 27Mar45; 4 (C) OTU 5Apr45; damaged 15Apr46; repaired on site by SBL; Wig Bay 16Jul46; SB&HL 8Sep52; test-flown 1Sep53 as **NZ4117**; to FBSU storage 3Oct53 as RNZAF **NZ4117** (see Part 3)

RN287   TOC Calshot 2Apr45; 4 (C) OTU 5Apr45; SOC 26Aug46

RN288   TOC 57 MU 10Apr45; 302 FTU 15May45; despatched to ACSEA 26May45, arrived 20Jun45; 205 Sqn [S]; 209 Sqn 29Dec47; returned to UK; SB&HL for mods 28Oct48 to 4Aug49, test-flown Jul49; 57 MU 11Aug49; Sydenham - Wig Bay and return 16Nov49 as crew ferry for PP155; 235 OCU 24Nov49; SB&HL for mods 5Apr51; 235 OCU [TA:J] del 13Apr51; delivered to SB&HL 29Feb52; delivered to FBSU 4Jul52; 201 Sqn [A:C] 18Sep53; Pembroke Dock to Sydenham 17Feb54 [M] and again 2-3 and 29Apr54; bounced on alighting off Eastbourne, Sussex, 4Jun55 during demonstration for RAF Association conference, nosed in and sank (4 killed, 6 injured); rear hull recovered from sea

RN289   TOC 57 MU 19Apr45; 302 FTU 25May45; despatched to ACSEA 5Jun45, arrived 22Jun45; 205 Sqn [P]; returned to UK; 57 MU 7Oct46; SOC 6Nov47

RN290   TOC 57 MU 10Apr45; 302 FTU 25May45; despatched to ACSEA 1Jun45, arrived 22Jun45; 205 Sqn [C]; returned to UK; 57 MU 1Jun46; SB&HL for mods 12Aug48 to 25Nov48; 57 MU same day; 230 Sqn [B:Z] 30Jun51; SB&HL for mods 6Dec51 to 19Dec51; 230 Sqn

209 Squadron operated Sunderland MR.5 RN293 [V] from Seletar during the latter half of 1953. (Roy Green collection)

Flying low over the jungle in Ceylon in 1945 was Sunderland Mk.V RN294 [R] of 205 Squadron. (R C Sturtivant collection)

Sunderland GR.5 RN297 on hardstanding at Cowes, IoW, where it was utilised by Saunders Roe Ltd 1948-52 for testing Princess flying boat Trial Installations. (R C Sturtivant collection)

Seen at Koggala in Ceylon, Sunderland Mk.V RN298 [F] of 240 Squadron eventually found its way back to the UK for scrapping. (P H T Green collection)

Visiting the Pool of London for BoB week in September 1949 was 230 Squadron's Sunderland GR.5 RN299 [4X:P]. (P H T Green collection)

[B:Z] same day; Castle Archdale to Wig Bay 27Feb52 [Z]; BoB Pool of London Sep53; alighted in Angle Bay 30Jan54 after engine caught fire in air; float broke off and aircraft destroyed by fire; SOC same day

RN291 TOC 57 MU 19Apr45; 302 FTU 29May45; despatched to ACSEA 31Jun45, arrived 16Jul45; 240 Sqn [G] 8.45; returned to UK; 57 MU 26Jan50; FBSU 15Apr52; delivered to SB&HL 3Nov52; test-flown 6Feb54 as **NZ4120**; to Wig Bay 15Feb54 for RNZAF as **NZ4120**; to SB&HL and return 24Feb54 (see Part 3)

RN292 TOC 57 MU 25Apr45; 302 FTU 30May45; despatched to ACSEA 27Jun45, arrived 12Jul45; 240 Sqn [C] 8.45; returned to UK; 57 MU 12Feb47; SB&HL for mods 29Jul48; destroyed by fire in works at Belfast14Oct48

RN293 TOC 57 MU 29Apr45; 302 FTU 29May45; despatched to ACSEA 9Jun45, arrived 20Jun45; 205 Sqn [B]; returned to UK; 57 MU 24Feb49; Pembroke Dock to Sydenham 10Apr51 and 14Dec51 [S];delivered Wig Bay to SB&HL for mods 5Feb52; delivered to FBSU 3Jul52 (crew ferry by PP130); despatched to Far East via Pembroke Dock 10Aug53; 209 Sqn [F, V] 22Aug53; 88 Sqn [F] 9Nov53; 209 Sqn 9Oct54; 205/209 Sqn 1Jan55; SOC 17Aug56

RN294 TOC 57 MU 4May45; 302 FTU 30May45; despatched to ACSEA 27Jun45, arrived 16Jul45; 205 Sqn [R]; struck debris on alighting at Cocos Is 29Aug45; repaired on site; returned to UK; 57 MU 8Aug47; Shorts 1Oct47; 57 MU 21Apr48; despatched to Far East via Calshot 8Jul48; 205 Sqn [P, later G:D] 29Jul48; returned to UK; delivered to SB&HL 11Oct50; delivered to 57 MU 25Oct51; sank at Wig Bay moorings 20Dec51; SOC 13Jun52

RN295 TOC 57 MU 24May45; 302 FTU 5Jun45; despatched to South Africa 25Jul45, arrived 31Jul45; to SAAF, later **1714** (see Part 4)

RN296 TOC 57 MU 25May45; 302 FTU 25Jun45; despatched to South Africa 15Jul45, arrived 27Jul45; to SAAF, later **1705** (see Part 4)

RN297 TOC 57 MU 25May45; 302 FTU 19Jun45; despatched to ACSEA 13Jul45, arrived 5Aug45; 240 Sqn [L] 8.45; 88 Sqn [H] by 28Feb47; left for UK after 30Nov47; 57 MU 22Dec47; SB&HL 27Feb48; 57 MU 3Jul48; Saunders Roe Ltd 28Jul48 for flight trials of power-operated controls for Saro 10/46 flying-boat; MAEE 13Sep51 for crew training; returned to Saunders Roe Ltd 27Sep51 for continuation of task; damaged in accident 20May52; sold to Aquila Airways 30Jun53 for spares

RN298 TOC 57 MU 3Jun45; 302 FTU; despatched to ACSEA 1Aug45, arrived 12Aug45; 240 Sqn [F] by Aug45; 209 Sqn [WQ:R, Y] 5Jan48; struck by launch while moored at Jesselton (N Borneo) 7Mar49; repaired on site; returned to UK; test-flown SB&HL Jul49; 57 MU Dec49; to non-effective stock 16Jun50; sold for scrap to Enfield Rolling Mills Ltd 15Sep50

RN299 TOC 57 MU 9Jun45; 302 FTU 13Jul45; despatched to ACSEA 6Aug45, arrived 21Aug45; 230 Sqn [P] 25Apr46; returned to UK; 57 MU 1Aug46; SB&HL for mods 22Apr48 to 26Aug48; 57 MU 9Sep48; 230 Sqn [4X:P] 21Oct48; crew ferry SB&HL for PP117 12May49; SB&HL for mods 19May49 to 16Jun49; 230 Sqn [B:P] same day; delivered to SB&HL 29Jul54; test-flown 5Sep55; delivered to FBSU 16Sep55; 201 Sqn [A:D] 30Nov55; FBSU 6Jun56; to non-effective stock 19Oct56; noted at FBSU, still coded A:D in black, 9Feb57 and 17Aug57; sold for scrap to International Alloys Ltd, Aylesbury, 4Oct57

RN300 TOC 10 (RAAF) Sqn [RB:Q] 15Jun45 and delivered 16Jun45; 201 Sqn [T] 20Oct45; 57 MU 16Feb46; SB&HL for mods 15Apr48 to 19Aug48; 57 MU 20Aug48; to Far East 30Jun49; 205 Sqn 28Jul49; returned to UK; Pembroke Dock - SB&HL and return 19Jul50 as crew ferry for RN270; 57 MU 31Oct50; FBSU 20Oct52; despatched to Far East via Pembroke Dock 11Feb54; FEFBWg reserve 6Mar54; 209 Sqn [X] 30Apr54; 205/209 Sqn 1Jan55; SOC 30Apr57

RN301 Delivered Rhu to 57 MU 20Jun45; TOC 57 MU 22Jun45; 302 FTU 3Aug45; despatched to ACSEA 29Aug45, arrived 9Sep45; 205 Sqn [D]; returned to UK; 57 MU 12Aug48; SB&HL for mods 7Oct48 to 25May49; 57 MU same day; to non-effective stock 22Feb54; sold for scrap to BKL Alloys Ltd, Birmingham, 30Jun55

RN302 TOC 57 MU 28Jun45; 302 FTU 9Aug45; despatched to ACSEA 1Sep45, arrived 1Sep45; 205 Sqn [B]; Station Flight Koggala; engine caught fire on take-off from Koggala 29Sep45; repaired on site; returned to UK; 57 MU 15Jan48; SB&HL for mods 20Jan48; 57 MU 21May48; 235 OCU [TA:H] 25Feb49; SB&HL for mods 1Nov51 to

CHAPTER 5 : INDIVIDUAL AIRCRAFT HISTORIES

Sunderland MR.5 RN303 [R] of 209 Squadron, seen here at Seletar, was not SOC until 24th January 1959.   (P H T Green collection)

Sunderland GR.5 RN304 was coded B:V when serving with 230 Squadron.   (Late Charles Waterfall via Dave Welch)

Sunderland MR.5 [V] at Kai Tak about 1954 was SZ560 of 209 Squadron, probably on deployment from Seletar as a result of the recent hostilities in Korea.   (P H T Green collection)

Coded [WQ:S] this Sunderland Mk.V of 209 Squadron appears to be SZ565 which remained in service post-war with 201 Squadron and 235 OCU before being written-off in 1951.   (via R A Walker)

31Mar52; FBSU 3Apr52; despatched to Far East via Pembroke Dock 2Jan53; delivered to 88 Sqn [C, later F] 17Jan53; force-landed in sea 22 mls E of Tsushima Island (Japan) 27Dec53 after engine caught fire; SOC 1Jan54

RN303   Delivered Rhu to 57 MU 29Jun45; TOC 57 MU 1Jul45; 302 FTU 3Aug45 despatched to ACSEA 3Sep45, arrived 11Sep45; 230 Sqn [W]; returned to UK; still with 230 Sqn 16Apr46; delivered to 57 MU 2Sep46; SB&HL for mods 29Jan48; 57 MU 27May48; to Far East; 209 Sqn [X] 10May50; 88 Sqn [C] by 30Sep51; left for UK 15Dec52, delivered to Wig Bay 22Dec52; FBSU 22Jan53; test-flown at SB&HL 11Mar54; FBTS [D:K] 30Sep55; 230 Sqn [230:T] 1Oct56; FBSU 11Feb57; to Far East; 205/209 Sqn [R] 23Aug57; made last recorded touch-down at Kalafrana 12Sep57 while on ferry flight en route to FEAF via Tripoli; SOC 24Jan59; believed scrapped at Seletar

RN304   Delivered Rhu to 57 MU 6Jul45; TOC 57 MU 11Jul45; 302 FTU 9Aug45; despatched to ACSEA 16Oct45, arrived 23Oct45; 230 Sqn [4X:L] 1Nov45; returned to UK; still with 230 Sqn 20Apr46; delivered to 57 MU 2Sep46; SB&HL for mods 24Jan48; 57 MU 3Jun48; 201 Sqn [NS:L, NS:C] 11Nov48; SB&HL for mods to sonobuoy equipment 14Apr49 to 2Jun49; accident 29Jul49; repaired on site by SB&HL 11Aug49; 201 Sqn 24Nov49; 230 Sqn 29Dec49; 201 Sqn [Q] 31Jul50; 230 Sqn [B:V] 22Nov50; 235 OCU [D:M]; delivered to SB&HL 19Dec52; test-flown 20 & 21Oct53; delivered to FBSU 5Nov53; FBTS 22Nov53; FBSU 3Mar54; FBTS 26Apr54; to non-effective stock 8Aug56; noted at FBSU 9Feb57 and 17Aug57; sold for scrap to International Alloys Ltd, Aylesbury, 20Sep57

RN305   Delivered Rhu to 57 MU 23Jul45; TOC 57 MU 24Jul45; 302 FTU 24Aug45; despatched to South Africa 21Sep45; delivered to Congella 18Oct45 via Khartoum (24Sep45) and Kisumu (12Oct45); to SAAF arr Durban 12Oct45, later **1706** (see Part 4)

RN306   TOC 57 MU 3Aug45; 302 FTU 1Sep45; despatched to ACSEA 23Sep45, arrived 1Oct45; 205 Sqn [J/P]; returned to UK; 57 MU 24Mar50; FBSU 30Sep52; delivered to SB&HL 9Oct52; test-flown 1Dec53 as **NZ4118** for RNZAF; to FBSU storage 15Dec53 as **NZ4118**; from Pembroke Dock to Belfast return 17Jun55 (see Part 3)

30 Sunderlands Mk.V built by Short & Harland Ltd, Belfast under Contract Acft.4067:

SZ559   c/n SH.1462; TOC 57 MU 24Jun45; 302 FTU 22Jul45; Desp ACSEA 12Aug45, arrived 24Aug45; 209 Sqn [S]; dragged moorings in typhoon and beached in Sana Bay, Hainan Province (China) 18Jul46

SZ560   c/n SH.1467; TOC 57 MU 30Jun45; 302 FTU 3Aug45; despatched to ACSEA 29Aug45, arrived 6Sep45; 205 Sqn [Q]; returned to UK; 57 MU 25Mar48; SB&HL for mods 13Jan49 to 20Oct49; delivered to 57 MU 31Oct49; crew ferry Wig Bay - Belfast for ML779 5.5.50; to Far East; delivered to SB&HL 21Mar53; test-flown 16 & 21Apr54; delivered to FBSU 5May54; 209 Sqn [D, W, V] 30Oct54; returned to UK; FBTS; Station Flight Pembroke Dock 1Oct56; 230 Sqn [230:R] 9Nov56; FBSU 20Feb57; to non-effective stock 11Mar57; noted at FBSU, still coded 230:R, 9Feb57 and 17Aug57; sold for scrap to International Alloys Ltd, Aylesbury,5 15Oct57

SZ561   c/n SH.1473; TOC 57 MU 3Jul45; 302 FTU 24Aug45; despatched to ACSEA 6Sep45, arrived 16Sep45; 230 Sqn 5Dec45; 209 Sqn [M, later S and W] 31Aug46; TRE (FE); returned to UK; 57 MU 28Mar49; FBSU 2Apr52; delivered to SB&HL 21Aug52; delivered to Wig Bay for RNZAF as **NZ4114** 18Nov53 (see Part 3)

SZ562   c/n SH.1483; TOC 57 MU 27Jul45; 302 FTU 1Sep45; despatched to ACSEA 23Sep45, arrived 30Sep45; 209 Sqn; SOC 18Aug46

SZ563   c/n SH.1485; TOC 57 MU 3Aug45; 302 FTU 4Sep45; despatched to ACSEA 17Sep45, arrived 26Sep45; 230 Sqn; bounced on alighting at Seletar 1Dec45 and damaged spar; SOC 25Apr46

SZ564   c/n SH.1496; TOC 57 MU 5Aug45; 302 FTU 8Sep45; despatched to ACSEA 2Oct45; engine changed at Kasfareet; arrived ACSEA 19Feb46; delivered to 1430 Flt [A] 23Aug46; 88 Sqn 1Sep46; fell off beaching trolley at Kai Tak 26Sep46 and damaged beyond repair; BBOC 28Nov46; SOC 31Dec46

SZ565   c/n SH.1501; TOC 57 MU 8Sep45; 302 FTU 22Sep45; despatched to ACSEA 6Oct45, arrived 15Oct45; 209 Sqn [S]; returned to UK; 57 MU 12May48; SB&HL for mods 14Apr49 to 22Dec49; 57 MU 12Jan50; delivered to 201 Sqn 10Mar50; SB&HL for mods 17Nov50 to 7Dec50, using radio call-sign MKMQM; 235 OCU 11Dec50; crashed on alighting off Hillhead, Southampton Water, 16Nov51 and sank (2 killed); salvaged and scrapped 1Feb52

SZ566   c/n SH.1503; TOC 57 MU 6Sep45; 302 FTU 31Oct45; despatched to ACSEA 1Mar46, arrived 4Apr46; 205 Sqn [F]; 1430

Seen at FBSU Wig Bay in 1957 shortly before scrapping in October that year was Sunderland MR.5 SZ567 [230:P], indicating that its last operator was 230 Squadron.
(Ron Campbell via Phil Butler)

SZ566, a Sunderland GR.5, saw much service in the Far East including periods with 205 Squadron.
(P H T Green collection)

Above the clouds, Sunderland Mk.V SZ568 [TA:C] whilst in use with 4 (C) OTU in 1946-47.
(P H T Green collection)

Another view of Sunderland Mk.V SZ568 [TA:C], this time probably with 235 OCU during 1947. (R C Sturtivant collection)

Flt; 88 Sqn [F] 1Sep46; left for UK 18Mar48; 57 MU 29Apr48; SB&HL for mods 13Jan49 to 15Sep49; delivered to 57 MU 29Sep49; to Far East; 205 Sqn [Z] 3Aug50; 209 Sqn [F, Z] 1Jan53; FEFBWg 15May53; 205 Sqn 1Aug53; FEFBWg reserve 14Dec53; 88 Sqn [C *Eastern Princess*] 15Jan54; left for UK 1Jul54; FBSU 27Jul54; to non-effective stock 18Aug56; noted at FBSU, still coded C in black, 9Feb57 and 17Aug57; sold for scrap to International Alloys Ltd, Aylesbury, Bucks, 20Sep57

SZ567 c/n SH.1504; TOC 57 MU 17Sep45; 302 FTU 10Nov45; despatched to ACSEA 19Dec45, arrived 29Dec45; 230 Sqn; returned to UK; 230 Sqn [N, B:P] 24Apr46; delivered to 57 MU 9Sep46; S&HL for mods 1Nov46; delivered to 201 Sqn [NS:B, later A:B] 6Apr47; repaired on site by SB&HL 19May49; SB&HL for mods to sonobuoy equipment 21Jul49 to 4Aug49; collided with buoy at Pembroke Dock 1Jan51; repaired on site; damaged 19May52; repaired on site by SB&HL; damaged 31Jan53; SB&HL 3Jul53 (crew ferry by PP122); test-flown at SB&HL 4Jun54; delivered to FBSU 22Jun54; 230 Sqn [B:P, 230:P] 30Jun54; despatched via Kalafrana to Far East May55, returned Jul55; Biggin Hill BoB 17Sep55; FBSU 6Feb57; noted there 9Feb57; to non-effective stock 11Mar57; noted at FBSU, coded 230:P in red, 17Aug57; sold for scrap to International Alloys Ltd, Aylesbury, 15Oct57

SZ568 c/n SH.1515; TOC 57 MU 26Sep45; 302 FTU 10Nov45; 4 (C) OTU [TA:C] 9Apr46; ground accident 4Feb47; repaired on site by S&HL 21Feb47; 235 OCU [TA:C] 31Jul47; 57 MU 25Sep47; SB&HL for mods 3Jun48 to 21Oct48; 57 MU 26Oct48; 235 OCU 23Feb50; bounced on alighting at Calshot 20Mar50 and lost float; repaired on site by SB&HL 13Apr50; damaged 29Feb52 to SB&HL 4Mar52 [G] (crew ferry by RN284); repaired on site by SB&HL 13Mar52; FBSU 1Sep52; to non-effective stock 29Apr54; sold for scrap to "? Ave Engine Servicing" 19Oct56

SZ569 c/n SH.1517; TOC 57 MU 5Oct45; 302 FTU 13Dec45; 4 (C) OTU [TA:T] 9Apr46; damaged 24Apr47; repaired on site by S&HL; 235 OCU 31Jul47; delivered to 57 MU 24Sep47; SB&HL for mods 1Jul48 to 11Nov48; 57 MU 17Nov48; despatched to Far East via Calshot 10Mar49, arrived 31Mar49; delivered to 205 Sqn [Z] same day; grounded while being taxied by a 201 Sqn crew in Malay Cove, Trincomalee (Ceylon) 3Oct50, and damaged beyond repair; SOC 31Oct50

SZ570 c/n SH.1518; TOC 57 MU 22Oct45; 302 FTU 28Jan46; despatched to ACSEA 9Mar46, arrived 21Mar46; 1430 Flt; 88 Sqn [D] 1Sep46; left for 57 MU 7Feb48; during ferry flight, broke away from moorings at Kalafrana 28Feb48 and was wrecked on rocks

SZ571 c/n SH.1520; TOC 57 MU 22Oct45; 302 FTU 26Feb46; 4 (C) OTU 9Apr46; damaged 31Dec46; 57 MU 27Feb47; S&HL for mods 1May47 to 24Oct47; 57 MU 27Oct47; 201 Sqn [C, 201:D] 24Jun48; strained planing hull during Berlin airlift; delivered to SB&HL 18Feb49; test-flown 1Mar50; delivered to 57 MU 7Mar50; crew ferry Wig Bay - Belfast for ML757 19.5.50; despatched to Far East 31May50; 209 Sqn [Y, W] 30Jun50; 88 Sqn [B] by 11Jul52; FEFBWg 31Jan53; 88 Sqn [B]; returned to UK; delivered to SB&HL from Wig Bay 15Dec53; test-flown 22Sep54 and 25Jan55; delivered to FBSU 7Feb55; FBTS; to non-effective stock 30Apr57; sold to SB&HL 31Jul57; to Brest for Aéronautique navale 15Nov57 using radio call-sign FYBUD (see Part 5)

SZ572 c/n SH.1527; TOC 57 MU 5Nov45; S&HL for mods 17Jan47; 230 Sqn [4X:P] 20Jun47; ground accident 9Sep47; repaired on site by S&HL 11Sep47; repair transferred to RAF 2Oct47; struck by refueller at Calshot moorings 25Mar48; 57 MU 4May48; delivered to SB&HL 23May52; delivered to FBSU 7Nov52; despatched to Far East via Pembroke Dock 3May54; FEFBWg reserve 11May54; delivered to 88 Sqn [C] 12Jul54; 205 Sqn 9Oct54; 205/209 Sqn [M] 1Jan55; SOC 27Jul57

SZ573 c/n SH.1533; TOC BOAC, Poole, 14Nov45; 57 MU 2Apr46; S&HL for mods 22Mar47 to 20Sep47; 57 MU 26Sep47; 230 Sqn [W] 24Jun48; struck submerged object while taxying at Finkenwerder, Hamburg, 5Aug48; SB&HL 26Aug48; 57 MU 21Jan49; despatched to Far East via Calshot 29Dec49; 209 Sqn [Y]; bomb fell off rack while being loaded at Seletar 26Mar50 and exploded, sinking aircraft (2 killed, 9 injured)

SZ574 c/n SH. 1542; TOC 57 MU 30Nov45; Shorts for mods 22Mar47 to 10Jul47; delivered to 201 Sqn [NS:K] 11Jul47; flying accident 21Aug47; repaired on site by S&HL 28Aug47; damaged beyond repair on hitting underwater obstruction in Lough Erne on take-off from Castle Archdale 31May48 and beached; SOC 16Dec48

SZ575 c/n SH.1543; TOC 57 MU 13Dec45; 302 FTU 4Mar46; 4 (C) OTU [TA:K] 9Apr46; struck by tender at Pembroke Dock moorings 13Sep46; repaired on site by S&HL 26Sep46; 57 MU 13Nov47; SB&HL for mods 23Sep48 to 24Feb49; delivered to 57 MU 10Mar49; struck by tender in Belfast Lough 10Apr51; repaired on site; 235 OCU [D:H] 30Apr51; SB&HL for mods 22Nov51; returned to 235 OCU 6Dec51; damaged 16May53; repaired on site by SB&HL; FBSU 5Oct54; 230 Sqn 24Nov54; 201 Sqn [201:E] 3Feb55; collided with RN299 near Pembroke Dock 8Dec55; repaired on site; FBSU 6Feb57; noted there, coded 201:E in blue, 9Feb57; to non-effective stock 11Mar57; noted at FBSU 17Aug57; sold for scrap to International Alloys Ltd, Aylesbury, 15Oct57

SZ576 c/n SH.1544; TOC 57 MU 22Dec45; S&HL for mods 26Jun47 to 2Oct47; 57 MU 15Oct47; 235 OCU [TA:H] 13May48; struck by refueller at Calshot moorings 5Jan49; repaired on site; struck by ship in fog at Calshot moorings 28Jan49; repaired on site by SB&HL 8Sep49; FBSU 14May52; SB&HL for mods 24Oct52 to 27Nov52; delivered to FBSU 27Nov52; 201 Sqn [A:A/201:A] 31Mar53; FBSU 18Mar57; sold to SB&HL 11Jun57; test-flown 18 & 27Jun57, 4Jul57; to Brest for Aéronautique navale 5Jul57 using radio call-sign FYBUA (see Part 5)

SZ577 c/n SH.1545; TOC 57 MU 9Jan46; S&HL for mods 12Jun47 to 11Sep47; 230 Sqn [4X:Z] 17Sep47; repaired in works SB&HL 16Sep48; test-flown 1.49; to Pembroke Dock 27Jan49 using radio call-sign MKQQD; 57 MU 22Feb49; despatched to Far East via Calshot 2May49; delivered to 88 Sqn [A] 6May49; still there 31Aug50; returned to UK; 57 MU 31Dec50; delivered to SB&HL 4Jun52; test-flown 7Nov52; delivered to FBSU 28Nov52; despatched to Far East via Pembroke Dock 6Apr54; FEFBWg reserve 15Apr54; 209 Sqn [Y] 14Jul54; 205/209 Sqn [S] 1Jan55; SOC 24May57

While other views of Sunderlands on visits to the Pool of London have been taken from the opposite bank, this classic image of MR.5 SZ576 [A:A] of 201 Squadron includes the Tower of London itself and probably dates from September 1953.   (R C Sturtivant collection)

Sunderland Mk.V SZ579 never entered service, as a result of an altercation with rocks on the South shore of Belfast Lough near Grey Point Fort when she broke away from her moorings on or about 10th January 1946.
(Shorts/Bombardier Aerospace)

Used by 235 OCU during 1947-49, Sunderland GR.5 SZ580 [TA:G] is seen with 57 MU Wig Bay after withdawal in May 1949 due to damage.   (K Wilson-Clark)

SZ578   c/n SH.1546; TOC 57 MU 11Feb46; S&HL for mods 2Apr47 to 31Jul47; delivered to 201 Sqn [C] 6Aug47; damaged while being slipped at Calshot 25Aug47; repaired on site by S&HL 28Aug47; 57 MU 29Apr48; test-flown at SB&HL 4.50; to FE; 209 Sqn [Z] 30Sep50; 205 Sqn [L]; converted to VVIP configuration 10.52 for Royal tour of Borneo and Sarawak; FEFBWg 1Aug53; 88 Sqn [A/B] 4Oct53; 205 Sqn [B] 9Oct54; FEFBWg reserve 19Oct54; despatched to UK 18Nov54; FBSU 6Dec54; to non-effective stock 8Aug56; noted at FBSU, coded B in black, 9Feb57 and 17Aug57; sold for scrap to International Alloys Ltd, Aylesbury, 4Oct57

SZ579   c/n SH.1547; whilst at S&HL before delivery broke from Belfast Lough moorings on or about 10Jan46 and went aground on rocks on the South shore of Lough near Grey Point Fort and could not be refloated; tides and wind broke her back; dismantled for salvage and scrap

SZ580   c/n SH.1548; TOC 57 MU 14Feb46; S&HL for mods 24Apr47; 235 OCU [TA:G] 14Aug47; damage found on inspection 31May49; 57 MU 25Aug49; sold for scrap to S Collins Ltd (?) 13Apr50

SZ581   c/n SH.1549; TOC 57 MU 11Mar46; S&HL for mods 11Mar47 to 11Jul47; 230 Sqn [4X:Y] same day; SB&HL for mods 9Jun49 to 20Jun49; 230 Sqn [B:Y] 28May52; repaired in works by SB&HL 29Jul54; sank at moorings, Wig Bay, 2Nov55; SOC 8Aug56

SZ582   c/n SH.1550; TOC 57 MU 26Mar46; S&HL for mods 1Feb47 to 26Jun47; 230 Sqn [4X:O] 9Jul47; crane gave way during propeller change at Finkenwerder, Hamburg, 8Oct48 and damaged mountings; repaired in works by SB&HL 11Nov48; test-flown 3May49; delivered to 57 MU 9May49; to non-effective stock 8Aug56; noted uncoded at FBSU 9Feb57 and 17Aug57; sold for scrap to International Alloys Ltd, Aylesbury, 20Sep57

SZ583   c/n SH.1551; TOC 57 MU 6Apr46; S&HL for mods 3Apr47; while in works, SOC 18Aug49

SZ584   c/n SH.1552; delivered to BOAC, Poole, on loan 3May46; registered **G-AHJR** 27Jun46 (see Chapter 6); returned to RAF at 57 MU 16Apr48 **SZ584**; FBSU 2Apr52; delivered to SB&HL 1Sep52; test-flown 23Aug53 as **NZ4115**; to Wig Bay 4Sep53 for RNZAF as NZ4115; test-flown Wig Bay to Belfast return 14Oct53 (see Part 3)

SZ598   c/n SH.1553; TOC 57 MU 16May46; SB&HL for mods 2Mar50 to 2Nov50; 57 MU same day; flew into hill in cloud near Beja (Tunisia) 16Feb51 while on ferry flight to Far East for 201 Sqn

SZ599   c/n SH.1554; first flight 14Jun46; TOC 57 MU 15Jun46; MAEE [B] 18Jun46 for boundary layer experiments and trials of safety glass canopy; 57 MU 31Jan51; SB&HL for mods 17Apr51 to 31Mar52; crew ferry 5Jan53 Wig Bay - Sydenham for RN280; despatched to Far East via Pembroke Dock 6Feb53; 209 Sqn 10Feb53; 88 Sqn [F] 11Apr53; FEFBWg reserve 9Nov53; 209 Sqn 14Dec53; hit swell on alighting at Christmas Island 21Jun54 and lost engine and float; scuttled off Christmas Island 56

1 Sunderland Mk.V built by Short Bros Ltd, Rochester under Contract Acft.2226:

TX293   TOC MAEE 15Dec45; ground accident 7Jan46; repaired on site by SBL 14Jan46; lost float on alighting at Felixstowe 3Apr46; damage found on inspection 2Aug46; delivered to 57 MU 10Sep46; blown over on ramp in gale at Wig Bay 9Feb48 and beaching leg collapsed; sold for scrap to J Connell 12Aug48

10 Sunderlands Mk.V built by Blackburn Aircraft Ltd, Dumbarton under Contract Acft.2228:

VB880   TOC 57 MU 20Aug45; 302 FTU 21Aug45; despatched to ACSEA 6Oct45, arrived 20Oct45; delivered to 88 Sqn [A] 6Jul47; left for UK 14Apr49; 57 MU Apr49; FBSU 2Apr52; SB&HL 26Jun52; test-flown 26Jun53 and 3Jul53 as **NZ4111**; to Wig Bay 7Jul53 for RNZAF as **NZ4111** (see Part 3)

VB881   TOC 201 Sqn [F, A, NS:A] 2Aug45; Victory Flypast. London 8Jun46; struck launch at Wilhelmshaven 19Jun46; repaired on site; struck debris on take-off from Pembroke Dock 26Jul46; repaired on site by SBL 8Aug46; blew off tail trolley at Calshot 18Nov46 while on compass swing, damaging keelson; repaired on site by SBL 6Dec46; 57 MU 13Nov47; FBSU on formation; SB&HL 3Jul52; to Wig Bay 10Aug53 for RNZAF as **NZ4112** (see Part 3)

VB882   TOC 57 MU 2Aug45; 302 FTU 21Sep45; despatched to ACSEA 13Oct45, arrived 3Nov45; 230 Sqn [X] 30Apr46; returned to UK; still with 230 Sqn delivered to 57 MU 9Sep46; SB&HL for mods 15Jan48; 57 MU 7May48; crew ferry for NJ267 Sydenham to Wig Bay

CHAPTER 5 : INDIVIDUAL AIRCRAFT HISTORIES

The remains of Sunderland MR.5 SZ582 at Wig Bay on 7th June 1956. It was SOC on 30th September 1957. The seemingly ramshackle corrugated-steel shed was to provide cover to mechanics working on Sunderlands' engines.   (R C Sturtivant collection)

"Two, six!" A gang of airmen ready themselves for hauling Sunderland GR.5 VB880 [A] of 88 Squadron up the slipway.   (P H T Green collection)

*Sunderland GR.5 VB887 took part in the Berlin airlift in 1948 in the hands of 230 Squadron. It is seen here coded [4X:X] on the Havel Lake in Berlin.
(R C Sturtivant collection)*

Sunderland MR.5 VB888 [Z] of 209 Squadron seen in 1953 moored near Seletar.   (P H T Green collection).

*Moored on the Havel Lake during the Berlin airlift is 201 Squadron's Sunderland GR.5 VB889 [NS:D]
(P H T Green collection)*

The first of six Sunderlands Mk.III which were flown in pairs from England to Australia in early 1944, ML730 / A26-1 receives some engine care via the folding leading edge platforms. For delivery the aircraft were painted 'extra dark sea grey' and 'dark slate grey' with 'sky S' undersides and both British and Australian serials were carried.
(RAAF via JM Collection)

5Apr49; to Far East via Calshot 28Apr49; 209 Sqn [W] 26May49; returned to UK (? date); bounced on alighting at Pembroke Dock 8Sep49 and lost float; returned to Far East; Seletar 25Nov49; SOC 5Jun50

VB883 TOC 57 MU 8Sep45; 302 FTU 10Nov45; despatched to ACSEA 31Dec45, arrived16Jan46; 1430 Flt; 88 Sqn [B] 1Sep46; left for UK 12Dec48; 57 MU 12.48; FBSU 2Apr52; delivered to SB&HL 12May52; test flight Wig Bay to Belfast return 6May53 as **NZ4107**; to SB&HL Belfast 10Jul53 as NZ4107 and test-flown 15 and 19Oct53; to Wig Bay 3Nov53 for RNZAF as **NZ4107** (see Part 3)

VB884 TOC 57 MU 24Sep45; 302 FTU 14Nov45; despatched to ACSEA 31Dec45; delivered to 209 Sqn [WQ:X] 16Jan46; returned to UK; 57 MU 26Aug48; FBSU 31May52; SOC 31Aug52

VB885 TOC 57 MU 26Sep45; 302 FTU 10Nov45; while attempting to regain flare path off Calshot in bad weather on three engines 13Feb46, hit sea in turn and broke up (10 killed); SOC 4Apr46

VB886 TOC 57 MU 9Nov45; 4 (C) OTU 22Oct45; 57 MU; deld to Pembroke Dock 22Oct46; sank in gale at Pembroke Dock moorings 16Mar47

VB887 TOC 57 MU 14Dec45; S&HL for mods 19Dec46 to 5Jun47; 230 Sqn [4X:X] 9Jun47; SB&HL for mods 16Jun49 to 30Jun49; returned to 230 Sqn 30Jun49; ran aground while taxying at Castle Archdale 17Oct49; repaired on site; 230/240 Sqn 30Jun50; FBSU 12May52; despatched to Far East via Pembroke Dock 7Jan54; delivered to 88 Sqn [A] 18Jan54; hit swell on take-off from Kai Tak 18Jul54, wing dug in and aircraft capsized near Cheung Chau Is (crew rescued)

VB888 TOC 57 MU 19Oct45; 302 FTU 30Jan46; 4 (C) OTU 4Apr46; damaged 24Apr47; repaired on site by SBL 26Apr47; 235 OCU 31Jul47; 57 MU 26Sep47; SB&HL for mods 25Nov48 to 28Apr49; 57 MU 3May49; to Far East; 88 Sqn [B] by 12.51; FEFBWg 2Jan52; 88 Sqn 1Jan53; FEFBWg 11Apr53; 209 Sqn[Z] 15May53; FEFBWg reserve 19Oct54; left for UK via Kalafrana (15Jan55); FBSU 15Feb55; to non-effective stock 8Aug56; noted at FBSU, coded Z in black, 9Feb57 and 17Aug57; sold for scrap to International Alloys Ltd, Aylesbury, 20Sep57; remains seen there 15Feb58

VB889 launched 19Oct45; FF 8Nov45; TOC 57 MU 3Nov45; S&HL for mods 17Dec46; 201 Sqn [NS:D] 11Jun47; SB&HL for mods to sonobuoy equipment 19May49 to 16Jun49; 201 Sqn [A:D] 17Jun49; struck by tender while refuelling at Pembroke Dock 4Apr50; repaired on site by SB&HL 27Apr50; 57 MU 10Nov50; Pembroke Dock 4Feb52; FBSU 17Oct55; to non-effective stock 8Aug56; noted at FBSU, coded [A:D], 9Feb57 and 17Aug57; sold for scrap to International Alloys Ltd, Aylesbury, 20Sep57; remains seen there 15Feb58

1 Solent 3 on loan from BOAC

WM759 ex G-AKNS, originally Seaford Mk.I NJ205; owned by MCA; loaned to BOAC; loaned to MAEE 13Nov50 for take-off and water stability trials at high all-up weights; serial number allocated 15Jan51; returned to MCA; SB&HL 16Feb52; restored to MCA

---

83 Short Sunderland Mk.III to Mk.V conversions 1944 - 1952

DP191, 195, 198, 199, 200 : **EJ153**, 155, 167, 170, 171, 172 : **EK579**, EK592 : **JM667**, 681, 714, 715, 717, 718, 719, 720.
ML739, 741, 745, 747, 757, 758, 761, 763, 764, 765 (**Prototype**), 768, 772, 778, 780, 781, 783, 784, 807, 809, 812, 814, 815, 816, 817, 818, 819, 820, 821, 824, 826, 827, 828, 838, 840, 866, 872, 873, 875, 877, 881, 882
NJ170, 171, 172, 176, 177, 179, 180, 182, 187, 188, 190, 191, 192, 193, 194, 253, 254, 255, 257, 258

Note: ML839 omitted: although it had the P&W engines it was the 10 (RAAF Squadron) concept aircraft and only a partial conversion.

The conversion work was largely shared between Scottish Aviation Ltd at Greenock, Short Brothers at Windermere and Short & Harland at Belfast, although one example, EJ171, was modified at RAF Sullom Voe, a very wild and lonely place.....

Of the 83 conversions, these included the prototype, ML765, and five (ML817, ML820, ML824, ML826 and NJ258) which were modified at the factories and not taken on RAF charge for the first time until after their conversion.
JM717 modified to MR.5, not GR.5. Probably intended for RNZAF, but replaced by one in better condition – see DP191, EJ167 below.

The last two, DP191 and EJ167, were modified in 1952 at Belfast for delivery to the RNZAF after long-term storage as Mk. III at Wig Bay. DP191 was also the oldest airframe, and the last of the 83, to undergo the conversion. By this time (post 1st February 1951) this pair would have been designated, MR.5 and not Mk.V or GR.5.

Summary table of conversions from Sunderland Mk.III to Mk.V - with thanks to Phil Butler and Douglas Rough.

CHAPTER 5 : INDIVIDUAL AIRCRAFT HISTORIES

Sunderland Mk.III ML733 moored at Rochester prior to preparation for delivery to Australia where it became A26-4. The RAAF aircraft had the dorsal turret removed. (via J D Oughton collection)

The first pair of Sunderlands Mk.III for the RAAF, the former ML730 and ML732, flying past the Sydney Harbour Bridge on arrival on 12th March 1944. (via JM Collection)

Sunderlands Mk.III A26-1 and A26-3 are seen here moored at Sydney after delivery in March 1944. (via JM Collection)

Damage assessment taking place on Sunderland Mk.III A26-6 after its collision with the mooring mast at Townsville on 28th November 1944 and subsequent sinking. (V A Hodgkinson)

Part 2: ROYAL AUSTRALIAN AIR FORCE

A26-1 ex ML730 11Nov43; left Mount Batten 27Jan44, delivered to QANTAS 12Mar44; 2 FBRD 9May44; QANTAS 23Jul44; 40 Sqn 24Aug44; radio call-sign VHCOA; QANTAS 23Jan45; returned to 40 Sqn 13May45; QANTAS 10Jul45; returned to 40 Sqn 23Aug45; 2 FBRD 18Dec45; sold to Capt B W Monkton 4Oct46; released to purchaser 10Apr47 and registered **VH-ARQ**, later **VH-BKO** (both not taken up) (see Chapter 6)

A26-2 ex ML731 11Nov43; left Mount Batten 14Feb, delivered to QANTAS 19Mar44; 2 FBRD 26Mar44; QANTAS 25Apr44; 2 FBRD 29May44; 40 Sqn 1Jul44; radio call-sign VHCOB; QANTAS 3Aug44; returned to 40 Sqn 9Sep44; QANTAS 30Nov44; returned to 40 Sqn 22Dec44; QANTAS 9Mar45; returned to 40 Sqn 26Apr45; QANTAS 19Jun45; returned to 40 Sqn 23Jul45; 2 FBRD 30Oct45; damaged in storm at Cairns, Queensland, 4Mar46; stored; made final flight of RAAF Sunderland 12Mar46; sold to Capt B W Monkton 4Oct46; released to purchaser 3Apr47 and registered **VH-BKQ** (see Chapter 6)

A26-3 ex ML732 11Nov43; left Mount Batten 27Jan44, delivered to QANTAS 12Mar44; 2 FBRD 27Apr44; QANTAS 25Aug44; 40 Sqn 30Sep44; radio call-sign VHCOC; QANTAS 26Dec44; returned to 40 Sqn 15Jan45; QANTAS 23Apr45; returned to 40 Sqn 8Jun45; 2 FBRD 8Feb46; stored; sold to Capt B W Monkton 3Apr47; released to purchaser 3Jun47 and registered **VH-BFX**, later **VH-BKP** (both not taken up) (see Chapter 6)

A26-4 ex ML733 11Nov43; left Mount Batten 1Mar44, delivered to QANTAS 12Apr44; 40 Sqn 7Aug44; radio call-sign VHCOD; QANTAS 2Nov44; returned to 40 Sqn 27Nov44; QANTAS 7Feb45; returned to 40 Sqn 23Feb45; QANTAS 22May45; returned to 40 Sqn 25Jun45; QANTAS 27Oct45; Commander Task Unit, Rathmines 18Apr46 for storage; sold to Capt B W Monkton 14Oct46; released to purchaser 3Jun47 and registered **VH-AKO** (see Chapter 6)

A26-5 ex ML734 11Nov43; left Mount Batten 1Mar44, delivered to 2 FBRD 12Apr44; QANTAS 7May44; 2 FBRD 29Jun44; 40 Sqn 3Jul44; radio call-sign VHCOE; damaged while taxiing 29Aug44; repaired in works by QANTAS 12Sep44; returned to 40 Sqn 7Nov44; QANTAS 15Jan45; returned to 40 Sqn 26Jan45; QANTAS 10Apr45; returned to 40 Sqn 7May45; QANTAS 7Aug45; returned to 40 Sqn 27Sep45; 2 FBRD 12Mar46; stored; sold to Capt B W Monkton 14Oct46; released to purchaser 3Apr47 and registered **VH-AKP** (see Chapter 6)

A26-6 ex DP192 15Feb44; left Mount Batten Feb44, delivered to QANTAS 19Mar44; 2 FBRD 26Mar44; QANTAS 29May44; 40 Sqn 23Jul44; radio call-sign VHCOF; QANTAS 18Oct44; returned to 40 Sqn 6Nov44; collided with mooring post at Townsville, Queensland, 28Nov44; engines were restarted to taxy to beach but aircraft sank in 18 feet (5.5 m) of water; 5 Repair & Salvage Unit 7Dec44 for salvage; SOC 19Dec44

The top photo on this page illustrates Sunderland Mk.III ML792 being hauled up the slipway at RNZAF Station Hobsonville near Auckland on 5th December 1944 after its transfer from Mechanics Bay where it had arrived from the UK on 2nd December 1944. The photo on the left, taken on the same occasion, shows ML792 on the hard-standing and ML793 protruding from the hangar. They were the first of four Mk.IIIs (ML792 - ML795) delivered, ex RAF stock and were fitted out primarily for transport duties, notably initially for ferrying personnel and cargo between New Zealand and the important American Pacific bases such as Segond Channel on Espiritu Santo in the New Hebrides. The aircraft retained their camouflage for the

CHAPTER 5 : INDIVIDUAL AIRCRAFT HISTORIES

duration of the war but after their arrival in December 1944, at Mechanics Bay, their British serials were overpainted with RNZAF ones and Maori canoe names applied: NZ4101 (ex ML792) Tainui, NZ4102 (ex ML793) Tokomaru, NZ4103 (ex ML794) Mataatua and NZ4104 (ex ML795) Takitimu. At the same time the RNZAF 'Pacific Roundel' was applied, having an RNZAF Roundel Blue centre and outer ring separated by white. Fin markings were RAF-style matt red-white-blue. The fuselage roundels had white bars added on either side, to which, under the wings, a blue border was added. These markings followed a uniform system adopted for Allied aircraft in the South Pacific. Following VJ-Day 15th August 1945 the four Sunderlands were stripped of their camouflage back to bare metal and post-WW2 RNZAF markings were applied, with names retained. The lower photograph opposite shows NZ4101 Tainui (ex ML792) on its take-off run in idyllic surroundings; note the faired-off nose and the South Pacific bars just visible under the wing. On this page at the top is NZ4101 wearing camouflage, name and very clearly the Pacific roundels with bars. We have a close-up view of the Port wing of NZ4103 Mataatua and two of its Bristol Pegasus 38 engines, troublesome until the 1946 fitment of featherable propellers. Below is the rear fuselage and tail unit of NZ4103 with "Sunderland III" clearly written above the door. On 1st July 1948 the RNZAF kept in step with British military aircraft designations, changing from Roman to Arabic numerals, and the four flying boats became Sunderland Mk.3. Meanwhile they had been allotted civil identities for operation by NZNAC. In 1951 the remaining three were returned but not to active duty, as detailed in the histories which follow.

Credits: ML792, ML793 (RNZAF Official: Air Force Museum of New Zealand); NZ4101 this page via P H Butler, others via JM Collection)

Part 3: ROYAL NEW ZEALAND AIR FORCE

The first four aircraft were new-build **Sunderland Mk.III**s converted by "Shorts" at Rochester to BOAC standards without turrets and with other variations. The UK Government proposed the transfer on 6Mar1944 in order to allow the creation of a transport service in the South Pacific area using British types. Initial US Navy objections to the use on non-US types (as the RNZAF was at the time attached to the US Navy) were eventually overcome on 3rd August. RNZAF Catalina crews from 490 Squadron flew their aircraft from Jui, Sierra Leone to the UK to convert to Sunderlands at 4 (C) OTU Alness in June 1944. After technical training they moved, with their aircraft from Rochester to Wig Bay in September 1944. There, as a result of a UK Air Ministry Directive, the featherable propellers which had been fitted from new were removed and constant-speed ones installed, a move which blighted the RNZAF Mk.IIIs throughout their operational life. The crews then went to 302 FTU at Oban for further experience, then in October positioned to Mount Batten to prepare for thier month-long ferry flight. The first pair departed Plymouth on 21st October, the second pair on the 28th. Their route was from Mount Batten via Bathurst, Natal, Belem, Trinidad, NAS Banana River, NAS Corpus Christi, San Diego, Kaneohe Bay (Hawaii), Palmyra, Canton Island, Suva, Whangarei, to Mechanics Bay, Auckland for service with the Sunderland FBTF. RNZAF serials were allotted on 21Nov44 and applied at No.1 Air Depot Hobsonville following arrival. Camouflaged at first in RAF Temperate Sea Scheme, with RNZAF serials and with South Pacific Area markings in common with US Navy aircraft, they commenced passenger and freight services on 15th January 1945 mostly to Lauthala Bay (Fiji), Segond Channel(New Hebrides) via Noumea, and occasionallt Sydney. Post VJ-Day, 15th September 1945, they changed to natural metal finish. Temporarily withdrawn from service due to the engine/propeller problems in October 1945, they were revived in 1946 and, except NZ4101, fitted with fully-feathering propellers. Operations were transferred to civilian operators TEAL and NZNAC in March 1947 and began in November in civil markings. The four Mk.IIIs were transferred back to the RNZAF for disposal from 1949.

Additional abbreviations used in the Aircraft Histories:
GSB Government Stores Board (NZ); **HB** Hobsonville, Auckland; **LB** Lauthala Bay, Fiji; **MB** Mechanics Bay, TEAL maintenance base; **TTS** Technical Training School (RNZAF).

NZ4101 Mk.III; ex ML792 at Rochester; flown to 57 MU Wig Bay 20Aug44 for service issue prep and TOC RAF same day; transferred to RNZAF 9Sep44; flown same day to 302 FTU Oban for Ferry Flight work-up; dep to Calshot 18Oct44; Mount Batten 19Oct44; fitted with 600 gal long-range tank; Captained by Flt Lt Brian Layne RNZAF departed (with ML794) 21Oct44 for Bathurst; serial NZ4101 allotted 21Nov44 to be applied asap after arrival in NZ; 2Dec44 en route LB to Aucklandand provided cover while ML794 was towed to Urquhart's Bay for repairs; arr MB 2Dec44 but after ML793 & ML795; TOC 1 AD Auckland 4Dec44; (Note: officially transferred to Sunderland FBTF 28Dec44 to be based at HB but made retrospective as of 21Nov44); hangared HB 5Dec44 for 90hr check & seats, NZ serial and name *Tainui* applied; flew first passenger service to Fiji 19Jan45 returning 20Jan; MB for major inspection and camouflage removal 16Jul - 9Sep45; in service 15Sep45; to new SFBTS 29Nov45; MB to HB 22Jan46 and beached for 120hr inspection; not selected for new props, test flown 22May46 and that day to TEAL at MB for training crews for Sandringham operations, also 9/10/20Jul46; to MB 15Aug46 for Ground Instructional use; intended **ZK-AMJ** Nov46 for NZNAC but ntu and used for spares (see Chapter 6); SOC 16Dec47 HB; for sale by GSB Tender 10Oct49; sold for scrap 10Nov49; noted in pieces 29Dec49

NZ4102 Mk.III; ex ML793 at Rochester; 57 MU Wig Bay 18Sep44 and TOC RAF that day for service issue prep; transferred to RNZAF 6Oct44; same day to 302 FTU Oban for Ferry Flight work-up, fitted with 600 gal long-range tank; Captained by Flt Lt Keith Patience RNZAF departed (with ML795) 28Oct44 for Bathurst; serial NZ4102 allotted 21Nov44 to be applied asap after arrival in NZ; 2Dec44 en route LB to Auckland it broke off with ML795 from 4 Sunderland formation and the pair landed at MB for official arrival reception; TOC 1 AD Auckland 4Dec44; (Note: officially transferred to Sunderland FBTF 28Dec44 to be based at HB but made retrospective as of 21Nov44); hangared HB 4Dec44 for 90hr check, NZ serial and name *Tokomaru* applied; test-flown 15Dec44; to HB for seats 9Jan45; flew first passenger service HB to Segond Channel via Noumea 15Jan45, return 16Jan; serious engine problems 23Feb45; to new SFBTS 29Nov45 but services suspended wef 30Sep45 until cMay46 to rectify engine problems and fit featherable props; recommenced Auckland - Suva route from 6Jun46.until RNZAF's last Fiji service 4Mar47; last flown with RNZAF 11Sep47; SOC 30Sep47; regd 16May47 to NZNAC as **ZK-AMF** *Tokomaru* 16May47, but held as reserve aircraft still marked as NZ4102; regn cancelled 22Dec47(see Chapter 6); returned to RNZAF 9Feb49 still as NZ4102; tail and fin damaged in storm HB c2Aug49; for sale by GSB Tender 28May51, unsold; GSB Tender 2May55; sold to NZ Metal Smelters Ltd for £350 and broken up at HB.

NZ4103 Mk.III; ex ML794 at Rochester; flown to 57 MU Wig Bay 9Sep44 for service issue prep; TOC RAF 12Sep44; transferred to RNZAF 6Oct44; flown same day to 302 FTU Oban for Ferry Flight work-up; dep to Calshot 18Oct44; Mount Batten 19Oct44; fitted with 600 gal long-range tank; Captained by Flt Lt Joe Shepherd RNZAF departed (with ML792) 21Oct44 for Bathurst; serial NZ4103 allotted 21Nov44 to be applied asap after arrival in NZ; 2Dec44 en route LB to Auckland port outer propeller damaged in collision with RNZAF Lodestar NZ3514 photographing formation over Hens & Chickens Islands off North Island and was forced to land at Bream Bay, Whangarei; towed by boat to Urquhart's Bay where new propeller fitted 3Dec44, flown to MB 4Dec44 and TOC 1 AD Auckland 4Dec44; (Note: officially transferred to Sunderland FBTF 28Dec44 to be based at HB but made retrospective as of 21Nov44); hangared HB 15Dec44 for repairs and 90hr check, NZ serial and name *Mataatua* applied; flew first HB - Sydney service 14Feb45, returning 16Feb; service suspended until 14-16Aug45; MB for major service 14Sep45; to SFBTS 29Sep45 but services suspended wef 30Sep45 to rectify engine problems and fit featherable props; props fitted May46 but not test flown until 6Oct46; commenced weekly Evans Bay, Wellington to Chatham Islands service 2Nov46; regd 16May47 to NZNAC as **ZK-AMG** *Mataatua*; test flown MB 12Sep47 after overhaul; SOC 30Sep47 and transferred to NZNAC; 28Oct47 MB to HB for removal RNZAF markings; to MB 31Oct47 as ZK-AMG for TEAL by arrangement with NZNAC, entered service on Fiji route 1Nov47; (see Chapter 6); last flight 31Mar49; returned to RNZAF 9Feb51; GSB Tender 28May51 and 23Nov53 but unsold; SOC 3Nov54 and scrapped HB

NZ4104 Mk.III; ex ML795 at Rochester; 57 MU Wig Bay 27Sep44 and TOC RAF that day for service issue prep; transferred to RNZAF 6Oct44; and to 302 FTU Oban for Ferry Flight work-up, fitted with 600 gal long-range tank; Captained by Flt Lt Jack Pettit RNZAF departed (with ML793) 28Oct44 for Bathurst; serial NZ4104 allotted 21Nov44 to be applied asap after arrival in NZ; 2Dec44 en route LB to Auckland it broke off with ML793 from 4 Sunderland formation and the pair landed at MB for official arrival reception; TOC 1 AD Auckland 4Dec44; (Note: officially transferred to Sunderland FBTF 28Dec44 to be based at HB but made retrospective as of 21Nov44); hangared HB 12Jan45 for repairs and 90hr check, NZ serial and name *Takitimu* applied, and into reserve; to TEAL hangar MB 28Apr45 for major maintenance prior to entering service; to new SFBTS 29Nov45 but grounded 30Nov45 until cMay46 to rectify engine problems and fit featherable props; SOC RNZAF16Dec47 on transfer to NZNAC; regd to NZNAC as **ZK-AMK** *Takitimu* 22Dec47, converted to civil standard 1948; entered service Mar49; operated last NAC Sunderland service Suva - Auckland 31May50; returned to RNZAF 9Feb51; for sale by GSB Tender 28May51; unsold; 6 (Territorial) Sqn HB May52-mid53 as **NZ4104** for water taxying and beaching training of MR.5 crews; GSB Tender 23Nov53 but unsold; declared surplus 3Nov54 and scrapped HB

As early as 28th February 1945, the RNZAF made an initial enquiry in London about either returning the Sunderlands Mk.III to the UK in exchange for Mk.Vs, or obtaining P&W R-1830-92 engines in place of the Pegasus XVIII. Nothing transpired from that enquiry. In August 1951 the RNZAF firmed up its requirement for **16 Sunderlands MR.5** and on 14th December 1951 a UK Air Ministry Order was issued for 16 refurbished aircraft, fitted with P&W R-1830-90D engines, of which 12 were in good condition but the other four required considerable refurbishment. All the aircraft would feed through "Shorts" in Belfast for airframe, engines and internal equipment modification and installation work
The RNZAF wished to equip two maritime reconnaissance/transport capable squadrons with four in reserve. On 1st May 1952 the serials NZ4105 to 4120 were allotted and on 15th May 1953 the RNZAF was notified that the first aircraft, NZ4105, would be handed over on the 18th and, along with NZ4108, was scheduled to depart Calshot on 25th May, routing via Kalafrana (Malta), Fanarah (Canal Zone), Bahrein, Korangi Creek, Trincomalee, Seletar, Soerbaja, Darwin, Cairns, Noumea to Lauthala Bay (Suva, Fiji) on 6th June 1953; 13 days in all. Their departure delayed, they arrived on 13th June. The route would be common to most, if not all 16. Initial deliveries were to the RNZAF base at Lauthala Bay, Fiji, for 5 Squadron (KN codes). The majority of later ones went to the RNZAF flying-boat base at Hobsonville for 6 Squadron (XX codes) or reserve storage.
There were delivery problems caused by a) assimilating too many aircraft in a short period of time, b) insufficient ferry and trained crews, c)

Chapter 5 : Individual Aircraft Histories

A trio of Sunderland MR.5s of 5 Squadron RNZAF featuring NZ4117 [KN:K] in the foreground. On its starboard side is [KN:G] which is probably NZ4116. The presence of NZ4117 dates the picture between 1955 and 1961. (Roy Green collection)

Former 5 Squadron Sunderland MR.5 NZ4109 [KN:C] at Hobsonville in December 1964 after years of storage. (R A Walker collection)

On its hardstanding at Mechanics Bay, New Zealand in June 1960 was Sunderland MR.5 NZ4115 [Q] of 5 Squadron. (R A Walker collection)

Flying over Suva Town in Fiji, NZ4117 [T] is about to alight at nearby Lauthala Bay. This Sunderland MR.5 was the last one delivered to the RNZAF, in May 1955, and was retired from service following an alighting incident of 15th April 1961. (Andrew Hendrie collection)

Sunderland MR.5 NZ4116 [S] of 5 Squadron was in good condition when photographed in 1959. (R C Sturtivant collection)

Sunderland MR.5 NZ4118 [XX:A] formerly with MOCU was another example in storage in 1964. (R C Sturtivant collection)

equipment availability delays and d) lack of storage facilities for more than four aircraft. Instead of having to cancel four Sunderlands, the 16 deliveries were staggered. In delivery order: **Batch 1, 1953 = 8**: NZ4105, 08, 09, 16, 11, 10, 12, 15. **Batch 2, 1954 = 7**: NZ4119, 06, 20, 18, 13, 14, 07. **Batch 3, 1955 = 1**: NZ4117. To achieve this many of the MR.5s went from Belfast to Wig Bay for temporary storage from where the majority were collected by RNZAF crews who were flown into nearby RAF West Freugh.

"Fern leaf" roundels were officially introduced in June 1957. From c1958 Sunderlands for Squadrons were drawn from an amalgamated aircraft pool and all were single-letter coded. Sunderlands were progressively withdrawn from use from mid-1956 and by December 1963 only eight remained on inventory. In reducing numbers the MR.5 served well until the last (NZ4107) was taken out of service in April 1967 by which time five Lockheed P-3B Orions, ordered in August 1964, had started coming into service with 5 Squadron.

NZ4105 ex PP110 12May53; dep Calshot for Fiji 28May53 (call-sign MOVLA, Flt Lt H B Thompson) with NZ4108; arr uncoded LB 13Jun53; to 5 Sqn LB by 28Jul53 [KN:A]; later [KN:C] unconfirmed; in storage HB at least Dec56 - Dec58; by Dec59 with TEAL MB for major servicing; with 5 Sqn [A] by Dec60 and LB-based at least Dec61 - Dec62; LB/HB based until wfs to outside storage HB 22Jan65; SOC 2Aug66; GSB Tenders Aug66 and May67;gradually dismantled HB Dec66 - Jan67 still [A]; scrapped HB during Aug67

NZ4106 ex RN280 Dec52; arr HB 23Apr54; BOC 24Apr54; to 5 Sqn LB by 21Aug54 [KN:G] later [KN:B]; 5 Sqn until at least Dec56 when noted with TEAL MB for servicing; 5 Sqn at least Jun-Dec57; to TEAL MB for major service in .58; at HB in reserve or temporary storage at least Dec58 - Dec59; 5 Sqn by Dec60 [B] and LB-based at Dec61; wfs as surplus 20Mar62; flown HB for storage 20Apr62; SOC 2Oct62 and after spares stripping sold by GSB Tender dated 11Jan63; broken up HB Aug-Sep63 still coded [B]

NZ4107 ex VB883 3Nov53; arr HB 22Sep54; BOC same day and into storage at HB until to TEAL MB May56 for major service; to 5 Sqn LB Jul56 [KN:F] (replaced NZ4110); with TEAL MB by Dec57 for service and to HB in reserve or temporary service by Dec58; 5 Sqn at least Dec59 - Dec60 [D]; HB at least Dec61 - Dec63 believed in reserve or stored; last Sunderland to have major refit TEAL MB .64; 5 Sqn LB by Jan64 [D]; flypast at opening Auckland Airport 31Jan66 [D]; wfs and flown LB to HB [D] 2Apr67 (last RNZAF MR.5 flight); GSB Tender 3May67; noted moored HB 1Jul67; sold Australian Aircraft Sales, Sydney in Aug67 for spares recovery scrappin at HB Aug67

NZ4108 ex ML814 21May53; departed Calshot 28May53 with NZ4105; arr LB 13Jun53 and BOC; air-tested 10Aug53 on issue to 5 Sqn [KN:B]; with 5 Sqn until at least Dec55; LB to HB 5Jan56 for 6 Sqn; with 6 Sqn/MOCU (shared usage) 5Jan - 20Aug56 [XX:D]; to LTS at HB 20Aug56, its last RNZAF flight; SOC 12Dec63 sold to Ansett Airways to become **VH-BRF**; overhauled and stripped to bare metal at MB, flown Auckland - Rose Bay, Sydney 18Dec63 as VH-BRF with original 6 Sqn code outlines still discernable on fuselage (see Chapter 6)

NZ4109 ex DP191 19Jun53; arr LB 21Jul53 and BOC same day; to 5 Sqn LB [KN:C] by 29Jul53; wfs and flown LB to HB 5Dec56 and into reserve LTS at HB [KN:C]; downgraded to parts/salvage early .64; soc Feb65; sold by GSB Tender to Ingot Metals, Auckland; noted derelict HB May65, still [KN:C] and scrapped 1965-66

NZ4110 ex PP129 19Jun53; arr LB 5Oct53 and BOC 14Oct53;air-tested 27Oct53 on issue to 5 Sqn LB [KN:F]; grounded Apr54 (reason unknown) but test-flown as serviceable 12Feb55, still 5 Sqn until at least Dec56; LB to HB 26Feb57 for major overhaul with TEALMB then into LTS at HB still as [KN:F]; became GI airframe **INST183** 14Oct59 on land at No.1 TTS, HB; SOC 14Apr64 GSB Tender Apr64 and sold to Ingot Metals, Auckland; broken up HB Feb65

NZ4111 ex VB880 6Jul53; arr LB 6Sep53 and BOC same day; airtested 14Sep53 on issue to 5 Sqn LB [KN:D]; struck floating object in Lauthala Bay and holed 30Oct53; repaired on beach, test flown 10Dec53; fitted as VIP aircraft for Vice-Regal tour of Fijian islands 21May54 to 20Jun54; struck coral reef in Nukunonu lagoon, on an atoll in the Tokelau Is, N of Samoa, 24Aug55 but temporarily repaired; returned LB 12Sep55 for proper repair; later named *Nukunonu Baby*; with 5 Sqn until at least Dec56; by Jun57 in reserve storage at HB; to MOCU HB late sep57 [XX:B] replacing NZ4119; back to reserve storage HB at least Dec57 - Dec58; to 5 Sqn cMar59 [K]; in flypast for opening of Auckland Harbour Bridge 30May59; while operating TEAL service struck an uncharted rock at Te Whanga lagoon, Chatham Is 4Nov59; declared not repairable and useful items removed, hulk dragged ashore by locals; SOC 9Dec59; some parts recovered by RNZAF Museum team in early 1994 and taken to Museum at Wigram, Christchurch; other parts still extant in Chatham Islands 2012

NZ4112 ex VB881 10Aug53; arr HB 2Nov53 and BOC same day; stored at HB until Jul56 then to TEAL MB for major service and issued to 5 Sqn LB Sep56 as [KN:A] (replacing NZ4105); recoded [KN:L] c.58 and then [L] in 1959 and still noted as such 1963; with MRSU HB by Jan64 [L]; last flight mid-66 and wfs; SOC 2Aug66; GSB Tenders Aug66 and May67; sold to Australian Aircraft Sales, Sydney, as spares source; hulk noted at HB 1Jul67 [L] and used by Hobsonville Yacht Club until 1970; cut up and disposed of as scrap at HB Nov73 except for cockpit and part of nose section reportedly airlifted by RNZAF Hercules NZ7005 to Ferrymead Aeronautical Society, Christchurch; extant, stored 2012

NZ4113 ex PP124 14Oct53; arr HB 7Aug54 and BOC same day; into storage until issued to 6 Sqn HB 15Feb44 - 23Mar56 reportedly as [KN:D] for a short while before becoming [XX:D]; to TEAL for major service Mar56; to 6 Sqn/MOCU HB 21May56 - Aug57 and MOCU Aug57 - 17Oct57 [XX:D]; TEAL servicing cJun - Dec57, then reserve HB at least Dec57 - Dec60 [KN:M], then [M] by 1959; in low flypast at official opening of Rongotai Airport, Wellington 25Oct59 downdraught caused keel to scrape along runway, puncturing the hull, temporarily shored up in flight, returned to HB and beached for repairs; with TEAL MB on 15Mar61; 5 Sqn LB pre-Dec61 [M]; believed HB-based from at least Dec62; with MRSU/5 Sqn as [M]; at HB by Jan64 until wfs Mar67 on completion of final Chatham Is run 22Mar67 to Evans Bay, Wellington; last flight to, or at, HB 30Mar67; SOC as surplus 3May67; sold by GSB Tender May67 to Australian Aircraft Sales, Sydney, as a spares source and scrap; seen moored HB 1Jul67; scrapped at HB

NZ4114 ex SZ561 cOct53; arr HB 2Aug54, BOC same day; into storage until issued to 6 Sqn HB 17Feb55 [XX:C]; later coded [XX:A]; to 6 Sqn/MOCU HB(shared usage) May55 - 25Jun56 [XX:A]; storage at HB at least Dec56 - Dec58; with 5 Sqn [KN:P], by Dec 59 [P]; in reserve or storage by Dec60 to Dec63; with MRSU HB by Jan64 until wfs 1965-6; GSB Tender Jan66 and SOC 6Feb67; sold Australian Aircraft Sales, Sydney, as spares source; noted engineless docked at HB braby (servicing pontoon) 11Jul67; hulk donated to become HQ of North District Volunteer Coastguard Service at Whangarei/Onerahi; towed HB to Onerahi by tug *Rata* 11Jul67 and beached; hauled ashore and by 1971 in a fenced enclosure [P]; later vandalised, deemed uneconomic to remove or restore, demolished and parts taken to Council dump at Pohe Island by 1972

CHAPTER 5 : INDIVIDUAL AIRCRAFT HISTORIES

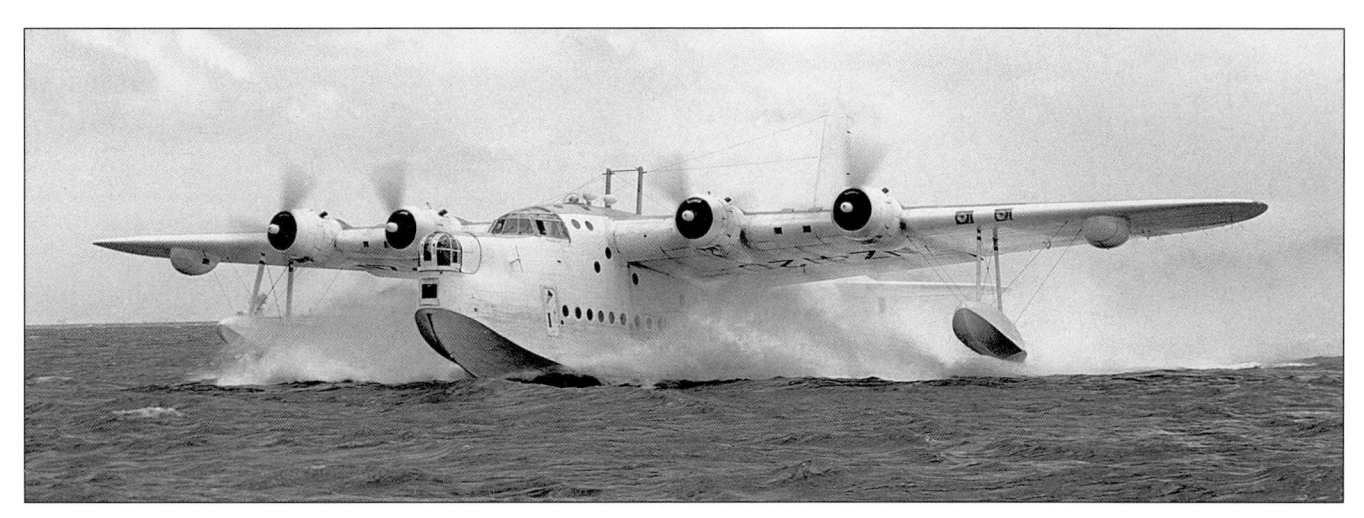

A great deal of spray being generated by 5 Squadron's Sunderland MR.5 NZ4120 at Lauthala Bay, Fiji. (Andrew Hendrie collection)

NZ4115 ex SZ584 4Sep53; arr HB 17Nov53 and BOC same day; into storage until Oct56 then TEAL MB for major servicing; to 5 Sqn LB [KN:B] Nov56; later [KN:Q]; with 5 Sqn until at least Dec59, [Q] in .59; noted HB in reserve or storage Dec60 and Dec61; 5 Sqn LB by Dec62 [Q]; until Dec63/Jan64 with TEAL MB for major inspection, overhaul and into immediate reserve at HB [Q]; wfs 8Dec66 and SOC 9Dec66; gifted to MOTAT, Auckland, in full airworthy condition, for preservation; formal ownership 22Dec66; towed HB to Meola Creek 22Feb67 and winched overland to MOTAT; extant Jan13

NZ4116 ex EJ167 4Jun53; arr HB 27Jul53 and BOC same day; into storage until Jan57; to TEAL MB for major service before delivery to 5 Sqn LB [KN:C] Mar57, with 5 Sqn until at least Dec61; unconfirmed codes [KN:G; KN:S] before [S] in 1959; at HB in reserve or storage in Dec62 and Dec63; with MRSU HB by Jan64; to 5 Sqn 1964 [S]; LB to HB 2Nov66; last flight, local10Nov66; wfs and into storage; GSB Tender; SOC 6Feb67; sold to Australian Aircraft Sales, Sydney, for spares; noted derelict at HB [S] 10Oct67

NZ4117 ex RN286 3Oct53; last MR.5 delivery; test-flown Belfast 24, 28, 29Mar55; to and from Castle Archdale 25 and 31Mar55; to Pembroke Dock 6Apr55; transitted through Kalafrana 20/24Apr55; arrived HB 9May55 and BOC same day; into storage 31May55; to TEAL MB for major service 2Aug55; to HB 29Sep55; HB to LB 15Oct55 for 5 Sqn [KN:K]; reportedly later [KN:T]; coded [T] by 1959; remained with 5 Sqn [T] until damaged on alighting in rough seas at Tarawa, Gilbert & Ellice Is, 15Apr61; temporary repair and ferried to LB c29Apr61 but SOC 10Aug61 and scrapped at LB; remains were melted down by local scrap merchant and ingots sold to Colmaco in Australia

NZ4118 ex RN306 15Dec53; arr HB 13May54 and BOC same day; allocated to 6 Sqn HB 18May54 and with Sqn by 20Jul54 to 14Dec55 [XX:A]; major service TEAL MB Dec55 - Mar56; 6 Sqn/MOCU HB 7Mar56 - Aug57 then MOCU Aug57 - 11Oct57 [XX:A]; wfs Oct57to , to LTS at HB 11Oct57; noted derelict [XX:A]; noted at HB May65; SOC Oct65; sold by GSB Tender for scrap to Ingot Metals, Auckland and scrapped post-Jan66

NZ4119 ex PP143 19Jan54; arr HB 22Apr54 and BOC same day; allocated to 6 Sqn HB [XX:B] 27Apr54; with 6 Sqn 17Jun54 - 23Sep55; to TEAL MB for major inspection Sep - Nov55; 6 Sqn; with 6 Sqn/MOCU at HB [XX:B] 25Nov55 to 9Aug57; into LTS at HB 9Aug57; declared surplus 20Mar62; GSB Tender .62; SOC 2Oct62 to be cannibalised for spares and sold Jan63; noted HB 11Jan63 still as [XX:B]

NZ4120 ex RN291 6Feb54; arr HB 6May54 and BOC that day; 6 Sqn HB [XX:C] May54; to TEAL MB 2Jun54 for unidentified repairs, then into storage HB 1Jul54; to TEAL MB for major inspection 3Jun56, back to HB 28Aug56; 6 Sqn/MOCU HB 1956 to 2Sep57 [XX:C] when flown into reserve/storage at HB; to 5 Sqn LB sometime between Dec57 and Dec58 [KN:Z]; back into storage HB but by Dec61 was with 5Sqn LB [Z]; LB to HB24Sep64 for storage; wfs 65 and noted derelict HB May65 as [Z]; SOC 2Aug66 and sold by GSB Tender Oct66; scrapped HB post 29Jan67

Note: RNZAF Sunderlands used radio call-signs ZMZGA to ZMZGZ, with the final letter usually corresponding with the individual aircraft code letter

Part 4: SOUTH AFRICAN AIR FORCE

35 Squadron SAAF was formed on 15th February 1945 out of 262 Squadron (RAF) at Congella, Durban and received 15 Sunderlands Mk.V, 12 of which were gifted by the UK including a no-cost replacement for the loss of PP153 on 26th April1945. In addition three were purchased by the SAAF (PP104, PP125 & RN305). The initial deliveries were sourced from 259 Squadron which disbanded at Dar-es-Salaam, Tanganyika in April 1945 and later augmented by others ex-storage at 57 MU Wig Bay, Scotland. All arrived in RAF markings and were either single-letter coded before delivery or immediately after arrival. RN305 was the last to be delivered, on 12th October 1945.

VJ-Day 15th August 1945 negated any rumoured Far East deployment and the Squadron made ready their flying-boats to repatriate South African troops from North Africa and the Suez Canal Zone. A proving flight was made between Durban and Cairo in early September 1945. The "Repat" flights to/from Kasfareet, Egypt, commenced on 2nd November and during this period the Sunderlands were individually named. On 12th November 1945 a Directive from the SAAF required Squadron identification letters [RB] to be applied to prefix the individual aircraft code letters which did not change. The concluding repatriation flight arrived at Congella on 2nd March 1946. As of August 1948 SAAF serials were allotted to replace RAF serials but whether they were actually applied to those in storage at Congella has yet to be confirmed. As far as roundels and fin-flashes are concerned it remains unconfirmed whether Orange centre spots in lieu of Red were applied but a Directive of 24th August 1950 introduced the Orange *Springbok* roundel which was gradually introduced on the extant operational aircraft. When first delivered the Sunderlands were referred to as Mk.V and there are mentions of GR.5 and then plain Mk.5. To date the use of MR.5 has not been confirmed. By late 1947 the need for so many aircraft had receded and the operational requirement was reduced to five, plus one immediate reserve. The six thus retained were given SAAF serials but exactly when is not known. The last Sunderland flight was made on 8th October 1957 marking the end of one era and the start of another with the delivery to South Africa in August 1957 of the first of 35 Squadron's eight Shackletons MR.3 to be based at Ysterplaat, Cape Town.

In this view of SAAF Congella in 1948 nine [RB]-coded Sunderlands Mk.5 may be seen outside, many already in long term storage, and a further example is hangared. Catalinas scrapped earlier feature on a dump on the left. (via the late Dave Becker)

Built as a Sunderland V, SAAF 1714 [RB:N] wearing Springbok roundel, was written-off in an attempted night landing on Lake Umsingazi in a storm following a navigation exercise to Europa Island in the Mozambique Channel on 1st November 1956. Night landings at Congella were forbidden due to the number of fishing boats using this section of the Durban coastline.   (via the late Dave Becker)

An unidentified Sunderland GR.5 of 35 Squadron SAAF, Durban, seen making an impressively low pass at a Pietermaritzburg event, more remarkable because the starboard engines are both feathered.
(via JM Collection)

1701   Allotted SAAF May45 as **NJ262**; arr Congella 31May45; TOC for 35 Sqn [Q]; named *Quis Keteer;* recoded [RB:Q] wef 12Nov45; made first non-stop round the Union flight, 29/30Jul48 (2880 mls / 4637 km in 19 hrs 50 mins); allotted **1701** wef Aug48 and applied; stored Congella from 1950; sold for scrap to J Newark & Co Ltd 24Mar55

1702   Allotted SAAF 24May45 as **PP125**; arr Congella Oct45; TOC 35 Sqn [K] named *King*; recoded [RB:K] wef 12Nov45; allotted **1702** wef Aug48 and applied (?); stored Congella from 49; sold for scrap to J Newark & Co Ltd 24Mar55

1703   Allotted SAAF May45 as **PP109**; arr Congella 13Jun45; TOC 35 Sqn [H] named *House Mouse*; recoded [RB:H] wef 12Nov45; allotted **1703** wef Aug48 and applied; due to make last flight 29Aug57 but dbr on 28Aug57 when during take-off from Durban Bay both port engines failed, aircraft swung towards wharf, straightened in time but port wing swept above wharf striking several bollards; portion of wing outboard of radome and float was taken off in collision; scrapped at Congella Apr58

1704   Allotted SAAF 21May45 as **RN279**; arr Congella 13Jun45; TOC 35 Sqn [F] named *Umzinfirkin Fifi*; recoded [RB:F] wef 12Nov45; stored Congella from .48; allotted **1704** wef Aug48 and applied (?); sold for scrap to Non-Ferrous Metal Works (SA) (Pty) Ltd, Durban 24Mar55

1705   Allotted SAAF 16Jul45 as **RN296**; arr Congella 27Jul45; TOC 35 Sqn [M] replacing PP153; no known name; recoded [RB:M] wef 12Nov45; made the last repatriation flight from Kasfareet, Egypt, to Congella 2Mar46; allotted **1705** wef Aug48 and applied; stored Congella from 49; sold for scrap to Non-Ferrous Metal Works (SA) (Pty) Ltd, Durban 24Mar55

1706   Allotted SAAF 17Sep45 as **RN305**; arr Congella 12Oct45; TOC 35 Sqn [O]; no known name; recoded [RB:O] wef 12Nov45; allotted **1706** wef Aug48 and applied; struck submerged object in Durban Bay during take-off 13Apr50; broke in half during salvage attempt; SOC 12Jan51; sold for scrap 12Jan57

1707   Allotted SAAF 23Apr45 as **NJ258**; arr Congella 31May45; TOC 35 Sqn [A]; no known name; recoded [RB:A] wef 12Nov45; stored Congella from 46; allotted **1707** wef Aug48 and applied (?); sold for scrap to Non-Ferrous Metal Works (SA) (Pty) Ltd, Durban 24Mar55

1708   Allotted SAAF 28Apr45 as **NJ263**; via Kisumu 21Apr45, arr Congella Apr45; TOC 35 Sqn [B]; no known name; recoded [RB:B] wef 12Nov45; stored from 46 Congella; allotted **1707** wef Aug48 and applied (?); sold for scrap to J Newark & Co Ltd 24Mar55

1709   Allotted SAAF 6May45 as **ML798**; arr Congella 31May45; TOC 35 Sqn [C]; named *Crooch Macree*; recoded [RB:C] wef 12Nov45; stored Congella from 47; allotted **1709** wef Aug48 and applied (?); sold for scrap to J Newark & Co Ltd 24Mar55

1710   Allotted SAAF 18May45 as **RN281**; arr Congella 1Jun45; TOC 35 Sqn [D]; named *Dynamite Daisy* (*Dinammmite Baby* has also been quoted); recoded [RB:D] wef 12Nov45; allotted **1710** wef Aug48 and applied; made final SAAF Sunderland flight 8Oct57 piloted by Capt A J Cooney; earmarked to become floating café but scrapped

1711   Allotted SAAF May45 as **NJ266**; arr Congella 1Jun45; TOC 35 Sqn [G]; no known name; recoded [RB:G] wef 12Nov45; allotted **1711** wef Aug48 and applied; stored Congella from 51; sold for scrap to Non-Ferrous Metal Works (SA) (Pty) Ltd, Durban 24Mar55

1712   Allotted SAAF 28Apr45 as **PP156**; arr Congella 31May45; TOC 35 Sqn [J]; named *My Lucky Star*; dep Cogella 1Sep45 for a repatriation survey flight to Cairo arriving 9Sep; recoded [RB:J] wef 12Nov45 allotted **1712** wef Aug48 and applied; stored Congella from 51; sold 10Mar55

1713   Allotted SAAF 23Apr45 as **NJ259**; arr Congella 26Apr45; TOC 35 Sqn [L]; named *Little Zulu Lulu;* recoded [RB:L] wef 12 Nov45; stored Congella from 47; allotted **1713** wef Aug48 and applied (?); sold for scrap to J Newark & Co Ltd 24Mar55

1714   Allotted SAAF 26Jul45 as **RN295**; arr Congella 31Jul45; TOC 35 Sqn [N]; no known name; recoded [RB:N] wef 12Nov45; allotted **1714** wef Aug48 and applied; returning from a navigation exercise on 1Nov56, dazzled by lightning during night touch-down on Lake Umsingazi, the pilot opened the throttles to go round again, but aircraft stalled under full power, struck the water and sank (2 killed); SOC 4Oct57; salvaged and sold for scrap 8Apr58

1715   Allotted SAAF 30Apr45 as **PP104**; arr Congella 31May45; TOC 35 Sqn [P]; no known name; recoded [RB:P] wef 12Nov45; stored Congella from 46; allotted **1715** wef Aug48 and applied (?); sold for scrap to J Newark & Co Ltd 24Mar55

——   Allotted SAAF 23Apr45 as **PP153**; arr Congella 24Apr45; TOC 35 Sqn [M]; commenced crew conversion training 26Apr45 but that day hit submerged object on alighting at Lake Umsingazi; pilot took off immediately but two hull compartments had been ripped open; to avoid sinking on landing, and possibly enable salvage or repair, crew decided to beach it on soft sand; however aircraft was SOC and cannibalised; no SAAF serial allotted

Few military Sunderlands were named; 35 Squadron SAAF aircraft were exceptions as recorded here on 1704.

Retaining its former British serial as its identity and French unit code 27.F-3, ML778 Sunderland 5 is seen in the Musgrave Channel on arrival at Belfast for major servicing on 11th October 1955 after storage at Berre. (Shorts/Bombardier via Noel Lynch)

Part 5: AÉRONAUTIQUE NAVALE

T9074 briefly on loan to Aéronautique navale, Dakar; 343 Squadron 19Apr43; replaced in Jun43 by JM674; SOC by RAF 25Oct43

W6080 allocated to Aéronautique navale at Dakar, Sénégal, 20Jul43; in the first batch of three Sunderlands leaving the UK for West Africa; TOC 7Aug43; Flottille 7F [7E-7]; accident on alighting 7Aug43, no casualties but wfu; SOC 3Sep43

DD833 one of two offered on loan 17Jan43 by Air Ministry (and Gp Capt R H Carter) to French Navy in Dakar; to Escadrille 4E coded 4E1 18Mar43; in use at Dakar from Mar43 to Aug43 (when overhauled); returned to RAF and damaged Wig Bay 10Sep43; SOC

DP182 allocated to Aéronautique navale at Dakar Sep43; 343 Sqn 29Nov43; Flottille 7FE coded 4E1 and later 3E9 with single code [I], later [J]; ditched in South Atlantic 2Feb44, capsized and sank (crew saved)

DP187 allocated to Aéronautique navale Jul43; 343 Sqn; Escadrille 3E [3E-6, code F; also reported 3E-7] 29Nov43; Flottille 7FE [G in late 1943]; SOC 21Jun45, official administrative date of transfer to France

DV965 allocated to Aéronautique navale Oct43; there is no evidence of DV965 in French service, probable confusion with DV985 (qv)

DV985 allocated to Aéronautique navale 9Aug43; 343 Sqn [3E-8 code H] 29Nov43; Flottille 7FE [I]; crashed off Gorée Island (Dakar) on night of 26-27Apr44 (13 killed); believed in-flight fire and sudden loss without distress signal being sent

DV986 allocated to Aéronautique navale 27Aug43; 343 Sqn [3E-5 code E]; Flottille 7FE [E]; crashed into sea off Port Etienne 19Sep43 (11 killed) following in-flight fire in port wing

DV987 allocated to Aéronautique navale 1Sep43; 343 Sqn [3E-3 code H uncertain, became C Sep43]; Flottille 7FE [3C] 29Nov43; administrative transfer to France Jun45; SOC by French Navy Jul45

EJ135 one of six transferred to Aéronautique navale 21Jun45; Flottille 7.F [7F-2B] coded 7.F-2, 1946-48; to storage Karouba, Tunisia 1949; TT1009 hours; returned to Dakar Sep49; repairs suspended and SOC 25Mar50; TT 1031 hours

EJ163 to Aéronautique navale 21 Jun45; Flottille 7.F [7.F-6, 1947-49]; smashed hull on take-off at Saint-Mandrier flying-boat base near Toulon 3Nov49 and crashed (4 killed); SOC 13Mar50

EJ168 343 Sqn/Flottille 7F 29Mar44 possibly [J]; to Aéronautique navale 21Jun45; Flottille 7.F [7.F-8]; SOC 7May48

EK587 to Aéronautique navale 21Jun45; Flottille 7.F [7.F-4]; to Tunisia for overhauls and mods second half 1947 until SOC 4Feb49 at Karouba repair base

JM674 allocated to Aéronautique navale 30Apr43; Escadrille 4E believed coded 4E5; Escadrille 3E [3E11] after Sep43; 343 Sqn/Flottille 7F [7F-11K]; official transfer to Aéronautique navale 21Jun45; war weary and SOC Jul45

JM688 allocated to Aéronautique navale 24Jul43; 343 Sqn/ Flottille 7F Escadrille 3E [3E-4 coded D] 29Nov43; minor incident at sea 19Jan44; administrative transfer to Aéronautique navale 21 Jun45; war weary and SOC Jul45

JM689 allocated to Aéronautique navale 1Sep43; 343 Sqn/Flottille 7F 29Nov43; Escadrille 3E [3E-7 coded G, later H] Dec43; administrative transfer to Aéronautique navale 21Jun45; Flottille 7.F [7.F-7]; major inspection Tunisia mid-48, TT 1061 hours; fitted with Pegasus 38 engines and returned to Dakar, still as 7.F-7 until SOC 26Mar50

JM704 alocated to Aéronautique navale 7Aug43; 343 Sqn/Flottille 7F 29Nov43; Escadrille 3E [3E-2 apparently without individual letter but B expected but not confirmed]; on night flight stalled and crashed on alighting at Bel Air, Dakar, 5Feb44; (4 killed, 9 survived)

JM705 allocated to Aéronautique navale 1Sep43; Escadrille 3E [3E1 later code letter A]; later 7FE coded 1 (for Squadron CO); spun into sea on approach to Bel Air, Dakar 22Oct43 (no casualties)

JM706 allocated to Aéronautique navale 25Jul43; one of the first three delivered from UK to West Africa; on ferry flight 17Jul43 made forced alighting off Cadiz, Spain, assisted by Spanish sailing boat and later British launch No.181; 343 Sqn/Flottille 7F 29Nov43 [coded 3E-5], later 7FE [coded F and possibly B but unconfirmed]; administrative transfer to France Jun45 and one of five SOC by French Navy Jul45

ML739 to Aéronautique navale 19Feb52, MR.5 deld via Pembroke Dock 20Feb52; 7.F-19; became 27.F-19 summer .53; SOC 9Dec55 due to excessive corrosion; hull remained at Dakar for some time.

ML750 apparently the only Sunderland transferred to France 1947 under the 'Nomy-West agreement' of 1946; intended ferry by RAF crew to River Seine at Les Mureaux 2Apr47 but delayed until transfer to Aéronautique navale 26Jul47; Flottille 7.F [7.F-12]; fitted with Pegasus 38 engines in 1948; major inspection at Dakar-Bel Air early .49 at 443 hrs TT; damaged beyond repair on ground at Dakar and SOC 18Jul50 with 882 hrs TT

Showing signs of intensive operation, Sunderland 5 ML799 / 27.F-5 of Aéronautique navale taxies in Belfast Lough on arrival at Short Bros & Harland's works on 5th March 1956 from Dakar via Berre for major servicing. (Shorts/Bombardier via Noel Lynch)

A close-up view of the tail markings on Aéronautique navale Sunderland 5 ML800 in a hangar at FBSU Wig Bay on 15th June 1957 just eleven days before delivery to Brest. (Bill Broadfoot)

ML757 to Aéronautique navale 19Jun51; Flottille 7.F [7.F-6]; Flottille 27.F [27.F-6] in 1953; in storage at Berre Naval Air Station 1954; delivered to SB&HL from Marignane 25Apr56, using radio call-sign FYBDE; test-flown 6 & 9Nov56; to Brest 8Dec56, using radio call-sign FYBUA; TT at 1Feb50 was 1,658 hrs; SOC 20Jun59

ML764 to Aéronautique navale 26Jul51;accepted 29Jul51; to storage at Berre then to Flottille 7.F [7.F-7] Oct51; to Flottille 27.F [27.F-7/5] summer 1953; Escadrille 12.S [12.S-5]; Escadrille 50.S [50.S-3]; delivered to SB&HL from Berre 10Jan57, using radio call-sign FYBDE; test-flown 4Oct57; to Brest 22Oct57; Flottille 27.F; SOC 23Feb60

ML778 to Aéronautique navale 12May51; deld via Pembroke Dock 12May51, using radio call-sign FXCGC; TOC 12May51; Flottille 7.F [7.F-3] 1951-53; Flottille 27.F [27.F-3] Oct53; [53.S-2] FBTU Sep55 to May56 but to SB&HL 11Oct55 for maintenance; test-flown 17 & 27Apr56; to Brest 28Apr56; then [27.F-3] arriving Dakar-Bel Air 27May56; TT 2,140 hrs 1Feb57; [53.S-2] FBTU until flying accident at sea 7Jul58 (4 killed); SOC 29Sep58

ML779 to Aéronautique navale 27Apr51; deld via Pembroke Dock 14Apr51, using radio call-sign FXGCB; Flottille 7.F [7.F-1] 1951-53; Flottille 27.F [27.F-2]; Escadrille 50.S [50.S-1]; delivered to SB&HL from Berre 4Dec56, using radio call-sign FYBDA; test-flown 22Aug57; to Brest 5Sep57, using radio call-sign FYBUE; [50.S-1]; SOC 24May60

ML781 to Aéronautique navale 14May51; deld via Pembroke Dock 14Apr51, using radio call-sign FXGCA; Flottille 7.F [7.F-1] 1951-53; Flottille 27.F [27.F-1] 1953-54; Escadrille 23.S Feb55 Saint-Mandrier; SOC Dakar 17Aug56 for spares

ML796 to Aéronautique navale 3Aug51 after modification for Sono-Buoy training by SB&HL; acceptance 4Aug51 Brest; Flottille 7.F [7.F-8] 16Aug51; ferried Brest - Port Lyautey - Dakar 18-20Aug51; Flottille 27.F [2.7F-8] 1953; Escadrille 12.S [12.S-1] Saint-Mandrier 17Dec54; Escadrille 50.S [50.S-3]; to UK for inspection survey Oct56; Wig Bay to SB&HL 19Oct56, using radio call-sign FYBDE; test-flown 29May57; to Brest 8Jun57, using radio call-sign FYBUG; Escadrille 50.S; SOC 30Jan62 at Lanvéoc/Poulmic, beached and stored; sold to M.Robert Bertin 1965 for use as bar at Moisden-la-Riviere, moved in 1969 to La Baule and parked in car park as "Le Mister Blue" nightclub; in 1976 a proposed road development required removal of the Sunderland which was donated to the Imperial War Museum, arriving at Duxford via Dunkirk and Harwich on five lorries 9Jul76; restored for exhibition and currently on display at IWM, Duxford as ML796 [NS:F]

ML799 to Aéronautique navale; deld via Pembroke Dock 25May51, using radio call-sign FXCGD; acceptance 4Jun51; TOC 6Jun51; Flottille 7.F [7.F-5] 1951-53; Flottille 27.F [27.F-5] 1953]; to storage at Berre; delivered to SB&HL from Berre 5Mar56, using radio call-sign FYBDE; test-flown 20 & 30Aug56; to Lanvéoc 31Aug56, using radio call-sign FYBDD; Escadrille 53.S [53.S-2] FBTU; SOC Dakar-Bel Air 29Sep58

ML800 to Aéronautique navale as a late transfer tp France; deld to Brest 26Jun57 using call-sign FYBUA; TOC 28Jul57; Flottille 2.7F [27.F-6]; Escadrille 50.S [50.S-4]; SOC 21Dec60 due to excessive corrosion

ML816 to Aéronautique navale 10Aug51; Flottille 7.F [7.F-9] 1951-53; then Flottille 27.F [27.F-9]; storage at Berre 1954; Escadrille 12.S [12.S-4]; Escadrille 50.S [50.S-8]; Escadrille 12.S [12.S-4] arrived Jan56 with equipment for sono-buoy school; delivered to SB&HL from Lanvéoc-Poulmic 28Aug56, using radio call-sign FYBDD; test-flown 8 & 25 Feb57; to Brest 26Feb57, using radio call-sign FYBYU; SOC 17Apr61 due to corrosion

ML819 to Aéronautique navale 30Aug51; accepted on same day; Flottille 7.F [7.F-10] 1951-53; then Flottille 27.F [27.F-10]; SOC 9Dec55 due to corrosion, spares and equipment recovered by technical department at Dakar

CHAPTER 5 : INDIVIDUAL AIRCRAFT HISTORIES

After service with 201 Squadron and 235 OCU, Sunderland MR.5 RN284 was delivered as a Sunderland 5 to the Aéronautique navale from Belfast en route Brest on 21st December 1957 and spent the next four years with Escadrille 12.S and Flottille 50.S. In service the French did not use the GR or MR rôle prefixes.
(Peter Davis collection)

ML820 to Aéronautique navale; acceptance flight 22Nov51; deld via Pembroke Dock 23Nov51, using radio call-sign FYBAC; TOC 23 or 26Nov51; Flottille 7.F [7.F-13]; Flottille 27.F [27.F-13]; storage at Berre Jun54; back to [27.F-13}; Escadrille 12.S [12.S-2] from Dec54; to FBTU Dakar [53.S-1]; TT on 1Feb57 1,000 hrs; possible repairs uneconomical; delivered to SB&HL from Berre for scrapping 21Feb57, using radio call-sign FYBDD; SOC 26Sep57, scrapped and hulk noted 2Mar58 (Note: has been reported as 10S-4 and 53.S-8 but dates uncertain)

ML821 to Aéronautique navale;acceptance flight 19Sep51; deld via Pembroke Dock 26Sep51, using radio call-sign FYBAA; TOC 26Sep51; Flottille 7.F [7.F-16] allocated late, confirmed by early.53; reserve boat Berre Oct54; Flottille 27.F [27.F-16]; Escadrille 53.S [53.S-1]; believed Sep56 to May57 after engine change Dakar; delivered to SB&HL 5Jun57 from Berre for scrapping, using radio call-sign FYBAG; after examination overhaul and repair considered uneconomical; SOC Belfast 27Sep57, noted less inner engines 2Mar58

ML824 to Aéronautique navale; deld via Pembroke Dock 26Oct51, using radio call-sign FYBAB; to storage Berre; late delivery to Flottille 7.F [7.F-14]; then [27.F-14]; Escadrille 12.S [12.S-5] Dec54 after storage at Berre; sonobuoy training equipment; Escadrille 50.S [50.S-9]; (reported [12.S-3 in Sep55 ?]); delivered to SB&HL 6Mar56 from Berre, using radio call-sign FYBAA; test-flown 26Sep56 & 4Oct56; to Lanvéoc 5Oct56, using radio call-sign FYBUE; TT 2,005 hrs 1Feb57; SOC 22Feb61 and delivered to Pembroke Dock from Brest 24Mar61for preservation escorted by two RAF Shackletons (last flight); beached 25Mar61 and hangared for cleaning etc; donated to Sunderland Trust .61; placed in outdoor dockyard site 2Jun62 [A:Z]; formally handed over to RAF Museum 11Jan71; dismantled and fuselage taken by landing craft to Dagenham arr 16Mar71, other parts by road; arr Hendon 21Mar71 for assembly and restoration; moved to permanent home in Battle of Britain Museum, RAFM, Hendon in 1978, marked ML824 [NS:Z]

ML835 343 Sqn; to Aéronautique navale 21Jun45; ferried Freetown - Dakar 4Jul45; Flottille 7.F [7.F-10]; stored as such, Karouba NAS, Tunisia 1947; reserve boat after overhaul and mods, Pegasus 38s, from 11Mar48; Dakar 1949-51; last Mk.III operational with Flottille 7.F 21Apr51; SOC 20Jul51

ML841 test-flown at 302FTU Oban by French crew 27-30May44; ferried Oban - Gibraltar 11-18Jun44; TOC Gibraltar 16Feb45 (possibly on loan); 343 Sqn; to Aéronautique navale 21Jun45; Flottille 7.F [7F-M]; crashed on take-off from Dakar 20Jul45, 10 fatalities

ML851 343 Sqn; to Aéronautique navale 21Jun45; Flottille 7.F [7F-A, then 7.F-1] 1946-49; lost at sea 16Sept49 off Almadies, French West Africa, during depth charge training possibly due to ricocheting depth charge; 10 fatalities; SOC 22Dec49; TT 760 hrs

ML854 343 Sqn; to Aéronautique navale 21Jun45; Flottille 7.F [7.F-9] 1946 until 22Dec48 when DBF afloat at Dakar-Bel Air; SOC 1Oct49

ML866 deld via Pembroke Dock 19Nov51; to storage then Flottille 7.F [7.F-11] Aug52; Flottille 27.F [27.F-11] 1953-56; delivered to SB&HL from Berre 20Jun56, using radio call-sign FYBDA; test-flown 17Dec56; to Brest 15Jan57, using radio call-sign FYBUE; wrecked at Lanvéoc-Poulmic when port float hit sea on arrival 16Jan57; drifted and sank in poor weather 20Jan57; SOC 29Mar57

Sunderland 5 ML824 with spurious code [A:Z] and still wearing the unit badge of Escadrille 50.S, was parked in the open at Pembroke Dock from 2nd June 1962 until formally handed over to the RAF Museum on 11th January 1971.

ML870   343 Sqn 21Jun45; believed 7FE [N]; Flottille 7.F [7.F-5] 1946-50; Pegasus 38 fitted 1947-48, Karouba; inspected 3Aug50 and allocated 80 hrs flying before SOC; SOC Dakar 2Jan51

ML871   343 Sqn [L]; to Aéronautique navale 2Jul44; Flottille 7FE [7FE-L] unconfirmed; Flottille 7.F [7.F-3] 1946-47; mods and overhaul, Pegasus 38 fitted, Karouba 1948; [7.F-3] Dakar 1949-50; SOC 29Nov50

ML872   test-flown Belfast 11Dec51; deld Brest via Pembroke Dock 13Dec51; reserve boat at Berre, in storage; to Flottille 7.F [7.F-17] Apr53; then Flottille 27.F [27.F-27]; accident due to engine trouble, Port-Etienne, Mauritania Sep55; later towed, engineless, to Dakar by tender *Paul Goffeny* F754; SOC 12Jul56

ML874   343 Sqn; to Aéronautique navale 21 Jun45; Flottille 7.F [7.F-11] 1946-48; mods and Pegasus 38 at Karouba 1947; destroyed by fire at Port-Etienne 16Nov48 when supply launch exploded (3 or 4 killed); TT 808 hrs; SOC on paper 1Jul49 and again at Dakar 1Oct49

ML877   deld via Pembroke Dock 12Jan52 (acceptance 8Jan52); Flottille 7.F [7F-12] Jan53; later [27.F-12] and stored at Berre 1955; redelivered as [27.F-12]; at SB&HL Apr57; to Brest 19Apr57, using radio call-sign FYBUA; to Escadrille 53.S FBTU [53.S-2] 1956; apparently back to 27.F May-Jun57 [27.F-1], then [53.S-1] Jul57; SOC 26Jan59

NJ170   TOC 25May51; Flottille 7.F [7.F-4] 1951-early53; Flottille 27.F [27.F-4]; Escadrille 53.S [53.S-1] 1953-54; again [27.F-4]; at SB&HL Feb56; test-flown 2 & 9Mar56; to Berre 10Mar56; accident while afloat at Port-Etienne 1Jun56; TT 1,315 hrs 1Feb57; SOC 26Jan59

NJ182   deld via Pembroke Dock 12Jan52 (acceptance 8Jan53); Flottille 7.F [7.F-15] Apr53; later Flottille 27.F [27.F-15] 1953-54; delivered to SB&HL from Berre 16Apr57, using radio call-sign FYBDA; test-flown 28Nov57, 5 & 6Dec57; to Brest 12Dec57, using radio call-sign FYBUA; Escadrille 12.S [12.S-2]; (was also 27.F-15, date unknown); SOC 17Apr61 due to corrosion

NJ190   deld via Pembroke Dock 20Feb52; TOC 19Feb52; storage at Berre; Flottille 27.F [27.F-18] 1953-54; Escadrille 53.S [53.S-2]; Escadrille 50.S [50.S-7]; at SB&HL 6.56; test-flown 13 & 22Jun56; to Lanvéoc 23Jun56; back to Flottille 27.F [27.F-8] 1956-57; then [27.F-2] when minor incident at sea 28Jun57; allocated to 53.S [53.S-2] spring 1958-Aug60; SOC 23Aug60

RN284   deld Belfast to Pembroke Dock 21Dec57 en route to Brest using radio call-sign FYBUG (acceptance 18Dec57); Escadrille 12.S [12.S-3]; Escadrille 50.S [50.S-5]; SOC 30Jan62, kept for some time for seamanship instruction

SZ571   TOC at SB&HL 31Jul57; test-flown 6 and 14Nov57; to Brest 15Nov57, using radio call-sign FYBUD; Escadrille 50.S [50.S-2]; SOC 17Apr61 due to corrosion

SZ576   TOC at SB&HL 11Jun57; test-flown 18 and 27Jun57 and 4Jul57 (final acceptance date); to Brest 5Jul57, using radio call-sign FYBUA; sank at Port-Etienne 23Oct57; SOC 31Dec57

Below is the enigma, wearing serial 120 and national markings. No propellers are fitted and it is difficult to tell whether the aircraft is being displayed or undergoing maintenance at Bom Sucesso. Perhaps 136 was repainted as 120 for some unknown reason? (Luis Tavares)

Part 6: PORTUGUESE NAVY (Aviação Naval)

136   ex P9623; taken over by Portuguese Navy when it force-landed near Troia beach south of Lisbon on 15Feb41 due to hurricane-strength winds; overhauled at Bom Sucesso NAS, test flown 2Sep42 and made several training flights; repaired and all engines replaced .44; took off 8Mar44 on flight to Portuguese Guinea with crew of nine; after 3 hours 10 minutes, near Canary Islands, No.3 propeller disengaged and No.4 engine had to be shut down; pilot decided to return to base on two engines, and after 9 hours 20 minutes aircraft alighted on River Tagus near Lisbon; never flew again and scrapped 44/45

"120"   identity unknown; photographic evidence of a second Sunderland in Portuguese Navy colours only serves to fuel contention about its possible origins. Favourite was W6065 which ditched off Oporto on 5Mar43 on a ferry flight to Bathurst, crew members were rescued and interned; but the aircraft is said to have been destroyed in heavy seas. The aircraft shown in the photograph is not on beaching gear but looks as if it is supported in position and may be on display. Possibly it could be 136 repainted for some unknown reason or occasion. Serial 136 was the last in the Navy's sequential series which changed after 1943; this implies that 120 was an earlier serial although some were duplicated and 120 should have belonged in a batch of Grumman Widgeons. It remains a mystery at the time of writing.

Two views (above and below) showing the Aviação Naval (Portuguese Navy) Sunderland Mk.I ex P9623 at some time prior to its final flight in 1944, see also page 70. In the upper picture the aircraft is still in its RAF camouflage. (via Luis Tavares)

G-AGER, ex JM660, the first of the modified Mk.III Sunderlands which were put into service on routes from Hamworthy (Poole) to Lagos and to Karachi in 1943. Here beaching wheels are being attached in order to bring the flying-boat ashore. The background has clearly been removed from the original print by the censor. (via JM Collection)

Chapter 6
CIVILIAN CONVERSIONS AND NEW BUILD AIRCRAFT

UNITED KINGDOM

British Overseas Airways Corporation

A number of Sunderlands had been loaned briefly to BOAC by the RAF in 1940/41, without alterations being made for passenger service. In 1942, however, RAF Transport Command, faced with an ever-increasing demand for long-distance freight and passenger aircraft, arranged for a batch of six Sunderlands Mk.III (JM660 to JM665) to be suitably modified. This involved removing all armament, fairing over the turrets, and fitting rudimentary bench seating, the nose fairing remaining retractable so that the anchor could be deployed.

On 1st March 1943 these Sunderlands were put into service on scheduled flights from RAF Hamworthy on Poole Harbour to Lagos (Nigeria) via Foynes and Lisbon. On 25th October, however, they were withdrawn from this route and switched to a longer service to Karachi via Cairo, which was extended to Calcutta on 10th May 1944. This route was the result of a proving flight of 5039 miles (8113 km) to Karachi in 28 hours flying time, in which the Sunderland carried seven passengers and freight.

The original routing from Poole for the service was via Gibraltar, Djerba (Tunisia), Cairo, Lake Habbaniya (Iraq), Bahrein, Jiwani, Karachi and Gwalior. The Sunderlands carried prominent RAF Transport Command four-letter codes as this BOAC operation was at the time part of Transport Command and used several RAF bases as staging posts. Following the Allied invasion of France, the route was shortened to avoid the long detour to Gibraltar, and from 20th February 1945 Augusta in Sicily became an intermediate stopping-place.

Six more Sunderlands (JM722 and ML725 to ML729) joined the fleet from 1 September 1943, followed by six more (ML 751 to ML756) in January and February 1944 and a final six (ML786 to ML791) in July and August 1944. Three of these aircraft flew the Poole-Foynes-Poole shuttle service until 20th February 1944, when Dakotas took over, flying from Croydon to Rineanna (Shannon).

The Hamworthy alighting area was transferred to 116 Wing of Transport Command on 13th January 1944, but the RAF vacated the site on 1st May and it was renamed Poole by the DGCA, who then took over its operation on behalf of BOAC. On 20th April, however, BOAC was notified that flying from Poole would have to be curtailed temporarily from 28 April due to the large number of landing craft gathering there in readiness for the invasion of France.

With the war in Europe over, the camouflage on BOAC Sunderlands was removed and silver finish substituted, and their engines were uprated, G-AGJM being the first to be so treated. In readiness for the reopening of the Empire routes to the Far East and Australasia, the passenger and cargo accommodation was rebuilt in three versions. Types H1 and H2 allowed for sixteen passengers and 3.5 tons (3.56 tonnes) of cargo, while in type H3 the number of passengers increased to 22 but the cargo was limited to 2.0 tons (2.04 tonnes). There was a crew of six: Captain, First Officer, navigator, radio officer, engineer and steward. As such, the aircraft became known as the

G-AGIA, formerly ML728, was one of the second batch of Mk.III Sunderlands to be converted to unarmed transports to supplement BOAC operations in 1943. Transport Command code OQZA is not yet applied in this view which shows the wartime civil marks underlined with a tricolour band and a just-discernable Speedbird symbol above the crew door. (Capt J E Hackett via JM Collection)

Hythe Class, and eighteen were converted by BOAC at Hythe and four by Short & Harland at Belfast.

In January 1946 two routes were being flown from Poole: to Rangoon via Biscarosse, Augusta, Cairo, Bahrein, Karachi and Calcutta and to Baltimore via Lisbon, Bathurst, Natal, Belem, Trinidad and Bermuda. The Rangoon route, flown four times per week and known as Line 4, was extended to Singapore on 7th February, with an additional stop at Lake Habbaniya in Iraq and an overall flying time of 57 hours.

On 22nd February a proving flight to Sydney (Rose Bay) was completed in the record time of 54 flying hours, paving the way for the Poole to Calcutta service to be extended to Sydney on 25th May 1946 by G-AGJN *Hudson*. This was the first through flying-boat service from the UK to Sydney since 1940, and the total time on the route was five and a half days, very slow by today's standards but excellent then! Between Singapore and Sydney QANTAS crews handled the flight, but for the remainder of the flight BOAC crews were in charge.

Another major proving flight was made between February and April 1946, when G-AGJM *Hythe* flew a 35,313 miles (56,854 km) round trip from Poole to Australia, New Zealand, Hong Kong, Shanghai (where it was the first British civil airliner to touch down on the river Wangpoo) and Tokyo, where it created another 'first'.

At the end of April 1946, BOAC vacated the Pottery Works at Poole, which had been used as a passenger terminal since the outset of operations during the war, and moved to more amenable surroundings in the Poole Yacht Club, where appropriate passenger facilities were installed. Adjacent to this building was the jetty from where passengers were taken by tender to their waiting aircraft. Later, on 24th August, Sunderland G-AGHW *Hamilton* reopened the Singapore to Hong Kong route for BOAC and early in August the Australian service was increased to three per week, departing from Poole on Sundays, Tuesdays and Thursdays.

It was soon realised that the converted Sunderlands were neither comfortable

The first BOAC Sunderland to have wartime camouflage removed was G-AGJM Hythe *which gave its name to the whole class of rebuilt civil transports and carried out a significant proving flight to Tokyo in 1946.* (R C Sturtivant collection)

CHAPTER 5 : INDIVIDUAL AIRCRAFT HISTORIES

nor economical enough to fulfil the obvious potential of the Empire air routes, so in 1945 G-AGKX returned to Short Bros at Rochester to be upgraded. The interior was completely rebuilt with two decks to provide a dining saloon and cocktail bar and seating for up to 24 passengers by day and 16 by night. As such, it was the first example of the Short S.25 Sandringham, and it was shown to the general public at the Victory Air Pageant at Southampton (Eastleigh) on 22nd June 1946 and at the SBAC display at Farnborough a week later. In 1947/48, thirteen more Sunderlands Mk.V were similarly converted by Short Bros & Harland, ten of them becoming Sandringhams Mk.5 (the Plymouth Class) and the other three Mk.7 (the Bermuda Class), which carried 30 passengers.

Towards the end of the war, the RAF had placed an order for 102 Sunderlands Mk.IV (later known as the Seaford Mk.I), which was radically different from the Mk.III and Mk.V then in service. In the end, only ten were built, and in 1946 one was loaned to BOAC as G-AGWU for evaluation. After successful trials, an order was placed by the Ministry of Civil Aviation for twelve similar aircraft, to be known as the Short S.45 Solent 2, for leasing to BOAC. Up to thirty passengers could be accommodated on two decks, and there were dining room facilities, a cocktail bar and space to 'promenade'. Construction was by Short Bros at Rochester, where the first of these aircraft, G-AHIL, was launched on 11th November 1946. The final Solent 2, G-AHIY, was the last aircraft built at the Rochester factory.

Another service, from Poole to Bahrein, was opened on 2nd May 1947, and three days later was extended to Karachi, all flown by Sandringhams of the Plymouth Class once a week. By September, BOAC was operating the 'Plymouth' class three times per week from Poole to Karachi, continuing twice weekly to Calcutta, Rangoon, Bangkok and Hong Kong. For this service, two-thirds of the 22 seats were allocated to 'non-priority' passengers, who paid £170 for the seven-day one-way flight or £306 return, a year's salary for many people! 'Hythes' flew once a week from Poole to Rangoon and Singapore and three times weekly to Rangoon and Singapore, from where QANTAS (qv) carried on to Sydney. All services called at Augusta, Cairo, Basra, Bahrein and Karachi. An additional connecting service was flown by 'Hythes' from Singapore to Bangkok and Hong Kong once a week. 'Sandringhams' flew

Capt Hackett flew the Sandringham I G-AGKX at the Victory Air Pageant at Eastleigh in June 1946. New windows clearly visible in this view emphasise the two-deck interior conversion.
(Aeroplane via JM Collection)

Sandringham interior, November 1945: (Above) on the lower deck, a two-place cabin area which converted into bunks for overnight services and (Below) on the upper deck looking forward to the bar and pantry from the dining saloon. *(Aeroplane via JM Collection)*

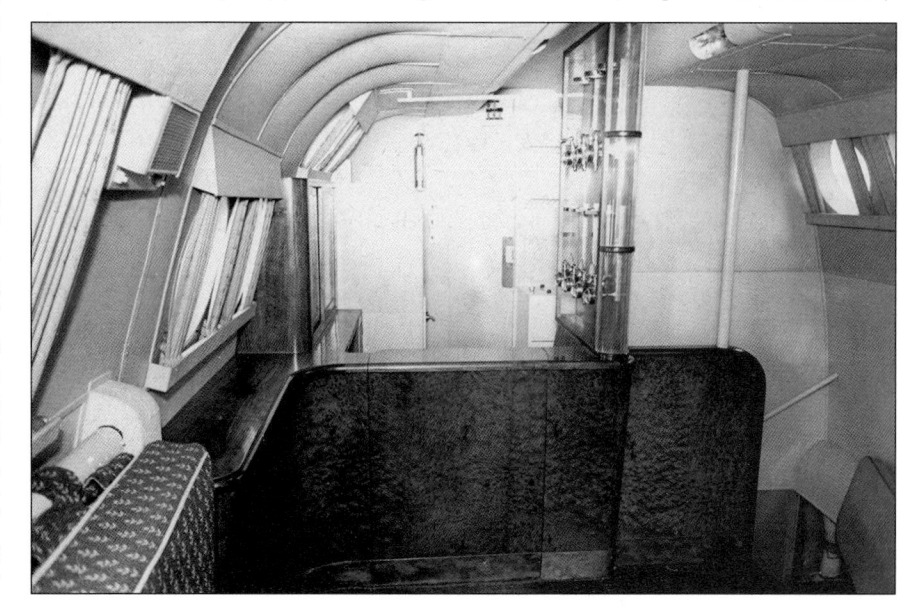

The first Solent 2, originally laid down as a Seaford, seen during trials at Rochester early in 1947 and already marked as G-AHIL for BOAC bearing the name Salisbury *below the cockpit window.* (Aeroplane via JM Collection)

an additional service from Poole to Cairo via Marseilles and Augusta.

By January 1948, Line 4 consisted of a route from Poole to Marseilles, Cairo, Karachi, Calcutta, Rangoon, Singapore, Darwin, Bowen, Sydney and Auckland, with a branch from Rangoon to Hong Kong. There were six flights per week on these routes, in partnership with QANTAS, but all were operated at a loss. During January, Poole handled 940 passengers in 41 inbound and 36 outbound aircraft. On 19th March, the Hong Kong route was extended once a week to Iwakuni in Japan, where there was an RAF Station.

A proving flight for a proposed service to Johannesburg in South Africa was made at the end of 1947, but on 5th December the aircraft, G-AHIT *Severn*, was delayed at Port Bell on Lake Victoria with engine trouble. On that occasion there was a crew of eight and 26 BOAC officials. A route-proving flight by Solent 2 G-AHIN on 1st May 1948 (the last BOAC flight from Poole) heralded the opening of the thrice-weekly service on 4th May, superseding their Avro York landplanes.

From Southampton, which on 31st March had replaced Poole as BOAC's UK flying-boat terminal, the Solents staged through Marseilles, Augusta, Cairo, Khartoum, Port Bell and Victoria Falls to reach Vaaldam Lake, near Johannesburg, in four and a half days. However, technical problems with wing-tip floats meant the withdrawal of the Solents between 22nd July and 17th October 1948.

At BOAC's new terminal at Southampton, Berth 50, the passenger building was opened officially by Lord Nathan, the Minister of Civil Aviation, on 14th April 1948, and on the same day new Solent G-AHIN was christened *Southampton* by the Mayor and Mayoress of the town. It was soon found possible for arriving passengers to disembark at the new terminal in no more than twenty minutes after touch-down. A launch then towed the empty flying-boat across the Solent to Hythe for maintenance. The new South Africa route meant that there would be 22 movements a week at Berth 50.

In 1949 four of the ex-RAF batch of Seafords were converted for BOAC as Solents Mk.3, with accommodation for 39 passengers, and joined the purpose-built Solents on the South Africa route. From 15th May 1949 the Solents also operated a service to Lake Naivasha near Nairobi in Kenya, replacing Yorks and reducing the journey time from 48 hours to 27 hours 30 minutes. From 25th May, Solents relieved Sandringhams on the Karachi service.

As during 1948 BOAC had been taking delivery of landplanes such as the Lockheed 749 Constellation to operate its Australia route, (the service starting on 1st December) and chartered Douglas DC-4 Skymasters to operate the Persian Gulf services, the days of flying-boats in the airline's service were becoming numbered. The last BOAC scheduled flying-boat service was flown by Solent 2 G-AHIO, which left Berth 50 at Southampton on 3rd November 1950 for Vaaldam in South Africa, where it arrived on 7th November. After its return flight, which included an additional stop at Marseilles (Marignane) all BOAC flying-boat operations ceased on 14th November, although other operators were only too keen to continue flying Sunderlands and their modified successors.

Aquila Airways Ltd

Formed on 18th May 1948 by Wg Cdr Barry T Aikman DFC, a former 210 Squadron Sunderland pilot, Aquila Airways' first task after taking delivery of two Sunderlands from BOAC was to work on the Berlin airlift. From the airline's maintenance base at Hamble on Southampton Water, the Sunderlands, G-AGEU and G-AGIA, flew to Hamburg (Finkenwerde) and began flying sorties to the Havel Lake in Berlin on August 4th. Like their RAF counterparts, the Aquila aircraft carried mainly salt, and before being withdrawn on 15th December made 265 sorties, carrying 1409 tons (1434 tonnes) of freight in 700 hours flying time. A third Sunderland, G-AHEO, also took part in the airlift, but made only six sorties.

After the airlift, Aquila acquired nine more Sunderlands from BOAC and either made them ready for service or dismantled them for spare parts. The intention was to use the aircraft on long-range charter work, but the demise of other companies who ventured into this sphere encouraged a change of mind. Aquila then applied for the right to operate a scheduled service between Southampton (where Aquila had taken over BOAC's terminal at Berth 50) and Funchal, the capital of Madeira, under a BEA Associate Agreement. Approval was soon received, and a proving flight was made on 24th March 1949 by G-AGEU. On board, in addition to Barry Aikman, were two other directors of the company, Geoffrey Howland-Jackson and Harold Rattle, and as they decided that the potential for such a service was good the service was inaugurated on 14th May. Mr Courtenay Edwards, editor of the aviation supplement

CHAPTER 6 : CIVIL CONVERSIONS AND NEW-BUILD AIRCRAFT

of the *Daily Mail*, was also on board, and wrote in the *Diário de Notícias*, the local newspaper, "We were extraordinarily impressed to find a large crowd awaiting the landing and mooring of our *Hampshire* seaplane [sic] in the waters of the Bay of Funchal. We knew beforehand that this gesture by Aquila Airways to bring to the island this aircraft, the first commercial craft of its kind to visit, would make a great step forward in Madeiran history. Nevertheless, we did not expect that this trial flight would arouse so much interest and enthusiasm among the population."

Aquila's new service was flown once a week during that summer, the outbound flight taking off from Southampton at 08.00 on Saturdays and arriving at Funchal at 16.45, returning on Thursdays at 18.00 after a take-off at Funchal at 07.15. For this the return fare was £79-4s-0d (£79.20), which for the ordinary person was several weeks' wages. As no refuelling facilities were available at Funchal, this had to be done at Lisbon. A shuttle service from Funchal to Lisbon and back was flown on Mondays at a fare of £32-8s-0d (£32.40).

The route proved very popular, but in order to make better use of its large fleet of Sunderlands Aquila undertook charter flights to and from places not otherwise served by airlines. Of particular significance were flights between Aden and the UK with the crew of a tanker; a return trip from Hull to Helsinki in Finland to collect a ship's crew; and a party of travel agents from Southampton to Le Havre. Among other destinations were the Isles of Scilly, to which Aquila operated a number of flights from Falmouth for holiday-makers in the summer of 1949. It had been hoped that a series of 5000-mile (8050 km) 'aerial cruises' around the Mediterranean Sea for Thomas Cook would begin in 1949, but sufficient support was not forthcoming.

With the success of the Funchal route, which had carried nearly 3,000 passengers, boosting the company's optimism, Aquila investigated further route possibilities. A route between Falmouth and Leith, near Edinburgh, and on to Glasgow was proposed, and a few bookings were taken. A proving flight from Southampton was made on 1st June 1950, when Sunderland 3 G-AGJN alighted at Albert Dock in Leith and then continued to the River Clyde at Greenock. The new service to Greenock (for Glasgow) opened on 4th July, the Sunderland taking just over two hours for the journey. Each destination enjoyed one

Sunderland 3 G-AGJN 'Hudson' of Aquila Airways, seen at Hamble in 1952, made the survey flight to the Falkland Islands in April/May that year but was written off at Funchal, Madeira on 21st January 1953. *(P H T Green collection)*

Aquila's G-AGJN moored in Stanley Harbour following its flight from Southampton to investigate the practicalities of a service to the Falkland Islands. Arriving on April 28th and departing on May 5th 1952, the experiment was a success but was not followed by any regular commercial service from the UK until 1985. *(via Douglas Rough)*

round trip per week, Glasgow on Tuesdays and Leith on Fridays, the fares being £9-0s-0d (£9.00) single and £16-4s-0d (£16.20) return, which were comparable to first-class rail fares. Unfortunately, passengers failed to appear in sufficient numbers, and the services were very soon cancelled, with heavy financial losses to Aquila.

However, a route to be flown under a BEA Associate Agreement between Southampton and Jersey opened on 7th July 1950. Two flights were flown every Saturday, using St Aubin's Bay at St Helier as the island terminal, until the end of the 1951 season.

Aquila's first Solent aircraft, G-AKNU, was introduced into service in the winter of 1951/52, and was fitted with 41 seats. This enabled the Funchal service to be extended to Las Palmas in the Canary Islands in 1952. British competitors in the Olympic Games that year were flown to Helsinki by Aquila Airways.

In 1952 a long-planned survey of a proposed service between the Falkland Islands and Montevideo was carried out for the Falkland Islands Company, whose managing director, L W H Young, had asked about the possibility of such a service. The aircraft, G-AGJN *Hudson*, was in the hands of Capt Douglas Pearson, and left Southampton on 20th April. It carried nine passengers, who each paid a single fare of £289-10s-0d (£289.50), airmail, diphtheria serum, eggs and clocks. Intermediate landings were made at Funchal, Cape Verde, Natal (Brazil), Rio de Janeiro and Montevideo, where there was a 40-hour stopover, before the aircraft reached Port Stanley harbour at 18.00 hours on 28th April. The stage from Montivideo had taken 7 hours 45 minutes, during which time a listening watch had been maintained by the Falklands radio station. An approach control procedure was carried out by Mr Halls, formerly the Falklands Islands Company's pilot, who operated a R/T set in the Town Hall! On the return journey 6,726 items of mail were carried, specially franked for the occasion. However, the proposed service was not considered viable and no further action was taken.

Unfortunately, Sunderland 3 G-AGJN was destroyed in an accident at Funchal

MADEIRA

FOUR-ENGINED FLYING BOAT SERVICE

BY

AQUILA AIRWAYS

(OPERATING UNDER AN ASSOCIATE AGREEMENT WITH BRITISH OVERSEAS AIRWAYS CORPORATION)

FARES
·
TIMETABLES
·
GENERAL INFORMATION

THE AIRCRAFT

It is not our intention here to eulogise on the high standard of comfort afforded by the Flying Boat. Seasoned travellers will be aware of the great comfort and roominess of this type of aircraft. Everything possible is done to ensure our passengers' comfort. Two stewards and one hostess minister to your needs. Full course hot meals are served and the touch of a button brings refreshments at any time, all at no charge to you except for alcoholic drinks, which of course are duty free. The aircraft is divided into cabins for four, five, six or seven people and meals are served on fixed tables. There is a cocktail bar at the rear of the aircraft —usually the most crowded spot on board— where complete strangers become friends in a matter of minutes. However you wish to spend your time, the four powerful engines will take you swiftly and surely to the finest holiday you will ever have.

GENERAL INFORMATION

Passports. All passengers must hold a valid passport.

Visas. Passengers spending more than four days in Lisbon or Madeira must have a Portuguese visa. We shall be pleased to obtain this on your behalf if you will forward your passport either direct or through your travel agent. The inclusive fee is £1 2s. 9d. each visa. British subjects do not need photographs or forms for this but other nationals should inquire of their travel agent who will give them full particulars.

Passengers will not be allowed to board the aircraft unless they are in possession of a valid Portuguese visa endorsed for Madeira.

Currency. The Bank of England allowance for holiday expenditure in Portugal and Madeira is £100 (Children under 16 £70). Payment for alcoholic drinks and cigarettes on board the aircraft and of course the fare and any excess baggage charges may be made in sterling All food and soft drinks are provided free of charge.

We would bring to the notice of passengers the currency concession granted to Reid's Hotel and The New Avenue Hotel whereby only 30/- per day per person is charged against the foreign currency allowance. The balance of the daily hotel rate may be paid in sterling.

Passengers travelling on business or for health reasons should consult their banks regarding special currency allowances.

Clothing. Summer clothing should be taken, and a warm coat for excursions into the mountains. Evening dress is essential at Reid's Hotel; optional, but usually worn, at the Savoy; and optional at the other hotels.

Shopping. There are good supplies of most things in the shops at prices below those prevailing in this country. The famous Madeira wines are cheap and plentiful. English cigarettes and tobacco are cheaper than here and in good supply. Madeira is world famous for exquisite embroidery and intricate basket work which can be purchased at extraordinarily low prices.

Postal Arrangements. Letters posted in Madeira are delivered in this country two days later and vice versa.

WINTER SCHEDULE 1951/52

Southampton/Madeira

Dep. Southampton	...	23.00	Monday and Friday
Arr. Madeira	...	08.00	Tuesday and Saturday
Dep. Madeira	...	07.00	Sunday and Thursday
Arr. Lisbon	...	12.15	,, ,, ,,
Dep. Lisbon	...	13.45	,, ,, ,,
Arr. Southampton	...	19.45	,, ,, ,,

Madeira/Lisbon

Dep. Madeira	...	10.00	Tuesday
Arr. Lisbon	...	15.15	,,
Dep. Lisbon	...	11.30	Wednesday
Arr. Madeira	...	14.45	,,

All times local

FARES

Southampton to Madeira: Return **£89 2s. 0d.**
Single **£49 10s. 0d.**
Excess baggage: **8s. 9d.** per kilo.

Lisbon to Madeira: Return **£40 10s. 0d.**
Single **£22 10s. 0d.**
Excess baggage: **4s. 5d.** per kilo.

Children: Under **12**, 50% of the fare; under **2**, 10% of the fare

The free baggage allowance is 44 lbs. (no free baggage for Children under 2)

Aquila Airways timetable of services to Madeira in the winter of 1951-52. (Ron Roberts collection)

CHAPTER 6 : CIVIL CONVERSIONS AND NEW-BUILD AIRCRAFT

on 21st January 1953 and G-AGKY sank off Calshot a week later. In March Aquila was taken over by the British Aviation Services Group (Britavia), which made further capital available for expansion. No new routes were added in 1953, but the Coronation of Queen Elizabeth presented an opportunity for Aquila to arrange flights over Spithead for passengers wishing to see the Navy's fleet lined up for inspection. Aquila was also occupied on trooping charters to and from Freetown and Lagos in West Africa.

In 1954, the Funchal service was flown twice each week and the extension to the Canary Islands once. Among the passengers to and from Funchal were many well-known people, such as Gracie Fields, Harry Secombe and Joe Louis, all remembered well by Norman Hull, then a Traffic Officer at Berth 50. Freight was also carried in both directions, and many freight charters were flown. A direct weekly service from Southampton to Capri via Marseilles was inaugurated on 3rd June by Solent G-ANAJ, taking eight and three quarter hours, which boosted Aquila's passenger numbers to over 8,000 that year. Application was made in October for a freight service to Perth in Western Australia, with a number of intermediate stops, but this proposal came to nothing.

Encouraged by the success of its scheduled services, Aquila opened routes from Southampton to Santa Margherita on 4th June 1955 and to Genoa next day. Both these services left Southampton before dawn to enable passengers to enjoy almost an extra day of their holidays. 1956 proved equally rewarding, with a new direct route from Southampton to Las Palmas in the Canary Islands opening on 8th January, operated by two Solents Mark 4 purchased from Tasman Empire Airways and ferried back to England by Aquila crews. On this service, designed to reduce the load on the popular Madeira route, the aircraft took off from Southampton at 20.30 on Sundays and arrived at Las Palmas at 08.15 next day, after a refuelling stop at Lisbon. The return flight left Las Palmas at 11.00 on Mondays and arrived at Southampton at 22.15 the same day. The fare for the return trip was £103.10.0 (£103.50).

During the Suez crisis of 1956, almost 900 civilians, mainly women and children, were evacuated by Aquila's aircraft from Fanara on the Great Bitter Lake, a former RAF Station, commencing on 14th August. They flew either direct to Southampton or to RAF Kalafrana in Malta, from where the passengers transferred to a Hermes aircraft of Britavia at RAF Luqa. In the opposite direction, troops, mainly Royal Marines and naval ratings, were taken out to Egypt.

G-AOBL was one of the three Aquila Airways Solent 2 and 4s being broken up on the Lisbon dock in 1971 after thirteen years of storage. (P H T Green collection)

By the end of that year, however, services were gradually being run down, although another route, a weekly service to Montreux on Lake Geneva, was inaugurated on 1st June 1957 for the exclusive benefit of package-deal holiday companies, eliminating a long coach drive. However, the Capri service was suspended at the end of the holiday season.

The situation was made worse when Solent 3 G-AKNU crashed on Chessel Down on the Isle of Wight on 15th November 1957, with the loss of 35 lives. In 1958 it was announced that Aquila Airways, the last operator of large flying boats in the UK, would go out of business at the end of the season, and all flying duly ceased on 30th September. The three Solents which then formed the airline's fleet were flown to the estuary of the River Tagus near Lisbon with the proposal that they would be reconditioned for service by another airline, Aerovias Aquila, on flights from Portugal to Madeira, but nothing came of this and they were finally broken up after thirteen years of deterioration.

International Aircraft Sales

This company purchased eleven Solents located at Sydenham and elsewhere from the MCA in competition with Aquila, who were notified of the transfer of ownership on 9th February 1953. The proprietors of International Aircraft Sales were American citizens, Col David Miller & Hugh Walker; the UK agent was Capt Jack Alcock; other directors included Swiss and French nationals. The Solents involved were G-AHIL, M, N, R, S, T, U, W, Y and G-AKNS, T. Of these, G-AHIN was later sold to Aquila, G-AKNT sold to the USA, G-AHIT scrapped at Belfast, and G-AHIL, U and KNS scrapped at Hamworthy. The remainder, then located at Felixstowe, were advertised for sale in *Flight* on 16th March 1956 by A King & Sons of Norwich and subsequently sold as scrap.

SOUTH AMERICA

Dodero (Compañía Argentina de Aeronavegación Dodero SA)

After the end of the Second World War, Argentine airlines were in a state of turmoil, but had plenty of money with which to re-equip. Although the new government of Juan Perón did not favour private enterprise, some businessmen were determined to pursue their own projects. Among them were Alberto and José Dodero, who had major shipping interests in Argentina and Uruguay. Without having acquired the necessary traffic rights, they set up the airline and ordered two Mk.2 and two Mk.3 Sandringhams late in 1945, at a cost of $1,250,000 each. The Mk.2 aircraft were fitted with 28 seats on the lower deck and 17 seats and a bar on the upper deck, while the Mk.3s, destined for longer routes, had seats for 21 on the lower deck and a dining room and bar above.

The first of Dodero's Sandringhams, G-AGPZ, was named *Argentina* by Senora Dodero at Belfast on 1st November 1945. Carrying a crew of seven and twelve passengers, with Geoffrey Tyson, chief test pilot of Short & Harland Ltd, at the controls, *Argentina* left Poole for Buenos Aires on 19th November 1945 and staged through Lisbon, Bathurst, Natal and Rio de Janiero, a journey of 7,330 miles (11,801 km). The total time

A mixed bag of Short Brithers' products, moored at Buenos Aires in the early sixties. In the foreground is Sandringham LV-AHH, formerly a Sunderland 5, of Cooperativa Aeronavigantes with port outer engine missing and company titles removed. On the far right is Sandringham 3 LV-AAQ of the same owner and on the far left is another Mk.V conversion LV-AHG still in Aerolineas Argentinas titles. (P H T Green collection)

Sandringham 2 LV-AAO towards the end of its career in the markings of Cooperativa Argentina de Aeronavegantes, and named Rio Aguilera. (P H T Green collection)

in the air was 45 hours 57 minutes at an average speed of 159 mph (256 kph). Following this, the second to be delivered was G-AGPT, which left Poole on 21st December in the hands of Capt E J Moreton and arrived five days later.

The Dodero company engaged fifteen ex-RAF crews on a temporary basis, but planned to recruit Argentine nationals to replace them. Before taking up their positions, the British crews underwent training by BOAC.

Next to be delivered was G-AGPY, which was fitted with 21 seats for long-range work, and left Poole early in February 1946, followed by G-AGTZ on 22nd February, arriving four days later. All the Sandringhams made the journey carrying their British registrations and were re-registered some time after arrival.

José Dodero struggled with the authorities for permission to launch his services, and in order to make a start he took control of Corporación Sudamericana de Servicios Aereos (CSSA), which had permission to operate routes to Montevideo in Uruguay and Asunción in Paraguay. The government, however, introduced a regulation to create 'mixed economy companies' with government and private assets, so in May 1946 Dodero became one of the constituent companies of Aviación del Litoral Fluvial Argentino (ALFA), to which the Sandringhams were transferred.

ALFA (Soc Mixta Aviación del Litoral Fluvial Argentino)

ALFA was formed in May 1946 and received Argentine Government approval to operate airline services. In August, when Dodero withdrew from active participation in Argentine aviation, ALFA began preparations to operate all the services allocated to it by charter. On 8th January 1947 ALFA began operations with a fleet of six Sunderland/Sandringham aircraft from Buenos Aires to Asunción, Montevideo and, during the summer, Punta del Este in Uruguay. Operating from the Puerto Nuevo (new port) at Buenos Aires, the flying-boats' route to Asunción was along the Paraná river, with calls at Paraná, Corrientes and Formosa.

The aircraft were operated in a 45-seat 'air-bus' configuration and by 1948/49 were carrying over 30,000 passengers on the Montevideo route alone. Unfortunately, the company lost Sandringham LV-AAP when the captain tried to land in fog at Buenos Aires on 29th July 1948, killing eighteen of the 23 passengers and crew on board. In May 1949, ALFA ceased operations, which were then operated under Ministry of Transportation supervision pending the formal foundation of Aerolineas Argentinas (q.v.) on 7th December 1950.

Aerolineas Argentinas

After taking over ALFA, Aerolineas Argentinas continued to operate the Sandringhams it had inherited, as well as two converted Sunderlands which had been delivered in 1947. The main route flown continued to be from Buenos Aires to Montevideo in Uruguay, which was operated in pool with CAUSA (q.v.). By 1953, the following routes were being flown from Buenos Aires: to Montevideo (nine or ten times per week but not Sundays); to Colonia (twice weekly); to Concordia (twice weekly); to Posadas (once weekly); to Corrientes (twice weekly); to Rosario, Corrientes and Formosa (twice weekly); and to Posadas and Corrientes (once weekly). An additional route was opened between Buenos Aires and Concepción in Paraguay in 1955, but was closed in 1956, in which year the Colonia service was also abandoned.

Routes to Asuncion via Rosario, Corrientes and Formosa were added in 1956 and to Punta del Este in 1957, the latter on a three flights per week schedule. That year a hub was established at Corrientes for services to Formosa and Asunción, rather than operating a through service from Buenos Aires.

When in November 1959 Aerolineas Argentinas announced that the Sandringhams would cease flying in 1960 there was considerable protest, as most destinations lacked land airports. The airline took notice, and withdrew flying-boats from only the Montevideo route.

In 1960, the Sandringhams were still giving excellent service, albeit at reduced frequency after the opening of landplane routes. This development brought about the demise of flying-boat operations on

1st May 1962 however, and the five surviving aircraft (the sixth had already been used for spares) were put into store at Puerto Nuevo. In 1963 they were put back into service and leased to a company known as Co-operativa Argentina de Aeronavegantes (q.v.) for a domestic freight service. The aircraft were scrapped in January 1967.

Co-operativa Argentina de Aeronavegantes

Formed in 1963 by former Aerolineas Argentinas aircrew, this company planned to operate that airline's five remaining flying-boats on domestic non-scheduled freight services to points on the Paraná and Uruguay rivers. Operations began by August, mainly between Buenos Aires and Posadas, but were short-lived, due to the increasing availability of airports and the difficulty of keeping the old flying-boats airworthy.

Corporacion Sudamericana de Servicios Aereos SA (CSSA)

This Argentinian company, which had been purchased by Dodero in 1945, took delivery of Sunderland 3 G-AGWX in March 1946, but it seems to have been passed on to ALFA (by then owner of Dodero) at once. Services commenced on 16th May 1946 using this aircraft as LV-AAS and also chartering LV-AAO and -AAP from ALFA with infrastructure provided by Dodero, a complex legal arrangement. Alberto Dodero is said to have used LV-AAS as a personal transport at times.

Cia Aeronáutica Uruguayana SA (CAUSA)

CAUSA was incorporated in 1936 and began operating a route from Buenos Aires to Montevideo in 1938. Services were maintained throughout the Second World War with Ju.52/3m floatplanes.

Two Sunderlands Mk.III were acquired by CAUSA with the encouragement of the British government after conversion to passenger configuration: G-AGWW, which left Poole on 29th March 1946 and after arrival became CX-AFA; and G-AGWX, which was initially loaned to CSSA as LV-AAS pending traffic growth and availability of crews. It became CX-AKF in 1948 with CAUSA. The Sunderlands were placed into service on the Montevideo route and to Colonia, both operated daily except Sundays. During the 1950s, with the addition of a third Sandringham, the Montevideo route could be flown ten times per week. By 1957, services were pooled with Aerolineas Argentinas, and by 1960 flights on the Montevideo route had been increased to fifteen per week. However, in 1961, with the introduction of Curtiss C-46 Commando landplanes on both routes, the flying-boat services were run down and closed.

Flota Aerea Mercante Argentina (FAMA)

This organisation, Argentine Merchant Air Fleet, chartered a Sandringham aircraft from Dodero and made a proving flight from Buenos Aires in May 1946. A once-weekly service to Europe began on 27th May but was closed on 26th September, when FAMA switched to York landplanes. The route taken was via Rio de Janiero, Natal, Bathurst, Lisbon and Biscarosse, where it is believed the route terminated, although an extension to Poole is possible.

AUSTRALASIA and the PACIFIC

Réseau Aérien Interinsulaire

This company was formed as Air Tahiti in 1950, was bought by the colonial government in 1953 and in the mid-1950s the French long-haul airline TAI acquired a substantial interest. One Sandringham 7 was acquired in 1958 by RAI to supplement and then replace a Catalina on services from its base at Papeete to Utuora (on the island of Raiatea) and from there to Bora Bora several times weekly. Flagstops were made also on Huahine Island. The flying-boat was configured for 30 to 40 passengers, depending on the type of service being operated. When TAI opened a through service from Paris to Bora Bora (at that time the only landplane airfield in the Society Islands) in 1959, the Sandringham (referred to as a 'Bermuda') was used to open a non-stop twice-weekly connecting flight from Bora Bora to Papeete, with TAI passengers given priority. This service closed down in 1960, however, after a land airfield was opened at Papeete.

Sandringham 7 F-OBIP moored at Papeete, Tahiti when operated by RAI. It was referred to as a 'Bermuda' after the BOAC class in which it originally served. (via JM Collection)

During the early 1960s, apart from the main route to Raiatea and Bora Bora, the Sandringham was used on regular schedules to Tiputa and Rangiroa (in the Tuamoto Islands), and charter flights were undertaken from the Society Islands to other island groups in French Polynesia. In 1965, with the addition of a Douglas DC-4 to the fleet, RAI operated the Sandringham only on the scheduled route from Papeete to Moorea five times weekly and to Huahine, Raiatea and Bora Bora and back once a week. The flying-boat era ended after airstrips had been built on the remaining islands, and the Sandringham was withdrawn by 1973. In 1975 it was sold to Douglas Pearson, a former Aquila Airways Captain.

Tasman Empire Airways Ltd

Formed in 1940 to operate flying-boat services between Sydney and Auckland, Tasman Empire Airways was a joint enterprise of BOAC, Qantas Empire Airways and Union Airways of New Zealand. Its route opened on 30th April 1940, flown by Short S.30 Empire boat ZK-AMA, previously operated by Imperial Airways as G-AFDA.

To replace the Empire flying-boats, the airline acquired four Sandringhams Mk.4 in 1946, but in service they proved to be inadequate. Unsuited to the route, they suffered badly from overheating of the cylinder heads, and after an engine failure on 3rd December 1947 they had to be withdrawn until June 1948. While the problems were being dealt with, DC-4 airliners were chartered in Australia.

ZK-AMD "Australia" was a Sandringham 4 of Tasman Empire Airways which ended its days with Ansett. (P H T Green collection)

Solent 4 ZK-AML of TEAL taking off at Queen's Island, Belfast later went to Aquila as G-AOBL. (via Phil Butler)

Solent 3 G-AKNP in Trans Oceanic Airways colours at Rose Bay, Sydney after delivery in April 1951. It still wears the UK registration and former BOAC name "City of Cardiff but soon became VH-TOB. (via JM Collection)

Late in 1949, the 45-passenger Solent was introduced to TEAL, and flew routes to and from Evans Bay in Wellington, where calm water was (and is) a rarity. First to be delivered was ZK-AML, and flying on the Auckland to Sydney service began on 14th November. Flight time was now reduced to six hours thirty minutes. Delivery of further Solents allowed the Sandringhams to be withdrawn after a final flight from Sydney to Auckland on 19th December 1949. The TEAL Solents originally accommodated 45 passengers in seven lounges on two decks, in contrast to the Sandringhams, which carried 30 passengers in five lounges on two decks.

With Solents in service, new routes could be opened. On 6th June 1950 a route between Auckland and Fiji was introduced, and this was followed by services from Wellington to Sydney on 2nd October 1950 and from Christchurch to Melbourne. Of prime importance to TEAL was the 'Coral Route' to Tahiti via Fiji, Samoa and Aitutaki, opened in December 1951. Equipped with wing de-icers and automatic hot air shutters on the air intakes, the Solents were found to be adequate, although they were not pressurised and were thus subject to low-altitude turbulence.

During the final year of full flying-boat operations (1953), the Solents flew seven services weekly from Auckland to Sydney and five weekly from Wellington to Sydney. In addition, a monthly service from Wellington and Auckland served Chatham Island. The 'Coral Route' was flown every two weeks from Auckland to Fiji (Suva), Samoa (Apia), Cook Island (Aitutaki) and Tahiti (Papeete), where it connected with the 'Bermuda' flying-boat of RAI (qv). In 1954, however, TEAL decided to replace their flying-boats with a fleet of second-hand DC-6s, a move which the crews greeted with much pleasure.

After two (out of the three planned) Solents had been sold to Aquila Airways (q.v.) in the United Kingdom late in 1954, one Solent (ZK-AMO) remained to carry out TEAL's schedules. From 1955, this aircraft continued to uphold the Pacific islands services, based at Suva and returning to New Zealand only for major overhauls. A fortnightly service went from Suva to Apia, Aitutaki and Papeete, while once a month a flight was operated from Suva to Nukualofa. These routes were maintained until 1960, when the Nukualofa service was dropped and the Papeete service was increased to once weekly until 14th September of that year, when all TEAL flying-boat services ceased. Solent ZK-AMO was then donated to the Museum of Transport & Technology in Auckland.

New Zealand National Airways Corporation

The result of a merger between Union Airways, Cook Strait Airways and Air Travel (NZ), NZNAC came into being on 1st April 1947. Four former RNZAF Sunderland Mk.3s were transferred in November 1947, (although one was soon reduced to spare parts for the other three), and, fitted out with 26 seats, operated a route from Sydney to Fiji (Suva) until

June 1950, when the route was taken over by Tasman Empire Airways (qv).

Trans Oceanic Airways

Founded by Capt Brian Monkton and incorporated on 24th February 1947, TOA began operations in May 1947 on regular and charter services from Sydney (Rose Bay). Regular services were flown to Grafton (NSW) (the 'Jacaranda' route), Lord Howe Island, the Solomon Islands, New Hebrides, New Caledonia, the Santa Cruz Islands and Port Macquarie on the Hastings River with three former RAAF Sunderlands which became known as Short 'Hythes'. Two more were acquired at the same time but were reduced to spares. On 16th August 1950 a service from Sydney to Hobart in Tasmania (the 'Ambassador' route) was started, cutting 90 minutes off the time taken by existing landplane service via Melbourne. A scheduled service between Sydney and Port Moresby in New Guinea began in May 1951, dubbed the 'Chieftain' route, prior to which charter flights had been operated to this destination. At the end of 1950, three Solents were acquired, the last being delivered in December 1951. In addition to scheduled services, charter flights were operated during the late 1940s and early 1950s to Fiji, Samoa, Tahiti, the Caroline Islands and the Marshall Islands.

By early 1953, however, the only scheduled service still appearing in the timetable were a weekly flight from Sydney to Lord Howe Island by 'Hythes' and a two or three times a week service with Solents from Sydney to Hobart. In April 1953 Trans Oceanic Airways went into liquidation. Dollar Lines Inc, of Reno, Nevada, agreed on 17th April to purchase the two airworthy Solents plus the third (unserviceable) aircraft on the Brisbane River for a reported £A70,000 for operation by South Pacific Airlines, though this project came to nothing, and one 'Hythe' was sold to Ansett Flying Boat Services.

Ansett Flying Boat Services

Ansett Airways took over Barrier Reef Airways (qv) in 1952 and acquired some of the routes of Trans Oceanic Airways (qv) in March 1953. 'Hythe' class boat VH-AKP was taken over from Trans Oceanic and flown until 12th March 1954, after which it was scrapped.

By April 1953, Ansett was operating Sandringhams on the Brisbane - Southport - Grafton - Sydney route two or three times per week, Brisbane to Hayman Island weekly, Brisbane - Hayman Island - Townsville - Cairns weekly, and Brisbane - Gladstone - Lindeman Island - South Molle Island - Hayman Island weekly. After the move of the airline's main base to Sydney, the latter route was dropped and extra services were operated from Sydney. By mid-1954, services were being flown to Lord Howe Island, to Hobart and to Brisbane, Hayman Island and Cairns once a week. Hayman Island was served by an additional two weekly services via Brisbane, while the Sydney to Brisbane service via Grafton and Southport was flown three or four times per week. All routes, however, apart from twice-weekly services from Sydney to Lord Howe Island and to Hobart, had been closed by April 1955, and the fleet remained at two Sandringhams for the next twenty years.

In 1957, Ansett acquired Australian National Airways (ANA), and in March 1958 control of Butler Air Transport Pty Ltd and its Queensland Airlines subsidiary also passed to Ansett Transport Industries Ltd, Ansett Airways' parent company. Butler Air Transport was renamed Airlines of New South Wales from 19th December 1959, and the flying-boat division of Ansett-ANA was subsequently integrated into Airlines of New South Wales, which resulted in the two Sandringhams being repainted with these titles early in 1960.

The only scheduled route at this stage was from Sydney to Lord Howe Island, which was flown between one and three times per week, depending on the season. However, one-day tourist flights were operated during the Australian summer of 1959/60 from Sydney to the dam on Lake Eucumbene, south-west of Canberra, which was part of the Snowy Mountain Authority's hydro-electric power scheme. In addition, a Sydney to Hayman Island service was reinstated briefly around 1960.

Ansett Flying Boat Services operated this Sandringham 4 VH-BRE after it had served with QANTAS and TEAL. Here it is being refuelled at a jetty, adjacent to which is a large slipstream deflector. The registration VH-BRE indicates that it was intended for Barrier Reef Airways but that company was taken over by Ansett shortly after the aircraft's delivery.
(P H T Green collection)

One of the Sandringhams was lost in July 1963 and was replaced by a former RNZAF Sunderland 5. The two machines reverted to Ansett Flying Boat Services titles in 1968. The Lord Howe Island service remained the only regular flying-boat service in Australia until the final return flight on 21st May 1974.

Barrier Reef Airways

Barrier Reef Airways was formed in 1946 at Brisbane by Capts Chris Poulson and Stewart Middlemiss, but Poulson lost his life soon afterwards. The company started operations with two former RAAF Catalinas in April 1947, flying from the Brisbane River to the Lindeman and Daydream Islands. Two former TEAL Sandringhams joined the Catalinas in 1950. A controlling interest was gained by Ansett Airways (qv) in 1952 and in the following year the Barrier Reef name disappeared from the Australian airline scene.

P G Taylor (Pty) Ltd

Captain Gordon Taylor became famous for his pioneering long-distance flights in Catalinas. Before the Second World War he surveyed routes across the Indian Ocean from Australia to East Africa, during the war a route between Australia and Mexico, and post-war from Australia to South America. In March 1954 he pur-

Sandringham 7 G-AKCO went to P G Taylor (Pty) Ltd as VH-APG "Frigate Bird III" and is seen here still in British marks at Cowes before delivery to Australia. It was intended to operate luxury air cruises in the Pacific islands but the demand did not achieve expected levels.   (P H T Green collection)

Seen at Oakland, California in 1956, this pair of Solent 3s were intended for South Pacific Air Lines. In the foreground is N9947F, ex G-AKNT, "Singapore" and behind ids the engineless N9945F ex VH-TOD. After purchase by Howard Hughes and years of inactivity they were scrapped in 1974.   (Howard Levy via JM Collection)

chased former BOAC 'Bermuda' Class Sandringham G-AKCO, which, after conversion to his specifications at the Saunders Roe works at Cowes he named *Frigate Bird III* and had the frigate bird logo of his company, P G Taylor (Pty) Ltd, painted on the fin. The Sandringham was fitted with a luxury 35-seat interior on two decks, a beautifully panelled promenade deck complete with bar, and carpeted stairs, and was handed over at Cowes on 14th October 1954.

Sir Gordon Taylor took off from Cowes in the Sandringham on 20th October 1954 on his way to his native Australia, via Kalafrana (Malta), where he picked up servicemen on their way home. He planned to use the aircraft on air cruises around the Pacific islands, carrying fourteen passengers on the upper deck and 21 below. However, the cruises were not as successful as he had hoped, and in 1958 the aircraft was sold to Réseau Aérien Interinsulaire (q.v.).

South Pacific Air Lines Ltd

Formed in 1953 as Dollar Airlines Inc, this airline was a subsidiary of the Robert Dollar Company, whose ships formerly operated trans-Pacific services. The airline bought out Trans Oceanic Airways (qv) with this company's three Solents (including one for spares), and subsequently acquired a fourth from Great Britain. On 15th August 1953 a certificate was issued covering the operation for two years of the Honolulu - Christmas Island - Tahiti (Papeete) route, extended for five years on 22nd November 1955, with irregular services in the Pacific area added. Some time after this, Dollar Airlines was renamed South Pacific Air Lines.

Dollar Associates, a subsidiary of Dollar Air Lines, agreed on 17th April 1953 to purchase Trans Oceanic's two airworthy Solents, which were at Sydney, and the third aircraft, lying unserviceable on the Brisbane River, for £A70,000 (thus beating Aquila Airways' bid of £A62,500 for the aircraft). By September 1953, the third aircraft, VH-TOC, had been stripped for spare parts, but it was not until 26th May 1954 that the first airworthy Solent (formerly VH-TOB) was handed over to the Robert Dollar Co at Oahu in Hawaii and registered N9946F. US certification of the type, involving inspections, taxying trials and flights, took from July 1954 until 24th January 1955.

N9946F eventually left Honolulu for NAS Alameda in California on 29th April 1955, and on 1st May it proceeded to Oakland North Field/San Leandro Bay.

The aircraft purchased in Great Britain, which became N9947F, was acquired on 15th November 1955 at Poole and was taxied a few days later around the south coast to Aquila Airways' base at Hamble for overhaul. This was completed and the aircraft was test-flown on 26th April 1956 before being ferried to California.

The planned start of the services was delayed several times, hope for the original summer 1956 date being dashed when it was announced that the intermediate staging-post at Christmas Island was unavailable indefinitely due to hydrogen bomb tests in the area. Further delays were caused by modifications deemed necessary by the US authorities which were carried out by Transocean Airlines and lasted until 23rd September 1957. After N9946F was flown to San Francisco on 24th September further test flights were made at intervals, but as another planned start-up date of summer 1958 approached, landings at Christmas Island were still banned.

After an inspection by the FAA on 25th July 1958, a US type certificate was finally issued on 29th October, nearly four years after delivery! As the refuelling point on the route was still closed to the airline in 1959, South Pacific Air Lines asked for a variation and renewal of its authority with the transfer of the route to Super Constellation landplanes, which was eventually granted, with the first flight on 26th July 1960.

Meanwhile, the three Solents were still stored in California, the last flight being made, it is believed, on 2nd November 1958, immediately after receipt of the US CoA. Aviation millionaire Howard Hughes gained ownership of all three Solents in 1959 (after it had become obvious that the route via Christmas Island was unlikely to become available), and immediately placed an armed guard on the aircraft.

Eight years later, in October 1967, two of the Solents were transferred by barge from the edge of Oakland airport to Shoal Point, Richmond, California on the orders of Hughes, followed several years later by the one stored at San Francisco. At Richmond they continued to be guarded by Hughes personnel until late 1972, when all three aircraft were purchased for $1,500. N9945F and N9947F were scrapped by 1974, but the third of the trio, N9946F, has fortunately been preserved for posterity.

WEST INDIES

Antilles Air Boats

This company was formed by the famous pioneer aviator Charles Blair, and for many years has served the Caribbean islands of St Thomas, St Croix and St John (US Virgin Islands) and San Juan, Puerto Rico, with a large fleet of Grumman Goose and Mallard amphibians. The scheduled services were very successful and several attempts were made to introduce larger aircraft, for example the last surviving Sikorsky VS-44A and the Catalina.

When Ansett (q.v.) ceased their flying-boat services in 1974, Capt Blair purchased both aircraft, a Sandringham 4, VP-LVE, and a modified Sunderland 5, N158J. The two aircraft were ferried from Sydney to St Croix between October and December 1974. After modifications to FAA standard, the Sandringham entered service in 1975 on the inter-island network, but the Sunderland remained stored in Puerto Rico.

A calm scene with Sandringham 4 N158C "Southern Cross" of Antilles Air Boats at anchor somewhere in the Virgin Islands in the 1970s. When its flying days ended, this aircraft became one of the few to be preserved and is now at the Solent Sky museum, Southampton.
(P H T Green collection)

Sandringham 6 LN-IAU "Bamse Brakar" of the Norwegian company DNL wears the titles 'Norwegian Air Lines' in English above the cheat-line. This aircraft crashed near Harstad on 15th May 1950 with severe loss of life. *(P H T Green collection)*

Capt Blair was married to actress Maureen O'Hara, and when she wished to visit Ireland he decided to make the trip in the Sandringham. In 1976 and 1977, therefore, the aircraft operated a series of memorable pleasure flights on the south coast of England (from Poole Harbour) and in Ireland, but unfortunately Blair was killed in a Grumman Goose accident shortly after returning to the Virgin Islands in 1977. Within a few months of his death the Sandringham was withdrawn from service and was stored in Puerto Rico with the Sunderland.

After a period of dereliction, Sandringham 4 N158C arrived at Calshot on 2 February 1981 from the Virgin Islands via Killadeas in Northern Ireland. The other aircraft flew from Bermuda to Calshot on 1st May 1981, now owned by Edward Hulton, and was then registered G-BJHS. N158C was moved to East Docks in Southampton, dismantled and taken in pieces to Southampton Hall of Aviation on 27/28th August 1981. It was reassembled there, painted in Ansett livery as VH-BRC, and now forms a major exhibit in what is now known as Solent Sky.

EUROPE

DNL (Det Norske Luftfartselskap A/S: Norwegian Air Lines)

Three Sandringhams were acquired in 1946 for DNL's seasonal Arctic route from Stavanger (Sola) to Tromsø in the Arctic Circle. This service started on 1st April 1947 and was nicknamed the 'Flying Coastal Express Steamboat'! The route was via Bergen, Oslo and Trondheim, alternately Bronnesund or Sandnessjøn, then Bodø and Harstad. Two aircraft were needed for the service, which operated six times per week from

The first three Sandringhams flown by DNL were all written-off but their replacements, LN-LAI and LN-LMK were still current when the airline was absorbed into Scandinavian Airlines System (SAS) in 1951. LN-LAI, seen here before the merger, was named "Jutulan" and the following year it was leased to France-Hydro but unfortunately it sank at its moorings at Bangui shortly afterwards.
(P H T Green collection)

April to August and three times in September and October, and one was kept as reserve. After the first season the stops at Bronnesund and Sandnessjøn were eliminated. The Sandringhams were fitted with 37 seats on two decks and a crew of seven.

Unfortunately, all three Sandringhams were lost in accidents, with some fatalities. The first incident was on 28th August 1947, when the aircraft struck a mountain, and the second on 2nd October 1948, a landing accident. Two replacements were acquired, but the last of the original aircraft crashed on take-off on 15th May 1950, fortunately without injury to passengers or crew.

In 1951 DNL became part of Scandinavian Airlines and the flying-boat services ceased. One of the two remaining aircraft was leased to France-Hydro (q.v.) in 1952, with whom it was written-off, while the second was sold to Aerolineas Argentinas (q.v.) in May 1955.

France-Hydro

France-Hydro was formed in 1952 to continue Latecoere LAT.631 flying-boat operations as cargo carriers after Air France had stopped doing so following three fatal crashes. France-Hydro operated charter flights from for example, France to Indo-China and the Northern Cameroons to France. A Sandringham was leased from DNL/SAS in 1952 but sank in French Equatorial Africa while on an Air France charter later that year.

BOAC Solent II G-AHIN "Southampton" moored at Augusta, Sicily, circa 1948-49. (via JM Collection)

CHAPTER 6 : CIVIL CONVERSIONS AND NEW-BUILD AIRCRAFT

INDIVIDUAL CIVIL AIRCRAFT HISTORIES

Sunderland 3

G-AGER ex **JM660**; regd (CofR 9374) 12Nov42 to BOAC; first flight 26Dec42; delivered 8Jan43; CofA (6955) issued 26Jan43; entered service by 18Mar43; used radio call-sign **OQZR** .45; later named *Hadfield*; damaged on alighting at Calcutta 18Oct46 but repaired; registered 6Dec 48 to Aquila Airways, retaining name; entered service Apr49; CofA expired 19Jul55 and withdrawn from use at Hamble; scrapped at Hamble Jul56; registration cancelled 26Jul 56

G-AGES ex **JM661**; registered (CofR 9375) 12Nov42 to BOAC; first flight 31Dec42; delivered 15Jan43; CofA (6953) issued 19Jan43; entered service 28May43; inbound from Lisbon to Foynes on 28Jul43, fog was encountered, and pilot tried to pinpoint position visually, but found that he was flying up a mountain valley; attempting to make a tight turn, the aircraft crashed at 2000 ft (610 m) on Slieveglass, Mount Brandon, on the Dingle peninsula, Co Kerry, Eire, and was destroyed by fire (captain and nine passengers killed, six crew and nine passengers survived); registration cancelled 28Jul43

G-AGET ex **JM662**; registered (CofR 9376) 12Nov42 to BOAC; first flight 5 Jan43; delivered 16 Jan43; CofA (6954) issued 5Feb43; entered service 1Mar43, when it was first BOAC Sunderland to visit Foynes; used radio call-sign **OQZT**; destroyed by fire on River Hooghly at Calcutta 15Feb46 while refuelling (1 killed); registration cancelled 20Feb46

G-AGEU ex **JM663**; registered (CofR 9377) 12Nov42 to BOAC; first flight 10Jan43; delivered 21Jan43; CofA (6958) issued 15Feb43; entered service 3Mar43; later named *Hampshire*; used radio call-sign **OQZU**; registered 19Jan49 to Aquila Airways, retaining name; entered service Mar49; CofA expired 6Aug51 and withdrawn from use at Hamble; registration cancelled 18Aug53 as 'destroyed' but extant beached at Hamble end Sep53; scrapped

G-AGEV ex **JM664**; registered (CofR 9378) 12Nov42 to BOAC; first flight 15Jan43; delivered 29Jan43; CofA (6957) issued 10Feb43; entered service by 21Mar43; later named *Hailsham*; used radio call-sign **OQZV**; damaged beyond repair in heavy landing at Poole Harbour 4Mar46; registration cancelled 4May46

G-AGEW ex **JM665**; registered (CofR 9379) 12Nov42 to BOAC; first flight 20Jan43; delivered 29Jan43; CofA (6959) issued 8Mar43; entered service 11Mar43; later named *Halton*, renamed *Hanwell*; used radio call-sign **OQZW**; capsized on take-off from Sourabaya, Java (now Indonesia) 5Sep48 and sank; registration cancelled 5Sep48

G-AGHV ex **JM722**; registered (CofR 9453) 1Jul43 to BOAC; delivered 21Aug43; CofA (7005) issued 31Aug43; entered service 1Sep43; used radio call-sign **OQZB**; later named *Hamble*; broke away from moorings, rammed RAF Sunderland PP112 and capsized during sandstorm at Rod-el-Farag, Cairo, 9/10Mar46; registration cancelled 4May46

G-AGHW ex **ML725**; registered (CofR 9454) 1Jul43 to BOAC; delivered 27Aug43; CofA (7006) issued 4Sep43; entered service 5Sep43; used radio call-sign **OQZC**; later named *Hamilton*; crashed on Brighstone Down, Isle of Wight, 19Nov47 while on positioning flight from Hythe to Poole (1 crew killed, 3 injured - no passengers on board); registration cancelled 16Feb48

G-AGHX ex **ML726**; registered (CofR 9455) 1Jul43 to BOAC; delivered 2Sep43; CofA (7007) issued 11Sep43; entered service 12Sep43; used radio call-sign **OQZX**; later named *Harlech*, renamed *Harlequin*; CofA expired 12Jun48 and withdrawn from use at Hythe; scrapped at Hythe Oct48; registration cancelled 18Oct48

G-AGHZ ex **ML727**; registered (C of R 9456) 1Jul43 to BOAC; delivered 3Sep43; CofA (7008) issued 14Sep43; entered service 14Sep43; used radio call-sign **OQZZ**; later named *Hastings*, renamed *Hawkesbury*; registered to Aquila Airways 19Jan49, but did not enter service; CofA expired 8Feb49 and withdrawn from use at Hamble; scrapped at Hamble 7Jan50; registration cancelled 17Jan50

G-AGIA ex **ML728**; registered (CofR 9457) 1Jul43 to BOAC; delivered 8Sep43; CofA (7009) issued 17Sep43; entered service 18Sep43; used radio call-sign **OQZA**; later named *Haslemere*; withdrawn from use 14May48; registered 23Jul48 to Aquila Airways, retaining name; CofA expired 23Mar49 and withdrawn from use at Hamble; registration cancelled 9Feb51; broken up for spares Jul52

Originally BOAC's first civil-registered Sunderland 3, G-AGER passed to Aquila Airways in 1948 and was scrapped in 1956 at Hamble where it is seen here. (P H T Green collection)

Against the backdrop of Funchal Harbour, Madeira, in March 1949, Sunderland 3 G-AGEU Hampshire *of Aquila Airways is the centre of attention.* (via JM Collection)

Sunderland 3 G-AGHW Hamilton, *the former ML725, sadly ended its days when it crashed on the Isle of Wight on 19th November 1947.*

G-AGIB ex **ML729**; registered (CofR 9458) 1Jul43 to BOAC delivered 15 Sep43; CofA (7010) issued 23Sep43; entered service 26Sep43; crashed in Libyan desert 130 mls (209 km) S of Tobruk at El Taurub Tawaali 5Nov43; registration cancelled 6Nov43

G-AGJJ ex **ML751**; registered (CofR 9490) 24Nov43 to BOAC; delivered 13Jan44; CofA (7037) issued 21Jan44; entered service 20Mar44; used radio call-sign **OQZJ** .45; later named *Henley*; registered 5Feb49 to Aquila Airways, retaining name, but did not enter service; CofA expired 9Feb49 and withdrawn from use at Hythe; scrapped Jan52; registration cancelled 7Jan52

G-AGJK ex **ML752**; registered (CofR 9491) 24Nov43 to BOAC; delivered 21Jan44; CofA (7038) issued 5Feb44; entered service 7Feb44; used radio call-sign **OQZK** .45; later named *Howard*; withdrawn from use 15Jan49; CofA expired 6Feb49 and withdrawn from use at Hamble; registered 24Mar49 to Aquila Airways, but did not enter service; scrapped at Hamble Jan52; registration cancelled 7Jan52

G-AGJL ex **ML753**; registered (CofR 9492) 24Nov43 to BOAC; delivered 23Jan44; CofA (7039) issued 19Apr44; entered service 18Mar44; used radio call-sign **OQZL**; later named *Hobart*; withdrawn from use 15Jan49; CofA expired 13Feb49 and withdrawn from use at Hamble; registered 24Mar49 to Aquila Airways, but did not enter service; scrapped at Hamble Jan52; registration cancelled 7Jan52

Launching BOAC "Hythe" Class boat G-AGHX initially named Harlech, *at Hythe, with a tractor fore and aft.*   *(P H T Green collection)*

G-AGJM ex **ML754**; registered (CofR 9493) 24Nov43 to BOAC; delivered 2Feb44; CofA (7040) issued 16Feb44; entered service 2Mar44; used radio call-sign **OQZM**; later named *Hythe*; withdrawn from use 31Dec48; registered 17Feb49 to Aquila Airways but did not enter service; C of A expired 20Feb49; scrapped at Hamble Jan52; registration cancelled 7Jan52

G-AGJN ex **ML755**; registered (CofR 9494) 24Nov43 to BOAC; delivered 3Feb44; CofA (7041) issued 10Mar44; entered service 12Mar44; used radio call-sign **OQZN**; later named *Hudson*; withdrawn from use 31Jan49; registered 25Feb49 to Aquila Airways, retaining name; entered service on CofA renewal 18May50; damaged beyond repair in Funchal Harbour, Madeira, 20Jan53 when it broke from moorings and was beached on rocks; registration cancelled 27Jan53 as 'destroyed by gale'

G-AGJO ex **ML756**; registered (CofR 9495) 24Nov43 to BOAC; delivered 3Feb44; CofA (7042) issued 21Feb44; entered service 2Mar44; used radio call-sign **OQZO**; later named *Humber*, renamed *Honduras*; withdrawn from use 16Feb49; struck by unknown vessel, broke away from mooring at Hythe and damaged beyond repair 21Feb49; registration cancelled same day

G-AGKV ex **ML786**; registered (CofR 9526) 28Jun44 to BOAC; delivered 13Jul44; CofA (7076) issued 31Oct44; entered service 11Nov44; used radio call-sign **OQZD**; later named *Huntingdon*; CofA expired 15Dec48; withdrawn from use at Hamble; registered 30Dec48 to SB&HL, Belfast and used for spares; registration cancelled 18May51 as 'presumed withdrawn from use'

G-AGKW ex **ML787**; registered (CofR 9527) 28Jun44 to BOAC; delivered 21Jul44; CofA (7077) issued 28Jul44; entered service 15Aug44; used radio call-sign **OQZQ**; later named *Hereford*, renamed *Hotspur*; CofA expired 30Nov48 and withdrawn from use at Hamble; registered 30Dec48 to SB&H, Belfast; registration cancelled 18May51 as 'presumed withdrawn from use'

G-AGKX ex **ML788**; registered (CofR 9528) 28Jun44 to BOAC; delivered 27Jul44; CofA (7078) issued 23Aug44; entered service 26Aug44 to 10Sep44 and flown Pembroke Dock - Karachi - Cairo - Poole as ML788 [F]; ferried to Rochester 23Sep44 and converted to prototype Sandringham 1; relaunched at Rochester as **ML788** 28Nov45; returned to BOAC 19Dec45 and reverted to **G-AGKX** Jan46; CofA renewed 2Jan46; re-entered BOAC service 17Feb46 for Poole - Athens - Cairo survey as **ML788**; using radio call-sign **OQZF**; operated from May46

After conversion from Sunderland 3 to Sandringham 1, G-AGKX reverted to its former serial ML788 and with call-sign OQZF externally worn carried out a route survey to Cairo early in 1946 for BOAC.   *(via JM Collection)*

Chapter 6 : Civil Conversions and New-Build Aircraft

A number of lucky passengers boarding Sunderland 3 G-AGJO Honduras of BOAC, probably at Southampton. (P H T Green collection)

G-AGKX was the prototype Sandringham 1 conversion for BOAC and was named Himalaya. *It demonstrated at Farnborough in June 1946 and ended its days with Aquila Airways. (P H T Green collection)*

Sunderland 3 G-AGKY being refurbished at Hamble by Air Service Training for Aquila Airways in 1949. This aircraft sank while under tow off Calshot in January 1953 and was scrapped after being salvaged. (R C Sturtivant collection)

as **G-AGKX**, named *Himalaya*; demonstrated at Farnborough 27-29Jun46 in hands of Capt R F Stone; withdrawn from use 8May48; registered 28May49 to Aquila Airways, retaining name; CofA expired 16Mar50 and withdrawn from use at Hamble; scrapped Hamble Aug53; registration cancelled 18Aug53 as 'destroyed'

G-AGKY ex **ML789**; registered (CofR 9529) to BOAC 28Jun44; delivered 28Jul44; CofA (7079) issued 17Aug44; entered service 23Aug44; used radio call-sign **OQZG** .45; later named *Hungerford*; withdrawn from use 28Dec48; registered 10Jan49 to Aquila Airways, retaining name; damaged when wing struck water on take-off from Southampton Water 28Jan53 and sank off Calshot while being towed for salvage; beached but scrapped May53; registration cancelled 5May53 as 'destroyed'

G-AGKZ ex **ML790**; registered (CofR 9530) 28Jun44 to BOAC; delivered 3Aug44; CofA (7080) issued 1Sep44; entered service 3Sep44; used radio call-sign **OQZH** .45; later named *Harwich*; withdrawn from use 20Jan49 although CofA extended to 25Jun49; scrapped Hythe May49; registration cancelled 24May49 as 'presumed withdrawn from use'

G-AGLA ex **ML791**; registered (CofR 9531) 28Jun44 to BOAC; delivered 12Aug44; CofA (7081) issued 7Sep44; entered service 12Oct44; used radio call-sign **OQZY**.45; later named *Hunter*; CofA expired 2Jan 49 and withdrawn from use at Hamble; registered 10Jan49 to Aquila Airways, but did not enter service; scrapped at Hamble Aug49; registration cancelled 11Aug49 as 'broken up'

G-AHEO ex **JM716**; delivered to BOAC 2Mar45; registered (CofR 9988) 20 Mar46 to BOAC; CofA (7553) issued 24Feb47; bought by BOAC 20Apr47; named *Halstead*; registered 23Jul48 to Aquila Airways, retaining name; CofA expired 26Feb49 and withdrawn from use at Hamble; scrapped at Hamble Nov49; registration cancelled 10Nov49

Languishing at Hamble with engines already removed prior to being scrapped in 1952 is Aquila's Sunderland 3 G-AHER Helmsdale. *(P H T Green collection)*

G-AHEP ex **DD860**; delivered to BOAC 2Mar45; registered (CofR 9989) 20Mar46 to BOAC but not converted; named *Hanbury*; CofA (7554) prepared but not issued; registration cancelled 22Sep47; returned to RAF at Wig Bay 24Sep47 as **DD860**; registered 6Dec48 as **G-AHEP** to Aircraft & Engineering Services Ltd, Croydon; no CofA issued; registration cancelled 11Sep52

G-AHER ex **PP142**; delivered to BOAC 1Mar46; registered (CofR 9990) 20Mar46 to BOAC; CofA (7555) issued 17Apr46; entered service 19Apr46; named *Helmsdale*; purchased by BOAC 22Jun49; CofA expired 11Sep49; registered 22Oct49 to Aquila Airways, but did not enter service; scrapped at Hamble Jan52; registration cancelled 7Jan52

Trans-Oceanic Airways Sunderland 3 VH-AKO Australis *lies at anchor, its bow showing little modification since its RAAF days. While routine maintenance continues one occupant appears anxious to leave before the tender arrives! (via JM Collection)*

ZK-AMK Takitimu *was the Sunderland 3 which operated the last Suva to Auckland service for NZNAC on 31st May 1950.*
(via JM Collection)

VH-AKO ex **A26-4**; registered 5May47 to Trans-Oceanic Airways Ltd; CofA (1251) issued 5May47; named *Australis*; first service 20May47; inaugurated Sydney - Lord Howe Island service 1Aug47; broke free from moorings at Lord Howe Island 27Aug47 but apparently undamaged; withdrawn from service 17May to 1Oct48; used on migrant flights from Europe to Australia from 25Oct48; renamed *Australia Star*, inaugurated Sydney - Grafton service 24Dec48; renamed *Samoa Star* 1949; final revenue service 23Nov50; officially withdrawn from use 19Dec50 on CofA expiry; registration cancelled 6Aug51; scrapped at Rose Bay

VH-AKP ex **A26-5**; registered 24Oct47 to Trans-Oceanic Airways Ltd; CofA (1350) issued and entered service 24Oct47; named *Antilles* 21Jan48, later *Tahiti Star* 1949; converted to 36-seats Dec49 to Dec50; company in liquidation 1Jul52 but VH-AKP maintained Lord Howe Island route; leased to Barrier Reef Airways 16-18Aug52; leased to Ansett Flying Boat Services 1Nov52 to 27Dec52 and sold to them 20May53 and regd 25May53; last revenue flight 12Mar54; officially withdrawn from use 24Mar54; registration cancelled 9May54; scrapped at Rose Bay Oct55 [TT 5,919 hours]

(VH-ARQ) ex **A26-1**; sold to Capt B W Monkton 4Oct46 and registration allotted but not taken up; re-registered **VH-BKO** allotted 24Feb47 but again not taken up; ferried Rathmines - Rose Bay 28Apr47 using call-sign VHCKR; not converted, used for spares for Trans-Oceanic Airways aircraft at Sydney (Rose Bay); scrapped 1953

(VH-BFX) ex **A26-3**; sold to Capt B W Monkton 4Oct46 and registration allotted but not taken up; re-registered **VH-BKP** allotted Jan 47 but again not taken up; ferried Rathmines - Rose Bay 27Janr47 using call-sign VHCKS; not converted, used for spares for Trans-Oceanic Airways aircraft at Sydney (Rose Bay); scrapped 1953

(VH-BKO) see VH-ARQ

(VH-BKP) see VH-BFX

VH-BKQ ex **A26-2**; converted to 36 seater Hythe-class; registered 5Nov49 to Trans-Oceanic Airways Ltd; named *Pacific Star*, CofA (1644) issued 5Nov49; first service 7Nov49; inaugurated Sydney - Hobart service 16Aug50 and Sydney - Brisbane -Townsville - Port Moresby service 29Oct50; lost port outer propeller and force-landed during flight from Sydney (Rose Bay) to Grafton 16Apr51; returned to Sydney but officially withdrawn from use 28Jun51, repairs abandoned due to main spar corrosion; scrapped .52 Rose Bay; registration cancelled 28Jun54

ZK-AMF ex **NZ4102**; registered 16May47 to New Zealand National Airways Corp; named *Tokomaru*; not taken up; registration cancelled 22Dec47; returned to RNZAF as **NZ4102** 9Feb 51; SOC 3Nov54 and sold for scrap from Hobsonville May55 (see Chapter 5)

ZK-AMG ex **NZ4103**; registered 16May47 to New Zealand National Airways Corp; named *Mataatua*; inaugurated TEAL Auckland-Suva service 1Nov47 and Auckland - Chatham Islands service Jan49; wfu May50; returned to RNZAF as **NZ4103** 9Feb 51; for sale Nov53 at Hobsonville; SOC 3Nov54 and broken up (see Chapter 5)

ZK-AMJ ex **NZ4101**; to New Zealand National Airways Corp Nov46; named *Tainui*; ntu, registration cancelled; scrapped (see Chapter 5)

ZK-AMK ex **NZ4104**; registered 22Dec47 to New Zealand National Airways Corp; named *Takitimu*; last service Suva - Auckland 31May50; wfu at Hobsonville 2Jun50; returned to RNZAF as **NZ4104** 9Feb51 for instructional use until 1953; SOC 3Nov54; scrapped (see Chapter 5)

CHAPTER 6 : CIVIL CONVERSIONS AND NEW-BUILD AIRCRAFT

CAUSA's second Sandringham 3 CX-AKF converted from Sunderland Mk.III ML876 / G-AGWX, was initially used by ALFA before it went into service in Uruguay. (via JM Collection)

Still wearing its RAF fin-flash, Sunderland 5 G-ANAK had been intended for the Aquila fleet in 1953 but was not converted and was later damaged in a gale at Hamble. (P H T Green collection)

Sunderland Mk.V DP195 was rebuilt to Sandringham standard for CAUSA of Uruguay as CX-AKR. (via Alan J King)

Sunderland 5

G-AHJR   ex **SZ584**; c/n SH.1552; delivered to BOAC at Poole on loan for freighting 2May46; registered (CofR 10114) 27Jun46 to BOAC; CofA (8056) issued 16Jul46; registration cancelled 15Apr48; returned to RAF at 57 MU, Wig Bay, 16Apr48 **SZ584** and later to New Zealand as **NZ4115** (see Chapter 5, Part 3)

G-ANAK   ex **PP162**; registered 25Jun53 to Aquila Airways; delivered to Hamble 18Jun53 and beached; not converted; damaged beyond repair in gale at Hamble 26-27Nov54; registration cancelled 5Apr55

G-BJHS   see VH-BRF

CX-AKR   ex **DP195**; to SB&HL 22Jan48; converted to Sandringham status (c/n SH.60C); CofA (10267) issued 20Aug48; registered to Compania Aeronautica Uruguaya SA (CAUSA), Montevideo; 48; named *Capitan Bosio Lanza*; withdrawn from use at Montevideo (25Jan56?); still extant Feb65; presumed scrapped

LV-AHG   ex **EK579**; to SB&HL 22Jan48; converted to Sandringham status (c/n SH.70C); CofA (10372) issued undated late 48; registered to Aviación del Litoral Fluvial Argentina (ALFA) 48; named *Uruguay*; absorbed into Aerolineas Argentinas regd 16Nov51; damaged in accident at Montevideo 11Feb59; under repair mid-60 but subsequently withdrawn from use; registration cancelled 11Jan61; reported scrapped by early 62 but also reported taken over by Cooperativa Argentina de Aeronavegantes 12Aug63 and scrapped at Buenos Aires Jan67

LV-AHH   ex **EJ171**; c/n SH.869; to SB&HL 22Jan48; converted to Sandringham status (c/n SH.69C); CofA (10371) issued undated late 48; registered to Aviación del Litoral Fluvial Argentina (ALFA) 48, named *Rio de la Plata*; absorbed into Aerolineas Argentinas regd 6Aug51.; test-flown at SB&HL 22Jun51; to Lisbon 8Jul51; badly damaged when ran aground in Uruguay River near Concordia 21Mar52; reported scrapped and registration cancelled but also reported taken over by Cooperativa

Aerolineas Argentinas Sandringham 5 LV-AHG being reduced to spare parts at Buenos Aires in April 1960. (ATPH)

Argentina de Aeronavegantes 12Aug63; embargoed 11Jun65 - 3Oct66, lifted 20Feb67 but cancelled and broken up .67

N158J   see VH-BRF

N814ML   see VH-BRF

VH-BRF   ex **NZ4108**; registered to Ansett Airways 13Dec63 (with c/n "SH.113") for use by Ansett Flying Boat Services, named *Islander*; ferried Hobsonville to Rose Bay for Ansett 19Dec63; converted by Ansett at Sydney to 42-seat configuration but not to Sandringham specification, remaining a Sunderland 5; launched 26Oct64; operated 400-mile (644 km) route between Sydney (Rose Bay) and Lord Howe Island; damaged by gale at Lord Howe Island Jun65; flew Ansett final Lord Howe Island to Sydney service 31Mar74; registration cancelled 24Sep74 as 'sold in USA'; to Antilles Air Boats, St Thomas, BVI 25Sep74 as **N158J**, named *Excalibur VIII*, for use in Virgin Islands, but US authorities would not grant CofA; registration **VP-LVF** reserved .78 but not taken up; stored at San Juan, Puerto Rico until May79, when overhauled for sale to Ed-

Sunderland 5 G-BJHS was a post-war survivor which has operated in a number of guises. Here it is wearing Ryanair titles and the name The Spirit of Foynes *in August 1989 when it was intended to operate sponsored pleasure flights from Lough Derg but the scheme failed to get approval and the titles were removed early in 1990. The aircraft is now a feature of Kermit Weeks' Fantasy of Flight Museum in Polk City, Florida and wears its orifinal identity as ML814.*
(via JM Collection)

The first civil operator of Sunderland 5 ML814 was Ansett Flying Boat Services who registered it VH-BRF with the name Islander.
(P H T Green collection)

ward Hulton Jul79 registered 8Oct80 to Juliett Flying Boats Inc, Miami; reflown Nov80; named *Juliet* and flown from either San Juan or St Croix 27Mar81 via Azores to Calshot for Edward Hulton; ferried Calshot to Marseilles 24May81; registered 11Sep81 to Sunderland Ltd (Edward Hulton) as Sunderland 5 (mod) **G-BJHS** and named *Sir Arthur Gouge*; landed on River Thames 6Aug82 and moored near Tower Bridge; to Calshot Oct82 and stored; named *Islander* while at Calshot; flew Calshot to Rochester 20Nov84 and thence to Chatham Historic Dockyard; late Aug85 painted to resemble PAA Clipper NC16806 for use in film 'Mr and Mrs Edgehill'; launched 27Sep85 and next day towed to nearby pier for filming of 'Tenko Reunion', simulating BOAC Sunderland; painted in full Ryanair colours and named *The Spirit of Foynes* Aug89 for pleasure flights but not operated and Ryanair markings soon obliterated; visited Windermere 15Jul90; registration N158J not cancelled until 3 May93!; registered to Personal Plane Services Ltd 5May93; sold to Kermit Weeks/Fantasy of Flight Museum, Polk City FL; registered as candidate for US CAR 14Jul93 as **N814ML**; UK regn cancelled 12Aug93; registered as N814ML 16Sep93 to Kermit Weeks, Polk City, FL; left Southampton 20Jul93 for Polk City; TT 6,329 hrs at 31Dec93; CofA issued 30May96 ; extant as ML814 but in civilian colours

VP-LVF   see VH-BRF

Sandringham 1

G-AGKX (see Sunderland 3)

Sandringham 2

G-AGPT ex Sunderland III **DD834**; registered (CofR 9648) to SB(R&B)L 19Jul45; converted to Sandringham 2 (c/n SH.2C); registered 24Nov45 to Cia Argentina de Aeronavigación Dodero SA, Buenos Aires; launched Belfast 5Dec45; named *Uruguay*; CofA (7272) issued 5Dec45; left Poole 21Dec45, arrived at Buenos Aires 26Dec45; UK registration cancelled 29May46; registered **LV-AAP** to Dodero 2May46; transferred 6Feb47 to Aviación del Litoral Fluvial Argentina (ALFA) *Uruguay*; hit dredger when alighting in fog on River Plate at Buenos Aires 29Jul48 (23 on board of whom 4 crew and 13 passengers were killed)

G-AGPZ ex Sunderland III **DV964**; registered (CofR 9654) to SB(R&B)L 19Jul45; converted to Sandringham 2 (c/n SH.1C); launched at Belfast by Senora Dodero 17Nov45 and named *Argentina*; CofA (7266) issued 17Nov45; left Poole 19Nov45, arrived at Buenos Aires 29Nov45; UK registration cancelled 26Apr46; registered **LV-AAO** to Cia Argentina de Aeronavigación Dodero SA, Buenos Aires 29Dec45; transferred 22Jan47 to Aviación del Litoral Fluvial Argentina (ALFA) *Argentina*; to Aerolineas Argentinas 7Dec50; damaged on alighting at Capilla del Senor (75 km SE of Posadas) 16Oct54 but repaired; stored without engines by early 62; to Cooperativa Argentina de Aeronavegantes 12Aug63, named *Rio Aguilera*; withdrawn from use 64; registration cancelled 2Oct66; scrapped at Buenos Aires Jan67

G-AHRE ex Sunderland III **ML843**; registered (CofR 10276) 21May46 to Cia Argentina de Aeronavigación Dodero SA, Buenos Aires; converted to Sandringham 2 (c/n SH.43C); named *Paraguay* at Belfast 31Oct46; CofA (8515) issued 12Nov46; launched 12Nov46; UK registration cancelled 31Dec46; registered **LV-ACT** 4Dec46, transferred 26Dec47 to Aviación del Litoral Fluvial Argentina (ALFA) *Paraguay*; to Aerolineas Argentinas regd 7Dec50; to Cooperativa Argentina de Aeronavegantes 12Aug63; withdrawn from use 64; scrapped at Buenos Aires Jan67

CHAPTER 6 : CIVIL CONVERSIONS AND NEW-BUILD AIRCRAFT

The three Sandringham 2s were all supplied to Argentina, initially for the Dodero company, and delivered in UK marks. G-AGPT, actually the second to arrive in Argentina, is seen at an unidentified location during its ferry flight. (The late Guy Ashenden)

The first Sandringham 2 conversion for Dodero, G-AGPZ, the appropriately named Argentina, *passes low over Belfast Lough during a test flight. (Shorts/Bombardier Aerospace via Jennifer M Gradidge)*

Sandringham 2, formerly G-AGPZ, in full Aerolineas Argentinas titles as LV-AAO Argentina *in the mid-1950s. Note the two D/F loops above the cockpit which had now replaced the single fitting in the earlier photograph above.* (via JM Collection)

Clearly nearing the end of its career and looking the worse for it, LV-ACT Paraguay *is seen at Buenos Aires in the later Aerolineas Argentinas scheme and with at least two of its engines missing.*
(via JM Collection)

LV-AAO see G-AGPZ

LV-AAP see G-AGPT

LV-ACT see G-AHRE

Sandringham 3

G-AGPY ex Sunderland III **DD841**; registered (CofR 9653) 19Jul45 to SB(R&B)L; converted to Sandringham 3 (c/n SH.3C); registered 24Nov45 to Cia Argentina de Aeronavigación Dodero SA, Buenos Aires; named *Brasil* by HE Senhora Isabel de Aragao, wife of Brazilian Ambassador, at Hythe; CofA (7273) issued 21Jan46; arr Buenos Aires early Feb46; carried out survey flight Buenos Aires to Baltimore MD 15-18Feb46; UK registration cancelled 20Aug46 as 'sold in Argentina'; registered **LV-AAR** to Dodero 9May46; overhauled by SB&HL 47 and new c/n SH.54C issued; transferred 30Dec47 to Aviación del Litoral Fluvial Argentina (ALFA) *Brasil*; to Aerolineas Argentinas 7Dec50; after takeoff from Buenos Aires harbour 31Dec57, turned back with engine trouble; on alighting, bounced in rough water and sank (1 steward and 8 passengers drowned, 5 crew and 36 passengers rescued); registration cancelled 12Jun62; TT 7,905 hours

G-AGTZ ex Sunderland III **EJ170**; registered (CofR 9729) to SB(R&B)L 25Sep45; converted to Sandringham 3 (c/n SH.4C); registered 24Nov45 to Cia Argentina de Aeronavigación Dodero SA, Buenos Aires; named *Inglaterra*; CofA (7274) issued 26Feb46; arrived at Buenos Aires 26Feb46; UK registration cancelled 29May46; registered **LV-AAQ** 9May46 to Dodero; overhauled by SB&HL 47 and new c/n SH.53C issued; transferred 2Jan48 to Aviación del Litoral Fluvial Argentina (ALFA) *Inglaterra*; to Aerolineas Argentinas 7Dec50; to Cooperativa Argentina de Aeronavegantes 18Nov63 with aid of loan from Provincia Formosa; withdrawn from use 64; scrapped at Buenos Aires Jan67

Sandringham 3 G-AGPY on the snow-covered hardstanding at Belfast awaiting delivery to Dodero. Here the aircraft name is spelt as the anglicised version 'Brazil', rather than Spanish 'Brasil'.
(P H T Green collection)

Another Sandringham 3 for Dodero, G-AGTZ at Belfast in May 1946, named Inglaterra *and wearing the full airline titling beneath the tailplane.*   (Shorts/Bombardier Aerospace via Jennifer M Gradidge)

Unforgettable Buenos Aires harbour scene in the mid-1950s with four of the Aerolineas Argentinas Sandringham fleet. On the left is LV-ACT Paraguay, *in the centre still in the older paint scheme is LV-AAO* Argentina, *on the right is Sandringham 6 LV-AHM Almirante Zar, with an unidentified example hidden behind it.*
(Jennifer M Gradidge collection)

CHAPTER 6 : CIVIL CONVERSIONS AND NEW-BUILD AIRCRAFT

Following the naming ceremony launch and launch of Sandringham 4 ZK-AMB Tasman of TEAL at Belfast on 1st July 1946, the official party is seen boarding the flying boat for a flight. The streamlined nose of the converted Sunderland is evident while in the background an aircraft carrier lies at the finishing berth; at this time almost certainly the Canadian HMCS Magnificent.
(via JM Collection)

Tasman ZK-AMB returning to Belfast harbour immediately after alighting with the official party on board on 1st July 1946.
(via JM Collection)

G-AGWW ex Sunderland III **EJ156**; registered (CofR 9799) 3Jan46 to SB(R&B)L; converted to Sandringham 3 with c/n SH.5C; registered 26Feb46 to Compania Aeronautica Uruguaya SA (CAUSA), Montevideo; CofA (7506) issued 14Mar46; delivered to Uruguay 29Mar46 and UK registration cancelled 29May46 as sold in Uruguay; registered May46 as **CX-AFA** to CAUSA and named *General Artigas*; sank at moorings in Montevideo harbour in high winds 11Sep56; salvaged but not repaired as already withdrawn from use

G-AGWX ex Sunderland III **ML876**; registered (CofR 9800) 3Jan46 to SB(R&B)L; converted to Sandringham 3 with c/n SH.6C; registered 26Feb46 to Compania Aeronautica Uruguaya SA (CAUSA), Montevideo; not delivered; cancelled and registered 28Mar46 to Corporación Sudamericana de Servicios Aereas SA (CSSA), Buenos Aires; CofA (7507) issued 28Mar46; diverted to Aviación del Litoral Fluvial (ALFA), Argentina, owners of Dodero which had bought CSSA; registered as **LV-AAS** 7May46, named *Rio de la Plata*; UK registration cancelled 12May46 as 're-registered in Buenos Aires'; also used as personal transport by Alberto Dodero; replaced by LV-AHH .48; registration cancelled 16Apr48; taken over by CAUSA and registered Mar48 as **CX-AKF**; named *San Martin*; fate unknown, presumed scrapped

CX-AFA see G-AGWW

CX-AKF see G-AGWX

LV-AAQ see G-AGTZ

LV-AAR see G-AGPY

LV-AAS see G-AGWX

Sandringham 4

ZK-AMB ex Sunderland V **ML761**; sold to Tasman Empire Airways 18Mar46; converted to Sandringham 4 (c/n SH.30C); CofA (7964) issued 1Jul46; launched and named *Tasman* at Belfast 1Jul46; handed over at Hythe 5Jul46 and left for Auckland 10Jul46, arrived 17Jul46; registered 25Jul46 to TEAL; last service 14Dec49; sold to QANTAS 13Apr50 and delivered to Australia 18Apr50; registration cancelled 24Apr50; registered **VH-EBW** to QANTAS 24Apr50 *Tasman*; damaged beyond repair when it struck uncharted coral reef at Port Vila in New Hebrides 10Jun51; registration cancelled 19Jul51

ZK-AMD ex Sunderland III **NJ255**; c/n SH.1173; sold to Tasman Empire Airways 9Apr46; converted to Sandringham 4 (c/n SH.32C); registerd 5Jul46; CofA (8093) issued 20Jul46; named *Australia*; left Poole for Auckland 25Jul46, arrived 5Aug46; first Auckland - Sydney service 25Aug46; last service 12Sep49; sold to QANTAS 13Apr50; registration cancelled 24Apr50; registered **VH-EBX** to QANTAS Empire Airways Ltd 24Apr50; named *Pacific Chieftain;* collided with safety launch at Rose Bay 3Sep51; sold to Barrier Reef Airways 10Dec54; registered **VH-BRE** to Ansett Flying Boat Services Ltd 22Dec54 (Ansett bought out Barrier Reef); regd to Ansett Airways (Pty) Ltd; chartered to TEAL 18-29Sep58; transferred to Ansett Flying Boat Services (Pty) Ltd .60; broke from

Sandringham 4 ZK-AMD became VH-EBX Pacific Chieftain with QANTAS in 1950 before sale to Barrier Reef / Ansett in 1954.
(QANTAS via JM Collection)

Another TEAL Sandringham 4, ZK-AMR New Zealand, captured immediately after lifting off from Waitemata Harbour, Auckland in late 1946.
(via JM Collection)

moorings in storm at Lord Howe Island 3Jul63 and sank; salvaged and spares removed before being scuttled Dec63; registration cancelled 5Dec63; TT 15,308 hours

ZK-AME   ex Sunderland V **NJ179**; sold to Tasman Empire Airways Ltd 11Apr46; converted to Sandringham 4 (c/n SH.33C); registered to TEAL 25Jul46, named *New Zealand*; CofA (8094) issued 22Aug46; left Poole for Auckland 26Aug46 with BOAC crew and 12 passengers, arrived 4Sep46; first Auckland - Sydney service 11Sep46; loaned to RNZAF 16-17May47 for Fiji service; withdrawn from use after last TEAL flight 19Dec49; ferried to Australia 27Apr50; registered to Barrier Reef Airways Pty Ltd as **VH-BRD** 12Mar51;named *Capricorn*; transferred to Ansett Flying Boat Services Ltd 1May52 and re-named *Princess of Cairns*; badly damaged by ship while moored on Brisbane River overnight and sank 31Oct52; salvaged to become night club at Coolangatta, but capsized while under tow and sank; registration cancelled 16Apr53

ZK-AMH   ex Sunderland V **JM715**; sold to Tasman Empire Airways Ltd 30Apr47; converted to Sandringham 4 (c/n SH.55C); registered to TEAL 29May47; named *Auckland*; CofA (9580) issued 10Oct47; left Poole for Auckland 15Oct47, arrived 29Oct47; last service 16Dec49; delivered to Australia 27Apr50; registered to Barrier Reef Airways Pty Ltd as **VH-BRC** 22May50; named *Coral Clipper*; last service 12Nov50; registered 15Dec52 to Ansett Flying Boat Services Ltd; named *Beachcomber*; converted to 41-passenger layout; registered to Ansett Airways .54; then to Ansett Transport Industries (Operations) Ltd 1Mar70 ; damaged at Lord Howe Island 9Jun74 but repaired; last passenger service 10Sep74; sold to Antilles Air Boats, Virgin Islands, date unknown; ferried from Sydney 28Nov74, arrived at St Croix 9Dec74; registered **N158C**; named *Southern Cross* (initially intended as *Southern Star*); re-registered **VP-LVE** Apr75 due to FAA restrictions; departed St Croix 6Jul76 for Boston then flew Atlantic to Foynes, Irish Republic, arriving 9Jul76; based at Killaloe on Lough Derg; visited Belfast 19Aug76; arrived at Poole 23Aug76, made nine passenger flights from Studland Bay to 28Aug76; returned St Croix; chartered to Aer Arann Aug77 and again based Lough Derg; visited Calshot 5Sep77 and made 17 passenger flights from mouth of Beaulieu River to 9Sep77; reverted to **N158C** 17Jun78 with change of ownership to AAT Inc, c/o Antilles Air Boats, Christansted, Virgin Islands; ferried from dereliction at San Juan, Puerto Rico, 9Oct80 by Capt Ron Gillies, to whom registered 5Sep80; flown St Croix - Boston - Port Washington - Oyster Bay - Sydney (Nova Scotia) - Gander Lake to Killaloe, Irish Republic arriving 24Oct80; stored until final flight to Calshot 2Feb81; airframe hours then approximately 19,500 (highest of any Sunderland type); beached; launched 6Jul81 and taxied 7Jul81 to RNAS Lee-on-Solent; purchased by The Science Museum .82; following conservration work transferred to Eastern Docks, Southampton, 1Mar83 on self-propelled Army barge, partially dismantled and and stored in secure compound; moved into semi-completed Hall of Aviation 27/28Aug83 and reassembled; restored in Ansett Flying Boat Services livery as VH-BRC *Beachcomber*; aircraft extant (museum re-titled Solent Sky from 2005); US registration expired 30Sep12

N158C   see ZK-AMH

VH-BRC   see ZK-AMH

VH-BRD   see ZK-AME

VH-BRE   see ZK-AMD

VH-EBW   see ZK-AMB

VH-EBX   see ZK-AMD

VP-LVE   see ZK-AMH

1. As ZK-AMH at Belfast before delivery to TEAL as Auckland, 1947.   *(P H T Green collection)*

Four stages of one Sandringham's history

2. As VH-BRC with Ansett Flying Boat Services from 1950 to 1974.   *(P H T Green collection)*

3. As VP-LVE Southern Cross with Antilles Air Boats flying passenger charters in the UK in 1976.   *(via JM Collection)*

4. Arriving by barge on the River Itchen as N158C in March 1983 en route to preservation in Southampton.   *(Science Museum)*

CHAPTER 6 : CIVIL CONVERSIONS AND NEW-BUILD AIRCRAFT

The first of ten Sandringham 5 "Plymouth" Class flying boats for BOAC, G-AHYY Portsmouth *was converted from Sunderland V ML838.*
(BOAC via JM Collection)

Sandringham 5

G-AHYY ex Sunderland V **ML838**; registered (CofR 10469) 15Jul46 to MoS; later re-registered to MCA; converted to Sandringham 5 (c/n SH.31C); CofA (8229) issued 4Mar 47; delivered to BOAC 6Mar47; registered to BOAC 13Mar47; named *Portsmouth*; entered service 2May47; withdrawn from use 8Jun49 but CofA renewed 2Oct 51; CofA expired 1Oct52; withdrawn from use and moored off Hamble until Jul53; towed to Hamworthy Aug53; stored at Solway Morgan's boatyard, Poole [Feb54]; sold 31Mar54 and registered 15Apr54 to Mentra Ltd, (London W1); extant at Hamworthy Quay Sep55; registration cancelled 15Apr57; scrapped at Hamworthy Mar59

G-AHYZ ex Sunderland V **ML784**; registered (CofR 10470) 15Jul46 to MoS; later re-registered to MCA; for conversion to Sandringham 5 (c/n SH.35C); allocated for BOAC, to be named *Perth* and CofA (8230) prepared but destroyed by fire while undergoing conversion at Belfast 18Jan47; registration cancelled 12Mar47

G-AHZA ex Sunderland V **ML783**; registered (CofR 10471) 15Jul46 to MoS; later re-registered to MCA; converted to Sandringham 5 (c/n SH.34C); registered to BOAC 18Apr47; named *Penzance*; CofA (8231) issued and delivered to BOAC 22Apr47; entered service 9May47; withdrawn from use 31Aug49 but CofA renewed 3Nov50; CofA expired 2Nov51 and wfu Hamworthy; moored off Hythe until Jul53; towed to Hamworthy Aug53; stored at Solway Morgan's boatyard, Poole [Feb54]; sold 31Mar54 and registered 15Apr54 to Mentra Ltd, (London W1); extant at Hamworthy Quay Sep55; registration cancelled 15Apr57; scrapped at Hamworthy Mar59

G-AHZB ex Sunderland V **NJ171**; registered (CofR 10472) 15Jul46 to MoS; later re-registered to MCA; converted to Sandringham 5 (c/n SH.38C); CofA (8232) issued 25Apr47; delivered to BOAC 26Apr47; registered to BOAC 2May47; named *Portland*; entered service 16May47; on arriving at Bahrain from Hong Kong and Karachi en route to Poole 23Aug47 (Capt R F Stone) alighted heavily, bounced and swung to starboard before settling nose-down (2 crew and 6 passengers killed, 16 survived); registration cancelled same day

G-AHZC ex Sunderland V **NJ253**; c/n SH.1159; registered (CofR 10473) 15Jul46 to MoS, later re-registered to MCA; converted to Sandringham 5 (c/n SH.39C); CofA (8233) issued 17May47; delivered to BOAC 17May47; registered to BOAC 21May47; named *Pembroke*; in service 30May47; withdrawn from use on expiry of CofA 26Jul 49, but renewed 18Jun51 to 17Jun52; withdrawn from use and moored off Hamble until towed to Hamworthy Aug53; stored at Solway Morgan's boatyard, Poole [Feb54]; sold 31Mar54 and registered 16Apr54 to Mentra Ltd, (London W1); extant at Hamworthy Quay Sep55; registration cancelled 15Apr57; scrapped at Hamworthy Mar59

G-AHZD ex Sunderland V **NJ257**; c/n SH.1195; registered (CofR 10474) 15Jul46 to MoS, later re-registered to MCA; converted to Sandringham 5 (c/n SH.40C); CofA (8234) issued 28May47; delivered to BOAC 28May47; registered to BOAC 31May47; named *Portmarnock*; entered service 13Jun47; withdrawn from use 13Aug49; CofA expired 25Aug49; stored at Hythe; sold to QANTAS 2Jun51; CofA renewed 28Jun51; registered to QANTAS Empire Airways Ltd 3Jul51; UK registration cancelled 10Aug 51; registered **VH-EBV** 10Aug51 to QANTAS; named *Pacific Warrior*; withdrawn from use at Rose Bay, Sydney, 6Jun55; broken up Aug55; registration cancelled 3Aug55

BOAC Sandringham 5 G-AHZC Pembroke *about to lift off from Hythe in 1947. Clearly visible above the cockpit are the pitot bipod, starsight bubble and D/F aerial loop.*
(BOAC via JM Collection)

QANTAS Sandringham 5 VH-EBV Pacific Warrior *beached at Rose Bay, Sydney during maintenance in 1952.* (Stephen Piercy collection)

This view of Sandringham 5 G-AHZE clearly shows the engine nacelles set at right angles to the swept-back wing leading edge. This 'toed-out' feature was said to reduce asymmetric effects in the event of an engine failure. (via JM Collection)

Sandringham 5 G-AJMZ Perth *was the first example to dock at BOAC's new Berth 50 at Southampton on 31st March 1948. It is being towed in by cable after arriving from Iwakuni, Japan with 21 passengers on board.* (via JM Collection)

G-AHZE ex Sunderland V **ML818**; registered (CofR 10475) 15Jul46 to MoS, later re-registered to MCA; converted to Sandringham 5 (c/n SH.36C); CofA (8235) issued 16Jun 47; delivered to BOAC 17Jun47; registered to BOAC 19Jun47; named *Portsea*; entered service 23Jun47; withdrawn from use 4Sep49; CofA expired 15Sep49; CofA renewed 12Jun51 to 11Jun52; withdrawn from use and moored off Hamble until Jul53; towed to Hamworthy Aug53 for continued storage; stored at Solway Morgan's boatyard, Poole [Feb54]; sold 31Mar54 and registered 16Apr54 to Mentra Ltd; extant Hamworthy Quay Sep55; registration cancelled 15Apr57; scrapped at Hamworthy Mar59

G-AHZF ex Sunderland V **NJ188**; registered (CofR 10475) 15Jul46 to MoS, later re-registered to MCA; converted to Sandringham 5 (c/n SH.41C); CofA (8236) issued 11Jul47; delivered to BOAC 11Jul47; registered to BOAC 22Jul47; named *Poole*; entered service 1 Aug47; withdrawn from use 25Aug49; CofA expired 29Sep49; stored at Hythe; sold to QANTAS 2Jun51; CofA renewed 12Jun51; registered 3 Jul51 to QANTAS Empire Airways Ltd; UK registration cancelled 31Dec51; registered **VH-EBY** 31Dec51 to QANTAS; named *Pacific Voyager*; damaged on take-off from Rose Bay, Sydney, 31Jan52 but repaired; holed on reef on take-off from Lindenhafen 8Oct53 but landed successfully and beached at Port Moresby, New Guinea; repaired; withdrawn from use 5Jul55 at Rose Bay and scrapped; registration cancelled 3Aug55

G-AHZG ex Sunderland V **ML828**; c/n SH.1115; registered (CofR 10477) 15Jul46 to MoS, later re-registered to MCA; converted to Sandringham 5 (c/n SH.37C); CofA (8237) issued 23Sept47; delivered to BOAC 23Sep47; registered 25Sep47 to BOAC; named *Pevensey*; entered service 6Oct47; withdrawn from use 3Sep49; CofA expired 17Nov49; stored at Hythe; sold to QANTAS 2Jun51; CofA renewed 18Jun51; registered 3Jul51 to QANTAS; UK registration cancelled 10Dec51; registered **VH-EBZ** 10Dec51 to QANTAS; named *Pacific Explorer*; operated final QANTAS Sandringham service 5Jun55; withdrawn from use 23Jun55 at Rose Bay and scrapped; registration cancelled 3Aug55

G-AJMZ ex Sunderland V **JM681**; registered (CofR 11438) 1Apr47 to MCA; converted to Sandringham 5 (c/n SH.56C); CofA (9473) issued 18Dec47; delivered to BOAC 19Dec47; registered 23Dec47 to BOAC; named *Perth*; entered service 24Feb48; withdrawn from use 28Aug49; CofA expired 2Feb50; CofA renewed 16Nov 50 to 15Nov51; withdrawn from use and moored off Hythe; towed to Hamworthy Aug53 for continued storage; stored at Solway Morgan's boatyard, Poole [Feb54]; sold

CHAPTER 6 : CIVIL CONVERSIONS AND NEW-BUILD AIRCRAFT

31Mar54 and registered 16Apr54 to Mentra Ltd; extant Hamworthy Quay Sep55; registration cancelled 15Apr57; scrapped at Hamworthy Mar59

VH-EBV   see G-AHZD

VH-EBY   see G-AHZF

VH-EBZ   see G-AHZG

Sandringham 6

LN-IAU   ex Sunderland V **ML807**; c/n SH.915; to S&HL 19Sep46; converted to Sandringham 6 (c/n SH.51C); CofA (8998) issued 13Jun47; registered 16Jun47 to Det Norske Luftfartselsskap A/S (DNL), Oslo; named *Bømse Brakar*; crashed on take-off from Harstad in snow-storm 15May50 after multiple engine failure (crew of 8 and 26 passengers killed); registration cancelled 31Aug50

LN-IAV   ex Sunderland V **ML809**; c/n SH.882; to S&HL 7Sep46; converted to Sandringham 6 (c/n SH.48C); CofA (8999) issued 17Apr47; registered 24Apr47 to Det Norske Luftfartselsskap A/S (DNL), Oslo; named *Kvitbjørn*; crashed at Tjelesund 28Aug47 when aircraft flew into side of cloud-covered mountain near Lødingen and caught fire (27 passengers and 8 crew killed); registration cancelled 19Sep47

LN-IAW   ex Sunderland V **JM720**; to S&HL 1Oct46; converted to Sandringham 6 (c/n SH.52C); CofA (9000) issued 16May47; registered 22May47 to Det Norske Luftfartselsskap A/S (DNL), Oslo; named *Bukken Bruse*; crashed on alighting in rough seas at Hommelvik, 20km North of Trondheim, 2Oct48 (19 of 45 crew and passengers killed); registration cancelled 26Sep49

LN-LAI   ex Sunderland III **W4037**; c/n S.1209; to S&HL; converted to Sandringham 6 (c/n SH.62C); CofA (9939) issued 29Apr48; registered 4May48 to Det Norske Luftfartselsskap A/S (DNL), Oslo; intended *Blessomen* but not used and named *Jutulen*; absorbed into Scandinavian Airlines System 51; leased to France-Hydro SA, Biscarosse, 52; sank after hitting mooring buoy on lake near Bangui, French Equatorial Africa, 16Nov52 while on charter to Air France; registration cancelled 4Jul53

LN-LMK   ex Sunderland V **JM714**; to S&HL 25Aug47; converted to Sandringham 6 (c/n SH.71C); test-flown 2/3Jun49; CofA (10375) issued 4Jun49 and delivered to Stavanger same day; registered 11Jun49 to Det Norske Luftfartselsskap A/S (DNL), Oslo; named *Polarbjørn*; absorbed into Scandinavian Airlines System 51; sold to to Aerolineas Argentinas and registered **LV-PAE** Apr55 for delivery; ferry flight to Argentina began 28Apr55 but noted at Southampton 22/23May55; Norwegian registration cancelled 25May55 as sold in Argentina; re-registered **LV-AHM** 28Jun55 after arrival and named *Almirante Zar*; CoR expired 16Apr63; to Cooperativa Argentina de Aeronavegantes 12Aug63; scrapped at Buenos Aires Jan67

LV-AHM   see LN-LMK

LV-PAE   see LN-LMK

Sandringham 7 ('Bermuda' class with BOAC)

G-AKCO   ex Sunderland V **JM719**; registered (CofR 11803) 29Jul47 to BOAC; converted to Sandringham 7 (c/n SH.57C); CofA (10008) issued 18Mar48; delivered to BOAC same day, originally named *Saint George*, later *St George*; entered service 2Apr48; withdrawn from use 22Aug49; CofA expired 15Mar50 but renewed 9Aug50; reported stored at Solway Morgan's yard at Poole Feb51; CofA again expired 8Nov51 but renewed 11Jul52 to 10Jul53; from moorings at Hamble, towed to Hamworthy early Jul53 for further storage; at Salway Morgan's yard Feb54; sold to W S Shackleton Ltd 5Mar54; registered 9Mar54; CofA renewed 8Apr54; registered 15Apr54 to P G Taylor (Pty) Ltd, Sydney; converted by Saunders-Roe Ltd at Cowes to luxury 35-seater interior for Sir Gordon P G Taylor; left Cowes 20Oct54 after refurbishment and called at Kalafrana (Malta) to collect Australian servicemen bound for home; registered 9May55 as **VH-APG** *Frigate Bird III* to Sir Gordon P G Taylor; UK registration cancelled 10May55; Australian registration cancelled 23 May58 as 'sold in France'; registered **F-OBIP** 4Jul58 to Transports Aériens Intercontinentaux, Papeete, Tahiti, and 13Apr63 to Réseau Aérien Interinsulaire, Papeete, a subsidiary of TAI; used on services between Tahiti, Huakine and Raiatea in French Polynesia; registered to Air Polynesie-RAI 70; CofA expired 13Mar70; last flight SAR mission 29Sep70; with-

All five Sandringham 6s were ordered initially by the Norwegian airline DNL but the first three were all written off in extreme weather conditions, including LN-IAV Kvitbjørn *(White Bear) seen above.*
(P H T Green collection)

The only French civil-registered Sunderland derivative was Sandringham 7 F-OBIP operated by TAI and RAI in the Pacific islands, seen after restoration by the Musée de l'Air.   *(P H T Green collection)*

Sandringham 7 G-AKCP St David, *probably photographed at Hythe, was one of two 'Bermuda' Class flying boats sold to CAUSA.*
(APN via P H T Green collection)

drawn from use 71 and beached; stored engineless; ownership transferred to Territoire de la Polynesie Française; auctioned at Papeete 74; acquired Mar75 by Douglas Pearson (son of former Aquila Airways Capt); proposed donation to Queensland Air Museum fell through due to cost and time constraints; donated to Musée de L'Air at Le Bourget; dismantled and shipped to Brest by French military Jul78; restored at Le Bourget in RAI colours winter 78/79 but badly damaged in gales Feb84; repaired, extant in store at Dugny

G-AKCP   ex Sunderland V **EJ172**; registered (CofR 11804) 31Jul47 to BOAC; converted to Sandringham 7 (c/n SH.58C); CofA (10009) issued 15Apr48; delivered to BOAC 15Apr48; named *St David*; entered service 23Apr48; withdrawn from use 11Sep49; CofA expired 7Jun50; CofA renewed 4Aug50 but cancelled 1Mar51 as 'sold abroad'; registered Mar51 to CAUSA as **CX-ANI**; damaged beyond repair when it struck an obstruction on take-off from Montevideo 25Jan56; beached and wreck still extant in Montevideo harbour early .64 but later scrapped

G-AKCR   ex Sunderland V **ML840**; registered (CofR 11805) 31Jul47 to BOAC; converted to Sandringham 7 (c/n SH.59C); CofA (10010) issued 1May48; delivered to BOAC 1May48; named *St Andrew*; entered service 14May48; withdrawn from use 5Sep49; CofA expired 5May50 but renewed 21Jul50; CofA cancelled 12Dec50 as 'sold to CAUSA'; registered to CAUSA Dec50 as **CX-ANA**; damaged beyond repair when it struck a dredger while taxying for take-off in Montevideo harbour 22Oct55; presumed scrapped

BRITAIN TO SOUTH AFRICA / SOUTH AFRICA TO BRITAIN

SOLENT SPEEDBIRD (FLYING-BOAT)

BO103 to Vaal Dam			BO104 to Southampton	
G.M.T. L.T.			L.T. G.M.T.	
Tue., Fri.				
10.45 11.45	dep. SOUTHAMPTON	arr.	16.00	15.00
17.15 19.15	arr. AUGUSTA	dep.	10.15	08.15
Wed., Sat.			Sat., Mon.	
06.00 08.00	dep. AUGUSTA	arr.	16.10	14.10
10.35 12.35	arr. CAIRO	dep.	10.15	08.15
			Fri., Sun.	
12.30 14.30	dep. CAIRO	arr.	17.20	15.20
14.15 16.15	arr. LUXOR	dep.	—	—
Thu., Sun.				
03.30 05.30	dep. LUXOR	arr.	—	—
07.15 09.15	arr. KHARTOUM	dep.	12.00	10.00
08.15 10.15	dep. KHARTOUM	arr.	10.55	08.55
14.00 17.00	arr. PORT BELL	dep.	06.30	03.30
Fri., Mon.			Thu., Sat.	
04.00 07.00	dep. PORT BELL	arr.	15.05	12.05
10.50 12.50	arr. VICTORIA FALLS	dep.	07.00	05.00
Sat., Tue.			Wed., Fri.	
05.00 07.00	dep. VICTORIA FALLS	arr.	15.10	13.10
08.35 10.35	arr. JOHANNESBURG (Vaal Dam)	dep.	11.30	09.30
			Tue., Thu.	

BRITAIN TO PAKISTAN & INDIA / INDIA & PAKISTAN TO BRITAIN

HYTHE SPEEDBIRD (FLYING-BOAT)

BO758 to Karachi			BO759 to Southampton	
G.M.T. L.T.			L.T. G.M.T.	
Thu.				
10.45 11.45	dep. SOUTHAMPTON	arr.	13.00	12.00
14.45 15.45	arr. MARSEILLES	dep.	09.00	08.00
			Wed.	
15.45 16.45	dep. MARSEILLES	arr.	16.30	15.30
20.00 22.00	arr. AUGUSTA	dep.	12.50	10.50
Fri.				
07.30 09.30	dep. AUGUSTA	arr.	11.50	09.50
13.35 15.35	arr. CAIRO	dep.	05.00	03.00
Sat.			Tue.	
05.45 07.45	dep. CAIRO	arr.	18.00	16.00
11.45 14.45	arr. BASRA	dep.	12.45	09.45
12.45 15.45	dep. BASRA	arr.	11.45	08.45
15.00 19.00	arr. BAHREIN	dep.	10.20	06.20
Sun.				
04.30 08.30	dep. BAHREIN	arr.	08.50	04.50
11.00 16.30	arr. KARACHI	dep.	04.00	22.30
			Mon.	

Extracts from BOAC timetable of 15th June 1948 showing selected flying-boat services

BRITAIN TO FAR EAST / FAR EAST TO BRITAIN

PLYMOUTH SPEEDBIRD (FLYING-BOAT)

BO900 to Iwakuni			BO901 to Southampton	
G.M.T. L.T.			L.T. G.M.T.	
Fri.				
11.30 12.30	dep. SOUTHAMPTON	arr.	15.00	14.00
15.20 16.20	arr. MARSEILLES	dep.	—	—
Sat.				
05.00 06.00	dep. MARSEILLES	arr.	—	—
09.10 11.10	arr. AUGUSTA	dep.	07.45	05.45
			Thu.	
10.10 12.10	dep. AUGUSTA	arr.	16.30	14.30
16.10 18.10	arr. CAIRO	dep.	09.30	07.30
Sun.			Wed.	
03.30 05.30	dep. CAIRO	arr.	18.00	16.00
10.45 14.45	arr. BAHREIN	dep.	12.15	08.15
11.45 15.45	dep. BAHREIN	arr.	11.15	07.15
18.15 23.45	arr. KARACHI	dep.	06.15	00.45
Mon.			Tue.	
01.30 07.00	dep. KARACHI	arr.	19.15	13.45
10.00 15.30	arr. CALCUTTA	dep.	10.50	05.20
Tue.				
00.01 05.30	dep. CALCUTTA	arr.	09.50	04.20
04.20 10.50	arr. RANGOON	dep.	06.30	00.01
			Mon.	
05.20 11.50	dep. RANGOON	arr.	14.00	07.30
07.50 14.50	arr. BANGKOK	dep.	12.00	05.00
Wed.				
23.30 06.30	dep. BANGKOK	arr.	11.00	04.00
06.30 15.30	arr. HONG KONG	dep.	06.00	21.00
Thu.			Sun.	
22.00 07.00	dep. HONG KONG	arr.	16.00	07.00
07.30 17.30	arr. IWAKUNI	dep.	07.30	21.30
			Sat.	

BRITAIN TO FAR EAST / FAR EAST TO BRITAIN

PLYMOUTH SPEEDBIRD (FLYING-BOAT)

BO902 to Hong Kong			BO903 to Southampton	
G.M.T. L.T.			L.T. G.M.T.	
Tue.				
11.30 12.30	dep. SOUTHAMPTON	arr.	15.00	14.00
15.20 16.20	arr. MARSEILLES	dep.	—	—
Wed.				
05.00 06.00	dep. MARSEILLES	arr.	—	—
09.10 11.10	arr. AUGUSTA	dep.	07.45	05.45
			Mon.	
10.10 12.10	dep. AUGUSTA	arr.	16.30	14.30
16.10 18.10	arr. CAIRO	dep.	09.30	07.30
Thu.			Sun.	
03.30 05.30	dep. CAIRO	arr.	18.00	16.00
10.45 14.45	arr. BAHREIN	dep.	12.15	08.15
11.45 15.45	dep. BAHREIN	arr.	11.15	07.15
18.15 23.45	arr. KARACHI	dep.	06.15	00.45
Fri.			Sat.	
01.30 07.00	dep. KARACHI	arr.	19.15	13.45
10.00 15.30	arr. CALCUTTA	dep.	10.50	05.20
Sat.				
00.01 05.30	dep. CALCUTTA	arr.	09.50	04.20
04.20 10.50	arr. RANGOON	dep.	06.30	00.01
			Fri.	
05.20 11.50	dep. RANGOON	arr.	14.00	07.30
07.50 14.50	arr. BANGKOK	dep.	12.00	05.00
Sun.				
23.30 06.30	dep. BANGKOK	arr.	11.00	04.00
06.30 15.30	arr. HONG KONG	dep.	06.00	21.00
			Thu.	

Frequent connections by Hong Kong Airways Ltd. to Canton and Shanghai.

AUSTRALIA TO NEW ZEALAND / NEW ZEALAND TO AUSTRALIA

OPERATED BY T.E.A.L.

Frequent connecting services between Sydney and Auckland are operated by Tasman Empire Airways Limited in association with B.O.A.C.

(British Airways Archives)

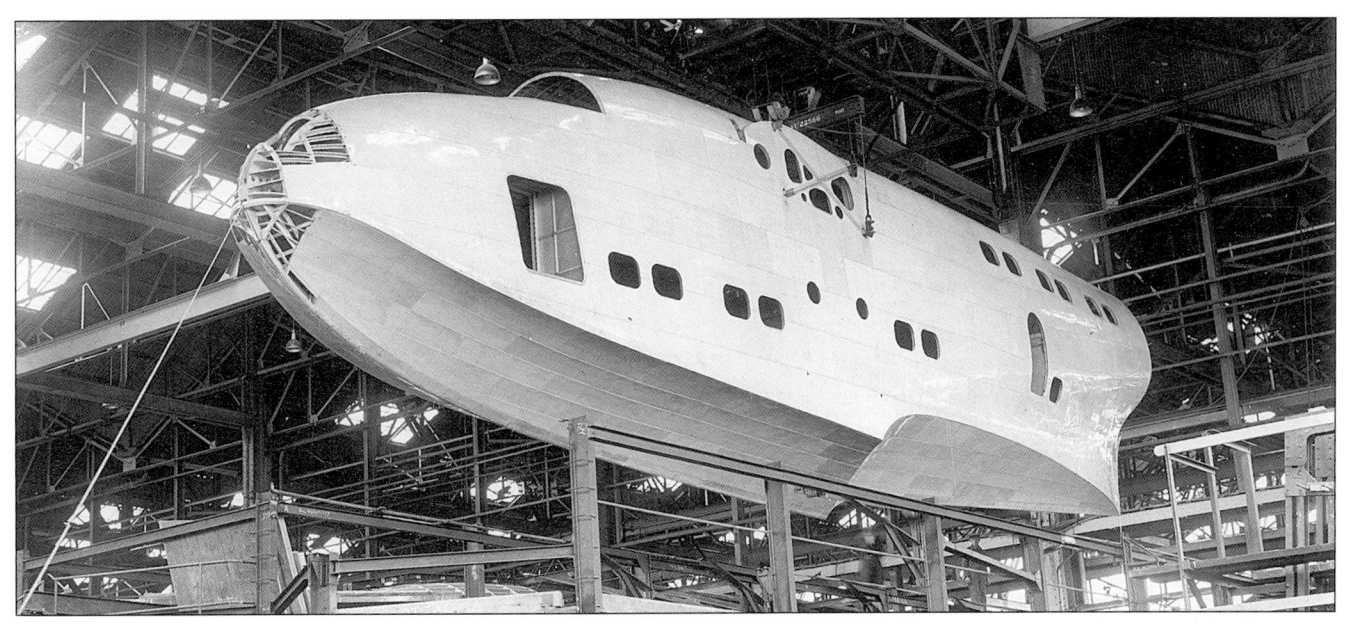

CHAPTER 6 : CIVIL CONVERSIONS AND NEW-BUILD AIRCRAFT

A dramatic view of a Solent fuselage for TEAL on the production line at Rochester in 1947. (Stephen Piercey collection)

CX-ANA see G-AKCR

CX-ANI see G-AKCP

F-OBIP see G-AKCO

VH-APG see G-AKCO

Seaford 1

G-AGWU ex **NJ201**; c/n S.1293; registered (CofR 9797) 31Dec45 to MoS&AP for evaluation by BOAC at Hythe;no CofA issued; registration cancelled as returned to RAF 19Feb46 reverted to **NJ201**; issued to BOAC on loan 24Apr46 as NJ201; returned to RAF at 57 MU, Wig Bay, 30Jun47; to Shorts, Belfast 19Dec47; flew Hythe to RAF Felixstowe 7Nov50 for storage; converted to Solent 3 **G-ANAJ** 1953-54

G-ALIJ ex **NJ200**; c/n S.1292; sold to Russell L Whyham, Blackpool, trading as Air Navigation & Trading Co Ltd, 17Feb49 but not collected from RAF Felixstowe and scrapped there; registration cancelled Oct49

Solent 2

Note: these twelve aircraft had originally been laid down as Seafords NJ208 to 219

G-AHIL c/n S.1300; ex (**NJ208**); registered (CofR 10085) 23Apr46 to MoS; first flight 11 Nov46; registered 3Jun48 to MCA; leased to BOAC and delivered 15Jun48; CofA (10147) issued 16Jun48; named *Salisbury*; converted to Solent 3 Sep49; renamed *City of Salisbury*; withdrawn from use at Belfast 29Sep50; returned to MCA at SB&HL 3Oct50; CofA expired 1Sep51 (total hours 3,515); sold to International Aircraft Sales, test-flown 9Apr53; ferried to Southampton 14Apr53 then to Poole Aug53; stored at Solway Morgan's boatyard, Poole [Feb54]; extant Hamworthy Quay Sep55 and partly dismantled by May58; registration cancelled 14Feb56 as 'sold', presumably for scrap

G-AHIM c/n S.1301; ex (**NJ209**); registered (CofR 10086) 23Apr46 to MoS; registered 24Sep47 to MCA; leased to BOAC and delivered 21May48; named *Scarborough*; CofA (10133) issued 24May48; entered service 28May48; flying display at SBAC Farnborough Sep48; withdrawn from use at Belfast 26Dec49; returned to MCA at SB&HL

The graceful lines of the Sunderland family are clear in this view of Solent 2 G-AHIL Salisbury *of BOAC.* (P H T Green collection)

JUNE 10TH, 1948   FLIGHT   Advertisements 5.

Some Short jottings for airline operators and their crews

The trend to the flying boat...

The new Short-Solent route on the Springbok Service

SOUTHAMPTON
AUGUSTA
CAIRO
LUXOR
KHARTOUM
PORT BELL
VICTORIA FALLS
JOHANNESBURG

New Springbok Route

Four and a half days of travel in comfort and luxury, over scenes of incredible beauty, are promised by the new B.O.A.C. Springbok service.

After taking over from landplanes at present used on the route, Short Solents will fly from the new flying boat terminal, Berth 50, Southampton; they will call at Augusta, Cairo, Luxor, Khartoum, Port Bell, Victoria Falls, and Vaaldam (Johannesburg). Making an overnight stop at Victoria Falls, passengers will have an opportunity of seeing the panorama of which Dr. Livingstone said, "scenes so lovely must have been gazed upon by angels in their flight."

Livingstone's amazing 'Shangwe,' renamed Victoria Falls

Passenger Comfort at Berth 50...

Passenger comfort has been catered for with all the ingenuity of modern design at B.O.A.C.'s new flying boat terminal. In addition to the well-appointed bar-lounge and restaurant, features of the new terminal are the two flying-boat floating docks approached along covered ways by outward and inward bound passengers.

...at Night-Stops on flying-boat Routes

For long-distance travellers the new B.O.A.C. night-stop accommodation will be a masterpiece of design for maximum comfort. Each air-conditioned bedroom will be self contained, connected by sliding doors to its own shower and toilet. There are extra-large divan beds, dressing tables, bedside tables, recessed lighting, and radio in every room.

FLYING BOAT PERSONALITIES

CAPT. H. L. M. GLOVER
No. 4 Line, B.O.A.C.

IN 1930 Captain Glover "worked his passage" from New Zealand and entered the R.A.F.

He was with No. 18 Squadron, Upper Heyford, when they escorted the Prince of Wales to the funeral of King Albert of Belgium. In 1937 he joined Imperial Airways, and by July 1938 he was First Officer on Short's Empire Flying Boats on the Durban and Singapore routes. In 1940 he was back with the R.A.F. at Kalafrana, operating in Short Sunderlands.

In 1942 Captain Glover was with B.O.A.C., and he has now logged over 10,000 hours, mostly in flying boats. He now regularly flies "down the routes" on B.O.A.C.'s Hythes and Plymouths.

Shorts

THE FIRST MANUFACTURERS OF AIRCRAFT IN THE WORLD

SHORT BROTHERS AND HARLAND LTD., QUEEN'S ISLAND, BELFAST

Enquiries to 17 GROSVENOR STREET, LONDON, W.1

STOP PRESS

Good news for the many who have sent in orders for and enquiries about the Sealand, is that her maiden flight and preliminary tests at Belfast were an unqualified success.

Tasman Empire Airways, who use only Short flying boats on their services, have announced that their enterprise has regularly paid a dividend of three per cent. T.E.A.'s fares have been among the lowest for international airlines, and the airline has been maintained without Government subsidies.

The bar-lounge, Berth 50, Southampton

The Southampton to Johannesburg Solent route as advertised by Short Brothers and Harland in Flight magazine dated 10th January 1948.
(via Peter J Marson)

CHAPTER 6 : CIVIL CONVERSIONS AND NEW-BUILD AIRCRAFT

A posed photograph of Solent 2 G-AHIO Somerset, apparently being waved farewell from the berth at Southampton but in fact moored to a buoy and with the engines closed down. After two and a half years with BOAC G-AHIO was sold to TOA. (P H T Green collection)

28Mar50; CofA expired 28Jun50 (total hours 2,156); test-flown 28Apr53; ferried to RAF Felixstowe for storage 8Jun53; derelict by Mar55; registration cancelled 14Feb 56 as 'sold'; 'for sale' in *Flight* 16Mar56 by agents A King & Sons, Norwich; stored May56; later scrapped

G-AHIN c/n S.1302; ex (**NJ210**); registered (CofR 10087/2) 21Apr46 to MoS; registered 21Apr48 to MCA; CofA (10087) issued 22Apr48; leased to BOAC and delivered 22Apr48; originally allocated name *Seaforth* but named *Southampton* by Mayoress of Southampton 14Apr48; entered service 18May48; made final BOAC flight from Poole 1May48 when it left on route-proving flight to South Africa; SB&HL 24Nov 49; converted to Solent 3 Feb50; CofA renewed 12Oct50 but withdrawn from use at Belfast 6Nov50; returned to MCA 10Nov50 (total hours 3,912); CofA expired 11Oct51; sold to International Aircraft Sales; ferried to Southampton 16Marr53 then to Poole Aug53; stored at Solway Morgan's boatyard, Poole [Feb54]; extant Hamworthy Quay Sep55 registration cancelled 14Feb56 as sold; to Aquila Airways for major overhaul and registered to them 17Jun57, still named *Southampton;* CofA renewed 13Jul57; sold to Aerovias Aquila Oct58; registration cancelled 5Dec58 as 'sold to Portugal' (notified 8Mar63}; test-flown 17Dec58; CofA renewed 19Dec58; ferried from Southampton to Lisbon 20Dec58; wfu and stored in Tagus estuary until at least .65; reportedly scrapped there May71

G-AHIO c/n S.1303; ex (**NJ211**); registered (CofR 10088) 23Apr46 to MoS; registered 8Jun48 to MCA; CofA (10167) issued 27Jan49; test-flown Mar49; to Southampton 26Mar49; leased to BOAC and delivered 19May49; named *Somerset*; entered service 20May49; damaged alighting at Hythe 2Aug49 but repaired; converted to Solent 3 Jan50; CofA renewed 5Oct50 but withdrawn from use 14Nov50; flown Southampton to Belfast and returned to MCA 17Nov50; registration cancelled 17Jul51; CofA renewed 12Oct51 for 2 months; registered 20Oct51 to Trans-Oceanic Airways (Pty) Ltd, Sydney; test-flown 9Nov51; left Belfast 12Nov51 on ferry flight via Southampton and Darwin;UK registration cancelled 10Dec51; registered **VH-TOD** 10Dec51 to TOA; named *Star of Samoa*; last service 12Nov52; stored Rose Bay; agreement 17Apr53 for purchase by Dollar Associates, Oakland CA for operation by South Pacific Air Lines, Oakland, CA; registered to South Pacific Air Lines 17Apr55 as **N9945F**; test flown 24May55; delivered May/Jun55; arrived Oakland 22Jun55 but never entered service and stored at Oakland; re-registered to Dollar Lines Ltd, Reno NV Jul63 to Jan66; although Howard Hughes is reported to have taken over all three South Pacific Air Lines Solents in 1959, they were never officially listed as owned by him personally, but rather by nominees; officially registered to Robert A Collier, Washington DC Jul66 to Jul71; remained stored at Oakland until 23Oct67, when transferred by barge to Shoal Point, Richmond CA; remained there under armed guard until sold to scrap dealer Virgil Martin, trading as H & M Airline Services Co, Feb73; listed as 'registration pending' at Houston TX Jul72 to Jul74; scrapped 74;registration cancelled 10Jun75; *Note: registration pending Jul95 wef 14Feb66 for owner in Houston, TX and not cancelled until Apr99 - a paper exercise only!*

G-AHIR c/n S.1304; ex (**NJ212**); registered (CofR 10089) 23Apr46 to MoS; registered 17Mar48 to MCA; CofA (10097) issued 4May48; leased to BOAC and delivered 5May48; named *Sark*; damaged alighting at Vaaldam 12May48 (probably on first service) but repaired; withdrawn from use at Belfast 24Dec49; returned to MCA at SB&HL 4Jan50; CofA expired 25May50 (total hours 2,000); test-flown 10Dec53;ferried to Felixstowe for storage 4Jan54; still stored Mar55; registration cancelled 14Feb56 as 'sold'; 'for sale' in *Flight* 16Mar56 by agents A King & Sons, Norwich; noted stored May56 but later scrapped

G-AHIS c/n S.1305; ex (**NJ213**); registered (CofR 10090) 23Apr46 to MoS; registered 14Apr48 to MCA; CofA (10168) issued 8Jul48; leased to BOAC and delivered 7Jul48; named *Scapa*; entered service 19Nov48; converted to Solent 3 Oct49; renamed *City of York*; withdrawn from use at Belfast 26Sep50; returned to MCA at SB&HL 2Oct50; CofA expired 10Sep51 (total hours 3,474); sold to International Aircraft Sales Mar53, test-flown 24Apr53; ferried to RAF Felixstowe for storage 4May53; registration cancelled 14Feb56 as 'sold'; 'for sale' in *Flight* 16Mar56 by agents A King & Sons, Norwich but later scrapped

G-AHIT c/n S.1306; ex (**NJ214**); registered (CofR 10091) 23Apr46 to MoS; registered 27Aug47 to MCA; CofA (9864) issued 10Nov47; registered to BOAC 10Nov47; delivered 30Apr48; named *Severn*; entered service 4May48; registered to MCA 4Jun48; withdrawn from use and ferried to Belfast for storage 22Nov49; CofA expired 17Dec49 (total hours 1,893); sold to International Aircraft Sales Mar53 scrapped for spares at SB&HL 1955-56; registration cancelled 14Feb56 as 'sold'

The big flying boats were regularly featured in the early post-war SBAC flying displays at Farnborough. Here Solent 2 G-AHIU Solway makes a low pass during the 1949 event.   (Air-Britain)

Solent 3 N9945F, the former G-AHIO and VH-TOD, was owned by South Pacific Airlines of Oakland, California but remained there unused for twelve years including time in the hands of Howard Hughes' nominees. Note the Boeing B-29 in the background.
(P H T Green collection)

G-AHIU   c/m S.1307; ex (**NJ215**); registered (CofR 10092) 23Apr46 to MoS; registered 24Feb48 to MCA; leased to BOAC for crew training 29Feb48 and delivered 1Mar48; CofA (9997) issued 2Mar48; entered service 6Feb49; named *Solway*; withdrawn from use at Poole 20Aug49; returned to MCA 21Aug49; demonstration flight at SBAC Farnborough show Sep49; to BOAC 9Sep49 and returned to MCA 17Oct49; flown to Belfast 29Nov49; CofA expired 4Feb50 (total hours 1,331); noted Belfast Dec52 with tail unit and control surgaces removed; sold to International Aircraft Sales Mar53; test-flown 4Sep53; ferried Belfast to Poole 7Sep53; noted stored at Solway Morgan's boatyard, Poole Oct53 and Sep55; registration cancelled 14Feb56 as 'sold'; planned conversion into coffee bar with G-AKNS fell through; scrapped at Hamworthy Apr59

G-AHIV   c/n S.1308; ex (**NJ216**); registered (CofR 10093) 23Apr46 to MoS; registered 12Feb48 to MCA; leased to BOAC and delivered 9Feb48; CofA (9967) issued 18Feb48; named *Salcombe*; entered service 11May48; converted to Solent 3 Jan50; withdrawn from use 15Sep50; CofA renewed 3Oct50; returned (ex-Southampton 4Oct50) to MCA at SB&HL 5Oct50; registration cancelled 22May51 as 'sold abroad'; registered 22Jun51 to Trans-Oceanic Airways (Pty) Ltd, Sydney; left SB&HL on delivery flight via Southampton 5Jul51arriving Sydney 14Jul51; registration cancelled 20Jul51 as 'sold in Australia'; registered **VH-TOC** 20Jul51 to TOA; named *Star of Papua*; collided with dredger on flarepath at Brisbane 28Oct51, losing 22 feet (6.7 m) of wing; beached but not repaired; sold in non-airworthy condition to Dollar Associates Apr53; spares removed and hulk sold for scrap at Colmslie, Brisbane for £A400; registration cancelled 28Jun54

G-AHIW   c/n S.1309; ex (**NJ217**); registered (CofR 10094) 23Apr46 to MoS; registered 16Mar48 to MCA; leased to BOAC for crew training and delivered 26Mar48; CofA (10037) 25Mar48; entered service 14May48; named *Stornoway*; withdrawn from use and returned to MCA 1Sep49; briefly restored to BOAC 9Sep49 to 23Oct49 then flown to Belfast for storage 24Nov49; CofA expired 24Mar50 (total hours 1,907); to Belfast 4Oct50; sold to International Aircraft Sales Mar53;ferried to RAF Felixstowe for storage 23Jun53, registration cancelled 14Feb56 as 'sold'; 'for sale' in *Flight* 16Mar56 by agents A King & Sons, Norwich; later scrapped at Felixstowe

G-AHIX   c/n S.1310; ex (**NJ218**); registered (CofR 10095) 23Apr46 to MoS; registered 9Apr48 to MCA; leased to BOAC and delivered 19Oct48; CofA (10169) 20Oct48; entered BOAC service 24Oct48; named *Sussex*; converted to Solent 3 Nov49; renamed *City of Edinburgh*; crash-landed in gale on Southampton Water and sank off Netley 1Feb50; registration cancelled 5Apr50 as 'reduced to spares following accident'

G-AHIY   c/n S.1311; ex (**NJ219**); last aircraft built at Rochester; registered (CofR 10096) 23Apr46 to MoS; first flown 8Apr48 as the last aircraft built at Rochester by Shorts; registered 24Apr48 to MCA; leased to BOAC and delivered 23Nov48; CofA (10170) 25Nov48; entered service 28Nov48; named *Southsea*; converted to Solent 3 Dec49; damaged between Augusta and Hythe 21Sep50; repaired; CofA renewed 16Sep50 but wfu Belfast 27Sep50; returned to MCA at SB&HL 12Oct50; CofA expired 15Sep51 (total hours 3,173); sold to International Aircraft Sales Mar53 and ferried to RAF Felixstowe for storage 28May53,registration cancelled 14Feb56 as 'sold'; 'for sale' in *Flight* 16Mar56 by agents A King & Sons, Norwich but later scrapped at Felixstowe

Solent 2 G-AHIY Southsea was the last flying boat to be built at the Short Brothers factory at Rochester on the River Medway and is seen here flying overhead the works in an appropriate farewell.
(via JM Collection)

VH-TOC   see G-AHIV

VH-TOD   see G-AHIO

N9945F   see G-AHIO

Solent 3 (ex Seaford Mk.I)

G-AGWU ex **NJ201** Dec45; returned to RAF Feb46; later registered **G-ANAJ** (see also under Solent 1 and below)

G-AHIL, G-AHIN, G-AHIO, G-AHIS, G-AHIV, G-AHIX, G-AHIY see Solent 2

CHAPTER 6 : CIVIL CONVERSIONS AND NEW-BUILD AIRCRAFT

BOAC Solent 3 G-AKNO, formerly Seaforth, *alighted on the Thames on 5th May 1949 and moored in the Pool of London in preparation for a re-naming ceremony to commemorate the 40th Anniversary of the commencement of British Civil Aviation. Its new name, still covered in this view, was revealed as* City of London *by the Lord Mayor on 10th May.* (Aeroplane via JM Collection)

G-AKNO ex **NJ202**; c/n S.1294; registered 2Dec47 to MCA; CofA (10242) issued 1Apr49; leased to BOAC and delivered to Hythe 1Apr49; originally named *Seaforth*; renamed *City of London* by Lord Mayor at Limehouse Reach 10May49; entered service 1Jun49; withdrawn from use 10Nov50; returned to MCA at SB&HL 17Nov50; registration cancelled 20Dec50 as 'sold abroad'; test-flown 22Jan51; sold to Trans-Oceanic Airways Pty Ltd and registered **VH-TOA** Jan51; left Belfast on delivery flight via Southampton 23Jan51; during delivery flight, lost float on take-off from Marsaxlokk Bay, Malta 28Jan51 and sank

G-AKNP ex **NJ203**; c/n S.1295; registered 2Dec47 to MCA; CofA (10243) 19Mar49; leased to BOAC and delivered to Hythe 18Mar49; entered service 12Apr49; named *City of Cardiff*; inaugurated Southampton to Nairobi (Lake Naivasha) service 15May49; CofA renewed 23Oct50; operated last scheduled BOAC flight by a Solent, from Augusta to Southampton 2Nov50; withdrawn from use 2Nov50; ferried to Belfast and returned to MCA 8Nov50; sold through W S Shackleton Ltd as replacement for VH-TOA (see G-AKNO);registration cancelled 5Feb51 as sold abroad; registered 20Mar51 to Trans-Oceanic Airways (Pty) Ltd as **VH-TOB**; named *Star of Papua*; delivered from Belfast 24Mar51 in TOA colours but as **G-AKNP**; arrived Sydney 3Apr51; registered **VH-TOB** 1May51; in service 22May51; damaged at Brisbane 19Jun51 and repaired at Sydney; damaged in Bass Strait 11Feb52 but repaired; again damage at Brisbane 22Mar52 and repaired; last TOA service 16Apr53; agreement for purchase by Dollar Associates 17Apr53 for operation by South Pacific Air Lines Inc, Oakland, and test-flown 4Jan54; ferried Australia to Honolulu and handed over at Oahu, Hawaii, 26May54; flew Honolulu to NAS Alameda CA 29Apr55; delivered to Oakland CA 1May55 and registered **N9946F**; to Dollar Lines Ltd Jun56 (?); named *Isle of Tahiti*; flew Oakland to San Francisco 24Sep57; US CofA issued after mods 29Oct58; last flight 2Nov58; never entered service with South Pacific Air Lines; beached and stored at San Francisco in full South Pacific colours; ownership reportedly transferred to Howard Hughes' nominees in .59 but remained officially registered to Dollar; registered to Robert A Collier, Washington DC Jul63 and "registration pending, Houston TX"; moved to Richmond CA by barge 73; offered to City of Rochester, Kent, for preservation if City paid for dismantling, shipping and reassembly, estimated at $150,000, but offer refused; sold late 72 (officially Feb73) to Virgil Martin, trading as H & M Airline Services Co, for scrap, but rescued, as best of three Solents, by R & H Grottelli; sold Nov76 to Rick and Randy Grant at Richmond CA, trading as PREFLITE (Program for Research & Education through Flying Long-range Investigations on Trans-oceanic Explorations)!; slow restoration to flying condition carried out; painted all white with name *Halcyon* c.78; first engine run-ups Apr81 but finance ran out; cockpit used in filming of '*Raiders of the Lost Ark*' 80; donated to Western Aerospace Museum, Oakland, and moved from Richmond to Oakland 12Aug87; painted in RAF colours with genuine Seaford serial NJ203 and on display from Nov88; extant; US registration expired 30Jun12

G-AKNR ex **NJ204**; c/n S.1296; registered 2Dec47 to MCA; CofA (10244) 27Apr49; leased to BOAC and delivered 17May49; entered service 18May49; named *City of Belfast*; withdrawn from use 27Oct50; CofA renewed 8Nov50; returned to MCA at SB&HL 9Nov50; registration cancelled 28May51 as sold abroad; registered 4Jul51 to Tasman Empire Airways Ltd, Auckland; left Belfast 22Aug51 on delivery flight via Southampton, arrived at Auckland 12Sep51; UK registration cancelled 6Nov51 as 'sold in New Zealand'; registered to TEAL as **ZK-AMQ** 27Nov51; named *Aparima*; withdrawn from use at Mechanics Bay, Auckland, after last flight 22Sep57; scrapped at Auckland 30Sep57

G-AKNS ex **NJ205**; c/n S.1297; registered 2Dec47 to MCA; CofA (10245) issued 24Jun49; leased to BOAC and delivered 27Jul49; entered service 28Jul49; named *City of Liverpool*; withdrawn from use 1Nov50; loaned to MAEE 7Nov50 for stability trials at overload weights as **WM759**; CofA expired 6Jul51 (total time 2,433 hours); allotted to SB&HL on completion of MAEE trials 16Feb52; test-flown as **G-AKNS** 1Apr53; sold to International Aircraft Sales Mar53; ferried Belfast to Poole Jan54; noted stored at Solway Morgan's boatyard, PooleFeb54 and Sep55; registration cancelled 14Feb56 as 'sold'; planned conversion into coffee bar with G-AHIU fell through; scrapped at Hamworthy Apr59

G-AKNT ex **NJ206**; c/n S.1298; registered 2Dec47 to MCA; CofA (10246) prepared but not issued; intended for BOAC, to be named *Singapore* but rejected Jul49; test-flown 9Mar50; stored Belfast after conversion 29Mar50 on behalf of MoS; test-flown 18Mar53; sold to International Aircraft Sales Mar53; ferried to Hamworthy for further storage 22Mar53 (total time 5 hours);to Poole Jan54 and stored at Solway Morgan's boatyard, Poole [Feb54];stored at Hamworthy Quay Sep55; bought by South Pacific Airlines Inc, Oakland, CA, 15Nov55; UK registration cancelled same day; registered **N9947F** and taxied to Hamble for rework by Aquila Airways 18Nov55 and beached; test-flown 26Apr56; delivered from Southampton to Oakland 1-8May56; never entered service with South Pacific; stored at Oakland in red protective paint; registered to Dollar Lines Ltd, Reno NV Jul63 to Jan66; ownership

Trans Oceanic Airways Solent 3 VH-TOB Star of Papua *beached at Rose Bay, Sydney, in 1952. In this view the Vee struts supporting the floats, a feature of this model, are clearly visible.* (Stephen Piercey collection)

Solent 3 VH-TOB was sold to South Pacific Air Lines and registered N9946F in May 1955. Named Isle of Tahiti, *it wears the airline's second colour scheme when beached at Oakland in 1958.* (via JM Collection)

Solent 3 G-AKNR was appropriately named City of Belfast *in BOAC service, 29th July 1949.* (Short Bros & Harland via JM Collection)

Seaford NJ205, at rest on the Medway, before conversion to become Solent 3 G-AKNS. (P H T Green collection)

transfer to Howard Hughes' nominees reported in .59 but remained officially registered to Dollar Lines; registered to Robert A Collier, Washington DC Jul66 and 'registration pending' Jul 72; moved by barge from Oakland to Richmond CA 23-25Oct67 and put into storage under armed guard; sold late 72 (officially Feb73) to Virgil Martin trading as H & M Airline Services Co for scrap; scrapped by 75; registration cancelled 10Jun75 *(Note: Paper exercise followed as for N9945F)*

G-AKNU ex **NJ207**; c/n S.1299; registered 2Dec47 to MCA; rejected by BOAC Jul49; held in storage at SB&HL after conversion 29Mar50 on behalf of MoS;cancelled 23Oct51 and registered to Aquila Airways Ltd 16Nov51; named *Sydney*; CofA (10247) issued 12Dec51 and flown to Southampton on same day; damaged between Lisbon and Funchal 2Feb53 but repaired; crashed on Chessell Down, Shalcombe, Isle of Wight, 15Nov57 while attempting to return to Southampton for emergency landing following engine failure;43 killed, 15 survivors; registration cancelled 9Apr58 as destroyed

G-ANAJ ex Solent 1 **NJ201**, **G-AGWU**, **NJ201** ; c/n S.1293; registered 25Jun53 (CofR R.4058/1) to Aquila Airways Ltd; ferried from RAF Felixstowe to Hamble late Jun53 for conversion and beached; CofA issued 30Apr54; entered service 1May54; named *City of Funchal*; driven ashore in gale and wrecked at Santa Margherita, Italy 25-26Sep56; registration cancelled 15Oct56

VH-TOA see G-AKNO

VH-TOB see G-AKNP

Aquila Airways Solent 3 G-ANAJ on the beach at Santa Margherita in Italy after being driven ashore in a gale on 26th September 1956. Not surprisingly, it never flew again. (R C Sturtivant collection)

ZK-AMQ see G-AKNR

CHAPTER 6 : CIVIL CONVERSIONS AND NEW-BUILD AIRCRAFT

Formating with a Short Sealand 1, Solent 4 G-ANYI Awatere *of Aquila Airways was initially owned by TEAL as ZK-AMN. Note the very large spinners fitted to the 2040hp Bristol Hercules 733 engines which were aligned parallel to the fuselage.* *(R C Sturtivant collection)*

N9946F see G-AKNP

N9947F see G-AKNT

Solent 4

ZK-AML c/n S.1556; to Tasman Empire Airways Ltd; test-flown 20Apr49; named *Aotearoa II* by HRH Princess Elizabeth at SB&HL 6May49; UK CofA (10665) issued 2Jul49 and re-issued 22Nov49; used for certification trials plus research and test work; left Belfast for New Zealand via Southampton 26Nov49, arrived 7Dec49; used by HM the Queen and HRH Prince Phillip during 1953 New Zealand tour; to Aquila Airways Ltd 12Apr55 as **G-AOBL**; CofA (A4957) issued 5May55; retained name; sold to Aerovias Aquila 27Oct58; ferried from Southampton to Lisbon 30Nov58; CofA lapsed 5Dec58; stored in Tagus estuary; registration cancelled 27Oct61 as 'sold in Portugal'; scrapped May 71

ZK-AMM c/n S.1557; to Tasman Empire Airways Ltd; UK CofA (10712) issued 20Sep49; left Southampton for Auckland 22Sep49, arrived 29Sep49; named *Ararangi*; inaugurated Wellington to Sydney service 30Oct50; engine caught fire while being cleaned at Mechanics Bay 28May54, leading to starboard wing being destroyed; not repaired; scrapped 12Jun56 for spares

ZK-AMN c/n S.1558; to Tasman Empire Airways Ltd; UK CofA (10717) issued 11Oct49; named *Awatere*; Belfast to Southampton Water 11Oct49;arrived Auckland 18Oct49; to Aquila Airways Ltd 16Jan55 as **G-ANYI**; CofA (A4837) issued 17Jan55; retained name; last flying-boat to operate commercially from UK, returning to Southampton 30Sep58; sold to Aerovias Aquila 27Oct58; ferried from Southampton to Lisbon 22Nov58; stored in Tagus estuary; CofA expired 17Apr59; registration cancelled 27Oct61 as 'sold in Portugal'; scrapped Aug71

ZK-AMO c/n S.1559; to Tasman Empire Airways Ltd; CofA (10718) issued 15Nov49; Belfast to Southampton Water 18Nov49; left Southampton for Auckland 21Nov49, arrived 29Nov49; named *Aranui*; damaged on alighting at Fiji 8May56 but repaired; flew final flying-boat service from Fiji to Tahiti 14Sep60; total time 14,500 hours; returned to Auckland 15Sep60, ending TEAL's flying-boat era; donated to Museum of Transport & Technology, Western Springs, Auckland, 8Dec60 but stored at Hobsonville until May66; fully restored and repainted for 50th anniversary of TEAL/Air New Zealand 90; extant

G-ANYI see ZK-AMN

G-AOBL see ZK-AML

Tasman Empire Airways Solent 4 ZK-AMO Aranui *in the airline's later colour scheme, taking off from Lauthala Bay, Suva, Fiji on a service to Samoa, Aitutaki and Tahiti in May 1958. This Solent flew TEAL's last flying-boat service in September 1960 and was subsequently preserved at MOTAT in Auckland.*
(Mike Hooks collection)

A page from the Log Book of Captain José M Carreras ATA (Air Transport Auxiliary) who had a Class 6 ATA Classification to fly flying boats. A most experienced pilot, he was a very charismatic Catalan from Barcelona who, throughout his ATA career, served with No.4 Ferry Pool based at Prestwick, Scotland. Many of his flying boat deliveries were of Sunderlands from the Blackburn Aircraft Ltd Clyde Factory at Dumbarton to locations throughout the UK. Dumbarton-built Sunderlands were collected from RAF Helensburgh (wartime home of the MAEE) which was often referred to simply as, Rhu. Places mentioned in his log appear throughout this book. The highlighted Sunderland entries refer to serials RN304, ML781, NJ171, RN305, NJ179 and JM681 all during July 1945. (ATA Museum Maidenhead Heritage Centre, Berkshire UK)

An interesting letter from H W C Alger, Manager of BOAC's No.4 Line, to Miss M E Luke regarding a flight she was about to make to New Zealand. Enclosed were detailed itineraries of the outward and return journeys. This was a special flight departing from Poole on 21st February 1946 in a BOAC Hythe, identified as "Hobart" (ie G-AGJL) commanded by Capt G G Stead, with delegates for a Civil Aviation Conference to be held in New Zealand. Miss Luke would appear to have been Secretary to Lord Winster, the then Minister of Civil Aviation. Also present on the flight were Lord Knollys, Chairman of BOAC, and Lady Knollys, seen above before the final leg from Sydney in a Sydney Sunday Morning Herald newspaper report dated 27th February 1946. An example of legendary BOAC customer service? (Bryan Savage)

COLOUR IMAGES 195

Sunderland MR.5 DP198 [W] of 205/209 Squadron, photographed when last operated in the Far East, was the longest-serving RAF example when it was struck off charge in June 1959 after almost fifteen years and sold to Chinese scrap dealers. (David Scott)

ML824 [NS:Z] the Sunderland Mk.V preserved at the RAF Museum, Hendon in its former 201 Squadron period markings displayed outside in 1964 before moving indoors in 1978. (Dave Welch)

Sunderland 5 ML796 [50.S-3] of Aéronautique navale was used as a nightclub at La Baule where it was photographed on 24th June 1976 prior to transfer to the UK for the IWM. (Trevor Davies)

ML796 is now restored and displayed in the crowded AirSpace hangar at the Imperial War Museum collection, Duxford as a Sunderland Mk.V wearing the code [NS:F] of 201 Squadron in which it initially served in 1945-46. later being transferred to the French Navy in 1951.

Seen at Mount Batten in 1945, this well-worn Sunderland Mk.III ML828 [RB:C] was based there with 10 (RAAF) Squadron. It was subsequently converted to Mk.V and was later civilianised as a Sandringham 5 and sold to the Ministry of Civil Aviation for BOAC as G-AHZG Pevensey. *In a final career move it became VH-EBZ with Qantas as* Pacific Explorer, *operating as such until retirement in 1955. (P H T Green collection)*

Sunderland MR.5 PP112 [O] had seen active service with several squadrons, commencing with 228 Squadron, then 201, 209 and finally 205/209 Squadron which it joined in February 1956. By mid-1958 the Sunderlands were being replaced by Shackletons and PP112 was redundant, being struck off charge on 27th June 1958 to linger on the scrapheap at Seletar where it was photographed on 7th December 1958. Note the scrapping bid number LOT 209 just below the serial.

(David Scott)

Colour Images 197

Sunderland MR.5 NZ4115 [Q], of 5 Squadron RNZAF, ex SZ584, on outside display and under restoration, at MOTAT, Auckland, New Zealand on 26th March 2012. (Ian W Shaw via Douglas A Rough)

Seen here in one of its several guises, Sunderland 5 N158J, the former ML814, belonged to Antilles Air Boats but failed to achieve US certification and following seven years of storage was sold to Edward Hulton to become G-BJHS. (P H T Green collection)

Sunderland 5 (mod) G-BJHS, owned by Edward Hulton, landed on the Thames on 6th August 1982 and moored at the Pool of London close to HMS Belfast for two months. Formerly ML814, NZ4108, VH-BRF, N158J and (VP-LVF), in 1993 it was cancelled in August 1993 on sale to Kermit Weeks' Fantasy of Flight Museum at Polk City, Florida where it still resides in 2012. (Author)

Sandringham 4 VH-BRC Beachcomber in the final colour scheme it carried when with Ansett Flying Boat Services. It is seen here at Rose Bay, Sydney in September 1974, shortly before it left for the Caribbean where it was operated by Antilles Air Boats as N158C and VP-LVE. (Stephen Piercey collection)

Sandringham 4 VP-LVE Southern Cross *of Antilles Air Boats moored in Studland Bay, Dorset, in August 1976 when it made a series of nine passenger flights. It returned to the south coast at the end of its flying career in 1983 and in 2012 resides in the Solent Sky Museum.*
(P H T Green collection)

Réseau Aérien Interinsulaire's Sandringham 7 F-OBIP resting off Papeete, Tahiti, between flights in the mid-1960s. One of only three of this Mark of Sandringham built, it was donated to the Musée de l'Air in Paris in 1978.
(Stephen Piercey collection)

BOAC's Solent 2 G-AHIY Southsea *on a photographic sortie in 1948. Later converted to Solent 3 with the addition of an extra top-deck cabin which increased the payload to 39 passengers and repositioning of the floats, G-AHIY was the last complete aircraft to be built at Short Brothers' Rochester works.* (Stephen Piercey collection)

Solent 3 N9946F Halcyon *was photographed in July 1982 after being lovingly restored over several years at Richmond, California, for the Grant brothers. Being uneconomical to operate, it was donated to the Western Aerospace Museum, Oakland CA, and moved there in August 1987 after which it was painted in RAF colours with genuine Seaford serial NJ203.* (Stephen Piercey collection)

COLOUR IMAGES

Seen moored at Las Palmas in the Azores is Solent 4 G-AOBL of Aquila Airways, formerly ZK-AML. The airline operated a weekly service as an extension of its route to Madeira in the mid-1950s.
(P H T Green collection)

Under restoration while on outside display at MOTAT, Auckland, New Zealand on 26th March 2012 is ZK-AMO a Solent 4 of TEAL The last of four Solent 4s, ZK-AMU flew the company's final flying-boat service from Fiji to Tahiti on 14th September 1960.
(Ian W Shaw via Douglas A Rough)

*First delivered to 210 Squadron in September 1938, Sunderland Mk.I
L5798 [DA:A] in typically weather-beated condition*

*Later, Sunderland Mk.I L5798 [KG:B] served with 204 Squadron in West
Africa between February 1942 and September 1943*

*Sunderland Mk.II W3985 [RB:U] of 10 (RAAF) Squadron showing an array
of ASV aerials and with depth charges rolled out on underwing racks*

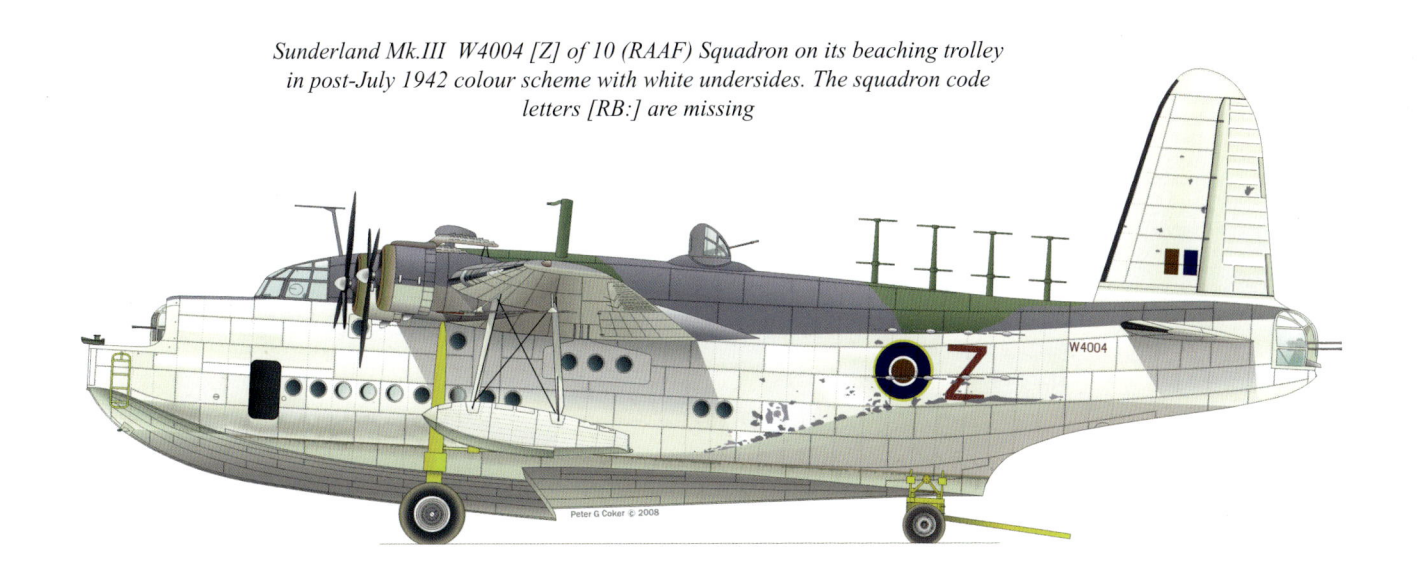

Colour Images

Sunderland Mk.III W4004 [Z] of 10 (RAAF) Squadron on its beaching trolley in post-July 1942 colour scheme with white undersides. The squadron code letters [RB:] are missing

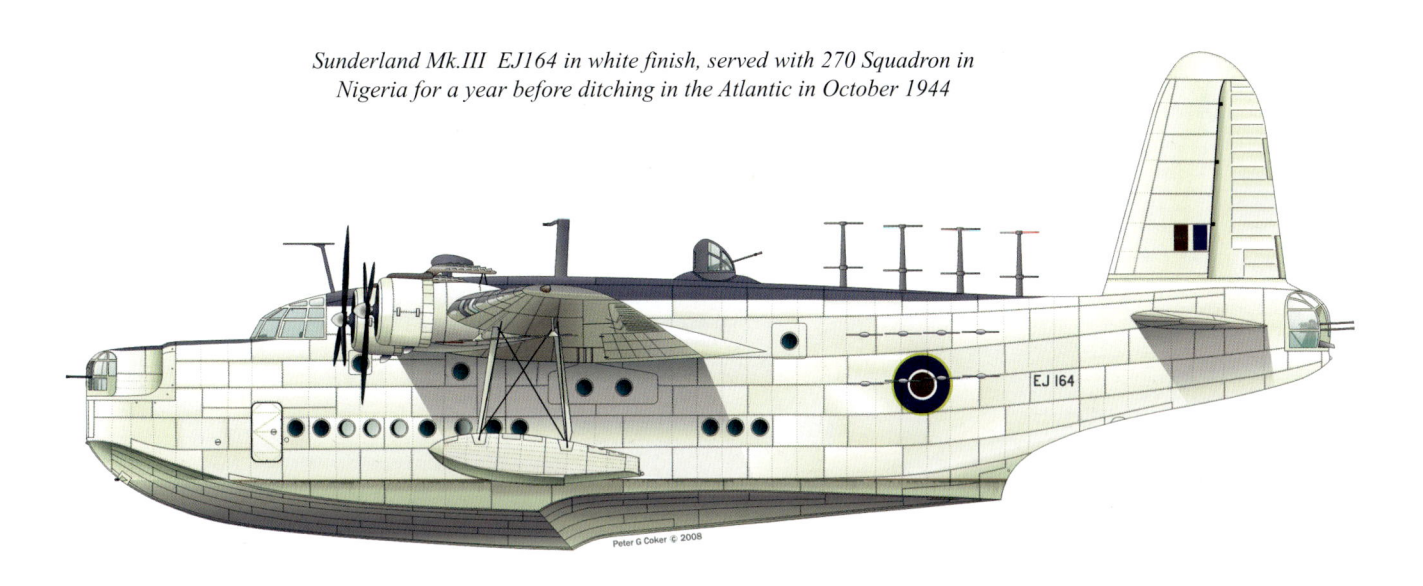

Sunderland Mk.III EJ164 in white finish, served with 270 Squadron in Nigeria for a year before ditching in the Atlantic in October 1944

Distinctive Sunderland Mk.III JM673 [P] was the personal aircraft of the 230 Squadron CO and was known as Black Peter

*Supplied direct to BOAC and carrying radio call-sign OQZT externally,
Sunderland Mk.III JM662 was later registered G-AGET*

*Sunderland 3 G-AGIA, ex ML728, wearing wartime civil marks with BOAC,
was transferred to Aquila Airways in 1948*

*ML788 was the Sandringham I prototype which joined BOAC after conversion
and used the Transport Command call-sign OQZF before becoming G-AGKX*

COLOUR IMAGES

Sunderland Mk.V ML796 [NS:F] of 201 Squadron was transferred to the Aéronautique navale in 1951 but later returned to the UK to be preserved in the Imperial War Museum at Duxford

RNZAF Sunderland MR.5 NZ4115 [Q] wearing the post-war paint scheme in which it is preserved at MOTAT, Auckland

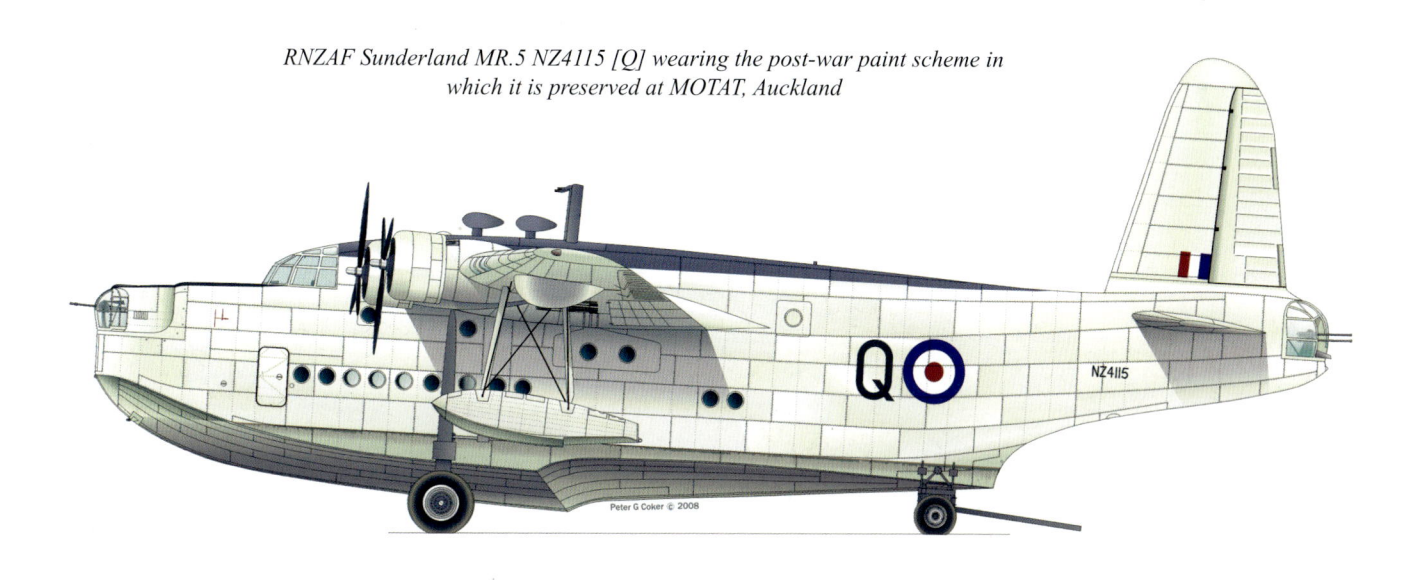

Sunderland 5 ML824 [27.F-14] of the Aéronautique navale which is now displayed at the RAF Museum, Hendon in its earlier 201 Squadron marks as [NS:Z]. Inset: The badge of Flotille 7.F later 27.F

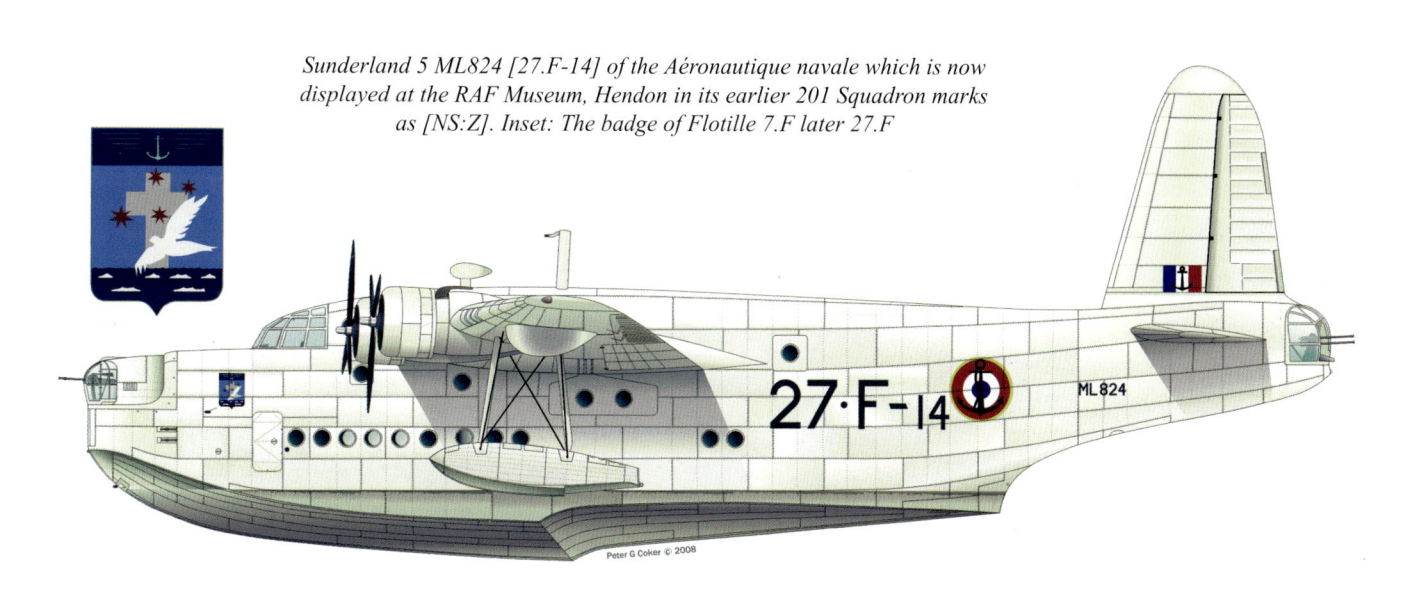

ZK-AME was a Sandringham 4 of TEAL, appropriately named New Zealand, *which later became VH-BRD with Barrier Reef Airways and Ansett*

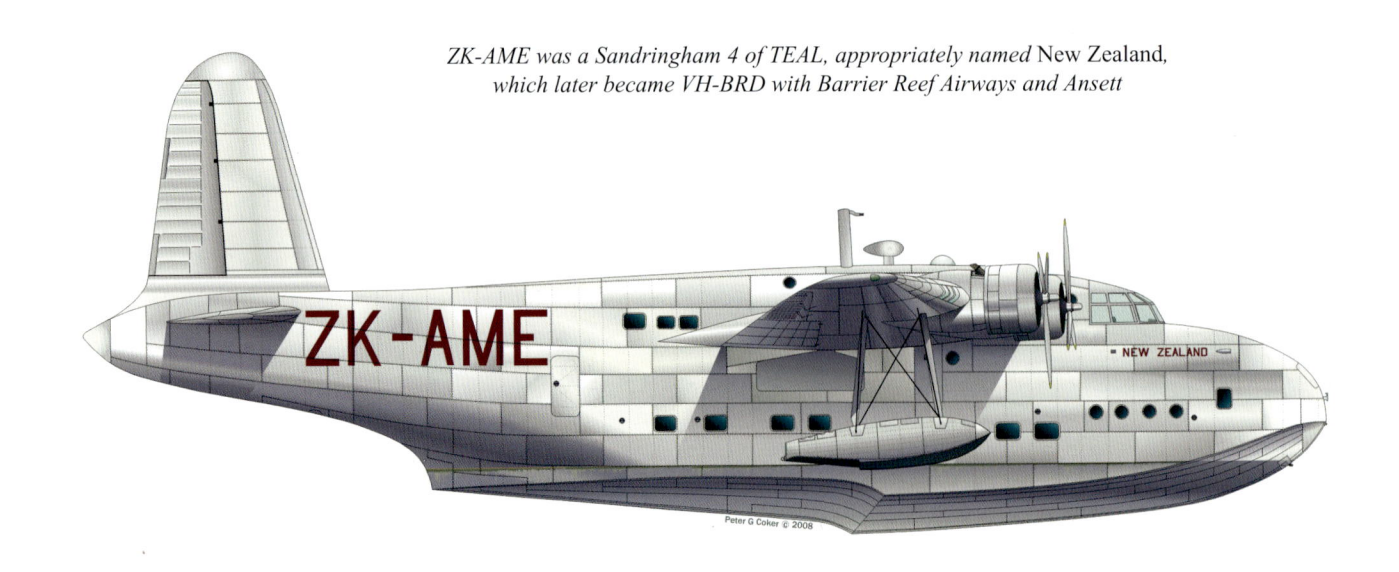

Sandringham 5 VH-EBV Pacific Warrior *of Qantas had previously been operated by BOAC as G-AHZB* Portmarnock

Sandringham 7 G-AKCO Saint George *of BOAC originated as Sunderland III / V JM719 and after two years service and three years storage subsequently became VH-APG and F-OBIP*

Colour Images

BOAC Sandringham 7 G-AKCR St Andrew *was sold to CAUSA in Uruguay in 1950, becoming CX-ANA*

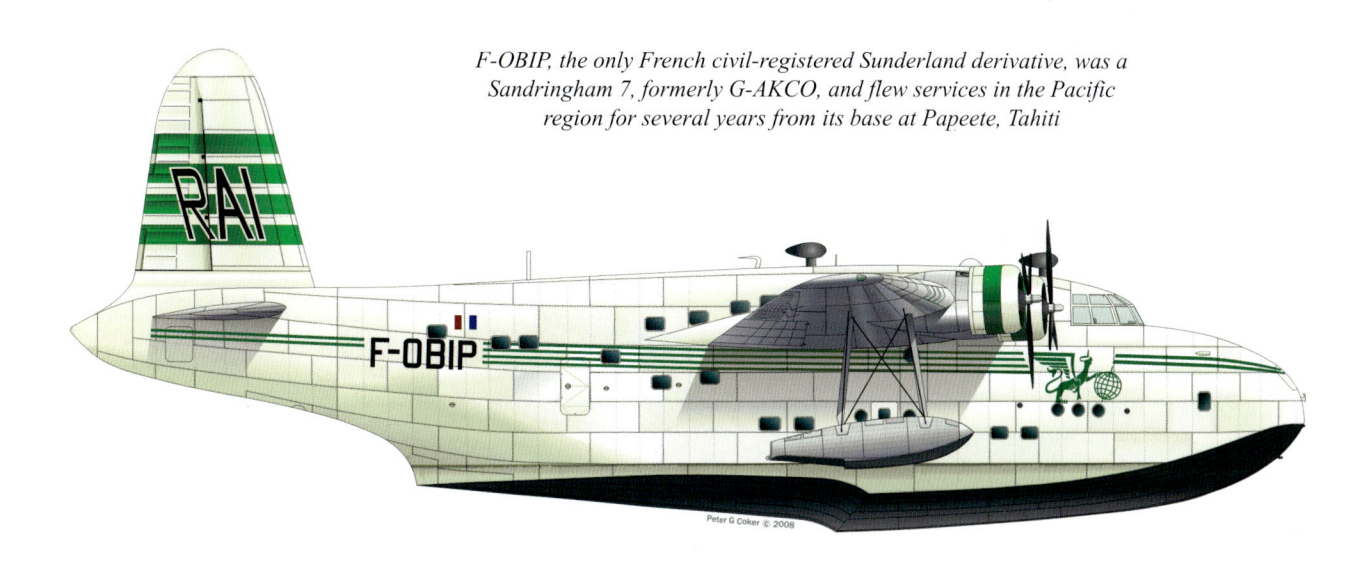

F-OBIP, the only French civil-registered Sunderland derivative, was a Sandringham 7, formerly G-AKCO, and flew services in the Pacific region for several years from its base at Papeete, Tahiti

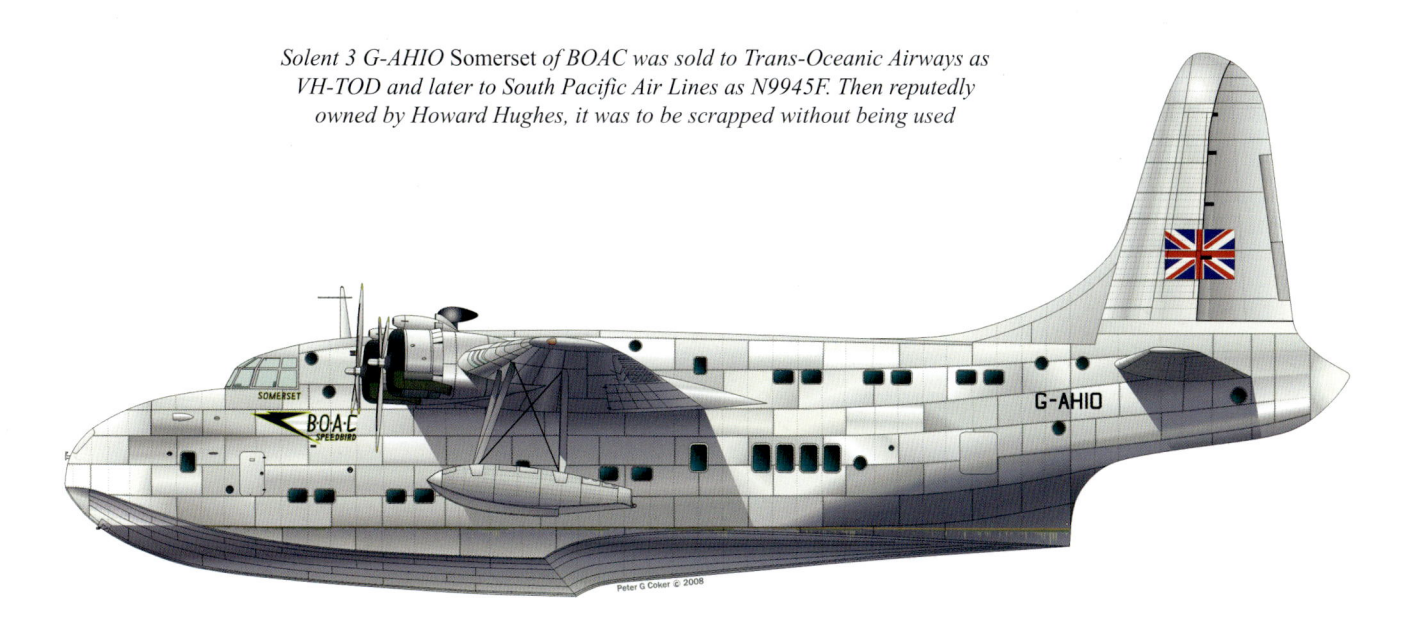

Solent 3 G-AHIO Somerset *of BOAC was sold to Trans-Oceanic Airways as VH-TOD and later to South Pacific Air Lines as N9945F. Then reputedly owned by Howard Hughes, it was to be scrapped without being used*

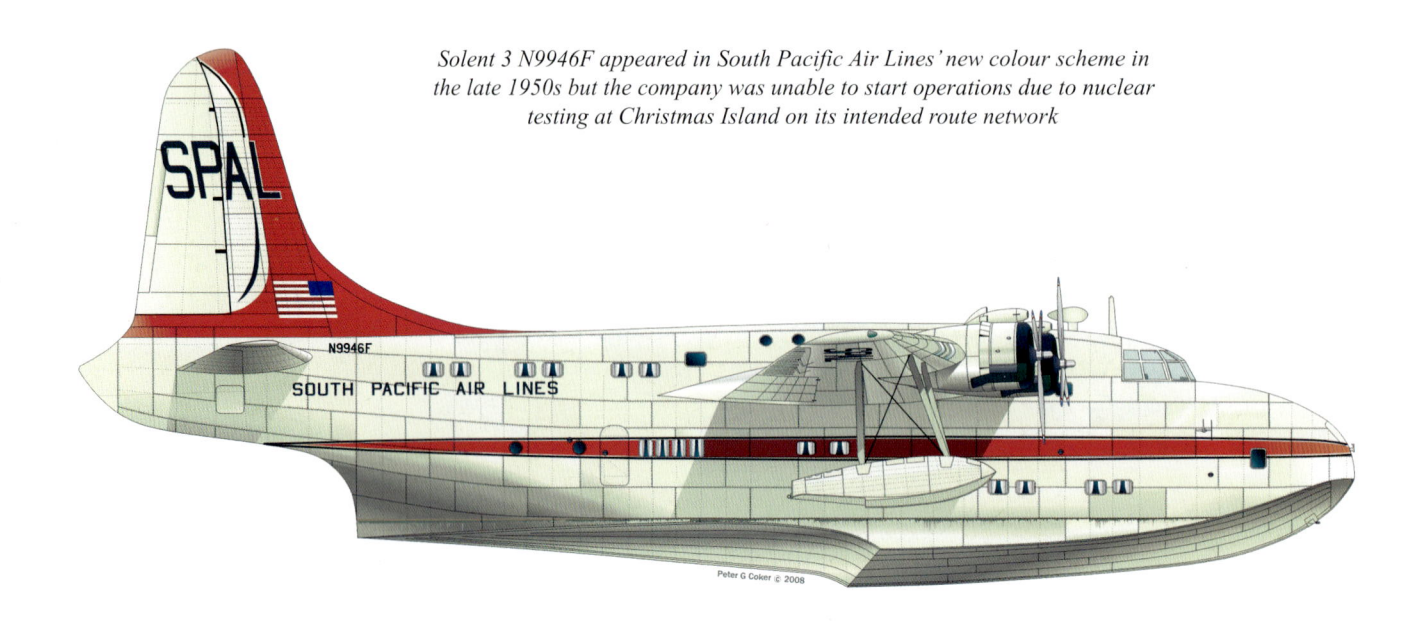

Solent 3 N9946F appeared in South Pacific Air Lines' new colour scheme in the late 1950s but the company was unable to start operations due to nuclear testing at Christmas Island on its intended route network

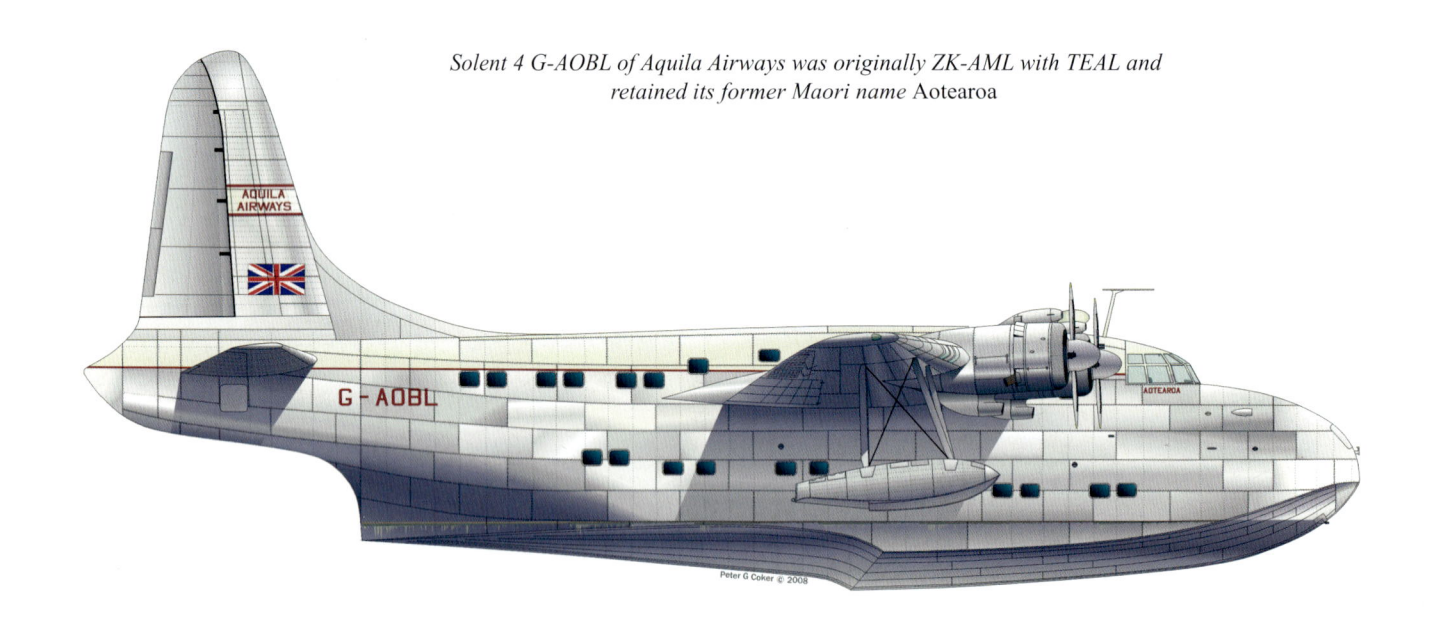

Solent 4 G-AOBL of Aquila Airways was originally ZK-AML with TEAL and retained its former Maori name Aotearoa

ZK-AMO, the last Solent 4, which was operated solely by TEAL and was donated to MOTAT, Auckland after it was withdrawn from use

Appendix 1
SUNDERLANDS BY MILITARY UNIT

This Appendix is intended to be a useful cross-reference to the information contained in Chapter 5, and lists by unit all RAF-serialled aircraft known to have been on charge to that unit. Maintenance Units and Ferry Training Units are not included.

The dates given are either dates of arrival on the unit or of allocation to that unit. It will be seen that some aircraft were with a unit for more than one period. Sometimes a unit was allocated more than one code at a time, for example 201 Squadron; if it is unclear which code was carried, only the individual aircraft letter is shown in the lists.

Serial	Code	Date

88 Squadron

Serial	Code	Date
DP199	C	19.5.48
EJ155	D	31.12.52
ML745	B	31.8.50
ML772	D	7.4.48
ML882	A	20.12.50
NJ176	F	15.5.48
NJ272	A	1.9.46
	F	30.11.50
NJ275	C	1.9.46
PP114	B	12.12.48
PP144	A	by 9.52
PP148	F	1.8.52
PP155	D	8.1.50
	D, F	15.10.51
RN271	G	1.9.46
RN277	D	23.4.50
RN282	C	by 30.6.50
RN293	F	9.11.53
RN297	H	by 28.2.47
RN302	C, F	17.1.55
RN303	C	by 30.9.51
SZ564		1.9.46
SZ566	F	1.9.46
	C	15.1.54
SZ570	D	1.9.46
SZ571	B	by 11.7.52
SZ572	C	12.7.54
SZ577	A	6.5.49
SZ578	A, B	4.10.53
SZ599	F	11.4.53
VB880	A	6.7.47
VB883	B	1.9.46
VB887	A	18.1.54
VB888	B	by 12.51
		1.1.53

95 Squadron

Serial	Code	Date
L5802	SE:F	
P9623	SE:E	16.1.41
T9040		16.4.41
	SE:E	16.9.41
	J	26.2.43
T9041	SE:D	16.1.41
T9046	SE:J	21.8.41
T9073	SE:G	3.5.41
T9074		3.1.42
T9078	SE:A	3.4.41
W6015	M	2.12.42
W6016		21.11.42
W6062	H	8.1.43
W6063	N	9.4.43
W6065		11.2.43
W6076	D	1.7.43
DP186	J	1.9.43
DP194	F	by 3.5.44
DV956	L	7.7.42
	H	by 21.4.45
DV957	K	17.7.42
DV963	B	21.8.42
DV964	C	20.8.42
DV973	J, P	15.10.42
DV974		28.9.42
DV975	H	15.10.42
DW105	T	22.10.43
DW107	R	14.12.43
EJ144	A	10.1.43
EJ163	K	15.5.44
EK581		7.9.43
EK587	F	27.10.43
JM670	M	4.3.43
JM671	Z	7.3.43
JM677	S	11.4.43
ML837	G	by 7.44
ML847	C	by 7.44

119 Squadron

Serial	Code	Date
W4024	J	12.9.42
W4028	O	20.9.42
W4030	C	16.9.42
W6001		29.11.42
W6002	R	29.9.42
DP176	D	1.10.42
DP179	V	30.1.43
DV958		29.9.42
DV962	Q	28.9.42
DV971	A	16.9.42
DV972		16.9.42
EJ133	F	11.11.42
EJ142	B	18.12.42
JM676	H	6.4.43

201 Squadron

Serial	Code	Date
L2168	ZM:Z	13.5.40
L5798	ZM:Z	22.4.41
L5800	ZM:S	by 1.5.40
L5802	ZM:U	3.6.40
L5805	ZM:Y	16.7.40
N6133	ZM:Y	6.8.40
N6138	ZM:V	12.4.40
N9021		19.10.40
N9024		
P9604	ZM:S	29.10.41
P9606	ZM:R	13.4.40
P9621	ZM:W	30.9.40
P9622	ZM:W	27.10.40
T9041		24.6.41
T9046		6.11.40
T9049	ZM:O	16.11.40
	ZM:S	7.8.41
T9074		1.4.41
T9076	ZM:O	23.4.41
T9077	ZM:Y	30.3.41
T9083	ZM:Q	31.10.42
T9084		10.12.41
T9087	ZM:O	23.3.42
W3977	ZM:Q	26.5.41
W3978	ZM:Z	27.7.41
W3980	ZM:P	16.10.41
W3981	ZM:R	1.8.41
	ZM:W	5.10.41
W3982		22.7.41
W3987		7.9.41
W3988	ZM:P	1.10.41
W3997	ZM:S	3.12.41
W3998		10.12.41
W4000	ZM:R	9.1.42
W4001	ZM:V	5.2.42
W4002	ZM:U	16.2.42
W4003	ZM:Y	7.2.42
W4018	ZM:Z	10.3.42
	ZM:O	1.4.43
W4028	ZM:P	14.6.42
W4036	ZM:W	7.7.42
W6005	ZM:P	21.8.42
W6010	ZM:V	16.10.42
W6014	ZM:S	9.11.42
W6051	ZM:T	3.8.42
W6055	ZM:R	18.9.42
	ZM:X	5.6.43
W6059	ZM:R	27.10.42
DD828	ZM:N	30.6.43
DD829	ZM:Z	22.12.42
DD835	ZM:R	6.5.43
DD848	ZM:N	20.4.43
DD855		30.5.43
DD857	ZM:V	24.6.43
DD858	ZM:Y	12.6.43
DD860	ZM:O	25.9.43
DP185	ZM:V	12.9.43
DP193		21.11.43
DP196	NS:K	16.9.44
DP198	A:B, 201:A	2.5.56
EJ137	ZM:T	8.5.43
EJ150	NS:W	30.3.44
EJ151		6.4.44
EK579	ZM:U	29.8.43
EK590	ZM:Y	30.9.43
EK594	W	8.12.43
EK595		4.4.44
JM666	ZM:Q	23.5.43
ML739	NS:N, NS:X	6.4.44
ML742	NS:Q	30.3.44
ML743	NS:A	16.9.44
ML749	O	26.3.44
ML759	T	17.4.44
ML760	S	24.4.44
ML764	NS:V	22.4.44
ML768	NS:B	23.5.44
ML769	NS:C	23.5.44
ML772	NS:S	17.6.44
ML778	NS:Z	10.5.45
ML782	NS:X	by 30.7.44
ML783		23.7.44
	H	20.3.45
ML784		15.3.45
ML796	F	by 30.9.45
ML812		27.4.45
ML813	NS:U	22.4.44
ML814	NS:R	24.4.44
ML817	NS:O	12.2.45
ML821	NS:C	6.45

ML824	NS:Z, NS:T	11.2.45	W4024	TQ:N	31.5.42	JM667	M, Q	11.7.53
ML875	NS:M	10.4.44	W4028	TQ:B	7.6.42	ML745	M	1.1.53
ML876	NS:O	17.4.44	W4029	A, M	4.6.42	NJ193	P	24.6.53
ML881	NS:P	18.5.44	W4030		16.6.42	NJ268	B	29.7.48
ML882	NS:Y	18.5.44	W4037		3.7.42	NJ270	K	
NJ187	201:W		W6002	AX:R	17.7.42	NJ271		
NJ192	L	15.5.45	W6003	S	8.7.42	NJ272	N	15.3.54
NJ193	X	30.10.45	DV958	AX:T	12.7.42	NJ274	B	
NJ194	NS:F	9.10.44	DV962	TQ:Q	14.8.42	PP106		28.4.46
NJ264	R	by 31.10.45				PP107		31.5.50
NJ267	P	19.10.45	**204 Squadron**			PP123	M	
	A:B	4.6.53				PP124	O	
NJ268	Z	1.11.45	L2158	KG:M	30.5.41	PP128	V	
PP112	G, X	16.6.45	L2161		19.8.40	PP129	L, Q	
PP113	W, Z	20.10.45	L5798	Z	31.7.41	PP137	O	27.5.53
PP114	Q	by 31.10.45	L5799	KG:D	19.6.39	PP144	P	25.12.50
PP115	NS:C, A:C	27.1.49	L5800	KG:L	1.8.41	PP148	L	31.10.50
PP117	A:D	15.6.45		KG:J	22.1.42	PP154	X, N	30.4.51
	A:W	4.1.51	L5802	RF:F, KG:F,	19.6.39	RN268	R	
	201:W	26.4.54		KG:D		RN269	P	
PP118	J	17.6.45	L5803		30.1.42		M	27.9.50
PP119	Y, V	by 31.10.45	N9021	KG:C, KG:G	19.8.39	RN273		14.12.53
PP120	Y	1.11.45	N9022		19.6.39	RN278	N	29.4.54
PP121	B	15.6.45	N9023		16.7.40	RN280		
PP122	O	by 31.10.45	N9024	KG:A	10.2.40	RN288	S	
	A:D, A:E	30.10.52		KG:H	11.11.40	RN289	P	
PP144	NS:O	16.6.45	N9028	KG:A	10.6.39	RN290	C	
PP162	S	20.12.45	N9044	KG:C	11.7.39	RN293	B	
PP163	N, D	16.6.45	N9045	KG:J	24.7.39	RN294	R, P	
PP164	A:L	16.6.45	N9046	KG:F	2.8.39	RN300		28.7.49
RN266	NS:M, M	16.12.45	N9047	KG:B		RN301	D	
RN269	K	29.7.48	P9620	KG:K	4.4.40	RN302	B	
RN270	K	28.8.45	T9040		21.8.40	RN306	J, P	
RN271	A:E	16.3.54	T9041	KG:V; KG:A	11.9.41	SZ560	Q	
RN272	G	19.8.46	T9045	KG:K	30.9.40	SZ566	F	
RN273	NS:W, L	3.9.47	T9048		6.11.40		Z	3.8.50
	A:A	24.6.49	T9049		14.11.40	SZ569	Z	31.3.49
RN277	NS:S, NS:O,	15.6.45	T9070	KG:E	9.12.40	SZ572		9.10.54
	A:F		T9072	KG:F	4.1.41	SZ578	L	
	A:D	26.10.45	T9074	KG:L	2.6.41		B	9.10.54
RN278	M	17.6.45	W3978		9.6.41			
RN282	U	20.10.45	W3981		4.7.41	**209 Squadron**		
RN284	NS:C	15.6.45	W6012	KG:E	22.10.42			
	A:C, A:G	15.6.51	W6015		21.11.42	DP198	V, W	5.8.50
	A:F, 201:F	20.6.55	W6063		10.1.43	EJ155		9.10.54
RN285	NS:H	15.6.45	W6079	KG:C	10.5.43	JM667	M	29.5.53
RN288	A:C	18.9.53	DD833	KG:M	24.1.43	ML881	X	6.8.48
RN299	A:D	30.11.55	DD834		30.3.43	ML882	X	1.1.53
RN300	T	20.10.45	DP182	KG:J		NJ177		29.4.53
RN304	NS:L, NS:C	11.11.48	DP188	KG:L, KG:C	20.8.43		V	5.6.53
	Q	31.7.50	DV959	KG:F	17.7.42	NJ191	W	1.12.53
SZ565		10.3.50	DV965	A	17.8.42	NJ254	V	6.8.48
SZ567	NS:B, A:B	6.8.47	DV966	KG:D	16.9.42	NJ260	V	
SZ571	C, 201:D	24.6.48	DV974		21.9.42	NJ261	T	
SZ574	NS:K	11.7.47		KG:G	14.10.42	NJ265	WQ:M	
SZ575	201:E	3.2.55	DV991	KG:G; KG:Q	1.11.43	NJ267	W, WQ:S	
SZ576	A:A, 201:A	31.3.53	DW104	KG:K	12.11.43	NJ272	Z	29.4.48
SZ578	C	6.8.47	EJ145	KG:P	4.3.43	NJ273		
VB881	F, NS:A	2.8.45	EK580	KG:B	7.9.43	NJ276	U	11.11.47
VB889	NS:D	11.6.47	EK582	KG:L	4.12.43	PP103	U	
	A:D, Q	17.6.49	EK587	KG:J	9.11.43	PP105	Y	
			EK593	KG:P	12.6.44	PP106	X	
202 Squadron			JM669	KG:A	7.3.43	PP107	W	
			JM672	KG:E	12.4.43	PP108	Z	
L5805		7.5.42	JM674	KG:X	11.4.43	PP112	Q	3.5.51
N9050		10.2.42	JM680	KG:J	25.4.43	PP130	A, N	
T9040		7.5.42	JM682	KG:H	10.5.43	PP131	F, WQ:J	
T9084		22.12.41	JM687		11.6.43	PP132		
W3989		20.12.41	JM710	KG:L	8.8.43	PP148	B	
		4.1.42	ML854	KG:M	by 4.6.44	PP150	S	
W3990		20.12.41	ML872	KG:B	?	PP151	R	
		4.1.42				PP152		
W3994		17.6.42	**205 Squadron**			PP154		1.1.53
W3998		17.12.41				PP159	Q	
W4004		14.5.42	DP198	O	1.1.53	PP164	Z	
W4019		29.3.42	EJ141		1.3.45	RN264	R	

Sunderlands by Military Unit

RN265	WQ:S	
RN266	Q	
RN277	X	
RN282		12.3.53
RN288		29.12.47
RN293	F, V	22.8.53
RN298	Y, WQ:R	5.1.48
RN300	X	30.4.54
SZ559	S	
SZ560	D, W, V	
SZ561	M, S, W	31.8.46
SZ564	A	
SZ565	S	
SZ566	F, Z	1.1.53
SZ571	Y, W	30.6.50
SZ573	Y	
SZ577	Y	14.7.54
SZ578	Z	30.9.50
SZ599		10.2.53
VB882	W	26.5.49
VB884	WQ:X	16.1.46
VB888	Z	15.5.53

205/209 Squadron

DP198	W	10.7.57
EJ155	U	1.1.55
ML745	V	21.2.57
ML797	P	9.3.57
NJ191	W	1.1.55
NJ193		1.1.55
NJ272	N	10.55
PP112	O	27.2.56
PP127	L, W	1.4.57
PP137	O	1.1.55
RN270	K	26.10.56
RN273	L	21.4.55
RN277	D	8.51
RN278	N	1.1.55
RN282	N	6.10.56
RN293		1.1.55
RN300		1.1.55
RN303	R	23.8.57
SZ572	M	1.1.55
SZ577	S	1.1.55

210 Squadron

L2162	DA:C	21.6.38
L2163	DA:G, C	24.6.38
L2165		16.7.38
L2167	DA:H	12.8.38
L2168		27.8.38
L5798	DA:A	8.9.38
L5799		19.9.38
L5800		29.9.38
L5802		24.10.38
L5803		3.11.38
L5806		13.7.39
L5807		17.8.39
N6135		13.7.39
N9022		29.3.39
	DA:B	26.9.39
N9024		21.4.39
N9025		18.7.39
N9026	DA:D	17.5.39
N9027	DA:J	19.6.39
N9047		18.8.39
N9048		5.9.39
N9049		9.8.39
N9050		3.10.39
P9600		27.10.39
P9623	DA:E	
P9629	DA:H	19.4.40
T9041		9.9.40
T9043		20.8.40

T9044		9.9.40
T9073		19.1.41
T9075		15.2.41
T9076		7.3.41

228 Squadron

L2160	DQ:X, DG:T	1.10.40
L2161	DQ:P	by 10.40
L2163		18.12.41
L2164	DQ:Z, DQ:M	by 10.40
L2168		28.1.42
L5803	DQ:T	6.11.40
L5805		24.11.38
L5806		10.12.38
	DQ:Q, BH:Q	22.8.39
L5807		14.1.39
	DQ:R	22.8.39
	DQ:F	18.10.40
N6133		12.2.39
N6135	TO:U, BH:U	17.2.39
N6138		22.2.39
N9020	TO:W, DQ:W	9.3.39
N9023		6.4.39
N9025		6.5.39
	DQ:Y	10.8.39
N9027		30.5.39
P9600	DQ:T	19.11.41
P9621		7.6.40
P9622		7.6.40
T9046		6.12.40
T9048	DQ:N, DQ:X	9.11.40
T9077		26.1.42
T9084	DQ:N	16.2.42
T9085		10.2.42
T9086		3.2.42
	DQ:S	13.8.42
T9088	DQ:R	9.3.42
T9089	DQ:O	26.3.42
T9109		28.9.43
T9112	DQ:N	13.5.42
W3986		19.2.42
W3989	DQ:L	3.11.41
W3990		7.11.41
W3991	DQ:P	11.11.41
W3992		11.11.41
W3995	DQ:P	28.11.41
W3996	DQ:R	28.11.41
W4017	DQ:T	19.3.42
W4026	DQ:M	13.5.42
W4032	DQ:O	31.5.42
W6004	DQ:U	6.8.42
DD830		30.12.42
DD834	S	15.4.43
DD835		27.5.44
DD836		25.2.43
DD837	DQ:V	8.3.43
DD838	DQ:X	3.2.43
DD847		29.3.43
DD864	K	1.8.43
DV958		19.10.43
DV967	U	2.4.43
DV970	DQ:E	17.9.42
DV977	DQ:V	29.10.42
DV978		5.5.43
DV980	DQ:G	5.5.43
DV988		20.6.43
DW110		20.11.43
EJ139		
EJ151		20.4.44
EK572	V	12.8.43
EK575		1.3.44
JM678	V	21.5.43
JM679	DQ:R	1.5.43
JM685		27.11.43
JM708	N	10.7.43

JM709		23.7.43
JM720	P	3.12.43
ML745	Z	27.4.44
ML749	O	22.4.44
ML762		30.4.44
ML763	UE:J, UE:R	4.5.44
ML766	R	22.5.44
ML767		24.4.44
ML769		16.9.44
ML770	UE:P, 1:P	22.5.44
ML774		15.6.44
ML782	UE:X	16.9.44
ML812	K	15.8.44
ML815	W	26.4.44
ML877	G	26.4.44
ML878		27.4.44
ML879	UE:M	10.5.44
ML880	U	10.5.44
NJ171	UE:A	20.6.44
NJ191	E	5.10.44
NJ192	Y	13.10.44
PP112	UE:U	11.2.45
PP117	UE:P	24.2.45
PP118	UE:P	28.2.45
PP120		14.3.45
PP121	UE:W	21.3.45
PP136		9.10.44
PP144	A	30.4.45
PP163		30.5.45
PP164		9.2.45
RN277		9.2.45
RN278		22.2.45
RN283	DQ:F	28.3.45
RN285		28.3.45

230 Squadron

L2159	FV:W, NM:W	22.6.38
L2160	NM:X	4.7.38
L2161	NM:Y	26.7.38
	NM:P	24.8.40
L2164	FV:Z, NM:Z	16.8.38
	NM:R	
L2166		5.9.38
	NM:U	17.8.40
L5801		15.11.38
L5803	NM:T	5.12.38
L5804	NM:S	22.12.38
L5806	DX:Q	.41
N9029	NM:V	25.7.39
T9050	NM:Y	9.12.40
T9071	NM:M	9.41
T9083		7.7.43
W3987	NM:X	30.9.41
W4021	NM:W	15.4.42
W4022	NM:Z	16.4.42
W4023	NM:U	25.4.42
W6078	DX:N	19.8.43
DD866	NM:T	18.12.44
DP180	NM:O	13.5.43
DP189	NM:L	16.11.43
DP200	B:Z, 230:Z	11.2.54
DW112		
EJ131	NM:T	11.12.42
EJ132	NM:X	31.12.42
EJ135	N	29.11.42
EJ136	NM:Y	4.12.42
EJ140	NM:V	10.12.42
EJ141	NM:R	10.12.42
EJ143	NM:S	10.2.43
EJ153	B:R, 230:R	7.1.55
EK595	NM:Q	by 13.12.44
JM659	NM:Q	24.3.43
JM673	NM:P	1.5.43
JM711	NM:M	by 7.10.43
	Z	4.46

Serial	Code	Date
JM718	B:Y, 230:Y	10.3.50
ML763	B:R	13.11.52
ML797	NM:Q	3.2.45
ML799	W	4.6.45
ML800	X	
ML817	B:X, 230:X	
ML846	W	13.12.44
ML861	NM:K	19.7.44
ML865	NM:J	
ML868	NM:H	
NJ264	B:R	19.7.46
NJ277		
PP115	4X:X	12.8.48
PP117	P	21.7.46
	4X:K, 4X:W,	13.6.49
	B:W	
PP118	Z	30.9.48
PP122	4X:O, O	19.7.46
PP145	NM:O	28.1.45
PP146	U, V	.45
PP147	V	.45
PP148	NM:P	28.1.45
PP149	R	.45
PP152		5.45
PP154	Y	.45
PP155	Z	.45
PP157	S	.45
PP158	T	.45
PP161		30.10.47
PP164	4X:X, X	19.7.46
RN269	T	23.4.46
RN270	4X:O, 4X:V	11.11.48
	B:O	9.6.49
	4X:O	15.12.51
RN278	S	17.7.46
RN290	B:Z	30.6.51
RN299	4X;P, P	25.4.46
	B:P	16.6.49
RN303	W	.45
	T	1.10.56
RN304	4X:L	1.11.45
	B:V	22.11.50
SZ560	230:R	9.11.56
SZ561		5.12.45
SZ563		
SZ567	N, B:P	.45
	230:P	30.6.54
SZ572	4X:P, P	20.6.47
SZ573	W	24.6.48
SZ575		24.11.54
SZ577	4X:Z, Z	17.9.47
SZ581	4X:Y, Y	11.7.47
	B:Y	28.5.52
SZ582	4X:O, O	9.7.47
VB882	X	30.4.46
VB887	4X:X, X	9.6.47

230/240 Squadron

Serial	Code	Date
RN270		20.7.50
VB887		30.6.50

240 Squadron

Serial	Code	Date
NJ272	B, N	8.45
NJ273	D	9.45
NJ275	N	
NJ276	M	8.45
PP126	K	1.7.45
PP130	A	8.45
PP131	J	8.45
RN291	G	8.45
RN292	C	8.45
RN297	L	8.45
RN298	F	8.45

246 Squadron

Serial	Code	Date
W6056	A	16.9.42
W6057	B	16.9.42
W6058	O	28.10.42
W6060	D	16.10.42
W6066	F	4.3.43
DD845		30.3.43
DD846		23.4.43
DV978	E	18.2.43
DV979	F	27.10.42
DV980	G	27.10.42
EJ137	K	24.11.42
EJ139	L	3.1.43

270 Squadron

Serial	Code	Date
DP190	G	11.1.44
DW108		5.12.43
	Y	14.2.44
DW109	Q	5.1.43
DW111		8.12.43
EJ164	E	16.2.44
EK584	D	4.2.44
EK585	A, V	28.12.43
EK588		5.12.43
EK589	V	9.1.44
EK592		5.12.43
ML844	X, H	4.3.44
ML849	K	4.44
ML853	B	6.6.44
ML857		
ML867	N	
ML874	L	

330 Squadron

Serial	Code	Date
T9083		
T9112		
W6030	WH:M	19.6.43
W6052	WH:D	8.5.43
W6053	WH:E	6.5.43
W6059	WH:P	29.4.43
W6061	WH:X	9.5.43
W6064	WH:R	9.2.43
W6067	WH:I	16.3.43
	WH:T	20.10.43
W6068		20.4.43
W6075	WH:Z	2.4.43
DD835	WH:H, WH:P	11.2.43
DD843	WH:S	14.3.43
DD844	WH:Y	9.3.43
DD851	WH:Z	17.5.43
DD856	WH:G	6.6.43
DP178	WH:L	7.6.44
DP181	WH:U	16.3.43
DP183	WH:W	6.6.43
DP184	WH:F	6.6.43
DV992	WH:H	23.9.43
EJ137		1.5.43
EJ138	WH:Y	21.4.45
EJ155	WH:O	11.7.44
JM666	WH:Q	1.3.43
JM667	WH:V	1.3.43
ML758	WH:O	2.5.43
ML780	WH:A	6.7.44
ML814	WH:A	18.4.45
ML817	WH:X	17.4.45
ML818	WH:X	21.7.44
ML819	WH:V	28.7.44
ML824	WH:Z, WH:T	17.4.45
ML827	WH:G	18.4.45
ML878	WH:R	14.5.45
NJ170		20.5.45
NJ172	WH:F	10.5.45
NJ177	WH:F	6.7.44
NJ178	WH:H, WH:L	21.7.44
NJ179	WH:Y	21.7.44
NJ180	WH:R	21.7.44
NJ181	WH:Z	27.7.44
NJ188	WH:G	15.10.44
NJ190		14.4.45
PP140	WH:V	19.12.44
RN267		9.8.45

343 Squadron

Serial	Code	Date
DP187	G	29.11.43
DV956		22.3.44
DV965		29.11.43
DV985		29.11.43
DV987	C	29.11.43
EJ135		4.7.44
EJ163		
EJ168		29.3.44
EJ169		
EK587		
JM670		17.7.44
JM674		7.43
JM688		29.11.43
JM689		29.11.43
JM704		29.11.43
JM706		29.11.43
ML835		
ML841		
ML851		
ML854		
ML870		
ML871	L	
ML874		

422 Squadron

Serial	Code	Date
W6026	DG:A	17.11.42
	2:A, 2:C	23.10.43
W6027	DG:B	19.11.42
	2:N	29.11.43
W6028	DG:C	1.11.42
	2:C	26.6.43
W6029	DG:D, 2:D	30.11.42
W6030	2:F	2.12.42
W6031	2:G	12.12.42
W6032	2:H	9.12.42
W6033	2:J	27.12.42
W6066	2:F	30.4.43
DD831	2:K	2.1.43
DD835		12.3.45
DD845	2:B	30.4.43
DD846	2:O	30.4.43
DD850	2:M	18.5.43
DD854	2:P	30.5.43
DD855	2:Y	12.2.44
DD861	2:P	26.6.43
DP178	2:L	21.12.42
DV970	2:T	15.5.44
DV988	2:D	15.5.44
DV990	2:R	8.9.43
DV994	2:T	5.10.43
EJ151	DG:H, H	11.11.44
EK576	2:Q	30.8.43
EK590		21.9.43
EK591	2:U	3.10.43
EK594	2:W	6.4.44
EK595		6.4.44
JM679	2:E	20.5.44
JM712	2:S	3.9.43
ML741		2.6.45
ML744	2:B	11.3.45
ML750	J	6.45
ML759	M, G	15.12.44
ML769	S	12.3.45
ML773	2:R	16.6.44

Sunderlands by Military Unit

ML777	2:M, 2:N	18.6.44
ML778	2:S	23.6.44
ML781	Q	3.7.44
ML814	2:N	1.12.44
ML816	2:X	30.6.44
ML821	T	21.7.44
ML836	S	24.11.43
ML879	P	13.2.45
ML883	V	9.6.44
ML884	2:Z	7.6.44
NJ170	Y	17.6.44
NJ172	2:O	18.6.44
NJ173	2:W	21.6.44
NJ174	2:U	29.6.44
NJ175	2:T	29.6.44
NJ176	2:P	23.6.44
NJ182	2:N	27.7.44
NJ189	2:V	3.10.44

423 Squadron

W6000	AB:A, 3:A	18.7.42
W6001	B	17.7.42
W6006	AB:F	26.8.42
	3:F	17.4.43
W6007	AB:G	8.9.42
W6008	AB:H	3.9.42
	3:H	29.6.43
W6009	AB:J	14.10.42
	3:J	6.4.43
W6011	3:F	3.10.42
W6013	3:B	12.11.42
W6052	AB:D	22.7.42
W6053	AB:E	7.8.42
W6061	3:K	?
W6064		26.1.43
W6068	3:N	9.5.43
DD828	3:B	16.12.42
DD838	3:X	12.5.44
DD843	3:E	10.5.43
DD849	3:M	28.4.43
DD853	3:K	30.5.43
DD859	3:G	14.6.43
DD860	3:J	19.6.43
DD862	AB:A	5.7.43
DD863	3:J	30.7.43
DD867	3:G	20.8.43
DP181	3:D	3.5.43
DP191	3:L	24.10.43
DP193		1.12.43
DP198	J	3.9.44
DP200		9.6.45
DV978	3:N, 3:P	15.5.44
DV980	A	11.5.44
DW111	3:S	13.5.44
DW112		8.12.43
EJ156		25.7.44
EJ157	YI:K	14.8.44
EJ158	YI:M	9.9.44
EK575		12.5.44
EK581	3:D	19.11.43
EK583	3:J	15.11.43
JM666		10.5.44
ML742	YI:P	by 1.45
ML746	O	18.12.44
ML777	F	24.12.44
ML783	3:H	25.7.44
ML784	L	30.7.44
ML817	X	20.2.45
ML823		27.7.44
ML825	YI:D, 3:D	14.8.44
ML883	F	8.8.44
NJ182	N, 3:G	by 12.44
NJ184	C	9.8.44
NJ185	E	14.8.44
NJ186	A	5.8.44
NJ187	B	9.8.44

461 Squadron

L5802		26.7.42
T9085	UT:A	24.4.42
T9086		2.5.42
T9088		by 2.5.42
T9090	UT:B	22.4.42
T9109	UT:D	24.4.42
T9111	UT:C	30.5.42
T9113	UT:F, K	12.7.42
T9114	UT:E	7.7.42
T9115	UT:G, UT:K	1.8.42
W4003		31.3.43
W6014		25.4.44
W6050	UT:L	14.8.42
W6077	UT:U	5.5.43
DD853	Y	6.3.45
DD866	B	14.8.43
DP196	K	16.2.44
DP199	UT:U	27.3.44
DP200	2:X	28.3.44
DV960	UT:H	26.7.42
DV961	A, I	18.7.42
DV962		26.4.43
DV968	2:M	24.9.42
	UT:M	27.4.43
DV985		9.5.43
DV986		19.5.43
DV989	F	3.8.43
EJ132		27.10.42
EJ133	T	26.4.43
EJ134	N	31.12.42
EJ138	J	6.11.43
EJ142	UT:S	26.4.43
EJ153	S	12.6.44
EJ154	T	31.7.44
EK575	2:C	20.8.43
EK577	D	21.8.43
EK590	D	14.5.44
JM675	UT:O	23.8.43
JM676	P	26.4.43
JM678	G, 2:G	28.9.43
JM683	W	6.6.43
JM685	X	6.6.43
JM686	Y	1.6.43
JM707	Z	13.6.43
ML735	A	27.3.44
ML739	W	11.11.44
ML740	M	19.2.44
ML741	2:P, X	17.3.44
ML743	O	24.3.44
ML744	UT:B	6.4.44
ML746	R	17.3.44
ML747	UT:N, 2:N	24.2.44
ML748	C	6.4.44
ML757	2:Z	6.4.44
ML758	E	6.4.44
ML771	UT:G	28.5.44
ML774	F	11.11.44
ML778	R	24.12.44
ML781	Q	21.1.45
ML827	C	5.10.44
ML831	UT:H	30.11.44
ML879	Y	10.11.44
NJ193	F	14.3.45
NJ264	G	14.3.45
NJ267		19.3.45
NJ268	M	3.4.45
PP113		11.2.45
PP115		3.3.45
PP116	K	16.2.45
PP119	E	10.3.45
PP122		5.4.45
PP162		19.2.45

RN279		24.2.45
RN280		24.2.45
RN282	UT:N	21.3.45

490 Squadron

EJ135	N	7.44
EJ165	R	by 11.6.44
EJ169	Y	by 2.6.44
JM717	O	15.3.45
ML810	W	25.5.44
ML835	Z	12.5.44
ML850	S, B	by 17.5.44
ML852	P	by 12.6.44
ML855	R	
ML857		17.1.45
ML859	T	
ML862	Q	6.44
ML863	X	27.6.44
ML864		25.7.44
ML869	V, N	26.6.44
ML870	V	8.44

1430 Flight

NJ272		
NJ275		
RN271		
SZ564	A	23.8.46
SZ566		
SZ570		
VB883		

ASWDU

ML763	P9:Q, Q	6.9.49
ML785		12.1.45
		(or 4.2.45?)
NJ182		26.10.45
PP122	P9:S	15.9.49

CCFIS/CCIS

ML781		22.2.46
NJ268		4.3.46

4 (C) OTU

L2168		22.4.42
L5800	TA:U	22.4.43
L5802	TA:J	16.11.42
N6138		19.12.41
N9024	HH	4.7.43
N9044	CC	3.7.43
N9050	TA:C	16.4.43
P9600		2.3.42
P9604	TA:A	19.12.41
P9605		14.3.42
P9606	TA:E	29.12.41
T9040		23.12.43
T9042		6.3.44
T9049	TA:A	3.12.41
T9076		3.12.41
	TA:D	10.1.43
T9077		19.2.42
T9078	TA:B	18.7.43
T9083		19.5.44
T9088		25.8.43
T9115		10.7.43
W3980	TA:S	5.6.42
W3989		5.9.43
W3990	TA:V	2.10.42
W3992	TA:R	7.42
W3997	TA:R	31.12.42
W4027	TA:M	6.6.42
W4028	AI	28.6.43

W4031	TA:N	8.6.42	ML801		18.7.45	RN208	TA:J	
W4033	TA:O	8.6.42	ML812		8.7.45	RN266	D:K	
W4034		8.6.42	ML816		16.6.45	RN284	D:G	
W4035	TA:Q	8.6.42	ML820		6.3.45	RN302	TA:H	
W4037		28.7.43	ML821		15.7.45	RN304	D:M	
W6001		5.12.42	ML826		7.3.45	SZ568	TA:C	
W6002		30.4.43	ML841		3.1.44	SZ575	D:H	30.4.51
W6005		18.5.44	ML866		20.3.45	SZ576	TA:H	13.5.48
W6006		4.7.43	ML873		12.1.45	SZ580	TA:G	14.8.47
W6009	DD	4.7.43	ML875		14.6.45	VB888		31.7.47
W6010	AA	8.7.43	ML882		2.6.45	VA889	TA:K	
W6012		28.7.43	NJ191		11.7.45			
W6014		25.4.44	NJ192			**FBTS**		
W6015	Q	28.7.43	NJ257	B:I	28.10.44			
W6026	V	18.7.44	NJ258		26.12.44	PP163		19.8.54
W6027	AD	8.7.44	NJ269		5.4.45	RN266	K	16.10.53
W6051		2.6.43	PP111		13.1.45	RN303	D:K	30.9.55
W6056		19.5.43	PP112		5.2.45	RN304		22.11.53
W6060		10.5.43	PP113		6.2.45	SZ560		
W6064		28.2.44	PP137		28.5.45	SZ571		
DD828		13.4.44	PP141	TA:B	20.6.45			
DD832	V	18.2.43	PP160		16.1.45	**MAEE**		
DD838	AB	28.7.44	PP161		17.1.45			
DD839		23.3.43	RN272	TA:D	4.4.47	K4774		11.4.38
DD840		24.2.43	RN285		24.4.47	L2158		2.6.38
DD841	J	2.3.43	RN286		5.4.45	N9021		17.3.39
DD842	AL	2.3.43	RN287		5.4.45	P9604		17.12.41
DD843	F	23.8.44	SZ568	TA:C	9.4.46	T9042		31.12.42
DD844	BE	15.7.44	SZ569	TA:T	9.4.46	T9083		1.11.41
DD850		16.8.44	SZ571		9.4.46	W3976		16.7.41
DD851		20.7.44	SZ575	TA:K	9.4.46	W4037		21.9.44
DD855	AJ	12.7.44	VB886		22.10.45	W6050		17.4.42
DD856	AR	21.7.44	VB888		4.4.46	W6051		4.6.42
DP178		6.7.44				DV967		12.9.42
DP184	AG	6.7.44	**131 (C) OTU**			DV976		13.11.46
DP185		28.4.44				JM681		19.6.43
DP195			W6007		29.5.44	JM713		31.3.44
DP197		30.3.44	W6011		8.9.44	JM714		4.7.43
DP200	TA:T	30.6.45	W6032		31.10.44	ML735		27.11.43
DV970		11.7.44	W6056		10.5.44	ML750		
DV988		9.9.44	W6066	C:U	30.5.44	ML765		22.4.44
DV992	AA	29.8.44	W6068		31.8.44	ML817		27.10.44
DV994		29.4.44	DD829		10.5.44	ML866		4.3.44
DW111		29.8.44	DD835		10.8.44	MZ269		
EJ133	AQ	13.4.44	DD843		25.6.44	MZ271	C	1.9.50
EJ137		12.4.44	DD845		25.6.44	NJ201	D	1.9.50
EJ142		12.5.44	DD847		12.6.44	PP109		17.1.45
EJ149	RR	29.4.44	DD849	C:K	28.7.44	PP136		
EJ152	TT	3.5.44	DD853		27.10.44	PP142		9.7.45
EJ155		6.7.45	DD854		25.6.44	PP153		7.12.44
EK573		17.5.45	DD867		2.8.44	PP154		7.12.44
EK576		23.7.44	DP191		29.7.44	PP155		11.12.44
EK577		12.4.44	DP193		6.9.44	PP162		20.10.48
EK581		23.8.44	DV960		9.8.44	RN297		13.9.51
EK590	AW	21.7.44	DV978		31.7.44	SZ599	B	18.6.46
EK591		22.7.44	DV980		4.8.44	TX293		15.12.45
JM668		1.8.43	DV989		27.10.44	WM759		11.50
JM679		29.8.44	EK579		4.8.44			
JM683		13.4.44	EK583		3.8.44	**AHQ Iraq CF/Iraq & Persia Comm Flight**		
JM686		22.4.44	JM666		26.5.44			
JM713		10.7.44	ML808		22.4.44	DW112		
JM718	BY	3.2.45	ML836		25.6.44	EK595		30.9.44
ML736	AY	20.11.43	ML842		22.4.44	JM711		
ML737	R	24.11.43						
ML738	B:H	20.11.43	**235 OCU**			**Station Flight Koggala**		
ML739		19.6.45						
ML741		16.6.45	JM718	D:L		RN280		
ML747		15.6.45	ML817	D:P		RN302		
ML749	B:J	5.9.44	NJ265	TA:D, D:J,				
ML757		26.5.45		D:F		**Station Flight Pembroke Dock**		
ML767	B:W	28.10.44	PP118	TA:G				
ML778	TA:P	15.7.45	PP131	TA:N		SZ560		1.10.56
ML779		17.5.45	PP141	TA:B				
ML780		22.6.45	PP163	D:K		**10 (RAAF) Squadron**		
ML781		8.7.45	RN271	TA:H, TA:J,				
ML796		4.3.46		D:L		N9048	RB:A	30.11.39

N9049	RB:B	18.9.39	W4003		10.1.42	ML822	RB:D	17.10.44
N9050	RB:D	30.11.39	W4004	RB:Z	6.2.42	ML828	RB:C	15.10.44
P9600	RB:E	27.10.39		RB:Z	31.12.42	ML829	RB:K	11.12.44
P9601	RB:F	3.11.39	W4019	RB:A	17.2.42	ML830	RB:A	14.10.44
P9602	RB:G	13.11.39		RB:A	24.4.42	ML831		15.10.44
P9603	RB:H	28.11.39	W4020	RB:B	7.3.42	ML839	RB:A	8.12.43
P9604	RB:J	15.12.39		RB:R	8.4.43		RB:A	1.7.44
P9605	RB:K	21.12.39	W4024	RB:G	16.4.43	ML848	RB:X	22.2.44
P9606		2.1.40	W4030	RB:H	16.4.43	ML856	RB:Y	19.3.44
T9041		28.2.41	W6054	RB:D	29.8.42	NJ193	RB:F	15.6.45
T9047	RB:L	21.10.40	DD852	RB:J	24.5.43	NJ253	RB:B	19.10.44
T9071	RB:M	23.12.40	DD865	RB:L	11.8.43	NJ254	RB:J	1.11.44
T9072	RB:V	29.9.41	DD867		8.8.43	NJ255	RB:G	21.11.44
T9075	RB:N	4.4.41	DP177	RB:K	31.12.42	NJ256	RB:F	28.10.44
T9086		2.3.42	DP179	RB:M	12.8.43	NJ264	RB:G	18.6.45
T9110	RB:C	7.7.42	DP192		11.11.43	NJ267	RB:H	18.6.45
W3979	RB:Q	19.6.41	DV958	RB:E	24.7.44	NJ268	RB:M	19.6.45
W3980		11.6.41	DV969	RB:E	6.9.42	PP113	RB:D	16.6.45
W3983	RB:R	27.7.41	DV993	RB:T	23.9.43	PP114	RB:A	15.6.45
W3984	RB:S	1.8.41	DW113	RB:V	10.1.44	PP115	RB:B	19.6.45
		28.2.42	EK573	RB:P	14.8.43	PP119		19.6.45
W3985	RB:U, RB:T	11.8.41	EK574	RB:Q	16.8.43	PP122	RB:L	19.6.45
W3986		29.8.41	EK575	RB:G	24.9.44	PP135	RB:E	30.11.44
	RB:U	8.4.42	EK586	RB:U	6.10.43	PP138	RB:M	9.11.44
W3993	RB:W, RB:G	15.11.41	EK594	RB:D	24.6.44	PP139	RB:H	30.11.44
W3994	RB:X	15.11.41	JM678	RB:B	14.5.44	PP142	RB:L	31.12.44
	RB:X	6.7.42	JM684	RB:K	28.5.43	PP162	RB:C	16.6.45
W3997		13.2.42	JM685	RB:Z	10.5.44	RN282	RB:N	19.6.45
W3999	RB:Y	5.1.42	JM721	RB:W	20.1.44	RN300	RB:Q	16.6.45

By the slipway ready for its initial launching on a rather wet 17th October 1941 at Blackburn Aircraft Ltd's Clyde Factory, is the first Dumbarton-produced Sunderland, T9083. The Sunderland II is sitting near P5154, a Lockheed Hudson I hulk used by MAEE for hull water pressure comparison trials with a Blackburn Botha. (R C Sturtivant collection)

U-625 was destroyed by 422 Squadron Sunderland Mk.III EK591 [2:U] on 10th March 1944 flown by Flt Lt S W Butler. Two depth charges exploded around the submarine's stern as the rear gunner raked the conning tower.

The Ocean Sentinels Strike Hard

Above, U-106 undergoing a joint attack from DV968 [UT:M] of 461 Squadron (Flt Lt I Clarke) and JM708 [N] of 228 Squadron (Flt Lt R D Hanbury) on 2nd August 1943, as a result of which it exploded and sank.

Above, Sunderland Mk.III EK586 [RB:U] of 10 (RAAF) Squadron (F/O J P Roberts) depth-charged U-426 which sank by the stern on 8th January 1944.

Left, U-71 attacked by an earlier [RB:U], 10 Squadron's W3986 on June 5th 1942. Seriously damaged, it managed to put in at La Pallice for repairs. (Top via E Cromie, others JM Collection)

Appendix 2
CIVIL-REGISTERED SUNDERLANDS, SANDRINGHAMS AND SOLENTS

Regn   Serial   Remarks

UNITED KINGDOM

Sunderland 3:
Regn	Serial	Remarks
G-AGER	JM660	Radio call-sign OQZR
G-AGES	JM661	Radio call-sign OQZS
G-AGET	JM662	Radio call-sign OQZT
G-AGEU	JM663	Radio call-sign OQZU
G-AGEV	JM664	Radio call-sign OQZV
G-AGEW	JM665	Radio call-sign OQZW
G-AGHV	JM722	Radio call-sign OQZB
G-AGHW	ML725	Radio call-sign OQZC
G-AGHX	ML726	Radio call-sign OQZX
G-AGHZ	ML727	Radio call-sign OQZZ
G-AGIA	ML728	Radio call-sign OQZA
G-AGIB	ML729	
G-AGJJ	ML751	Radio call-sign OQZJ
G-AGJK	ML752	Radio call-sign OQZK
G-AGJL	ML753	Radio call-sign OQZL
G-AGJM	ML754	Radio call-sign OQZM
G-AGJN	ML755	Radio call-sign OQZN
G-AGJO	ML756	Radio call-sign OQZO
G-AGKV	ML786	Radio call-sign OQZD
G-AGKW	ML787	Radio call-sign OQZE
G-AGKX	ML788	Radio call-sign OQZF
G-AGKY	ML789	Radio call-sign OQZG
G-AGKZ	ML790	Radio call-sign OQZH
G-AGLA	ML791	Radio call-sign OQZI
G-AGWW	EJ156	to CX-AFA
G-AGWX	ML876	to LV-AAS, CX-AKF
G-AHEO	JM716	
G-AHEP	DD860	
G-AHER	PP142	

Sunderland 5:
Regn	Serial	Remarks
G-AHJR	SZ584	
G-ANAK	PP162	
G-BJHS	NZ4108	ex N158J, N814ML

Sandringham 2:
Regn	Serial	Remarks
G-AGPT	DD834	to LV-AAP
G-AGPZ	DV964	to LV-AAO
G-AHRE	ML843	to LV-ACT

Sandringham 3:
Regn	Serial	Remarks
G-AGPY	DD841	to LV-AAR
G-AGTZ	EJ170	to LV-AAQ

Sandringham 5:
Regn	Serial	Remarks
G-AHYY	ML838	
G-AHYZ	ML784	
G-AHZA	ML783	
G-AHZB	NJ171	
G-AHZC	NJ253	
G-AHZD	NJ257	to VH-EBV
G-AHZE	ML818	
G-AHZF	NJ188	to VH-EBY
G-AHZG	ML828	to VH-EBZ
G-AJMZ	JM681	

Sandringham 7:
Regn	Serial	Remarks
G-AKCO	JM719	to VH-APG, F-OBIP
G-AKCP	EJ172	to CX-ANI
G-AKCR	ML840	to CX-ANA

Seaford 1:
Regn	Serial	Remarks
G-AGWU	NJ201	Radio call-sign OZZA; restored to RAF; to G-ANAJ (Solent 3)
G-ALIJ	NJ200	

Solent 2:
Regn	Serial	Remarks
G-AHIL	—	conv to Solent 3
G-AHIM	—	
G-AHIN	—	conv to Solent 3
G-AHIO	—	to VH-TOD; to N9945F
G-AHIR	—	
G-AHIS	—	conv to Solent 3
G-AHIT	—	
G-AHIU	—	
G-AHIV	—	to VH-TOC
G-AHIW	—	
G-AHIX	—	conv to Solent 3
G-AHIY	—	conv to Solent 3

Solent 3:
Regn	Serial	Remarks
G-AGWU	NJ201	to G-ANAJ
G-AKNO	NJ202	to VH-TOA
G-AKNP	NJ203	to VH-TOB, N9946F
G-AKNR	NJ204	to ZK-AMQ
G-AKNS	NJ205	to MoS as WM759
G-AKNT	NJ206	to N9947F
G-AKNU	NJ207	
G-ANAJ	NJ201	ex G-AGWU (Seaford 1)

Solent 4:
Regn	Serial	Remarks
G-ANYI	—	ex ZK-AMN
G-AOBL	—	ex ZK-AML

ARGENTINA

Sunderland 3:
Regn	Serial	Remarks
LV-AAS	ML876	ex G-AGWX; to CX-AKF

Sunderland 5:
Regn	Serial	Remarks
LV-AHG	EK579	
LV-AHH	EJ171	

Sandringham 2:
Regn	Serial	Remarks
LV-AAO	DV964	ex G-AGPZ
LV-AAP	DD834	ex G-AGPT
LV-ACT	ML843	ex G-AHRE

Sandringham 3:
Regn	Serial	Remarks
LV-AAQ	EJ170	ex G-AGTZ
LV-AAR	DD841	ex G-AGPY

Sandringham 6:
Regn	Serial	Remarks
LV-AHM	JM714	ex LV-PAE, LN-LMK
LV-PAE	JM714	ex LN-LMK; to LV-AHM

AUSTRALIA

Sunderland 3:
Regn	Serial	Remarks
VH-AKO	A26-4	
VH-AKP	A26-5	
VH-ARQ	A26-1	ntu; to VH-BKO but ntu
VH-BFX	A26-3	ntu; to VH-BKP but ntu
VH-BKQ	A26-2	

Sunderland 5:
Regn	Serial	Remarks
VH-BRF	NZ4108	to N158J, G-BJHS, N814ML

Sandringham 4:
Regn	Serial	Remarks
VH-BRC	JM715	ex ZK-AMH; to N158C, VP-LVE
VH-BRD	NJ179	ex ZK-AME
VH-BRE	NJ255	ex VH-EBX, ZK-AMD
VH-EBW	ML761	ex ZK-AMB
VH-EBX	NJ255	ex ZK-AMD; to VH-BRE

Sandringham 5:
Regn	Serial	Remarks
VH-EBV	NJ257	ex G-AHZD
VH-EBY	NJ188	ex G-AHZF
VH-EBZ	ML828	ex G-AHZG

Sandringham 7:
Regn	Serial	Remarks
VH-APG	JM719	ex G-AKCO; to F-OBIP

Solent 2:
Regn	Serial	Remarks
VH-TOC	—	ex G-AHIV
VH-TOD	—	ex G-AHIO; to N9945F

Solent 3:
Regn	Serial	Remarks
VH-TOA	NJ202	ex G-AKNO
VH-TOB	NJ203	ex G-AKNP; to N9946F

FRENCH DEPENDENCIES

Sandringham 7:
Regn	Serial	Remarks
F-OBIP	JM719	ex VH-APG; ex G-AKCO

NEW ZEALAND

Sunderland 3:
Regn	Serial	Remarks
ZK-AMF	NZ4102	
ZK-AMG	NZ4103	
ZK-AMJ	NZ4101	
ZK-AMK	NZ4104	

Sandringham 4:
Regn	Serial	Remarks
ZK-AMB	ML761	to VH-EBW
ZK-AMD	NJ255	to VH-EBX, VH-BRE
ZK-AME	NJ179	to VH-BRD
ZK-AMH	JM715	to VH-BRC

Solent 3:
Regn	Serial	Remarks
ZK-AMQ	NJ204	ex G-AKNR

Solent 4:
Regn	Serial	Remarks
ZK-AML	—	to G-AOBL
ZK-AMM	—	
ZK-AMN	—	to G-ANYI
ZK-AMO	—	

NORWAY

Sandringham 6:
Regn	Serial	Remarks
LN-IAU	ML809	
LN-IAV	ML807	
LN-IAW	JM720	
LN-LAI	W4037	
LN-LMK	JM714	to LV-PAE, LV-AHM

UNITED STATES OF AMERICA

Sunderland 5
N158J	NZ4108	ex VH-BRF; to (VP-LVF), G-BJHS, N814ML
N814ML	NZ4108	ex G-BJHS

Solent 2:
N9945F	—	ex VH-TOD; ex G-AHIO

Solent 3:
N9946F	NJ203	ex VH-TOB; ex G-AKNP
N9947F	NJ206	ex G-AKNT

Sandringham 4:
N158C	JM715	ex VH-BRC; to VP-LVE, N158C

URUGUAY

Sunderland 3:
CX-AFA	EJ156	ex G-AGWW
CX-AKF	ML876	ex LV-AAS, G-AGWX

Sunderland 5:
CX-AKR	DP195	

Sandringham 7:
CX-ANA	ML840	ex G-AKCR
CX-ANI	EJ172	ex G-AKCP

VIRGIN ISLANDS

Sandringham 4
VP-LVE	JM715	ex N158C, VH-BRC, ZK-AMH; to N158C

CIVIL AIRCRAFT NAMES

Name	Reg	Name	Reg	Name	Reg
Almirante Zar	LV AHM	Harlech	G AGHX	Portmarnock	G AHZD
Antilles	VH-AKP	Harlequin	G AGHX	Portsea	G AHZE
Aotearoa II	ZK AML/G AOBL	Harwich	G AGKZ	Portsmouth	G AHYY
Aparima	ZK AMQ	Haslemere	G AGIA	Princess of Cairns	VH-BRD
Aranui	ZK AMO	Hastings	G AGHZ	Rio Aguilera	LV AAO
Ararangi	ZK AMM	Hawkesbury	G AGHZ	Rio de la Plata	LV AAS
Argentina	G AGPZ/LV AAO	Helmsdale	G AHER	Rio de la Plata	LV AHH
Auckland	ZK AMH	Henley	G AGJJ	St Andrew	G AKCR
Australia	ZK AMD	Hereford	G AGKW	St David	G AKCP
Australia Star	VH-AKO	Himalaya	G AGKX	St George	G AKCO
Australis	VH AKO	Hobart	G AGJL	Salcombe	G AHIV
Awatere	ZK AMN/G ANYI	Honduras	G AGJO	Salisbury	G AHIL
Bamse Brakar	LN IAU	Hotspur	G AGKW	Samoa Star	VH-AKO
Beachcomber	VH BRC	Howard	G AGJK	San Martin	CX-AKF
Brasil	G AGPY/LV AAR	Hudson	G AGJN	Sark	G AHIR
Bukken Bruse	LN IAW	Humber	G AGJO	Scapa	G AHIS
Capitan Bosio Lanza	CX AKR	Hungerford	G AGKY	Scarborough	G AHIM
Capricorn	VH-BRD	Hunter	G AGLA	Severn	G AHIT
City of Belfast	G AKNR	Huntingdon	G AGKV	Singapore	G AKNT
City of Cardiff	G AKNP	Hythe	G AGJM	Sir Arthur Gouge	G-BJHS
City of Edinburgh	G AHIX	Inglaterra	G AGTZ/LV AAQ	Solway	G AHIU
City of Funchal	G ANAJ	Islander	VH BRF	Somerset	G AHIO
City of Liverpool	G AKNS	Isle of Tahiti	N9946F	Southampton	G AHIN
City of London	G AKNO	Juliet	N158J	Southern Cross	N158C/VP LVE
City of Salisbury	G AHIL	Jutulen	LN LAI	Southsea	G AHIY
City of Southampton	G AHIN	Kvitbjorn	LN IAV	Star of Hobart	VH TOC
City of York	G AHIS	Mataatua	ZK AMG	Star of Papua	VH TOB
Coral Clipper	VH-BRC	New Zealand	ZK AME	Star of Samoa	VH TOD
Excalibur VIII	N158J	Pacific Chieftain	VH EBX/BRE	Stornaway	G AHIW
Frigate Bird III	VH APG	Pacific Explorer	VH EBZ	Sussex	G AHIX
General Artigas	CX AFA	Pacific Star	VH BKQ	Sydney	G AKNU
Hadfield	G AGER	Pacific Voyager	VH EBY	Tahiti Star	VH AKP
Hailsham	G AGEV	Pacific Warrior	VH EBV	Tainui	ZK-AMJ
Halcyon	N9946F	Paraguay	G AHRE/LV ACT	Takitimu	ZK AMK
Halstead	G AHEO	Pembroke	G AHZC	Tasman	ZK AMB
Halton	G AGEW	Penzance	G AHZA	The Spirit of Foynes	G-BJHS
Hamble	G AGHV	Perth	G AHYZ/G AJMZ	Tokomaru	ZK AMF
Hamilton	G AGHW	Pevensey	G AHZG	Uruguay	G AGPT/LV AAP
Hampshire	G AGEU	Polarbjorn	LN LMK	Uruguay	LV AHG
Hanbury	G AHEP	Poole	G AHZF		
Hanwell	G AGEW	Portland	G AHZB		

EXTANT AIRFRAMES

Complete aircraft:

Sunderland MR.5	ML786	Imperial War Museum, Duxford
Sunderland MR.5	ML824	Royal Air Force Museum, Hendon
Sunderland 5	N814ML (ML814)	Fantasy of Flight, Polk City, Florida
Sunderland MR.5	NZ4115 (SZ584)	MOTAT, Auckland, NZ
Sandringham 4	VH-BRC (JM715)	Solent Sky, Southampton
Sandringham 7	F-OBIP (JM719)	Musée de l'Air et de l'Espace, Paris
Solent 3	N9946F	Oakland, California
Solent 4	ZK-AMO	MOTAT, Auckland, NZ

Nose section and flight deck only:

Sunderland MR.5	NZ4112 (VB881)	Ferrymead Aeronautical Society, Christchurch, NZ

Appendix 3
ROLL OF HONOUR
'We will remember them'

In this Roll of Honour an attempt has been made to include the name of every person who lost his or her life in a Sunderland, whether in action, in a flying accident or in an incident on the ground. It is realised however, that as a small number of accident reports are missing, a few names are unavoidably omitted.

Name	Rank	Date	Unit	Aircraft
Abbott, H	Flt Sgt	1Aug42	201 Sqn	W4000
Adam, R J	Plt Off RAAF	11Aug43	10 (RAAF)	DP177
Adams, N K	Plt Off	22Aug42	202 Sqn	W4029
Agur, R J	Flg Off RCAF	13Jun43	228 Sqn	DV967
Ainslie, A S, DFC	Flt Lt	29Jun40	210 Sqn	N9026
Aldridge, A R	Sgt RAAF	18Aug43	10 (RAAF)	W3985
Alecock, N J	AC1	1Sep42	461 Sqn	T9113
Allan, W A	LAC RCAF	19Dec42	422 Sqn	W6029
Allen, J	Plt Off	31Jul42	201 Sqn	W4025
Allen, S	Sgt	5Jun43	330 Sqn	W6052
Ambler, G G	Sgt	13Apr43	204 Sqn	JM669
Amos, C O W	Cpl RAAF	28Apr41	10 (RAAF)	T9075
Anderson, D D	Sgt RCAF	29Nov42	204 Sqn	W6016
Anderson, R M	Flt Sgt	13Feb46	302 FTU	VB885
Andreassen	Sgt RNorAF	12Oct43	4 (C) OTU	W3997
Applegate, J S	Sgt	22Aug43	201 Sqn	DD848
Armstrong, R C	Flt Sgt RNZAF	12Jul43	228 Sqn	DV977
Audsley, J S	AC1	27Dec40	210 Sqn	N9022
Austin, D	Sgt	17Feb44	4 (C) OTU	T9088
Bailey, F E G	Sgt	29Jun40	210 Sqn	N9026
Baker, D R H	Sgt	16Feb51	201 Sqn	SZ598
Baker, R E	Flg Off	28Jan51	205 Sqn	PP107
Bardsey, V	LMM	18Jul43	Royal Navy	JM687
Barker, H	Flt Sgt	13Feb46	302 FTU	VB885
Barnard, J	Cpl	1Jan43	230 Sqn	N9029
Barraclough, R	Sgt	3Mar54	201 Sqn	NJ267
Barter, J A C	Sgt	9Apr40	210 Sqn	L2167
Bartlet, J P	Plt Off	5Feb42	201 Sqn	W3977
Battersby, L	Flt Sgt	1Aug42	201 Sqn	W4000
Beane, F A	Plt Off	29Nov42	204 Sqn	W6016
Beare, E S	Sgt	16Feb51	201 Sqn	SZ598
Beavis, K W	AC1	28Oct40	204 Sqn	P9620
Becker, R D A	Wt Off RCAF	14Mar45	201 Sqn	ML743
Beesley, K W	Flg Off	13Apr43	204 Sqn	JM669
Behr, R A C	Cdr	29Nov42	Royal Navy	W6016
Belderson, J B	AC1	9Jul40	201 Sqn	N6133
Bell, R D	LAC RAAF	28Apr41	10 (RAAF)	T9075
Benison, P M	Sgt	21Jun42	10 (RAAF)	W3999
Bennett, A E	AC1	3Dec41	201 Sqn	W3988
Bennett, J W	Flt Lt	28Nov44	230 Sqn	JM673
Bennett, K W	AC1	20Dec41	201 Sqn	W3998
Bennett, L C	AC1	21Jul40	204 Sqn	N9028
Bennington, D E	Sgt RAAF	11Aug43	10 (RAAF)	DP177
Biggin, G M	Plt Off RAAF	8Aug42	10 (RAAF)	W4019
Bill, W J	Sgt	21Nov43	4 (C) OTU	L2168
Birrell, D M	Flt Lt	20Nov49	88 Sqn	NJ176
Bjerche, L	QM RNorAF	12Oct43	4 (C) OTU	W3997
Black, W	Sgt	31Jul42	201 Sqn	W4025
Blacklock, E F	Sgt RNZAF	25Aug42	4 (C) OTU	W4036
Blackwell, C A	Sgt	29May42	228 Sqn	T9089
Bluck, W	Sgt	31Jul42	201 Sqn	W4025
Boddy, T I	Master Eng	4Jun55	201 Sqn	RN288
Bonner, A J	Flt Sgt	28Nov44	230 Sqn	JM673
Booth, G F H	Flg Off	12Oct43	4 (C) OTU	W3997
Borgen, A	Sgt RNorAF	12Oct43	4 (C) OTU	W3997
Bowd, D M	Sgt	1Sep42	461 Sqn	T9113
Bowen, I W	Flg Off RAAF	11Aug43	10 (RAAF)	DP177
Bowley, R G, DFC	Flg Off RAAF	17May43	10 (RAAF)	W4004
Bradley, E	Plt Off RAAF	21Jan43	461 Sqn	T9085
Brant, G W	Plt Off	17Sep39	210 Sqn	L2168
Baxter, B	Sgt	17Feb44	4 (C) OTU	T9088
Britton, R D	Sgt	22Sep43	204 Sqn	JM710
Brock, C D E	Cdr	29Nov42	Royal Navy	W6016
Brookes, P E T	Flt Sgt	28Jan51	205 Sqn	PP107
Bryers, R B	Sgt RCAF	25May43	422 Sqn	DD846
Buckland, A N	Flg Off RAAF	21Sep43	10 (RAAF)	DV969
Budd, H R D	Flg Off RAAF	1Aug43	10 (RAAF)	W4020
Bulmer, B V H	AC1	8Apr40	204 Sqn	L5799
Buls, B L	A/Flt Lt RAAF	21Jan43	461 Sqn	T9085
Burbridge, H E	Flt Sgt RAAF	18Aug43	10 (RAAF)	W3985
Burley, J E	Sgt	10Jun42	95 Sqn	L5805
Burrows, J W	Sgt	7Apr43	4 (C) OTU	W6001
Burt-Gerrans, H F	Wt Off RCAF	19Dec42	422 Sqn	W6029
Burton, J W	Flt Sgt	22Aug43	201 Sqn	DD848
Bushell, G J	Flg Off RAAF	30Aug43	461 Sqn	JM707
Butcher, V	Flt Sgt	1Jan43	230 Sqn	N9029
Butler, A	Sgt	20Aug43	230 Sqn	EJ131
Butler, P J	Sgt	11Aug41	201 Sqn	W3978
Cameron, C S	Flt Sgt RAAF	21Sep43	10 (RAAF)	DV969
Cameron, D M	Flg Off	19Dec42	422 Sqn	W6029
Campbell, D M	Sgt	5Jan44	95 Sqn	DW105
Capes, F W	Flt Sgt	24May43	228 Sqn	EJ139
Carmichael, A	Sgt	13Jun43	228 Sqn	DV967
Carpenter, A J	Sgt	28Jan51	205 Sqn	PP107
Carpenter, J C	Sgt	9Apr40	210 Sqn	L2167
Carson, J L	Sgt	29Oct40	201 Sqn	P9622
Carson, R C	Plt Off RAAF	8Aug42	10 (RAAF)	W4019
Cary, C L	Flg Off	28Nov44	230 Sqn	JM673
Catt, A R	Sgt	25Aug42	4 (C) OTU	W4036
Cave, E N	Flg Off	14Mar45	201 Sqn	ML743
Chadwick, B W	LAC	3Mar54	201 Sqn	NJ267
Challinor, J E	Sgt RAAF	11Aug43	10 (RAAF)	DP177
Chaplin, E F	Sgt	22Aug42	202 Sqn	W4029
Chataway, C C	Plt Off	21Jun42	10 (RAAF)	W3999
Chelman, W O	AC1 RAAF	8Aug42	10 (RAAF)	W4019
Chinnery, R V	Sgt RAAF	1Sep42	461 Sqn	T9113
Church, G A	Flt Lt	15May43	228 Sqn	DD837
Clare, N	Flt Sgt	5Feb42	201 Sqn	W3977
Clark, D H	Flg Off	5Jul47	201 Sqn	PP113
Clark, E A	Flt Lt	16Feb51	201 Sqn	SZ598
Clark, P	AC1	9Jul40	201 Sqn	N6133
Clarke, G D	Flt Sgt	15Oct45	230 Sqn	NJ277
Clarke, J W	Plt Off RCAF	25May43	422 Sqn	DD846
Clayton, L S	Plt Off	1Jan43	230 Sqn	N9029
Cleland, W R	Flg Off RAAF	20May43	10 (RAAF)	W3986
Clive-Davies, A C S	Sgt	1Aug42	201 Sqn	W4000
Codd, R D E	Sgt	12Jul43	228 Sqn	DV977
Coleman, F J A	Lt	13Jun43	Can Army	DV967
Collins, J A	Flt Sgt	31Jul42	201 Sqn	W4025
Collins, V D W	Flg Off RAAF	18Aug43	10 (RAAF)	W3985
Comer, V	Sgt	10Jun42	95 Sqn	L5805
Connell, W H	Sgt RCAF	17Aug42	204 Sqn	L2158
Cook, W	Sgt	23Apr41	204 Sqn	N9023
Coomes, A L	Flg Off RAAF	21Sep43	10 (RAAF)	DV969
Cooper, E A	LAC	28Jan51	205 Sqn	PP107
Cooper, J L R	Flt Sgt	24May43	228 Sqn	EJ139
Copping, A J T	Sgt	23Apr41	204 Sqn	N9023
Corcoran, J M	Flt Sgt	22Aug42	202 Sqn	W4029
Cordrey, R E	Sgt	13Nov42	10 (RAAF)	W6054
Corless, V J	Flg Off RAAF	17May43	10 (RAAF)	W4004
Coster, J R	Flt Sgt	22Aug43	201 Sqn	DD848
Couchman, R B	Flg Off	13Feb46	302 FTU	VB885
Cox, J S, MC	Major	19Dec42	Black Watch	W6029
Cox, T G H	Wt Off	15Oct45	230 Sqn	NJ277
Cox, W L	A/Flt Lt	1Aug42	201 Sqn	W4000
Craig, F B	Flt Sgt	22Sep43	204 Sqn	JM710
Crate, R S	Cpl	5Jan44	95 Sqn	DW105
Crawford, N D	Flt Sgt	28Nov44	230 Sqn	JM673
Crawshaw, L E	Sgt	27Dec40	210 Sqn	N9022
Crockart, W	Sgt	16Nov51	235 OCU	SZ565
Crockett, D T	Sgt	29Jun40	210 Sqn	N9026
Crockett, R F	Flt Lt	7Sep42	230 Sqn	W3987
Croft, C R	Flg Off RAAF	30Aug43	461 Sqn	JM707
Crombie, G	Wt Off	29Dec43	230 Sqn	EJ140
Cronk, A F	Sgt	23Oct54	230 Sqn	PP155
Crosbie, J J	Sgt	28Nov45	95 Sqn	DV975
Crosland, D E T	Flt Sgt	24May43	228 Sqn	EJ139
Crossman, E F	Sgt	13Apr43	204 Sqn	JM669
Croxford, D S	Flt Sgt	18Aug43	10 (RAAF)	W3985
Cryer, G E	Plt Off	11Jun42	4 (C) OTU	P9604
Cunningham, R	AC1	20Dec41	201 Sqn	W3998
Currie, D J, DFM	Flt Sgt	12Jun44	201 Sqn	ML760
Curtis, J M	Flg Off RAAF	1Aug43	10 (RAAF)	W4020
Curtis, R C	LAC	28Jan51	205 Sqn	PP107
Cutchie, J W	AC1	11Aug41	201 Sqn	W3978
Cuthbert, S B	Flg Off	22Sep43	204 Sqn	JM710

Name	Rank	Date	Unit	Serial
Daley, J D T	Sgt RAAF	21Sep43	10 (RAAF)	DV969
Dallas, J R	Sgt RAAF	11Aug43	10 (RAAF)	DP177
Daniels, A G	Sgt	1Jan43	230 Sqn	N9029
Darge, W H	Sgt	1Jan43	230 Sqn	N9029
Davidson, E	Sgt	12Jul43	228 Sqn	DV977
Davies, A	Sgt	22Aug43	201 Sqn	DD848
Davies, C	Sgt	1Aug42	201 Sqn	W4000
Davies, D D	Flt Lt	16Feb51	201 Sqn	SZ598
Davies, D G	Sgt	29Nov42	204 Sqn	W6016
Davies, D M	Wt Off	15Oct45	230 Sqn	NJ277
Davies, D M	Sgt	13Jun43	228 Sqn	DV967
Davies, E	Flt Sgt	23Oct54	230 Sqn	PP155
Davis, E S C, OBE, AFC	Wg Cdr	21Jul40	204 Sqn	N9028
Davies, F S	P.II	5Jul47	201 Sqn	PP113
Davies, L J	Flt Lt	15Apr43	119 Sqn	DP176
Davies, T I.	Flt Lt	17Sep39	210 Sqn	L2168
Davis, W A	Sgt	17Aug42	204 Sqn	L2158
Davison, N	Flt Sgt	14Mar45	201 Sqn	ML743
De Wit, E	Lt SAAF	Nov56	35 Sqn SAAF	1714
Deacon, R L	Sgt	15May43	228 Sqn	DD837
Dean, J	Sgt RCAF	1Jan43	230 Sqn	N9029
Debnam, H J H	Flg Off	24May43	228 Sqn	EJ139
Dent, H I C	Plt Off RAAF	21Jan43	461 Sqn	T9085
Devlin	Cdr RN	13Nov42	Royal Navy	W6054
Dewhurst, E	Sgt RAAF	20May43	10 (RAAF)	W3986
Dixon, D P	Sgt	21Jul40	204 Sqn	N9028
Dodge, M D	Sgt	3Mar54	201 Sqn	NJ267
Dods, W S E	Flt Lt RAAF	29May43	461 Sqn	JM675
Dolley, W H U	AC2	8Apr40	204 Sqn	L5799
Dollin, K	Plt Off	13Feb46	302 FTU	VB885
Donaldson, D W	Eng	20Nov49	88 Sqn	NJ176
Doncaster, A	LAC	3Dec41	201 Sqn	W3988
Doran, A E	Flg Off	4Jun55	201 Sqn	RN288
Doran, T H	Sgt RAAF	17May43	10 (RAAF)	W4004
Douglas, J W	LAC	20Dec41	201 Sqn	W3998
Dowell, R W B	Sgt RAAF	20May43	10 (RAAF)	W3986
Dummigan, F W	LAC	7Apr43	4 (C) OTU	W6001
Dunford, R J	Flg Off	7Apr43	4 (C) OTU	W6001
Dunn, R E	Flg Off	2Oct43	204 Sqn	W9079
Durney, T	AC1	21Jun42	10 (RAAF)	W3999
Dutton, E A	Flt Sgt	18Jul43	204 Sqn	JM687
Dwyer, J G	Sgt RAAF	11Aug43	10 (RAAF)	DP177
Easson, W	Sgt	24May43	228 Sqn	EJ139
Eaton, J E	AC1	20Nov49	88 Sqn	NJ176
Eddy, H E	Sgt RCAF	5Jun43	330 Sqn	W6052
Edwards, A	Flg Off	25Sep45	230 Sqn (fell overboard)	PP157
Edwards, K T	Sgt RAAF	8Aug42	10 (RAAF)	W4019
Edwards, L P	Sgt RCAF	5Jun43	330 Sqn	W6052
Elder, C F	Flg Off	29Jun40	210 Sqn	N9026
Elomgrem, E	Sgt RNorAF	12Oct43	4 (C) OTU	W3997
Elrick, A	AC1 RAAF	21Jan43	461 Sqn	T9085
Emmett, W S	Plt Off RNZAF	3Dec41	201 Sqn	W3988
Emrys-Jones, L G	Flg Off RAAF	1Sep42	461 Sqn	T9113
Epps, S J	Sgt	3Dec41	201 Sqn	W3988
Espley, A G	Flt Lt	29Nov42	204 Sqn	W6016
Eva, R	Sgt RAAF	1Sep42	461 Sqn	T9113
Evans, B S	Flt Sgt RAAF	22Sep43	204 Sqn	JM710
Evans, D J	Flg Off	27Mar46	209 Sqn	PP103
Evans, P	Sgt RAAF	21Jan43	461 Sqn	T9085
Everrett, F H	Flg Off	16Nov51	235 OCU	SZ565
Eveson, G	AC2	9Apr40	210 Sqn	L2167
Ewen, T W	Sgt	5Jan44	95 Sqn	DW105
Ewens, R W	Cpl	17Sep39	210 Sqn	L2168
Faulkner, E	Cpl	11Jun42	4 (C) OTU	P9604
Fazl Husain	Dvr	15Oct45	Indian Army	NJ277
Ferrett, H J	Sgt	30Aug43	461 Sqn	JM707
Fiddock, W H	AC2	15Oct39	204 Sqn	N9030
Field, P R	Cpl	1Aug42	201 Sqn	W4000
Filmer, O S	Flt Sgt RAAF	21Jan43	461 Sqn	T9085
Finney, J C	Flg Off	22Sep43	204 Sqn	JM710
Fletcher, A W	Sgt	17Feb44	4 (C) OTU	T9088
Fletcher, D J	Flt Lt	20Dec41	201 Sqn	W3998
Ford, D	Flg Off	15Oct39	204 Sqn	N9030
Ford, F N G	Flt Sgt	14Mar45	201 Sqn	ML743
Form, G	Sgt	22Aug43	202 Sqn	W4029
Fort, C G	Sgt RAAF	31Jul42	201 Sqn	W4025
Foster, F	Flt Sgt	12Jun44	201 Sqn	ML760
Fowell, L J	AC1	8Apr40	204 Sqn	L5799
Fox, M W G	Sgt	3Dec41	201 Sqn	W3988
Frame, D J	LAC	21Jul40	204 Sqn	N9028
Francis, A P D	Sgt	29Nov42	204 Sqn	W6016
Francis, J C	AC1 RAAF	28Apr41	10 (RAAF)	T9075
Franklin, A C	Nav.II	5Jul47	201 Sqn	PP113
Fraser, J W	Sgt	13Jun43	228 Sqn	DV967
French, E A	Sgt	24May43	228 Sqn	EJ139
French, J R	Sgt	12Jun44	201 Sqn	ML760
Frith, S B	Flt Sgt	14Mar45	201 Sqn	ML743
Fry, K G	Flt Lt RAAF	1Aug43	10 (RAAF)	W4020
Fryer, J E	Sgt RAAF	1Aug43	10 (RAAF)	W4020
Fuller, A E DFM	Flt Sgt	13Aug43	461 Sqn	DV968
Gallagher, T	Sgt	15Dec42	119 Sqn	DV971
Galt, D T	Flg Off RAAF	13Aug43	461 Sqn	DV968
Gamble, J	Wt Off RAAF	30Aug43	461 Sqn	JM707
Garrard, J P	Flt Lt RAAF	14Mar45	201 Sqn	ML743
Gash, T R	Flt Lt	4Jun55	201 Sqn	RN288
Gaylard, G N	Plt Off	29Jun40	210 Sqn	N9026
Galloway, T	Sgt	15Apr43	119 Sqn	DP176
Gerrard, N C	Flg Off RAAF	11Aug43	10 (RAAF)	DP177
Gerrard, M J	Sgt	17Feb44	4 (C) OTU	T9088
Ghulam Ali	Gnr	15Oct45	Indian Army	NJ277
Gibbs, R A	Flt Sgt RAAF	18Aug43	10 (RAAF)	W3985
Gibson, G C	Sgt	5Jan44	95 Sqn	DW105
Gibson, J C F	Flt Lt	14May45	209 Sqn	NJ260
Gibson, T M	Flg Off RAAF	8Aug42	10 (RAAF)	W4019
Gilbert, A B	Flt Lt	28Nov44	230 Sqn	JM673
Gilbert, B N	Plt Off	21Jun42	10 (RAAF)	W3999
Gill, J H C	P.II	5Jul47	201 Sqn	PP113
Gill, J W J	Sgt RAAF	21Jan43	461 Sqn	T9085
Gillett, I J	AC1	26Mar50	209 Sqn	SZ593
Goldstein, V M	Sgt RCAF	13Jun43	228 Sqn	DV967
Gooch, A H N	Flt Lt	18Jul43	204 Sqn	JM687
Goode, R M	Wt Off RAAF	13Aug43	461 Sqn	DV968
Goodings, J R	Sgt	31Jul42	201 Sqn	W4025
Gossop, H	Sgt	4Aug43	423 Sqn	DD859
Goyen, F McK	Flt Lt	25Aug42	4 (C) OTU	W4036
Gracie, J	LAC	28Jan51	205 Sqn	PP107
Graham, J B	Sgt	12Jul43	228 Sqn	DV977
Grainger, J C	Flg Off RAAF	13Aug43	461 Sqn	DV968
Granger, G	Sgt	13Feb46	302 FTU	VB885
Gray, A D H	Flg Off	17Feb44	4 (C) OTU	T9088
Greatz, W P	Sgt RAAF	18Aug43	10 (RAAF)	W3985
Green, C A	Flt Sgt	15Oct45	230 Sqn	NJ277
Greenwood, J	Sgt	18Jul43	204 Sqn	JM687
Greenman, R G	Sgt	10Jun42	95 Sqn	L5805
Griffin, A C	Flt Lt	22Aug43	201 Sqn	DD848
Griffith, C J	Flg Off	12Jun44	201 Sqn	ML760
Griffiths, D G	Sgt	18Jul43	204 Sqn	JM687
Grinham, N F	Flt Lt	3Mar54	201 Sqn	NJ267
Grossan, G S	Sgt	15Dec42	119 Sqn	DV971
Grossey, C S	Flt Lt	22Aug43	201 Sqn	DD848
Grosvenor, T	Sgt	30Jun43	201 Sqn	DD857
Guiton, K R	Flg Off	17Feb44	4 (C) OTU	T9088
Gunson, A W	Plt Off RAAF	21Sep43	10 (RAAF)	DV969
Gurdin, R A	AC2	21Oct47	MAEE	DV976
Gurnett, F H W	Sgt	1Aug42	201 Sqn	W4000
Guy, A	LMM	18Jul43	Royal Navy	JM687
Hadcroft, F	Sgt	4Aug43	423 Sqn	DD859
Hadwell, C W	Sgt	28Nov42	95 Sqn	DV975
Haines, R C		25Mar53	88 Sqn	PP148
Hakim Ali	Gnr	15Oct45	Indian Army	NJ277
Halls, J W	LAC	25Aug42	4 (C) OTU	W4036
Hamilton, D	Sgt	12Jul43	228 Sqn	DV977
Hamilton, G	Sgt	15Dec42	119 Sqn	DV971
Hammond, R H F	LAC	9Jul40	201 Sqn	N6133
Hardan Singh	Hvdr	15Oct45	Indian Army	NJ277
Harding, P E	Flt Sgt	12Jul43	228 Sqn	DV977
Harman, G	Sgt	11Jun42	4 (C) OTU	P9604
Harnwell, J R	Flg Off	21Nov43	4 (C) OTU	L2168
Harris, D	Flt Sgt RAAF	21Sep43	10 (RAAF)	DV969
Harris, R G	Flt Sgt RAAF	30Aug43	461 Sqn	JM707
Harrison, R P A	Flt Lt	8Apr47	204 Sqn	L5799
Harrott, H	AC2	8Apr40	204 Sqn	L5799
Harry, D M	Plt Off	9Jul40	201 Sqn	N6133
Hart, N H	Flt Sgt RAAF	21Jan43	461 Sqn	T9085
Hatton, D J	Flg Off	27Mar46	209 Sqn	PP103
Hatton, D R	Flt Lt	14Mar45	201 Sqn	ML743
Hawthorne, F	Flt Sgt	15Oct45	230 Sqn	NJ277
Hayes, A G N	Sgt	29Jun40	210 Sqn	N9026
Haylock, W C	Flg Off	24May43	228 Sqn	EJ139
Hayward, C E	Sgt	1Sep42	461 Sqn	T9113
Hayward, J H	AC2	15Oct39	204 Sqn	N9030
Hazard, J	Plt Off	21Jun42	10 (RAAF)	W3999
Heath, W E C	Sgt	24Jan43	246 Sqn	DV979
Henderson, J M	Flg Off RAAF	10Jun42	95 Sqn	L5805
Hewerdine, E J	Flt Sgt	25Aug42	4 (C) OTU	W4036
Hewitt, F	Cpl RAAF	28Apr41	10 (RAAF)	T9075
Hibberd, A J	Flg Off	15May43	228 Sqn	DD837
Hick, A N	Sqn Ldr RAAF	24Jun41	10 (RAAF)	P9603
Hides, J B	LAC	20Dec41	201 Sqn	W3998
Hill, D F	Flg Off	13Jun43	228 Sqn	DV967
Hill, J R	Flt Lt	23Oct54	230 Sqn	PP155

ROLL OF HONOUR

Name	Rank	Date	Unit	Aircraft
Hill, W N	Flg Off RAAF	18Aug43	10 (RAAF)	W3985
Hindle, J F	LAC	9Jul40	201 Sqn	N6133
Hird, J	Sgt	25May43	422 Sqn	DD846
Hird, R A	Sgt	29Nov42	204 Sqn	W6016
Hobbins, E C	Flt Sgt RAAF	22Sep43	204 Sqn	JM710
Hobday, D R	Flt Lt	28Jan51	205 Sqn	PP107
Hobson, J S	Flt Sgt	12Jun44	201 Sqn	ML760
Hodge, R F	Flt Sgt	28Jan51	205 Sqn	PP107
Hodgson, J L	Flg Off	30Jun43	201 Sqn	DD857
Hogg, J H	Sgt RAAF	17May43	10 (RAAF)	W4004
Hogg, W A	Sgt	28Nov42	95 Sqn	DV975
Holcombe, R H	Flg Off	1Jan43	230 Sqn	N9029
Holmes, W C	Flt Lt	16Feb51	201 Sqn	SZ598
Hood, A V	LAC	29Dec43	230 Sqn	EJ140
Hopkinson, E	AC	5Feb42	201 Sqn	W3977
Hopps, W G	Sgt RCAF	25May43	422 Sqn	DD846
Horsburgh, J B	Flt Sgt	4Aug43	423 Sqn	DD859
Hosband, R H H	Plt Off RAAF	1Sep42	461 Sqn	T9113
Hoskins, R F	Plt Off	8Apr40	204 Sqn	L5799
Houedard, C L	Flg Off	24May43	228 Sqn	EJ139
Howarth, D	Sgt	24Jan43	246 Sqn	DV979
Howatson, A A	Flg Off	23Oct54	230 Sqn	PP155
Howell, A F	Flt Lt	7Sep42	230 Sqn	W3987
Howkins, V	Flg Off	14Mar45	201 Sqn	ML743
Hudson, F E	AC1	17Sep39	210 Sqn	L2168
Hughes, C A	AC1	8Apr40	204 Sqn	L5799
Hughes, J R	Flt Sgt	29May42	228 Sqn	T9089
Humphrey, H J	Flt Sgt	28Jun42	204 Sqn	T9041
Humphrey, J C L	Flt Sgt	12Jun44	201 Sqn	ML760
Humphreys, D E	LAC	28Jan51	205 Sqn	PP107
Hunt, P A C	Flg Off	12Jun44	201 Sqn	ML760
Hunter, I	Sgt RAAF	20May43	10 (RAAF)	W3986
Hunter, R J	Flt Sgt RAAF	30Aug43	461 Sqn	JM707
Ingham, F L	Flg Off	29Dec43	230 Sqn	EJ140
Ingham, K V	Sqn Ldr	28Nov44	230 Sqn	JM673
Irvine, R	Sgt	28Nov42	95 Sqn	DV975
Isaac, T J	Flt Sgt	29May42	228 Sqn	T9089
Isle, W H	Sgt RAAF	8Aug42	10 (RAAF)	W4019
Jabour, R J	Sgt	24Jan43	246 Sqn	DV979
Jackman, E C G	Flt Sgt	17Aug42	204 Sqn	L2158
Jackman, G H	Flt Lt	29Nov42	204 Sqn	W6016
Jackson, E N	Flg Off RNZAF	15Dec42	119 Sqn	DV971
Jackson, E W	Sgt	3Dec41	201 Sqn	W3988
Jackson, J E	Flt Sgt RAAF	17May43	10 (RAAF)	W4004
Jackson, L	Flg Off	21Nov43	4 (C) OTU	L2168
Jacobson, G W E	Sgt	5Feb42	201 Sqn	W3977
Jagmal Singh	Gnr	15Oct45	Indian Army	NJ277
James, R S S	Flt Sgt	29May42	228 Sqn	T9089
Jarvis, M J E	LAC	9Jul40	201 Sqn	N6133
Jebson, S	Plt Off	5Jun43	330 Sqn	W6052
Jennison, A G	Flg Off RAAF	21Sep43	10 (RAAF)	DV969
Jensen, J	Sub Lt RNorNavy	12Oct43	4 (C) OTU	W3997
Johnson, W A	Sgt RCAF	24Jan43	246 Sqn	DV979
Jones, H	Sgt	5Feb42	201 Sqn	W3977
Jones, F H	Wt Off RAAF	11Aug43	10 (RAAF)	DP177
Jones, L E	Sgt	13Apr43	204 Sqn	JM669
Jones, W A	Flt Sgt	15May43	228 Sqn	DD837
Jones, W R	Flt Sgt	25Aug42	4 (C) OTU	W4036
Joyce, T G	Flg Off RAAF	28Apr41	10 (RAAF)	T9075
Judell, M L	Flt Lt	21Jun42	10 (RAAF)	W3999
Juffs, R F	Flt Sgt	28Nov44	230 Sqn	JM673
Kearney, W H J	Flt Lt	26Mar50	209 Sqn	SZ573
Kelly, J C	Flt Sgt RAAF	17May43	10 (RAAF)	W4004
Kelly, J S	Flt Sgt RCAF	4Aug43	423 Sqn	DD859
Kennedy, G R	Flt Sgt	14Mar45	201 Sqn	ML743
Kennedy, T A	LAC	27Dec40	210 Sqn	N9022
Kent, A J	LAC	28Jan51	205 Sqn	PP107
Kent, Duke of	Air Cdre	25Aug42	—	W4036
Kenyon, D	Sgt	1Aug42	201 Sqn	W4000
King, B D	Plt Off	15Dec42	119 Sqn	DV971
King, S	Flt Sgt	1Sep42	461 Sqn	T9113
Kinnish, W M	AC1	11Aug41	201 Sqn	W3978
Kitchin, H	Flg Off	5Feb42	201 Sqn	W3977
Kite, P W H	Flt Lt	9Apr40	210 Sqn	L2167
Kjellstrup, I W H	Sub Lt RNorNavy	12Oct43	4 (C) OTU	W3997
Knutzen, E	Sgt RNorAF	12Oct43	4 (C) OTU	W3997
Kul Man Pun	Naik	15Oct45	Indian Army	NJ277
La Nauze, P C	Flt Sgt	27Mar46	209 Sqn	PP103
Lane, A	Flt Sgt RAAF	13Aug43	461 Sqn	DV968
Lane, J H	LAC	9Jul40	201 Sqn	N6133
Lauder, R	Sgt	29Oct40	201 Sqn	P9622
Law, J T	Sgt RAAF	21Sep43	10 (RAAF)	DV969
Law, R I	Flt Sgt	15Dec42	119 Sqn	DV971
Le Maistre, A F	Plt Off	9Apr40	210 Sqn	L2167
Lea, F W	LAC	3Dec41	201 Sqn	W3988
Leadbitter, B F	Sub Lt	27Dec40	Royal Navy	N9022
Lee, C J	Sgt	22Aug42	202 Sqn	W4029
Lee, L B	Flt Lt	13Jun43	228 Sqn	DV967
Leech, S C E	Sgt RAAF	21Sep43	10 (RAAF)	DV969
Leeman, W L	Flg Off	15May43	228 Sqn	DD837
Lester, N F	Plt Off	5Jun43	330 Sqn	W6052
Levy-Haarscher, R S	Flt Lt	15Oct45	230 Sqn	NJ277
Lewis, C N	Flt Sgt	25Aug42	4 OTU	W4036
Lewis, E	Sgt	29May42	228 Sqn	T9089
Lewis, V	Sgt RAAF	31Jul42	201 Sqn	W4025
Lewis, W R	Sgt	20Aug43	230 Sqn	EJ131
Lillie, W G DFM	Sgt	21Jul40	204 Sqn	N9028
Lloyd, D S	LAC	8Apr40	204 Sqn	L5799
Longson, C D L	Flt Sgt RAAF	13Aug43	461 Sqn	DV968
Looms, A H	Flt Sgt	18Jul43	204 Sqn	JM687
Lord, E W	Sgt	13Apr43	204 Sqn	JM669
Lough, G	Plt Off	13Jun43	228 Sqn	DV967
Lowther, J	Lt	25Aug42		W4036
Luke, J	Sgt	19Dec42	422 Sqn	W6029
Lumsden, D E	Flg Off	29Dec43	230 Sqn	EJ140
Lydeamore, H B	Sgt RAAF	1Aug43	10 (RAAF)	W4020
MacDonald, G E	Plt Off	21Jul40	204 Sqn	N9028
MacDonald, S H	Sgt	28Oct40	204 Sqn	P9620
MacDonald, T	Flt Sgt	16Feb51	201 Sqn	SZ598
MacDougall, A K	Flg Off RCAF	13Jun43	228 Sqn	DV967
MacLaren, W R	Flt Lt	3Mar54	201 Sqn	NJ267
Maconnell, W D	Sgt RCAF	17Aug42	204 Sqn	L2158
Mahony, B T	Sgt	16Feb51	201 Sqn	SZ598
Maile, G H	AC1	9Apr40	210 Sqn	L2167
Major, G C	Sgt	24Jan43	246 Sqn	DV979
Makens?	Flt Sgt	29Dec43	230 Sqn	EJ140
Malmoe, A	Sgt RNorAF	12Oct43	4 (C) OTU	W3997
Manphul Singh	Hvdr	15Oct45	Indian Army	NJ277
Mansbridge, W J	Sgt	1Aug42	201 Sqn	W4000
Marker, E G	Plt Off	3Dec41	201 Sqn	W3988
Marsh, G	Wt Off	15Oct45	Indian Army	NJ277
Marshall, A J	Sgt	29Nov42	204 Sqn	W6016
Marshall, J	AC2	12Oct43	4 (C) OTU	W3997
Martin, J H	Cpl	20Dec41	201 Sqn	W3998
Martin, R J	Sgt	12Jul43	228 Sqn	DV977
Mason, H S	Wt Off	5Feb42	201 Sqn	W3977
Massam, E T	Sgt	11Jun42	4 OTU	P9604
Matthews, R E G	Sgt RAAF	11Aug42	10 (RAAF)	DP177
Mawasi Ram	Gnr	15Oct45	Indian Army	NJ277
Maycock, E J	Wt Off	15May43	228 Sqn	DD837
McAllister, P C	LAC	28Jan51	205 Sqn	PP107
McAuley, B	Sgt	29Nov42	204 Sqn	W6016
McAvoy, J	Sgt	14Mar45	201 Sqn	ML743
McCallum, A R	Flg Off RCAF	15Dec42	119 Sqn	DV971
McCarroll, W	Flt Lt	21Nov43	4 (C) OTU	L2168
McCarthy, G G M	Flt Sgt RNZAF	12Oct43	4 (C) OTU	W3997
McCombie, H K	AC1	10Jun42	95 Sqn	L5805
McCombie, P	Sgt RAAF	20May43	10 (RAAF)	W3986
McDonald, R S	RCAF	5Jun43	330 Sqn	W6052
McGregor, M W	Flg Off	20Aug43	230 Sqn	EJ131
McKaig, R A	Flt Sgt	27Mar46	209 Sqn	PP103
McKenzie, M K	Flt Lt RAAF	17May43	10 (RAAF)	W4004
McLean J V	Sgt	21Jun42	10 (RAAF)	W3999
McLean, W	Sgt	22Aug43	201 Sqn	DD848
McLeod Nibbs	Plt Off	17Feb44	4 (C) OTU	T9098
McLeod, N J	Plt Off RAAF	17May43	10 (RAAF)	W4004
McNeill, G McL	LAC	10Jun42	95 Sqn	L5805
Meaton, R W	Flg Off RAAF	1Jan43	230 Sqn	N9029
Meggitt, I H	Flt Lt	27Dec40	210 Sqn	N9022
Mehaffey	RN Nurse	18Jul43	R Navy	JM687
Meldrum, K M	Flt Sgt RAAF	18Aug43	10 (RAAF)	W3985
Menzies, D J	Sgt	20Aug43	230 Sqn	EJ131
Menzies, W E	AC1 RAAF	8Aug42	10 (RAAF)	W4019
Middleton, J D	Flt Lt	9Jul40	201 Sqn	N6133
Miles, E C	Plt Off	2Jun43	461 Sqn	EJ134
Millar, R L	AC1	9Apr40	210 Sqn	L2167
Millgate, J L	Flt Sgt	25Mar53	88 Sqn	PP148
Mills, R J A	Flg Off	29Dec43	230 Sqn	EJ140
Milne, W G	Plt Off RCAF	15Dec42	119 Sqn	DV971
Mitchell, A L	Flt Lt	29Nov42	204 Sqn	W6016
Mitchell, H F	Flt Sgt	20Dec41	201 Sqn	W3998
Mitchell, M C B	Flt Lt	25Mar53	88 Sqn	PP148
Moll, C	Sgt	20Aug43	230 Sqn	EJ131
Monson, W H	A/Sqn Ldr	22Jul45	230 Sqn (fell overboard)	PP197
Moodie		Nov.56	35 SAAF	1714
Moore, J H	Plt Off RAAF	21Jan43	461 Sqn	T9085
Moore, R S	Sgt RAAF	20May43	10 (RAAF)	W3986
Morgan, A	Sgt	22Aug42	202 Sqn	W4029
Morgan, A M	Sgt	15May43	228 Sqn	DD837

Name	Rank	Date	Unit	Serial
Morris, E R	LAC	29Jun40	210 Sqn	N9026
Morris, G	AC1	15Mar41	210 Sqn	P9624
Morrison, F A	LAC	9Apr40	210 Sqn	L2167
Moseley, T L	Wg Cdr	25Aug42	4 (C) OTU	W4036
Moss, J	AC2	17Sep39	210 Sqn	L2168
Muir, G F	Sgt	1Aug42	201 Sqn	W4000
Mullett, K G	Flt Lt	5Jan44	95 Sqn	DW105
Murdoch, J	LAC RAAF	17May43	10 (RAAF)	W4004
Murphy, M	AC1	17Sep39	210 Sqn	L2168
Murray, A T J	Sgt	5Jun43	330 Sqn	W6052
Nangle, G A	AC1	29Oct40	201 Sqn	P9622
Nek Muhammad	Hvdr	15Oct41	Indian Army	NJ277
Newbery, T A	Flg Off	15May43	228 Sqn	DD837
Nicholas, E A	Cpl	1Jan43	230 Sqn	N9029
Nishan Singh	Sepoy	15Oct45	Indian Army	NJ277
(Non-RAF 7persons)		7Mar46	209 Sqn	PP103
Norris, C E	Sgt	5Jan44	95 Sqn	DW105
Nutt, K C	Sgt	5Feb42	201 Sqn	W3977
O'Brien, W A	AC2	17Sep39	210 Sqn	L2168
O'Donoghue, M	Sgt	13Feb46	302 FTU	VB885
O'Dowd, D A	Sgt	25May43	422 Sqn	DD846
O'Keefe, H	Sgt	13Feb46	302 FTU	VB885
Ogg, L T	AC1 RAAF	8Aug42	10 (RAAF)	W4019
Ogston, D	Sgt	27Dec40	210 Sqn	N9022
Olley, J S	LAC	28Jan51	205 Sqn	PP107
Orford, N H	Sgt RAAF	18Aug43	10 (RAAF)	W3985
Orr, C J B	Sgt	22Aug42	202 Sqn	W4029
Osborne, H	Plt Off RAAF	21Jan43	461 Sqn	T9085
Ovens, E W	Sgt	21Jul40	204 Sqn	N9028
Owen, D T	Sgt	11Aug41	201 Sqn	W3978
Owen, N J	Sgt RAAF	20May43	10 (RAAF)	W3986
Owens, W	Sapper	15Oct45	Royal Eng	NJ277
Paige, E F DFC	Flg Off RCAF	25May43	422 Sqn	DD846
Palmer, E G	Sgt RAAF	24Jan43	246 Sqn	DV979
Pareezer, R T	Plt Off	21Jul40	204 Sqn	N9028
Parkes, H J	Sgt	11Aug41	201 Sqn	W3978
Parliament, H B	Flg Off RCAF	4Aug43	423 Sqn	DD859
Patrick, T W	Flt Lt RAAF	17May43	10 (RAAF)	W4004
Patston, V J	Flg Off	20May43	10 (RAAF)	W3986
Paulsen, A	RNorNavy Q/M	5Jun43	330 Sqn	W6052
Peacock, E	LAC	29Jun40	210 Sqn	N9026
Peacock, W	Flt Sgt	27Mar46	209 Sqn	PP103
Peaker, G C	Flt Sgt	29Dec43	230 Sqn	EJ140
Pearce, J A	Sgt RAAF	17May43	10 (RAAF)	W4004
Pearce, W H N	Flg Off	13Apr43	204 Sqn	JM669
Pelham-Clinton, A G	Flg Off	24May43	228 Sqn	EJ139
Penney, A S	Sgt	13Apr43	204 Sqn	JM669
Perkins, A K	Sgt	27Dec40	210 Sqn	N9022
Peters, F T RN	Capt	13Nov42	R Navy	W6054
Phelps, R W J	Sgt	29Oct40	201 Sqn	P9622
Phillips, S G	Flg Off	5Jan44	95 Sqn	DW105
Phillips, F DFC	Flt Lt	21Jul40	204 Sqn	N9028
Phillips, G C	Sgt	24Jan43	246 Sqn	DV979
Philp, A V	Flg Off	12Jun44	201 Sqn	ML760
Pickford, N	Flt Sgt	22Aug43	201 Sqn	DD848
Pitts, W	Sgt	22Aug43	201 Sqn	DD848
Pollock, N D	Sgt RAAF	20May43	10 (RAAF)	W3986
Potter, J K	Flg Off RCAF	19Dec42	422 Sqn	W6029
Prescott, G G	Sgt	15Mar41	210 Sqn	P9624
Pritchard, J H	Sgt	5Jun43	330 Sqn	W6052
Purkiss, W L	LAC	1Jan43	230 Sqn	N9029
Purvis, D	Sgt	25May43	422 Sqn	DD846
Pybus, J	Flg Off RNZAF	10Jun42	95 Sqn	L5805
Quinn, R J	Sgt	18Jul43	204 Sqn	JM687
Rae, W S DFC	Flt Lt	5Dec41	10 (RAAF)	T9072
Rahmut Ullah	Gnr	15Oct45	Indian Army	NJ277
Raine, A	Cpl	11Jun42	4 (C) OTU	P9604
Raine, N	LAC RAAF	28Apr41	10 (RAAF)	T9075
Rees, A C	Sgt RAAF	19Dec42	422 Sqn	W6029
Reilly, J J	Wt Off	15Oct45	230 Sqn	NJ277
Revell, H	Sgt	22Sep43	204 Sqn	JM710
Rheuben, C A	AC1 RAAF	8Aug42	10 (RAAF)	W4019
Richardson, D H	Sgt	25May43	422 Sqn	DD846
Riddell, G R S	Sgt	21Nov43	4 OTU	L2168
Rideout, E E	Flt Lt	5Jul47	201 Sqn	PP113
Ridge, S	Sgt	20Aug43	230 Sqn	EJ131
Ridings, K L	Flg Off RAAF	17May43	10 (RAAF)	W4004
Rimmington, C A	Plt Off RAAF	22Aug42	202 Sqn	W4029
Ritchie, W	AC1	12Oct43	4 (C) OTU	W3997
Roberts, A F	LAC	8Apr40	204 Sqn	L5799
Roberts, C C I	Sgt	27Dec40	210 Sqn	N9022
Roberts, T W	S.II	5Jul47	201 Sqn	PP113
Robinson, J	AC2	20Dec41	201 Sqn	W3998
Robinson, J G	Flt Sgt	14Mar45	201 Sqn	ML743
Robinson, R W	Flt Sgt	28Nov42	95 Sqn	DV975
Robjohns, E	Sgt	20Aug43	230 Sqn	EJ131
Rohtas Singh		15Oct45	Indian Army	NJ277
Rolfe, A A	Sgt	5Feb42	201 Sqn	W3977
Rolfe, J A	Flt Sgt	15May43	228 Sqn	DD837
Roper, D A	Flg Off	5Jan44	95 Sqn	DW105
Ross, M S	Sgt	28Oct40	204 Sqn	P9620
Rothwell, J K	LAC	4Jun55	201 Sqn	RN288
Rowe, D	Sgt	25May43	422 Sqn	DD846
Rowland, J I	Flg Off RAAF	11Aug43	10 (RAAF)	DP177
Rowlands, A J	LAC	3Mar54	201 Sqn	NJ267
Rundle, D C	Plt Off RCAF	18Jul43	204 Sqn	JM687
Rustad, L W	RNorNavy	12Oct43	4 (C) OTU	W3997
Ryan, J J	LAC	21Oct47	MAEE	DV976
Sadleir, T W	Flt Sgt	5Jan44	95 Sqn	DW105
Sales, J	Sgt	24May43	228 Sqn	EJ139
Sandison, H I	Flt Sgt	13Feb46	302 FTU	VB885
Saunders, D	Flt Lt RAAF	20May43	10 (RAAF)	W3986
Saunders, G R	Plt Off	25Aug42	4 (C) OTU	W4036
Savidge, J	LAC	1Jan43	230 Sqn	N9029
Scarce, H	Sgt	31Jul42	201 Sqn	W4025
Schmok, A J W	Sgt (RCAF)	5Jun43	330 Sqn	W6052
Scott, F D'A	Sgt (RAAF)	22Aug42	202 Sqn	W4029
Scott, J		25Mar53	88 Sqn	PP148
Scrace, K	Sgt	31Jul42	201 Sqn	W4025
Scutts, R B	Flg Off RAAF	24Jan41	10 (RAAF)	P9603
Searl, W F	Sgt	28Nov42	95 Sqn	DV975
Seeds, J	Plt Off	9Jul40	201 Sqn	N6133
Shand, E E	Flt Lt	16Feb51	201 Sqn	SZ598
Sharland, D E	Flt Sgt	12Jun44	201 Sqn	ML760
Shaw, R A	Sgt RCAF	13Jun43	228 Sqn	DV967
Shears, G K J	Sgt	29Dec43	230 Sqn	EJ140
Sheppard, C E	Sgt	15May43	228 Sqn	DD837
Sherwood, R	Sgt	25May43	422 Sqn	DD846
Short, J D	Sgt	29Nov42	204 Sqn	W6016
Shum, A G	Sgt	15Dec42	119 Sqn	DV971
Simpson, K M DFC	Flt Lt RAAF	13Aug43	461 Sqn	DV968
Simpson, W	Sgt	24Jan43	246 Sqn	DV979
Skinner, H W	Flg Off RAAF	18Aug43	10 (RAAF)	W3985
Slater, W	Sgt RAAF	18Aug43	10 (RAAF)	W3985
Smart, D	Flt Sgt	15May43	228 Sqn	DD837
Smedley, H	Flt Sgt	30Aug43	461 Sqn	JM052
Smith, A	S.II	5Jul47	201 Sqn	PP113
Smith, E B	Sgt	13Apr43	204 Sqn	JM669
Smith, F W	Flt Lt	5Feb42	201 Sqn	W3977
Smith, G L T	Flg Off RAAF	20May43	10 (RAAF)	W3986
Smith, K D	Flg Off RAAF	11Aug43	10 (RAAF)	DP177
Smith, R	Sgt	13Apr43	204 Sqn	JM669
Smith, R E J	Sgt	13Jun43	228 Sqn	DV967
Smith, R M	Plt Off	5Feb42	201 Sqn	W3977
Smith, S J	Cpl	20Nov49	88 Sqn	NJ176
Sneyd, E	AC2	21Jul40	204 Sqn	N9028
Snook, L E	Flt Sgt	13Feb46	302 FTU	VB885
Soanes, W A	AC1	17Sep39	210 Sqn	L2168
Soden, L	Sgt	15Mar41	210 Sqn	P9624
Soffe, F J	AC1	17Sep39	210 Sqn	L2168
South, D E DFM	Flt Sgt	12Jun44	201 Sqn	ML760
Southall, H L	Sgt	20Dec41	201 Sqn	W3998
Sowerby, J H	Sgt	12Jul43	228 Sqn	DV977
Sparks, A	Sgt	12Jul43	228 Sqn	DV977
Spencer, S A	Sgt	21Nov43	4 (C) OTU	L2168
Stendtvedt, D J	Sgt RNorAF	12Oct43	4 (C) OTU	W3997
Stevens, R C	Flt Sgt	13Feb46	302 FTU	VB885
Stewart, D I	Plt Off RAAF	1Sep42	461 Sqn	T9113
Stewart, W	Flt Sgt	30Aug43	461 Sqn	JM707
Stone, P A H	Wt Off	14May45	209 Sqn	NJ260
Strutt, M	Plt Off RCAF	25Aug42	4 (C) OTU	W4036
Sturdy, J W	Plt Off	20Aug43	230 Sqn	EJ131
Sutton, G W	Plt Off	17Sep39	210 Sqn	L2168
Svendsen, K	Sgt RNorAF	12Oct43	4 (C) OTU	W3997
Swain, F J	Flg Off	15Mar41	210 Sqn	P9624
Sweet, L E	Sgt	25Aug42	4 (C) OTU	W4036
Swinson, R R	Flg Off RAAF	18Aug43	10 (RAAF)	W3985
Swinton, N D K	Flt Sgt RAAF	21Sep43	10 (RAAF)	DV969
Tamsett, J A	Plt Off RAAF	30Aug43	461 Sqn	JM707
Tasker, H J	Sgt	24Jan43	246 Sqn	DV979
Taylor, E J	Sgt	21Jun42	10 (RAAF)	W3999
Taylor, H W	Sgt	23Apr41	204 Sqn	N9023
Taylor, M E	Flt Sgt RCAF	28Nov42	95 Sqn	DV975
Thompson, A	Sgt	18Jul43	204 Sqn	JM687
Thompson, J	Sgt	28Jun42	204 Sqn	T9041
Thompson, W	Sgt	28Jan51	205 Sqn	PP107
Thompson, W R	Wt Off RAAF	25May43	422 Sqn	DD846
Thomson, N E	Sgt RNZAF	27Dec40	210 Sqn	N9022
Thomson, S	Flt Lt RAAF	5Dec41	10 (RAAF)	T9072
Thorpe, W	AC1	20Nov49	88 Sqn	NJ176
Tilt, G F W	Sgt	22Aug43	201 Sqn	DD848
Tinkler, J W	Flt Lt	27Mar46	209 Sqn	PP103

Roll of Honour

Name	Rank	Date	Unit	Serial
Tipping, F W	AC1	21Jun42	10 (RAAF)	W3999
Titchie, G F	Flt Sgt RAAF	30Aug43	461 Sqn	JM707
Todd, A M	Flt Lt	20Aug43	230 Sqn	EJ131
Tomley, M J	Flt Sgt	31Jul42	201 Sqn	W4025
Towe, M E	LAC	28Oct40	204 Sqn	P9620
Tozer, A J	Sgt	18Jul43	204 Sqn	JM687
Traill, J R	Flg Off	31Jul42	201 Sqn	W4025
Trickey, T P J	LAC	21Jul40	204 Sqn	N9028
Trood, D D	Sgt RAAF	8Aug42	10 (RAAF)	W4019
Tucker, R A S	Sgt RAAF	21Jan43	461 Sqn	T9085
Turner, P K	Flt Sgt RAAF	13Aug43	461 Sqn	DV968
Twist, D J	Flt Sgt	14Mar45	201 Sqn	ML743
Underwood, D W	Sgt	28Nov44	230 Sqn	JM673
Upham, D W B	LAC	9Apr40	210 Sqn	L2167
Vaughan, R J DFC	Flt Lt	5Dec41	10 (RAAF)	T9072
Vogel, F W	Brig	13Nov42	Army	W6054
Waddington, L E	Flt Sgt RAAF	21Sep43	10 (RAAF)	DV969
Wadham, G W	Capt	13Nov42	Royal Navy	W6054
Wainwright, J H	Surg.Lt	18Jul43	Royal Navy	JM687
Wakefield, W H	Flt Lt	31Jul42	201 Sqn	W4025
Walker, A P	LAC	3Dec41	201 Sqn	W3988
Walker, G M	Sgt RAAF	20May43	10 (RAAF)	W3986
Walker, J J	Sgt	5Jun43	330 Sqn	W6052
Wallace, J H	LAC	20Dec41	201 Sqn	W3998
Wallike, R F	Wt Off	28Nov44	230 Sqn	JM673
Wallis, H	Sgt	22Aug42	202 Sqn	W4029
Walters, G L	Sgt	29Jun40	210 Sqn	N9026
Waring, J W	Sgt	5Jun43	330 Sqn	W6052
Waterman, D A	Sgt	12Jul43	228 Sqn	DV977
Waters, J H	Flt Sgt	29Dec43	230 Sqn	EJ140
Waters, K R	Flg Off RCAF	15Apr43	119 Sqn	DP176
Watkins, H C	Plt Off	3Mar54	201 Sqn	NJ267
Watkinson, H R	Sgt	15Dec42	119 Sqn	DV971
Watson, E	Flt Sgt	12Jun44	201 Sqn	ML760
Watson, L S	Sgt RAAF	13Aug43	461 Sqn	DV968
Watson, W	AC2	20Dec41	201 Sqn	W3998
Watts, E L	Wt Off	13Apr43	204 Sqn	JM669
Webber, H J	AC1 RAAF	5Dec41	10 (RAAF)	T9072
Webber, L J	Flt Sgt	1Jan43	230 Sqn	N9029
Webster, A A	Plt Off	1Aug42	201 Sqn	W4000
Webster, J G H	Wt Off RAAF	11Aug43	10 (RAAF)	DP177
Welch, A M	Flg Off RAAF	1Aug43	10 (RAAF)	W4020
Wennholm, O L	Plt Off RAAF	1Sep42	461 Sqn	T9113
Weston, G	Sgt	22Sep43	204 Sqn	JM710
Whale, R G	Sgt	12Jul43	228 Sqn	DV977
Whalley, D J	Plt Off	10Jun42	95 Sqn	L5805
Whatley, L R	Sgt	24May43	228 Sqn	EJ139
White, J A McL G	AC1	21Jul40	204 Sqn	N9028
White, J I	Sgt	1Sep42	461 Sqn	T9113
Whitford, J D	AC2	15Oct39	204 Sqn	N9030
Wilkins, S L	Lt	1Aug42	201 Sqn	W4000
Wilkins, R W	Lt	1Aug42	Som Lt Inf	W4000
Wilkinson, E	Plt Off	22Aug43	201 Sqn	DD848
Wilkinson, G N	Flg Off	22Aug43	201 Sqn	DD848
Williams, E R J	Flt Sgt	28Nov44	230 Sqn	JM673
Williams, R M H	Flt Sgt	14May45	209 Sqn	NJ260
Willians, N	Sgt	31Jul42	201 Sqn	W4025
Willis, R G	LAC	21Jun42	10 (RAAF)	W3999
Wilson, A G E	Sgt	15Dec42	119 Sqn	DV971
Wilson, G H	Sgt	29Nov42	204 Sqn	W6016
Winterflood, W L	Sgt	21Jun42	10 (RAAF)	W3999
Worthington, L E	Sgt	9Jul40	201 Sqn	N6133
Wright, D R	LAC	21Oct47	MAEE	DV976
Yeomans, W	Flt Sgt	30Aug43	10 (RAAF)	W4019
Zaman Ali	Dvr	15Oct45	Indian Army	NJ277

The Short Scion Senior L9786, seen here at Rochester in October or November 1939, was fitted with a central float which was used to test the main step design for the Sunderland Mk.III and for later wartime experiments to reduce drag and improve the stability and handling of flying-boat hulls.
(Crown via Phil Butler)

The end. A rather sad sight of seven or more Sandringhams and Solents withdrawn from use and awaiting scrapping, beached at Hamworthy in the mid-1950s.
(Peter Amos)

AUGUST 4TH, 1949   FLIGHT   Advertisements. I

> Some Short jottings for airline operators, charter companies, and V.I.P.s

Adaptability means long service

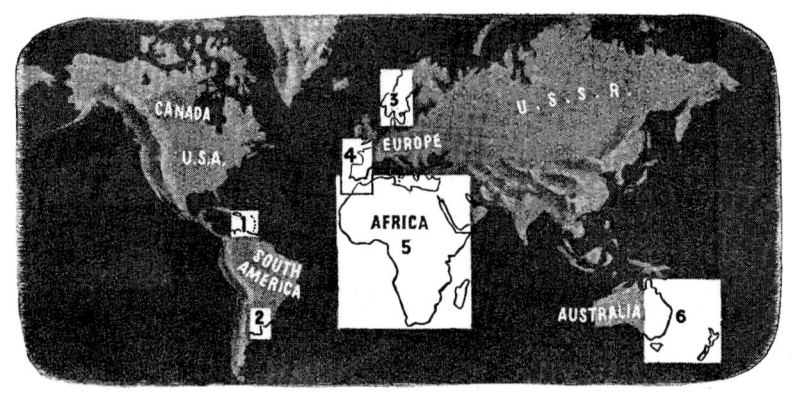

Made to Measure

There is no more versatile aircraft than the amphibian Short Sealand, which will soon be flying over the Caribbean.

British West Indian Airways chose this plane of many parts to inaugurate their "Sea Island Service," which links scattered islands from Trinidad to St. Kitts. The Sealand meets exactly the needs of small feeder lines and charter companies, and can double the scope of their services.

Its use makes even jungle areas accessible to the transport of freight, for the Sealand is in its element on lakes and rivers, needing only 900 yards of water on which to operate.

The simplicity of its design allows conversion to many usages. Basically fitted for 5-8 passengers, the Sealand can be adapted to carry stores of considerable bulk: it will serve as an air ambulance or a flying office. A normal range, with 7 passengers and luggage, would be 350 miles; but a reduced payload can increase this to 765 miles, and the amphibian is converted easily into a flying boat proper, with a doubling of the payload.

Sandringhams around the World

The Short Sandringhams have appeared in no less than seven versions. In many parts of the world these Short boats, modified internally to meet particular needs and conditions, are building up the traditions of reliable service that mean so much to passengers and crews.

In South America, A.L.F.A. and C.A.U.S.A. are operating Sandringhams round the estuary of the River Plate. A.L.F.A's 45-seater air-buses carry 30,000 passengers a year between Buenos Aires and Montevideo alone — an example of the successful use of a 60,000 lb. aircraft over short hauls in difficult country.

In Norway, 37-seater Sandringhams of S.A.S. are in daily use during the summer, carrying 1,000 passengers a week beween Oslo and Tromso.

In every case the flexibility of the flying boat and its practical value in severe conditions, have been profitably proved.

More millions of Miles

There seems no limit to the active life of Short aircraft. Now 12 of the famous "Hythe"-class boats, part of the fleet which completed 22,000,000 miles of service on B.O.A.C's England-Australia route, are being refitted for new duties in the European area. Aquila Airways, who purchased these remarkable aircraft, have already used some of these Hythes as freighters on the Berlin air-lift. Others will be used on a regular weekly service from Southampton to Funchal in Madeira, with a shuttle run between this holiday island and Lisbon.

Aquila's Hythe "Hampshire," which made the proving flight over this new route, was the largest and the first commercial aircraft to visit the island. It carried in Madeira's first airmail.

Passenger-preference shows the Trend

The latest Short Solent, with its luxurious bar, its library and its "promenade," is delighting passengers on B.O.A.C.'s "Springbok" service to South Africa.

Recently, a party of travellers, offered alternative accommodation by landplane, preferred, unanimously, to accept delay rather than forfeit the amenities of the flying boat.

Soon, four of the long-range Solents will leave to operate for T.E.A.L. in Australasia, between Sydney and Auckland.

Shorts   THE FIRST MANUFACTURERS OF AIRCRAFT IN THE WORLD

SHORT BROTHERS & HARLAND LIMITED, Queens Island, Belfast
London Office: 17 Grosvenor Street, W.1

Shorts flying-boat operations throughout the world, as advertised in Flight *magazine dated 24th August 1949.*   *(via Peter J Marson)*